Accessible Design Review Guide

Accessible Design Review Guide

An ADAAG Guide for Designing and Specifying Spaces, Buildings, and Sites

The Accessible Space Team

Robert R. Grist

Mary Joyce Hasell

Rocke Hill

James L. West

Tony R. White

Sara Katherine Williams

McGraw-Hill

New York   San Francisco   Washington, D.C.   Auckland   Bogotá
Caracas   Lisbon   London   Madrid   Mexico City   Milan
Montreal   New Delhi   San Juan   Singapore
Sydney   Tokyo   Toronto

Library of Congress Cataloging-in-Publication Data

Accessible design review guide / by the Accessible Space Team, Robert
Grist ... [et al.].
      p.   cm.
    ISBN 0-07-000189-8 (hardcover)
    1.   Architecture and the physically handicapped—United States.
2. Architectural design.   I. Grist, Robert R.   II. University of
Florida. College of Architecture. Accessible Space Team.
NA2545.A1A2X5   1996
720'.42'0973—dc20   96-5437
                                                       CIP

McGraw-Hill

A Division of The McGraw·Hill Companies

    3 4 5 6 7 8 9 0   BBC/BBC   9 0 1 0 9 8 7

ISBN 0-07-000189-8

*The sponsoring editor for this book was Wendy Lochner, the editing supervisor was
Fred Dahl, and the production supervisor was Donald F. Schmidt. It was set in
Century by Inkwell Publishing Services.*

Printed and bound by Braceland.

To:

Kenneth Caudle
Wanda Hasell and Craig Forrest
Virginia R. Grist
Evelyn, Alicia, Gladys, Vernon, and Sandy Hill
Peggy, Leah, Lindsay, Meagan, and Wilson West
Hope, Skye, and Leona White
T. G. and Sara Anne Williams

and

Challenged Persons Everywhere

Contents

ILLUSTRATIONS

Preface

In 1992, the Accessible Space Team obtained a research contract to survey nine universities for compliance with the Americans with Disabilities Act Accessibility Guidelines (ADAAG) for the State University System, Board of Regents, State of Florida. The two-year contract involved surveying 120 individual sites across the state, with over 4000 buildings and more than 100,000 spaces totaling over 43 million square feet of interior space along with accessible exterior routes to each of those buildings. As we became familiar with the Americans with Disabilities Act (ADA) and the companion ADAAG, we realized that our needs for using these documents as an efficient survey tool were not met by the organization of the legal documents or by other existing survey documents.

The primary objective of the ADAAG is to provide specific, enforceable requirements for evaluating a facility's accessibility. The ADA states clearly that any facility in compliance with the ADAAG is deemed to meet the requirements of the ADA for accessibility, even if some individuals still find certain barriers to their own use of the facility. However, neither the organization nor the legal purpose of ADAAG are suited to the needs of a building-related professional whose job includes a compliance review and evaluation of new and altered building and site plan drawings and specifications. Furthermore, extensive review of available resources revealed the lack of a design-targeted guide suitable for an ADAAG evaluation of new and altered spaces, buildings, and sites. Our book meets this challenge and provides an ADAAG guide tailored specifically for the tasks of the building-related professions.

Accessible Design Review Guide: An ADAAG Guide for Designing and Specifying Spaces, Buildings, and Sites presents ADAAG guidelines in an understandable yet technically reliable format to aid professionals in reviewing drawings and specifications of proposed or existing buildings and sites. The format parallels the design and production process through the stages of schematic design, design development, and construction documents in new construction and in building alteration.

Accessible Design Review Guide is based on both the tools developed by the Accessible Space Team for successfully completing a State University System research contract for the State of Florida and their academic and professional consulting experience. Whether the reader of this reference book is a professional designer, codes enforcer, or an upper level student in one of the building-related professions, the information is clearly attuned to the need to understand ADAAG within the framework of functioning spaces.

The *Accessible Design Review Guide*'s authors—The Accessible Space Team—are an interdisciplinary team of design faculty in the College of Architecture at the University of Florida. In addition, they are all licensed practicing professionals.

- Robert Grist, associate professor, Department of Landscape Architecture
- Mary Joyce Hasell, associate professor, Department of Interior Design
- Rocke Hill, associate professor, Department of Architecture
- James L. West, associate professor, Department of Interior Design
- Tony R. White, associate professor, Department of Architecture
- Sara Katherine Williams, associate professor, Department of Landscape Architecture

Significant contributions were made by Charles F. Morgan, associate professor, Department of Architecture, to the original research project and to the early conceptual organization of this book.

The partnership between academics who also practice design in the fields of architecture, interior design, and landscape architecture makes this book usable by numerous building-related professionals. The individual viewpoints of the various authors have been woven together to show how the ADAAG information can help make buildings and sites accessible for disabled users.

ACKNOWLEDGMENTS

Many people contributed their time, energy, ideas, and support to the research project that led to the development and testing of the review guide presented here. First, the Dean of the College of Architecture Wayne Drummond, and associate dean Richard Schneider helped us secure and monitor the research contract with the State of Florida Board of Regents. Many times they stepped in with advice and phone calls that made the project run smoothly. The department chairs of Architecture, Interior Design, and Landscape Architecture worked hard to replace their faculty members to free their time for the grant. Thank you, Robert McCarter, Jerry Nielson, and Herrick Smith. The SUS Board of Regents and the Division of Sponsored Research at the University of Florida believed in our ability to structure this large project and to carry it out. Bob Friedman, associate vice chancellor,

Phillip Turner and Terri Tabor at the State of Florida Board of Regents, and Tom Walsh at the University of Florida, Division of Sponsored Research, all made significant contributions.

This list only begins to mention some of the people involved in the research project. Thomas Pugh, Craig Huffman, and Rolando Guiterez at Florida A & M University, James Moore and Trent Green at the University of South Florida, and Gisela Lopez-Mata at Florida International University were project coordinators who organized the surveys of State University System Facilities within their universities. In addition, we enlisted and worked with graduate and undergraduate students across the State University System of Florida. Over 100 students were involved in this grant as surveyors during the course of the research contract. Many times they were away from home and on the move for weeks at a time. Often they had to fit a couple of hours of survey time between classes and into their weekends. Their dedication to the project and their overall belief in its importance for improving accessibility across Florida's universities were exemplary. To all who contributed and helped we thank you.

THE ACCESSIBLE SPACE TEAM

Accessible Design Review Guide

Introduction

The primary purpose of the *Accessible Design Review Guide* is to facilitate the review of plans, specifications, and other drawings in meeting ADAAG compliance. It may also be used for evaluating existing buildings and sites for ADAAG compliance or as a prelude to renovations and alterations. This book is based on the ADA and ADAAG; however, repeated use of these documents in a research project led the authors to extensively reorganize them as detailed below.

The *ADA Accessibility Guidelines for Buildings and Facilities (ADAAG)* (Federal Register, Vol. 56, No. 144, July 26, 1991, Rules and Regulations) is primarily organized according to building and site elements. Conversely, in this book, the elements have been incorporated into a guide tailored to individual space-types in buildings and sites. For example, certain elements in ADAAG must be compliant in a toilet room (water closets, lavatories, grab bars, etc.); different ones must be compliant in a parking lot (van parking requirements, signage, etc.). In this book, typical elements pertinent to a toilet room are organized as a review guide specifically for toilet rooms while typical elements pertinent to a parking lot are organized as a review guide specifically for parking lots. By grouping these elements into unique "Space-type Review Guides," we have reduced the necessity to remember all elements in ADAAG. The result is a room, building, or site review that is simple and comprehensive. In addition, a major benefit of this book is that one learns about ADAAG as one reviews and corrects drawings, specifications, or existing space.

WHO SHOULD USE THE BOOK?

State and local building codes and regulations must conform to the ADAAG. Thus, the following design and building-related professionals can use our guide as a comprehensive tool for reviewing compliance:

- Architects, interior designers, and landscape architects involved in schematic, design development, and construction document phases of a proposed building project as well as adaptive reuse of existing facilities.
- Mechanical, electrical, and civil engineers in their specific design roles within the building design process (e.g., mechanical and electrical controls, fire safety, site planning).
- Specialty consultants involved in the building design process (e.g., kitchen and restaurant consultants, acoustical and auditorium consultants).
- Specification writers responsible for the preparation of ADAAG-compliant project specifications.

- Building officials, including code enforcement officials, responsible for adopting and enforcing building code compliance.
- Facilities managers responsible for the ongoing maintenance and rehabilitation of buildings or building groups, including bringing those buildings into compliance with the ADAAG.
- Educators and students within building programs, including individuals in architecture, interior design, landscape architecture, and building construction.

Designers and building-related professionals with a working knowledge of accessibility issues can use the book as a working manual, a reference, and a survey guide to *review proposed drawings and specifications* as well as *for the survey of existing facilities and sites.*

This book provides a simple but effective review method consistent with conventional practices used by designers, specifiers, and other site and building reviewers. Each "Space-type Review Guide" contains a plan drawing, a preliminary design overview, and both abbreviated and detailed compliance checklists. Both the professional who is naive with respect to the ADAAG, and an experienced user who requires a systematic process for review, can be accommodated by this presentation. The *ADAAG Guide* can influence the project and subsequent decisions, not just during the production of drawings and specifications or the conducting of compliance surveys, but also in conceptual and preliminary design phases.

BOOK ORGANIZATION

Chapter 1, "Building Design, the ADA, and the ADAAG" presents a brief overview of the Americans with Disabilities Act of 1990 (ADA), its history, and the ADA Accessibility Guidelines (ADAAG), as well as how this legislation impacts the design and renovation of buildings and sites. Chapter 2, "Development of the Space-type Review Guides and the Master Guidelines," explains how the "Space-type Review Guides" and "Master Guidelines" are organized for use by designers. Chapter 3, "Space-type Review Guides," contains 26 review guides necessary to evaluate the plan drawings for a building or site. Drawings are presented along with a preliminary design overview that lists the typical and special compliance issues in the space. The "Space-type Review Guides" are grouped under the following headings:

- Exterior Spaces
- Interior Spaces
- Transient Lodging

- Transportation (specific areas within)
- Site and Building Summary

Many micro decisions are only detailed and specified in the final phase of design. Likewise, numerous ADAAG compliance elements do not appear on a plan drawing, but instead are presented elsewhere—in specifications, on various schedules, or in enlarged details using a section, elevation, or plan. Chapter 4, "Specifications, Schedules, and Details," provides an alphabetically arranged sequence of such categories and identifies the *ADAAG Guide*'s coded elements and necessary technical

requirements. These alpha-numeric codes are listed in App. C, "Master Guidelines," which is a complete list of all compliance guidelines.

The final section of the book includes the appendices that contain ADA resources and bibliography, and several sample recording worksheets to check drawings or to survey existing sites, buildings, and space types. Also included are the "Master Guidelines"—a complete and reformatted listing of all ADAAG compliance items—as well as a complete set of ADAAG figures which are referenced in the "Master Guidelines."

1

Building Design, the ADA, and the ADAAG

THE AMERICANS WITH DISABILITIES ACT OF 1990 (ADA)

The Americans with Disabilities Act was signed into law in July, 1990, as federal civil rights legislation to prohibit discrimination against persons with disabilities. It became the most important civil rights legislation to be passed since the Civil Rights Act of 1964, which mandated equal rights to all citizens of the United States. The unique aspect of this legislation is its extensive coverage of individuals who have a disability that limits one or more of their major life activities. ADA legislation affects over 43 million people with mobility, visual, hearing, or other physical or mental disabilities that limit their access to opportunities and resources. Passage of this legislation was a lengthy process that evolved incrementally over three decades.

In 1961, the American National Standard Institute's (ANSI) "Specifications for Making Buildings and Facilities Accessible to and Usable by the Physically Handicapped" was implemented. The ANSI Standard was followed in 1969 by the Architectural Barriers Act, which required buildings to be accessible when federal funds were used for their construction. The Rehabilitation Act of 1973 (Section 504) required organizations receiving federal financial assistance to make their programs accessible to persons with disabilities. In 1984, the Uniform Federal Accessibility Standards (UFAS) were developed as the mandatory standards for all federal agencies. UFAS established the minimum accessibility standards for any organization required to adhere to Section 504 of the Rehabilitation Act of 1973. Until the ADA was passed, most state and local codes were based on the ANSI and UFAS. The development and implementation of codes and accessibility standards is a continual process at the state and local levels.

Despite early efforts to implement reforms, many services, opportunities, and built facilities remained closed to persons with disabilities. The limited success of pre-ADA standards and guidelines can be traced to the following factors.

- Many standards and codes were inexact and/or targeted selectively to particular disabilities.
- Frequently the uneven enforcement of standards was followed by an inability of officials to enforce corrective measures upon builders and owners.
- More importantly, there was a limited definition of disabilities related only to building codes.
- Access had not yet been defined as a civil right issue for individuals with disabilities in

The Americans with Disabilities Act of 1990 represents significant changes in philosophy from the numerous standards passed over the previous three decades. The ADA is no longer an option for local municipalities or state agencies; it is a law, not a building code, required to be uniformly applied throughout the country. The ADA addresses the total spectrum of access from employment, to communications and transportation, and finally building accessibility. Additionally, centralization of compliance enforcement within the federal government allows an individual to use the U.S. Department of Justice's civil rights enforcement structure. The consequences for any regulated institution or business that does not comply with the ADA can involve severe financial penalties. Indeed, the consequences of prosecution are consistent with the ADA legislation, because its primary goal is to empower disabled individuals. The underlying assumption of the ADA is that individuals with equal access to resources and opportunities can increase their ability to make social and economic contributions to society as well as to themselves.

ORGANIZATION OF THE AMERICANS WITH DISABILITIES ACT

The ADA itself is organized into five "titles," each with a different focus and intention:

Title I—Employment Section: This section addresses general definitions and effective dates relating to employment of a qualified individual with a disability. It also describes the main employer constraints of the ADA, especially as they relate to hiring practices.

Title II—Public Services and Public Transportation Section (public entities include any state or local government agency, department, etc.): Public entities must facilitate the participation of individuals with disabilities in all programs, services, or other activities. In simplest form, this title prohibits public entities from excluding an individual from any offered program or service just because that individual has a disability. This title covers the full spectrum of governmental agencies and facilities including agriculture, education, housing, justice, social services, and transportation, among others.

Title III—Public Accommodations and Services Section (private entities that own, lease, lease to, or operate a facility whose operations affect commerce and fall within at least one of the twelve specified categories): Public accommodations owned and operated by private entities may not discriminate in the providing of goods and services to individuals with disabilities. Title III requires the removal of all barriers in existing facilities that are "readily achievable." This term has been defined by the Department of Justice to mean "easily accomplished and able to be carried out without much difficulty or expense" (Federal Register, July 26, 1996, Sec. 36-304). New construction, including alterations to existing facilities, is required to comply with the standards for accessible design as delineated by the Americans with Disabilities Act Accessibility Guidelines (ADAAG). The goal is to provide all individuals the same level of use and enjoyment of all goods, services, privileges, and advantages provided by the private entity.

Title IV—Telecommunications Section: This section requires telephone companies to provide appropriate telecommunications relay equipment to the hearing-impaired and speech-impaired.

Title V—Miscellaneous Provisions Section: Among other miscellaneous items, this section states that federal, state, and local laws that are more stringent take precedence over the ADA.

The requirements and constraints addressed in Titles II and III are the main subjects of this book. Title II and Title III of the ADA do not contain any specific information delineating minimum standards that are to be used to judge the accessibility of facilities affected by these two titles. Rather, the ADAAG, the companion document included within the ADA, establishes the minimum physical criteria necessary to provide accessibility to facilities and sites.

Building designers, site designers, managers, and code enforcers have a direct time-based interest in the demands of these titles. Title II became effective on January 26, 1992. It required services, programs, and activities offered and operated by public entities, when viewed in their entirety, to be accessible and usable by individuals with disabilities. Any new construction, including building alterations, for which a building permit was issued after January 26, 1992 has to be accessible. The last structural changes required to provide access to existing Title II facilities were to be completed by January 26, 1995.

Title III has a similar set of effective dates, depending on the size of the private entities. For the largest, the date by which the removal of all barriers in existing facilities must be accomplished was January 26, 1992; for the smallest entities the date was January 26, 1993. Any new construction with first occupancy after January 26, 1993 must be compliant upon opening, including those for which the last application for a building permit was after January 26, 1992.

UNDERSTANDING THE AMERICANS WITH DISABILITIES ACT ACCESSIBILITY GUIDELINES (ADAAG)

Public entities and places of public accommodation must meet the requirements of Title II and Title III of the ADA. The detailed spatial, visual, textural, and aural requirements are presented in the Americans with Disabilities Act Accessibility Guidelines (ADAAG). The ADAAG—which continues to be modified, augmented, and refined—provides the specifics that are of interest to building designers, site designers, evaluators, and code enforcement personnel.

The ADAAG addresses both large-scale features, such as technical requirements for accessible routes in auditoriums, and small-scale elements that prescribe the location, size, and color contrast of permanent room identification signs. There are over 400 different elements and technical requirements addressed in the ADAAG regarding building and site accessibility. ADAAG is explained and presented in a ten-chapter document. The first three chapters introduce the basic purposes, definitions, and miscellaneous instructions for use of the document. Chapter 4, "Accessible Elements and Spaces: Scope and Technical Requirements," specifically addresses architectural elements (e.g., doors, protruding objects, alarms, signage) and general space-types or usage areas (e.g., toilet rooms, assembly areas). The final six chapters address specific space-types one by one (e.g., restaurants and cafeterias, libraries, health care facilities, and so on). Finally, an appendix contains "materials of advisory nature." The organizing principle in the ADAAG is primarily the individual elements used to define the specific requirements (from large- to small-scale) upon which a facility can be judged to be ADA compliant.

Limitations of the ADAAG Document for Design and Evaluation

The ADAAG is not organized to follow a logical process of moving through a site or space that exists either in reality or on paper. If one tries to review a single space-type, it is necessary to shift from one part of the ADAAG document to another in order to include all pertinent elements. For example, an auditorium is likely to include a ramp, signage, wheelchair spaces, stairs, and handrails. In the ADAAG, all of these compliance elements are addressed in different sections, with some aspects of them detailed in more than one. Such a review process can be very time-consuming and unwieldy, as well as prone to errors and omissions, especially for anyone not using the ADAAG on a regular basis. To further complicate the process, most exceptions and explanations concerning the technical requirements for equipment, such as audible alarms, are included in introductory chapters and are not referenced within the technical sections. This could easily cause a designer to overlook a legitimate exception to which the project client is entitled, or to incorrectly interpret a guideline within a particular context.

The design and evaluation of contemporary buildings and sites is an increasingly complex process. Add to this the problems of interpretation, inconsistency, and even internal conflict in accessibility standards for new construction and existing facilities, and the complexity multiplies. Even though ADAAG provides useful, specific information, occasionally the requirements are ambiguous or nonspecific. For example:

- The ADAAG does not make it clear whether a 10-ft long corridor less than 60 in. wide requires the same wheelchair passing space required in a corridor over 200 ft long. The ADAAG requirement is to provide passing space "at reasonable intervals not to exceed 200 feet." Does this mean a corridor of 190 ft does not need a passing space?

- The ADAAG requires an 80-in. minimum vertical clearance for any point along an accessible route, yet almost all door stops and thresholds reduce the actual vertical clearance of a door opening by some fraction of an inch. Is this a noncompliant item, or an acceptable construction tolerance? If it is a violation of the standard it will render the vast majority of existing doors and those currently being manufactured for new construction as noncompliant.

Experienced users of the ADAAG will find many other unavoidable anomalies of these types. Each situation must be carefully evaluated case by case. (The Department of Justice and the Transportation Access Board are available for interpretation of ADAAG—please see App. A for resources, phone numbers, and internet addresses.)

Given the complexity created by the many possible space-type and accessibility relationships within a project, it seems inevitable that conflicts will arise between requirements for the different elements regulated by ADAAG. The ADAAG makes allowances for conflicting goals within some projects by allowing for certain degrees of freedom. For example, buildings with historic significance are granted exemption from some guidelines in order to preserve historically significant features of buildings and sites.

Conflicts and Misconceptions

Sometimes ambiguous technical requirements within ADAAG may solve an accessibility problem for persons with one type of disability while creating yet another problem for other users. For example, retrofitting stairs and ramps with ADAAG compliant railings may make the stairs or ramp more usable for persons with mobility impairment, but the new railings may protrude into an accessible route. This protruding railing could be dangerous for persons with vision impairment. In another example, an apparently "compliant" ramp edge protection may channel storm water down an accessible ramp and onto landings. Fast-running rainwater may unintentionally cause a slippery surface and pooling of water at edge protectors. This situation could be dangerous for disabled and nondisabled persons alike. It is critical to maintain an awareness of these potential conflicts throughout the design process.

Similar to codes or standards, the ADAAG, a guideline, is about establishing minimum requirements. This means that the Americans with Disabilities Act Accessibility Guidelines does not cover all possibilities and situations. For example, ADAAG's list describing where detectable warnings and edge protections are mandatory does not specifically mention many common hazardous situations, such as an unprotected vertical drop-off along the edge of a sidewalk. A vertical change of even 2 inches may be a hazard to chair, walker, or cane users.

Ramps are an example of how common misconceptions based on other codes or standards, or an incomplete understanding of the ADAAG, may affect function, aesthetics, and even compliance. According to the ADAAG, a fully compliant ramp (complete with railings, level landings, etc.) is needed whenever the running slope is 1:20 or greater (except curb ramps). This single technical requirement may significantly impact design of circulation spaces, site planning, and costs. The familiar ramp running slope of 8.33 percent or 1:12 may be neither compliant nor the maximum allowed. According to ADAAG, 1:12 is the maximum slope allowable (in most cases), but ADAAG also clearly directs that if the slope is 1:20 or greater, a ramp must be used, and its slope should be *as slight as possible.* This implies that compliant ramp design should not automatically assume the running slope to be 1:12. It also sensitizes one to the increased length of ramps and the increase in number if ramps were installed each and every time the running slope exceeds 1:20. This is especially true for exterior routes. However, the ADAAG allows some exceptions, and some ramps may exceed 1:12. For example, if the structure is historic, it may fall under ADAAG exceptions for historic preservation, thus potentially allowing some flexibility in ramp and certain other requirements. As these types of problems are brought to light, the ADAAG will continue to evolve. In the suggested revisions currently under review by the Access Board, some leniency is being considered for ramps incorporated into sidewalks (pedestrian circulation along a vehicular way)—no handrails would be required for sidewalks that also function as a ramp.

Changes in the ADAAG

Some technical requirements for specific architectural elements (windows, opening force of exterior doors), and several general space-types (judicial, detention centers, and wilderness areas) were not completed in time for publication in the July 26, 1991, Federal Register. They are "reserved" until final decisions are made at a later date. Specifications for the design and use of detectable warnings were published in the original ADAAG, but, in 1994, they were suspended (in most situations) until July 26, 1996. These changes illustrate the ongoing reevaluation of specific issues already published, and suggest more changes yet to come.

In this book typical requirements related to a particular space-type are presented together with an overview section for each space that will alert the reviewer to potential problem areas and relevant exceptions. Atypical requirements are organized so they can be easily found. Beginning reviewers, as well as experts, will find the self-prompting method convenient and useful. Chapter 2 explains how the "Space-type Review Guides" were developed and Chap. 3 explains how to use them.

2

Development of the Space-type Review Guides and the Master Guidelines

The ADAAG is organized primarily as elements found within a building or site, such as doors, signs, alarms, ramps, parking, and so on. However, most building-related professionals design and review buildings as a series of spaces, not as categories of elements. The review process presented here explicitly reformats the ADAAG requirements, first by identifying the space usage, and second by selecting those typical elements within each space-type.

Additionally, since most buildings and sites are comprised of a series of related spaces, this ADAAG Guide is organized in two somewhat different formats: "Space-type Review Guides" and the "Master Guidelines." The primary organizational element is the "Space-type Review Guide." There are 26 occupancy-based space-types including assembly areas, business and mercantile, toilet rooms, laboratories, corridors, cafeterias, parking lots, transportation facilities, and so on. Chapter 3 contains all these "Space-type Review Guides." The secondary organizational element is the "Master Guidelines," an alphabetical listing of the more than 400 ADAAG requirements, including both elements and space-type designations, reformatted into simple direct questions. The "Master Guidelines" are located in App. C.

Each "Space-type Review Guide" is composed of a unique selection of pertinent compliance questions from the "Master Guidelines." These compliance questions lead the user through a self-prompting process, to address the ADAAG requirements generally found in that space-type. The narrow focus of each "Space-type Review Guide" removes the task of working through all possible noncompliant elements in the ADAAG and reduces the total number of possible issues for a given space. Thus, the design approach and review process becomes manageable. Additionally, the number of inadvertent compliance misses is reduced for any space undergoing review. Whenever an unusual element is included within a space-type—such as a sink in an office—then the "Master Guidelines" (App. C) are available with the alphabetical listing of more than 400 direct questions to facilitate review of an "out of context" element.

Chapter 3 includes the review process for the ADAAG items most likely to appear in the schematic phase of the design process or on contract document plan drawings. Chapter 4 explains how to use this system to write specifications and schedules. Chapter 4 may also be used to evaluate ADAAG compliance in detail drawings.

ADAAG REVIEW: WHEN TO USE IT

Individual design offices, building officials, or facilities managers have different procedures for reviewing both design documents and existing facilities. We have made every effort to make the ADAAG review guides accommodate a variety of styles, procedures, and new situations since accessibility must be addressed at different levels of detail in all phases of the design process. The review procedure described in this book will occur at different points in the building or site design process. For example, the toilet room layout, at a schematic design stage, may involve accessible routes, clear floor space, and basic fixture locations. The details for grab bars and dispensers for this space will be resolved during later design development and construction document stages. The construction document review often includes ADAAG compliance items in plans of varying scale, from site plans to detailed enlargements of particular areas. Other items are drawn in section or elevation, and a significant number appear only in schedules or specifications. By providing both the "Space-type Review Guides" and the "Master Guidelines," we have enhanced the flexibility of the system.

NONCOMPLIANT ITEMS: THE CODES

The questions included in the "Space-type Review Guides" faithfully cover all the detailed accessibility requirements of the original ADAAG document. Each question contains the specific, related ADAAG reference number (e.g., 4.13.6) and, where appropriate, an associated ADAAG graphic [e.g., Fig. 25 (a-f)]. A complete set of separate ADAAG graphics is included in App. D. The "Master Guidelines" found in App. C are organized either by element or space usage types that have been reformatted from the ADAAG document. Beginning with "Accessible Routes (AR)" and proceeding through "Water Closets (WC)," all categories of entries are listed alphabetically.

We created a coding scheme for the ADAAG questions in the "Master Guidelines" to facilitate recording noncompliant elements. Individual compliance questions are designated by a four-character code. The two beginning characters of the code indicate the element type; "DF" is an abbreviation for drinking fountain requirements, "BR" for bathrooms and elements associated with that space type, and so on. These abbreviations are followed by a two-digit number indicating the specific element or requirement within the guideline question. The following two examples have all the elements included in the specific guidelines. In the first example, "Drinking Fountains: clearances," the original ADAAG criteria are stated first, followed by the reformatted coded question, an ADAAG "Note," and the "Author's Interpretation," which we have included to help clarify the different issues involved. The second example, "(EX) Exits and Areas of Rescue Assistance," includes not only the reformatted coded question but also the pertinent "Definitions," "Exceptions," and "Allowances" that have been collected from different locations within the ADAAG.

Example 1

Drinking Fountains: clearances

4.15.5 Clearances (Original ADAAG)
Wall- and post-mounted cantilevered units shall have a clear knee space between the bottom of the apron and the floor or ground at least 27 in. high, 30 in. wide, and 17 to 19 in. deep [see ADAAG Fig. 27(a) and (b)].

DF-05 Does the knee clearance space for wall- and post-mounted cantilevered accessible drinking fountains meet required criteria? (4.15.5; Fig. 27)

- Height: at least 27 in. high from the floor to the apron bottom and maintaining that height for at least 8 in. under the equipment.
- Width: at least 30 in. wide.
- Depth: between 17 in. and 19 in. deep.

NOTE:

- Wall-mounted fountains with leading edges between 27 and 80 in. are protruding objects if they project more than 4 in. into the accessible route. A leading edge at 27 in. or below can project any amount as long as it does not restrict the required clear width of the route. (4.4.1)

AUTHOR'S INTERPRETATION:

- If a water fountain is going to protrude more than 4 in. into an accessible route, then it must be mounted at exactly 27 in. in order to comply with required knee clearances and not be considered a protruding object.

Example 2

(EX) Exits and Areas of Rescue Assistance (4.3.11)

DEFINITIONS:

- *Area of Rescue Assistance:* An area with direct access to an exit where people who are unable to use stairs may remain temporarily in safety to await further instructions or assistance during emergency evacuation.
- *Means of Egress:* A continuous and unobstructed way of exit travel from any point in a building or facility to a public way. A means of egress comprises vertical and horizontal travel and may include intervening room spaces, doorways, hallways, corridors, passageways, balconies, ramps, stairs, enclosures, lobbies, horizontal exits, courts and yards. An accessible means of egress is one that complies with these guidelines and does not include stairs, steps, or escalators. Areas of rescue assis-

tance or evacuation elevators may be included as part of accessible means of egress.

EXCEPTIONS:

- *New Construction:* Areas of rescue assistance are not required in buildings or facilities having a supervised automatic sprinkler system. [4.1.3(9)]
- *Alterations:* Alterations are not required to provide an area of rescue assistance. [4.1.6(1)(g)]

ALLOWANCES:

- *New Construction:* A horizontal exit can be used as an area of rescue assistance when the exit is designed in accordance with the local building code. [4.1.3(9)]

Exits: number required

EX-01 Does each occupiable level of a building or facility that is required to be accessible have accessible means of egress equal to the number of exits required by local building/life safety regulations? [4.1.3(9)]

- Where a required exit is not accessible, areas of rescue assistance shall be provided equal to the number of inaccessible required exits. [4.1.3(9)]

The direct question following each code acts as a prompt to the reader in the evaluation of each specific element. This short code attached to the question makes the recording system simple and convenient, whether one is redlining drawings or editing specification drafts or schedules.

Each specific space-type ("Offices," "Restaurants and Cafeterias," "Health Care Facilities," and so on) has its own unique list of compliance questions referred to as "Comprehensive Criteria." The "Comprehensive Criteria" include the questions and any "Exceptions," "Notes," "Allowances," or "Author's Interpretation," as illustrated in the examples above.

A brief list of each item from the "Comprehensive Criteria" is referred to as the "Checklist." It includes the alpha-numeric codes and a very brief description for each question in the "Comprehensive Criteria." This "Checklist" provides an overview of the typical accessibility items to be considered within a specific space, and is a convenient format for someone experienced with the review process who does not need to read the full question and associated notes. A complete explanation of all the parts of the "Space-type Review Guide" is included in Chap. 3.

NONCOMPLIANCE RECORDING

When conducting a review of any type, we suggest that the reviewer first select an appropriate method for recording and keeping records of the ADAAG noncompliances, space by space. We have found that the following alternatives work to cover a variety of situations:

- The most direct system is *redlining*. By recording the codes of the noncompliances directly onto the documents specific locations, possible ambiguities, and any other questions can be easily addressed. This method can be enhanced by making detailed notations along with the code to ensure that the appropriate issues are addressed as they develop throughout the design process. A sample of annotated design development drawings is shown in Fig. 2-1.

- The second alternative is more comprehensive. It involves establishing a set of *recording sheets,* apart from the construction documents, that are used to explicitly record each noncompliance. A recording system separate from the construction documents will also facilitate the development of a computerized database using the recording sheets for input data. Appendix B includes blank copies of five different recording sheets that the authors have developed. In addition to the two illustrated here in Figs. 2-2 and 2-3, there is one sheet that includes all the compliance codes, one specifically for exterior spaces, and one for the overall building and site questions. You may want to make copies of the sheets or use them as a starting point for developing a more individualized system. Figures 2-2 and 2-3 are completed sample "Toilet Room Recording Sheets" for the previously redlined example in Fig. 2-1.

- Figure 2-2 illustrates a scheme for recording noncompliances by code, along with making pertinent notations. We have found this scheme to be very flexible in terms of options and tracking of spaces and their development over time.

- Figure 2-3 suggests a more rigorous recording scheme to track individual spaces. The authors used a modification of this system in a research project for the State of Florida involving the survey of more than 100,000 rooms and over 40,000,000 square feet of space. There

are four types of recording sheets developed around the different general categories of the "Space-type Review Guides." The first is for use with exterior routes and spaces. The second, illustrated in Fig. 2-3, is for interior spaces excluding lodging and transportation facilities. These two space-types are included in the third recording sheet, "All Spaces." The final recording sheet is for the overall building and site issues.

Each recording sheet lists every potential ADAAG noncompliance code within that group, with a space for entering the number of noncompliances adjacent to each code. Since a separate recording sheet is filled out for each space, no matter which atypical element might be found in a space, there is a place to record that noncompliance. The blank space on the recording sheets may be used to locate noncompliant items as well as detail sketches or miscellaneous notes. When all the interior space sheets are completed, the "Building and Site Recording Sheet" should be filled out for the building as a whole, since some compliance items refer to building-wide issues. Recording sheets for the exterior routes and activity areas, parking lots, and other similar exterior areas associated with the building complete the facility review package.

When all data have been entered, a database of project noncompliances can be produced. With the data compiled and tabulated, the document becomes a guide for the coordination of design alterations. Because the database is comprehensive, it may be used to guide a final project review of construction documents. It could also be used in

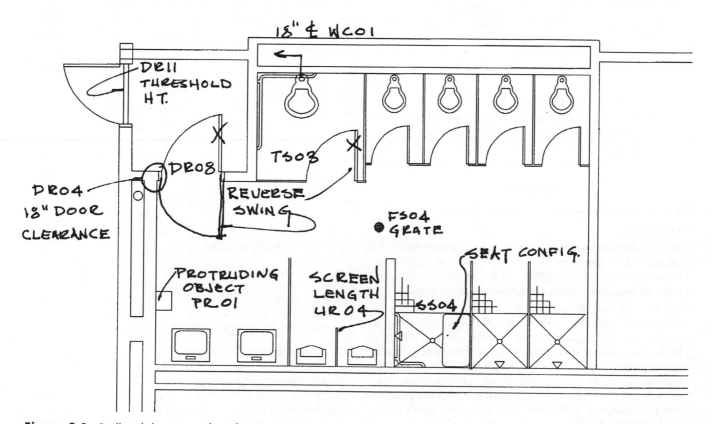

Figure 2-1. Redlined drawing with codes.

ADAAG Recording Sheet

ROOM/SPACE	CODE	REMARKS	COST
01-1995 **JOB NUMBER**	*ACME ELECTRONICS* **PROJECT NAME**		*6/15/95* **DATE**	*Xw/* **REVIEWER**
TOILET #2 SHEET A·4	DR11 DR08 DR04 PR01 TS03 FS04 SS04 WC01 UR04	THRESHOLD TOO HIGH REVERSE 2ND DOOR MOVE DOOR TO PROVIDE 18" CLEAR USE RECESSED P.T HOLDER SWING TOILET DOOR OUT CHECK GRATE OPENING SIZE SHOWER SEAT CONFIG. IS WRONG WATER CLOSET TO BE 18" ₵ to WALL URINAL SCREEN ONLY TO FRONT OF URINAL	

Figure 2-2. General coding sheet.

ADAAG Recording Sheet

Interior Spaces (excluding Lodging and Transportation Facilities)

PROJECT NAME	ACME ELECTRONICS	DATE 4/15/95	REVIEWER *(signature)*

JOB NUMBER 01-1995	ROOM NUMBER-USE TOILET 216	FLOOR 2	SHEET 22 OF 36

NOTES

AA 01	AR 09	BR 16	DL 05	EL 20	HR 05	PL 01	RP 09	SR 01	TL 10
AA 02	AR 10	BR 17	DL 06	EL 21	HR 06	PL 02	RP 10	SR 02	TL 11
AA 03	AR 11	BR 18	DL 07	EL 22	HR 07	PL 03	RP 11	SR 03	TL 12
AA 04	AR 12	BR 19	DL 08	EL 23	HR 08	PL 04	RP 12	SR 04	TL 13
AA 05	AR 13	BR 20	DL 09	EL 24	HR 09	PL 05	RP 13	SR 05	TL 14
AA 06	AR 14		DL 10	EL 25	HR 10	PL 06	RP 14		TL 15
AA 07		BT 01		EL 26		PL 07	RP 15	SS 01	TL 16
AA 08	AT 01	BT 02	DR 01	EL 27	LB 01	PL 08	RP 16	SS 02	TL 17
AA 09	AT 02	BT 03	DR 02	EL 28	LB 02	PL 09	RP 17	SS 03	TL 18
AA 10	AT 03	BT 04	DR 03	EL 29	LB 03			SS 04 ✓	TL 19
AA 11	AT 04	BT 05	DR 04 ✓	EL 30	LB 04	PR 01 ✓	SA 01	SS 05	TL 20
AA 12	AT 05	BT 06	DR 05	EL 31	LB 05	PR 02	SA 02	SS 06	TL 21
AA 13	AT 06	BT 07	DR 06		LB 06	PR 03	SA 03	SS 07	
AA 14		BT 08	DR 07	EN 01	LB 07	PR 04	SA 04	SS 08	TS 01
AA 15	BM 01		DR 08 ✓	EN 02		PR 05	SA 05	SS 09	TS 02
AA 16	BM 02	CT 01	DR 09	EN 03	LV 01			SS 10	TS 03 ✓
	BM 03	CT 02	DR 10	EN 04	LV 02	RC 01	SE 01		TS 04
AL 01	BM 04	CT 03	DR 11 ✓	EN 05	LV 03	RC 02	SE 02	ST 01	TS 05
AL 02	BM 05	CT 04		EN 06	LV 04	RC 03	SE 03	ST 02	TS 06
AL 03	BM 06	CT 05	EL 01	EN 07	LV 05	RC 04	SE 04	ST 03	TS 07
AL 04	BM 07	CT 06	EL 02		LV 06	RC 05		ST 04	TS 08
AL 05	BM 08	CT 07	EL 03	EX 01	LV 07	RC 06	SG 01	ST 05	TS 09
AL 06			EL 04	EX 02	LV 08	RC 07	SG 02	ST 06	TS 10
AL 07	BR 01	DF 01	EL 05	EX 03	LV 09	RC 08	SG 03	ST 07	TS 11
AL 08	BR 02	DF 02	EL 06	EX 04		RC 09	SG 04	ST 08	
AL 09	BR 03	DF 03	EL 07	EX 05	MD 01	RC 10	SG 05	ST 09	UR 01
AL 10	BR 04	DF 04	EL 08	EX 06	MD 02	RC 11	SG 06	ST 10	UR 02
AL 11	BR 05	DF 05	EL 09	EX 07	MD 03	RC 12	SG 07	ST 11	UR 03
AL 12	BR 06	DF 06	EL 10		MD 04	RC 13	SG 08		UR 04 ✓
	BR 07	DF 07	EL 11	FS 01	MD 05		SG 09	TL 01	UR 05
AR 01	BR 08	DF 08	EL 12	FS 02	MD 06	RP 01	SG 10	TL 02	
AR 02	BR 09	DF 09	EL 13	FS 03	MD 07	RP 02	SG 11	TL 03	WC 01 ✓
AR 03	BR 10	DF 10	EL 14	FS 04 ✓	MD 08	RP 03	SG 12	TL 04	WC 02
AR 04	BR 11		EL 15		MD 09	RP 04	SG 13	TL 05	WC 03
AR 05	BR 12	DL 01	EL 16	HR 01	MD 10	RP 05	SG 14	TL 06	WC 04
AR 06	BR 13	DL 02	EL 17	HR 02	MD 11	RP 06		TL 07	WC 05
AR 07	BR 14	DL 03	EL 18	HR 03		RP 07		TL 08	WC 06
AR 08	BR 15	DL 04	EL 19	HR 04		RP 08		TL 09	WC 07

Figure 2-3. Comprehensive recording sheet—interior spaces.

a design project that includes existing buildings slated to be rehabilitated or altered. For alteration projects, a facilities management database may be appropriate. These more comprehensive recording sheets also may be appropriate for use in the accessibility survey of existing buildings, for inventory, and for assessment.

COMPLIANCE SURVEYS

In addition to serving as a design guide for new construction and alterations, the "Space-type Review Guides" in this book may be used for surveying existing buildings. The "Comprehensive Criteria" and "Checklist" described earlier provide a self-prompting, survey-efficient format for conducting a compliance survey of any facility. The comprehensive criteria for each space-type are arranged in a manner that allows the surveyor to evaluate elements when encountered upon entering and moving through spaces. Such an assessment survey can provide a client with an accurate description of the ADAAG noncompliances within a given facility and site. While the effective dates for this type of survey for both public and private entities have passed, many more surveys have yet to be completed. The explicit, comprehensive nature of the more detailed "Coding Sheet," used in conjunction with the comprehensive criteria for each space, provide complete tools for such surveys. The system also may be used as part of a detailed preliminary analysis, for finding the noncompliances in historic structures or other existing facilities as a part of the process of determining how to attain legal accessibility.

While the primary use of this book in professional offices is directed toward the review and survey of designs and space for compliance with the ADAAG, this format has proven to be an excellent teaching tool for students in the design disciplines. Most design studio projects address specific function types (restaurants, health care facilities, offices, hotels, homeless shelters, etc.). It can be over-whelming to introduce students or educators to the entirety of a document such as the ADA Accessibility Guidelines. It is far better to have the guidelines organized by space-type in manageable segments. Educators and students will find it more efficient to address the information specific to their project focus, and in the process gradually gain an understanding of the ADAAG.

FINAL NOTES AND REMINDERS

The process and techniques presented in this book are advisory only, even though the authors have made every attempt at accuracy. The system presented here has been used for a significant number of design review and building surveys and has proven to be an effective and efficient resource. However, there is no intention that the specific language used or techniques presented have any legal standing. The users of the methods and techniques presented here should consult with the Access Board, the Department of Justice, or an attorney familiar with the requirements of the ADA. They should also familiarize themselves with the variety of state and local codes that may preempt the ADAAG in their locales. For example, the state of Florida has adopted the ADAAG into its accessibility code, but has made certain requirements more stringent. These changes are as broad as the removal of the exemption for religious organizations and as detailed as requiring an accessible lavatory within the accessible toilet stall.

This book is written and intended to be used along with the *ADA Accessibility Guidelines for Buildings and Facilities (ADAAG),* as published in the Federal Register, Vol. 56, No. 144, July 26, 1991 which, in conjunction with the ADA, are the legal documents.

To address the variety of review procedures and information types, "Space-type Review Guides" for building and site design review, and "Specifications, Schedules, and Details" are presented in the next two chapters.

3

Space-type Review Guides

INTRODUCTION

Using the Review Guides

The twenty-six "Space-type Review Guides" presented in this chapter are the engine that drives this *ADAAG Guide.* "Space-type Review Guides" are organized within the following five broad categories:

- Exterior Spaces
- Interior Spaces
- Transient Lodging
- Transportation
- Site and Building Summary

Each category has a general "Overview" of definitions, anomalies of the ADAAG, and so on. Within these categories, each "Space-type Review Guide" is divided into five parts—"Introduction," "Preliminary Design Overview," "Plan Drawing," "Checklist," and "Comprehensive Criteria" (please see discussion and illustrations below). Each of these parts presents compliance information for designers and reviewers to use at different phases during concept formation, schematic design, and construction document stages of the design process. The "Introduction," "Preliminary Design Overview," and "Plan Drawing" contain general planning criteria and may be most useful at the concept and schematic stages of design. The "Checklist" and "Comprehensive Criteria" contain all the ADAAG requirements that must be addressed during the construction document phase. Descriptions and illustrations of the parts of the review guides follow:

- *Introduction:* Although ADAAG elements, like doors, floor surfaces, and controls are common to many space-types, a unique combination of ADAAG compliance items is necessary for each different space. Each "Space-type Review Guide" has a brief introduction that describes design issues and accessibility concerns specific to that space-type. Also, in some cases, ADAAG has "Exceptions" and "Allowances" that a designer must understand at the outset of a project. Thus, the "Introduction" establishes the broad compliance issues important to the schematic design phase of a facility, especially when used in combination with the "Preliminary Design Overview" and the "Plan Drawings." The following quote is a segment taken from the toilet room introduction:

    ... "Toilet rooms often have a vestibule connected to a main corridor by two doors in a series. Adequate space for a person in a wheelchair to open these two doors and to pass into the lavatory and toilet stall areas must be provided" ...

- *Preliminary Design Overview:* This section provides a synopsis by ADAAG elements or issues of the compliance requirements unique to the space-type. These ADAAG elements are provided with a two-character code and listed alphabetically. This list works in tandem with the plan drawing. This is not a detailed discussion of all possible compliance items, but rather an abbreviated outline of special concerns. When the phrase "Typical requirements" appears after a code, then the ADAAG concerns are the same as for all space-types. The following quote is taken from the toilet room preliminary design overview and indicates the different format used to alert the designer to a typical ADAAG compliance requirement in toilet rooms:

    #### ... (DR) Doors
    - Two doors in a series must meet both clear space and door swing requirements (e.g., vestibules, toilet room entries, etc.) ...

- *Plan Drawing(s):* Most of the "Space-type Review Guides" are illustrated by an annotated plan drawing that is "prototypical." Labels indicate particular compliance issues encountered in the prototypical space. Examine these drawings carefully, because they illustrate particular concerns listed in the "Preliminary Design Overview." Note that these drawings may illustrate more elements than one might normally expect to find in such a space. In other words, we have exaggerated the quantity and combination of compliance issues in many drawings to provide rich examples. The drawing in Fig. 3-1 is a detail from the toilet room drawing illustrating the vestibule with two doors in a series. Note the abbreviated code and compliance issue.

- *Checklist:* An abbreviated, single-sheet version of the "Comprehensive Criteria" contains all the compliance criteria items. It provides the reviewer with an overview of the elements in a particular space-type. As you become familiar with the review process, this single-sheet "Checklist" can replace the more comprehensive multipage guide and greatly speed up the review process. This part of the guide may be used at the construction document stage of the design process or for conducting a survey of an existing facility by a reviewer familiar with ADAAG and this *Guide.* The example below is taken from the toilet room checklist and illustrates the abbreviated format used to present the compliance issues.

    #### ...DOORS
DR04	Doors: maneuvering clearances
DR05	Doors: handle type
DR06	Doors: opening force (interior only)

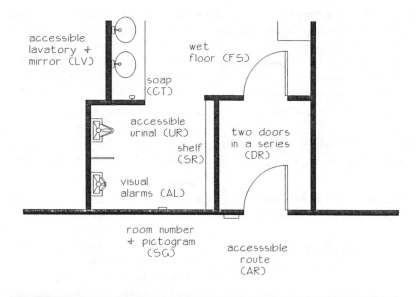

Figure 3-1. Two doors in a series.

DR07   Doors: closing speed
DR08   Doors: thresholds
DR09   Doors: clear width and height
DR10   Openings (no door): clear width/height
DR11   Doors in series: clear space between ...

- *Comprehensive Criteria:* This part of the guide is the full-blown version of the ADAAG compliance elements and requirements for the given space-type. It is written as a series of direct questions. The items are organized in a manner that begins at the entry point of a room or most important issues of a site, then moves through all elements in the space. For example, signage and doors are reviewed first in most rooms, then the accessible route into the space, then protruding objects, and finally more detailed items in the space. Don't be tempted to skip over the subheadings in the "Comprehensive Criteria," since even as you gain experience, it is possible to omit an element targeted by ADAAG for compliance. The "Comprehensive Criteria" are technically accurate and systematically organized to facilitate the review of construction drawings and specifications.

  - A number of explanatory items are included when necessary within the "Comprehensive Criteria" to explain items that are complex.

  - *Author's Interpretation:* Collectively the authors have a great deal of experience in surveying and reviewing design drawings. These notes represent our interpretation of complex situations. These are not legal opinions or references to rulings made by the Department of Justice.

  - *Notes:* We included them as points of clarification for you since they are also included in the ADAAG document.

  - *Exceptions* and *Allowances:* These items are compiled directly from the ADAAG and are included to clarify a particular issue or element.

The following segment is taken from the Comprehensive Criteria for Toilet Rooms.

...(DR) Doors (4.13)

NOTE:

- Included in this category are doors, revolving doors, turnstiles, and gates.

AUTHOR'S INTERPRETATION:

- It is suggested, for purposes of documentation and review, that a door be assigned to the space it swings into. Corridors are an exception to this rule and include only entry doors into the corridor or intermediate fire doors.

Doors: two doors in a series

DR-11 If there are two doors in a series, is the required clear space between the doors provided and do the doors swing in the appropriate direction? (4.13.7; Fig. 26)

- Clear space between the doors: not less than 48 in. plus the width of any door swinging into the space.

- Door swing: must swing in the same direction or away from the space between the doors ...

Organizing the Project Review

Now that we have introduced all of the pieces of the review system, we recommend a strategy for organizing an entire project review. First, look over the "Space-type Review Guides" to consider how they will work with your overall drawing and review process. We realize that the way you use the review guides may vary according to the phase of your project, because of style and preferences, or with specific office practices. Nonetheless, we suggest the following general steps:

Establish a Review Strategy for the Entire Project:

- Determine the procedures for recording noncompliance elements throughout the entire project.
- Build in flexibility so that details and changes along the way can be included in the final review.
- Choose one of the methods for recording elements previously discussed in Chap. 2, Figs. 2-1 through 2-3.
  — Redlining the drawings
  — Recording sheet for noncompliant elements by room
  — Systematic computerized database facility coding scheme

Establish Overall Organization of the Site and Building

- Preview the site plans associated with the building project.
- Establish the primary and secondary entrances and exits (50 percent of the entrances must be accessible).
- Identify exterior activity areas.
- Define the interior and exterior space interfaces (e.g., areas under roof but not enclosed).
- Organize a system for recording the noncompliant items, space by space, as reviewed. This will help assure that no interior or exterior spaces are inadvertently omitted.

Establish Exterior Accessible Routes

- Designate the "Exterior Accessible Route(s)." For a discussion of how to establish this exterior route, see the "Exterior Spaces" section in this chapter. Once the "Exterior Accessible Route" has been established, a detailed review of the exterior spaces may proceed using the "Exterior Space-type Review Guides."

Establish Interior Accessible Routes

- Establish the "Interior Accessible Routes" so that logical sections can be designated for dividing a large building into manageable parts.

- Identify and complete the review of the "Interior Accessible Routes" using the "Building Summary" and the "Space-type Review Guide," "Lobbies, Corridors, Interior Accessible Routes and Exits."
- Identify and review elevators, stairs, and ramps that must comply with the "Interior Accessible Routes."

Review the Exterior Spaces

- Exterior routes and activity spaces, parking lots, and passenger loading zones must be in compliance with the ADAAG: See the "Exterior Spaces" section.

Review Individual Spaces

- Begin a systematic review of all interior spaces. Group the individual spaces by space-type to increase accuracy, efficiency, and speed as you become familiar with specific compliance items and elements typical of a particular space-type.
- Review each of the spaces, even if it seems redundant, just in case there is some item unique to that space-type. For example, a design change as small as a door recess or the inclusion of a control device such as a thermostat shared by several spaces can result in a noncompliance in a room that is otherwise identical to other rooms.

Review Items Relating to the Entire Building

- Complete the "Site and Building Summary" after all facility spaces have been reviewed for compliance. Several of the entire building compliance items require information about all individual spaces in a building as well as spaces between related buildings. For example, the ADAAG requires that all publicly used spaces connect to an accessible route. This is easily determined after the spaces and the interior routes have been individually reviewed. See the "Site and Building Summary" section of this chapter.

EXTERIOR SPACES: OVERVIEW

This section provides four "Space-type Review Guides" to aid in determining compliance for exterior spaces, parking, and exterior routes:

- Exterior Accessible Routes
- Exterior Activity Areas
- Parking Lots and Passenger Loading Zones
- Parking Structures

The minimum ADAAG requirements for an accessible site include:

1. Connection(s) to adjacent sites, facilities, and circulation systems
2. Connections to all accessible elements and spaces within the site itself
3. Removal or compliant mitigation of all protruding objects
4. Compliant ground surfaces
5. If provided, compliant accessible parking and passenger loading
6. If provided, compliant toilet facilities
7. Compliant signage as needed

Additional elements (such as seating, drinking fountains, etc.) are not specifically mentioned in ADAAG's minimum requirements for an accessible site, but if provided they, too, must comply.

How much of any exterior use area and its routes must be accessible—and how to make them so—is not always clearly answered in ADAAG. Character of the site (as in a wilderness area or historic site), services and facilities offered, feasibility, and other issues must be considered. Compliance may be technically infeasible in some areas, such as mountainous terrain, valleys, or caves. Historic sites and structures may be allowed certain exceptions to maintain historic integrity. The ADA does not demand compliance if it would radically change the experience or use (as in wilderness trails, primitive camping, historic sites, or cultural landscapes); however, ADAAG gives no clear advice as to how such decisions are to be made. While it could be argued that a particular amusement park ride need not be accessible, a public swimming pool should be made as accessible as possible, even if ADAAG does not yet present specific guidelines for that particular element. For certain limited situations, alternative routes, access, and/or experience may be considered (audio-visuals, special entrances or routes not available or used by the general public, etc.). ADAAG does not explain procedures or criteria for evaluating acceptable options. Interpretations on these subjects vary and must be addressed on an individual basis. ADAAG suggests consultation with "interested persons" (state or local accessibility officials, individuals with disabilities, and organizations representing individuals with disabilities). Legal advice is wise in such cases. It is not within the scope of this book to determine which or how many facilities and elements must be accessible. Nor will this book attempt to describe how spaces and elements not specifically covered in ADAAG are to be made legally or functionally accessible.

Exterior spaces specifically covered in the Americans with Disabilities Act Accessibility Guidelines include parking, passenger loading zones, and accessible routes. However, the diversity of elements, functions, and relationships found in exterior sites complicates consistent and objective assessment. Many elements in exterior sites are designed for that specific project; these will require an understanding of the basic logic behind ADAAG's many technical requirements. The lack of exact ADAAG technical requirements for other common elements or spaces (swimming pools, grills, play equipment, etc.) further underscores the need for a creative understanding of the ADA Accessibility Guidelines and how the baseline criteria of those guidelines may be applied to varied situations (reach ranges, maneuvering clearances, clear width, knee clearances, etc.). If specific elements are not to be made accessible, access *to* them is recommended. For example, a chair user should minimally be able to accompany family or friends to play equipment in a park, participating socially if not physically.

Exterior Accessible Routes

Introduction. Use this review guide to evaluate routes through exterior spaces, particularly path and sidewalk systems. "Parking Lots and Passenger Loading Zones," "Bus Stops," and "Exterior Activity Areas" are separate review guides.

Exterior accessible routes must provide continuous and unobstructed circulation to and through all accessible areas and entrances within and immediately adjacent to the site. If an element is not accessible, then access to it should be considered to the maximum extent practicable. Evaluations of accessible routes must therefore address the use of accessible elements (particularly reach ranges and maneuvering clearances) as well as passage to them.

Accessible routes include elements that contribute directly to the accessibility of the route, such as signage, ramps, parking access aisles, and curb cuts. Additionally, accessible routes may include or connect to other elements within or along the route (i.e., storage, seating,

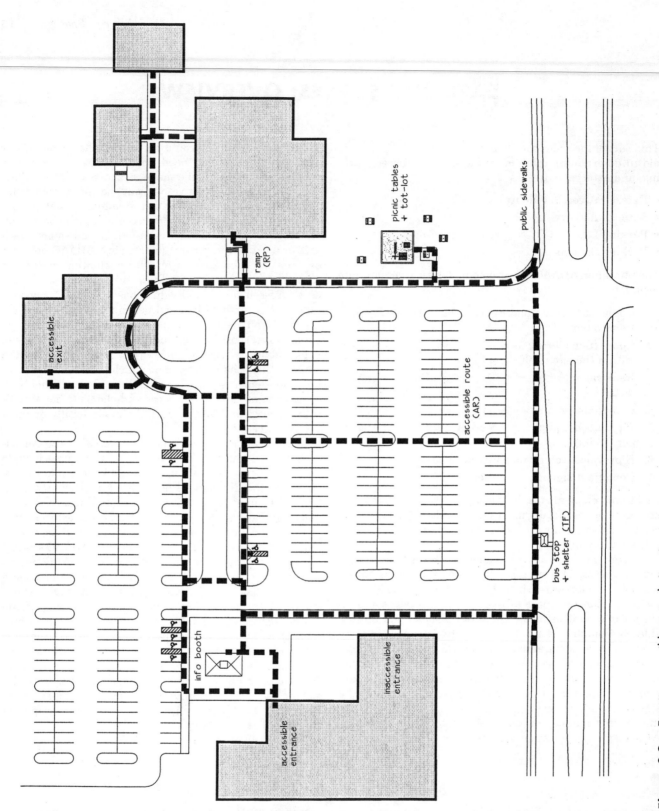

Figure 3-2. Exterior accessible route designation.

accessible exit

ramp (RP)

picnic tables + tot-lot

public sidewalks

accessible route (AR)

bus stop + shelter (IF)

info booth

accessible entrance

inaccessible entrance

telephones, vending machines, and drinking fountains). If provided, these must be compliant. Please refer to the "Master Guidelines" for any elements not included in this review guide.

Designation of the Exterior Accessible Route. Minimally, an exterior accessible route (or network of accessible routes):

- Must connect all accessible buildings, facilities, spaces, and elements within the site in a continuous and unobstructed manner
- Must connect to any public transportation stops, accessible parking, passenger loading zones, and public streets and sidewalks immediately adjacent to the site
- Should coincide with the route used by the general public as much as possible

The accessible route(s) should be identified prior to any compliance evaluations. This designation is critical to meeting compliance concerns if the entire site is not to maintain universal design or barrier-free standards. In setting minimum requirements for an accessible site, ADAAG refers to "at least one accessible route"; therefore, ADAAG may be interpreted as not mandating universal design or barrier-free access. Designation of accessible exterior routes within the larger network of site circulation is an alternative to barrier-free access which may or may not be viable—each project must be evaluated individually. While designation of a network of accessible routes within a larger circulation system may be the most feasible way to approach site accessibility, the ideal of barrier-free access should remain strong, particularly in new construction.

In designating the accessible route, consider functions and activities within the site, all structures or facilities served, and the immediate adjacencies. Begin by identifying the following:

- Spaces and facilities that must be linked (including but not limited to accessible parking, transportation stops, passenger loading zones, etc.)
- Accessible entrances to structures and use areas (accessible building entrances, picnic areas, swimming pools, tennis courts, etc.)
- Elements on or immediately adjacent to the accessible route (telephones, seating, ATM's, drinking fountains, informational and directional signage, etc.)
- Routes used by the general public
- Routes that are the most direct
- Routes that are most feasible to bring into compliance
- Possible conflicts and exceptions (such as historic preservation)

An understanding of building and site functions and their individual accessibility is vital. All entrances to a structure or activity area might not be accessible. Interior layout or functions may require multiple accessible entrances which must be included in the exterior accessible route.

The accessible route may be the simple connection of a few elements and spaces, or it may be a complex network involving numerous buildings, multiple accessible entries, multiple parking lots, off-site circulation systems, and various accessible facilities and use areas within the site. The ADAAG definition of accessible route demands access to "all accessible elements of a building or facility." *Facility* should be interpreted as site or activity area; it must not be seen as structure only.

Topography and other physical issues often limit or dictate where accessible routes may go. ADAAG recognizes that full compliance may be "structurally impracticable." Compliance to the fullest extent possible is then expected. ADAAG also recognizes exceptions for historic structures and facilities. However, "historic" is not synonomous with "old"—a federal, state, or local agency must have designated the site as "historic." Other design concerns, such as experience (including equal or equivalent experience for disabled users), ecological concerns, and general safety issues such as avoidance of vehicular/pedestrian conflicts may influence the actual configuration of the accessible route.

Common Exterior Accessible Route Issues. The accessible route is primarily concerned with providing access through the site, permitting use of accessible elements and spaces, and protecting users from hazards. Specific signage may also need to be compliant.

ADAAG 4.3.7 states "an accessible route with a running slope greater than 1:20 is a ramp and must comply." Note that it specifies *accessible* route, thus not *all* slopes greater than 1:20 must be ramps if they are not part of the designated accessible route. All such slopes on the accessible route must, however, be treated as ramps, with compliant handrails, length of run, landings, and so on. Nowhere on the accessible route may the cross slope exceed 1:50.

The criteria for curb cuts, ramps, and other elements presented in ADAAG are generally the minimums and maximums. Occasionally, a specific dimension will be mandated. In many cases, more generous dimensions should be considered. For example, a gentler slope and longer flared sides will make curb cuts more accessible and safer for all users. ADAAG clearly states that "the *least possible* slope shall be used for any ramp" (italics by the authors). Site constraints, the specific needs of the users, and other considerations must come into play.

Passing spaces are necessary, but their function may be met by intersections, gathering spaces, or changes in width of paving instead of clearly defined passing spaces. ADAAG gives only a maximum distance between such spaces, stating that they be placed at "reasonable" intervals. A reasonable interval between passing spaces in a public park in flat terrain may not be the same interval as that used in an adult congregate living facility complex or in path systems in the mountains. Consider site character, user, and activities/functions.

Noncompliant ground surfaces are a serious concern. Grates that work well for drainage are often noncompliant in design and/or location. Choice and placement of tree grates are of particular concern as many projects have traditionally treated them as part of the pedestrian circulation. Common paving materials (such as decking and individual pavers) may be noncompliant as installed. Others, like pavers on sand, may become noncompliant over time. Rustic or naturalistic paving materials such as mulch, crushed shells, gravel, or sand are not usually stable or firm; consider not only chair users but those who use a cane, crutches, or a walker. Well-compacted soil is a questionable choice that must consider specific soil type characteristics and the maintenance of the surface. Water flowing across or collecting on ground surfaces can make an otherwise compliant surface hazardous.

Access must be considered whenever elements or services are provided, even if they are not specifically covered in ADAAG. Site fixtures (such as trash receptacles, brochure racks, and parking meters) should be on the accessible route and installed in accordance with reach range and clear floor space criteria. Please refer to the "Master Guidelines" for detailed compliance criteria for specific elements. If an element is not mentioned in ADAAG, minimally provide clear floor space, maneuvering clearances, and reach ranges. Many elements not described in ADAAG (such as trash cans) can be made accessible with little extra effort.

Not all elements must be accessible. Sometimes only a portion must be compliant. Fixed seating, such as benches or picnic tables, must provide minimum compliant seating opportunities for chair users. Elements used by the public (telephones, ATM's, drinking fountains, etc.) must also provide a minumum number or percentage that are accessible. These generally should be dispersed throughout the site if more than one are compliant.

Many projects (such as scenic areas, historic or ecological preservation sites, and cultural landscapes) challenge designers to provide safe and compliant use while maintaining the character of the site. For example, scenic overlooks often do not provide protective railings at all, or they are kept to a minimum to avoid impacting either the view or the character of the site. Compliant slopes on nature trails may be infeasible in mountainous areas—is there some way of offering equivalent experience, interpretation, or education? Compliance that is compatible with visual and ecological concerns requires a creative understanding of the basic logic and intent of both ADA and ADAAG.

Hazards must be removed (the problem is fixed) or mitigated (the user is protected from the hazard). To add to the difficulty of identifying and dealing with hazards in exterior spaces, site hazards vary greatly from project type to project type, hazards may be difficult to forsee based solely upon the drawings at hand, and the severity of hazards may vary over time.

Vertical drop-offs and uneven or unstable surfaces along paths can be hazardous. In ADAAG, detectable warnings, edge protection, railings, and other means of mitigation are prescribed for a limited number of situations, but ADAAG by no means identifies all such hazardous situations. ADAAG specifically mandates detectable warnings for just a few hazardous situations (such as edges of reflecting pools and pedestrian/vehicular conflicts), but many other potentially hazardous situations exist. Drop-offs along pedestrian paths or use areas may be as dangerous as unprotected ramp edges or pools. Areas of particular concern include planting beds abutting paved areas; changes in grade immediately adjacent to and along paved areas; and severe changes in grade along trails, scenic overlooks, docks, and boardwalks. With the suspension of detectable warnings, ADAAG-compliant mitigation is not clear on this issue.

Protruding objects are common hazards along the exterior accessible route. These may be permanent fixed problems (signage, utility guy wires, etc.) or temporary (vegetation, moveable fixtures, the overhang of parked vehicles, etc.). Site sculptures, banners, decorative lighting fixtures, and other site elements should be scrutinized carefully for the actual design of the element and its placement within the design.

Parks, plazas, amphitheaters, and other exterior spaces may have both accessible and inaccessible entrances. If all entrances to a facility or building are not accessible, then compliant signage must direct users to the accessible entrances. This signage may be part of the building, or it may be somewhere along the accessible route, thus entry signage concerns may be part of site work and the exterior accessible route.

Not all site signage is required to be compliant; review ADAAG carefully to determine which signs must comply. Interpretation and other signage are an important aspect of many path systems. Criteria for exhibits, document display, and signage for historic sites are given in ADAAG 4.1.7 (e). These guidelines are useful in other situations as well.

PRELIMINARY DESIGN OVERVIEW

(AR) Accessible Routes

- Cross slope requirements easily are exceeded. Of particular concern are slopes in parking areas, passenger loading zones, aisles, and cross aisles in amphitheaters.
- Frequently overlooked maneuvering space problems include approaches to information displays, operable gates, bollards, and security devices.
- Parked vehicles or bikes must not reduce the clear width of the accessible route.
- Route surfaces must meet criteria for vertical changes in level. Problem areas may include transitions between materials, construction and expansion joints, wood decks, and individual pavers.
- At turns around obstructions, width of the accessible route may need to increase according to the size of the obstruction.

(CT) Controls and Operating Mechanisms

- Controls and operating mechanisms have clear floor space and reach range requirements. Frequently overlooked in this space-type are street crossing controls, trash receptacles, communication devices (intercoms, emergency phones, etc.).

(CR) Curb Ramps

- Frequently overlooked problems include transitions from ramp to street or gutter, traffic islands, and storm water accumulation.
- If a curb ramp is located so that pedestrians must walk across it, provide protection or flared sides.
- There are several acceptable options for the design and placement of curb ramps. Review ADAAG graphics to determine the best alternative for specific situations.

(DR) Doors

- Gates, openings in fences or walls, and other passageways must meet door criteria.

(DT) Detectable Warnings

- Detectable warnings are suspended for most space-types as of April 24, 1994 until July 26, 1996.

(SE) Fixed or Built-in Seating and Tables and/or Counters

- If fixed tables or counters are provided, a minimum of 5 percent of the total number but not fewer than one of either type must be accessible.
- An accessible route must lead to and through accessible seating at fixed tables or counters.

(FS) Floor and Ground Surfaces

- In most areas ground surfaces should be evaluated as if wet. Consider irrigation overspray onto paving, surface flow of stormwater, and spray from fountains.
- Vertical changes in levels along the accessible route can be an unforeseen barrier, e.g., transition between floor materials, construction and expansion joints, uneven planks in wood decks. Also of concern are raised objects in the path of travel (e.g., electrical and communication outlets, etc.)
- Grates located on the accessible route must meet accessibility requirements. This includes tree grates, lighting grates, and drainage grates.

(PR) Protruding Objects

- Common wall-mounted elements can be protruding objects, e.g., shelves and other storage devices, drinking fountains, public telephones, ATM's, signs, mail boxes, display cases, and lighting fixtures.
- Overhead clearances can be an unforeseen compliance problem, e.g., signs and banners, utility guy wires, open space under stairs, low ceilings, and roof overhangs (such as at concession stands, rest room facilities, and information booths).

(RP) Ramps

- Any slope along an accessible route greater than 1:20 (5 percent) is considered a ramp and must meet all ramp criteria.
- Handrail extensions are possible protruding objects, especially where the extensions intersect another accessible route.
- Required ramp and landing edge protection should be designed so that they do not collect storm water runoff or debris.
- Exterior ramps and their approaches must not allow water to accumulate on their surfaces.

(SG) Signage

- If all entrances to a parking lot, building, exterior activity area, or other facility are not accessible, the accessible entrance(s) must be identified by the I.S.A. symbol; inaccessible entrances must have signage indicating the accessible route to an accessible entrance. This signage may occur on or at the building or activity area entrance or along the exterior accessible route.
- Permanent directional and informational signage must meet accessibility criteria; letter height varies with mounting height of sign.
- Building directories, menus, and temporary signs are not required to comply.
- Displays, exhibits, and interpretive signage should be displayed so that they can be seen by a seated person.

(ST) Stairs

- Only stairs that connect levels not connected by an elevator or other accessible means of vertical access are required to comply.
- Exterior stairs and their approaches must not allow water to accumulate on their surfaces.
- Open risers are not permitted on accessible stairs.
- Handrail extensions are possible protruding objects, especially where the extensions intersect another accessible route.

ADAAG APPENDIX

The ADAAG Appendix includes additional advisory information pertinent to this space-type.

- A4.3: Accessible Route

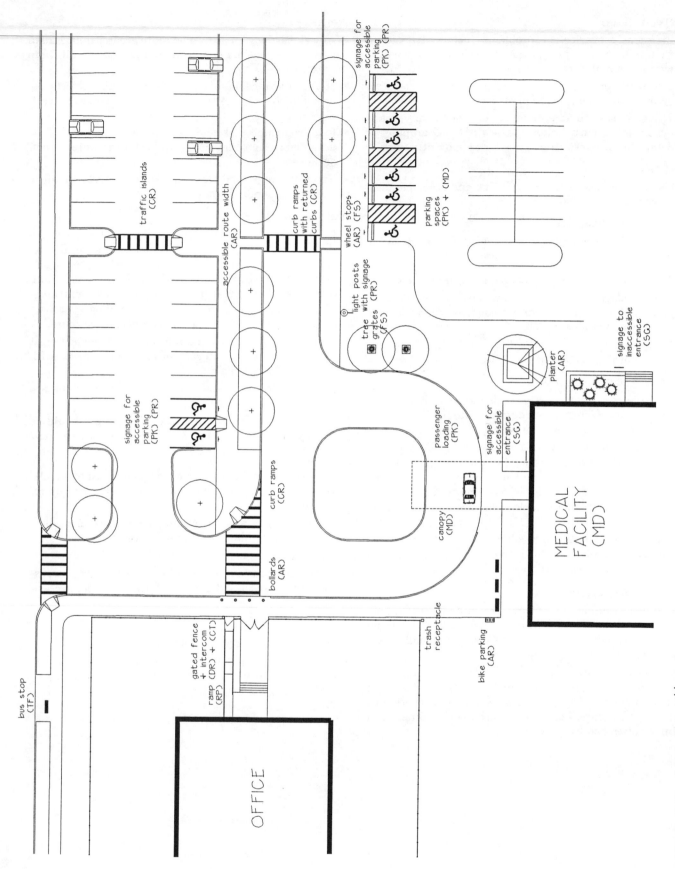

Figure 3-3. Exterior accessible route.

20

Exterior Accessible Route Checklist

ACCESSIBLE ROUTES

AR01	Bldg entry: from parking
AR02	Bldg entry: from public streets
AR03	Bldg entry: from public transit stops
AR04	Bldg entry: from passenger zone
AR05	Bldg entry: from other buildings
AR06	Bldg entry to accessible spaces/elements
AR07	Dwelling unit entry to int./ext. spaces
AR08	Route: clear width
AR09	Route width: U-turns
AR10	Route: passing space
AR11	Route: maneuvering clearances
AR12	Route: running slope
AR13	Route: cross slope
AR14	Route: changes of level

FLOOR AND GROUND SURFACES

FS01	Surface: firm, stable, and slip-resistant
FS02	Vertical changes in level
FS04	Floor gratings

PROTRUDING OBJECTS

PR01	Wall-mounted
PR02	Freestanding/suspended on posts/pylons
PR03	Clear route width maintained
PR04	Overhead clearance
PR05	Vertical clearance: cane detection barrier

CURB RAMPS

CR01	Accessible route: crossing at curb
CR02	Curb ramp: running slope
CR03	Curb ramp to walkway/road transition
CR04	Running slopes of adjoining surfaces
CR05	Curb ramp: width w/o flared sides
CR06	Curb ramp: surface stability
CR07	Curb ramp: required flared sides
CR08	Return curb cuts: nonwalking surfaces
CR09	Built-up curb ramps: criteria
CR10	Curb ramp: detectable warnings
CR11	Detectable warning: criteria
CR12	Curb ramp not blocked by parked vehicles
CR13	Curb ramp within marked crossings
CR14	Diag. curb ramp: edges and traffic flow
CR15	Diag. curb ramp: clear space in crosswalk
CR16	Diag. curb ramp w/flared sides: design
CR17	Raised traffic islands: acc. route options

RAMPS

RP01	Maximum running slopes and lengths
RP02	Maximum cross slope
RP03	Minimum clear width
RP04	Landings: location
RP05	Landings: size
RP06	Landings used to change direction
RP07	Handrails: when required
RP08	Handrails: switchbacks
RP09	Handrails: extensions past ramp
RP10	Handrails: clear space to wall
RP11	Handrails: mounting height
RP12	Handrails: continuous gripping surface
RP13	Handrails: rounded end or returned
RP14	Handrails: no rotation
RP15	Ramp edge protection
RP16	Floor surface stability
RP17	Water does not accumulate

STAIRS

ST01	Riser/tread: criteria
ST02	Stair nosing: criteria
ST03	Handrails: location and continuity
ST04	Handrails: extensions
ST05	Ext. handrail is not a protruding object
ST06	Handrails: clear space to wall
ST07	Handrails: mounting height
ST08	Handrails: gripping surface uninterrupted
ST09	Handrails: rounded ends or returned
ST10	Handrails: no rotation
ST11	Water does not accumulate

HANDRAILS

HR01	Handrails and grab bars: diameter
HR02	Handrails and grab bars: edge radius
HR04	Handrails in recess: criteria
HR05	Handrails and grab bars: no rotation
HR06	Handrails and grab bars: structural strength
HR07	Mounting devices: structural stength
HR10	Wall adjacent to handrail abrasion free

DETECTABLE WARNINGS

DW01	Pedestrian/vehicular conflict: warning
DW02	Reflecting pools: warning
DW03	Truncated dome: criteria

CONTROLS AND OPERATING MECHANISMS

CT01	Clear floor space
CT02	Reach ranges: elec./comm. systems
CT04	Reach ranges: other controls
CT05	Reach ranges: life safety devices
CT06	Controls: operation
CT07	Controls: exterior routes

SIGNAGE

SG08	Directional/informational signage: criteria
SG09	Suspended/projected signs: location

FIXED OR BUILT-IN SEATING AND TABLES

SE01	Fixed seating: number required
SE02	Wheelchairs: clear floor space at tables
SE03	Tables/counters: heights
SE04	Tables/counters: knee clearance criteria

See **DF, TL,** and other sections as needed.

EXTERIOR ACCESSIBLE ROUTE
COMPREHENSIVE CRITERIA

Any element not included in this review guide but necessary to complete the evaluation of the site should be selected from the "Master Guidelines." These may include passenger loading and drop-off zones, ATM's, storage, bus stops, drinking fountains, telephones, etc.

(AR) Accessible Routes (4.3)

NOTES:

- All walks, paths, decks, routes through plazas, skywalks, tunnels, and other spaces that are part of a designated accessible route shall comply with accessible requirements.

- Any slope on the accessible rate that is greater than 1:20 is required to meet all ramp criteria.

- The accessible route shall, to the maximum extent feasible, coincide with the route for the general public.

- In historic buildings, accessible routes from an accessible entrance shall be provided to all publicly used spaces on at least the level of the accessible entrance. Access shall be provided to all levels of a building or facility whenever practical. [4.1.7(3)(d)]

AUTHOR'S INTERPRETATION:

- An accessible route "generally coincides" with the route used by the public if:
  — It does not force the user to go out of the way
  — It is most like the route chosen by the general public
  — It is direct
  — It gives the same basic experience as the route preferred by the public

Accessible Routes: site

AR-01 If on-site parking is provided, does at least one accessible route within the boundaries of the site connect accessible parking spaces to the accessible building entrance? [4.1.2(1), 4.3.2(1)]

AR-02 Does at least one accessible route within the boundaries of the site connect public streets and sidewalks to the accessible building entrance? [4.1.2(1), 4.3.2(1)]

AR-03 If public transportation stops are available, does at least one accessible route within the boundaries of the site connect public transportation stops to the accessible building entrance? [4.1.2(1), 4.3.2(1)]

AR-04 If passenger loading zones are provided, does at least one accessible route within the boundaries of the site connect a passenger loading zone to the accessible building entrance? [4.1.2(1), 4.3.2(1)]

AR-05 Is there an accessible route connecting all accessible buildings, facilities, elements and spaces on the same site? [4.1.2(2), 4.3.2(2)]

Accessible Routes: interior

AR-06 Is the building entrance space connected by an accessible route to all accessible spaces, elements, and all accessible dwelling units within the building or facility? [4.3.2(3)]

Accessible Routes: dwelling units

AR-07 Does an accessible route connect at least one accessible entrance of each accessible dwelling unit with those exterior and interior spaces and facilities that serve the accessible unit? [4.3.2(4)]

Accessible Routes: width

AR-08 Is the minimum clear width along the accessible route adequate for continuous or point passage? (4.2.1, 4.3.3, Fig. 1, Fig. 8e, Fig. 24e)

- Continuous passage (greater than 24 in. long): at least a 36-in. clear width.

- Point passage (not more than 24 in. long): at least a 32-in. clear width.

AUTHOR'S INTERPRETATION:

- Noncompliance with this question generally relates to permanent elements that encroach on the accessible route. Large, heavy equipment that is not readily movable might be considered permanent. If the space is designed so that temporary elements (such as bikes in a bike rack or car bumpers) will consistently encroach, the situation might also be considered a permanent barrier.

AR-09 Is the minimum clear width along the accessible route adequate at a U-turn around an obstruction? (4.3.3, Fig. 7a–b)

- Obstruction 48 in. or greater: at least a 36-in. clear width around the obstruction.

- Obstruction less than 48 in.: at least a 42-in. clear width at each side with at least a 48-in. clear width in the turn.

Accessible Routes: passing space

AR-10 Does the accessible route provide at least 60 in. of clear width for two wheelchairs to pass and, if not, is the required passing space provided? (4.2.2, 4.3.4)

- A 60-in. × 60-in. passing space or "T" intersection should be provided at reasonable intervals not to exceed 200 ft.

AUTHOR'S INTERPRETATION:

- Accessible routes more than 5 ft long (e.g., routes in short hallways, aisles in laboratories, and work/storage areas) should have passing spaces provided. In exterior sites, the specific situation and users should suggest "reasonable" intervals.

DEFINITION:

- A *"T" intersection* is defined as the intersection of two corridors or walks, each at least 36 in. wide providing at least a 60-in. depth at the intersection. (Fig. 3b)

Accessible Routes: maneuvering clearances

AR-11 Is the minimum clear floor space for an unobstructed 180° wheelchair turning space or a "T"-shaped turning space provided? (4.2.3, Fig. 3a–b)

- 180° turning space: at least a 60-in. diameter.

- "T"-shaped turning space: at least 36-in. wide legs with a minimum length of 60 in.

Accessible Routes: slopes

AR-12 Is the running slope on the accessible route 1:20 or less? (4.3.7)

- Any slope on the accessible route that is greater than 1:20 is required to meet all ramp criteria.

AR-13 Is the cross slope on the accessible route 1:50 or less? (4.3.7)

Accessible Routes: changes in level

AR-14 Are changes in level greater than 1/2 in. accomplished by means of a curb ramp, ramp, elevator, or platform lift (as permitted in ADAAG 4.1.3 and 4.1.6)? (4.3.8)

(FS) Floor and Ground Surfaces (4.5)

Floor Surfaces: general

FS-01 Are the floor/ground surfaces on the accessible route stable, firm, and slip-resistant? (4.5.1)

AUTHOR'S INTERPRETATION:

- Exterior spaces, interior circulation, bathrooms, and other spaces where water can collect on the floor around an element (sinks, drinking fountains, hose bibbs, etc.) are reviewed as if wet.
- High gloss surfaces without significant textures that are regularly maintained with waxing (smooth tiles, waxed concrete, etc.) could be considered noncompliant.
- Accessible criteria are not specified for nonpermanent floor surfaces such as mats or rugs.

Floor Surfaces: changes in level

FS-02 Are vertical changes in level between 1/4 in. and 1/2 in. beveled with a slope of 1:2 or less? (4.5.2)

- Changes in level up to 1/4 in. may be vertical without edge treatment.
- Changes in level greater than 1/2 in. should be accomplished by means of a curb ramp, ramp, elevator, or platform lift (as permitted in ADAAG 4.1.3 and 4.1.6).

Floor Surfaces: gratings

FS-04 Do floor gratings in the path of travel comply with accessible criteria? (4.5.4, Fig. 8g–h)

- Opening size: no greater than 1/2 in. in one direction.
- Opening direction: the long dimension is perpendicular to the dominant direction of travel.

(PR) Protruding Objects (4.4)

Protruding Objects: general

PR-01 Do wall-mounted objects having leading edges between 27 in. and 80 in. high project less than 4 in. into walkways, corridors, aisles, or paths of travel? (4.4.1, Fig. 8a–e)

- Objects mounted with their leading edge at or below 27 in. can protrude any amount, as long as they do not reduce the required clear width of an accessible route.

AUTHOR'S INTERPRETATION:

- Protruding objects might include signage, ATM's, telephones, drinking fountains, shelving, counters, built-in equipment overhangs, or various dispensers.

PR-02 Do free-standing objects, suspended or mounted on posts or pylons with leading edges between 27 in. and 80 in. high, project less than 12 in. into the perpendicular route of travel? (4.4.1, Fig. 8a–e)

AUTHOR'S INTERPRETATION:

- These might include telephone enclosures, drinking fountains, or free-standing signage kiosks.

PR-03 Is the minimum clear route width or maneuvering space still maintained even with the projection of a protruding object? (4.4.1, Fig. 8a–e)

Protruding Objects: overhead clearance

PR-04 Is the minimum overhead clearance of 80 in. provided in accessible areas or along accessible routes? (4.4.2, Fig. 8a)

AUTHOR'S INTERPRETATION:

- Overhead objects that can reduce the required clearance might include structures, pipes, ducts, or light fixtures.

PR-05 Where the vertical clearance of a space adjoining the accessible route is less than 80 in. high, is a cane detection barrier less than 27 in. from the floor provided for blind or visually impaired persons? (4.4.2, Fig. 8c-1)

AUTHOR'S INTERPRETATION:

- This condition might be found under a stair, at a sloped ceiling space, or with guy wires from telephone poles along an exterior accessible route.

(CR) Curb Ramps (4.7)

Curb Ramps: location

CR-01 Is there a curb ramp wherever an accessible route crosses a curb? (4.7.1)

Curb Ramps: slopes

CR-02 Is the running slope of the curb ramp 1:12 or less? (4.7.2)

- On existing sites where space limitations prohibit the use of a slope of 1:12 or less, the following slopes can be considered. [4.1.6(3)(a)(i-ii)]
  —Between 1:10 and 1:12 for a maximum rise of 6 in.
  —Between 1:8 and 1:10 for a maximum rise of 3 in.
  —A slope steeper than 1:8 is not allowed.

CR-03 Is the transition from the curb ramp to the walkway and to the road or gutter flush and free of abrupt changes? (4.7.2)

CR-04 Are the running slopes of the road, gutter, or accessible route adjoining the ramp no greater than 1:20? (4.7.2, Fig. 11)

Curb Ramps: width

CR-05 Is the width of the curb ramp, not including the flared sides, at least 36 in.? (4.7.3)

Curb Ramps: surface

CR-06 Is the surface of the curb ramp stable, firm, and slip-resistant? (4.5.1, 4.7.4)

Curb Ramps: side flares

CR-07 If the curb ramp is located where pedestrians must walk across it or where it is not protected by handrails or guardrails, does it have flared sides? (4.7.5, Fig. 12a)

- Flared sides shall have a slope of 1:10 or less.
- If the space at the top of the ramp is less than 48 in. and wheelchair users must use the side flares for access, the flared sides shall have a slope of 1:12 or less.

CR-08 If return curb cuts are provided, are the sides flanked by non-walking surfaces that prevent pedestrian cross traffic? (4.7.5, Fig. 12b)

AUTHOR'S INTERPRETATION:

- "Nonwalking surfaces" such as plantings, raised planters, or raised curbs prevent pedestrian movement. Signage, impermanent objects such as newspaper boxes, and movable planters do not qualify.

Curb Ramps: built-up

CR-09 If built-up curb ramps are provided, are they located so that they do not project into vehicular traffic lanes or parking access aisles? (4.7.6, Fig. 13)

Curb Ramps: detectable warnings

NOTE:

- Requirements for detectable warnings (truncated domes) at curb ramps (4.7.7) have been suspended until July 26, 1996.

CR-10 Does the curb ramp have a detectable warning? (4.7.7)

- **Suspended until July 26, 1996.**

CR-11 Does the detectable warning consist of raised truncated domes and do they comply with the required criteria? (4.29.2)

- Diameter: nominal 0.9 in.
- Height: nominal 0.2 in.
- Spacing: nominal 2.35 in., center to center, offset every other row.
- Contrast: contrast visually with adjoining surface (light-on-dark or dark-on-light).
- The material used to provide contrast shall be an integral part of the walking surface. Detectable warnings used on interior surfaces shall differ from adjoining walking surfaces in resiliency or sound-on-cane contact.
- **Suspended until July 26, 1996.**

Curb Ramps: obstructions

CR-12 Are curb ramps located or protected to prevent obstruction by parked vehicles? (4.7.8)

Curb Ramps: location at marked crossings

CR-13 Are curb ramps at marked crossings wholly contained (excluding flared sides) within the marked crossing? See Fig. 15. (4.7.9)

Curb Ramps: diagonal or corner type

CR-14 If diagonal (or corner type) curb ramps have returned curbs or other well-defined edges, are these curbs or edges parallel to the direction of pedestrian flow? (4.7.10)

CR-15 Is there at least 48 in. of clear space within the crosswalk lines at the bottom of a diagonal curb ramp? (4.7.10, Fig. 15c–d)

CR-16 If the diagonal curb ramp has flared sides, is there at least a 24-in. segment of straight curb located on each side of the diagonal curb ramp within the crosswalk lines? (4.7.10, Fig. 15c)

Curb Ramps: islands

CR-17 Are raised islands in crossings cut through level with the street or are curb ramps provided on each side of the island with at least 48 in. of level area between the curb ramps? (4.7.11, Fig. 15a–b)

(RP) Ramps (4.8)

NOTE:

- Any slope on the accessible route that is greater than 1:20 is considered a ramp and shall comply with accessible requirements.

Ramps: slopes and rises

RP-01 Is the running slope for the ramp within required parameters? (4.8.2, Fig. 16)

- New construction: 1:12 slope or less with not more than a 30-in. rise for any run.
  - 1:12 slope: 30-ft run between landings.
  - 1:16 slope: 40-ft run between landings.
- On existing sites where space limitations prohibit the use of a slope of 1:12 or less, the following slopes can be considered. [4.1.6(3)(a)(i-ii)]
  - Between 1:10 and 1:12 for a maximum rise of 6 in.
  - Between 1:8 and 1:10 for a maximum rise of 3 in.
  - A slope steeper than 1:8 is not allowed.

EXCEPTION:

- In historic buildings, a ramp with a slope no greater than 1:6 for a run not to exceed 2 ft may be used as part of an accessible route to an entrance. [4.1.7(3)(a)]

RP-02 Is the cross slope of the ramp 1:50 or less? (4.8.6)

Ramps: clear width

RP-03 Is the clear width (between handrails) of the ramp at least 36 in.? (4.8.3)

Ramps: landings

RP-04 Is there a level landing at the top and bottom of each ramp and each ramp run? (4.8.4)

- If a doorway is located at a landing, then the area in front of the doorway must meet door maneuvering clearance requirements.

RP-05 Does each ramp landing meet required dimensions? [4.8.4(1-2)]

- Landing width: at least equal to the ramp width.
- Landing length: at least 60 in. long.

RP-06 Where the ramp changes direction, is there a landing of at least 60 in. × 60 in.? [4.8.4(3)]

Ramps: handrails

NOTE:

- Additional criteria for handrails can be found in Section "HR, Handrails."

RP-07 If the ramp rises more than 6 in. or is longer than 72 in., does it have a handrail on each side? (4.8.5)

- Handrails are not required on curb ramps or adjacent to seating in assembly areas.

RP-08 Is the handrail provided on both sides of ramp segments and is the inside rail on switchback or dogleg ramps continuous? [4.8.5(1), Fig. 19a–b]

RP-09 At the end of the ramp handrails, is there at least 12 in. of handrail parallel to the floor or ground surface, extending beyond the top and the bottom of the ramp segments? [4.8.5(2), Fig. 17]

RP-10 Is the clearance between the ramp handrail and the wall exactly 1½ in.? [4.8.5(3)]

- For recesses, see ADAAG Fig. 39.

RP-11 Are the tops of ramp handrails between 34 in. and 38 in. above ramp surfaces? [4.8.5(5)]

RP-12 Is the ramp handrail gripping surface continuous without obstructions or missing segments? [4.8.5(4)]

RP-13 Are the ends of ramp handrails rounded or returned smoothly to the floor, wall, or post? [4.8.5(6)]

RP-14 Are the ramp handrails fixed so that they do not rotate within their fittings? [4.8.5(7)]

Ramps: edge protection and floor surfaces

RP-15 If a ramp or landing has a drop-off, is it protected by an acceptable option? (4.8.7, Fig. 17)

- Acceptable options include: a wall, a minimum 12-in. horizontal floor extension beyond the railing, a minimum 2-in. curb, or a railing design that prevents people from falling or rolling off.

RP-16 Is the ramp floor surface stable, firm, and slip-resistant? (4.5.1)

RP-17 Are outdoor ramps and their approaches designed so that water does not accumulate on walking surfaces? (4.8.8)

(ST) Stairs (4.9)

NOTE:

- Only stairs that connect levels not connected by an elevator, ramp, or other accessible means of vertical access are required to comply. [4.1.3(4)]

- In new construction, this condition may occur in facilities subject to the elevator exemption [4.1.3(5)— Exception 1] or where mezzanines are exempt in restaurants. (5.4)

Stairs: risers, treads, and nosings

ST-01 Do the stair treads and risers meet the required criteria? (4.9.2, Fig. 18a)

- Uniformity: riser heights and tread widths should remain uniform in any one flight of stairs.

- Treads: not less than 11 in. measured from riser to riser.

- Risers: no open risers are permitted.

ST-02 Do the stair nosings meet the required criteria? See ADAAG Fig. 18 for clarification. (4.9.3)

- Risers: risers slope toward the nosing.

- Radius of the curvature: not more than 1/2-in. radius at the leading edge of the tread.

- Angle nosing: angled underside on nosing is not less than 60° from the horizontal; underside of nosing should not be abrupt.

- Nosing projection: not more than 1½ in.

Stairs: handrails

NOTE:

- Additional criteria for handrails can be found in Section "HR, Handrails"

ST-03 Is the handrail provided on both sides of the stair and is the inside rail on switchback or dogleg stairs continuous at the landing? [4.9.4(1), Fig. 19a-b]

- The outside handrail along the perimeter wall does not have to be continuous around the landing.

ST-04 At the end of the stair handrails, is there at least 12 in. of handrail parallel to the floor beyond the top riser and is there at least one tread width of sloping handrail plus at least 12 in. of horizontal handrail beyond the bottom riser? [4.9.4(2), Fig. 19c–d.]

- See ADAAG Fig. 19c–d for extension design.

ST-05 If the handrail extension protrudes into an accessible route, is the handrail extension rounded to 27 in. or less from the floor so that it does not create a protruding object? [4.9.4(2)]

ST-06 Is the clearance between the stair handrail and the wall exactly 1½ in.? [4.9.4(3)]

ST-07 Are the tops of stair handrails between 34 in. and 38 in. above the stair nosing? [4.9.4(5)]

ST-08 Is the stair handrail gripping surface uninterrupted by newel posts, other obstructions, or missing segments? [4.9.4(4)]

ST-09 Are the ends of stair handrails rounded or returned smoothly to the floor, wall, or post? [4.9.4(6)]

ST-10 Are handrails fixed so that they do not rotate within their fittings? [4.9.4(7)]

Stairs: water accumulation

ST-11 Are outdoor stairs and their approaches designed so that water does not accumulate on walking surfaces? (4.9.6)

(HR) Handrails, Grab Bars, and Tub and Shower Seats (4.26)

NOTE:

- HR Guidelines may be repeated in other element-based guidelines: (RP) Ramps, (ST) Stairs, (WC) Water Closets, (TS) Toilet Stalls, (BT) Bathtubs, and (SS) Shower Stalls.

Handrails: size and spacing

HR-01 Is the gripping surface of the grab bars or handrails 1¼ to 1½ in. in outside diameter? (4.26.2, Fig. 39)

AUTHOR'S INTERPRETATION:

- Standard pipe sizes designated by the industry as 1¼ in. to 1½ in. are acceptable for purposes of this section.

HR-02 Do the grab bars or handrails have edges with a minimum radius of 1/8 in.? (4.26.4)

HR-04 If the handrail is located in a recess, is the recess a maximum of 3 in. deep extending at least 18 in. above the rail? (4.26.2, Fig. 39d)

Handrails: grab bar or handrail structural strength

HR-05 Are the grab bars or handrails secure so that they do not rotate in their fittings? [4.26.3(5)]

HR-06 Do the grab bars and handrails meet the structural strength requirements for bending stress and shear stress? (4.26.3)

- Actual bending stress in the grab bar induced by the maximum bending moment from the application of 250 lbf is less than the allowable bending stress for the material of the grab bar.
- Shear stress induced in a grab bar by the application of 250 lbf shall be less than the allowable shear stress for the material of the grab bar. If the connection between the grab bar and its mounting bracket or other support is considered to be fully restrained, then direct and torsional shear stresses shall be totaled for the combined shear stress, which shall not exceed the allowable shear stress.

HR-07 Do the fasteners and mounting devices for the grab bars or handrails meet the structural strength requirements for shear force and tensile force? (4.26.3)

- Shear force induced in a fastener or mounting device from the application of 250 lbf shall be less than the allowable lateral load of either the fastener or mounting device or the supporting structure, whichever is the smaller allowable load.
- Tensile force induced in a fastener by a direct tension force of 250 lbf plus the maximum moment from the application of 250 lbf shall be less than the allowable withdrawal load between the fastener and the supporting structure.

Handrails: hazards

HR-10 Are handrails or grab bars and any wall or other surfaces adjacent to them free of any sharp or abrasive elements? (4.26.4)

(DW) Detectable Warnings (4.29)

NOTE:

- Requirements for detectable warnings (truncated domes) at curb ramps (4.7.7), hazardous vehicular areas (4.29.5), and reflecting ponds (4.29.6) have been suspended until July 26, 1996. This action does not affect the requirement for detectable warnings (truncated domes) at transit platforms [10.3.1(8)], which remains in effect.

Detectable Warnings: hazardous vehicular areas

DW-01 If a walk crosses or adjoins a vehicular way, and the pedestrian and vehicular paths are not separated by curbs, railings, or other elements, is the boundary of the pedestrian path defined by a continuous detectable warning (truncated domes), 36 in. wide on the edge of the pedestrian area? (4.29.5)

- **Suspended until July 26, 1996.**

Detectable Warnings: reflecting pools

DW-02 Are edges of reflecting pools protected by railings, walls, curbs, or detectable warnings (truncated domes)? (4.29.6)

- **Suspended until July 26, 1996.**

Detectable Warnings: criteria

DW-03 Do detectable warnings consist of raised truncated domes and do they meet the required criteria? (4.29.2)

- Diameter: nominal 0.9 in.
- Height: nominal 0.2 in.
- Spacing: nominal 2.35 in., center to center, offset every other row.
- Contrast: contrast visually with adjoining surface (light-on-dark or dark-on-light).
- The material used to provide contrast shall be an integral part of the walking surface. Detectable warnings used on interior surfaces shall differ from adjoining walking surfaces in resiliency or sound-on-cane contact.

(CT) Controls and Operating Mechanisms (4.27)

NOTES:

- Controls or operating mechanisms can include elements such as light switches, latches, traffic light crossing controls, interpretive station buttons, dispensers, and hooks.
- If controls are to be operated by occupants of the space, they must be accessible. If controls are to be manipulated by maintenance staff only and not by occupants or other users of the space, they do not have to be accessible. For example, the buttons controlling traffic signals at street crossings would need to be accessible, as would controls on interpretive devices. Intercoms, security gates, and other equipment operated by staff would probably not need to be accessible.

Controls: clear floor space

CT-01 Is a clear floor space of at least 30 in. × 48 in. provided in front of controls, dispensers, receptacles, and other operable equipment for forward or parallel approach? (4.27.2, Fig. 4a–b)

Controls: reach ranges

NOTES:

- Accessible reach ranges for controls and operating mechanisms are:
  - Forward reach: not less than 15 in. high and not more than 48 in. high without any obstruction or where the obstruction is less than 20 in. deep. For obstructions from 20 in. to 25 in. deep, no forward reach higher than 44 in.

— Side reach: not less than 9 in. high and not more than 54 in. high. For obstructions not more than 34 in. high or 24 in. deep, no side reach higher than 46 in.

— Electrical outlets, switches, and communication system receptacles have a minimum outlet height of 15 in. regardless of forward or side reach. See CT-02 below.

CT-02 Are electrical outlets, switches, and communication system receptacles mounted within accessible forward or side reach ranges? (4.27.3)

EXCEPTION:

- These requirements do not apply where the use of special equipment dictates otherwise or where electrical and communications system receptacles are not normally intended for use by building occupants. (4.27.3)

CT-04 Are dispensers or other similar operable equipment mounted within accessible forward or side reach ranges? (4.2.5, 4.2.6, Fig. 5a–b, Fig. 6a–c)

CT-05 Are life safety devices or other similar operable equipment mounted within accessible forward or side reach ranges? (4.2.5, 4.2.6, Fig. 5a–b, Fig. 6a–c)

NOTE:

- This might include fire alarm pull stations, handles to extinguisher cabinets, or wall-mounted extinguishers.

Controls: operation

CT-06 Are controls, dispensers, receptacles, and other operable equipment operable with one hand without tight grasping, pinching, or wrist twisting, and requiring no more than 5 lbf of force? (4.27.4)

Controls: exterior conditions

CT-07 Are the controls for fixtures or equipment located on the exterior accessible route mounted within accessible forward or side reach ranges? (4.2.5, 4.2.6, Fig. 5a–b, Fig. 6a–c)

(SG) Signage (4.30)

NOTES:

- In historic buildings displays and written information, documents, etc., should be located where they can be seen by a seated person. Exhibits and signage displayed horizontally (e.g., open books) should be no higher than 44 in. above the floor surface. [4.1.7(3)(e)] While ADAAG requires this only for historic structures, it is a good guideline for other similar situations.
- Not all signage is required to be accessible.
- Signage directing users to accessible entrances may be part of the exterior route or part of the building. If this information is provided along the exterior accessible route, please refer to "entry signage" under "Signage" in the "Master Guidelines."

Signage: direction and information (where provided)

DEFINITION:

- Signs that provide direction to or information about functional spaces of the building.

EXCEPTION:

- Building directories, menus, and all other temporary signs are not required to comply. [4.1.3(16)]

SG-08 Do signs that provide direction to, or information about, functional spaces of the building comply with the criteria below? [4.1.2(7); 4.1.3(16); 4.30.1, 2, 3, 5]

- Character proportion: letters and numbers have a width to height ratio between 3:5 and 1:1 and a stroke width to height ratio between 1:5 and 1:10.
- Character height: sized according to viewing distance with characters on overhead signs at least 3 in. high.

NOTE:

- When the sign is mounted below 80 in., there are no prescribed character heights. Only when the sign is mounted 80 in. or higher are the characters required to be at least 3 in. high. (4.30.3)
- Finish: characters and backgrounds have a nonglare finish.
- Contrast: characters contrast with their background (light-on-dark or dark-on-light).

SG-09 Is a sign located so that the overhead clearance or the projection of a suspended or projected sign does not result in a protruding object (free-standing or wall-mounted)?

- Clear height: at least 80 in. (4.4.2, Fig. 8a)
- Overhang for free-standing signs on posts or pylons located between 27 in. and 80 in. high: no more than a 12-in. projection into accessible routes. (4.4.1, Fig. 8c)
- Overhang for wall-mounted signs between 27 in. and 80 in. high: no more than a 4-in. projection into accessible routes. (4.4.1, Fig. 8a)

(SE) Fixed or Built-in Seating and Tables (4.32)

Fixed or Built-in Seating and Tables: minimum number

SE-01 Is the minimum number of accessible wheelchair seating locations at fixed tables or counters provided? (4.1.3.18)

- Number required: 5 percent of total number of seats but not fewer than one.

AUTHOR'S INTERPRETATION:

- ADAAG is not clear about required number/percentage of accessible seating space for fixed seating (benches, seat walls, etc.) without tables. Five percent of the total number of seats but not fewer than one is recommended.

Fixed or Built-in Seating and Tables: clear floor space

AUTHOR'S INTERPRETATION:

- Where the accessible route leads to and through accessible seating adjacent to a wall or another table, the minimum required width for the accessible route will be 65 in. between the table edge and next parallel surface (e.g., wall or another table edge). (4.1.3.18, Fig. 45)

SE-02 Is the clear floor space for a wheelchair at a seating location adequate? (4.32.3, Fig. 4a, Fig. 45)

- Clear floor space: 30 in. × 48 in.

- This clear space can include up to 19 in. under the table/desk.

Fixed or Built-in Seating and Tables: clearances

SE-03 Are the tops of accessible tables and counters between 28 in. and 34 in. from the floor? (4.32.3, Fig. 45)

SE-04 Are the knee clearances at least 27 in. high, 30 in. wide, and 19 in. deep? (4.32.3, Fig. 45)

(DF) Drinking Fountains and Water Coolers (4.15)

NOTE:

- Please use the review guide "Drinking Fountains and Water Coolers."

(TL) Telephones (4.31)

NOTE:

- Please use the review guide "Telephones" if provided.

Exterior Activity Areas

Introduction. Use this review guide to assess exterior activity areas such as picnic facilities, amphitheaters, plazas, outdoor gathering spaces, swimming pools, and other recreational and general use facilities. Each site must be evaluated on a case by case basis to determine acceptable levels, percentages, and solutions for accessibility. Please refer to other review guides or sections of the "Master Guidelines" as needed to evaluate these diverse areas.

In evaluating exterior activity areas, begin at the site scale and work down to individual elements and spaces.

- First, determine all areas, elements, and activities that are or should be made accessible. All or only a portion may need to be accessible. For example, all scattered picnic tables within a park need not be compliant; a percentage dispersed throughout the site is acceptable. However, if an area for group picnicking is provided, it must be compliant.
- Second, if all elements, spaces, and routes are not to be accessible, designate the accessible route. Please refer to "Exterior Accessible Routes" and its introduction for a more detailed explanation of this process. Even if a major element is not accessible (e.g., play equipment, barbecue pit), an accessible route to it should be considered. Accessible routes must go both to and through use areas.
- Third, evaluate individual components—elements, routes, and spaces.

Unlike many space-types addressed in this book, the diversity among exterior activity areas makes a concise yet comprehensive review guide infeasible. The following areas of concern and the corresponding "Checklist" and "Comprehensive Criteria" are meant as a general basis. Using this book—not just this review guide—accessibility may be evaluated using several strategies:

- Adapting other review guides when the functions are similar.
- Incorporating individual "Master Guidelines" as needed.
- Using the element-based "Master Guidelines" to tailor a review guide for a particularly unusual site.
- Using reach ranges, maneuvering clearances, clear width, and other basic dimensions, ranges, minimums, and maximums as stated in Section 4.2, "Space Allowances and Reach Ranges" to assess accessibility for elements not discussed in ADAAG.

For example, "Auditoriums and Assembly Areas" may be adapted for amphitheaters, outdoor classrooms and lecture areas, and certain functional areas in outdoor gathering areas or plazas. "Restaurants and Cafeterias" contains guidelines pertinent to outdoor eating areas. Criteria for information booths, concession stands, etc., may be found in the "Business and Mercantile" review guide or in the "Master Guidelines." Outdoor showers, such as those commonly found at public pools and beach crossovers, should adhere to the pertinent standards presented in the "Master Guidelines" for shower stalls (control and operating mechanisms, approach and maneuvering space, floor surface, etc.). Compliant solutions demand logic and creativity, and ADAAG can educate designers and reviewers as to how any element may be made accessible. For example, ADAAG has no mention of the accessible chicken coop, but the authors of this text used basic understanding of ADAAG to determine minimal needs. The father of one of the authors constructed a deer stand for a chair user.

Unfortunately, using ADAAG unquestioningly may, in some cases, make a site or element inaccessible for the users. ADAAG 4.2, "Space Allowances and Reach Ranges," as well as all other dimensional criteria in ADAAG, are based on adults. Children may find "compliant" ramps impossible to maneuver. Often a simple adjustment or addition, such as a second, lower railing, may be adequate. While this is important in all space-types, it is crucial in school yards, camps, recreational areas, and many other exterior activity areas.

Many exterior activity areas contain structures that are not covered in other Space-type Review Guides. Structures such as gazebos, pavilions, decks, docks, interpretive stations, and entry gates must adhere to elemental criteria as needed, including but not limited to:

- All accessible route standards
- Doors and openings
- Overhead clearances and protruding objects
- Ground and floor surfaces
- Controls and operating mechanisms (buttons, levers, interpretation devices, etc.)
- Fixed seating
- Signage (including mounting height of interpretive materials)

The typical concerns of accessible route (ground surface, stability, slopes, clear width, etc.) are often more critical in exterior activity areas. Paved areas often have slopes that work well for drainage or original topography, but do not comply with ADAAG's maximum slope criteria. Paths in rustic parks and naturalistic areas are often not compliant. Accessibility to and through picnic areas, parks, nature trails, play areas, ball fields, and the like must be carefully planned. If seating is provided at these spaces (picnic tables, benches adjacent to recreational and play areas, etc.), and if an accessible route leads to such spaces, accessible seating should also be provided. Urban settings have many potential route problems (grates, slopes, clear width through and around bollards and other obstructions, selection of the most efficient and safest curb cuts, etc.). Refer to "Exterior Accessible Routes" for more detailed information.

ADAAG's definition of *assembly areas* implies that almost every exterior use area (plaza or gathering space, recreational facility, picnic area, amphitheater, etc.) be accessible. It may be infeasible to make every seating area or picnic table along a path accessible—or even to make every path accessible—but major gathering areas and use areas should be compliant. Reasonable judgment should be used to determine which areas and elements must be accessible. Refer to "Assembly Areas" for more detailed criteria.

Tables (with and without umbrellas), signage, and other permanent elements often interfere with overhead clearance or act as protruding objects. They also encroach on the minimum clear width of the accessible route. Temporary elements such as parked bikes or vehicles, vendor stands in plazas and along sidewalks, etc., may also present barriers.

Directional and informational signage must be compliant. Many activity areas, as well as structures within or adjacent to the activity area, may have one or more entrance that is not accessible; compliant signage must be provided to inform users of accessible and inaccessible entrances. Interpretation is a key feature of many recreational and historic sites. ADAAG 4.2(3)(e) covers displays and exhibits for historic preservation; that criteria will be useful for other signage and displays as well, particularly when interpretive materials are provided.

Public telephones have slightly different requirements and exceptions for exterior vs. interior spaces.

PRELIMINARY DESIGN OVERVIEW

This overview presents common issues of concern for this space-type as well as unusual issues. Not all issues addressed here are covered in the complete review guide. Because of the diversity of "Exterior Activity Areas," all issues one could find cannot be dealt with in this overview or the corresponding materials. Refer to the "Master Guidelines" and other review guides as appropriate.

(AA) Assembly Areas
- For amphitheaters, outdoor classrooms, and similar spaces, refer to "Assembly Areas." For fixed seating in plazas, along paths, picnic areas, etc., refer to "Fixed or Built-in Seating and Tables."

- An *assembly area* is defined in ADAAG as a "room or space accommodating a group of individuals for recreational, educational, political, social, or amusement purposes, or for the consumption of food and drink."

(AR) Accessible Routes
- Cross slope requirements for any sloped surface are often overlooked and easily exceeded (e.g., aisles, plazas). Positive drainage may be a problem in some situations.
- Frequently overlooked maneuvering space problems include approaches to elements such as trash receptacles, gates, or information displays; turns around an obstruction; intersections of narrow paths; bollards and turnstiles.
- Parked vehicles and other nonpermanent elements must not reduce the clear width of the accessible route. Consider bicycle parking, vendor booths, etc.
- Route surfaces must meet criteria for vertical changes in level. Problem areas may include transition between materials, construction and expansion joints, spacing between the boards of wood decks, and individual pavers.

(BM) Business and Mercantile
- Accessible counters are required at each different area offering sales or service such as ticket booths, reception desks, concession stands, information counters, etc. Consider different types of services as "different types."
- If sales and services are located in different parts of the site, then accessible counters must be dispersed throughout the site.
- In retail, self-service shelves or displays must be located on an accessible route. However, these self-service shelves or displays are not required to comply with accessible reach ranges.
- Sales service counters (both with and without cash registers) must meet height and length minimums. Equivalent facilitations may be considered for counters without cash registers.
- All accessible sales and service counters must be on the accessible route.

(CT) Controls and Operating Mechanisms
- Frequently overlooked are emergency telephones, interpretation systems, trash receptacle lids, etc.
- One of each type of control device for use by the general public should be accessible and operable.

(DF) Drinking Fountains
- Drinking fountains must serve two height requirements; this may require two different spout heights or other options.

(DR) Doors
- Revolving doors or turnstiles require an adjacent accessible door, gate, or opening.
- Gates, openings in walls and fences, and other passages must meet accessibility criteria.

(DW) Detectable Warnings

- Detectable warnings are suspended for most space-types until July 26, 1996.

(FS) Floor and Ground Surfaces

- In most areas surfaces should be evaluated as if wet even if they are roofed; in particular consider drinking fountains, concession stands, etc.
- Smooth floor surfaces should be evaluated for slip-resistance based on floor finish and maintenance.
- Vertical changes in levels along the accessible route can be an unforeseen barrier, e.g., transition between floor materials, construction and expansion joints, uneven planks in wood decks. Also of concern are raised objects in the path of travel (e.g., electrical and communication outlets, door stops, etc.)
- Grates located on the accessible route must meet accessibility requirements.

(PL) Platform Lifts

- Use platform lifts in lieu of elevators or ramps only under specific conditions.

(PR) Protruding Objects

- Common wall- or post-mounted elements can be protruding objects, e.g., drinking fountains, public telephones, ATM machines, signs, mailboxes, display cases.
- Overhead clearances can be an unforeseen compliance problem, e.g., signs and banners, open space under stairs, low ceilings around concession stands and information booths, utility guy wires, etc.

(RC) Restaurants and Cafeterias

- Refer to "Restaurants and Cafeterias" for outdoor eating areas.

(RP) Ramps

- Any slope along an *accessible* route greater than 1:20 (5 percent) is considered a ramp and must meet all ramp criteria.
- Aisles with slopes greater than 1:20 that are used as accessible routes must meet ramp requirements. Note exception for handrails.
- Handrail extensions are possible protruding objects, especially where the extensions intersect another accessible route.
- Required ramp edge protection should not inhibit storm water runoff and collect debris.
- Exterior ramps and their approaches must not allow water to accumulate on their surfaces.
- Some persons who use walking aids prefer stairs over ramps; consider including both.

(SE) Fixed or Built-in Seating and Tables and/or Counters

- If fixed tables or counters are provided, a minimum of 5 percent of the total number but not fewer than one of either type must be accessible. If seating has no tables, the same minimums are suggested.
- An accessible route must lead to and through accessible seating at fixed tables or counters.

(SG) Signage

- Activity areas may have both accessible and inaccessible entrances. If all entrances are not accessible, the accessible entrances must be identified by the ISA symbol; inaccessible entrances must have signage indicating the accessible route to an accessible entrance.
- Permanent directional and informational signage must meet accessibility criteria; letter height varies with mounting height of sign.
- Building directories, menus, and temporary signs are not required to comply.
- Displays, exhibits and interpretive signage should be displayed so that they can be seen by a seated person.

(SR) Fixed Storage, Closets, Lockers, and Shelves

- When provided, at least one of each type of storage unit (shelves, dispensers, hooks, etc.) must be accessible.
- Frequently overlooked storage units for this space-type include towel hooks around pools, brochure racks, lockers.

(SS) Shower Stalls

- If provided, outdoor showers must be on the accessible route and must meet pertinent compliance criteria: reach ranges, maneuvering space, controls and operating mechanisms, floor surface, etc.

(ST) Stairs

- Only stairs that connect levels not connected by an elevator or other accessible means of vertical access are required to comply.
- Exterior stairs and their approaches must not allow water to accumulate on their surfaces.
- Open risers are not permitted on accessible stairs.
- Handrail extensions are possible protruding objects, especially where the extensions intersect another accessible route.

(TL) Public Telephones

- Typical requirements.

ADAAG APPENDIX

The ADAAG Appendix includes additional advisory information pertinent to this space-type.

- A4.3 Accessible Route
- A4.32 Fixed or Built-in Seating and Tables

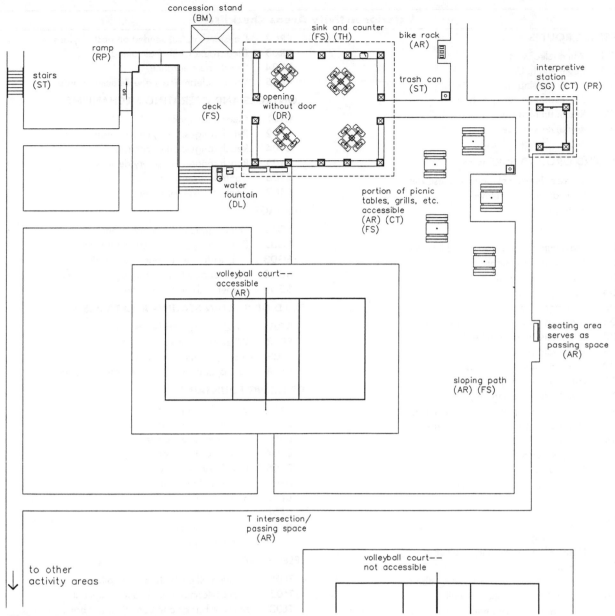

Figure 3-4. Exterior activity areas.

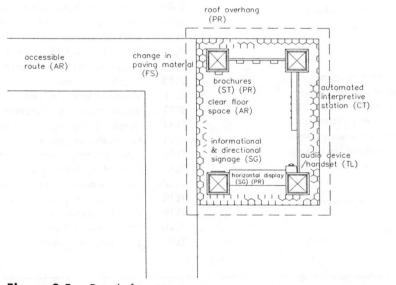

Figure 3-5. Detail of interpretive station.

Exterior Activity Areas Checklist

ACCESSIBLE ROUTES

AR08	Route: clear width
AR09	Route width: U-turns
AR10	Route: passing space
AR11	Route: maneuvering clearances
AR12	Route: running slope
AR13	Route: cross slope
AR14	Route: changes of level

FLOOR AND GROUND SURFACES

FS01	Surface: firm, stable, and slip-resistant
FS02	Vertical changes in level
FS04	Floor gratings

RAMPS

RP01	Maximum running slopes and lengths
RP02	Maximum cross slope
RP03	Minimum clear width
RP04	Landings: location
RP05	Landings: size
RP06	Landings used to change direction
RP07	Handrails: when required
RP08	Handrails: switchbacks
RP09	Handrails: extensions past ramp
RP10	Handrails: clear space to wall
RP11	Handrails: mounting height
RP12	Handrails: continuous gripping surface
RP13	Handrails: rounded end or returned
RP14	Handrails: no rotation
RP15	Ramp edge protection
RP16	Floor surface stability
RP17	Water does not accumulate

STAIRS

ST01	Riser/tread: criteria
ST02	Stair nosing: criteria
ST03	Handrails: location and continuity
ST04	Handrails: extensions
ST05	Ext. handrail is not a protruding object
ST06	Handrails: clear space to wall
ST07	Handrails: mounting height
ST08	Handrails: gripping surface uninterrupted
ST09	Handrails: rounded ends or returned
ST10	Handrails: no rotation
ST11	Water does not accumulate

HANDRAILS

HR01	Handrails and grab bars: diameter
HR02	Handrails and grab bars: edge radius
HR04	Handrails in recess: criteria
HR05	Handrails and grab bars: no rotation
HR06	Handrails and grab bars: structural strength
HR07	Mounting devices: structural strength
HR10	Wall adjacent to handrail abrasion free

DETECTABLE WARNINGS

DW01	Pedestrian/vehicular conflict: warning
DW02	Reflecting pools: warning
DW03	Truncated dome: criteria

PROTRUDING OBJECTS

PR01	Wall-mounted
PR02	Freestanding/suspended on posts/pylons
PR03	Clear route width maintained
PR04	Overhead clearance
PR05	Vertical clearance: cane detection barrier

CONTROLS AND OPERATING MECHANISMS

CT01	Clear floor space
CT02	Reach ranges: elec./comm. systems
CT04	Reach ranges: other controls
CT05	Reach ranges: life safety devices
CT06	Controls: operation
CT07	Controls: exterior routes

SIGNAGE

SG01	Entry signage: ISA requirement
SG02	Entry signage: inaccessible entrances
SG03	Inaccessible entry signage: criteria
SG08	Directional/informational signage: criteria
SG09	Suspended/projected signs: location

FIXED OR BUILT-IN SEATING AND TABLES

SE01	Fixed seating: number required
SE02	Wheelchairs: clear floor space at tables
SE03	Tables/counters: heights
SE04	Tables/counters: knee clearance criteria

DRINKING FOUNTAINS

DF01	Single unit requirements
DF02	Multiple unit requirements
DF03	Alcove location: criteria
DF04	Unit: clear floor space
DF05	Unit: knee clearance
DF06	Unit: toe clearance
DF07	Spout: height
DF08	Spout: location
DF09	Controls: location
DF10	Controls: operation

TELEPHONES

TL01	Single public telephone: compliance
TL02	Public telephone bank: one compliant
TL03	Multiple banks: one compliant per bank
TL04	Accessible telephone: clear floor space
TL05	Accessible telephone: accessible route
TL06	Wall- or post-mounted: protruding objects
TL07	Reach ranges
TL08	Push-button controls where available
TL09	Telephone book: reach ranges
TL10	Handset cord: length
TL11	Volume control: requirements
TL12	Volume control: amplification
TL13	Telephone: hearing aid compatible
TL14	Four public telephones: one text
TL15	Listed assembly areas: public text telephone
TL16	Hospital locations: public text telephone
TL17	No required text: equivalent facilitation
TL18	Text telephone: permanently mounted
TL19	Acoustic coupler: cord length
TL20	Three interior telephones: shelf/electrical outlet
TL21	Shelf: size requirements

EXTERIOR ACTIVITY AREAS
COMPREHENSIVE CRITERIA

Any element not included in this review guide but necessary to complete the evaluation of the site should be selected from the "Master Guidelines." These may include ATM's, curb ramps, etc. Other review guides, such as "Restaurants and Cafeterias," "Business and Mercantile," etc., should also be used as needed.

ADAAG defines an *assembly area* as "a room or space accommodating a group of individuals for recreational, educational, political, social, or amusement purposes, or for the consumption of food and drink." For amphitheaters, outdoor classrooms, or other outdoor gathering areas, see "Assembly Areas Review Guide." For seating along paths, scattered benches, etc., refer to the "Master Guidelines" for "Fixed or Built-in Seating and Tables."

(AR) Accessible Routes (4.3)

NOTES:

- All walks, decks, routes through plazas, skywalks, tunnels, and other spaces that are part of a designated accessible route shall comply with accessible requirements.
- Any slope on the accessible route that is greater than 1:20 is required to meet all ramp criteria.
- The accessible route shall, to the maximum extent feasible, coincide with the route for the general public.
- In historic buildings, accessible routes from an accessible entrance shall be provided to all publicly used spaces on at least the level of the accessible entrance. Access shall be provided to all levels of a building or facility whenever practical. [4.1.7(3)(d)]

AUTHOR'S INTERPRETATION:

- An accessible route "generally coincides" with the route used by the public if:
  — It does not force the user to go out of the way
  — It is most like the route chosen by the general public
  — It is direct
  — It gives the same basic experience as the route preferred by the public

Accessible Routes: width

AR-08 Is the minimum clear width along the accessible route adequate for continuous or point passage? (4.2.1, 4.3.3, Fig. 1, Fig. 8e, Fig. 24e)

- Continuous passage (greater than 24 in. long): at least a 36-in. clear width.
- Point passage (not more than 24 in. long): at least a 32-in. clear width.

AUTHOR'S INTERPRETATION:

- Noncompliance with this question generally relates to permanent elements that encroach on the accessible route. Large, heavy equipment that is not readily movable might be considered permanent. If the space is designed so that temporary elements (such as bikes in a bike rack or car bumpers) will consistently encroach, the situation might also be considered a permanent barrier.

AR-09 Is the minimum clear width along the accessible route adequate at a U-turn around an obstruction? (4.3.3, Fig. 7a–b)

- Obstruction 48 in. or greater: at least a 36-in. clear width around the obstruction.
- Obstruction less than 48 in.: at least a 42-in. clear width at each side with at least a 48-in. clear width in the turn.

Accessible Routes: passing space

AR-10 Does the accessible route provide at least 60 in. of clear width for two wheelchairs to pass, and if not, is the required passing space provided? (4.2.2, 4.3.4)

- A 60-in. × 60-in. passing space or "T" intersection should be provided at reasonable intervals not to exceed 200 ft.

AUTHOR'S INTERPRETATION:

- Accessible routes more than 5 ft long (e.g., routes in short hallways, aisles in laboratories, and work/storage areas) should have passing spaces provided. In exterior routes, the specific situation and users should suggest "reasonable" intervals.

DEFINITION:

- A *"T" intersection* is defined as the intersection of two corridors or walks, each at least 36 in. wide providing at least a 60-in. depth at the intersection. (Fig. 3b)

Accessible Routes: maneuvering clearances

AR-11 Is the minimum clear floor space for an unobstructed 180° wheelchair turning space or a "T"-shaped turning space provided? (4.2.3, Fig. 3a–b)

- 180° turning space: at least a 60-in. diameter.
- "T"-shaped turning space: at least 36-in. wide legs with a minimum length of 60 in.

Accessible Routes: slopes

AR-12 Is the running slope on the accessible route 1:20 or less? (4.3.7)

- Any slope on the accessible route that is greater than 1:20 is required to meet all ramp criteria.

AR-13 Is the cross slope on the accessible route 1:50 or less? (4.3.7)

Accessible Routes: changes in level

AR-14 Are changes in level greater than 1/2 in. accomplished by means of a curb ramp, ramp, elevator, or platform lift (as permitted in ADAAG 4.1.3 and 4.1.6)? (4.3.8)

(FS) Floor and Ground Surfaces (4.5)

Floor Surfaces: general

FS-01 Are the floor/ground surfaces on the accessible route stable, firm, and slip-resistant? (4.5.1)

AUTHOR'S INTERPRETATION:

- Exterior spaces, interior circulation, bathrooms, and other spaces where water can collect on the floor around an element (sinks, drinking fountains, hose bibbs, etc.) are reviewed as if wet.

- High gloss surfaces without significant textures that are regularly maintained with waxing (smooth tiles, waxed concrete, etc.) could be considered noncompliant.
- Accessible criteria are not specified for nonpermanent floor surfaces such as mats or rugs.

Floor Surfaces: changes in level

FS-02 Are vertical changes in level between 1/4 in. and 1/2 in. beveled with a slope of 1:2 or less? (4.5.2)

- Changes in level up to 1/4 in. may be vertical without edge treatment.
- Changes in level greater than 1/2 in. should be accomplished by means of a curb ramp, ramp, elevator, or platform lift (as permitted in ADAAG 4.1.3 and 4.1.6).

Floor Surfaces: gratings

FS-04 Do floor gratings in the path of travel comply with accessible criteria? (4.5.4, Fig. 8g–h)

- Opening size: no greater than 1/2 in. in one direction.
- Opening direction: the long dimension is perpendicular to the dominant direction of travel.

(RP) Ramps (4.8)

NOTE:

- Any slope on the accessible route that is greater than 1:20 is considered a ramp and shall comply with accessible requirements.

Ramps: slopes and rises

RP-01 Is the running slope for the ramp within required parameters? (4.8.2, Fig. 16)

- New construction: 1:12 slope or less with not more than a 30-in. rise for any run.
  — 1:12 slope: 30-ft run between landings.
  — 1:16 slope: 40-ft run between landings.
- On existing sites where space limitations prohibit the use of a slope of 1:12 or less, the following slopes can be considered. [4.1.6(3)(a)(i–ii)]
  — Between 1:10 and 1:12 for a maximum rise of 6 in.
  — Between 1:8 and 1:10 for a maximum rise of 3 in.
  — A slope steeper than 1:8 is not allowed.

EXCEPTION:

- In historic buildings, a ramp with a slope no greater than 1:6 for a run not to exceed 2 ft may be used as part of an accessible route to an entrance. [4.1.7(3)(a)]

RP-02 Is the cross slope of the ramp 1:50 or less? (4.8.6)

Ramps: clear width

RP-03 Is the clear width (between handrails) of the ramp at least 36 in.? (4.8.3)

Ramps: landings

RP-04 Is there a level landing at the top and bottom of each ramp and each ramp run? (4.8.4)

- If a doorway is located at a landing, then the area in front of the doorway must meet door maneuvering clearance requirements.

RP-05 Does each ramp landing meet required dimensions? [4.8.4(1-2)]

- Landing width: at least equal to the ramp width.
- Landing length: at least 60 in. long.

RP-06 Where the ramp changes direction, is there a landing of at least 60 in. × 60 in.? [4.8.4(3)]

Ramps: handrails

NOTE:

- Additional criteria for handrails can be found in Section "HR, Handrails."

RP-07 If the ramp rises more than 6 in. or is longer than 72 in., does it have a handrail on each side? (4.8.5)

- Handrails are not required on curb ramps or adjacent to seating in assembly areas.

RP-08 Is the handrail provided on both sides of ramp segments and is the inside rail on switchback or dogleg ramps continuous? [4.8.5(1), Fig. 19a–b]

RP-09 At the end of the ramp handrails, is there at least 12 in. of handrail parallel to the floor or ground surface, extending beyond the top and the bottom of the ramp segments? [4.8.5(2), Fig. 17]

RP-10 Is the clearance between the ramp handrail and the wall exactly 1½ in.? [4.8.5(3)]

- For recesses, see ADAAG Fig. 39.

RP-11 Are the tops of ramp handrails between 34 in. and 38 in. above ramp surfaces? [4.8.5(5)]

RP-12 Is the ramp handrail gripping surface continuous without obstructions or missing segments? [4.8.5(4)]

RP-13 Are the ends of ramp handrails rounded or returned smoothly to the floor, wall, or post? [4.8.5(6)]

RP-14 Are the ramp handrails fixed so that they do not rotate within their fittings? [4.8.5(7)]

Ramps: edge protection and floor surfaces

RP-15 If a ramp or landing has a drop-off, is it protected by an acceptable option? (4.8.7, Fig. 17)

- Acceptable options include: a wall, a minimum 12-in. horizontal floor extension beyond the railing, a minimum 2-in. curb, or a railing design that prevents people from falling or rolling off.

RP-16 Is the ramp floor surface stable, firm, and slip-resistant? (4.5.1)

RP-17 Are outdoor ramps and their approaches designed so that water does not accumulate on walking surfaces? (4.8.8)

(ST) Stairs (4.9)

NOTE:

- Only stairs that connect levels not connected by an elevator, ramp, or other accessible means of vertical access are required to comply. [4.1.3(4)]

— In new construction, this condition may occur in facilities subject to the elevator exemption [4.1.3(5)—Exception 1] or where mezzanines are exempt in restaurants (5.4)

Stairs: risers, treads, and nosings

ST-01 Do the stair treads and risers meet the required criteria? (4.9.2, Fig. 18a)

- Uniformity: riser heights and tread widths should remain uniform in any one flight of stairs.
- Treads: not less than 11 in. measured from riser to riser.
- Risers: no open risers are permitted.

ST-02 Do the stair nosings meet the required criteria? See ADAAG Fig. 18 for clarification. (4.9.3)

- Risers: risers slope toward the nosing.
- Radius of the curvature: not more than 1/2-in. radius at the leading edge of the tread.
- Angle nosing: angled underside on nosing is not less than 60° from the horizontal; underside of nosing should not be abrupt.
- Nosing projection: not more than 1½ in.

Stairs: handrails

NOTE:

- Additional criteria for handrails can be found in Section "HR, Handrails."

ST-03 Is the handrail provided on both sides of the stair and is the inside rail on switchback or dogleg stairs continuous at the landing? [4.9.4(1), Fig. 19a–b]

- The outside handrail along the perimeter wall does not have to be continuous around the landing.

ST-04 At the end of the stair handrails, is there at least 12 in. of handrail parallel to the floor beyond the top riser and is there at least one tread width of sloping handrail plus at least 12 in. of horizontal handrail beyond the bottom riser? [4.9.4(2), Fig. 19c–d.]

- See ADAAG Fig. 19c–d for extension design.

ST-05 If the handrail extension protrudes into an accessible route, is the handrail extension rounded to 27 in. or less from the floor so that it does not create a protruding object? [4.9.4(2)]

ST-06 Is the clearance between the stair handrail and the wall exactly 1½ in.? [4.9.4(3)]

ST-07 Are the tops of stair handrails between 34 in. and 38 in. above the stair nosing? [4.9.4(5)]

ST-08 Is the stair handrail gripping surface uninterrupted by newel posts, other obstructions, or missing segments? [4.9.4(4)]

ST-09 Are the ends of stair handrails rounded or returned smoothly to the floor, wall, or post? [4.9.4(6)]

ST-10 Are handrails fixed so that they do not rotate within their fittings? [4.9.4(7)]

Stairs: water accumulation

ST-11 Are outdoor stairs and their approaches designed so that water does not accumulate on walking surfaces? (4.9.6)

(HR) Handrails, Grab Bars, and Tub and Shower Seats (4.26)

NOTE:

- HR Guidelines may be repeated in other element-based guidelines: (RP) Ramps, (ST) Stairs, (WC) Water Closets, (TS) Toilet Stalls, (BT) Bathtubs, and (SS) Shower Stalls.

Handrails: size and spacing

HR-01 Is the gripping surface of the grab bars or handrails 1¼ to 1½ in. in outside diameter? (4.26.2, Fig. 39)

AUTHOR'S INTERPRETATION:

- Standard pipe sizes designated by the industry as 1¼ in. to 1½ in. are acceptable for purposes of this section.

HR-02 Do the grab bars or handrails have edges with a minimum radius of 1/8 in.? (4.26.4)

HR-04 If the handrail is located in a recess, is the recess a maximum of 3 in. deep extending at least 18 in. above the rail? (4.26.2, Fig. 39d)

Handrails: grab bar or handrail structural strength

HR-05 Are the grab bars or handrails secure so that they do not rotate in their fittings? [4.26.3(5)]

HR-06 Do the grab bars and handrails meet the structural strength requirements for bending stress and shear stress? (4.26.3)

- Actual bending stress in the grab bar induced by the maximum bending moment from the application of 250 lbf is less than the allowable bending stress for the material of the grab bar.
- Shear stress induced in a grab bar by the application of 250 lbf shall be less than the allowable shear stress for the material of the grab bar. If the connection between the grab bar and its mounting bracket or other support is considered to be fully restrained, then direct and torsional shear stresses shall be totaled for the combined shear stress, which shall not exceed the allowable shear stress.

HR-07 Do the fasteners and mounting devices for the grab bars or handrails meet the structural strength requirements for shear force and tensile force? (4.26.3)

- Shear force induced in a fastener or mounting device from the application of 250 lbf shall be less than the allowable lateral load of either the fastener or mounting device or the supporting structure, whichever is the smaller allowable load.
- Tensile force induced in a fastener by a direct tension force of 250 lbf plus the maximum moment from the application of 250 lbf shall be less than the allowable withdrawal load between the fastener and the supporting structure.

Handrails: hazards

HR-10 Are handrails or grab bars and any wall or other surfaces adjacent to them free of any sharp or abrasive elements? (4.26.4)

(DW) Detectable Warnings (4.29)

NOTE:

- Requirements for detectable warnings (truncated domes) at curb ramps (4.7.7), hazardous vehicular areas (4.29.5), and reflecting ponds (4.29.6) have been suspended until July 26, 1996. This action does not affect the requirement for detectable warnings (truncated domes) at transit platforms [10.3.1(8)], which remains in effect.

Detectable Warnings: hazardous vehicular areas

DW-01 If a walk crosses or adjoins a vehicular way, and the pedestrian and vehicular paths are not separated by curbs, railings, or other elements, is the boundary of the pedestrian path defined by a continuous detectable warning (truncated domes), 36 in. wide on the edge of the pedestrian area? (4.29.5)

- **Suspended until July 26, 1996.**

Detectable Warnings: reflecting pools

DW-02 Are edges of reflecting pools protected by railings, walls, curbs, or detectable warnings (truncated domes)? (4.29.6)

- **Suspended until July 26, 1996.**

Detectable Warnings: criteria

DW-03 Do detectable warnings consist of raised truncated domes and do they meet the required criteria? (4.29.2)

- Diameter: nominal 0.9 in.
- Height: nominal 0.2 in.
- Spacing: nominal 2.35 in., center to center, offset every other row.
- Contrast: contrast visually with adjoining surface (light-on-dark or dark-on-light).
- The material used to provide contrast shall be an integral part of the walking surface. Detectable warnings used on interior surfaces shall differ from adjoining walking surfaces in resiliency or sound-on-cane contact.

(PR) Protruding Objects (4.4)

Protruding Objects: general

PR-01 Do wall-mounted objects having leading edges between 27 in. and 80 in. high project less than 4 in. into walkways, corridors, aisles, or paths of travel? (4.4.1, Fig. 8a–e)

- Objects mounted with their leading edge at or below 27 in. can protrude any amount, as long as they do not reduce the required clear width of an accessible route.

AUTHOR'S INTERPRETATION:

- Protruding objects might include signage, shelving, counters, built-in equipment overhangs, various dispensers, or racks.

PR-02 Do free-standing objects, suspended or mounted on posts or pylons with leading edges between 27 in. and 80 in. high, project less than 12 in. into the perpendicular route of travel? (4.4.1, Fig. 8a–e)

AUTHOR'S INTERPRETATION:

- These might include telephone enclosures, drinking fountains, or free-standing signage kiosks.

PR-03 Is the minimum clear route width or maneuvering space still maintained even with the projection of a protruding object? (4.4.1, Fig. 8a–e)

Protruding Objects: overhead clearance

PR-04 Is the minimum overhead clearance of 80 in. provided in accessible areas or along accessible routes? (4.4.2, Fig. 8a)

AUTHOR'S INTERPRETATION:

- Overhead objects that can reduce the required clearance might include structural overhangs, signage, pipes, ducts, or light fixtures.

PR-05 Where the vertical clearance of a space adjoining the accessible route is less than 80 in. high, is a cane detection barrier less than 27 in. from the floor provided for blind or visually impaired persons? (4.4.2, Fig. 8c-1)

AUTHOR'S INTERPRETATION:

- This condition might be found under a stair, at a sloped ceiling space, or with guy wires from telephone poles along an exterior accessible route.

(CT) Controls and Operating Mechanisms (4.27)

NOTES:

- Controls or operating mechanisms can include elements such as light switches, latches, traffic light crossing controls, interpretive station buttons, dispensers, and hooks.
- If controls are to be operated by occupants of the space, they must be accessible. If controls are to be manipulated by maintenance staff only and not by occupants or other users of the space, they do not have to be accessible. For example, the buttons controlling self-service interpretive devices or light switches in pavilions would have to be accessible. Audio-visual equipment, security gates, and other equipment operated by staff would probably not need to be accessible.

Controls: clear floor space

CT-01 Is a clear floor space of at least 30 in. × 48 in. provided in front of controls, dispensers, receptacles, and other operable equipment for forward or parallel approach? (4.27.2, Fig. 4a–b)

Controls: reach ranges

NOTES:

- Accessible reach ranges for controls and operating mechanisms are:
  — Forward reach: not less than 15 in. high and not more than 48 in. high without any obstruction or where the obstruction is less than 20 in. deep. For obstructions from 20 in. to 25 in. deep, no forward reach higher than 44 in.
  — Side reach: not less than 9 in. high and not more than 54 in. high. For obstructions not more than 34

in. high or 24 in. deep, no side reach higher than 46 in.

— Electrical outlets, switches, and communication system receptacles have a minimum outlet height of 15 in. regardless of forward or side reach. See CT-02 below.

CT-02 Are electrical outlets, switches, and communication system receptacles mounted within accessible forward or side reach ranges? (4.27.3)

EXCEPTION:

- These requirements do not apply where the use of special equipment dictates otherwise or where electrical and communications system receptacles are not normally intended for use by building occupants. (4.27.3)

CT-04 Are dispensers or other similar operable equipment mounted within accessible forward or side reach ranges? (4.2.5, 4.2.6, Fig. 5a–b, Fig. 6a–c)

CT-05 Are life safety devices or other similar operable equipment mounted within accessible forward or side reach ranges? (4.2.5, 4.2.6, Fig. 5a–b, Fig. 6a–c)

NOTE:

- This might include fire alarm pull stations, handles to extinguisher cabinets, or wall-mounted extinguishers.

Controls: operation

CT-06 Are controls, dispensers, receptacles, and other operable equipment operable with one hand without tight grasping, pinching, or wrist twisting, and requiring no more than 5 lbf of force? (4.27.4)

Controls: exterior conditions

CT-07 Are the controls for fixtures or equipment located on the exterior accessible route or activity areas mounted within accessible forward or side reach ranges? (4.2.5, 4.2.6, Fig. 5a–b, Fig. 6a–c)

(SE) Fixed or Built-in Seating and Tables (4.32)

Fixed or Built-in Seating and Tables: minimum number

SE-01 Is the minimum number of accessible wheelchair seating locations at fixed tables or counters provided? (4.1.3.18)

- Number required: 5 percent of total number of seats but not fewer than one.

AUTHOR'S INTERPRETATION:

- ADAAG is not clear about required number/percentage of accessible seating space for fixed seating (benches, seat walls, etc.) without tables. Five percent of the total number of seats but not fewer than one is recommended.

Fixed or Built-in Seating and Tables: clear floor space

AUTHOR'S INTERPRETATION:

- Where the accessible route leads to and through accessible seating adjacent to a wall or another table, the minimum required width for the accessible route will be 65 in. between the table edge and next parallel surface (e.g., wall or another table edge). (4.1.3.18, Fig. 45)

SE-02 Is the clear floor space for a wheelchair at a seating location adequate? (4.32.3, Fig. 4a, Fig. 45)

- Clear floor space: 30 in. × 48 in.
- This clear space can include up to 19 in. under the table/desk.

Fixed or Built-in Seating and Tables: clearances

SE-03 Are the tops of accessible tables and counters between 28 in. and 34 in. from the floor? (4.32.3, Fig. 45)

SE-04 Are the knee clearances at least 27 in. high, 30 in. wide, and 19 in. deep? (4.32.3, Fig. 45)

(DF) Drinking Fountains and Water Coolers (4.15)

Drinking Fountains: minimum number

DF-01 Where only one drinking fountain is provided on a floor, is it on an accessible route and is it accessible to both wheelchair users and to persons having difficulty stooping or bending? [4.1.3(10)(a)]

- Drinking fountains are required to be accessible to both wheelchair users (accessible height fountain) and persons having difficulty stooping or bending (standard height fountain).

NOTE:

- Alternate solutions might include a high-low fountain or an accessible height fountain and a water cooler with cups. [4.1.3(10)(a)]

DF-02 Where more than one drinking fountain is provided on a floor, do at least 50 percent but not fewer than one of the fountains meet accessible criteria, and is each accessible fountain on an accessible route? [4.1.3(10)(b)]

- Drinking fountains are required to be accessible to both wheelchair users (accessible height fountain) and persons having difficulty stooping or bending (standard height fountain).

Drinking Fountains: clearances and clear floor space

DF-03 If the accessible drinking fountain is located in an alcove, is the alcove adequate in depth and width? (4.15.5, Fig. 27b)

- Depth: not more than 24 in. deep.
- Width: at least 30 in. wide.

DF-04 Is a clear floor space at least 30 in. × 48 in. provided at accessible drinking fountains? [4.15.5(1, 2), Fig. 27b]

DF-05 Does the knee clearance space for wall- and post-mounted cantilevered accessible drinking fountains meet required criteria? (4.15.5, Fig. 27)

- Height: at least 27 in. high from the floor to the apron bottom and maintaining that height for at least 8 in. under the equipment.
- Width: at least 30 in. wide.
- Depth: between 17 in. and 19 in. deep.

NOTE:

- Wall-mounted fountains with leading edges between 27 in. and 80 in. are protruding objects if they project more than 4 in. into the accessible route. A leading edge at 27 in. or below can project any amount as long as it does not restrict the required clear width of the route. (4.4.1)

AUTHOR'S INTERPRETATION:

- If a water fountain is going to protrude more than 4 in. into an accessible route, then it must be mounted at exactly 27 in. in order to comply with required knee clearances and not be considered a protruding object.

DF-06 Is toe clearance at the base of the accessible drinking fountain at least 9 in. high and not more than 6 in. deep? (4.15.5, Fig. 27)

- See ADAAG Fig. 27 for the permitted equipment or piping area.

Drinking Fountains: spout location

DF-07 Is the accessible drinking fountain spout outlet no higher than 36 in. from the ground or floor? (4.15.2, Fig. 27)

DF-08 Is the spout located near the front of the fountain and does it meet required water flow criteria? (4.15.3)

- Water flow trajectory: nearly parallel to the front edge and at least 4 in. high to allow the insertion of a cup or glass.
- Fountain with a round or oval bowl: flow of water is within 3 in. of the front edge.

Drinking Fountains: controls

DF-09 Are the accessible drinking fountain controls front-mounted and/or side-mounted near the front edge? (4.15.4)

DF-10 Are the accessible drinking fountain controls operable with one hand without tight grasping, pinching, or wrist twisting, and require no more than 5 lbf of force? (4.15.4)

(TL) Telephones (4.31)

DEFINITION:

- Telephone types include public pay telephones, public closed circuit telephones, or other public telephones.

NOTE:

- Signage related to telephones is found in Section "SG, Signage."

AUTHOR'S INTERPRETATION:

- Frequently, public pay telephones are provided by a contractual agreement with a vendor. The vendor, through the contract, might be made responsible for compliance with all applicable ADAAG criteria.

Telephones: number required

TL-01 If there is only one public telephone provided, does it comply with accessible criteria? [4.1.3(17)(a)]

- Unless otherwise specified, accessible telephones may be either forward or side reach telephones.

TL-02 If there is a single bank of public telephones, does at least one of the telephones in the bank comply with accessible criteria? [4.1.3(17)(a)]

- A bank consists of two or more adjacent public telephones, often installed as a unit.
- Unless otherwise specified, accessible telephones may be either forward or side reach telephones.

TL-03 Where two or more banks of public telephones are provided, is at least one accessible telephone provided at each bank or within proximity to the bank and does at least one of these accessible telephones comply with forward reach criteria? [4.1.3(17)(a)]

EXCEPTION:

- For exterior installations only, if dial tone first service is available, then a side reach telephone may be installed instead of the required forward reach telephone.

Telephones: clear floor or ground space

TL-04 Does the accessible telephone have at least a 30-in. × 48-in. clear floor or ground space that allows either a forward or side approach? (4.31.2, Fig. 44, 4.2.4)

- Bases, enclosures, and fixed seats shall not impede approaches to telephones.
- If this clear floor space is located in an alcove or confined space, see ADAAG Fig. 4d–e for additional maneuvering clearance requirements.

TL-05 Does an accessible route adjoin or overlap the clear floor space for the accessible telephone? (4.31.2, Fig. 44, 4.2.4)

Telephones: protruding object

TL-06 Do wall-mounted or post-mounted telephones with leading edges between 27 in. and 80 in. from the floor have projections that do not result in a protruding object? (4.31.4, 4.4.1)

- Wall-mounted: project less than 4 in. into the pathway.
- Post-mounted: project less than 12 in. into a perpendicular route of travel.

Telephones: mounting height

TL-07 Is the highest operable part of the telephone within forward or side reach ranges? (4.31.3, 4.2.6)

- Forward: not more than 48 in. above the floor.
- Side: not more than 54 in. above the floor.

Telephones: push-button controls

TL-08 Does the telephone have push-button controls where such service is available? (4.31.6)

Telephones: telephone book

TL-09 Is the telephone book, if provided, located in a position that complies with forward or side reach ranges? (4.31.7)

- Forward: not more than 48 in. above the floor.
- Side: not more than 54 in. above the floor.

Telephones: cord length

TL-10 Is the cord from the telephone to the handset at least 29 in. long? (4.31.8)

Telephones: volume control and hearing aid compatibility

TL-11 Do the public telephones comply with volume control requirements? [4.1.3(17)(b)]

- Each accessible telephone is equipped with a volume control.

- In addition, 25 percent, but not fewer than one, of all other public telephones should be equipped with volume controls and dispersed among all types of public telephones.

TL-12 Are volume controls capable of amplification between 12 dbA and 18 dbA above normal? [4.31.5(2)]

- If an automatic reset button is provided, the maximum of 18 dbA may be exceeded.

TL-13 Are telephones hearing aid compatible? [4.31.5(1)]

Telephones: text telephones

TL-14 If a total of four or more public pay telephones (including both interior and exterior phones) are provided at a site and at least one is in an interior location, is at least one interior public text telephone provided? [4.1.3(17)(c)(i)]

TL-15 If an interior public pay telephone is provided in a stadium or arena, convention center, a hotel with a convention center, or a covered mall, is at least one interior public text telephone provided in the facility? [4.1.3(17)(c)(ii)]

TL-16 If there is a public pay telephone in or adjacent to a hospital emergency room, a hospital recovery room, or a hospital waiting room, is there a public text telephone in each such location? [4.1.3(17)(c)(iii)]

TL-17 If a required text telephone is not provided, is equivalent facilitation provided? [4.31.9(3)]

- A portable text telephone may be made available in a hotel at the registration desk if it is available on a 24-hour basis for use with nearby public pay telephones that can accommodate the accessible requirements for a portable text telephone.

TL-18 Is a required text telephone permanently mounted within, or adjacent to, the telephone enclosure? (4.31.9)

TL-19 If an acoustic coupler is used, is the telephone cord long enough to allow connection of the text telephone to the telephone receiver? [4.31.9(1)]

TL-20 If there are three or more telephones in an interior bank of telephones, does at least one telephone have a shelf and electrical outlet for use with a portable text telephone? [4.1.3(17)(d)]

TL-21 Is the shelf large enough to accommodate a text telephone, provide at least 6 in. of vertical clearance, and allow the telephone handset to be placed flush on the surface of the shelf? [4.31.9(2)]

(SG) Signage (4.30)

NOTES:

- In historic buildings displays and written information, documents, etc., should be located where they can be seen by a seated person. Exhibits and signage displayed horizontally (e.g., open books) should be no higher than 44 in. above the floor surface. [4.1.7(3)(e)]. While ADAAG requires this only for historic structures, it is a good guideline for other similar situations.

- Signage concerning accessible and inaccessible entrances may be located on a structure (pavilions, rest rooms, etc.) along the accessible route, at the entrance to an activity area, or in the parking lot. Evaluate this requirement in the appropriate space-type.

Signage: entry

SG-01 Where a building or activity area has both accessible and inaccessible entrances, are the accessible entrances identified by the International Symbol of Accessibility? [4.1.2(7)(c), Fig. 43a–b]

SG-02 If an entrance is not accessible, is there a directional sign indicating the location of the nearest accessible entrance? [4.1.2(7)(c), 4.1.3(8)(d)]

SG-03 Does the directional sign indicating the location of the nearest accessible entrance comply with directional signage criteria? (4.30.2, 3, 5)

- Character proportion: letters and numbers have a width to height ratio between 3:5 and 1:1 and a stroke width to height ratio between 1:5 and 1:10.

- Character height: sized according to viewing distance with characters on overhead signs at least 3 in. high.

- Finish: characters and backgrounds have a nonglare finish.

- Contrast: characters contrast with their background (light-on-dark or dark-on-light).

Signage: direction and information (where provided)

DEFINITION:

- Signs that provide direction to or information about functional spaces of the building.

EXCEPTION:

- Building directories, menus, and all other temporary signs are not required to comply. [4.1.3(16)]

SG-08 Do signs that provide direction to, or information about, functional spaces of the building comply with the criteria below? [4.1.2(7); 4.1.3(16); 4.30.1, 2, 3, 5]

- Character proportion: letters and numbers have a width to height ratio between 3:5 and 1:1 and a stroke width to height ratio between 1:5 and 1:10.

- Character height: sized according to viewing distance with characters on overhead signs at least 3 in. high.

NOTE:

- When the sign is mounted below 80 in., there are no prescribed character heights. Only when the sign is mounted 80 in. or higher are the characters required to be at least 3 in. high. (4.30.3)

- Finish: characters and backgrounds have a nonglare finish.

- Contrast: characters contrast with their background (light-on-dark or dark-on-light).

SG-09 Is a sign located so that the overhead clearance or the projection of a suspended or projected sign does not result in a protruding object (free-standing or wall-mounted)?

- Clear height: at least 80 in. (4.4.2, Fig. 8a)
- Overhang for free-standing signs on posts or pylons located between 27 in. and 80 in. high: no more than a 12-in. projection into accessible routes. (4.4.1, Fig. 8c)

- Overhang for wall-mounted signs between 27 in. and 80 in. high: no more than a 4-in. projection into accessible routes. (4.4.1, Fig. 8a)

Signage: volume control telephones

SG-10 Are volume controlled telephones identified by a sign showing a handset with radiating sound waves? [4.30.7(2)]

Parking Lots and Passenger Loading Zones

Introduction. Use this review guide to evaluate general use or self-parking facilities, valet parking situations, and passenger loading zones. For parking garages, garages, carports, and other covered parking, refer to "Parking Structures" for additional information. Bus stops or shelters are often located in parking lots. Refer to "Transportation Facilities: Bus Stops" for additional compliance information.

Two types of accessible parking are required—accessible parking spaces and van accessible parking spaces. Size, number, signage requirements, and vertical clearance minimums are different for each. If only one accessible parking space is required, it must meet the van accessible criteria. The ADAAG Appendix gives criteria and rationale for universal parking spaces that may be used in lieu of ADAAG-compliant accessible and van accessible spaces.

The minimum number of accessible and van accessible parking spaces needed, as well as their location and dispersal, is influenced by the total number of parking spaces provided, the services offered in adjacent facilities and structures, the number of accessible entrances or facilities served, and other contextual issues. If a single lot serves a single facility, then the tables, graphics, and formulas given in ADAAG are relatively clear. Meeting ADAAG criteria is more complex if the lot serves several buildings, if there are multiple accessible entrances, if there is a series of parking lots (as in a campus or office complex), or if medical facilities are served.

Accessible parking spaces should be located as close to the facility or entrance served as possible. In lots serving several accessible entrances or structures, accessible parking must be dispersed. If the parking lot does not serve a particular building, as in a park or recreation facility, the accessible spaces should be located as close to the pedestrian entrance or path of travel as possible.

All passenger loading zones do not have to be accessible, but, if provided, at least one must meet ADAAG criteria. The separation of vehicular and pedestrian traffic may be problematic, because bollards, curbs, and other separation devices must not interfere with accessibility.

Accessible routes must connect the parking and loading areas to adjacent accessible facilities, routes, or spaces. Routes that move through parking lots must meet all accessible route criteria. Users should not be forced to travel behind parked cars or in the vehicular route of travel. Parking bays might be connected by pedestrian paths, or paths within the parking lot may connect various bays and parking spaces to facilities or routes adjacent to the parking lot. Depending on the situation, these routes will probably need to be compliant.

Pedestrian/vehicular conflicts are common in these spaces. As mandatory use of detectable warnings has been suspended until July 26, 1996, design responsibility for this critical issue is unclear and should be dealt with on an individual basis until new technical requirements are mandated. A form of detectable warning (visual and tactile) may be considered in certain situations, such as where the accessible route crosses vehicular routes, at curb ramps, and so on.

Temporary barriers such as parked vehicles must not encroach on the minimum clear width of the accessible route or hide required signage. Other temporary hazards or barriers include vegetation encroaching on minimum clear width or overhead clearance, plant litter, and banners. Parked bicycles must not encroach on the accessible route.

Overhead clearances and protruding objects are common problems in parking facilities. Parking access control devices, bollards, signage, wheel stops, and other elements must not encroach on the minimum clear width or overhead clearance of the accessible route, nor may they act as protruding objects. In van accessible parking spaces and loading zones, overhead clearances are greater than that required for interior spaces and exterior accessible routes. ADAAG requires vertical clearance for the entire vehicular path of travel, not just the pedestrian path of travel.

The very slight slopes and cross slopes mandated for accessible parking spaces and loading zones may increase storm water runoff problems; precise grading at and around these areas becomes critical if water is to be moved while still maintaining compliant slopes. Grates or catch basins may interfere with accessibility if they are in the loading zone or parking space or in the immediate accessible route.

Valet parking does not exempt the project from accessibility concerns, nor would "resident parking only" designations. Valet parking must adhere to loading zone criteria and must connect to an accessible route.

If provided, crossing controls, parking meters, and other equipment must be accessible. Design and operation of equipment is not within the scope of most design work; however, issues such as reach ranges and maneuvering clearances at such equipment are.

Directional and informational signage, telephones, and other elements often occur in these spaces. Any provided elements must adhere to the compliance criteria for those elements. Waiting areas are frequently included within or adjacent to parking lots and passenger loading zones. ADAAG is not clear about required number/percentage of accessible seating for fixed seating (benches, seat walls, etc.) without tables. Criteria for fixed seating with tables (5 percent of the total number of seats but not fewer than one) is recommended.

Pictograms are commonly used to convey information about available facilities, use areas, etc., that are served by the parking lot. According to the Access Board, only pictograms that are used for room or space identification must meet ADAAG criteria for pictograms, so recreational icons and the like would not have to be compliant. Both accessible and van accessible parking spaces need compliant signage located where vehicles cannot obscure the signage. Van accessible spaces need additional "Van Accessible" signage mounted below the ISA symbol.

PRELIMINARY DESIGN OVERVIEW

This overview includes ADAAG requirements that are unique to this space-type and may need special attention, as well as those that are typical. Not all issues included here occur in the comprehensive criteria for this space-type.

(AR) Accessible Routes

- Raised traffic islands on an accessible route must meet accessibility criteria.
- Frequently overlooked maneuvering space and clear width problems include security bollards, parking control devices, and access to various automated devices such as crossing controls, parking meters, pay parking and carded parking controls.
- Parked vehicles must not reduce the clear width of the accessible route. Consider bicycle parking as well.
- Route surfaces must meet criteria for vertical changes in level. Problem areas may include transition between materials, construction and expansion joints, individual pavers, and the transition from gutter to paved road surface.

(CR) Curb Ramps

- Frequently overlooked problems include transitions from ramp to street or gutter, traffic islands, and storm water accumulation.
- If a curb ramp is located so that pedestrians must walk across it, provide protection or flared sides.

(CT) Controls and Operating Mechanisms

- Frequently overlooked in this space type are reach range and clear space for parking meter controls.

(DW) Detectable Warnings

- Detectable warnings are suspended for most spaces until July 26, 1996.

(FS) Floor and Ground Surfaces

- In most areas ground surfaces should be evaluated as if wet.

- Grates located on the accessible route must meet accessibility requirements.
- Drop inlets and other storm water control devices are often hazards and/or barriers. Consider both location and design of the element.

(MC) Medical Care Facilities

- At least one accessible entrance must be protected from weather by canopy or roof overhang and incorporate a compliant passenger loading zone.

(PK) Parking and Passenger Loading Zones

- There are different minimum vertical clearances for passenger loading zones, van accessible parking, the vehicular route leading to van parking, and the accessible route.
- If provided, at least one passenger loading zone must meet accessibility requirements.
- Valet parking must meet accessibility requirements for passenger loading zones.
- A percentage or minimum number of accessible spaces is required for both vans and cars. The minimum number of spaces increases if the parking area is associated with a facility that serves the mobility-impaired or outpatients.
- The location of accessible parking must respond to the shortest accessible route of travel to the facility or facilities served. If there are multiple accessible entrances, facilities, or use areas, the parking must be dispersed and located closest to the entrances served.
- Access aisles between accessible parking spaces may be shared.
- Slopes in accessible parking and passenger loading zones must not exceed 1:50.
- Bumper overhangs of parked vehicles must not reduce the clear width of the accessible route.

(PR) Protruding Objects

- Overhead clearances can be an unforeseen compliance problem, e.g., parking control devices, signs and banners, low rooflines on structures (such as rest rooms, shelters, pay facilities, or information booths), utility guy wires, etc.

(RP) Ramps

- Pedestrian connections between parking bays may need to be accessible.
- Any slope along an accessible route greater than 1:20 (5 percent) is considered a ramp and must meet all ramp criteria.
- Handrail extensions are possible protruding objects, especially where the extensions intersect another accessible route.
- Required ramp edge protection may inhibit storm water runoff and collect debris.
- Exterior ramps and their approaches must not allow water to accumulate on their surfaces.

(SE) Fixed or Built-in Seating and Tables and/or Counters

- If fixed seating is provided (e.g., waiting areas), a minimum of 5 percent of the total number but not fewer than one must be accessible.

(SG) Signage

- Information about accessible entrances and/or routes may be placed in the parking lot, along the accessible route, or on the building itself. Signage must be compliant.

- Permanent directional and informational signage must meet accessibility criteria; letter height varies with mounting height of sign.

(ST) Stairs

- Pedestrian connections between parking bays may need to be accessible.

- Only stairs that connect levels not connected by a ramp or other accessible means of vertical access are required to comply.

- Exterior stairs and their approaches must not allow water to accumulate on their surfaces.

- Open risers are not permitted on accessible stairs.

- Handrail extensions are possible protruding objects, especially where the extensions intersect another accessible route.

(TF) Transportation Facilities (Bus Stops)

- Please refer to "Transportation Facilities (Bus Stops)."

ADAAG APPENDIX
The ADAAG Appendix includes additional advisory information pertinent to this space-type.

- A4.1.2(5)(e): Valet Parking
- A4.6: Parking and Passenger Loading Zones

Parking Lots and Passenger Loading Zones Checklist

PARKING AND PASSENGER LOADING ZONES

PK01	Car parking: number required
PK02	Van parking: number required
PK03	Accessible spaces provided in every lot
PK04	Outpatient facilities: number required
PK05	Mobility impairment facilities: number required
PK06	Specific bldg: parking space location
PK07	No specific bldg: parking space location
PK08	Multiple entrances: parking space location
PK09	Car parking spaces: criteria
PK10	Van parking spaces: criteria
PK11	Parking space and aisle: slope
PK12	Access aisle surface
PK13	Vertical clearance for vans
PK14	Access aisle connect to accessible route
PK15	Bumper overhang: clear width maintained
PK16	Car parking signage: I.S.A.
PK17	Van parking signage: I.S.A./van
PK18	Passenger loading zones: number required
PK19	Passenger loading signage: I.S.A.
PK20	Passenger loading: access aisle criteria
PK21	Passenger loading: slope requirements
PK22	Passenger loading: vertical clearance

ACCESSIBLE ROUTES

AR01	Bldg entry: from parking
AR03	Bldg entry: from public transit stops
AR04	Bldg entry: from passenger zone
AR05	Bldg: from other buildings
AR08	Route: clear width
AR09	Route width: U-turns
AR10	Route: passing space
AR11	Route: maneuvering clearances
AR12	Route: running slope
AR13	Route: cross slope
AR14	Route: changes of level

FLOOR AND GROUND SURFACES

FS01	Surface: firm, stable, and slip-resistant
FS02	Vertical changes in level
FS04	Floor gratings

PROTRUDING OBJECTS

PR01	Wall-mounted
PR02	Freestanding/suspended on posts/pylons
PR03	Clear route width maintained
PR04	Overhead clearance
PR05	Vertical clearance: cane detection barrier

CURB RAMPS

CR01	Accessible route: crossing at curb
CR02	Curb ramp: running slope
CR03	Curb ramp to walkway/road transition
CR04	Running slopes of adjoining surfaces
CR05	Curb ramp: width w/o flared sides
CR06	Curb ramp: surface stability
CR07	Curb ramp: required flared sides
CR08	Return curb cuts: nonwalking surfaces
CR09	Built-up curb ramps: criteria
CR10	Curb ramp: detectable warnings
CR11	Detectable warning: criteria
CR12	Curb ramp not blocked by parked vehicles
CR13	Curb ramp within marked crossings
CR14	Diag. curb ramp: edges and traffic flow
CR15	Diag. curb ramp: clear space in crosswalk
CR16	Diag. curb ramp w/flared sides: design
CR17	Raised traffic islands: acc. route options

DETECTABLE WARNINGS

DW01	Pedestrian/vehicular conflict: warning
DW02	Reflecting pools: warning
DW03	Truncated dome: criteria

CONTROLS AND OPERATING MECHANISMS

CT01	Clear floor space
CT04	Reach ranges: other controls
CT05	Reach ranges: life safety devices
CT06	Controls: operation
CT07	Controls: exterior routes

SIGNAGE

SG08	Directional/informational signage: criteria
SG09	Suspended/projected signs: location

FIXED OR BUILT-IN SEATING AND TABLES

SE01	Fixed seating: number required
SE02	Wheelchairs: clear floor space at tables
SE03	Tables/counters: heights
SE04	Tables/counters: knee clearance criteria

See **DF, TL, RP, ST, TF,** and other sections as needed.

PARKING AND PASSENGER LOADING ZONES
COMPREHENSIVE CRITERIA

Any element not included in this review guide but necessary to complete the evaluation of the site should be selected from the "Master Guidelines." These may include bus stops, telephones, ramps, stairs, drinking fountains, etc.

(PK) Parking and Passenger Loading Zones (4.6)

NOTE:

- Where only one accessible space is provided, it shall meet van accessible criteria. [4.1.2(5)(b)]

Parking: required number

PK-01 Where parking spaces are provided for self-parking by employees, visitors, or both, is the required number of accessible car parking spaces provided? [4.1.2(5)(a)]

- 1–25:1, 26–50:2, 51–75:3, 76–100:4, 101–150:5, 151–200:6, 201–300:7, 301–400:8, 401–500:9, 501–1000:2 percent of the total, greater than 1000:20+1 for each 100 over 1000.
- All or some of the accessible parking spaces may be in a different location if equivalent or greater accessibility is ensured.

PK-02 Is the minimum number of accessible van spaces provided? [4.1.2(5)(b)]

- One in every eight spaces must be served by an access aisle at least 96 in. wide and must be designated "van accessible." Where only one accessible space is provided, it must meet van accessible criteria.

PK-03 Are accessible parking spaces provided in every specific area/lot? [4.1.2(5)(a)]

- All or some of the accessible parking spaces may be provided in a different location if equivalent or greater accessibility (in terms of distance from an accessible entrance), cost, and convenience is ensured.

PK-04 If the parking lot serves an outpatient facility, are 10 percent of the total parking spaces accessible? [4.1.2(5)(d)(i)]

PK-05 If the parking lot serves a mobility impairment facility, are 20 percent of the total parking spaces accessible? [4.1.2(5)(d)(ii)]

Parking: location

NOTE:

- Van accessible spaces may be grouped on one level of a parking structure.

PK-06 Where accessible parking spaces serve a particular building, are the accessible parking spaces located on the shortest accessible route of travel to an accessible entrance? (4.6.2)

PK-07 In parking facilities that do not serve any particular building, are the accessible parking spaces located on the shortest accessible route of travel to an accessible pedestrian entrance of the parking facility? (4.6.2)

PK-08 If multiple accessible entrances in a building are served by adjacent parking, are the accessible parking spaces dispersed and located closest to the accessible entrances? (4.6.2)

Parking: space dimensions and clearances

PK-09 Do the designated accessible car parking spaces comply with accessible criteria? (4.6.3, Fig. 9, Fig. 10)

- Car parking space width: at least 96 in. wide with a clearly demarcated access aisle.
- Adjacent access aisle width: at least 60 in. wide.
- Two adjacent accessible parking spaces may share a common access aisle.

PK-10 Do the designated accessible van parking spaces comply with accessible criteria? [4.1.2(5)(b), 4.6.3, Fig. 9]

- Van parking space width: at least 96 in. wide with a clearly demarcated access aisle.
- Adjacent access aisle width: at least 96 in. wide.
- Two adjacent accessible parking spaces may share a common access aisle.

PK-11 Are the surface slopes of accessible parking spaces and access aisles 1:50 or less in all directions? (4.6.3)

NOTE:

- This means a curb ramp cannot project into the access aisle.

PK-12 Are the access aisles stable, firm, and slip-resistant? (4.6.3)

PK-13 Does the accessible van parking space have vertical clearance of at least 98 in. at the parking space and along one vehicular route to the parking space (including entry and exiting from the parking lot)? [4.6.5, 4.1.2(5)(b)]

NOTE:

- Van accessible spaces may be grouped on one level of a parking structure.

Parking: access aisle and accessible route

PK-14 Does the access aisle for each accessible parking space connect directly to the accessible route? (4.6.3)

PK-15 Is the clear width (36 in.) of the accessible route maintained and not reduced by potential vehicle bumper overhang? (4.6.3, Fig. 9)

AUTHOR'S INTERPRETATION:

- A bumper overhang of 30 in. is assumed. The 30 in. is measured from the curb or wheel stop.

Parking: signage

PK-16 Does each accessible car parking space have a vertical sign, not obscured by a parked vehicle, showing the International Symbol of Accessibility (ISA)? (4.6.4)

PK-17 Does each accessible van parking space have a vertical sign, not obscured by a parked vehicle, showing the International Symbol of Accessibility (ISA) and an additional sign, "Van Accessible," mounted below the ISA sign? (4.6.4)

Passenger Loading

PK-18 Where passenger loading zones are provided, does at least one meet accessibility requirements? [4.1.2(5)(c)]

PK-19 Is the accessible passenger loading zone marked by the International Symbol of Accessibility (ISA)? [4.1.2(7)(b)]

PK-20 Is there an access aisle adjacent and parallel to the vehicular pull-up space, and is it at least 60 in. wide and 20 ft long? (4.6.6, Fig. 10)

PK-21 Is the vehicle standing space and access aisle in accessible passenger loading zones level with no slope greater than 1:50 (2 percent) in all directions? (4.6.6)

PK-22 Is a minimum vertical clearance of 114 in. provided at the passenger loading zone (including vehicle pull-up space and access aisle) and along the vehicular route to the vehicle pull-up space from site entrances and exits? (4.6.5)

(AR) Accessible Routes (4.3)

NOTES:

- All walks, traffic islands, skywalks, tunnels, and other spaces that are part of a designated accessible route shall comply with accessible requirements.

- Any slope on the accessible route that is greater than 1:20 is required to meet all ramp criteria.

- The accessible route shall, to the maximum extent feasible, coincide with the route for the general public.

- In historic buildings, accessible routes from an accessible entrance shall be provided to all publicly used spaces on at least the level of the accessible entrance. Access shall be provided to all levels of a building or facility whenever practical. [4.1.7(3)(d)]

AUTHOR'S INTERPRETATION:

- An accessible route "generally coincides" with the route used by the public if:
  — It does not force the user to go out of the way
  — It is most like the route chosen by the general public
  — It is direct
  — It gives the same basic experience as the route preferred by the public

Accessible Routes: site

AR-01 If on-site parking is provided, does at least one accessible route within the boundaries of the site connect accessible parking spaces to the accessible building entrance? [4.1.2(1), 4.3.2(1)]

AR-03 If public transportation stops are available, does at least one accessible route within the boundaries of the site connect public transportation stops to the accessible building entrance? [4.1.2(1), 4.3.2(1)]

AR-04 If passenger loading zones are provided, does at least one accessible route within the boundaries of the site connect a passenger loading zone to the accessible building entrance? [4.1.2(1), 4.3.2(1)]

AR-05 Is there an accessible route connecting all accessible buildings, facilities, elements, and spaces on the same site? [4.1.2(2), 4.3.2(2)]

Accessible Routes: width

AR-08 Is the minimum clear width along the accessible route adequate for continuous or point passage? (4.2.1, 4.3.3, Fig. 1, Fig. 8e, Fig. 24e)

- Continuous passage (greater than 24 in. long): at least a 36-in. clear width.

- Point passage (not more than 24 in. long): at least a 32-in. clear width.

AUTHOR'S INTERPRETATION:

- Noncompliance with this question generally relates to permanent elements that encroach on the accessible route. Large, heavy equipment that is not readily movable might be considered permanent. If the space is designed so that temporary elements (such as bikes in a bike rack or car bumpers) will consistently encroach, the situation might also be considered a permanent barrier.

AR-09 Is the minimum clear width along the accessible route adequate at a U-turn around an obstruction? (4.3.3, Fig. 7a–b)

- Obstruction 48 in. or greater: at least a 36-in. clear width around the obstruction.

- Obstruction less than 48 in.: at least a 42-in. clear width at each side with at least a 48-in. clear width in the turn.

Accessible Routes: passing space

AR-10 Does the accessible route provide at least 60 in. of clear width for two wheelchairs to pass and, if not, is the required passing space provided? (4.2.2, 4.3.4)

- A 60-in. × 60-in. passing space or "T" intersection should be provided at reasonable intervals not to exceed 200 ft.

AUTHOR'S INTERPRETATION:

- Interior accessible routes more than 5 ft long (e.g., routes in short hallways, aisles in laboratories, and work/storage areas) should have passing spaces provided. In exterior sites, the specific situation should suggest similar "reasonable" intervals.

DEFINITION:

- A *"T" intersection* is defined as the intersection of two corridors or walks, each at least 36 in. wide providing at least a 60-in. depth at the intersection. (Fig. 3b)

Accessible Routes: maneuvering clearances

AR-11 Is the minimum clear floor space for an unobstructed 180° wheelchair turning space or a "T"-shaped turning space provided? (4.2.3, Fig. 3a–b)

- 180° turning space: at least a 60-in. diameter.
- "T"-shaped turning space: at least 36-in. wide legs with a minimum length of 60 in.

Accessible Routes: slopes

AR-12 Is the running slope on the accessible route 1:20 or less? (4.3.7)

- Any slope on the accessible route that is greater than 1:20 is required to meet all ramp criteria.

AR-13 Is the cross slope on the accessible route 1:50 or less? (4.3.7)

Accessible Routes: changes in level

AR-14 Are changes in level greater than 1/2 in. accomplished by means of a curb ramp, ramp, elevator, or platform lift (as permitted in ADAAG 4.1.3 and 4.1.6)? (4.3.8)

(FS) Floor and Ground Surfaces (4.5)

Floor Surfaces: general

FS-01 Are the floor/ground surfaces on the accessible route stable, firm, and slip-resistant? (4.5.1)

AUTHOR'S INTERPRETATION:

- Exterior spaces and other spaces where water can collect on the floor around an element (sinks, drinking fountains, hose bibbs, etc.) are reviewed as if wet.
- High gloss surfaces without significant textures that are regularly maintained with waxing (smooth tiles, waxed concrete, etc.) could be considered noncompliant.
- Accessible criteria are not specified for nonpermanent floor surfaces such as mats or rugs.

Floor Surfaces: changes in level

FS-02 Are vertical changes in level between 1/4 in. and 1/2 in. beveled with a slope of 1:2 or less? (4.5.2)

- Changes in level up to 1/4 in. may be vertical without edge treatment.
- Changes in level greater than 1/2 in. should be accomplished by means of a curb ramp, ramp, elevator, or platform lift (as permitted in ADAAG 4.1.3 and 4.1.6).

Floor Surfaces: gratings

FS-04 Do floor gratings in the path of travel comply with accessible criteria? (4.5.4, Fig. 8g–h)

- Opening size: no greater than 1/2 in. in one direction.
- Opening direction: the long dimension is perpendicular to the dominant direction of travel.

(PR) Protruding Objects (4.4)

Protruding Objects: general

PR-01 Do wall-mounted objects having leading edges between 27 in. and 80 in. high project less than 4 in. into walkways, corridors, aisles, or paths of travel? (4.4.1, Fig. 8a–e)

- Objects mounted with their leading edge at or below 27 in. can protrude any amount, as long as they do not reduce the required clear width of an accessible route.

AUTHOR'S INTERPRETATION:

- Protruding objects might include signage, telephones, drinking fountains, etc.

PR-02 Do free-standing objects, suspended or mounted on posts or pylons with leading edges between 27 in. and 80 in. high, project less than 12 in. into the perpendicular route of travel? (4.4.1, Fig. 8a–e)

AUTHOR'S INTERPRETATION:

- These might include telephone enclosures, drinking fountains, or free-standing signage kiosks.

PR-03 Is the minimum clear route width or maneuvering space still maintained even with the projection of a protruding object? (4.4.1, Fig. 8a–e)

Protruding Objects: overhead clearance

PR-04 Is the minimum overhead clearance of 80 in. provided in accessible areas or along accessible routes? (4.4.2, Fig. 8a)

AUTHOR'S INTERPRETATION:

- Overhead objects that can reduce the required clearance might include structural overhangs, parking control devices, signage, or light fixtures.

PR-05 Where the vertical clearance of a space adjoining the accessible route is less than 80 in. high, is a cane detection barrier less than 27 in. from the floor provided for blind or visually impaired persons? (4.4.2, Fig. 8c-1)

AUTHOR'S INTERPRETATION:

- This condition might be found under a stair, at a sloped ceiling space, or with guy wires from telephone poles along an exterior accessible route.

(CR) Curb Ramps (4.7)

Curb Ramps: location

CR-01 Is there a curb ramp wherever an accessible route crosses a curb? (4.7.1)

Curb Ramps: slopes

CR-02 Is the running slope of the curb ramp 1:12 or less? (4.7.2)

- On existing sites where space limitations prohibit the use of a slope of 1:12 or less, the following slopes can be considered. [4.1.6(3)(a)(i-ii)]
  — Between 1:10 and 1:12 for a maximum rise of 6 in.
  — Between 1:8 and 1:10 for a maximum rise of 3 in.
  — A slope steeper than 1:8 is not allowed.

CR-03 Is the transition from the curb ramp to the walkway and to the road or gutter flush and free of abrupt changes? (4.7.2)

CR-04 Are the running slopes of the road, gutter, or accessible route adjoining the ramp no greater than 1:20? (4.7.2, Fig. 11)

Curb Ramps: width

CR-05 Is the width of the curb ramp, not including the flared sides, at least 36 in.? (4.7.3)

Curb Ramps: surface

CR-06 Is the surface of the curb ramp stable, firm, and slip-resistant? (4.5.1, 4.7.4)

Curb Ramps: side flares

CR-07 If the curb ramp is located where pedestrians must walk across it or where it is not protected by handrails or guardrails, does it have flared sides? (4.7.5, Fig. 12a)

- Flared sides shall have a slope of 1:10 or less.
- If the space at the top of the ramp is less than 48 in. and wheelchair users must use the side flares for access, the flared sides shall have a slope of 1:12 or less.

CR-08 If return curb cuts are provided, are the sides flanked by nonwalking surfaces that prevent pedestrian cross traffic? (4.7.5, Fig. 12b)

AUTHOR'S INTERPRETATION:

- "Nonwalking surfaces" such as plantings, raised planters, or raised curbs prevent pedestrian movement. Signage, impermanent objects such as newspaper boxes, and movable planters do not qualify.

Curb Ramps: built-up

CR-09 If built-up curb ramps are provided, are they located so that they do not project into vehicular traffic lanes or parking access aisles? (4.7.6, Fig. 13)

Curb Ramps: detectable warnings

NOTE:

- Requirements for detectable warnings (truncated domes) at curb ramps (4.7.7) have been suspended until July 26, 1996.

CR-10 Does the curb ramp have a detectable warning? (4.7.7)

- **Suspended until July 26, 1996.**

CR-11 Does the detectable warning consist of raised truncated domes and do they comply with the required criteria? (4.29.2)

- Diameter: nominal 0.9 in.
- Height: nominal 0.2 in.
- Spacing: nominal 2.35 in., center to center, offset every other row.
- Contrast: contrast visually with adjoining surface (light-on-dark or dark-on-light).
- The material used to provide contrast shall be an integral part of the walking surface. Detectable warnings used on interior surfaces shall differ from adjoining walking surfaces in resiliency or sound-on-cane contact.
- **Suspended until July 26, 1996.**

Curb Ramps: obstructions

CR-12 Are curb ramps located or protected to prevent obstruction by parked vehicles? (4.7.8)

Curb Ramps: location at marked crossings

CR-13 Are curb ramps at marked crossings wholly contained (excluding flared sides) within the marked crossing? See ADAAG Fig. 15. (4.7.9)

Curb Ramps: diagonal or corner type

CR-14 If diagonal (or corner type) curb ramps have returned curbs or other well-defined edges, are these curbs or edges parallel to the direction of pedestrian flow? (4.7.10)

CR-15 Is there at least 48 in. of clear space within the crosswalk lines at the bottom of a diagonal curb ramp? (4.7.10, Fig. 15c–d)

CR-16 If the diagonal curb ramp has flared sides, is there at least a 24-in. segment of straight curb located on each side of the diagonal curb ramp within the crosswalk lines? (4.7.10, Fig. 15c)

Curb Ramps: islands

CR-17 Are raised islands in crossings cut through level with the street or are curb ramps provided on each side of the island with at least 48 in. of level area between the curb ramps? (4.7.11, Fig. 15a–b)

(DW) Detectable Warnings (4.29)

NOTE:

- Requirements for detectable warnings (truncated domes) at curb ramps (4.7.7), hazardous vehicular areas (4.29.5), and reflecting ponds (4.29.6) have been suspended until July 26, 1996. This action does not affect the requirement for detectable warnings (truncated domes) at transit platforms [10.3.1(8)], which remains in effect.

Detectable Warnings: hazardous vehicular areas

DW-01 If a walk crosses or adjoins a vehicular way, and the pedestrian and vehicular paths are not separated by curbs, railings, or other elements, is the boundary of the pedestrian path defined by a continuous detectable warning (truncated domes), 36 in. wide on the edge of the pedestrian area? (4.29.5)

- **Suspended until July 26, 1996.**

Detectable Warnings: reflecting pools

DW-02 Are edges of reflecting pools protected by railings, walls, curbs, or detectable warnings (truncated domes)? (4.29.6)

- **Suspended until July 26, 1996.**

Detectable Warnings: criteria

DW-03 Do detectable warnings consist of raised truncated domes and do they meet the required criteria? (4.29.2)

- Diameter: nominal 0.9 in.
- Height: nominal 0.2 in.
- Spacing: nominal 2.35 in., center to center, offset every other row.
- Contrast: contrast visually with adjoining surface (light-on-dark or dark-on-light).
- The material used to provide contrast shall be an integral part of the walking surface. Detectable warnings used on interior surfaces shall differ from adjoining walking surfaces in resiliency or sound-on-cane contact.

(CT) Controls and Operating Mechanisms (4.27)

NOTES:

- Controls or operating mechanisms can include elements such as street crossing controls, light switches, intercoms and other communication devices, interpretive devices, alarm pull stations, and parking ticket dispensers.

- If controls are to be operated by occupants of the space, they must be accessible. If controls are to be operated by maintenance staff only and not by occupants or other users of the space, they do not have to be accessible. For example, buttons allowing pedestrians to change a traffic light need to be accessible; similar buttons allowing parking attendants to raise and lower parking barriers might not need to be accessible.

Controls: clear floor space

CT-01 Is a clear floor space of at least 30 in. × 48 in. provided in front of controls, dispensers, receptacles, and other operable equipment for forward or parallel approach? (4.27.2, Fig. 4a–b)

Controls: reach ranges

NOTES:

- Accessible reach ranges for controls and operating mechanisms are:
  — Forward reach: not less than 15 in. high and not more than 48 in. high without any obstruction or where the obstruction is less than 20 in. deep. For obstructions from 20 in. to 25 in. deep, no forward reach higher than 44 in.
  — Side reach: not less than 9 in. high and not more than 54 in. high. For obstructions not more than 34 in. high or 24 in. deep, no side reach higher than 46 in.

CT-04 Are dispensers or other similar operable equipment mounted within accessible forward or side reach ranges? (4.2.5, 4.2.6, Fig. 5a–b, Fig. 6a–c)

CT-05 Are life safety devices or other similar operable equipment mounted within accessible forward or side reach ranges? (4.2.5, 4.2.6, Fig. 5a–b, Fig. 6a–c)

NOTE:

- This might include fire alarm pull stations, emergency telephones, handles to extinguisher cabinets, or wall-mounted extinguishers.

Controls: operation

CT-06 Are controls, dispensers, receptacles, and other operable equipment operable with one hand without tight grasping, pinching, or wrist twisting, and requiring no more than 5 lbf of force? (4.27.4)

Controls: exterior conditions

CT-07 Are the controls for fixtures or equipment located on the exterior accessible route mounted within accessible forward or side reach ranges? (4.2.5, 4.2.6, Fig. 5a–b, Fig. 6a–c)

(SG) Signage (4.30)

NOTE:

- In historic buildings displays and written information, documents, etc., should be located where they can be seen by a seated person. Exhibits and signage displayed horizontally (e.g., open books) should be no higher than 44 in. above the floor surface. [4.1.7(3)(e)] While ADAAG requires this only for historic structures, it is a good guideline for other similar situations.

- Signage concerning accessible and inaccessible entries may be located on the structure or entrance to the activity area, along the accessible route to the facility, and/or in the parking lot. Evaluate this requirement in the appropriate space-type.

Signage: direction and information (where provided)

DEFINITION:

- Signs that provide direction to or information about functional spaces of the building.

EXCEPTION:

- Building directories, menus, and all other temporary signs are not required to comply. [4.1.3(16)]

SG-08 Do signs which provide direction to, or information about, functional spaces of the building comply with the criteria below? [4.1.2(7); 4.1.3(16); 4.30.1, 2, 3, 5]
  - Character proportion: letters and numbers have a width to height ratio between 3:5 and 1:1 and a stroke width to height ratio between 1:5 and 1:10.
  - Character height: sized according to viewing distance with characters on overhead signs at least 3 in. high.

  NOTE:
  - When the sign is mounted below 80 in., there are no prescribed character heights. Only when the sign is mounted 80 in. or higher are the characters required to be at least 3 in. high. (4.30.3)

  - Finish: characters and backgrounds have a nonglare finish.
  - Contrast: characters contrast with their background (light-on-dark or dark-on-light).

SG-09 Is a sign located so that the overhead clearance or the projection of a suspended or projected sign does not result in a protruding object (free-standing or wall-mounted)?
  - Clear height: at least 80 in. (4.4.2, Fig. 8a)
  - Overhang for free-standing signs on posts or pylons located between 27 in. and 80 in. high: no more than a 12-in. projection into accessible routes. (4.4.1, Fig. 8c)
  - Overhang for wall-mounted signs between 27 in. and 80 in. high: no more than a 4-in. projection into accessible routes. (4.4.1, Fig. 8a)

(SE) Fixed or Built-in Seating and Tables (4.32)

Fixed or Built-in Seating and Tables: minimum number

SE-01 Is the minimum number of accessible wheelchair seating locations at fixed tables or counters provided? (4.1.3.18)

- Number required: 5 percent of total number of seats but not fewer than one.

AUTHOR'S INTERPRETATION:

- ADAAG is not clear about required number/percentage of accessible seating space for fixed seating (benches, seat walls, etc.) without tables. Five percent of the total number of seats but not fewer than one is recommended.

Fixed or Built-in Seating and Tables: clear floor space

AUTHOR'S INTERPRETATION:

- Where the accessible route leads to and through accessible seating adjacent to a wall or another table, the minimum required width for the accessible route will be 65 in. between the table edge and next parallel surface (e.g., wall or another table edge). (4.1.3.18, Fig. 45)

SE-02 Is the clear floor space for a wheelchair at a seating location adequate? (4.32.3, Fig. 4a, Fig. 45)

- Clear floor space: 30 in. × 48 in.
- This clear space can include up to 19 in. under the table/desk.

Fixed or Built-in Seating and Tables: clearances

SE-03 Are the tops of accessible tables and counters between 28 in. and 34 in. from the floor? (4.32.3, Fig. 45)

SE-04 Are the knee clearances at least 27 in. high, 30 in. wide, and 19 in. deep? (4.32.3, Fig. 45)

Parking Structures

Introduction. Use this review guide for parking structures and covered parking facilities, offered to or provided for members of the general public, such as:

- Parking garages
- Garages or covered parking associated with businesses, housing, or transient lodging (including covered parking or garages available to those renting or owning units in a multifamily housing complex)
- Small scale covered parking structures such as carports, porte-coucheres, and residential scale garages

Compliance includes but is not limited to parking space criteria, overhead clearances, clear width and maneuvering spaces, and reach ranges for controls or operating mechanisms. There are no ADAAG criteria for garage or vehicular doors, but other doors serving pedestrians must comply with typical door criteria. Nor does ADAAG describe compliance for self-service or attendant payment systems. If provided, other elements and spaces used by the general public must be accessible as well (elevators, rest rooms, offices, telephones, drinking fountains, etc.). Refer to the appropriate review guide or section of the "Master Guidelines" as needed. Open air parking lots are covered in "Parking Lots and Passenger Loading Zones."

Parking Garages. Basic parking issues must be met: dimensions, number, location, slopes, etc. As with parking lots, both van accessible and accessible spaces are needed; compliance criteria vary for each. Universal parking spaces may be used in lieu of ADAAG acessible parking spaces.

An accessible route must connect to other adjacent accessible spaces and routes, both within the parking garage and immediately adjacent to it. Consider sidewalks and streets that abut the site, adjacent public transportation facilities, and direct connections to facilities served by the structure (retail, housing, transportation facilities, etc.). If there are spaces or elements used by the general public within the garage (elevators, stairs, offices, rest rooms, etc.), they must connect to the accessible route. Many garages provide elevators, but if not provided, then the stairs must be compliant.

If the parking structure serves a single facility, then the tables, graphics, and formulas given in ADAAG are relatively simple. Meeting ADAAG's technical requirements is more complex if the parking structure serves several buildings, if there are multiple accessible entrances, or if the parking structure is part of a series of parking facilities. Additional accessible spaces are required if the lot serves specific types of medical facilities. "Parking and Passenger Loading Zones" contains a more detailed explanation of general parking issues.

Parking structures must be evaluated in the context of the facilities they serve to determine the number, location, and possible dispersal of accessible parking spaces. Accessible parking should be located to meet the general goals of accessible route (most direct, most like that of the general public, etc.) Some parking garages connect to adjacent facilities on more than one level; others have several accessible entrances or entrances that serve different facilities. In such cases, accessible parking must be dispersed; however, in parking garages, all van accessible parking spaces may be grouped on one level of the structure instead of dispersed.

If provided, at least one passenger loading zone must be accessible. However, if multiple loading zones are provided in the structure, it may be advisable to make more than one accessible, particularly if the loading zones serve different facilities (as occurs in many large airports, conference facilities, etc.).

Traditional parking garage design standards are often problematic. The typical slopes and cross slopes that efficiently accommodate vehicular circulation in a parking garage are too steep for compliant parking spaces, passenger loading zones, or accessible routes. Spatial efficiency and economics often result in low ceilings that are not compliant, especially for van accessible parking spaces and passenger loading zones. Since the overhead clearance must be maintained along the entire vehicular route, location of accessible spaces within the structure is important.

Pedestrian/vehicular conflicts are common. As mandatory use of detectable warnings has been suspended until July 26, 1996, design responsibility for this critical issue is unclear and should be dealt with on an individual basis until new technical requirements are mandated. Some form of detectable warning is advisable. Bollards, curbs, and other devices intended to separate vehicular traffic from pedestrian must not interfere with accessibility.

ADAAG does not address how ticketing and payment systems are to be made accessible. This is probably best dealt with on a case by case basis. Manufacturers may provide advice on various systems and their installation. Using the logic of ADAAG may not be feasible here, because reach ranges in ADAAG are based upon a user seated in a wheelchair, not a car or van. These dimensions may vary greatly.

Protruding objects and overhead clearance problems are common. The minimum overhead clearance for van accessible parking and passenger loading zones is greater than for other spaces and must be maintained along the entire vehicular route, not just at the parking space. Parking control devices (gates, control arms, ticket dispensers, etc.), life safety devices, telephones, and so on may protrude into the accessible route.

Accessible parking spaces need compliant signage. Other signage may need to be compliant as well. Consider directional and informational signage, directions to accessible entrances, signs that designate permanent rooms and spaces, building signage, etc.

Valet parking does not exempt the structure from accessibility concerns, nor would "resident parking only" designations. The space used for valet parking must adhere to passenger loading zone technical requirements and must connect to an accessible route. The suggested revisions to ADAAG amplify parking requirements, including accessible visitor parking and compliant assigned parking spaces.

Functions other than parking are common. If available to the general public toilet facilities, elevators, offices, etc. must be compliant. Refer to the appropriate "Space-type Review Guide." Elements such as emergency phones, public telephones, intercoms, and other communication devices must also comply.

Parking garages are buildings; it may be necessary to refer to "Building Review Guide."

If other codes or regulations mandate alarms in the parking garage, these must be compliant.

Carports and Garages. ADAAG requires that a carport, garage, or parking space, if provided as part of an accessible unit, sleeping room, or suite, be accessible and on an accessible route. ADAAG does not, however, address specific requirements of accessible garages or carports. Nor does ADAAG specifically address business-related covered parking or other banks of covered or enclosed parking. What if there are covered parking spaces and uncovered parking spaces available? Are these treated as one lump sum of parking, or must accessible parking be provided in each? ADAAG implies that a compliant number, not fewer than one, of each type be provided.

Basic parking issues such as dimensions, overhead clearances, slopes, etc. must be met. Accessible and van accessible spaces may be needed; compliance criteria vary for each. Universal parking spaces may be used in lieu of these (see ADAAG Appendix). If only one accessible space is needed, it should meet all van accessible requirements.

An accessible route must connect this space to other adjacent accessible spaces and routes, both within the project site and immediately adjacent to it. Consider sidewalks and streets that abut the site, direct connections to adjacent facilities (interior and exterior), accessible entrances, and all the other issues involved in determining the accessible route. The accessible route must also provide accessible use of elements and services offered in the space, such as storage. Many carports and garages include sinks, laundry machines, and other elements. While ADAAG does not describe the accessible washing machine, access to such elements is required.

The width between parked vehicles and walls or posts, as well as clear width of paved floor surface, must allow passage and egress/exit from the vehicle. Also consider passage in front of or behind the vehicle. Adequate paved area in a carport is critical as drop-offs and changes in ground surface around the paving may be hazardous. Doors, ceilings, roof overhangs, and so on must reflect overhead clearances suitable for van accessible parking, which is greater than the more familiar minimum required for interior spaces and exterior accessible routes. ADAAG requires this vertical clearance for the entire vehicular path of travel—not just at the parking space or loading zone—so consider door or opening height, roof overhangs, etc.

Easily overlooked are reach ranges and maneuvering clearances for controls and operating mechanisms such as doors, lights, intercoms, etc.

ADAAG does not provide accessibility criteria for garage doors. Remote controlled doors may not be suitable for all situations. An accessible door should be provided in addition to the garage door.

PRELIMINARY DESIGN OVERVIEW

This overview includes ADAAG requirements typical for this particular space-type as well as situations that are unusual and may need special attention. Refer to other review guides ("Building Review," "Elevators," "Laundry," etc.) and the "Master Guidelines" as needed.

(AR) Accessible Routes

- Cross slope requirements for accessible parking spaces, passenger loading zones, and accessible routes are easily exceeded.
- Frequently overlooked maneuvering space problems in this space-type are approach to payment devices, turns around obstructions, security or parking control gates, bollards, controls and operating mechanisms (light switches, intercoms, etc.).
- Parked vehicles must not reduce the clear width of the accessible route.

- Route surfaces must meet criteria for vertical changes in level. Problem areas may include transition between materials, construction and expansion joints, and individual pavers.

(AL) Alarms

- If alarms are required by local codes or building regulations, they must be compliant.

(CT) Controls and Operating Mechanisms

- Frequently overlooked in this space-type are light switches, intercoms, emergency phones, etc.
- One of each type of control device for use by the general public should be accessible and operable.
- ADAAG does not provide criteria for accessible payment systems or ticket dispensers.

(CR) Curb Ramps

- If a curb ramp is located so that pedestrians must walk across it, provide protection or flared sides.

(DR) Doors

- ADAAG does not give criteria for an accessible garage door. If provided, doors to storage, to other spaces, or to an accessible route must be compliant.

(DW) Detectable Warnings

- Detectable warnings are suspended for most space-types until July 26, 1996.

(EL) Elevators

- Please refer to "Elevators." If no elevators are provided in parking garages, stairs must meet compliance criteria.

(FS) Floor and Ground Surfaces

- In most areas floor surfaces should be evaluated as if wet. In particular consider exterior doors and entries, drinking fountains, vehicular entrances, areas where rain may blow in, etc.
- Smooth floor surfaces should be evaluated for slip-resistance based on floor finish and maintenance.
- Vertical changes in levels along the accessible route can be an unforeseen barrier, e.g., transition between floor materials, grates, construction and expansion joints. Also of concern are raised objects in the path of travel (e.g., wheel stops, electrical and communication outlets, etc.)
- Grates located on the accessible route must meet accessibility requirements.

(PK) Parking and Passenger Loading Zones

- There are different minimum vertical clearances for passenger loading zones, van accessible parking, accessible parking, the vehicular route leading to the van parking, and the accessible route for pedestrians.
- If provided, at least one passenger loading zone must meet accessibility requirements.
- Valet parking must meet accessibility requirements for passenger loading zones.

- A percentage or minimum number of accessible spaces is required for both vans and cars. The minimum number of spaces increases if parking serves the mobility-impaired or outpatients.
- Accessible parking requirements for cars and vans differ (e.g., access aisle width, signage, vertical clearances).
- The location of accessible parking must respond to the shortest accessible route of travel to the facility or facilities served. If there are multiple accessible entrances, facilities, or use areas, the parking must be dispersed and located closest to the entrances served. In parking garages, van accessible spaces may be grouped on one floor of the structure.
- Access aisles may be shared.
- Slopes in accessible parking spaces and passenger loading zones must not exceed 1:50.
- Parked vehicles must not reduce the clear width of the accessible route.

(PR) Protruding Objects

- Common wall-mounted elements might be protruding objects, e.g., drinking fountains, public telephones, ATM machines, signs, etc. Parking control gates, ticket dispensers, and other elements peculiar to parking facilities may also be a problem.
- Overhead clearances can be an unforeseen compliance problem, e.g., signs, open space under stairs, low ceilings, etc. Overhead clearance for van accessible parking is greater than that of most interior spaces or accessible routes; this clearance must be maintained for the entire vehicular route.
- Standard fire safety items are often protruding objects, e.g., permanently mounted fire hose cabinets, fire extinguishers and fire extinguisher cabinets, valves on standpipes, etc.

(SG) Signage

- If all entrances are not accessible, the accessible entrances must be identified by the ISA symbol; nonaccessible entrances must have signage indicating the accessible route to an accessible entrance.
- Permanent directional and informational signage must meet accessibility criteria; letter height varies with mounting height of sign.
- Building directories, menus, and temporary signs are not required to comply.

(SR) Fixed Storage, Closets, Lockers, and Shelves

- If provided in carports or garages, one of each type of storage unit must be accessible.

(ST) Stairs

- Only stairs that connect levels not connected by an elevator or other accessible means of vertical access are required to comply.
- Stairs and their approaches must not allow water to accumulate on their surfaces.
- Open risers are not permitted on accessible stairs.

- Handrail extensions are possible protruding objects, especially where the extensions intersect another accessible route.

(PT) Public Telephones

- When public telephones are provided, at least one must be on the accessible route and comply with all telephone requirements.
- Text telephones or equivalent facilitation may be required depending on the number of public telephones provided within the building.
- For text telephones, specific signage is required even if a telephone is not provided.

- An accessible shelf and electrical outlet must be provided for portable text telephone(s) if a bank of 3 or more interior public telephones is provided.

ADAAG APPENDIX

The ADAAG Appendix includes additional advisory information pertinent to this space-type.

- A4.1.2(5)(e): Valet Parking
- A4.6: Parking and Passenger Loading Zones

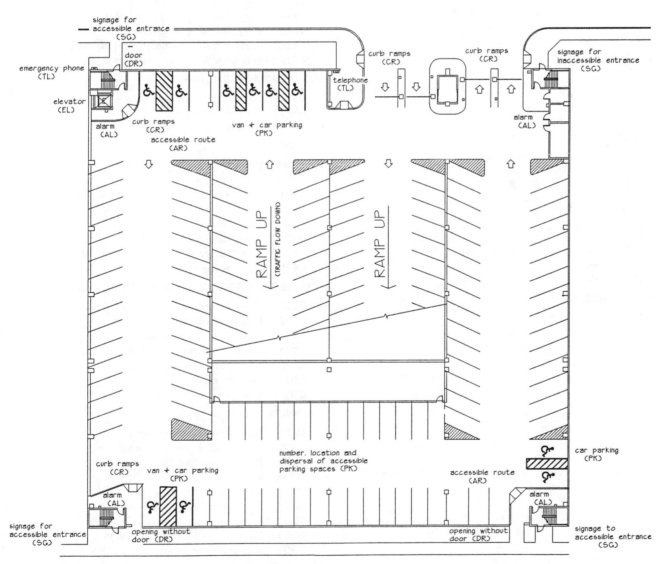

Figure 3-6. Parking structure.

PARKING AND PASSENGER LOADING ZONES

PK01	Car parking: number required
PK02	Van parking: number required
PK03	Accessible spaces provided in every lot
PK04	Outpatient facilities: number required
PK05	Mobility impairment facilities: number required
PK06	Specific bldg: parking space location
PK07	No specific bldg: parking space location
PK08	Multiple entrances: parking space location
PK09	Car parking spaces: criteria
PK10	Van parking spaces: criteria
PK11	Parking space and aisle: slope
PK12	Access aisle surface
PK13	Vertical clearance for vans
PK14	Access aisle connect to accessible route
PK15	Bumper overhang: clear width maintained
PK16	Car parking signage: I.S.A.
PK17	Van parking signage: I.S.A./van
PK18	Passenger loading zones: number required
PK19	Passenger loading signage: I.S.A.
PK20	Passenger loading: access aisle criteria
PK21	Passenger loading: slope requirements
PK22	Passenger loading: vertical clearance

ACCESSIBLE ROUTES

AR01	Bldg entry: from parking
AR06	Bldg entry to accessible spaces/elements
AR07	Dwelling unit entry to int./ext. spaces
AR08	Route: clear width
AR09	Route width: U-turns
AR10	Route: passing space
AR11	Route: maneuvering clearances
AR12	Route: running slope
AR13	Route: cross slope
AR14	Route: changes of level

FLOOR AND GROUND SURFACES

FS01	Surface: firm, stable, and slip-resistant
FS02	Vertical changes in level
FS04	Floor gratings

PROTRUDING OBJECTS

PR01	Wall-mounted
PR02	Freestanding/suspended on posts/pylons
PR03	Clear route width maintained
PR04	Overhead clearance
PR05	Vertical clearance: cane detection barrier

STAIRS

ST01	Riser/tread: criteria
ST02	Stair nosing: criteria
ST03	Handrails: location and continuity
ST04	Handrails: extensions
ST05	Ext. handrail is not a protruding object
ST06	Handrails: clear space to wall
ST07	Handrails: mounting height
ST08	Handrails: gripping surface uninterrupted
ST09	Handrails: rounded ends or returned
ST10	Handrails: no rotation
ST11	Water does not accumulate

HANDRAILS

HR01	Handrails and grab bars: diameter
HR02	Handrails and grab bars: edge radius
HR04	Handrails in recess: criteria
HR05	Handrails and grab bars: no rotation
HR06	Handrails and grab bars: structural strength
HR07	Mounting devices: structural strength
HR10	Wall adjacent to handrail abrasion free

CURB RAMPS

CR01	Accessible route: crossing at curb
CR02	Curb ramp: running slope
CR03	Curb ramp to walkway/road transition
CR04	Running slopes of adjoining surfaces
CR05	Curb ramp: width w/o flared sides
CR06	Curb ramp: surface stability
CR07	Curb ramp: required flared sides
CR08	Return curb cuts: nonwalking surfaces
CR09	Built-up curb ramps: criteria
CR10	Curb ramp: detectable warnings
CR11	Detectable warning: criteria
CR12	Curb ramp not blocked by parked vehicles
CR13	Curb ramp within marked crossings
CR14	Diag. curb ramp: edges and traffic flow
CR15	Diag. curb ramp: clear space in crosswalk
CR16	Diag. curb ramp w/flared sides: design
CR17	Raised traffic islands: acc. route options

DETECTABLE WARNINGS

DW01	Pedestrian/vehicular conflict: warning
DW02	Reflecting pools: warning
DW03	Truncated dome: criteria

DOORS

DR04	Doors: maneuvering clearances
DR05	Doors: handle type
DR06	Doors: opening force (interior only)
DR07	Doors: closing speed
DR08	Doors: thresholds
DR09	Doors: clear width/height
DR10	Openings (no door): clear width/height
DR11	Doors in series: clear space between

CONTROLS AND OPERATING MECHANISMS

CT01	Clear floor space
CT02	Reach ranges: elec./comm. systems
CT03	Reach ranges: thermostats
CT04	Reach ranges: other controls
CT05	Reach ranges: life safety devices
CT06	Controls: operation
CT07	Controls: exterior routes

SIGNAGE

SG01	Entry signage: ISA requirement
SG02	Entry signage: inaccessible entrances
SG03	Inaccessible entry signage: criteria
SG04	Room signage: criteria
SG05	Room signage: location
SG06	Pictograms: size requirements
SG07	Pictograms: verbal description criteria
SG08	Directional/informational signage: criteria
SG09	Suspended/projected signs: location

See **EL, DF, SE, TL,** and other sections as needed.

PARKING STRUCTURES
COMPREHENSIVE CRITERIA

This review guide addresses parking issues. Additional functions or spaces (rest rooms, elevators, laundry, etc.) should be evaluated using the appropriate review guide. Any element not included in this review guide but necessary to complete the evaluation should be selected from the "Master Guidelines." These may include ATM's, storage, drinking fountains, telephones, etc. The "Building Review Guide" should also be used.

(PK) Parking and Passenger Loading Zones (4.6)

NOTE:

- Where only one accessible space is provided, it shall meet van accessible criteria. [4.1.2(5)(b)]

Parking: required number

PK-01 Where parking spaces are provided for self-parking by employees, visitors, or both, is the required number of accessible car parking spaces provided? [4.1.2(5)(a)]

- 1–25:1, 26–50:2, 51–75:3, 76–100:4, 101–150:5, 151–200:6, 201–300:7, 301–400:8, 401–500:9, 501–1000:2 percent of the total, greater than 1000:20+1 for each 100 over 1000.
- All or some of the accessible parking spaces may be in a different location if equivalent or greater accessibility is ensured.

PK-02 Is the minimum number of accessible van spaces provided? [4.1.2(5)(b)]

- One in every eight spaces must be served by an access aisle at least 96 in. wide and must be designated "van accessible." Where only one accessible space is provided, it must meet van accessible criteria.

PK-03 Are accessible parking spaces provided in every specific area/lot? [4.1.2(5)(a)]

- All or some of the accessible parking spaces may be provided in a different location if equivalent or greater accessibility (in terms of distance from an accessible entrance), cost, and convenience is ensured.

PK-04 If the parking lot serves an outpatient facility, are 10 percent of the total parking spaces accessible? [4.1.2(5)(d)(i)]

PK-05 If the parking lot serves a mobility impairment facility, are 20 percent of the total parking spaces accessible? [4.1.2(5)(d)(ii)]

Parking: location

NOTE:

- Van accessible spaces may be grouped on one level of a parking structure.

PK-06 Where accessible parking spaces serve a particular building, are the accessible parking spaces located on the shortest accessible route of travel to an accessible entrance? (4.6.2)

PK-07 In parking facilities that do not serve any particular building, are the accessible parking spaces located on the shortest accessible route of travel to an accessible pedestrian entrance of the parking facility? (4.6.2)

PK-08 If multiple accessible entrances in a building are served by adjacent parking, are the accessible parking spaces dispersed and located closest to the accessible entrances? (4.6.2)

Parking: space dimensions and clearances

PK-09 Do the designated accessible car parking spaces comply with accessible criteria? (4.6.3, Fig. 9, Fig. 10)

- Car parking space width: at least 96 in. wide with a clearly demarcated access aisle.
- Adjacent access aisle width: at least 60 in. wide.
- Two adjacent accessible parking spaces may share a common access aisle.

PK-10 Do the designated accessible van parking spaces comply with accessible criteria? [4.1.2(5)(b), 4.6.3, Fig. 9]

- Van parking space width: at least 96 in. wide with a clearly demarcated access aisle.
- Adjacent access aisle width: at least 96 in. wide.
- Two adjacent accessible parking spaces may share a common access aisle.

PK-11 Are the surface slopes of accessible parking spaces and access aisles 1:50 or less in all directions? (4.6.3)

NOTE:

- This means a curb ramp cannot project into the access aisle.

PK-12 Are the access aisles stable, firm, and slip-resistant? (4.6.3)

PK-13 Does the accessible van parking space have vertical clearance of at least 98 in. at the parking space and along one vehicular route to the parking space (including entry and exiting from the parking lot)? [4.6.5, 4.1.2(5)(b)]

NOTE:

- Van accessible spaces may be grouped on one level of a parking structure.

Parking: access aisle and accessible route

PK-14 Does the access aisle for each accessible parking space connect directly to the accessible route? (4.6.3)

PK-15 Is the clear width (36 in.) of the accessible route maintained and not reduced by potential vehicle bumper overhang? (4.6.3, Fig. 9)

AUTHOR'S INTERPRETATION:

- A bumper overhang of 30 in. is assumed. The 30 in. is measured from the curb or wheel stop.

Parking: signage

PK-16 Does each accessible car parking space have a vertical sign, not obscured by a parked vehicle, showing the International Symbol of Accessibility (ISA)? (4.6.4)

PK-17 Does each accessible van parking space have a vertical sign, not obscured by a parked vehicle, showing the International Symbol of Accessibility (ISA) and an additional sign, "Van Accessible," mounted below the ISA sign? (4.6.4)

Passenger Loading

PK-18 Where passenger loading zones are provided, does at least one meet accessibility requirements? [4.1.2(5)(c)]

PK-19 Is the accessible passenger loading zone marked by the International Symbol of Accessibility (ISA)? [4.1.2(7)(b)]

PK-20 Is there an access aisle adjacent and parallel to the vehicular pull-up space, and is it at least 60 in. wide and 20 ft long? (4.6.6, Fig. 10)

PK-21 Is the vehicle standing space and access aisle in accessible passenger loading zones level with no slope greater than 1:50 (2 percent) in all directions? (4.6.6)

PK-22 Is a minimum vertical clearance of 114 in. provided at the passenger loading zone (including vehicle pull-up space and access aisle) and along the vehicular route to the vehicle pull-up space from site entrances and exits? (4.6.5)

(AR) Accessible Routes (4.3)

NOTES:

- All walks, halls, corridors, aisles, skywalks, tunnels, and other spaces that are part of a designated accessible route shall comply with accessible requirements.

- Any slope on the accessible route that is greater than 1:20 is required to meet all ramp criteria.

- The accessible route shall, to the maximum extent feasible, coincide with the route for the general public.

- Pedestrian accessible routes and vehicular routes may coincide in certain parking stucture situations. The typical minimums for overhead clearances will be increased for accessible van parking and for passenger loading zones.

- In historic buildings, accessible routes from an accessible entrance shall be provided to all publicly used spaces on at least the level of the accessible entrance. Access shall be provided to all levels of a building or facility whenever practical. [4.1.7(3)(d)]

AUTHOR'S INTERPRETATION:

- An accessible route "generally coincides" with the route used by the public if:
  — It does not force the user to go out of the way
  — It is most like the route chosen by the general public
  — It is direct
  — It gives the same basic experience as the route preferred by the public

Accessible Routes: site

AR-01 If on-site parking is provided for a specific facility, does at least one accessible route within the boundaries of the site and/or parking structure connect accessible parking spaces to the accessible building entrance? [4.1.2(1), 4.3.2(1)]

Accessible Routes: dwelling units

AR-07 Does an accessible route connect at least one accessible entrance of each accessible dwelling unit with those exterior and interior spaces and facilities (including parking) that serve the accessible unit? [4.3.2(4)]

Accessible Routes: width

AR-08 Is the minimum clear width along the accessible route adequate for continuous or point passage? (4.2.1, 4.3.3, Fig. 1, Fig. 8e, Fig. 24e)

- Continuous passage (greater than 24 in. long): at least a 36-in. clear width.

- Point passage (not more than 24 in. long): at least a 32-in. clear width.

AUTHOR'S INTERPRETATION:

- Noncompliance with this question generally relates to permanent elements that encroach on the accessible route. Large, heavy equipment that is not readily movable might be considered permanent. If the space is designed so that temporary elements (such as bikes in a bike rack or car bumpers) will consistently encroach, the situation might also be considered a permanent barrier.

AR-09 Is the minimum clear width along the accessible route adequate at a U-turn around an obstruction? (4.3.3, Fig. 7a–b)

- Obstruction 48 in. or greater: at least a 36-in. clear width around the obstruction.

- Obstruction less than 48 in.: at least a 42-in. clear width at each side with at least a 48-in. clear width in the turn.

Accessible Routes: passing space

AR-10 Does the accessible route provide at least 60 in. of clear width for two wheelchairs to pass and, if not, is the required passing space provided? (4.2.2, 4.3.4)

- A 60-in. × 60-in. passing space or "T" intersection should be provided at reasonable intervals not to exceed 200 ft.

AUTHOR'S INTERPRETATION:

- Accessible routes more than 5 ft long (e.g., routes in short hallways, aisles in laboratories, and work/storage areas) should have passing spaces provided. ADAAG does not define "reasonable intervals"; each situation should be evaluated individually.

DEFINITION:

- A *"T" intersection* is defined as the intersection of two corridors or walks, each at least 36 in. wide providing at least a 60-in. depth at the intersection. (Fig. 3b)

Accessible Routes: maneuvering clearances

AR-11 Is the minimum clear floor space for an unobstructed 180° wheelchair turning space or a "T"-shaped turning space provided? (4.2.3, Fig. 3a–b)

- 180° turning space: at least a 60-in. diameter.

- "T"-shaped turning space: at least 36-in. wide legs with a minimum length of 60 in.

Accessible Routes: slopes

AR-12 Is the running slope on the accessible route 1:20 or less? (4.3.7)

- Any slope on the accessible route that is greater than 1:20 is required to meet all ramp criteria.

AR-13 Is the cross slope on the accessible route 1:50 or less? (4.3.7)

Accessible Routes: changes in level

AR-14 Are changes in level greater than 1/2 in. accomplished by means of a curb ramp, ramp, elevator, or platform lift (as permitted in ADAAG 4.1.3 and 4.1.6)? (4.3.8)

(FS) Floor and Ground Surfaces (4.5)

Floor Surfaces: general

FS-01 Are the floor/ground surfaces on the accessible route stable, firm, and slip-resistant? (4.5.1)

AUTHOR'S INTERPRETATION:

- Exterior spaces, interior spaces where rain can blow in, vehicular entrances to garages, and other spaces where water can collect on the floor or around an element (sinks, drinking fountains, hose bibbs, etc.) are reviewed as if wet.
- High gloss surfaces without significant textures that are regularly maintained with waxing (smooth tiles, waxed concrete, etc.) could be considered noncompliant.
- Accessible criteria are not specified for nonpermanent floor surfaces such as mats or rugs.

Floor Surfaces: changes in level

FS-02 Are vertical changes in level between 1/4 in. and 1/2 in. beveled with a slope of 1:2 or less? (4.5.2)

- Changes in level up to 1/4 in. may be vertical without edge treatment.
- Changes in level greater than 1/2 in. should be accomplished by means of a curb ramp, ramp, elevator, or platform lift (as permitted in ADAAG 4.1.3 and 4.1.6).

Floor Surfaces: gratings

FS-04 Do floor gratings in the path of travel comply with accessible criteria? (4.5.4, Fig. 8g–h)

- Opening size: no greater than 1/2 in. in one direction.
- Opening direction: the long dimension is perpendicular to the dominant direction of travel.

(PR) Protruding Objects (4.4)

Protruding Objects: general

PR-01 Do wall-mounted objects having leading edges between 27 in. and 80 in. high project less than 4 in. into walkways, corridors, aisles, or paths of travel? (4.4.1, Fig. 8a–e)

- Objects mounted with their leading edge at or below 27 in. can protrude any amount, as long as they do not reduce the required clear width of an accessible route.

AUTHOR'S INTERPRETATION:

- Protruding objects might include fire extinguishers or cabinets, shelving, counters, built-in equipment overhangs, or various dispensers.

PR-02 Do free-standing objects, suspended or mounted on posts or pylons with leading edges between 27 in. and 80 in. high, project less than 12 in. into the perpendicular route of travel? (4.4.1, Fig. 8a–e)

AUTHOR'S INTERPRETATION:

- These might include telephone enclosures, drinking fountains, parking control devices, or free-standing signage kiosks.

PR-03 Is the minimum clear route width or maneuvering space still maintained even with the projection of a protruding object? (4.4.1, Fig. 8a–e)

Protruding Objects: overhead clearance

PR-04 Is the minimum overhead clearance of 80 in. provided in accessible areas or along accessible routes? (4.4.2, Fig. 8a)

- Minimum vertical clearance of 114 in. must be provided at the passenger loading zone (including vehicle pull-up space and access aisle) and along the vehicular route to the vehicle pull-up space from parking structure entrances and exits (4.6.5). Accessible van parking space must have vertical clearance of at least 98 in. at the parking space and along one vehicular route to the parking space (including entry and exiting from the parking structure). [4.6.5, 4.1.2(5)(b)]

AUTHOR'S INTERPRETATION:

- Overhead objects that can reduce the required clearance might include structures, pipes, ducts, parking control devices, or light fixtures.

PR-05 Where the vertical clearance of a space adjoining the accessible route is less than 80 in. high, is a cane detection barrier less than 27 in. from the floor provided for blind or visually impaired persons? (4.4.2, Fig. 8c-1)

AUTHOR'S INTERPRETATION:

- This condition might be found under a stair, at a sloped ceiling space, or with guy wires from telephone poles along an exterior accessible route.

(ST) Stairs (4.9)

NOTE:

- Only stairs that connect levels not connected by an elevator, ramp, or other accessible means of vertical access are required to comply. [4.1.3(4)]
  - In new construction, this condition may occur in facilities subject to the elevator exemption [4.1.3(5)—Exception 1] or where mezzanines are exempt in restaurants. (5.4)

Stairs: risers, treads, and nosings

ST-01 Do the stair treads and risers meet the required criteria? (4.9.2, Fig. 18a)

- Uniformity: riser heights and tread widths should remain uniform in any one flight of stairs.
- Treads: not less than 11 in. measured from riser to riser.
- Risers: no open risers are permitted.

ST-02 Do the stair nosings meet the required criteria? See ADAAG Fig. 18 for clarification. (4.9.3)

- Risers: risers slope toward the nosing.
- Radius of the curvature: not more than 1/2-in. radius at the leading edge of the tread.
- Angle nosing: angled underside on nosing is not less than 60° from the horizontal; underside of nosing should not be abrupt.
- Nosing projection: not more than 1½ in.

Stairs: handrails

NOTE:

- Additional criteria for handrails can be found in Section "HR, Handrails."

ST-03 Is the handrail provided on both sides of the stair and is the inside rail on switchback or dogleg stairs continuous at the landing? [4.9.4(1), Fig. 19a–b]

- The outside handrail along the perimeter wall does not have to be continuous around the landing.

ST-04 At the end of the stair handrails, is there at least 12 in. of handrail parallel to the floor beyond the top riser and is there at least one tread width of sloping handrail plus at least 12 in. of horizontal handrail beyond the bottom riser? [4.9.4(2), Fig. 19c–d.)

- See ADAAG Fig. 19c–d for extension design.

ST-05 If the handrail extension protrudes into an accessible route, is the handrail extension rounded to 27 in. or less from the floor so that it does not create a protruding object? [4.9.4(2)]

ST-06 Is the clearance between the stair handrail and the wall exactly 1½ in.? [4.9.4(3)]

ST-07 Are the tops of stair handrails between 34 in. and 38 in. above the stair nosing? [4.9.4(5)]

ST-08 Is the stair handrail gripping surface uninterrupted by newel posts, other obstructions, or missing segments? [4.9.4(4)]

ST-09 Are the ends of stair handrails rounded or returned smoothly to the floor, wall, or post? [4.9.4(6)]

ST-10 Are handrails fixed so that they do not rotate within their fittings? [4.9.4(7)]

Stairs: water accumulation

ST-11 Are outdoor stairs and their approaches designed so that water does not accumulate on walking surfaces? (4.9.6)

(HR) Handrails, Grab Bars, and Tub and Shower Seats (4.26)

NOTE:

- HR Guidelines may be repeated in other element-based guidelines: (RP) Ramps, (ST) Stairs, (WC) Water Closets, (TS) Toilet Stalls, (BT) Bathtubs, and (SS) Shower Stalls.

Handrails: size and spacing

HR-01 Is the gripping surface of the grab bars or handrails 1¼ to 1½ in. in outside diameter? (4.26.2, Fig. 39)

AUTHOR'S INTERPRETATION:

- Standard pipe sizes designated by the industry as 1¼ in. to 1½ in. are acceptable for purposes of this section.

HR-02 Do the grab bars or handrails have edges with a minimum radius of 1/8 in.? (4.26.4)

HR-04 If the handrail is located in a recess, is the recess a maximum of 3 in. deep extending at least 18 in. above the rail? (4.26.2, Fig. 39d)

Handrails: grab bar or handrail structural strength

HR-05 Are the grab bars or handrails secure so that they do not rotate in their fittings? [4.26.3(5)]

HR-06 Do the grab bars and handrails meet the structural strength requirements for bending stress and shear stress? (4.26.3)

- Actual bending stress in the grab bar induced by the maximum bending moment from the application of 250 lbf is less than the allowable bending stress for the material of the grab bar.
- Shear stress induced in a grab bar by the application of 250 lbf shall be less than the allowable shear stress for the material of the grab bar. If the connection between the grab bar and its mounting bracket or other support is considered to be fully restrained, then direct and torsional shear stresses shall be totaled for the combined shear stress, which shall not exceed the allowable shear stress.

HR-07 Do the fasteners and mounting devices for the grab bars or handrails meet the structural strength requirements for shear force and tensile force? (4.26.3)

- Shear force induced in a fastener or mounting device from the application of 250 lbf shall be less than the allowable lateral load of either the fastener or mounting device or the supporting structure, whichever is the smaller allowable load.
- Tensile force induced in a fastener by a direct tension force of 250 lbf plus the maximum moment from the application of 250 lbf shall be less than the allowable withdrawal load between the fastener and the supporting structure.

Handrails: hazards

HR-10 Are handrails or grab bars and any wall or other surfaces adjacent to them free of any sharp or abrasive elements? (4.26.4)

(CR) Curb Ramps (4.7)

Curb Ramps: location

CR-01 Is there a curb ramp wherever an accessible route crosses a curb? (4.7.1)

Curb Ramps: slopes

CR-02 Is the running slope of the curb ramp 1:12 or less? (4.7.2)

- On existing sites where space limitations prohibit the use of a slope of 1:12 or less, the following slopes can be considered. [4.1.6(3)(a)(i–ii)]
  — Between 1:10 and 1:12 for a maximum rise of 6 in.
  — Between 1:8 and 1:10 for a maximum rise of 3 in.
  — A slope steeper than 1:8 is not allowed.

CR-03 Is the transition from the curb ramp to the walkway and to the road or gutter flush and free of abrupt changes? (4.7.2)

CR-04 Are the running slopes of the road, gutter, or accessible route adjoining the ramp no greater than 1:20? (4.7.2, Fig. 11)

Curb Ramps: width

CR-05 Is the width of the curb ramp, not including the flared sides, at least 36 in.? (4.7.3)

Curb Ramps: surface

CR-06 Is the surface of the curb ramp stable, firm, and slip-resistant? (4.5.1, 4.7.4)

Curb Ramps: side flares

CR-07 If the curb ramp is located where pedestrians must walk across it or where it is not protected by handrails or guardrails, does it have flared sides? (4.7.5, Fig. 12a)

- Flared sides shall have a slope of 1:10 or less.
- If the space at the top of the ramp is less than 48 in. and wheelchair users must use the side flares for access, the flared sides shall have a slope of 1:12 or less.

CR-08 If return curb cuts are provided, are the sides flanked by nonwalking surfaces that prevent pedestrian cross traffic? (4.7.5, Fig. 12b)

AUTHOR'S INTERPRETATION:

- "Nonwalking surfaces" such as plantings, raised planters, or raised curbs prevent pedestrian movement. Signage, impermanent objects such as newspaper boxes, and movable planters do not qualify.

Curb Ramps: built-up

CR-09 If built-up curb ramps are provided, are they located so that they do not project into vehicular traffic lanes or parking access aisles? (4.7.6, Fig. 13)

Curb Ramps: detectable warnings

NOTE:

- Requirements for detectable warnings (truncated domes) at curb ramps (4.7.7) have been suspended until July 26, 1996.

CR-10 Does the curb ramp have a detectable warning? (4.7.7)

- **Suspended until July 26, 1996.**

CR-11 Does the detectable warning consist of raised truncated domes and do they comply with the required criteria? (4.29.2)

- Diameter: nominal 0.9 in.
- Height: nominal 0.2 in.
- Spacing: nominal 2.35 in., center to center, offset every other row.
- Contrast: contrast visually with adjoining surface (light-on-dark or dark-on-light).
- The material used to provide contrast shall be an integral part of the walking surface. Detectable warnings used on interior surfaces shall differ from adjoining walking surfaces in resiliency or sound-on-cane contact.
- **Suspended until July 26, 1996.**

Curb Ramps: obstructions

CR-12 Are curb ramps located or protected to prevent obstruction by parked vehicles? (4.7.8)

Curb Ramps: location at marked crossings

CR-13 Are curb ramps at marked crossings wholly contained (excluding flared sides) within the marked crossing? See ADAAG Fig. 15. (4.7.9)

Curb Ramps: diagonal or corner type

CR-14 If diagonal (or corner type) curb ramps have returned curbs or other well-defined edges, are these curbs or edges parallel to the direction of pedestrian flow? (4.7.10)

CR-15 Is there at least 48 in. of clear space within the crosswalk lines at the bottom of a diagonal curb ramp? (4.7.10, Fig. 15c–d)

CR-16 If the diagonal curb ramp has flared sides, is there at least a 24-in. segment of straight curb located on each side of the diagonal curb ramp within the crosswalk lines? (4.7.10, Fig. 15c)

Curb Ramps: islands

CR-17 Are raised islands in crossings cut through level with the street or are curb ramps provided on each side of the island with at least 48 in. of level area between the curb ramps? (4.7.11, Fig. 15a–b)

(DW) Detectable Warnings (4.29)

NOTE:

- Requirements for detectable warnings (truncated domes) at curb ramps (4.7.7), hazardous vehicular areas (4.29.5), and reflecting ponds (4.29.6) have been suspended until July 26, 1996. This action does not affect the requirement for detectable warnings (truncated domes) at transit platforms [10.3.1(8)], which remains in effect.

Detectable Warnings: hazardous vehicular areas

DW-01 If a walk crosses or adjoins a vehicular way, and the pedestrian and vehicular paths are not separated by curbs, railings, or other elements, is the boundary of the pedestrian path defined by a continuous detectable warning (truncated domes), 36 in. wide on the edge of the pedestrian area? (4.29.5)

- **Suspended until July 26, 1996.**

Detectable Warnings: reflecting pools

DW-02 Are edges of reflecting pools protected by railings, walls, curbs, or detectable warnings (truncated domes)? (4.29.6)

- **Suspended until July 26, 1996.**

Detectable Warnings: criteria

DW-03 Do detectable warnings consist of raised truncated domes and do they meet the required criteria? (4.29.2)

- Diameter: nominal 0.9 in.
- Height: nominal 0.2 in.
- Spacing: nominal 2.35 in., center to center, offset every other row.
- Contrast: contrast visually with adjoining surface (light-on-dark or dark-on-light).
- The material used to provide contrast shall be an integral part of the walking surface. Detectable warnings used on interior surfaces shall differ from adjoining walking surfaces in resiliency or sound-on-cane contact.

(DR) Doors (4.13)

NOTE:

- Included in this category are doors, revolving doors, turnstiles, and gates used by pedestrians. Parking control gates and overhead and other types of vehicular garage doors are not described in ADAAG.

AUTHOR'S INTERPRETATION:

- It is suggested that, for purposes of documentation and review, a door be assigned to the space it swings into. Corridors are an exception to this rule and include only entry doors into the corridor or intermediate fire doors.

Doors: maneuvering clearance

DR-04 If the door is not automatic or power assisted, does it have the required maneuvering clearance provided on the push and pull side, and is the floor level and clear within the maneuvering area? (4.13.6)

- A verbal description cannot adequately describe the requirements. See ADAAG Fig. 25a–f for a graphic description.

EXCEPTION:

- Entry doors to acute care hospital bedrooms for inpatients are exempt from maneuvering space at the latch side of the door if the door is at least 44 in. wide.

AUTHOR'S INTERPRETATION:

- While ADAAG does not describe what elements can reduce the required maneuvering clearance, they could include a narrow entry alcove, an adjacent wall, railing, or permanently installed shelving, or a deep recessed door jamb.

Doors: hardware

DR-05 Do all door handles, locks, latches, or other operable devices meet required operational criteria? (4.13.9)

- Hardware operation: operable with one hand without tight grasping, pinching, or wrist twisting.

- Force required to operate the controls: not greater than 5 lbf. This does not apply to the force required to retract latch bolts or to disengage other devices that only hold the door in a closed position.
- Hardware type: "U"-shaped handles, levers, and push type mechanisms are acceptable designs.
- Hardware height: not greater than 48 in. above the floor.
- Sliding doors: hardware is exposed and usable from both sides when the doors are fully open.

Doors: opening force

DR-06 Do interior hinged doors and sliding or folding doors have an opening force of 5 lbf or less? (4.13.11)

- At present, no accessible criteria exist for exterior doors or vehicular garage doors.
- Fire doors shall have the minimum opening force allowable by the appropriate administrative authority.

Doors: closing speed

DR-07 If the door has a closer, is the closer adjusted so that the door does not close too quickly? (4.13.10)

- From an open position of 70° the door will take at least 3 sec to move to a point 3 in. from the latch (measured to the leading edge of the door).

Doors: thresholds

DR-08 Where raised thresholds are provided, do they meet height limitations and are they beveled when required? (4.13.8, 4.5.2, Fig. 7)

- Threshold height: not more than 3/4 in. for exterior sliding doors or 1/2 in. for other types of doors.
- Threshold bevel: thresholds less than 1/4 in. high need no bevel; thresholds between 1/4 and 1/2 in. high shall be beveled at each edge with not more than a 1:2 slope.

EXCEPTION:

- A 3/4-in. high threshold is allowed in existing conditions. [4.1.6(3)(d)(ii)]

Doors: clear opening width and height

DR-09 Is the clear opening for the doorway adequate in width and height? (4.13.3, 4, 5, Fig. 24)

- Door width: at least 32 in. of clear width with the door open at 90°, measured between the face of the door and the door stop on the latch side. This also pertains to the active leaf of a double-leaf door or gate.
- Opening width: openings more than 24 in. deep must provide 36 in. of clear width.
- Height: at least 80 in. of vertical clearance.

EXCEPTIONS:

- Doors not requiring full user passage, such as shallow closets, may have the clear opening reduced to not less than 20 in.
- Where it is technically infeasible to comply with clear opening width requirements, a projection of 5/8 in. maximum will be permitted for the latch side. [4.1.6(d)(i)]

DR-10 Is the clear opening (when there is no door) adequate in width and height? (4.2.1, 4.3.3, 4.4.2)

- Width: at least 32 in. of clear width for depths 24 in. or less and at least 36 in. of clear width for depths greater than 24 in.
- Height: at least 80 in. of vertical clearance.

Doors: two doors in a series

DR-11 If there are two doors in a series, is the required clear space between the doors provided and do the doors swing in the appropriate direction? (4.13.7, Fig. 26)

- Clear space between the doors: not less than 48 in. plus the width of any door swinging into the space.
- Door swing: must swing in the same direction or away from the space between the doors.

(CT) Controls and Operating Mechanisms (4.27)

NOTES:

- Controls or operating mechanisms can include elements such as light switches, nonkeyed thermostats, alarm pull stations, fire extinguisher cabinets, towel dispensers, and wall hooks. ADAAG does not describe compliant ticket dispensers or payment devices that are accessed by drivers.
- If controls are to be operated by occupants of the space, they must be accessible. If controls are to be operated by maintenance staff only and not by occupants or other users of the space, they do not have to be accessible. For example, attendant-controlled parking gates usually do not have to be accessible, while intercoms would need to be accessible.

Controls: clear floor space

CT-01 Is a clear floor space of at least 30 in. × 48 in. provided in front of controls, dispensers, receptacles, and other operable equipment for forward or parallel approach? (4.27.2, Fig. 4a–b)

Controls: reach ranges

NOTES:

- Accessible reach ranges for controls and operating mechanisms are:
  - Forward reach: not less than 15 in. high and not more than 48 in. high without any obstruction or where the obstruction is less than 20 in. deep. For obstructions from 20 in. to 25 in. deep, no forward reach higher than 44 in.
  - Side reach: not less than 9 in. high and not more than 54 in. high. For obstructions not more than 34 in. high or 24 in. deep, no side reach higher than 46 in.
  - Electrical outlets, switches, and communication system receptacles have a minimum outlet height of 15 in. regardless of forward or side reach. See CT-02 below.

CT-02 Are electrical outlets, switches, and communication system receptacles mounted within accessible forward or side reach ranges? (4.27.3)

EXCEPTION:

- These requirements do not apply where the use of special equipment dictates otherwise or where electrical and communications system receptacles are not normally intended for use by building occupants. Such devices in residential scale garages or carports (in which the occupants use the devices) shall be compliant. (4.27.3)

CT-03 Are thermostats or other similar operable equipment mounted within accessible forward or side reach ranges? (4.2.5, 4.2.6, Fig. 5a–b, Fig. 6a–c)

CT-04 Are dispensers or other similar operable equipment mounted within accessible forward or side reach ranges? (4.2.5, 4.2.6, Fig. 5a–b, Fig. 6a–c)

CT-05 Are life safety devices or other similar operable equipment mounted within accessible forward or side reach ranges? (4.2.5, 4.2.6, Fig. 5a–b, Fig. 6a–c)

NOTE:

- This might include fire alarm pull stations, handles to extinguisher cabinets, or wall-mounted extinguishers.

Controls: operation

CT-06 Are controls, dispensers, receptacles, and other operable equipment operable with one hand without tight grasping, pinching, or wrist twisting, and requiring no more than 5 lbf of force? (4.27.4)

Controls: exterior conditions

CT-07 Are the controls for fixtures or equipment located on the exterior accessible route mounted within accessible forward or side reach ranges? (4.2.5, 4.2.6, Fig. 5a–b, Fig. 6a–c)

(SG) Signage (4.30)

NOTE:

- In historic buildings displays and written information, documents, etc., should be located where they can be seen by a seated person. Exhibits and signage displayed horizontally (e.g., open books) should be no higher than 44 in. above the floor surface. [4.1.7(3)(e)]

Signage: entry

SG-01 Where a building or space has both accessible and inaccessible entrances, are the accessible entrances identified by the International Symbol of Accessibility? [4.1.2(7)(c), Fig. 43a–b]

SG-02 If an entrance is not accessible, is there a directional sign indicating the location of the nearest accessible entrance? [4.1.2(7)(c), 4.1.3(8)(d)]

SG-03 Does the directional sign indicating the location of the nearest accessible entrance comply with directional signage criteria? (4.30.2, 3, 5)

- Character proportion: letters and numbers have a width to height ratio between 3:5 and 1:1 and a stroke width to height ratio between 1:5 and 1:10.
- Character height: sized according to viewing distance with characters on overhead signs at least 3 in. high.

- Finish: characters and backgrounds have a nonglare finish.
- Contrast: characters contrast with their background (light-on-dark or dark-on-light).

Signage: room identification (where provided)

DEFINITION:

- These signs designate permanent rooms and spaces.

AUTHOR'S INTERPRETATION:

- Signs that designate stairs, exit doors, and toilet rooms generally are associated with permanent spaces, while an "office" sign is not since the room function may change over time. Room numbers also must meet the ADAAG criteria as permanent designations, while personal names do not since the occupant may change over time.

SG-04 Do signs that designate permanent rooms and spaces comply with the following criteria? [4.1.2(7); 4.1.3(16); 4.30.4, 5, 6]

- Character type: raised and accompanied by Grade II Braille.
- Character size: between 5/8 in. and 2 in. high; raised at least 1/32 in.
- Character style: upper case, and sans or simple serif.
- Finish: characters and backgrounds have a nonglare finish.
- Contrast: characters contrast with their background (light-on-dark or dark-on-light).

SG-05 Is the room identification sign mounted in the required location? (4.30.6)

- Mounting location: installed on the wall adjacent to the latch side of the door or where wall space to the latch side of the door is not available, including double doors, placed on the nearest adjacent wall.
- Mounting height: 60 in. above the floor/ground to the centerline of the sign.
- Sign access: approach to within 3 in. of a sign without encountering protruding objects or standing within the swing of the door.

Signage: pictorial symbol signs (pictograms) (where provided)

AUTHOR'S INTERPRETATION:

- Because the criteria for pictograms are listed in ADAAG 4.30.4, they fall into the category of room identification signage and must meet those criteria that follow.
- While the ISA symbol might be considered to be a pictogram, it does not appear to have the same requirements as pictograms.

SG-06 Is the border dimension of a pictogram, where provided, at least 6 in. high? (4.30.4)

AUTHOR'S INTERPRETATION:

- A pictogram includes both a symbol and the field on which it is displayed. The 6-in. vertical dimension applies to the vertical field, not to the symbol. The required verbal description may not intrude on the 6-in. field.

SG-07 Is a pictogram, where provided, accompanied by the equivalent verbal description placed directly below the pictogram, and does the verbal description meet room identification signage criteria? (4.30.4)

- Character type: raised and accompanied by Grade II Braille.
- Character size: between 5/8 in. and 2 in. high; raised at least 1/32 in.
- Character style: upper case, and sans or simple serif.
- Finish: characters and backgrounds have a nonglare finish.
- Contrast: characters contrast with their background (light-on-dark or dark-on-light).

Signage: direction and information (where provided)

DEFINITION:

- Signs that provide direction to or information about functional spaces of the building.

EXCEPTION:

- Building directories, menus, and all other temporary signs are not required to comply. [4.1.3(16)]

SG-08 Do signs that provide direction to, or information about, functional spaces of the building comply with the criteria below? [4.1.2(7); 4.1.3(16); 4.30.1, 2, 3, 5]

- Character proportion: letters and numbers have a width to height ratio between 3:5 and 1:1 and a stroke width to height ratio between 1:5 and 1:10.
- Character height: sized according to viewing distance with characters on overhead signs at least 3 in. high.

NOTE:

- When the sign is mounted below 80 in., there are no prescribed character heights. Only when the sign is mounted 80 in. or higher are the characters required to be at least 3 in. high. (4.30.3)

- Finish: characters and backgrounds have a nonglare finish.
- Contrast: characters contrast with their background (light-on-dark or dark-on-light).

SG-09 Is a sign located so that the overhead clearance or the projection of a suspended or projected sign does not result in a protruding object (free-standing or wall-mounted)?

- Clear height: at least 80 in. (4.4.2, Fig. 8a)
- Overhang for free-standing signs on posts or pylons located between 27 in. and 80 in. high: no more than a 12-in. projection into accessible routes. (4.4.1, Fig. 8c)
- Overhang for wall-mounted signs between 27 in. and 80 in. high: no more than a 4-in. projection into accessible routes. (4.4.1, Fig. 8a)

The "Space-type Review Guides" were developed and organized to allow a designer to accurately and efficiently verify that a given three-dimensional design complies with the elements described and regulated by the ADAAG. The spaces listed in this category were selected to provide review guides of interior spaces representative of typologies so that, alone or in combination with individual ADAAG elements, these guides will facilitate the review of any space-type. The spaces selected were initially based on analysis of university environments. These initial space-types were expanded to include public accommodation and public municipalities. We have used these space-types to survey or review a wide range of spaces from classrooms and laboratories to student accessible pig farrowing barns, retail stores, hospital morgues, and city owned fire stations. There will be times when these interior forms will need to be combined. For example, the main areas of a dinner theater may require the use of "Lobbies, Corridors, Interior Accessible Routes, and Exits," "Restaurants and Cafeterias," and "Assembly Areas." These interior space-type forms may also be used for exterior functions, such as exterior dining or assembly spaces. For any element or situation not directly addressed by the ADAAG, it is hoped that the spirit of the law will be a guide to those responsible for designing interior spaces universally accessible to all.

Assembly Areas with Fixed Seating or Tables
(Auditoriums, Movie Theaters, Sports Arenas)

Introduction. Use this "Space-type Review Guide" to design or evaluate areas of assembly with *fixed* seats or tables. This would include general auditoriums, sports arenas, movie theaters, and lecture halls in schools and universities. Areas of assembly with *moveable* seating, such as conference rooms and classrooms, should be designed or surveyed using "Assembly Areas without Fixed Seating or Tables." Lobby spaces which generally occur with auditoriums and theaters should be evaluated using "Lobbies and Corridors."

Sports arenas and large auditoriums can be some of the most difficult spaces to make totally accessible. Sight lines in this type of assembly area usually dictate the programmatic need for sloped or stepped aisles to reach all seating areas. Both of these aisle types can be a challenge for people with mobility problems. These architectural needs are in conflict with two ADAAG requirements which state that:

- Wheelchair seating should not be in one location but dispersed throughout the seating area
- An accessible route needs to connect each wheelchair location to all areas of the facilities available to the general public, and also to serve as a means of emergency egress.

Basically the goal is to insure that disabled people with mobility problems are not grouped together but rather integrated into all seating areas. The first requirement provides people with a choice of seating areas depending on price categories or sight lines. The second requirement is meant to provide wheelchair users the same access as the general public to restrooms and concession areas, as well as performing areas, including stages or arena floors, dressing rooms, locker rooms, and other spaces used by performers. Both of these requirements are made even more demanding by the fact that a companion seat must be provided next to each wheelchair location. This, of course, allows a wheelchair user the opportunity to sit next to a spouse or friend who does not use a wheelchair. An exception to these criteria is allowed when viewing positions are located in bleachers, balconies, and other similar areas with sight lines that require slopes greater than 5 percent. Wheelchair locations may then be clustered in these viewing areas, and equivalent viewing positions may be located on differing levels provided an accessible route can be furnished to each level.

Another unique requirement of these spaces is their need for Assistive Listening Systems (ALS). These systems are intended to augment standard public address systems by providing signals which can be received with special receivers or personal hearing aids. The type of system appropriate for a particular space depends on the characteristics of the space, the nature of the program, and the particular needs of the hearing-impaired individual. There are a variety of different systems available and the designer will need to work with the manager of the facility to determine which system best meets all these needs.

PRELIMINARY DESIGN OVERVIEW

(AA) Assembly Areas

- The minimum number of wheelchair locations in facilities with fixed seating but no fixed writing surface (tables, counters, folding arms, etc.) is determined by using the table provided in ADAAG. For seating with fixed writing surfaces, see (SE) "Fixed Tables and/or Counters."
- A fixed companion seat must be located next to each wheelchair location.
- Facilities with 300 or more seats must provide wheelchair locations that offer variety in price and view.

- A percentage of all aisle seats must be seats without fixed armrests.
- Accessible viewing positions may be clustered for bleachers, balconies, and other areas having sight lines that require slopes greater than 5 percent.
- Assistive Listening Systems must be provided when there is fixed seating and the space seats more than 50 people or has audio amplification.
- An Assistive Listening System serving individual fixed seats needs to be located within a 50-ft viewing distance of the stage or platform and have a complete view of the stage or platform

(AL) Alarms

- Visual alarms must be provided in every general usage area (e.g., auditoriums, movie theaters, sports arenas, lobbies, and any other area of common use).

(AR) Accessible Routes

- An accessible route must connect each wheelchair seating location to all performance areas including stages, arena floors, dressing rooms, locker rooms, and other spaces used by performers.
- An accessible route from each wheelchair seating location must serve as a means of egress in an emergency.
- Running and cross slope requirements for any sloped floor are often overlooked and easily exceeded (e.g., aisles, cross aisles, theater lobbies).

(BM) Business and Mercantile

- An accessible counter is required at each different area offering sales or service such as ticket booths, reception desks, concession stands, information counters, coat check rooms, etc.
- All accessible sales and service counters must be on the accessible route.

(CT) Controls and Operating Mechanisms

- One of each type of control and operating mechanism used by the general public should be accessible and operable.
- Frequently overlooked control and operating mechanisms in this space-type are communication outlets; switches located on stage for lights, curtains, and projection screens; pull cords on overhead chalkboards and screens; and so on.

(DR) Doors

- Revolving doors or turnstiles require an adjacent accessible door, gate, or opening.
- Two doors in a series must meet both clear space and door swing requirements (e.g., lobby entrances, vestibules).
- Both interior and exterior doors may need to be accessible.
- Automatic or power assisted entry doors will need to meet accessibility requirements.

(EN) Entrances

- Half of all public entrances must be accessible and at least one must be accessible on the ground floor.

- The number of accessible entrances must be equal to the number of exits required by the building/fire code.

(FS) Floor and Ground Surfaces

- In some areas floor surfaces should be evaluated as if wet. In particular consider exterior doors, drinking fountains, concession stands, etc.
- Smooth floor surfaces should be evaluated for slip-resistance based on floor finish and maintenance.

(PL) Platform Lifts

- Platform lifts may be used in lieu of ramps for access to raised platforms or stages.

(PR) Protruding Objects

- Common wall-mounted elements can be protruding objects, e.g., pencil sharpeners, storage shelves, drinking fountains, public telephones, signs, display cases.
- Overhead clearances can be an unforeseen compliance problem, e.g., signs and banners, open space under stairs, low ceilings around concession stands and information booths, etc.
- Standard fire safety items are often protruding objects, e.g., permanently mounted fire hose cabinets, fire extinguishers and fire extinguisher cabinets, valves on standpipes, etc.

(RC) Raised Platforms (Stages)

- A raised platform or stage accessible by the general public must be accessible to wheelchair users from each wheelchair location.
- Access to the platform or stage will require a platform lift or a ramp with a handrail.
- Platforms and stages require edge protection.

(RP) Ramps

- Aisles with slopes greater than 1:20 that are used as accessible routes must meet ramp requirements. Note exception for handrails.
- Handrail extensions are possible protruding objects, especially where the extensions intersect another accessible route.
- Some persons who use walking aids prefer stairs over ramps; consider including both.

(SE) Fixed Tables or Folding Arm Seats

- If fixed writing tables (folding arm seats) or counters are provided, a minimum of 5 percent of the total number but not fewer than one of either type must be accessible.
- An accessible route must lead to and through accessible seating at fixed tables.

(SG) Signage

- If all entrances are not accessible, the accessible entrances must be identified by the ISA symbol; nonaccessible entrances must have signage indicating the accessible route to an accessible entrance.
- Permanent directional and informational signage, such as those indicating direction to restrooms, telephones, and seating, must meet accessibility criteria; letter height varies with mounting height of sign.

- Building directories, menus, and temporary signs are not required to comply.
- Accessible fixed aisle seats must be identified by a sign or marker. A sign at the ticket office must notify patrons that such seats are available.
- Signage indicating the availability of an Assistive Listening System is required and must include the International Symbol for hearing loss.

(SR) Fixed Storage, Lockers, and Shelves

- When provided, one of each type of storage unit (shelves, lockers, etc.) for use by the general public must be accessible.

(ST) Stairs

- Only stairs that connect levels not connected by an elevator or other accessible means of vertical access are required to comply.

- Some people who use walking aids have difficulty with ramps and prefer stairs.
- Open risers are not permitted on accessible stairs.
- Handrail extensions are possible protruding objects, especially where the extensions intersect another accessible route.

ADAAG APPENDIX

The ADAAG Appendix contains advisory information pertinent to this space-type.

- A4.30.7 Symbols of Accessibility for Different Types of Listening Systems

- A4.33 Assembly Areas

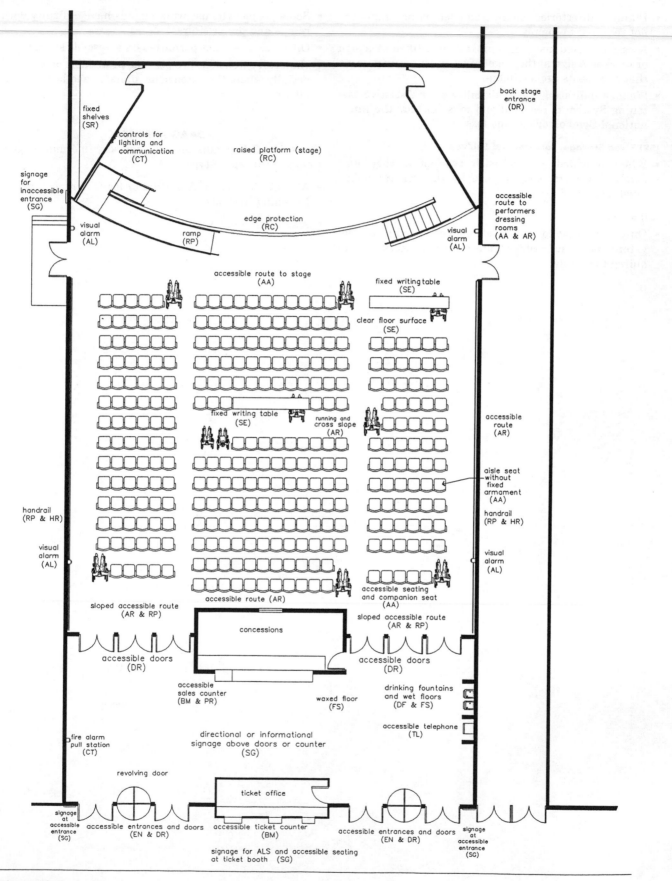

Figure 3-7. Auditorium.

Assembly Areas with Fixed Seating or Tables Checklist

SIGNAGE

SG01	Entry signage: I.S.A. requirement
SG02	Entry signage: inaccessible entrances
SG03	Inaccessible entry signage: criteria
SG04	Room signage: criteria
SG05	Room signage: location
SG06	Pictograms: size requirements
SG07	Pictograms: verbal description criteria
SG08	Directional/informational signage: criteria
SG09	Suspended/projected signs: location
SG14	Assistive Listening System: signage

DOORS

DR01	Revolving door/turnstile
DR02	Automatic doors: ANSI standards
DR03	Automatic doors: operation
DR04	Doors: maneuvering clearances
DR05	Doors: handle type
DR06	Doors: opening force (interior only)
DR07	Doors: closing speed
DR08	Doors: thresholds
DR09	Doors: clear width/height
DR10	Openings (no door): clear width/height
DR11	Doors in series: clear space between

ASSEMBLY AREAS

AA01	Wheelchair spaces: number required
AA02	Aisle seats w/o armrest: number required
AA03	Aisle seats: identified by signage
AA04	Signage for acc. seating at ticket office
AA05	Wheelchair locations: clear floor space
AA06	Wheelchair locations: choice in view/price
AA07	Wheelchair spaces: companion seating
AA08	Wheelchair locations: emergency egress
AA09	Accessible route to performer spaces
AA10	Wheelchair locations: floor surfaces
AA11	Assistive Listening System: signage
AA12	Assistive Listening System: integral
AA13	Assistive Listening System: portable units
AA14	Assistive Listening System: req'd receivers
AA15	Assistive Listening System: view distances
AA16	Assistive Listening System: operation

BUSINESS AND MERCANTILE

BM01	Sales/service counters: accessible route
BM02	Counters w/cash registers: criteria
BM03	Counters w/o cash registers: criteria

ACCESSIBLE ROUTES

AR06	Bldg entry to accessible spaces/elements
AR08	Route: clear width
AR09	Route width: U-turns
AR10	Route: passing space
AR11	Route: maneuvering clearances
AR12	Route: running slope
AR13	Route: cross slope
AR14	Route: changes of level

RAMPS

RP01	Maximum running slopes and lengths
RP02	Maximum cross slope
RP03	Minimum clear width
RP04	Landings: location
RP05	Landings: size
RP06	Landings used to change direction
RP07	Handrails: when required
RP08	Handrails: switchbacks
RP09	Handrails: extensions past ramp
RP10	Handrails: clear space to wall
RP11	Handrails: mounting height
RP12	Handrails: continuous gripping surface
RP13	Handrails: rounded end or returned
RP14	Handrails: no rotation
RP15	Ramp edge protection
RP16	Floor surface stability

HANDRAILS

HR01	Handrails and grab bars: diameter
HR02	Handrails and grab bars: edge radius
HR03	Clearance between handrail and wall
HR04	Handrails in recess: criteria
HR06	Handrails and grab bars: structural strength
HR07	Mounting devices: structural strength
HR10	Wall adjacent to handrail abrasion free

FLOOR SURFACES

FS01	Surface: firm, stable, and slip-resistant
FS02	Vertical changes in level
FS03	Carpet and tile floors

PROTRUDING OBJECTS

PR01	Wall-mounted
PR02	Freestanding/suspended on posts/pylons
PR03	Clear route width maintained
PR04	Overhead clearance
PR05	Vertical clearance: cane detection barrier

RAISED PLATFORMS

RC10	Raised platforms: accessible
RC11	Raised platforms: edge protection

CONTROLS AND OPERATING MECHANISMS

CT01	Clear floor space
CT02	Reach ranges: elec./comm. systems
CT03	Reach ranges: thermostats
CT04	Reach ranges: other controls
CT05	Reach ranges: life safety devices
CT06	Controls: operation

FIXED TABLES OR SEATING

SE01	Fixed seating: number required
SE02	Wheelchairs: clear floor space at tables
SE03	Tables/counters: heights
SE04	Tables/counters: knee clearance criteria

(continued)

Assembly Areas with Fixed Seating or Tables Checklist *(continued)*

STORAGE	**AL03** Single station audible and visual
SR01 Accessibility: one of each type	**AL04** Visual alarms: integration w/building alarm
SR02 Clear floor space	**AL05** Visual alarms: operation
SR03 Reach ranges	**AL06** Visual alarms: public restrooms
SR04 Storage closets w/o passage: criteria	**AL07** Visual alarms: common use areas
SR05 Storage hardware: operation	**AL08** Visual alarms: vertical placement
ALARMS	**AL09** Visual alarms: horizontal spacing
AL01 Emergency warning: audible/visual	
AL02 Audible alarms: operation	

ASSEMBLY AREAS WITH FIXED SEATING OR TABLES COMPREHENSIVE CRITERIA

General Note

- This "Space-type Review Guide" focuses on assembly areas with fixed seating such as auditoriums, movie theaters, and sports arenas.

(SG) Signage (4.30)

NOTE:

- In historic buildings displays and written information, documents, etc., should be located where they can be seen by a seated person. Exhibits and signage displayed horizontally (e.g., open books) should be no higher than 44 in. above the floor surface. [4.1.7(3)(e)]

Signage: entry

SG-01 Where a building or space has both accessible and inaccessible entrances, are the accessible entrances identified by the International Symbol of Accessibility? [4.1.2(7)(c), Fig. 43a–b]

SG-02 If an entrance is not accessible, is there a directional sign indicating the location of the nearest accessible entrance? [4.1.2(7)(c), 4.1.3(8)(d)]

SG-03 Does the directional sign indicating the location of the nearest accessible entrance comply with directional signage criteria? (4.30.2, 3, 5)

- Character proportion: letters and numbers have a width to height ratio between 3:5 and 1:1 and a stroke width to height ratio between 1:5 and 1:10.
- Character height: sized according to viewing distance with characters on overhead signs at least 3 in. high.
- Finish: characters and backgrounds have a nonglare finish.
- Contrast: characters contrast with their background (light-on-dark or dark-on-light).

Signage: room identification (where provided)

DEFINITION:

- These signs designate permanent rooms and spaces.

AUTHOR'S INTERPRETATION:

- Signs that designate stairs, exit doors, and toilet rooms generally are associated with permanent spaces, while an "office" sign is not since the room function may change over time. Room numbers also must meet the ADAAG

criteria as permanent designations, while personal names do not since the occupant may change over time.

SG-04 Do signs that designate permanent rooms and spaces comply with the following criteria? [4.1.2(7); 4.1.3(16); 4.30.4, 5, 6]

- Character type: raised and accompanied by Grade II Braille.
- Character size: between 5/8 in. and 2 in. high; raised at least 1/32 in.
- Character style: upper case, and sans or simple serif.
- Finish: characters and backgrounds have a nonglare finish.
- Contrast: characters contrast with their background (light-on-dark or dark-on-light).

SG-05 Is the room identification sign mounted in the required location? (4.30.6)

- Mounting location: installed on the wall adjacent to the latch side of the door or where wall space to the latch side of the door is not available, including double doors, placed on the nearest adjacent wall.
- Mounting height: 60 in. above the floor/ground to the centerline of the sign.
- Sign access: approach to within 3 in. of a sign without encountering protruding objects or standing within the swing of the door.

Signage: pictorial symbol signs (pictograms) (where provided)

AUTHOR'S INTERPRETATION:

- Because the criteria for pictograms are listed in ADAAG 4.30.4, they fall into the category of room identification signage and must meet those criteria that follow.
- While the ISA symbol might be considered to be a pictogram, it does not appear to have the same requirements as pictograms.

SG-06 Is the border dimension of a pictogram, where provided, at least 6 in. high? (4.30.4)

AUTHOR'S INTERPRETATION:

- A pictogram includes both a symbol and the field on which it is displayed. The 6-in. vertical dimension applies to the vertical field, not to the symbol. The required verbal description may not intrude on the 6-in. field.

SG-07 Is a pictogram, where provided, accompanied by the equivalent verbal description placed directly below the pictogram, and does the verbal description meet room identification signage criteria? (4.30.4)

- Character type: raised and accompanied by Grade II Braille.
- Character size: between 5/8 in. and 2 in. high; raised at least 1/32 in.
- Character style: upper case, and sans or simple serif.
- Finish: characters and backgrounds have a nonglare finish.
- Contrast: characters contrast with their background (light-on-dark or dark-on-light).

Signage: direction and information (where provided)

DEFINITION:

- Signs that provide direction to or information about functional spaces of the building.

EXCEPTION:

- Building directories, menus, and all other temporary signs are not required to comply. [4.1.3(16)]

SG-08 Do signs that provide direction to, or information about, functional spaces of the building comply with the following criteria? [4.1.2(7); 4.1.3(16); 4.30.1, 2, 3, 5]

- Character proportion: letters and numbers have a width to height ratio between 3:5 and 1:1 and a stroke width to height ratio between 1:5 and 1:10.
- Character height: sized according to viewing distance with characters on overhead signs at least 3 in. high.

NOTE:

- When the sign is mounted below 80 in., there are no prescribed character heights. Only when the sign is mounted 80 in. or higher are the characters required to be at least 3 in. high. (4.30.3)

- Finish: characters and backgrounds have a nonglare finish.
- Contrast: characters contrast with their background (light-on-dark or dark-on-light).

SG-09 Is a sign located so that the overhead clearance or the projection of a suspended or projected sign does not result in a protruding object (free-standing or wall-mounted)?

- Clear height: at least 80 in. (4.4.2, Fig. 8a)
- Overhang for free-standing signs on posts or pylons located between 27 in. and 80 in. high: no more than a 12-in. projection into accessible routes. (4.4.1, Fig. 8c)
- Overhang for wall-mounted signs between 27 in. and 80 in. high: no more than a 4-in. projection into accessible routes. (4.4.1, Fig. 8a)

Signage: Assistive Listening System (ALS)

SG-14 Where a permanently installed Assistive Listening System is provided, is there informational signage installed to notify patrons of the availability of such a system and does the signage include the International Symbol for hearing loss? [4.1.3(19)(b), 4.30.7(4), Fig. 43d]

(DR) Doors (4.13)

NOTE:

- Included in this category are doors, revolving doors, turnstiles, and gates.

AUTHOR'S INTERPRETATION:

- It is suggested that, for purposes of documentation and review, a door be assigned to the space it swings into. Corridors are an exception to this rule and include only entry doors into the corridor or intermediate fire doors.

Doors: revolving doors, turnstiles, and gates

DR-01 Where revolving doors or turnstiles are used on an accessible route, is an adjacent accessible gate or door provided that allows the same use pattern? (4.13.2)

Doors: automatic or power assisted

DR-02 If an automatic door or power assisted door is used, does it comply with the appropriate ANSI standard? (4.13.12)

- Automatic door: ANSI/BHMA A156.10-1985.
- Slow opening, low powered automatic door: ANSI A156.19-1984.
- Power assisted door: ANSI A156.19-1984.

DR-03 Do slow opening, low powered automatic doors or power assisted doors comply with opening and closing requirements? (4.13.12)

- Slow opening, low powered automatic doors: do not open to back-check faster than 3 sec and require no more than 15 lbf of force to stop door movement.
- Power assisted doors: no more than 5 lbf of opening force.

Doors: maneuvering clearance

DR-04 If the door is not automatic or power assisted, does it have the required maneuvering clearance provided on the push and pull side, and is the floor level and clear within the maneuvering area? (4.13.6)

- A verbal description cannot adequately describe the requirements. See ADAAG Fig. 25a–f for a graphic description.

EXCEPTION:

- Entry doors to acute care hospital bedrooms for inpatients are exempt from maneuvering space at the latch side of the door if the door is at least 44 in. wide.

AUTHOR'S INTERPRETATION:

- While ADAAG does not describe what elements can reduce the required maneuvering clearance, they could include a narrow entry alcove, an adjacent wall, railing, or permanently installed shelving, or a deep recessed door jamb.

Doors: hardware

DR-05 Do all door handles, locks, latches, or other operable devices meet required operational criteria? (4.13.9)

- Hardware operation: operable with one hand without tight grasping, pinching, or wrist twisting.

- Force required to operate the controls: not greater than 5 lbf. This does not apply to the force required to retract latch bolts or to disengage other devices that only hold the door in a closed position.
- Hardware type: "U"-shaped handles, levers, and push type mechanisms are acceptable designs.
- Hardware height: not greater than 48 in. above the floor.
- Sliding doors: hardware is exposed and usable from both sides when the doors are fully open.

Doors: opening force

DR-06 Do interior hinged doors and sliding or folding doors have an opening force of 5 lbf or less? (4.13.11)

- At present, no accessible criteria exist for exterior doors.
- Fire doors shall have the minimum opening force allowable by the appropriate administrative authority.

Doors: closing speed

DR-07 If the door has a closer, is the closer adjusted so that the door does not close too quickly? (4.13.10)

- From an open position of 70° the door will take at least 3 sec to move to a point 3 in. from the latch (measured to the leading edge of the door).

Doors: thresholds

DR-08 Where raised thresholds are provided, do they meet height limitations and are they beveled when required? (4.13.8, 4.5.2, Fig. 7)

- Threshold height: not more than 3/4 in. for exterior sliding doors or 1/2 in. for other types of doors.
- Threshold bevel: thresholds less than 1/4 in. in height need no bevel; thresholds between 1/4 and 1/2 in. in height shall be beveled at each edge with not more than a 1:2 slope.

EXCEPTION:

- A 3/4-in. high threshold is allowed in existing conditions. [4.1.6(3)(d)(ii)]

Doors: clear opening width and height

DR-09 Is the clear opening for the doorway adequate in width and height? (4.13.3, 4, 5, Fig. 24)

- Door width: at least 32 in. of clear width with the door open at 90°, measured between the face of the door and the door stop on the latch side. This also pertains to the active leaf of a double-leaf door or gate.
- Opening width: openings more than 24 in. deep must provide 36 in. of clear width.
- Height: at least 80 in. of vertical clearance.

EXCEPTIONS:

- Doors not requiring full user passage, such as shallow closets, may have the clear opening reduced to not less than 20 in.
- Where it is technically infeasible to comply with clear opening width requirements, a projection of 5/8 in. maximum will be permitted for the latch side. [4.1.6(d)(i)]

DR-10 Is the clear opening (when there is no door) adequate in width and height? (4.2.1, 4.3.3, 4.4.2)

- Width: at least 32 in. of clear width for depths 24 in. or less and at least 36 in. of clear width for depths greater than 24 in.
- Height: at least 80 in. of vertical clearance.

Doors: two doors in a series

DR-11 If there are two doors in a series, is the required clear space between the doors provided and do the doors swing in the appropriate direction? (4.13.7, Fig. 26)

- Clear space between the doors: not less than 48 in. plus the width of any door swinging into the space.
- Door swing: must swing in the same direction or away from the space between the doors.

(AA) Assembly Areas (4.33)

Assembly Areas: minimum number and notification

AA-01 In assembly areas with fixed seating, is the minimum number of required wheelchair spaces provided? [4.1.3(19)(a), 4.33.1]

- Number of spaces required: one per 4–25 seats, two per 26–50 seats, four per 51–300 seats, six per 301–500 seats, over 500 seats requires six plus one per additional 100 seats. [4.1.3(19)(a)]

AA-02 In addition to required wheelchair spaces, is the required number of aisle seats (without fixed armrests or with removable armrest on the aisle side) provided? [4.1.3(19)(a)]

- Number of spaces required: 1 percent of all fixed seating but not fewer than one.

AA-03 Is the aisle seating without fixed armrests or removable armrest on the aisle side identified by signage? [4.1.3(19)(a)]

AA-04 Is notification of accessible seating posted at the ticket office? [4.1.3(19)(a)]

Assembly Areas: wheelchair seating size

AA-05 Is the clear floor space adequate for forward, rear, or side access to a wheelchair space? (4.33.2, Fig. 46)

- Width: not less than 33 in. for an individual space or 66 in. for paired spaces.
- Depth: not less than 48 in. for forward and rear access or 60 in. for side access.

Assembly Areas: location

AA-06 Are wheelchair spaces located so that they provide variety in price and view comparable to those for the general public? (4.33.3)

- If the seating capacity is over 300, provide spaces in more than one location.

EXCEPTION:

- These spaces may be clustered for bleachers, balconies, and other areas where sight lines require slopes greater than 5 percent.

AA-07 Is a fixed companion seat provided next to a wheelchair space in each wheelchair area? (4.33.3)

AA-08 Do wheelchair locations adjoin an accessible route that also serves as a means of emergency egress? (4.33.3)

AA-09 Is there an accessible route connecting wheelchair seating locations and performance areas including stages, arena floors, dressing rooms, locker rooms, and other spaces used by performers? (4.33.5)

- In alterations, where it is technically infeasible to alter all performing areas to be on an accessible route, at least one of each type of performing area shall be made accessible. [4.1.6(3)(f)(ii)]

Assembly Areas: floor surfaces

AA-10 Is the floor surface at each wheelchair location level, stable, firm, and slip-resistant? (4.33.4; 4.5)

Assembly Areas: Assistive Listening System (ALS)

AA-11 Where a permanently installed Assistive Listening System is provided, is there informational signage installed to notify patrons of the availability of such a system and does the signage include the International Symbol for hearing loss? [4.1.3(19)(b), 4.30.7(4), Fig. 43d]

AA-12 In assembly areas where audible communications are integral to the use of the space (e.g., concert and lecture halls, playhouses, movie theaters, etc.), is there a permanently installed Assistive Listening System (ALS)? [4.1.3(19)(b)]

- The permanently installed ALS is required in assembly areas where there is fixed seating and one of the following:
  — the space seats more than 50 people, or
  — audio amplification is provided.

NOTE:
- See AA-13 if the assembly area does not meet the preceding criteria.

AA-13 For assembly areas not covered in AA-12, is there a permanently installed or portable Assistive Listening System (ALS) available? [4.1.3(19)(b)]

- This provision can be meet by a permanently installed ALS or by an adequate number of outlets for a portable ALS.
- A portable ALS might be an FM type broadcast system with volume controlled, portable headphones.

AA-14 Is the required number of Assistive Listening System (ALS) receivers provided? [4.1.3(19)(b)]

- Receivers required: 4 percent of total number of seats but not fewer than two receivers.

AA-15 If the Assistive Listening System (ALS) serves individual fixed seats, are these seats located within an unobstructed 50-ft viewing distance of the stage? (4.33.6)

AA-16 Does the Assistive Listening System (ALS) provided meet required operational criteria? (4.33.7)

- Operational criteria: provide signals that can be received directly by persons with special receivers or their own hearing aids and that eliminate or filter background noise.

- Magnetic induction loops, infrared, and radio frequency systems are types of listening systems that are appropriate for various applications.

(BM) Business and Mercantile (7.0)

Business: general

BM-01 Are all areas used for business transactions with the public, such as sales and service counters and/or self-service displays, on an accessible route? [4.1.3(12)(b), 7.2.2]

Business: sales counters with cash registers

BM-02 In retail stores where counters with cash registers are provided, is there at least one accessible cash register counter, and where more than one occurs, are they distributed throughout the facility? (7.2.1)

- Main counter: a portion of the counter is at least 36 in. long and is not more than 36 in. high.
- Alterations: where it is technically infeasible to provide an accessible counter, an auxiliary counter meeting these criteria may be provided.

Business: sales or service counters without cash registers

BM-03 At ticketing counters, teller stations, registration counters, and other counters for distributing goods or services to the public without cash registers, is there an accessible counter or alternative provided? (7.2.2)

- Main counter: a portion of the counter is at least 36 in. long and is not more than 36 in. high.
- Auxiliary counter: in close proximity to the main counter and not more than 36 in. high.
- Equivalent facilitation: might consist of a folding shelf attached to the main counter (for an individual with disabilities to write) and use of the space at the side of the counter for handing materials back and forth.

(AR) Accessible Routes (4.3)

NOTES:
- All walks, halls, corridors, aisles, skywalks, tunnels, and other spaces that are part of a designated accessible route shall comply with accessible requirements.
- Any slope on the accessible route that is greater than 1:20 is required to meet all ramp criteria.
- The accessible route shall, to the maximum extent feasible, coincide with the route for the general public.
- In historic buildings, accessible routes from an accessible entrance shall be provided to all publicly used spaces on at least the level of the accessible entrance. Access shall be provided to all levels of a building or facility whenever practical. [4.1.7(3)(d)]

AUTHOR'S INTERPRETATION:
- An accessible route "generally coincides" with the route used by the public if:
  — It does not force the user to go out of the way
  — It is most like the route chosen by the general public
  — It is direct
  — It gives the same basic experience as the route preferred by the public

Accessible Routes: interior

AR-06 Is the building entrance space connected by an accessible route to all accessible spaces, elements, and all accessible dwelling units within the building or facility? [4.3.2(3)]

Accessible Routes: width

AR-08 Is the minimum clear width along the accessible route adequate for continuous or point passage? (4.2.1, 4.3.3, Fig. 1, Fig. 8e, Fig. 24e)

- Continuous passage (greater than 24 in. long): at least a 36-in. clear width.
- Point passage (not more than 24 in. long): at least a 32-in. clear width.

AUTHOR'S INTERPRETATION:

- Noncompliance with this question generally relates to permanent elements that encroach on the accessible route. Large, heavy equipment that is not readily movable might be considered permanent. If the space is designed so that temporary elements (such as bikes in a bike rack or car bumpers) will consistently encroach, the situation might also be considered a permanent barrier.

AR-09 Is the minimum clear width along the accessible route adequate at a U-turn around an obstruction? (4.3.3, Fig. 7a–b)

- Obstruction 48 in. or greater: at least a 36-in. clear width around the obstruction.
- Obstruction less than 48 in.: at least a 42-in. clear width at each side with at least a 48-in. clear width in the turn.

Accessible Routes: passing space

AR-10 Does the accessible route provide at least 60 in. of clear width for two wheelchairs to pass and, if not, is the required passing space provided? (4.2.2, 4.3.4)

- A 60-in. × 60-in. passing space or "T" intersection should be provided at reasonable intervals not to exceed 200 ft.

AUTHOR'S INTERPRETATION:

- Accessible routes more than 5 ft long (e.g., routes in short hallways, aisles in laboratories, and work/storage areas) should have passing spaces provided.

DEFINITION:

- A *"T" intersection* is defined as the intersection of two corridors or walks, each at least 36 in. wide providing at least a 60-in. depth at the intersection. (Fig. 3b)

Accessible Routes: maneuvering clearances

AR-11 Is the minimum clear floor space for an unobstructed 180° wheelchair turning space or a "T"-shaped turning space provided? (4.2.3, Fig. 3a-b)

- 180° turning space: at least a 60-in. diameter;
- "T"-shaped turning space: at least 36-in. wide legs with a minimum length of 60 in.

Accessible Routes: slopes

AR-12 Is the running slope on the accessible route 1:20 or less? (4.3.7)

- Any slope on the accessible route that is greater than 1:20 is required to meet all ramp criteria.

AR-13 Is the cross slope on the accessible route 1:50 or less? (4.3.7)

Accessible Routes: changes in level

AR-14 Are changes in level greater than 1/2 in. accomplished by means of a curb ramp, ramp, elevator, or platform lift (as permitted in ADAAG 4.1.3 and 4.1.6)? (4.3.8)

(RP) Ramps (4.8)

NOTE:

- Any slope on the accessible route that is greater than 1:20 is considered a ramp and shall comply with accessible requirements.

Ramps: slopes and rises

RP-01 Is the running slope for the ramp within required parameters? (4.8.2, Fig. 16)

- New construction: 1:12 slope or less with not more than a 30-in. rise for any run.
  - 1:12 slope: 30-ft run between landings.
  - 1:16 slope: 40-ft run between landings.
- On existing sites where space limitations prohibit the use of a slope of 1:12 or less, the following slopes can be considered. [4.1.6(3)(a)(i–ii)]
  - Between 1:10 and 1:12 for a maximum rise of 6 in.
  - Between 1:8 and 1:10 for a maximum rise of 3 in.
  - A slope steeper than 1:8 is not allowed.

EXCEPTION:

- In historic buildings, a ramp with a slope no greater than 1:6 for a run not to exceed 2 ft may be used as part of an accessible route to an entrance. [4.1.7(3)(a)]

RP-02 Is the cross slope of the ramp 1:50 or less? (4.8.6)

Ramps: clear width

RP-03 Is the clear width (between handrails) of the ramp at least 36 in.? (4.8.3)

Ramps: landings

RP-04 Is there a level landing at the top and bottom of each ramp and each ramp run? (4.8.4)

- If a doorway is located at a landing, then the area in front of the doorway must meet door maneuvering clearance requirements.

RP-05 Does each ramp landing meet required dimensions? [4.8.4(1-2)]

- Landing width: at least equal to the ramp width.
- Landing length: at least 60 in. long.

RP-06 Where the ramp changes direction, is there a landing of at least 60-in. × 60-in.? [4.8.4(3)]

Ramps: handrails

NOTE:

- Additional criteria for handrails can be found in Section "HR, Handrails."

RP-07 If the ramp rises more than 6 in. or is longer than 72 in., does it have a handrail on each side? (4.8.5)

- Handrails are not required on curb ramps or adjacent to seating in assembly areas.

RP-08 Is the handrail provided on both sides of ramp segments and is the inside rail on switchback or dogleg ramps continuous? [4.8.5(1), Fig. 19a–b]

RP-09 At the end of the ramp handrails, is there at least 12 in. of handrail parallel to the floor or ground surface, extending beyond the top and the bottom of the ramp segments? [4.8.5(2), Fig. 17]

RP-10 Is the clearance between the ramp handrail and the wall exactly 1½ in.? [4.8.5(3)]

- For recesses, see ADAAG Fig. 39.

RP-11 Are the tops of ramp handrails between 34 in. and 38 in. above ramp surfaces? [4.8.5(5)]

RP-12 Is the ramp handrail gripping surface continuous without obstructions or missing segments? [4.8.5(4)]

RP-13 Are the ends of ramp handrails rounded or returned smoothly to the floor, wall, or post? [4.8.5(6)]

RP-14 Are the ramp handrails fixed so that they do not rotate within their fittings? [4.8.5(7)]

Ramps: edge protection and floor surfaces

RP-15 If a ramp or landing has a drop-off, is it protected by an acceptable option? (4.8.7, Fig. 17)

- Acceptable options include: a wall, a minimum 12-in. horizontal floor extension beyond the railing, a minimum 2-in. curb, or a railing design that prevents people from falling or rolling off.

RP-16 Is the ramp floor surface stable, firm, and slip-resistant? (4.5.1)

(HR) Handrails (4.26)

NOTE:

- HR Guidelines may be repeated in other element-based guidelines: (RP) Ramps, (ST) Stairs, (WC) Water Closets, (TS) Toilet Stalls, (BT) Bathtubs, and (SS) Shower Stalls.

Handrails: size and spacing

HR-01 Is the gripping surface of the grab bars or handrails 1¼ to 1½ in. in outside diameter? (4.26.2, Fig. 39)

AUTHOR'S INTERPRETATION:

- Standard pipe sizes designated by the industry as 1¼ in. to 1½ in. are acceptable for purposes of this section.

HR-02 Do the grab bars or handrails have edges with a minimum radius of 1/8 in.? (4.26.4)

HR-04 If the handrail is located in a recess, is the recess a maximum of 3 in. deep extending at least 18 in. above the rail? (4.26.2, Fig. 39d)

Handrails: grab bar or handrail structural strength

HR-06 Do the grab bars and handrails meet the structural strength requirements for bending stress and shear stress? (4.26.3)

- Actual bending stress in the grab bar induced by the maximum bending moment from the application of 250 lbf is less than the allowable bending stress for the material of the grab bar.
- Shear stress induced in a grab bar by the application of 250 lbf shall be less than the allowable shear stress for the material of the grab bar. If the connection between the grab bar and its mounting bracket or other support is considered to be fully restrained, then direct and torsional shear stresses shall be totaled for the combined shear stress, which shall not exceed the allowable shear stress.

HR-07 Do the fasteners and mounting devices for the grab bars or handrails meet the structural strength requirements for shear force and tensile force? (4.26.3)

- Shear force induced in a fastener or mounting device from the application of 250 lbf shall be less than the allowable lateral load of either the fastener or mounting device or the supporting structure, whichever is the smaller allowable load.
- Tensile force induced in a fastener by a direct tension force of 250 lbf plus the maximum moment from the application of 250 lbf shall be less than the allowable withdrawal load between the fastener and the supporting structure.

Handrails: hazards

HR-10 Are handrails or grab bars and any wall or other surfaces adjacent to them free of any sharp or abrasive elements? (4.26.4)

(FS) Floor and Ground Surfaces (4.5)

Floor Surfaces: general

FS-01 Are the floor/ground surfaces on the accessible route stable, firm, and slip-resistant? (4.5.1)

AUTHOR'S INTERPRETATION:

- Exterior spaces, interior circulation, bathrooms, and other spaces where water can collect on the floor around an element (sinks, drinking fountains, hose bibbs, etc.) are reviewed as if wet.
- High gloss surfaces without significant textures that are regularly maintained with waxing (smooth tiles, waxed concrete, etc.) could be considered noncompliant.
- Accessible criteria are not specified for nonpermanent floor surfaces such as mats or rugs.

Floor Surfaces: changes in level

FS-02 Are vertical changes in level between 1/4 in. and 1/2 in. beveled with a slope of 1:2 or less? (4.5.2)

- Changes in level up to 1/4 in. may be vertical without edge treatment.
- Changes in level greater than 1/2 in. should be accomplished by means of a curb ramp, ramp, elevator, or platform lift (as permitted in ADAAG 4.1.3 and 4.1.6).

Floor Surfaces: carpet

FS-03 Does carpet or carpet tile used on the floor comply with accessible criteria?

- Attachment: secured. (4.5.3, Fig. 8f)
- Exposed edges: fastened and trimmed along the entire length.
- Pile type: low pile (1/2 in. maximum).
- Padding: firm pad or no pad underneath.

(PR) Protruding Objects (4.4)

Protruding Objects: general

PR-01 Do wall-mounted objects having leading edges between 27 in. and 80 in. high project less than 4 in. into walkways, corridors, aisles, or paths of travel? (4.4.1, Fig. 8a–e)

- Objects mounted with their leading edge at or below 27 in. can protrude any amount, as long as they do not reduce the required clear width of an accessible route.

AUTHOR'S INTERPRETATION:

- Protruding objects might include fire extinguishers or cabinets, pencil sharpeners, shelving, counters, built-in equipment overhangs, or various dispensers such as for paper towels or soap.

PR-02 Do free-standing objects, suspended or mounted on posts or pylons with leading edges between 27 in. and 80 in. high, project less than 12 in. into the perpendicular route of travel? (4.4.1, Fig. 8a–e)

AUTHOR'S INTERPRETATION:

- These might include telephone enclosures, drinking fountains, or free-standing signage kiosks.

PR-03 Is the minimum clear route width or maneuvering space still maintained even with the projection of a protruding object? (4.4.1, Fig. 8a–e)

Protruding Objects: overhead clearance

PR-04 Is the minimum overhead clearance of 80 in. provided in accessible areas or along accessible routes? (4.4.2, Fig. 8a)

AUTHOR'S INTERPRETATION:

- Overhead objects that can reduce the required clearance might include structures, pipes, ducts, or light fixtures.

PR-05 Where the vertical clearance of a space adjoining the accessible route is less than 80 in. high, is a cane detection barrier less than 27 in. from the floor provided for blind or visually impaired persons? (4.4.2, Fig. 8c-1)

AUTHOR'S INTERPRETATION:

- This condition might be found under a stair, at a sloped ceiling space, or with guy wires from telephone poles along an exterior accessible route.

(RC) Raised Platforms (5.7)

Raised platforms:

AUTHOR'S INTERPRETATION:

- ADAAG addresses raised platforms only within the restaurant criteria. However, it would seem that raised platforms found in other space-types such as meeting rooms, classrooms, or auditoriums would be required to meet the same criteria.

RC-10 In banquet rooms or spaces where a head table or speakers' lectern is located on a raised platform, is the platform accessible by means of a ramp or platform lift? (5.7)

- Where applicable, review questions related to [(RP) Ramps] or [(PL) Platform Lifts].

RC-11 Are the open edges of a raised platform protected by the placement of tables, a curb, or some other form of edge protection? (5.7)

(CT) Controls and Operating Mechanisms (4.27)

NOTES:

- Controls or operating mechanisms can include elements such as light switches, pencil sharpeners, manual overhead screens, nonkeyed thermostats, alarm pull stations, fire extinguisher cabinets, A/C window units, microwave ovens, towel dispensers, and wall hooks.
- If controls are to be operated by occupants of the space, they must be accessible. If controls are to be operated by maintenance staff only and not by occupants or other users of the space, they do not have to be accessible. For example, thermostats in auditoriums usually do not have to be accessible, while thermostats in classrooms may need to be accessible.

Controls: clear floor space

CT-01 Is a clear floor space of at least 30 in. × 48 in. provided in front of controls, dispensers, receptacles, and other operable equipment for forward or parallel approach? (4.27.2, Fig. 4a–b)

Controls: reach ranges

NOTES:

- Accessible reach ranges for controls and operating mechanisms are:
  — Forward reach: not less than 15 in. high and not more than 48 in. high without any obstruction or where the obstruction is less than 20 in. deep. For obstructions from 20 in. to 25 in. deep, no forward reach higher than 44 in.
  — Side reach: not less than 9 in. high and not more than 54 in. high. For obstructions not more than 34 in. high or 24 in. deep, no side reach higher than 46 in.
  — Electrical outlets, switches, and communication system receptacles have a minimum outlet height of 15 in. regardless of forward or side reach. See CT-02 below.

CT-02 Are electrical outlets, switches, and communication system receptacles mounted within accessible forward or side reach ranges? (4.27.3)

EXCEPTION:

- These requirements do not apply where the use of special equipment dictates otherwise or where electrical and communications system receptacles are not normally intended for use by building occupants. (4.27.3)

CT-03 Are thermostats or other similar operable equipment mounted within accessible forward or side reach ranges? (4.2.5, 4.2.6, Fig. 5a–b, Fig. 6a–c)

CT-04 Are dispensers or other similar operable equipment mounted within accessible forward or side reach ranges? (4.2.5, 4.2.6, Fig. 5a–b, Fig. 6a–c)

CT-05 Are life safety devices or other similar operable equipment mounted within accessible forward or side reach ranges? (4.2.5, 4.2.6, Fig. 5a–b, Fig. 6a–c)

NOTE:
- This might include fire alarm pull stations, handles to extinguisher cabinets, or wall-mounted extinguishers.

Controls: operation

CT-06 Are controls, dispensers, receptacles, and other operable equipment operable with one hand without tight grasping, pinching, or wrist twisting, and requiring no more than 5 lbf of force? (4.27.4)

(SE) Fixed or Built-in Seating and Tables (4.32)

Fixed or Built-in Seating and Tables: minimum number

SE-01 Is the minimum number of accessible wheelchair seating locations at fixed tables or counters provided? (4.1.3.18)
- Number required: 5 percent of total number of seats but not fewer than one.

Fixed or Built-in Seating and Tables: clear floor space

AUTHOR'S INTERPRETATION:
- Where the accessible route leads to and through accessible seating adjacent to a wall or another table, the minimum required width for the accessible route will be 65 in. between the table edge and next parallel surface (e.g., wall or another table edge). (4.1.3.18, Fig. 45)

SE-02 Is the clear floor space for a wheelchair at a seating location adequate? (4.32.3, Fig. 4a, Fig. 45)
- Clear floor space: 30 in. × 48 in.
- This clear space can include up to 19 in. under the table/desk.

Fixed or Built-in Seating and Tables: clearances

SE-03 Are the tops of accessible tables and counters between 28 in. and 34 in. from the floor? (4.32.3, Fig. 45)

SE-04 Are the knee clearances at least 27 in. high, 30 in. wide, and 19 in. deep? (4.32.3, Fig. 45)

(SR) STORAGE (4.25)

NOTE:
- Accessible reach range requirements do not apply to shelves or display units allowing self-service by customers in mercantile occupancies but they must be located on an accessible route. [4.1.3(12)(b)]

Storage: general

SR-01 Does at least one of each type of fixed or built-in storage unit comply with accessible criteria? [4.1.3(12)(a), 4.25.1]

NOTE:
- Types of storage facilities might include cabinets, shelves, closets, and drawers.

Storage: clear floor space

SR-02 Is there a clear floor space at least 30 in. × 48 in. at fixed or built-in storage units that allows for either a forward or side approach? (4.25.2, Fig. 4a–b)

Storage: reach ranges

SR-03 Are forward or side reach for each type of accessible storage unit within acceptable reach ranges? (4.2.5–6, Fig. 5a–b, Fig. 6a–c, 4.25.3)
- Forward reach: not less than 15 in. high and not more than 48 in. high without any obstruction or where the obstruction is less than 20 in. deep. For obstructions from 20 in. to 25 in. deep, no forward reach higher than 44 in.
- Side reach: not less than 9 in. high and not more than 54 in. high. For obstructions not more than 34 in. high or 24 in. deep, no side reach higher than 46 in.

SR-04 In a closet where passage is not required to access storage (e.g., door opening is less than 32 in.), are the clothes rod or shelves within required reach ranges? (4.25.3, Fig. 38a–b)
- Door width: at least 20 in. (4.13.5)
- Horizontal reach: not more than 21 in. from the opening.
- Rod reach: if over 10 in. deep, then not more than 48 in. high.
- Shelf reach: if over 10 in. deep, then not more than 48 in. high or less than 9 in. high.

Storage: hardware

SR-05 Is the hardware on the storage unit doors or drawers operable with one hand without tight grasping, pinching, or wrist twisting, and requiring no more than 5 lbf of force? (4.25.4, 4.27.4)

(AL) Alarms (4.28)

NOTE:
- At a minimum, visual signal appliances shall be provided in buildings and facilities in restrooms and any other general usage areas. **The ADAAG does not define the number of occupants needed to establish a general or common use area.**

ALLOWANCE:
- Emergency warning systems in medical care facilities may be modified to suit standard health care alarm design practice. [4.1.3(14)]

Alarms: general

AL-01 If emergency warning systems are provided, do they include both audible alarms and visual alarms? [4.1.3(14)]

Audible Alarms: general

AL-02 If provided, do the audible alarms meet required operational criteria? (4.28.2)

- Sound level: exceeds the prevailing sound level in the room or space by at least 15 dbA or exceeds any maximum sound level with a duration of 60 sec by 5 dbA, whichever is louder.
- Sound levels for alarm signals shall not exceed 120 dbA.

AL-03 If single station audible alarms are provided, then are single station visual alarm signals also provided? (4.28.3)

Visual Alarms: general

AL-04 If provided, are the visual alarm signal appliances integrated into the building or facility alarm system? (4.28.3)

AL-05 If provided, do the visual alarm signals meet required operational criteria? [4.28.3(1, 2, 3, 4, 5)]

- Lamp: xenon strobe type or equivalent.
- Color: clear or nominal white (i.e., unfiltered or clear filtered white light).
- Pulse duration: maximum shall be 0.2 sec with a maximum duty cycle of 40 percent.
- Intensity: not less than 75 candela.
- Flash rate: not less than 1 Hz and not more than 3 Hz.

AL-06 Are visual alarm signal appliances provided in public and common use restrooms? (4.28.1)

AL-07 Are visual alarm signal appliances provided in general usage areas of the building (such as meeting rooms, corridors, and lobbies) or any other area for common use? (4.28.1)

AUTHOR'S INTERPRETATION:

- The authors identified three or more occupants as the minimum number to establish a common use area.

AL-08 Are the visual alarms placed at 80 in. above the highest floor level or 6 in. below the ceiling, whichever is lower? [4.28.3(6)]

AL-09 In spaces required to have visual alarms, are the alarms spaced properly? [4.28.3(7)]

- No place in any space should be more than 50 ft from a visual signal alarm.
- Where a space or large room exceeds 100 ft across, without obstructions 6 ft above the finished floor, visual alarms can be spaced a maximum of 100 ft apart at the perimeter, in lieu of suspending appliances from the ceiling.

Assembly Areas without Fixed Seating or Tables (Conference/Meeting Rooms, Classrooms)

Introduction. Use this "Space-type Review Guide" to design or evaluate areas of assembly in which the seating and the majority of furnishings are movable. This would include conference rooms, meeting rooms, and typical classrooms in schools and universities. Areas of assembly and classrooms with fixed seating should be reviewed using "Assembly Areas with Fixed Seating or Tables."

When reviewing drawings for this type of space, even small spaces will appear to have ample maneuvering room and large spaces such as classrooms, ballrooms, and convention halls seem to offer even fewer problems because of their large scale. While furniture placement in large spaces seldom restricts maneuvering room, it can be a major barrier in small meeting rooms. It is important to design smaller spaces with some idea as to the type and placement of furnishings such as large tables. Fixed work tables, lecterns, and raised platforms can sometimes pose maneuvering problems in classrooms, particularly in colleges and universities.

ADAAG addresses raised platforms for only a head table or speakers' lectern within the restaurant criteria. However, the authors feel that raised platforms used by teachers, speakers, and actors in other space-types such as classrooms, meeting rooms, and auditoriums would be required to meet the same accessibility criteria.

Once maneuverability within the space is resolved, the next major issues are reach ranges for storage, controls and operating mechanisms, and protruding objects. Storage would include shelves, cabinets, closets, coat

hooks, and even towel bars by sinks. The authors consider upper and lower cabinets of similar design (e.g., both with doors or both without doors) to be different types of storage units because one is mounted on the wall while the other is attached to the floor. Many of the above mentioned items can be protruding objects if they occur along the accessible path of travel and protrude more than 4 in. off the wall or do not provide a minimum overhead clearance of 80 in.

Controls and operating mechanisms include such things as light switches, electrical outlets, communication systems, pencil sharpeners, chalkboards, pull down projector screens, overhead fans, controls for A/C window units, and thermostats if they can be controlled by the occupants. Classrooms and large meeting rooms may include alarm pull stations and fire extinguisher cabinets which also must be accessible.

Two other items which sometimes occur in classrooms and conference/meeting rooms are fixed counters with sinks. If they are for use by the general public both the counter and the sink must be accessible.

PRELIMINARY DESIGN OVERVIEW

(AL) Alarms

- A visual alarm is required in every general usage area (e.g., meeting rooms, conference rooms, classrooms, etc.).

(AR) Accessible Routes

- Provide access to all sides of a conference table if possible (allow 65 in. between table and wall or perimeter furnishings).
- Provide access to speaking areas, chalkboards, and storage areas.

(CT) Controls and Operating Mechanisms

- Frequently overlooked control and operating mechanisms in this space-type are communication outlets, controls on window air conditioner units, thermostats, pull cords on overhead projection screens, fans, lights, etc.

(DR) Doors

- Both interior and exterior doors may need to be accessible.

(EN) Entrances

- Half of all public entrances must be accessible.
- The number of accessible entrances must be equal to the number of exits required by the building/fire code.

(SE) Fixed Tables and/or Counters

- If fixed counters are provided, a minimum of 5 percent, but not fewer than one, of each type must be accessible.

(FS) Floor Surfaces

- In some areas floor surfaces should be evaluated as if wet. In particular consider the areas around exterior doors, drinking fountains, etc.

(LV) Lavatories and/or Sinks

- If sinks and/or lavatories are provided and used for different purposes, then one of each use type must be accessible.

(PR) Protruding Objects

- Common wall-mounted elements can be protruding objects, e.g., pencil sharpeners, book shelves, upper cabinets, signs, mailboxes, display cases, fire extinguishers, etc.

(RC) Raised Platforms

- A raised platform or stage used by the general public must be accessible. A ramp or platform lift may be used to make the platform or stage accessible.
- An accessible platform or stage requires edge protection.

(SG) Signage

- If all entrances are not accessible, the accessible entrances must be identified by the ISA symbol; nonaccessible entrances must have signage indicating the accessible route to an accessible entrance.

(SR) Fixed storage, Closets, Lockers, and Shelves

- One of each type of storage unit provided for the general public such as cabinets, lockers, shelves, dispensers, hooks, towel bars, must be accessible.
- Hardware on accessible drawers, cabinets, and closets must be accessible.

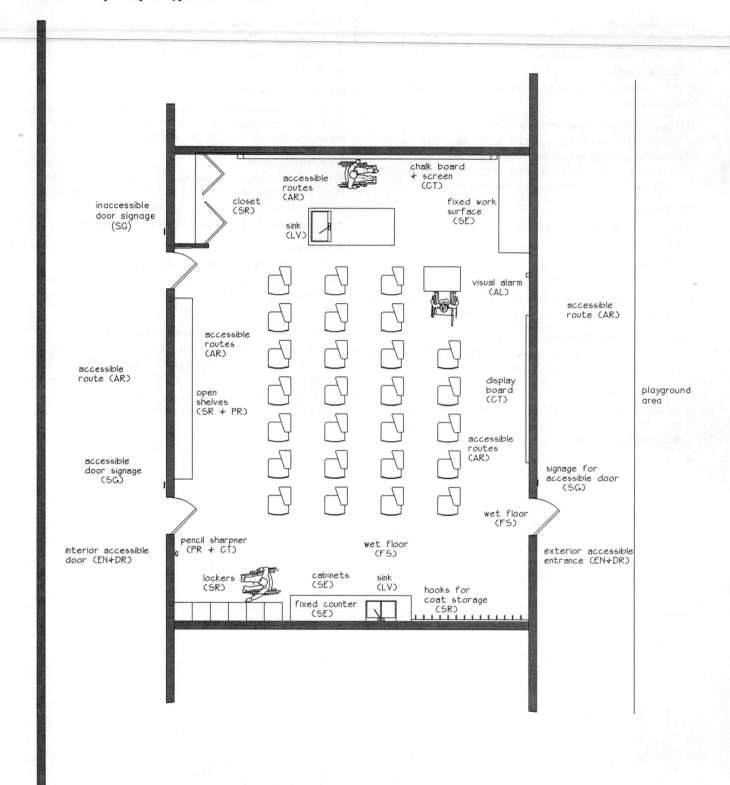

inaccessible
door signage
(SG)

closet
(SR)

accessible
routes
(AR)

sink
(LV)

chalk board
+ screen
(CT)

fixed work
surface
(SE)

accessible
route (AR)

accessible
routes
(AR)

open
shelves
(SR + PR)

accessible
route (AR)

visual alarm
(AL)

display
board
(CT)

accessible
routes
(AR)

accessible
door signage
(SG)

signage for
accessible door
(SG)

wet floor
(FS)

interior accessible
door (EN+DR)

pencil sharpner
(PR + CT)

wet floor
(FS)

exterior accessible
entrance (EN+DR)

lockers
(SR)

cabinets
(SE)

sink
(LV)

fixed counter
(SE)

hooks for
coat storage
(SR)

playground
area

Figure 3-8. Classroom.

Assembly Areas without Fixed Seating or Tables Checklist

SIGNAGE

SG01	Entry signage: I.S.A. requirement
SG02	Entry signage: inaccessible entrances
SG03	Inaccessible entry signage: criteria
SG04	Room signage: criteria
SG05	Room signage: location
SG06	Pictograms: size requirements
SG07	Pictograms: verbal description criteria
SG08	Directional/informational signage: criteria
SG09	Suspended/projected signs: location

DOORS

DR04	Doors: maneuvering clearances
DR05	Doors: handle type
DR06	Doors: opening force (interior only)
DR07	Doors: closing speed
DR08	Doors: thresholds
DR09	Doors: clear width/height
DR10	Openings (no door): clear width/height

ACCESSIBLE ROUTES

AR08	Route: clear width
AR09	Route width: U-turns
AR11	Route: maneuvering clearances

PROTRUDING OBJECTS

PR01	Wall-mounted
PR02	Freestanding/suspended on posts/pylons
PR03	Clear route width maintained
PR04	Overhead clearance

FLOOR SURFACES

FS01	Surface: firm, stable, and slip-resistant
FS02	Vertical changes in level
FS03	Carpet and tile floors

CONTROLS AND OPERATING MECHANISMS

CT01	Clear floor space
CT02	Reach ranges: elec./comm. systems
CT03	Reach ranges: thermostats
CT04	Reach ranges: other controls
CT05	Reach ranges: life safety devices
CT06	Controls: operation

RAISED PLATFORMS

RC10	Raised platforms: acc. requirements
RC11	Raised platforms: edge protection

FIXED TABLES AND/OR COUNTERS

SE01	Fixed seating: number required
SE02	Wheelchairs: clear floor space at tables
SE03	Tables/counters: heights
SE04	Tables/counters: knee clearance criteria

STORAGE

SR01	Accessibility: one of each type
SR02	Clear floor space
SR03	Reach ranges
SR04	Storage closets w/o passage: criteria
SR05	Storage hardware: operation

ALARMS

AL01	Emergency warning: audible/visual
AL02	Audible alarms: operation
AL03	Single station audible and visual
AL04	Visual alarms: integration w/building alarm
AL05	Visual alarms: operation
AL07	Visual alarms: common use areas
AL08	Visual alarms: vertical placement
AL09	Visual alarms: horizontal spacing

ASSEMBLY AREAS WITHOUT FIXED SEATING OR TABLES COMPREHENSIVE CRITERIA

General Note

- This "Space-type Review Guide" focuses on assembly areas without fixed seating such as conference/meeting rooms or classrooms.

(SG) Signage (4.30)

NOTE:

- In historic buildings displays and written information, documents, etc., should be located where they can be seen by a seated person. Exhibits and signage displayed horizontally (e.g., open books) should be no higher than 44 in. above the floor surface. [4.1.7(3)(e)]

Signage: entry

SG-01 Where a building or space has both accessible and inaccessible entrances, are the accessible entrances identified by the International Symbol of Accessibility? [4.1.2(7)(c), Fig. 43a-b]

SG-02 If an entrance is not accessible, is there a directional sign indicating the location of the nearest accessible entrance? [4.1.2(7)(c), 4.1.3(8)(d)]

SG-03 Does the directional sign indicating the location of the nearest accessible entrance comply with directional signage criteria? (4.30.2, 3, 5)

- Character proportion: letters and numbers have a width to height ratio between 3:5 and 1:1 and a stroke width to height ratio between 1:5 and 1:10.
- Character height: sized according to viewing distance with characters on overhead signs at least 3 in. high.
- Finish: characters and backgrounds have a nonglare finish.
- Contrast: characters contrast with their background (light-on-dark or dark-on-light).

Signage: room identification (where provided)

DEFINITION:

- These signs designate permanent rooms and spaces.

AUTHOR'S INTERPRETATION:

- Signs that designate stairs, exit doors, and toilet rooms generally are associated with permanent spaces, while an "office" sign is not since the room function may change over time. Room numbers also must meet the ADAAG criteria as permanent designations, while personal names do not since the occupant may change over time.

SG-04 Do signs that designate permanent rooms and spaces comply with the following criteria? [4.1.2(7); 4.1.3(16); 4.30.4, 5, 6]

- Character type: raised and accompanied by Grade II Braille.
- Character size: between 5/8 in. and 2 in. high; raised at least 1/32 in.
- Character style: upper case, and sans or simple serif.
- Finish: characters and backgrounds have a nonglare finish.
- Contrast: characters contrast with their background (light-on-dark or dark-on-light).

SG-05 Is the room identification sign mounted in the required location? (4.30.6)

- Mounting location: installed on the wall adjacent to the latch side of the door or where wall space to the latch side of the door is not available, including double doors, placed on the nearest adjacent wall.
- Mounting height: 60 in. above the floor/ground to the centerline of the sign.
- Sign access: approach to within 3 in. of a sign without encountering protruding objects or standing within the swing of the door.

Signage: pictorial symbol signs (pictograms) (where provided)

AUTHOR'S INTERPRETATION:

- Because the criteria for pictograms are listed in ADAAG 4.30.4, they fall into the category of room identification signage and must meet those criteria that follow.
- While the ISA symbol might be considered to be a pictogram, it does not appear to have the same requirements as pictograms.

SG-06 Is the border dimension of a pictogram, where provided, at least 6 in. high? (4.30.4)

AUTHOR'S INTERPRETATION:

- A pictogram includes both a symbol and the field on which it is displayed. The 6-in. vertical dimension applies to the vertical field, not to the symbol. The required verbal description may not intrude on the 6-in. field.

SG-07 Is a pictogram, where provided, accompanied by the equivalent verbal description placed directly below the pictogram, and does the verbal description meet room identification signage criteria? (4.30.4)

- Character type: raised and accompanied by Grade II Braille.
- Character size: between 5/8 in. and 2 in. high; raised at least 1/32 in.
- Character style: upper case, and sans or simple serif.
- Finish: characters and backgrounds have a nonglare finish.
- Contrast: characters contrast with their background (light-on-dark or dark-on-light).

Signage: direction and information (where provided)

DEFINITION:

- Signs that provide direction to or information about functional spaces of the building.

EXCEPTION:

- Building directories, menus, and all other temporary signs are not required to comply. [4.1.3(16)]

SG-08 Do signs that provide direction to, or information about, functional spaces of the building comply with the following criteria? [4.1.2(7); 4.1.3(16); 4.30.1, 2, 3, 5]

- Character proportion: letters and numbers have a width to height ratio between 3:5 and 1:1 and a stroke width to height ratio between 1:5 and 1:10.
- Character height: sized according to viewing distance with characters on overhead signs at least 3 in. high.

NOTE:

- When the sign is mounted below 80 in., there are no prescribed character heights. Only when the sign is mounted 80 in. or higher are the characters required to be at least 3 in. high. (4.30.3)
- Finish: characters and backgrounds have a nonglare finish.
- Contrast: characters contrast with their background (light-on-dark or dark-on-light).

SG-09 Is a sign located so that the overhead clearance or the projection of a suspended or projected sign does not result in a protruding object (free-standing or wall-mounted)?

- Clear height: at least 80 in. (4.4.2, Fig. 8a)
- Overhang for free-standing signs on posts or pylons located between 27 in. and 80 in. high: no more than a 12-in. projection into accessible routes. (4.4.1, Fig. 8c).
- Overhang for wall-mounted signs between 27 in. and 80 in. high: no more than a 4 in. projection into accessible routes. (4.4.1, Fig. 8a)

(DR) Doors (4.13)

NOTE:

- Included in this category are doors, revolving doors, turnstiles, and gates.

AUTHOR'S INTERPRETATION:

- It is suggested that, for purposes of documentation and review, a door be assigned to the space it swings into. Corridors are an exception to this rule and include only entry doors into the corridor or intermediate fire doors.

Doors: maneuvering clearance

DR-04 If the door is not automatic or power assisted, does it have the required maneuvering clearance provided on the push and pull side, and is the floor level and clear within the maneuvering area? (4.13.6)

- A verbal description cannot adequately describe the requirements. See ADAAG Fig. 25a–f for a graphic description.

EXCEPTION:

- Entry doors to acute care hospital bedrooms for in-patients are exempt from maneuvering space at the latch side of the door if the door is at least 44 in. wide.

AUTHOR'S INTERPRETATION:

- While ADAAG does not describe what elements can reduce the required maneuvering clearance, they could include a narrow entry alcove, an adjacent wall, railing, or permanently installed shelving, or a deep recessed door jamb.

Doors: hardware

DR-05 Do all door handles, locks, latches, or other operable devices meet required operational criteria? (4.13.9)

- Hardware operation: operable with one hand without tight grasping, pinching, or wrist twisting.
- Force required to operate the controls: not greater than 5 lbf. This does not apply to the force required to retract latch bolts or to disengage other devices that only hold the door in a closed position.
- Hardware type: "U"-shaped handles, levers, and push type mechanisms are acceptable designs.
- Hardware height: not greater than 48 in. above the floor.
- Sliding doors: hardware is exposed and usable from both sides when the doors are fully open.

Doors: opening force

DR-06 Do interior hinged doors and sliding or folding doors have an opening force of 5 lbf or less? (4.13.11)

- At present, no accessible criteria exist for exterior doors.
- Fire doors shall have the minimum opening force allowable by the appropriate administrative authority.

Doors: closing speed

DR-07 If the door has a closer, is the closer adjusted so that the door does not close too quickly? (4.13.10)

- From an open position of 70° the door will take at least 3 sec to move to a point 3 in. from the latch (measured to the leading edge of the door).

Doors: thresholds

DR-08 Where raised thresholds are provided, do they meet height limitations and are they beveled when required? (4.13.8, 4.5.2, Fig. 7)

- Threshold height: not more than 3/4 in. for exterior sliding doors or 1/2 in. for other types of doors.
- Threshold bevel: thresholds less than 1/4 in. high need no bevel; thresholds between 1/4 and 1/2 in. high shall be beveled at each edge with not more than a 1:2 slope.

EXCEPTION:

- A 3/4-in. high threshold is allowed in existing conditions. [4.1.6(3)(d)(ii)]

Doors: clear opening width and height

DR-09 Is the clear opening for the doorway adequate in width and height? (4.13.3, 4, 5, Fig. 24)

- Door width: at least 32 in. of clear width with the door open at 90°, measured between the face of the door and the door stop on the latch side. This also pertains to the active leaf of a double-leaf door or gate.

- Opening width: openings more than 24 in. deep must provide 36 in. of clear width.
- Height: at least 80 in. of vertical clearance.

EXCEPTIONS:

- Doors not requiring full user passage, such as shallow closets, may have the clear opening reduced to not less than 20 in.
- Where it is technically infeasible to comply with clear opening width requirements, a projection of 5/8 in. maximum will be permitted for the latch side. [4.1.6(d)(i)]

DR-10 Is the clear opening (when there is no door) adequate in width and height? (4.2.1, 4.3.3, 4.4.2)

- Width: at least 32 in. of clear width for depths 24 in. or less and at least 36 in. of clear width for depths greater than 24 in.
- Height: at least 80 in. of vertical clearance.

(AR) Accessible Route (4.3)

NOTES:

- The accessible route shall, to the maximum extent feasible, coincide with the route for the general public.
- In historic buildings, accessible routes from an accessible entrance shall be provided to all publicly used spaces on at least the level of the accessible entrance. Access shall be provided to all levels of a building or facility whenever practical. [4.1.7(3)(d)]

AUTHOR'S INTERPRETATION:

- An accessible route "generally coincides" with the route used by the public if:
  — It does not force the user to go out of the way
  — It is most like the route chosen by the general public
  — It is direct
  — It gives the same basic experience as the route preferred by the public

Accessible Routes: width

AR-08 Is the minimum clear width along the accessible route adequate for continuous or point passage? (4.2.1, 4.3.3, Fig. 1, Fig. 8e, Fig. 24e)

- Continuous passage (greater than 24 in. long): at least a 36-in. clear width.
- Point passage (not more than 24 in. long): at least a 32-in. clear width.

AUTHOR'S INTERPRETATION:

- Noncompliance with this question generally relates to permanent elements that encroach on the accessible route. Large, heavy equipment that is not readily movable might be considered permanent. If the space is designed so that temporary elements (such as bikes in a bike rack or car bumpers) will consistently encroach, the situation might also be considered a permanent barrier.

AR-09 Is the minimum clear width along the accessible route adequate at a U-turn around an obstruction? (4.3.3, Fig. 7a-b)

- Obstruction 48 in. or greater: at least a 36-in. clear width around the obstruction.

- Obstruction less than 48 in.: at least a 42-in. clear width at each side with at least a 48-in. clear width in the turn.

Accessible Routes: maneuvering clearances

AR-11 Is the minimum clear floor space for an unobstructed 180° wheelchair turning space or a "T"-shaped turning space provided? (4.2.3, Fig. 3a–b)

- 180° turning space: at least a 60-in. diameter;
- "T"-shaped turning space: at least 36-in. wide legs with a minimum length of 60 in.

(PR) Protruding Objects (4.4)

Protruding Objects: general

PR-01 Do wall-mounted objects having leading edges between 27 in. and 80 in. high project less than 4 in. into walkways, corridors, aisles, or paths of travel? (4.4.1, Fig. 8a–e)

- Objects mounted with their leading edge at or below 27 in. can protrude any amount, as long as they do not reduce the required clear width of an accessible route.

AUTHOR'S INTERPRETATION:

- Protruding objects might include fire extinguishers or cabinets, pencil sharpeners, shelving, counters, built-in equipment overhangs, or various dispensers such as for paper towels or soap.

PR-02 Do free-standing objects, suspended or mounted on posts or pylons with leading edges between 27 in. and 80 in. high, project less than 12 in. into the perpendicular route of travel? (4.4.1, Fig. 8a–e)

AUTHOR'S INTERPRETATION:

- These might include telephone enclosures, drinking fountains, or free-standing signage kiosks.

PR-03 Is the minimum clear route width or maneuvering space still maintained even with the projection of a protruding object? (4.4.1, Fig. 8a–e)

Protruding Objects: overhead clearance

PR-04 Is the minimum overhead clearance of 80 in. provided in accessible areas or along accessible routes? (4.4.2, Fig. 8a)

AUTHOR'S INTERPRETATION:

- Overhead objects that can reduce the required clearance might include structures, pipes, ducts, or light fixtures.

(FS) Floor and Ground Surfaces (4.5)

Floor Surfaces: general

FS-01 Are the floor/ground surfaces on the accessible route stable, firm, and slip-resistant? (4.5.1)

AUTHOR'S INTERPRETATION:

- Exterior spaces, interior circulation, bathrooms, and other spaces where water can collect on the floor around an element (sinks, drinking fountains, hose bibbs, etc.) are reviewed as if wet.
- High gloss surfaces without significant textures that are regularly maintained with waxing (smooth tiles, waxed concrete, etc.) could be considered noncompliant.
- Accessible criteria are not specified for nonpermanent floor surfaces such as mats or rugs.

Floor Surfaces: changes in level

FS-02 Are vertical changes in level between 1/4 in. and 1/2 in. beveled with a slope of 1:2 or less? (4.5.2)

- Changes in level up to 1/4 in. may be vertical without edge treatment.
- Changes in level greater than 1/2 in. should be accomplished by means of a curb ramp, ramp, elevator, or platform lift (as permitted in ADAAG 4.1.3 and 4.1.6).

Floor Surfaces: carpet

FS-03 Does carpet or carpet tile used on the floor comply with accessible criteria?

- Attachment: secured. (4.5.3, Fig. 8f)
- Exposed edges: fastened and trimmed along the entire length.
- Pile type: low pile (1/2 in. maximum).
- Padding: firm pad or no pad underneath.

(CT) Controls and Operating Mechanisms (4.27)

NOTES:

- Controls or operating mechanisms can include elements such as light switches, pencil sharpeners, manual overhead screens, nonkeyed thermostats, alarm pull stations, fire extinguisher cabinets, A/C window units, microwave ovens, towel dispensers, and wall hooks.
- If controls are to be operated by occupants of the space, they must be accessible. If controls are to be operated by maintenance staff only and not by occupants or other users of the space, they do not have to be accessible. For example, thermostats in auditoriums usually do not have to be accessible, while thermostats in classrooms may need to be accessible.

Controls: clear floor space

CT-01 Is a clear floor space of at least 30 in. × 48 in. provided in front of controls, dispensers, receptacles, and other operable equipment for forward or parallel approach? (4.27.2, Fig. 4a–b)

Controls: reach ranges

NOTES:

- Accessible reach ranges for controls and operating mechanisms are:
  - Forward reach: not less than 15 in. high and not more than 48 in. high without any obstruction or where the obstruction is less than 20 in. deep. For obstructions from 20 in. to 25 in. deep, no forward reach higher than 44 in.
  - Side reach: not less than 9 in. high and not more than 54 in. high. For obstructions not more than 34 in. high or 24 in. deep, no side reach higher than 46 in.
  - Electrical outlets, switches, and communication system receptacles have a minimum outlet height of 15 in. regardless of forward or side reach. See CT-02 below.

CT-02 Are electrical outlets, switches, and communication system receptacles mounted within accessible forward or side reach ranges? (4.27.3)

EXCEPTION:

- These requirements do not apply where the use of special equipment dictates otherwise or where electrical and communications system receptacles are not normally intended for use by building occupants. (4.27.3)

CT-03 Are thermostats or other similar operable equipment mounted within accessible forward or side reach ranges? (4.2.5, 4.2.6, Fig. 5a–b, Fig. 6a–c)

CT-04 Are dispensers or other similar operable equipment mounted within accessible forward or side reach ranges? (4.2.5, 4.2.6, Fig. 5a–b, Fig. 6a–c)

CT-05 Are life safety devices or other similar operable equipment mounted within accessible forward or side reach ranges? (4.2.5, 4.2.6, Fig. 5a–b, Fig. 6a–c)

NOTE:

- This might include fire alarm pull stations, handles to extinguisher cabinets, or wall-mounted extinguishers.

Controls: operation

CT-06 Are controls, dispensers, receptacles, and other operable equipment operable with one hand without tight grasping, pinching, or wrist twisting, and requiring no more than 5 lbf of force? (4.27.4)

(RC) RAISED PLATFORMS (5.7)

Raised Platforms:

AUTHOR'S INTERPRETATION:

- ADAAG addresses raised platforms only within the restaurant criteria. However, it would seem that raised platforms found in other space-types such as meeting rooms, classrooms, or auditoriums would be required to meet the same criteria.

RC-10 In banquet rooms or spaces where a head table or speakers' lectern is located on a raised platform, is the platform accessible by means of a ramp or platform lift? (5.7)

- Where applicable, review questions related to [(RP) Ramps] or [(PL) Platform Lifts].

RC-11 Are the open edges of a raised platform protected by the placement of tables, a curb, or some other form of edge protection? (5.7)

(SE) Fixed Tables or Counters (4.32)

Fixed or Built-in Seating and Tables: minimum number

SE-01 Is the minimum number of accessible wheelchair seating locations at fixed tables or counters provided? (4.1.3.18)

- Number required: 5 percent of total number of seats but not fewer than one.

Fixed or Built-in Seating and Tables: clear floor space

AUTHOR'S INTERPRETATION:

- Where the accessible route leads to and through accessible seating adjacent to a wall or another table, the minimum required width for the accessible route will be 65 in. between the table edge and next parallel surface (e.g., wall or another table edge). (4.1.3.18, Fig. 45)

SE-02 Is the clear floor space for a wheelchair at a seating location adequate? (4.32.3, Fig. 4a, Fig. 45)

- Clear floor space: 30 in. × 48 in.
- This clear space can include up to 19 in. under the table/desk.

Fixed or Built-in Seating and Tables: clearances

SE-03 Are the tops of accessible tables and counters between 28 in. and 34 in. from the floor? (4.32.3, Fig. 45)

SE-04 Are the knee clearances at least 27 in. high, 30 in. wide, and 19 in. deep? (4.32.3, Fig. 45)

(SR) STORAGE (4.25)

Storage: general

SR-01 Does at least one of each type of fixed or built-in storage unit comply with accessible criteria? [4.1.3(12)(a), 4.25.1]

NOTE:

- Types of storage facilities might include cabinets, shelves, closets, and drawers.

Storage: clear floor space

SR-02 Is there a clear floor space at least 30 in. × 48 in. at fixed or built-in storage units that allows for either a forward or side approach? (4.25.2, Fig. 4a–b)

Storage: reach ranges

SR-03 Are forward or side reach for each type of accessible storage unit within acceptable reach ranges? (4.2.5–6, Fig. 5a–b, Fig. 6a–c, 4.25.3)

- Forward reach: not less than 15 in. high and not more than 48 in. high without any obstruction or where the obstruction is less than 20 in. deep. For obstructions from 20 in. to 25 in. deep, no forward reach higher than 44 in.
- Side reach: not less than 9 in. high and not more than 54 in. high. For obstructions not more than 34 in. high or 24 in. deep, no side reach higher than 46 in.

SR-04 In a closet where passage is not required to access storage (e.g., door opening is less than 32 in.), are the clothes rod or shelves within required reach ranges? (4.25.3, Fig. 38a–b)

- Door width: at least 20 in. (4.13.5)
- Horizontal reach: not more than 21 in. from the opening.
- Rod reach: if over 10 in. deep, then not more than 48 in. high.
- Shelf reach: if over 10 in. deep, then not more than 48 in. high or less than 9 in. high.

Storage: hardware

SR-05 Is the hardware on the storage unit doors or drawers operable with one hand without tight grasping, pinching, or wrist twisting, and requiring no more than 5 lbf of force? (4.25.4, 4.27.4)

(AL) Alarms (4.28)

NOTE:

- At a minimum, visual signal appliances shall be provided in buildings and facilities in restrooms and any other general usage areas. **The ADAAG does not define the number of occupants needed to establish a general or common use area.**

  ALLOWANCE:

  - Emergency warning systems in medical care facilities may be modified to suit standard health care alarm design practice. [4.1.3(14)]

Alarms: general

AL-01 If emergency warning systems are provided, do they include both audible alarms and visual alarms? [4.1.3(14)]

Audible Alarms: general

AL-02 If provided, do the audible alarms meet required operational criteria? (4.28.2)

- Sound level: exceeds the prevailing sound level in the room or space by at least 15 dbA or exceeds any maximum sound level with a duration of 60 sec by 5 dbA, whichever is louder.
- Sound levels for alarm signals shall not exceed 120 dbA.

AL-03 If single station audible alarms are provided, then are single station visual alarm signals also provided? (4.28.3)

Visual Alarms: general

AL-04 If provided, are the visual alarm signal appliances integrated into the building or facility alarm system? (4.28.3)

AL-05 If provided, do the visual alarm signals meet required operational criteria? [4.28.3(1, 2, 3, 4, 5)]

- Lamp: xenon strobe type or equivalent.
- Color: clear or nominal white (i.e., unfiltered or clear filtered white light).
- Pulse duration: maximum shall be 0.2 sec with a maximum duty cycle of 40 percent.
- Intensity: not less than 75 candela.
- Flash rate: not less than 1 Hz and not more than 3 Hz.

AL-07 Are visual alarm signal appliances provided in general usage areas of the building (such as meeting rooms, corridors, and lobbies) or any other area for common use? (4.28.1)

AUTHOR'S INTERPRETATION:

- The authors identified three or more occupants as the minimum number to establish a common use area.

AL-08 Are the visual alarms placed at 80 in. above the highest floor level or 6 in. below the ceiling, whichever is lower? [4.28.3(6)]

AL-09 In spaces required to have visual alarms, are the alarms spaced properly? [4.28.3(7)]

- No place in any space should be more than 50 ft from a visual signal alarm.
- Where a space or large room exceeds 100 ft across, without obstructions 6 ft above the finished floor, visual alarms can be spaced a maximum of 100 ft apart at the perimeter, in lieu of suspending appliances from the ceiling.

Business and Mercantile

Introduction. Use this "Space-type Review Guide" for buildings, facilities, or portions thereof that contain one or more business and mercantile facility accessible to the public. Business and mercantile facilities may include, but are not limited to, department stores, shopping centers, sales rooms, bookstores, drug stores, markets, tellers' counters in banks, ticket offices, and retail stores of all types and sizes. If parking facilities are provided by the business for the general public, then accessible spaces must be provided for disabled customers as well. Refer to "Parking Lots and Passenger Loading Zones." If physically disabled persons are employed by a business, then all areas used by those employees in carrying out their jobs must be accessible and accommodate their needs.

Entrances to shops and businesses should meet the requirements for clear entry and maneuvering space. All doors, except the exterior doors, must comply with opening force requirements. Avoid designing security entries with bollards and turnstiles that unintentionally impede movement for persons who use wheelchairs or have mobility impairments. Revolving doors do not meet accessibility criteria, so an accessible door must be provided for users in wheelchairs. Level changes within shops should be avoid-

ed when possible and ramps should be provided where changes do occur. Changes of material from one section of a shop or store to another are common but must not result in an inaccessible level change. Take precautions when designing a change in materials from hard surfaces such as wood, tile, or marble onto soft surfaces like carpeting. Also, in marketplaces where floors may frequently be wet due to spills, dropped vegetables and fruit, and so on, give special attention to making the floor slip-resistant.

There is a large range of retail activity possible within the business and mercantile classification including those facilities with counters and cash registers, those with sales and service counters without registers, and those with checkout aisles. For example, at a food court in a mall, each different vendor with a service counter must meet accessibility requirements. In facilities under 5000 ft^2 of selling space, at least one sales, service, or transaction counter must be accessible in height and length for customers and employees. If a facility is large with over 5000 ft^2 of selling space, then at least one of each different type of checkout aisle or transaction counter must be accessible. In large stores, such as grocery and discount chains, ADAAG specifies the number of accessible aisles depending on the total number of checkout aisles. These types might be belted vs. nonbelted or permanently designated express lanes vs. regular lanes. In smaller facilities at least one checkout aisle must have accessible passage space for a person who uses a wheelchair. Accessible checkout aisles must be marked with the ISA symbol. These checkout aisles must comply with typical accessible route width requirements and the adjoining counter(s) must not exceed accessible height requirements.

In retail stores and businesses with self-service displays, the minimum accessible width requirements between aisles, switchbacks, turns around an obstruction, and intersections must meet requirements for accessible routes. While shelves or displays allowing self-service by customers must be located on an accessible route, requirements for accessible reach do not apply. In retail shops and department stores where dressing rooms are provided, 5 percent or not fewer than one accessible dressing room of each type (gender or use) must be provided. Refer to "Dressing, Fitting, and Locker Rooms."

PRELIMINARY DESIGN OVERVIEW

(AR) Accessible Route

- Maneuvering space requirements for accessible routes must be met at display aisles; minimum accessible width requirements between aisles, switchbacks, turns around an obstruction, and intersections where provided; and when security bollards and turnstiles are used accessible route must not be impeded.
- Route surfaces must meet criteria for vertical changes in level. Problem areas may include transition between materials.
- At turns around obstructions, widths of the accessible route may increase according to the size of the obstruction.

(AL) Alarms

- Visual alarms must be visible in general usage areas.

(BM) Business and Mercantile

- An accessible counter is required at each different area offering sales or services such as ticket booths, reception desks, concession stands, information counters, coat check rooms, etc. Consider different types of services such as pharmacy counters, courtesy service counters, deli counters, etc., as different types.
- If sales and service counters are located in different parts of the facility, then accessible counters must be dispersed throughout the facility.
- Sales service counters (both with and without cash registers) must meet height and length minimums. Equivalent facilitation may be considered for counters without cash registers.
- All accessible sales and service counters must be on the accessible route.
- The number of accessible checkout aisles is determined by the total number of checkout aisles provided (with an exception given for selling spaces under 5000 ft^2).

- Accessible checkout aisles must be identified by ISA symbol.
- Width of accessible checkout aisles must comply with typical accessible route criteria. In addition, the adjoining counter must comply with height criteria.
- In retail, self-service shelves or displays must be located on an accessible route.
- In retail, self-service shelves or displays are not required to comply with accessible reach ranges.

(CT) Controls and Operating Mechanisms

- Controls and operating mechanisms have clear floor space and reach range requirements. When there are controls such as credit card scanners mounted at transaction counters, provide clear floor space and required reach ranges.

(DR) Doors

- Revolving doors or turnstiles require an adjacent accessible door, gate, or opening.
- Automatic and power assisted doors must comply with appropriate ANSI standard for slow opening.
- Slow opening, low powered automatic doors or power assisted doors must comply with opening and closing requirements.
- Opening width at security bollards must be accessible.

(DL) Dressing Rooms

- See "Dressing, Fitting, and Locker Rooms."

(FS) Floor Surfaces

- In some areas floor surfaces should be evaluated as if wet. In particular consider spaces around exterior doors, drinking fountains, concession stands, food service areas, grocery produce counters, etc.
- Smooth floor surfaces should be evaluated for slip-resistance based on floor finish and maintenance.
- Vertical changes in levels along the accessible route can be an unforeseen barrier, e.g., transition between floor materials.

(PR) Protruding Objects

- Typical requirements.

(RP) & (ST) & (HR) Ramps and Stairs and Handrails

- Typical requirements.

(SG) Signage

- ISA symbols are required at accessible checkout aisles—see (BM).

(SR) Storage

- One of each type of storage unit (shelves, drawers, and hooks, if present) must be accessible.

ADAAG APPENDIX

The ADAAG Appendix contains advisory information pertinent to this space-type.

- A7.0 Business and Mercantile

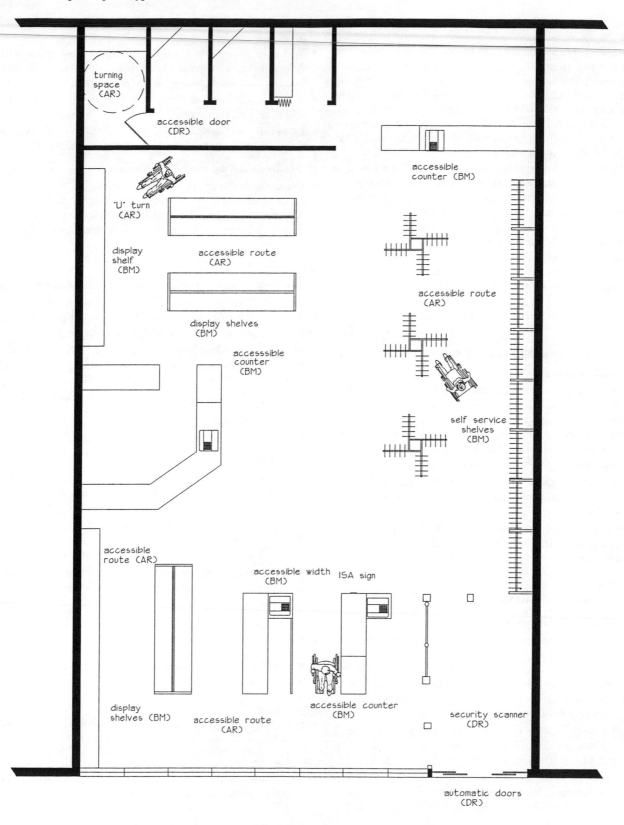

Figure 3-9. Business and mercantile.

Business and Mercantile Checklist

SIGNAGE

SG01	Entry signage: ISA requirement
SG02	Entry signage: inaccessible entrances
SG03	Inaccessible entry signage: criteria
SG04	Room signage: criteria
SG05	Room signage: location
SG08	Directional/informational signage: criteria
SG09	Suspended/projected signs: location

DOORS

DR01	Revolving door/turnstile
DR02	Automatic doors: ANSI standards
DR03	Automatic doors: operation
DR04	Doors: maneuvering clearances
DR05	Doors: handle type
DR06	Doors: opening force (interior only)
DR07	Doors: closing speed
DR08	Doors: thresholds
DR09	Doors: clear width/height
DR10	Openings (no door): clear width/height
DR11	Doors in series: clear space between

BUSINESS AND MERCANTILE

BM01	Sales/service counters: accessible route
BM02	Counters w/cash registers: criteria
BM03	Counters w/o cash registers: criteria
BM04	Acc. checkout aisle: ISA sign
BM05	Acc. checkout aisle: number req'd <5000 ft^2
BM06	Acc. checkout aisle: number req'd >5000 ft^2
BM07	Accessible checkout aisle: clear width
BM08	Security bollards: access and egress

ACCESSIBLE ROUTES

AR08	Route: clear width
AR09	Route width: U-turns

FLOOR SURFACES

FS01	Surface: firm, stable, and slip-resistant
FS02	Vertical changes in level
FS03	Carpet and tile floors

PROTRUDING OBJECTS

PR01	Wall-mounted
PR02	Freestanding/suspended on posts/pylons
PR03	Clear route width maintained
PR04	Overhead clearance
PR05	Vertical clearance: cane detection barrier

CONTROLS AND OPERATING MECHANISMS

CT01	Clear floor space
CT02	Reach ranges: elec./comm. systems
CT03	Reach ranges: thermostats
CT04	Reach ranges: other controls
CT05	Reach ranges: life safety devices
CT06	Controls: operation

STORAGE

SR01	Accessibility: one of each type
SR02	Clear floor space
SR03	Reach ranges
SR04	Storage closets w/o passage: criteria
SR05	Storage hardware: operation

Alarms

AL01	Emergency warning: audible/visual
AL02	Audible alarms: operation
AL03	Single station audible and visual
AL04	Visual alarms: integration w/building alarm
AL05	Visual alarms: operation
AL07	Visual alarms: common use areas
AL08	Visual alarms: vertical placement
AL09	Visual alarms: horizontal spacing

DRESSING, FITTING, AND LOCKER ROOMS

Use **DL** section when necessary.

RAMPS AND STAIRS AND HANDRAILS

Use **RP**, **ST**, and **HR** sections when necessary.

BUSINESS AND MERCANTILE COMPREHENSIVE CRITERIA

(SG) Signage (4.30)

NOTE:

- In historic buildings displays and written information, documents, etc., should be located where they can be seen by a seated person. Exhibits and signage displayed horizontally (e.g., open books) should be no higher than 44 in. above the floor surface. [4.1.7(3)(e)]

Signage: entry

SG-01 Where a building or space has both accessible and inaccessible entrances, are the accessible entrances identified by the International Symbol of Accessibility? (4.1.2(7)(c), Fig. 43a–b)

SG-02 If an entrance is not accessible, is there a directional sign indicating the location of the nearest accessible entrance? [4.1.2(7)(c), 4.1.3(8)(d)]

SG-03 Does the directional sign indicating the location of the nearest accessible entrance comply with directional signage criteria? (4.30.2, 3, 5)

- Character proportion: letters and numbers have a width to height ratio between 3:5 and 1:1 and a stroke width to height ratio between 1:5 and 1:10.
- Character height: sized according to viewing distance with characters on overhead signs at least 3 in. high.
- Finish: characters and backgrounds have a nonglare finish.
- Contrast: characters contrast with their background (light-on-dark or dark-on-light).

Signage: room identification (where provided)

DEFINITION:

- These signs designate permanent rooms and spaces.

AUTHOR'S INTERPRETATION:

- Signs that designate stairs, exit doors, and toilet rooms generally are associated with permanent spaces, while an "office" sign is not since the room function may change over time. Room numbers also must meet the ADAAG criteria as permanent designations, while personal names do not since the occupant may change over time.

SG-04 Do signs that designate permanent rooms and spaces comply with the following criteria? [4.1.2(7); 4.1.3(16); 4.30.4, 5, 6]

- Character type: raised and accompanied by Grade II Braille.
- Character size: between 5/8 in. and 2 in. high; raised at least 1/32 in.
- Character style: upper case, and sans or simple serif.
- Finish: characters and backgrounds have a nonglare finish.
- Contrast: characters contrast with their background (light-on-dark or dark-on-light).

SG-05 Is the room identification sign mounted in the required location? (4.30.6)

- Mounting location: installed on the wall adjacent to the latch side of the door or where wall space to the latch side of the door is not available, including double doors, placed on the nearest adjacent wall.
- Mounting height: 60 in. above the floor/ground to the centerline of the sign.
- Sign access: approach to within 3 in. of a sign without encountering protruding objects or standing within the swing of the door.

Signage: direction and information (where provided)

DEFINITION:

- Signs that provide direction to or information about functional spaces of the building.

EXCEPTION:

- Building directories, menus, and all other temporary signs are not required to comply. [4.1.3(16)]

SG-08 Do signs that provide direction to, or information about, functional spaces of the building comply with the following criteria? [4.1.2(7); 4.1.3(16); 4.30.1, 2, 3, 5]

- Character proportion: letters and numbers have a width to height ratio between 3:5 and 1:1 and a stroke width to height ratio between 1:5 and 1:10.
- Character height: sized according to viewing distance with characters on overhead signs at least 3 in. high.

NOTE:

- When the sign is mounted below 80 in., there are no prescribed character heights. Only when the sign is mounted 80 in. or higher are the characters required to be at least 3 in. high. (4.30.3)
- Finish: characters and backgrounds have a nonglare finish.
- Contrast: characters contrast with their background (light-on-dark or dark-on-light).

SG-09 Is a sign located so that the overhead clearance or the projection of a suspended or projected sign does not result in a protruding object (free-standing or wall-mounted)?

- Clear height: at least 80 in. (4.4.2, Fig. 8a)

- Overhang for free-standing signs on posts or pylons located between 27 in. and 80 in. high: no more than a 12-in. projection into accessible routes. (4.4.1, Fig. 8c).
- Overhang for wall-mounted signs between 27 in. and 80 in. high: no more than a 4-in. projection into accessible routes. (4.4.1, Fig. 8a)

(DR) Doors (4.13)

NOTE:

- Included in this category are doors, revolving doors, turnstiles, and gates.

AUTHOR'S INTERPRETATION:

- It is suggested that, for purposes of documentation and review, a door be assigned to the space it swings into. Corridors are an exception to this rule and include only entry doors into the corridor or intermediate fire doors.

Doors: revolving doors, turnstiles, and gates

DR-01 Where revolving doors or turnstiles are used on an accessible route, is an adjacent accessible gate or door provided that allows the same use pattern? (4.13.2)

Doors: automatic or power assisted

DR-02 If an automatic door or power assisted door is used, does it comply with the appropriate ANSI standard? (4.13.12)

- Automatic door: ANSI/BHMA A156.10-1985.
- Slow opening, low powered automatic door: ANSI A156.19-1984.
- Power assisted door: ANSI A156.19-1984.

DR-03 Do slow opening, low powered automatic doors or power assisted doors comply with opening and closing requirements? (4.13.12)

- Slow opening, low powered automatic doors: do not open to back-check faster than 3 sec and require no more than 15 lbf of force to stop door movement.
- Power assisted doors: no more than 5 lbf of opening force.

Doors: maneuvering clearance

DR-04 If the door is not automatic or power assisted, does it have the required maneuvering clearance provided on the push and pull side, and is the floor level and clear within the maneuvering area? (4.13.6)

- A verbal description cannot adequately describe the requirements. See ADAAG Fig. 25a–f for a graphic description.

EXCEPTION:

- Entry doors to acute care hospital bedrooms for inpatients are exempt from maneuvering space at the latch side of the door if the door is at least 44 in. wide.

AUTHOR'S INTERPRETATION:

- While ADAAG does not describe what elements can reduce the required maneuvering clearance, they could include a narrow entry alcove, an adjacent wall, railing, or permanently installed shelving, or a deep recessed door jamb.

Doors: hardware

DR-05 Do all door handles, locks, latches, or other operable devices meet required operational criteria? (4.13.9)

- Hardware operation: operable with one hand without tight grasping, pinching, or wrist twisting.
- Force required to operate the controls: not greater than 5 lbf. This does not apply to the force required to retract latch bolts or to disengage other devices that only hold the door in a closed position.
- Hardware type: "U"-shaped handles, levers, and push type mechanisms are acceptable designs.
- Hardware height: not greater than 48 in. above the floor.
- Sliding doors: hardware is exposed and usable from both sides when the doors are fully open.

Doors: opening force

DR-06 Do interior hinged doors and sliding or folding doors have an opening force of 5 lbf or less? (4.13.11)

- At present, no accessible criteria exist for exterior doors.
- Fire doors shall have the minimum opening force allowable by the appropriate administrative authority.

Doors: closing speed

DR-07 If the door has a closer, is the closer adjusted so that the door does not close too quickly? (4.13.10)

- From an open position of 70° the door will take at least 3 sec to move to a point 3 in. from the latch (measured to the leading edge of the door).

Doors: thresholds

DR-08 Where raised thresholds are provided, do they meet height limitations and are they beveled when required? (4.13.8, 4.5.2, Fig. 7)

- Threshold height: not more than 3/4 in. for exterior sliding doors or 1/2 in. for other types of doors.
- Threshold bevel: thresholds less than 1/4 in. high need no bevel; thresholds between 1/4 and 1/2 in. high shall be beveled at each edge with not more than a 1:2 slope.

  EXCEPTION:

  - A 3/4-in. high threshold is allowed in existing conditions. [4.1.6(3)(d)(ii)]

Doors: clear opening width and height

DR-09 Is the clear opening for the doorway adequate in width and height? (4.13.3, 4, 5; Fig. 24)

- Door width: at least 32 in. of clear width with the door open at 90°, measured between the face of the door and the door stop on the latch side. This also pertains to the active leaf of a double-leaf door or gate.
- Opening width: openings more than 24 in. deep must provide 36 in. of clear width.
- Height: at least 80 in. of vertical clearance.

  EXCEPTIONS:

  - Doors not requiring full user passage, such as shallow closets, may have the clear opening reduced to not less than 20 in.

- Where it is technically infeasible to comply with clear opening width requirements, a projection of 5/8 in. maximum will be permitted for the latch side. [4.1.6(d)(i)]

DR-10 Is the clear opening (when there is no door) adequate in width and height? (4.2.1, 4.3.3, 4.4.2)

- Width: at least 32 in. of clear width for depths 24 in. or less and at least 36 in. of clear width for depths greater than 24 in.
- Height: at least 80 in. of vertical clearance.

Doors: two doors in a series

DR-11 If there are two doors in a series, is the required clear space between the doors provided and do the doors swing in the appropriate direction? (4.13.7, Fig. 26)

- Clear space between the doors: not less than 48 in. plus the width of any door swinging into the space.
- Door swing: must swing in the same direction or away from the space between the doors.

(BM) Business and Mercantile (7.0)

Business: general

BM-01 Are all areas used for business transactions with the public, such as sales and service counters and/or self-service displays, on an accessible route? [4.1.3(12)(b), 7.2.2]

Business: sales counters with cash registers

BM-02 In retail stores where counters with cash registers are provided, is there at least one accessible cash register counter, and where more than one occurs, are they distributed throughout the facility? (7.2.1)

- Main counter: a portion of the counter is at least 36 in. long and is not more than 36 in. high.
- Alterations: where it is technically infeasible to provide an accessible counter, an auxiliary counter meeting these criteria may be provided.

Business: sales or service counters without cash registers

BM-03 At ticketing counters, teller stations, registration counters, and other counters for distributing goods or services to the public without cash registers, is there an accessible counter or alternative provided? (7.2.2)

- Main counter: a portion of the counter is at least 36 in. long and is not more than 36 in. high.
- Auxiliary counter: in close proximity to the main counter and not more than 36 in. high.
- Equivalent facilitation: might consist of a folding shelf attached to the main counter (for an individual with disabilities to write) and use of the space at the side of the counter for handing materials back and forth.

Business: checkout aisles

BM-04 Is there a sign identifying each accessible checkout aisle that is mounted above the checkout aisle and does the sign include the International Symbol of Accessibility (ISA)? (4.30.7, 7.3.3, Fig. 43a–b)

BM-05 For facilities (new or altered) with under 5000 ft² of selling space, is at least one accessible checkout aisle provided? (7.3.1)

BM-06 For facilities with 5000 or more ft^2 of selling space, is the required number of accessible checkout aisles provided? (7.3.1)

- New construction and alterations: minimum number for each type of checkout aisle design
  - One accessible aisle for each 1–4
  - Two accessible aisles for each 5–8
  - Three accessible aisles for each 9–15
  - Three plus 20 percent of additional aisles for over 15

NOTE:

- Types might be belted vs. nonbelted or permanently designated express lane vs. regular lane.

Business: checkout aisles

BM-07 Is the required clear aisle width provided for accessible checkout aisles and is the adjoining counter within the required height? (7.3.2)

- Aisle width: at least 36 in. for lengths greater than 24 in. and at least 32 in. for lengths 24 in. or less. (4.2.1, Fig. 1)
- Counter height: no more than 38 in. above the floor or no more than 40 in. above the floor if the counter has a lip on the edge.

Business: security bollards

BM-08 Are security bollards or other such devices installed so that accessible access and egress is provided? (7.4)

NOTE:

- An alternate accessible entry that is equally convenient to that provided for the general public is acceptable.

(AR) Accessible Routes (4.3)

NOTES:

- All walks, halls, corridors, aisles, skywalks, tunnels, and other spaces that are part of a designated accessible route shall comply with accessible requirements.
- Any slope on the accessible route that is greater than 1:20 is required to meet all ramp criteria.
- The accessible route shall, to the maximum extent feasible, coincide with the route for the general public.
- In historic buildings, accessible routes from an accessible entrance shall be provided to all publicly used spaces on at least the level of the accessible entrance. Access shall be provided to all levels of a building or facility whenever practical. [4.1.7(3)(d)]

AUTHOR'S INTERPRETATION:

- An accessible route "generally coincides" with the route used by the public if:
  - It does not force the user to go out of the way
  - It is most like the route chosen by the general public
  - It is direct
  - It gives the same basic experience as the route preferred by the public

Accessible Routes: width

AR-08 Is the minimum clear width along the accessible route adequate for continuous or point passage? (4.2.1, 4.3.3, Fig. 1, Fig. 8e, Fig. 24e)

- Continuous passage (greater than 24 in. long): at least a 36-in. clear width.
- Point passage (not more than 24 in. long): at least a 32-in. clear width.

AUTHOR'S INTERPRETATION:

- Noncompliance with this question generally relates to permanent elements that encroach on the accessible route. Large, heavy equipment that is not readily movable might be considered permanent. If the space is designed so that temporary elements (such as bikes in a bike rack or car bumpers) will consistently encroach, the situation might also be considered a permanent barrier.

AR-09 Is the minimum clear width along the accessible route adequate at a U-turn around an obstruction? (4.3.3, Fig. 7a–b)

- Obstruction 48 in. or greater: at least a 36-in. clear width around the obstruction.
- Obstruction less than 48 in.: at least a 42-in. clear width at each side with at least a 48-in. clear width in the turn.

(FS) Floor and Ground Surfaces (4.5)

Floor Surfaces: general

FS-01 Are the floor/ground surfaces on the accessible route stable, firm, and slip-resistant? (4.5.1)

AUTHOR'S INTERPRETATION:

- Exterior spaces, interior circulation, bathrooms, and other spaces where water can collect on the floor around an element (sinks, drinking fountains, hose bibbs, etc.) are reviewed as if wet.
- High gloss surfaces without significant textures that are regularly maintained with waxing (smooth tiles, waxed concrete, etc.) could be considered noncompliant.
- Accessible criteria are not specified for nonpermanent floor surfaces such as mats or rugs.

Floor Surfaces: changes in level

FS-02 Are vertical changes in level between 1/4 in. and 1/2 in. beveled with a slope of 1:2 or less? (4.5.2)

- Changes in level up to 1/4 in. may be vertical without edge treatment.
- Changes in level greater than 1/2 in. should be accomplished by means of a curb ramp, ramp, elevator, or platform lift (as permitted in ADAAG 4.1.3 and 4.1.6).

Floor Surfaces: carpet

FS-03 Does carpet or carpet tile used on the floor comply with accessible criteria?

- Attachment: secured. (4.5.3, Fig. 8f)
- Exposed edges: fastened and trimmed along the entire length.

- Pile type: low pile (1/2 in. maximum).
- Padding: firm pad or no pad underneath.

(PR) Protruding Objects (4.4)

Protruding Objects: general

PR-01 Do wall-mounted objects having leading edges between 27 in. and 80 in. high project less than 4 in. into walkways, corridors, aisles, or paths of travel? (4.4.1, Fig. 8a–e)

- Objects mounted with their leading edge at or below 27 in. can protrude any amount, as long as they do not reduce the required clear width of an accessible route.

AUTHOR'S INTERPRETATION:

- Protruding objects might include fire extinguishers or cabinets, pencil sharpeners, shelving, counters, built-in equipment overhangs, or various dispensers such as for paper towels or soap.

PR-02 Do free-standing objects, suspended or mounted on posts or pylons with leading edges between 27 in. and 80 in. high, project less than 12 in. into the perpendicular route of travel? (4.4.1, Fig. 8a–e)

AUTHOR'S INTERPRETATION:

- These might include telephone enclosures, drinking fountains, or free-standing signage kiosks.

PR-03 Is the minimum clear route width or maneuvering space still maintained even with the projection of a protruding object? (4.4.1, Fig. 8a–e)

Protruding Objects: overhead clearance

PR-04 Is the minimum overhead clearance of 80 in. provided in accessible areas or along accessible routes? (4.4.2, Fig. 8a)

AUTHOR'S INTERPRETATION:

- Overhead objects that can reduce the required clearance might include structures, pipes, ducts, or light fixtures.

PR-05 Where the vertical clearance of a space adjoining the accessible route is less than 80 in. high, is a cane detection barrier less than 27 in. from the floor provided for blind or visually impaired persons? (4.4.2, Fig. 8c-1)

AUTHOR'S INTERPRETATION:

- This condition might be found under a stair, at a sloped ceiling space, or with guy wires from telephone poles along an exterior accessible route.

(CT) Controls and Operating Mechanisms (4.27)

NOTES:

- Controls or operating mechanisms can include elements such as light switches, nonkeyed thermostats, alarm pull stations, fire extinguisher cabinets, A/C window units, microwave ovens, towel dispensers, and wall hooks.
- If controls are to be operated by occupants of the space, they must be accessible. If controls are to be operated by maintenance staff only and not by occupants or other users of the space, they do not have to be accessible.

Controls: clear floor space

CT-01 Is a clear floor space of at least 30 in. × 48 in. provided in front of controls, dispensers, receptacles, and other operable equipment for forward or parallel approach? (4.27.2, Fig. 4a–b)

Controls: reach ranges

NOTES:

- Accessible reach ranges for controls and operating mechanisms are:
  - Forward reach: not less than 15 in. high and not more than 48 in. high without any obstruction or where the obstruction is less than 20 in. deep. For obstructions from 20 in. to 25 in. deep, no forward reach higher than 44 in.
  - Side reach: not less than 9 in. high and not more than 54 in. high. For obstructions not more than 34 in. high or 24 in. deep, no side reach higher than 46 in.
  - Electrical outlets, switches, and communication system receptacles have a minimum outlet height of 15 in. regardless of forward or side reach. See CT-02 below.

CT-02 Are electrical outlets, switches, and communication system receptacles mounted within accessible forward or side reach ranges? (4.27.3)

EXCEPTION:

- These requirements do not apply where the use of special equipment dictates otherwise or where electrical and communications system receptacles are not normally intended for use by building occupants. (4.27.3)

CT-03 Are thermostats or other similar operable equipment mounted within accessible forward or side reach ranges? (4.2.5, 4.2.6, Fig. 5a–b, Fig. 6a–c)

CT-04 Are dispensers or other similar operable equipment mounted within accessible forward or side reach ranges? (4.2.5, 4.2.6, Fig. 5a–b, Fig. 6a–c)

CT-05 Are life safety devices or other similar operable equipment mounted within accessible forward or side reach ranges? (4.2.5, 4.2.6, Fig. 5a–b, Fig. 6a–c)

NOTE:

- This might include fire alarm pull stations, handles to extinguisher cabinets, or wall-mounted extinguishers.

Controls: operation

CT-06 Are controls, dispensers, receptacles, and other operable equipment operable with one hand without tight grasping, pinching, or wrist twisting, and requiring no more than 5 lbf of force? (4.27.4)

(SR) STORAGE (4.25)

NOTE:

- Accessible reach range requirements do not apply to shelves or display units allowing self-service by customers in mercantile occupancies but they must be located on an accessible route. [4.1.3(12)(b)]

Storage: general

SR-01 Does at least one of each type of fixed or built-in storage unit comply with accessible criteria? [4.1.3(12)(a), 4.25.1]

NOTE:
- Types of storage facilities might include cabinets, shelves, closets, and drawers.

Storage: clear floor space

SR-02 Is there a clear floor space at least 30 in. × 48 in. at fixed or built-in storage units that allows for either a forward or side approach? (4.25.2, Fig. 4a–b)

Storage: reach ranges

SR-03 Are forward or side reach for each type of accessible storage unit within acceptable reach ranges? (4.2.5-6, Fig. 5a–b, Fig. 6a–c, 4.25.3)

- Forward reach: not less than 15 in. high and not more than 48 in. high without any obstruction or where the obstruction is less than 20 in. deep. For obstructions from 20 in. to 25 in. deep, no forward reach higher than 44 in.
- Side reach: not less than 9 in. high and not more than 54 in. high. For obstructions not more than 34 in. high or 24 in. deep, no side reach higher than 46 in.

SR-04 In a closet where passage is not required to access storage (e.g., door opening is less than 32 in.), are the clothes rod or shelves within required reach ranges? (4.25.3, Fig. 38a–b)

- Door width: at least 20 in. (4.13.5)
- Horizontal reach: not more than 21 in. from the opening.
- Rod reach: if over 10 in. deep, then not more than 48 in. high.
- Shelf reach: if over 10 in. deep, then not more than 48 in. high or less than 9 in. high.

Storage: hardware

SR-05 Is the hardware on the storage unit doors or drawers operable with one hand without tight grasping, pinching, or wrist twisting, and requiring no more than 5 lbf of force? (4.25.4, 4.27.4)

(AL) Alarms (4.28)

NOTE:
- At a minimum, visual signal appliances shall be provided in buildings and facilities in restrooms and any other general usage areas. **The ADAAG does not define the number of occupants needed to establish a general or common use area.**

ALLOWANCE:
- Emergency warning systems in medical care facilities may be modified to suit standard health care alarm design practice. [4.1.3(14)]

Alarms: general

AL-01 If emergency warning systems are provided, do they include both audible alarms and visual alarms? [4.1.3(14)]

Audible Alarms: general

AL-02 If provided, do the audible alarms meet required operational criteria? (4.28.2)

- Sound level: exceeds the prevailing sound level in the room or space by at least 15 dbA or exceeds any max-imum sound level with a duration of 60 sec by 5 dbA, whichever is louder.
- Sound levels for alarm signals shall not exceed 120 dbA.

AL-03 If single station audible alarms are provided, then are single station visual alarm signals also provided? (4.28.3)

Visual Alarms: general

AL-04 If provided, are the visual alarm signal appliances integrated into the building or facility alarm system? (4.28.3)

AL-05 If provided, do the visual alarm signals meet required operational criteria? [4.28.3(1, 2, 3, 4, 5)]

- Lamp: xenon strobe type or equivalent.
- Color: clear or nominal white (i.e., unfiltered or clear filtered white light).
- Pulse duration: maximum shall be 0.2 sec with a maximum duty cycle of 40 percent.
- Intensity: not less than 75 candela.
- Flash rate: not less than 1 Hz and not more than 3 Hz.

AL-07 Are visual alarm signal appliances provided in general usage areas of the building such as meeting rooms, corridors, and lobbies or any other area for common use? (4.28.1)

AUTHOR'S INTERPRETATION:
- The authors identified three or more occupants as the minimum number to establish a common use area.

AL-08 Are the visual alarms placed at 80 in. above the highest floor level or 6 in. below the ceiling, whichever is lower? [4.28.3(6)]

AL-09 In spaces required to have visual alarms, are the alarms spaced properly? [4.28.3(7)]

- No place in any space should be more than 50 ft from a visual signal alarm.
- Where a space or large room exceeds 100 ft across, without obstructions 6 ft above the finished floor, visual alarms can be spaced a maximum of 100 ft apart at the perimeter, in lieu of suspending appliances from the ceiling.

(DL) Dressing and Fitting Rooms (4.35)

NOTE:
- Use the review guide "Dressing, Fitting, and Locker Rooms" if dressing or fitting rooms are provided.

(RP) Ramps (4.8)

NOTE:
- See "Master Guidelines" for ramp criteria if an accessible ramp is required.

(ST) Stairs (4.9)

NOTE:
- See "Master Guidelines" for stair criteria if an accessible stair is required.

(HR) Handrails, Grab Bars, and Tub and Shower Seats (4.26)

NOTE:
- See "Master Guidelines" for handrails criteria if an accessible handrail is required.

Dressing, Fitting, and Locker Rooms

Introduction. Use this "Space-type Review Guide" to design or evaluate accessible dressing and fitting rooms or areas used by the general public, patients, customers, or employees. This includes everything from simple fitting rooms or changing booths provided in clothing stores to individual dressing rooms in locker rooms such as those found in gymnasiums, swimming areas, athletic clubs, etc. It would also be used for dressing rooms in medical facilities used by patients, as well as locker rooms used by doctors, nurses, and other staff members. Since showers and lavatories are quite often part of dressing/locker areas, they must be accessible and can be evaluated using this review guide. Toilet areas should be reviewed using "Toilet Rooms."

In general, there are two types of dressing areas that must be accessible if provided. The first type is usually a small individual room or booth used for fitting or changing clothes, such as are found in department stores or medical facilities. A similar type of space can also be found in locker rooms or in bathing/shower facilities. The second type is not an individual room but simply a changing area located within a locker room or bathing/shower facility. The major difference in these two types depends on whether they are part of the design in new construction or part of an alteration. If individual rooms are provided in new construction, at least 5 percent, but not fewer than one of each type in each cluster of dressing rooms, must be accessible. Different types of dressing rooms would include those serving different genders or distinct and different functions, as in different treatment or examination facilities. In alterations, where it is technically infeasible to provide one of each type, or one in each cluster, a dressing room for each sex on each level must be accessible. If only unisex dressing rooms are provided, they may be used to meet this requirement. If a dressing area is part of a locker room or bathing/shower facility then certain parts of the locker room must be accessible.

Dressing/Fitting Rooms. In their simplest design, accessible dressing/fitting rooms are similar to any type of changing room except they must be large enough to accommodate a wheelchair and they must provide a wall-mounted bench on the room's longest dimension. If a mirror is provided, it must be a full length type mounted in a position to afford a view to a person seated on a bench or to a person standing. Lockers, clothes hooks, rods, and shelves must also be accessible if provided. Benches provided in most dressing/fitting rooms are usually not adequate for people with mobility problems who change their clothes in a supine position. ADAAG requires a minimum bench dimension of 24 in. × 48 in., although some experts feel a 30 in. × 72 in. bench is a more appropriate minimum size. Whatever size or type of bench is used, a clear floor space must be provided along the bench to allow a parallel transfer onto the bench. The bench surface must be slip-resistant if there is any chance that water might accumulate, such as near a shower or a swimming pool.

If access into the room is through a swinging or sliding door, a clear floor space must be provided to allow a 180° turning area for a wheelchair. No door, including the entry door or a closet door in the room, can swing into any part of the turning space. Dressing rooms entered through a curtained opening, which must be at least 32 in. wide, are not required to have the turning space as long as there is adequate maneuvering clearance for a wheelchair. Although ADAAG does not actually specify the dimension for "adequate maneuvering clearance" the authors feel that a dressing room with curtained opening is very similar to an alcove and should therefore at least meet the minimum ADAAG specifications for alcoves. This would mean that a curtained dressing room with a frontal approach would need a minimum clear floor space of 36 in. × 48 in. and those with side approaches would need a minimum clear floor space of 30 in. × 60 in. In each case, the clear floor space must be parallel to a wall-mounted bench. Again, if a mirror is provided it must be a full length type mounted in a position to afford a view to a person seated on a bench or to a person standing.

Locker Rooms. Locker rooms such as those in which employees change clothes, and those provided in gymnasiums and other recreational facilities, should be accessible. These rooms are usually large enough to accommodate a wheelchair but care must be taken to maintain an accessible route to other elements in the space, such as lavatories, showers, toilets, and urinals. If the route requires a U-turn around any fixed object such as lockers or fixed benches, a minimum turning clearance must be maintained. As with other types of changing areas, a bench must be provided and if a mirror is provided it must be full length to afford a view to a person seated on the bench or standing. Elements such as lockers, shelves, and clothes and towel hooks or rods must also be accessible.

In locker rooms attached to shower facilities, most people are undressed when moving between the lockers and the showers. Since many people might feel self-conscious making this trip, it is desirable, but not required, to provide a private dressing/shower room with a lavatory and a toilet if possible.

PRELIMINARY DESIGN OVERVIEW

(AL) Alarms

- Visual alarms must be provided in common use dressing, fitting, or locker rooms. The authors identified three or more occupants as the minimum number to establish a common use area

(AR) Accessible Routes

- Provide an accessible route to at least one of each type of element in the space (e.g., water closets, urinals, lavatories, showers, hooks, hanger rods, shelves, towel bars, electric hand dryers, etc.).
- At turns around obstructions, widths of the accessible route may increase according to the size of the obstruction.

(CT) Controls and Operating Mechanisms

- Frequently overlooked in this space-type are controls on window air conditioner units, thermostats, fans, electric hand dryers, etc.

(DL) Dressing and Fitting

- Five percent or not fewer than one accessible dressing room of each type (gender or use) must be provided.
- Individual dressing room or space must allow 180° wheelchair turn. Private dressing rooms entered through a 32 in. curtained opening do not require the turning space if adequate maneuvering clearance is provided.
- If doors are used, they must be compliant and must not open into the wheelchair turning space.
- A compliant bench, affixed to the wall, must be provided in accessible dressing rooms.
- Clear floor space and bench mounting must allow parallel transfer.
- In areas where floor surfaces may be wet (swimming pools, showers, etc.), water must not accumulate on the bench. The bench surface must be slip-resistant.
- If provided, mirrors must be full length and offer a view for someone seated at the bench or standing.

(DR) Doors

- If doors are used, they must meet typical door criteria and they must not swing into the wheelchair turning space.

(FS) Floor and Ground Surfaces

- Floor surfaces in locker rooms and some dressing rooms should be evaluated as if wet.
- Grates located on the accessible route must meet accessibility requirements.

(LV) Lavatories, Sinks, and Mirrors

- Hot pipes and sharp objects (e.g., valves and drains) must be shielded under lavatories and sinks.

- If sinks and/or lavatories are used for different purposes, then one of each use type must be accessible.
- Where mirrors are provided, one must be accessible. The bottom edge of the reflecting surface (slanted or flush-mounted) must meet accessibility requirements.

(PR) Protruding Objects

- Common wall-mounted elements can be protruding objects, e.g., hanger rods, shelves, paper towel and soap dispensers.

(SE) Fixed Counters

- If fixed counters are provided, one of each type must be accessible.

(SG) Signage

- If dressing or locker facilities are stand-alone buildings and all entrances are not accessible, the accessible entrances must be identified by the ISA symbol; nonaccessible entrances must have signage indicating the accessible route to an accessible entrance.

(SR) Fixed Storage, Closets, Lockers, and Shelves

- When provided, one of each type of storage unit (shelves, dispensers, hooks, towel bars, etc.) must be accessible.

(SS) Shower Stalls

- Accessible showers may be a transfer or roll-in type; requirements vary for each.
- Accessible shower seating may be mounted or folding; structural and dimensional requirements vary for each.
- Shower spray unit must be accessible for both fixed or hand-held operation. (In vandal-prone facilities, a fixed shower head may be used in lieu of a hand-held shower head. The fixed head must meet mounting height requirements.)

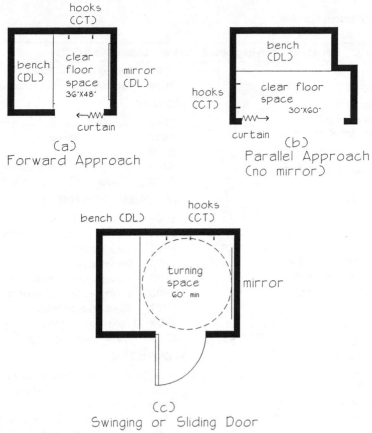

Figure 3-10. Dressing and fitting rooms.

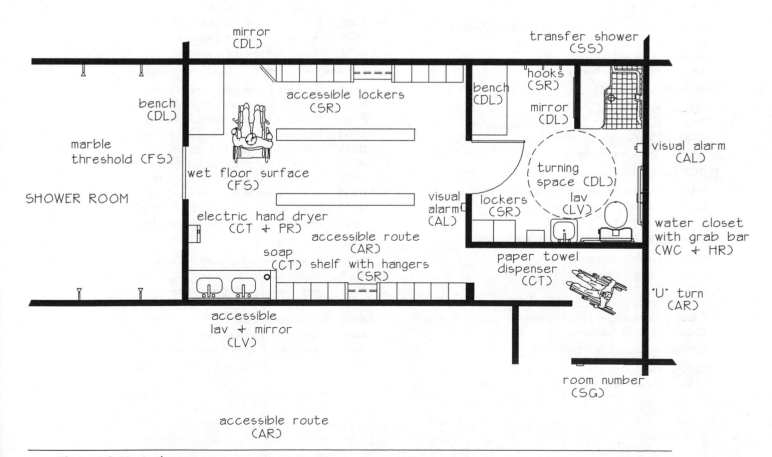

Figure: 3-11. Locker rooms.

Dressing, Fitting, and Locker Rooms Checklist

SIGNAGE

SG04	Room signage: criteria
SG05	Room signage: location
SG06	Pictograms: size requirements
SG07	Pictograms: verbal description criteria

DOORS

DR04	Doors: maneuvering clearances
DR05	Doors: handle type
DR06	Doors: opening force (interior only)
DR07	Doors: closing speed
DR08	Doors: thresholds
DR09	Doors: clear width/height
DR10	Openings (no door): clear width/height
DR11	Doors in series: clear space between

DRESSING, FITTING, AND LOCKER ROOMS

DL01	Rooms: number required
DL02	Rooms: on accessible route
DL03	Rooms: maneuvering space
DL04	Bench: size, height, and location
DL05	Bench: clear floor space
DL06	Bench: structurally stable
DL07	Bench: slip-resistant surface
DL08	Bench: water accumulation
DL09	Mirror: size and height
DL10	Mirror: location

ACCESSIBLE ROUTES

AR06	Building entry to accessible spaces/elements
AR08	Route: clear width
AR09	Route width: U-turns
AR11	Route: maneuvering clearances

PROTRUDING OBJECTS

PR01	Wall-mounted
PR02	Freestanding/suspended on posts/pylons
PR03	Clear route width maintained
PR04	Overhead clearance

FLOOR SURFACES

FS01	Surface: firm, stable, and slip-resistant
FS02	Vertical changes in level
FS03	Carpet and tile floors

CONTROLS AND OPERATING MECHANISMS

CT01	Clear floor space
CT02	Reach ranges: elec./comm. systems
CT03	Reach ranges: thermostats
CT04	Reach ranges: other controls
CT05	Reach ranges: life safety devices
CT06	Controls: operation

FIXED TABLES AND/OR COUNTERS

SE01	Fixed seating: number required
SE02	Wheelchairs: clear floor space at tables
SE03	Tables/counters: heights
SE04	Tables/counters: knee clearance criteria

STORAGE

SR01	Accessibility: one of each type
SR02	Clear floor space
SR03	Reach ranges
SR04	Storage closets w/o passage: criteria
SR05	Storage hardware: operation

LAVATORIES AND SINKS

LV01	Clear floor space
LV02	Rim/apron heights and extension from wall
LV03	Toe clearance
LV04	Insulated pipes
LV05	Controls and operation requirements
LV06	Lavatories: knee clearance
LV07	Sinks: knee clearance
LV08	Sinks: bowl depth
LV09	Mirror: mounting height

SHOWER STALLS

SS01	Where provided: at least one accessible
SS02	Min. size criteria and clear floor space
SS03	Shower stall seats: location
SS04	Shower stall seats: type and size
SS05	Shower stall grab bars: criteria
SS06	Shower controls: location
SS07	Shower controls: operation
SS08	Shower stall controls: spray unit criteria
SS09	Shower stall: floor curb criteria
SS10	Shower stall enclosure: criteria

GRAB BARS AND SHOWER SEATS

HR01	Handrails & grab bars: diameter
HR02	Handrails & grab bars: edge radius
HR03	Clearance between handrail and wall
HR04	Handrails in recess: criteria
HR05	Handrails and grab bars: no rotation
HR06	Handrails and grab bars: structural strength
HR07	Mounting devices: structural strength
HR08	Tub/shower seat: structural strength
HR09	Tub/shower fasteners: structural strength
HR10	Wall adjacent to handrail abrasion free

ALARMS

AL01	Emergency warning: audible/visual
AL02	Audible alarms: operation
AL03	Single station audible and visual
AL04	Visual alarms: integration with building alarm
AL05	Visual alarms: operation
AL07	Visual alarms: common use areas
AL08	Visual alarms: vertical placement

DRESSING, FITTING, AND LOCKER ROOMS
COMPREHENSIVE CRITERIA

NOTE

- This review guide focuses on dressing, fitting, and locker rooms which are typically found in stores and gymnasiums. Small dressing and locker rooms such as those found at tennis courts or public swimming pools can also be reviewed using this guide but they must also included the signage criteria for entries. (See "Signage" in the "Master Guidelines.")

(SG) Signage (4.30)

Signage: room identification (where provided)

DEFINITION:

- These signs designate permanent rooms and spaces.

AUTHOR'S INTERPRETATION:

- Signs that designate stairs, exit doors, and toilet rooms generally are associated with permanent spaces, while an "office" sign is not since the room function may change over time. Room numbers also must meet the ADAAG criteria as permanent designations, while personal names do not since the occupant may change over time.

SG-04 Do signs that designate permanent rooms and spaces comply with the following criteria? [4.1.2(7), 4.1.3(16), 4.30.4, 5, 6]

- Character type: raised and accompanied by Grade II Braille.
- Character size: between 5/8 in. and 2 in. high; raised at least 1/32 in.
- Character style: upper case, and sans or simple serif.
- Finish: characters and backgrounds have a nonglare finish.
- Contrast: characters contrast with their background (light-on-dark or dark-on-light).

SG-05 Is the room identification sign mounted in the required location? (4.30.6)

- Mounting location: installed on the wall adjacent to the latch side of the door or where wall space to the latch side of the door is not available, including double doors, placed on the nearest adjacent wall.
- Mounting height: 60 in. above the floor/ground to the centerline of the sign.
- Sign access: approach to within 3 in. of a sign without encountering protruding objects or standing within the swing of the door.

Signage: pictorial symbol signs (pictograms) (where provided)

AUTHOR'S INTERPRETATION:

- Because the criteria for pictograms are listed in ADAAG 4.30.4, they fall into the category of room identification signage and must meet those criteria that follow.
- While the ISA symbol might be considered to be a pictogram, it does not appear to have the same requirements as pictograms.

SG-06 Is the border dimension of a pictogram, where provided, at least 6 in. high? (4.30.4)

AUTHOR'S INTERPRETATION:

- A pictogram includes both a symbol and the field on which it is displayed. The 6-in. vertical dimension applies to the vertical field, not to the symbol. The required verbal description may not intrude on the 6-in. field.

SG-07 Is a pictogram, where provided, accompanied by the equivalent verbal description placed directly below the pictogram, and does the verbal description meet room identification signage criteria? (4.30.4)

- Character type: raised and accompanied by Grade II Braille.
- Character size: between 5/8 in. and 2 in. high; raised at least 1/32 in.
- Character style: upper case, and sans or simple serif.
- Finish: characters and backgrounds have a nonglare finish.
- Contrast: characters contrast with their background (light-on-dark or dark-on-light).

(DR) Doors (4.13)

Doors: maneuvering clearance

DR-04 If the door is not automatic or power assisted, does it have the required maneuvering clearance provided on the push and pull side, and is the floor level and clear within the maneuvering area? (4.13.6)

- A verbal description cannot adequately describe the requirements. See ADAAG Fig. 25a–f for a graphic description.

EXCEPTION:

- Entry doors to acute care hospital bedrooms for inpatients are exempt from maneuvering space at the latch side of the door if the door is at least 44 in. wide.

AUTHOR'S INTERPRETATION:

- While ADAAG does not describe what elements can reduce the required maneuvering clearance, they could include a narrow entry alcove, an adjacent wall, railing, or permanently installed shelving, or a deep recessed door jamb.

Doors: hardware

DR-05 Do all door handles, locks, latches, or other operable devices meet required operational criteria? (4.13.9)

- Hardware operation: operable with one hand without tight grasping, pinching, or wrist twisting.
- Force required to operate the controls: not greater than 5 lbf. This does not apply to the force required to retract latch bolts or to disengage other devices that only hold the door in a closed position.
- Hardware type: "U"-shaped handles, levers, and push type mechanisms are acceptable designs.
- Hardware height: not greater than 48 in. above the floor.
- Sliding doors: hardware is exposed and usable from both sides when the doors are fully open.

Doors: opening force

DR-06 Do interior hinged doors and sliding or folding doors have an opening force of 5 lbf or less? (4.13.11)

- At present, no accessible criteria exist for exterior doors.
- Fire doors shall have the minimum opening force allowable by the appropriate administrative authority.

Doors: closing speed

DR-07 If the door has a closer, is the closer adjusted so that the door does not close too quickly? (4.13.10)

- From an open position of 70° the door will take at least 3 sec to move to a point 3 in. from the latch (measured to the leading edge of the door).

Doors: thresholds

DR-08 Where raised thresholds are provided, do they meet height limitations and are they beveled when required? (4.13.8, 4.5.2, Fig. 7)

- Threshold height: not more than 3/4 in. for exterior sliding doors or 1/2 in. for other types of doors.
- Threshold bevel: thresholds less than 1/4 in. high need no bevel; thresholds between 1/4 and 1/2 in. high shall be beveled at each edge with not more than a 1:2 slope.

EXCEPTION:

- A 3/4-in. high threshold is allowed in existing conditions. [4.1.6(3)(d)(ii)]

Doors: clear opening width and height

DR-09 Is the clear opening for the doorway adequate in width and height? (4.13.3, 4, 5, Fig. 24)

- Door width: at least 32 in. of clear width with the door open at 90°, measured between the face of the door and the door stop on the latch side. This also pertains to the active leaf of a double-leaf door or gate.
- Opening width: openings more than 24 in. deep must provide 36 in. of clear width.
- Height: at least 80 in. of vertical clearance.

EXCEPTIONS:

- Doors not requiring full user passage, such as shallow closets, may have the clear opening reduced to not less than 20 in.
- Where it is technically infeasible to comply with clear opening width requirements, a projection of 5/8 in. maximum will be permitted for the latch side. [4.1.6(d)(i)]

DR-10 Is the clear opening (when there is no door) adequate in width and height? (4.2.1, 4.3.3, 4.4.2)

- Width: at least 32 in. of clear width for depths 24 in. or less and at least 36 in. of clear width for depths greater than 24 in.
- Height: at least 80 in. of vertical clearance.

Doors: two doors in a series

DR-11 If there are two doors in a series, is the required clear space between the doors provided and do the doors swing in the appropriate direction? (4.13.7, Fig. 26)

- Clear space between the doors: not less than 48 in. plus the width of any door swinging into the space.
- Door swing: must swing in the same direction or away from the space between the doors.

(DL) Dressing, Fitting, and Locker Rooms (4.35)

AUTHOR'S INTERPRETATION:

- ADAAG does not specifically address locker rooms within this category. However, it appears that a number of items identified below are applicable in locker room situations.
- Locker rooms that have toilet facilities within the same space would also have to meet the ADAAG bathroom criteria.

Dressing, Fitting, and Locker Rooms: general criteria

DL-01 Where dressing and fitting rooms are provided for use by the general public, patients, customers, or employees, is the minimum number of rooms complying with accessibility requirements provided? [4.1.3(21), 4.35.1]

- Number: 5 percent (but not fewer than one) of each type (gender or use) in each cluster.

DL-02 Are the accessible dressing and fitting rooms located on an accessible route? (4.35.1)

DL-03 In a dressing or fitting room with a swinging or sliding door, are required maneuvering clearances provided? (4.35.2)

- Turning space: 180° turning space with at least a 60-in. diameter or a "T"-shaped space with at least 36-in. wide legs.
- The clear turning space should not be obstructed by the door swing.

NOTE:

- Turning space is not required in a private dressing room entered through a curtained opening at least 32 in. wide and where clear floor space at least 30 in. × 48 in. is provided.

Dressing, Fitting, and Locker Rooms: benches

DL-04 Does every accessible dressing and fitting room have a bench that complies with accessible criteria? (4.35.4)

- Size: 24 in. × 48 in.
- Height: mounted 17 in. to 19 in. above the floor.
- Location: affixed to the wall along the longer dimension.

DL-05 Is a clear floor space at least 30 in. × 48 in. provided alongside the accessible bench to allow a person using a wheelchair to make a parallel transfer onto the bench? (4.35.4)

DL-06 Do the accessible bench and its attachments comply with structural strength requirements? (4.35.4)

- Actual bending stress in the seat induced by the maximum bending moment from the application of 250 lbf is less than the allowable bending stress for the material of the grab bar.

- Shear stress induced in a seat by the application of 250 lbf shall be less than the allowable shear stress for the material of the seat. If the connection between the seat and its mounting bracket or other support is considered to be fully restrained, then direct and torsional shear stresses shall be totaled for the combined shear stress, which shall not exceed the allowable shear stress.

- Shear force induced in a fastener or mounting device from the application of 250 lbf shall be less than the allowable lateral load of either the fastener or mounting device or the supporting structure, whichever is the smaller allowable load.

- Tensile force induced in a fastener by a direct tension force of 250 lbf plus the maximum moment from the application of 250 lbf shall be less than the allowable withdrawal load between the fastener and the supporting structure.

DL-07 When installed in conjunction with wet locations, does the surface of the accessible bench have a slip-resistant surface? (4.35.4)

DL-08 When installed in conjunction with wet locations, is the accessible bench constructed so that water does not accumulate on the surface? (4.35.4)

Dressing, Fitting, and Locker Rooms: mirrors

DL-09 Where a mirror is provided, is it a full length mirror at least 18 in. × 54 in. high? (4.35.5)

DL-10 Is the mirror mounted in a position affording a view to a person on the accessible bench as well as to a person in a standing position? (4.35.5)

(AR) Accessible Routes (4.3)

NOTE:

- The accessible route shall, to the maximum extent feasible, coincide with the route for the general public.

AUTHOR'S INTERPRETATION:

- An accessible route "generally coincides" with the route used by the public if:
  — It does not force the user to go out of the way
  — It is most like the route chosen by the general public
  — It is direct
  — It gives the same basic experience as the route preferred by the public

Accessible Routes: interior

AR-06 Is the building entrance space connected by an accessible route to all accessible spaces, elements, and all accessible dwelling units within the building or facility? [4.3.2(3)]

Accessible Routes: width

AR-08 Is the minimum clear width along the accessible route adequate for continuous or point passage? (4.2.1, 4.3.3, Fig. 1, Fig. 8e, Fig. 24e)

- Continuous passage (greater than 24 in. long): at least a 36-in. clear width.
- Point passage (not more than 24 in. long): at least a 32-in. clear width.

AUTHOR'S INTERPRETATION:

- Noncompliance with this question generally relates to permanent elements that encroach on the accessible route. Large, heavy equipment that is not readily movable might be considered permanent. If the space is designed so that temporary elements (such as bikes in a bike rack or car bumpers) will consistently encroach, the situation might also be considered a permanent barrier.

AR-09 Is the minimum clear width along the accessible route adequate at a U-turn around an obstruction? (4.3.3, Fig. 7a–b)

- Obstruction 48 in. or greater: at least a 36-in. clear width around the obstruction.
- Obstruction less than 48 in.: at least a 42-in. clear width at each side with at least a 48-in. clear width in the turn.

Accessible Routes: maneuvering clearances

AR-11 Is the minimum clear floor space for an unobstructed 180° wheelchair turning space or a "T"-shaped turning space provided? (4.2.3, Fig. 3a–b)

- 180° turning space: at least a 60-in. diameter;
- "T"-shaped turning space: at least 36-in. wide legs with a minimum length of 60 in.

(PR) Protruding Objects (4.4)

Protruding Objects: general

PR-01 Do wall-mounted objects having leading edges between 27 in. and 80 in. high project less than 4 in. into walkways, corridors, aisles, or paths of travel? (4.4.1, Fig. 8a–e)

- Objects mounted with their leading edge at or below 27 in. can protrude any amount, as long as they do not reduce the required clear width of an accessible route.

AUTHOR'S INTERPRETATION:

- Protruding objects might include fire extinguishers or cabinets, pencil sharpeners, shelving, counters, built-in equipment overhangs, or various dispensers such as for paper towels or soap.

PR-02 Do free-standing objects, suspended or mounted on posts or pylons with leading edges between 27 in. and 80 in. high, project less than 12 in. into the perpendicular route of travel? (4.4.1, Fig. 8a–e)

AUTHOR'S INTERPRETATION:

- These might include telephone enclosures, drinking fountains, or free-standing signage kiosks.

PR-03 Is the minimum clear route width or maneuvering space still maintained even with the projection of a protruding object? (4.4.1, Fig. 8a–e)

Protruding Objects: overhead clearance

PR-04 Is the minimum overhead clearance of 80 in. provided in accessible areas or along accessible routes? (4.4.2, Fig. 8a)

AUTHOR'S INTERPRETATION:

- Overhead objects that can reduce the required clearance might include structures, pipes, ducts, or light fixtures.

(FS) Floor and Ground Surfaces (4.5)

Floor Surfaces: general

FS-01 Are the floor/ground surfaces on the accessible route stable, firm, and slip-resistant? (4.5.1)

AUTHOR'S INTERPRETATION:

- Exterior spaces, interior circulation, bathrooms, and other spaces where water can collect on the floor around an element (sinks, drinking fountains, hose bibbs, etc.) are reviewed as if wet.
- High gloss surfaces without significant textures that are regularly maintained with waxing (smooth tiles, waxed concrete, etc.) could be considered noncompliant.
- Accessible criteria are not specified for nonpermanent floor surfaces such as mats or rugs.

Floor Surfaces: changes in level

FS-02 Are vertical changes in level between 1/4 in. and 1/2 in. beveled with a slope of 1:2 or less? (4.5.2)

- Changes in level up to 1/4 in. may be vertical without edge treatment.
- Changes in level greater than 1/2 in. should be accomplished by means of a curb ramp, ramp, elevator, or platform lift (as permitted in ADAAG 4.1.3 and 4.1.6).

Floor Surfaces: carpet

FS-03 Does carpet or carpet tile used on the floor comply with accessible criteria?

- Attachment: secured. (4.5.3, Fig. 8f)
- Exposed edges: fastened and trimmed along the entire length.
- Pile type: low pile (1/2 in. maximum).
- Padding: firm pad or no pad underneath.

(CT) Controls and Operating Mechanisms (4.27)

NOTES:

- Controls or operating mechanisms can include elements such as light switches, pencil sharpeners, manual overhead screens, nonkeyed thermostats, alarm pull stations, fire extinguisher cabinets, A/C window units, microwave ovens, towel dispensers, and wall hooks.
- If controls are to be operated by occupants of the space, they must be accessible. If controls are to be operated by maintenance staff only and not by occupants or other users of the space, they do not have to be accessible. For example, thermostats in auditoriums usually do not have to be accessible, while thermostats in classrooms may need to be accessible.

Controls: clear floor space

CT-01 Is a clear floor space of at least 30 in. × 48 in. provided in front of controls, dispensers, receptacles, and other operable equipment for forward or parallel approach? (4.27.2, Fig. 4a–b)

Controls: reach ranges

NOTES:

- Accessible reach ranges for controls and operating mechanisms are:
  - Forward reach: not less than 15 in. high and not more than 48 in. high without any obstruction or where the obstruction is less than 20 in. deep. For obstructions from 20 in. to 25 in. deep, no forward reach higher than 44 in.
  - Side reach: not less than 9 in. high and not more than 54 in. high. For obstructions not more than 34 in. high or 24 in. deep, no side reach higher than 46 in.
  - Electrical outlets, switches, and communication system receptacles have a minimum outlet height of 15 in. regardless of forward or side reach. See CT-02 below.

CT-02 Are electrical outlets, switches, and communication system receptacles mounted within accessible forward or side reach ranges? (4.27.3)

EXCEPTION:

- These requirements do not apply where the use of special equipment dictates otherwise or where electrical and communications system receptacles are not normally intended for use by building occupants. (4.27.3)

CT-03 Are thermostats or other similar operable equipment mounted within accessible forward or side reach ranges? (4.2.5, 4.2.6, Fig. 5a–b, Fig. 6a–c)

CT-04 Are dispensers or other similar operable equipment mounted within accessible forward or side reach ranges? (4.2.5, 4.2.6, Fig. 5a–b, Fig. 6a–c)

CT-05 Are life safety devices or other similar operable equipment mounted within accessible forward or side reach ranges? (4.2.5, 4.2.6, Fig. 5a–b, Fig. 6a–c)

NOTE:

- This might include fire alarm pull stations, handles to extinguisher cabinets, or wall-mounted extinguishers.

Controls: operation

CT-06 Are controls, dispensers, receptacles, and other operable equipment operable with one hand without tight grasping, pinching, or wrist twisting, and requiring no more than 5 lbf of force? (4.27.4)

(SE) Fixed or Built-in Seating, Tables or Counters (4.32)

NOTE:

- In theater dressing rooms and in some locker rooms, fixed counters are provided with mirrors. If the dressing room is used by the general public, the counter and the mirror should be accessible. If a lavatory is provided it must also be accessible.

Fixed or Built-in Seating and Tables: minimum number

SE-01 Is the minimum number of accessible wheelchair seating locations at fixed tables or counters provided? (4.1.3.18)

- Number required: 5 percent of total number of seats but not fewer than one.

Fixed or Built-in Seating and Tables: clear floor space

AUTHOR'S INTERPRETATION:

- Where the accessible route leads to and through accessible seating adjacent to a wall or another table, the minimum required width for the accessible route will be 65 in. between the table edge and next parallel surface (e.g., wall or another table edge). (4.1.3.18, Fig. 45)

SE-02 Is the clear floor space for a wheelchair at a seating location adequate? (4.32.3, Fig. 4a, Fig. 45)

- Clear floor space: 30 in. × 48 in.
- This clear space can include up to 19 in. under the table/desk.

Fixed or Built-in Seating and Tables: clearances

SE-03 Are the tops of accessible tables and counters between 28 in. and 34 in. from the floor? (4.32.3, Fig. 45)

SE-04 Are the knee clearances at least 27 in. high, 30 in. wide, and 19 in. deep? (4.32.3, Fig. 45)

(SR) STORAGE (4.25)

Storage: general

SR-01 Does at least one of each type of fixed or built-in storage unit comply with accessible criteria? [4.1.3(12)(a), 4.25.1]

NOTE:

- Types of storage facilities might include cabinets, shelves, closets, and drawers.

Storage: clear floor space

SR-02 Is there a clear floor space at least 30 in. × 48 in. at fixed or built-in storage units that allows for either a forward or side approach? (4.25.2, Fig. 4a–b)

Storage: reach ranges

SR-03 Are forward or side reach for each type of accessible storage unit within acceptable reach ranges? (4.2.5–6, Fig. 5a–b, Fig. 6a–c, 4.25.3)

- Forward reach: not less than 15 in. high and not more than 48 in. high without any obstruction or where the obstruction is less than 20 in. deep. For obstructions from 20 in. to 25 in. deep, no forward reach higher than 44 in.
- Side reach: not less than 9 in. high and not more than 54 in. high. For obstructions not more than 34 in. high or 24 in. deep, no side reach higher than 46 in.

SR-04 In a closet where passage is not required to access storage (e.g., door opening is less than 32 in.), are the clothes rod or shelves within required reach ranges? (4.25.3, Fig. 38a–b)

- Door width: at least 20 in. (4.13.5)
- Horizontal reach: not more than 21 in. from the opening.
- Rod reach: if over 10 in. deep, then not more than 48 in. high.

- Shelf reach: if over 10 in. deep, then not more than 48 in. high or less than 9 in. high.

Storage: hardware

SR-05 Is the hardware on the storage unit doors or drawers operable with one hand without tight grasping, pinching, or wrist twisting, and requiring no more than 5 lbf of force? (4.25.4, 4.27.4)

(LV) Lavatories, Sinks, and Mirrors (4.19, 4.24)

NOTE:

- Where lavatories or sinks are provided, at least one of each type must meet accessible requirements.

AUTHOR'S INTERPRETATION:

- While not specifically defined by ADAAG, it appears lavatories are for personal hygiene in bathrooms or toilet rooms, while sinks are for all other situations (e.g., laboratories or kitchens).

Lavatories or Sinks: clearances

LV-01 Is there a clear floor space not less than 30 in. × 48 in. in front of the accessible lavatory or sink allowing a forward approach, and does it adjoin or overlap the accessible route? (4.19.3, 4.24.5, Fig. 32)

- The clear floor space can extend up to 19 in. under the sink or lavatory if adequate knee clearance is provided.

LV-02 Are the accessible lavatory or sink rim or counter height, apron height, and extension from the wall adequate? (4.19.2, 4.24.2, Fig. 31)

- Rim height: not greater than 34 in. above the finish floor.
- Apron height: not less than 29 in. above the finish floor to the bottom of the apron.
- Lavatory extension: not less than 17 in. from the wall.

LV-03 Is toe clearance under the accessible lavatory or sink not less than 9 in. above the finish floor and not deeper than 6 in. from the back wall for the full length of the lavatory or sink? (4.19.2, Fig. 31)

Lavatories or Sinks: pipe shielding

LV-04 Are the hot water and drain pipes at the accessible lavatory or sink insulated or otherwise configured to protect against contact, and is the area below the lavatory or sink free of sharp or abrasive surfaces? (4.19.4)

Lavatories or Sinks: controls

LV-05 Do the accessible lavatory or sink controls meet operational requirements? (4.19.5)

- Operation: operable with one hand without tight grasping, pinching, or twisting of the wrist. Acceptable types might include lever operated, push type, touch type, or electronically controlled; no more than 5 lbf of force.
- Self-closing faucets, when used, remain open for at least 10 sec.

Lavatories Only

LV-06 Is adequate knee clearance provided underneath the accessible lavatory? (4.19.2, Fig. 31)

- Lavatory knee clearance: not less than 27 in. high from finish floor to the bottom of the lavatory when measured at a point not less than 8 in. from the front of the lavatory.

Sinks Only

LV-07 Is adequate knee clearance provided underneath the accessible sink? (4.24.3)

- Sink knee clearance: not less than 27 in. high, 30 in. wide, and 19 in. deep under the sink.

LV-08 Is the accessible sink bowl not more than 6½ in. deep? (4.24.4)

Lavatories or Sinks: mirrors

LV-09 Where mirrors are provided, does at least one mirror have a bottom edge of the reflecting surface no higher than 40 in. above the floor? (4.19.6, Fig. 31)

AUTHOR'S INTERPRETATION:

- Slanted mirrors located above 40 in. are not recognized as compliant by the ADAAG.

(SS) Shower Stalls (4.21)

NOTE:

- Bathtubs should be reviewed using "Bathtubs" in the "Master Guidelines."

DEFINITIONS:

- *Transfer stall:* a shower stall exactly 36 in. × 36 in.
- *Roll-in stall:* a shower stall at least 30 in. × by 60 in.

Shower Stalls: general

SS-01 Where showers are provided, does at least one comply with accessibility requirements? (4.21.1)

Shower Stalls: stall and clear floor space dimensions

SS-02 Does the accessible shower stall meet the minimum size criteria and provide the required clear floor space? (4.21.2, Fig. 35a–b)

- Transfer stall: a shower stall exactly 36 in. × 36 in. with a clear floor space at least 36 in. wide × 48 in. long extending at least 12 in. beyond the seat wall. A lavatory may not encroach into the clear floor space.
- Roll-in stall: a shower stall at least 30 in. × 60 in. with a clear floor space of at least 36 in. wide × 60 in. long. A lavatory may encroach into the clear floor space.
- Roll-in stall with folding seat: two configurations shown in ADAAG Fig. 57a–b. This type may be required in transient housing.

Shower Stalls: seats

NOTE:

- Depending on the situation, a seat (within a roll-in shower) may only be required if located in transient housing. For seating in a roll-in shower with folding seat, see ADAAG Fig. 57a–b.

SS-03 Is the seat required in the transfer type shower mounted in the required location? (4.21.3, Fig. 37)

- Height: between 17 in. and 19 in. from the floor.
- Location: mounted on the wall opposite the control wall.

SS-04 Does the seat required in the transfer type shower meet size and shape requirements? (4.21.3, Fig. 36)

- Extends the full width of the stall.
- See ADAAG Fig. 36 for dimensional criteria.

Shower Stalls: grab bars

NOTE:

- Additional criteria for grab bars can be found in Section "HR, Handrails."

SS-05 Do the shower stall grab bars comply with accessible criteria? (4.21.4, Fig. 37a–b)

- Height: between 33 in. and 36 in. above the floor.
- Transfer stall: bar runs along the control wall and is continuous for 18 in. on the back wall. Does not run behind the seat.
- Roll-in stall: continuous bar on all three walls.
- Roll-in stall with folding seat: see grab bar locations shown in ADAAG Fig. 57a–b.

Shower Stalls: controls

SS-06 Are the accessible shower faucets and other controls located in the required area? (4.21.5, Fig. 37a–b)

- Height: between 38 in. and 48 in. above the floor.
- Transfer stall: located on the side wall opposite the seat wall, within 18 in. from the outside edge of the stall.
- Roll-in stall: located on the back wall or on either side wall. If located on the back wall within 27 in. from either side wall with the controls offset to one side; controls located on the side wall are offset to the outside edge of the stall.
- Roll-in stall with folding seat: see control locations shown in ADAAG Fig. 57a–b.

SS-07 In accessible showers, are faucets and other controls operable with one hand without tight grasping, pinching, or wrist twisting, and requiring no more than 5 lbf of force? (4.21.5)

SS-08 In accessible showers, is a shower spray unit provided that can be used as both a fixed shower head and a hand-held unit and does the unit have a hose at least 60 in. long? (4.21.6)

EXCEPTION:

- In unmonitored facilities where vandalism is a consideration, a fixed shower head mounted at 48 in. above the floor may be used in lieu of the hand-held shower head.

Shower Stalls: curbs and enclosure

SS-09 Where floor curbs are provided, do they comply with accessibility requirements? (4.21.7)

- Transfer stall: curbs can be no higher than 1/2 in.
- Roll-in stall: no curb is allowed.

SS-10 Where a shower stall enclosure is provided, is it located so that it does not obstruct the controls or obstruct the transfer from a wheelchair to the shower seat? (4.21.8)

(HR) Grab Bars and Shower Seats (4.26)

NOTE:

- HR Guidelines may be repeated in other element-based guidelines: (RP) Ramps, (ST) Stairs, (WC) Water Closets, (TS) Toilet Stalls, (BT) Bathtubs, and (SS) Shower Stalls.

Handrails: size and spacing

HR-01 Is the gripping surface of the grab bars or handrails 1¼ to 1½ in. in outside diameter? (4.26.2, Fig. 39)

AUTHOR'S INTERPRETATION:

- Standard pipe sizes designated by the industry as 1¼ in. to 1½ in. are acceptable for purposes of this section.

HR-02 Do the grab bars or handrails have edges with a minimum radius of 1/8 in.? (4.26.4)

HR-03 Is the clearance between the grab bars or handrails and the wall exactly 1½ in.? (4.26.2, Fig. 39)

HR-04 If the handrail is located in a recess, is the recess a maximum of 3 in. deep extending at least 18 in. above the rail? (4.26.2., Fig. 39d)

Handrails: grab bar or handrail structural strength

HR-05 Are the grab bars or handrails secure so that they do not rotate in their fittings? [4.26.3(5)]

HR-06 Do the grab bars and handrails meet the structural strength requirements for bending stress and shear stress? (4.26.3)

- Actual bending stress in the grab bar induced by the maximum bending moment from the application of 250 lbf is less than the allowable bending stress for the material of the grab bar.
- Shear stress induced in a grab bar by the application of 250 lbf shall be less than the allowable shear stress for the material of the grab bar. If the connection between the grab bar and its mounting bracket or other support is considered to be fully restrained, then direct and torsional shear stresses shall be totaled for the combined shear stress, which shall not exceed the allowable shear stress.

HR-07 Do the fasteners and mounting devices for the grab bars or handrails meet the structural strength requirements for shear force and tensile force? (4.26.3)

- Shear force induced in a fastener or mounting device from the application of 250 lbf shall be less than the allowable lateral load of either the fastener or mounting device or the supporting structure, whichever is the smaller allowable load.
- Tensile force induced in a fastener by a direct tension force of 250 lbf plus the maximum moment from the application of 250 lbf shall be less than the allowable withdrawal load between the fastener and the supporting structure.

Handrails: tub and shower seat structural strength

HR-08 Do the tub and shower seats meet the structural strength requirements for bending stress and shear stress? (4.26.3)

- Actual bending stress in the seat induced by the maximum bending moment from the application of 250 lbf is less than the allowable bending stress for the material of the grab bar.
- Shear stress induced in a seat by the application of 250 lbf shall be less than the allowable shear stress for the material of the seat. If the connection between the seat and its mounting bracket or other support is considered to be fully restrained, then direct and torsional shear stresses shall be totaled for the combined shear stress, which shall not exceed the allowable shear stress.

HR-09 Do the fasteners and mounting devices for the tub and shower seats meet the structural strength requirements for shear force and tensile force? (4.26.3)

- Shear force induced in a fastener or mounting device from the application of 250 lbf shall be less than the allowable lateral load of either the fastener or mounting device or the supporting structure, whichever is the smaller allowable load.
- Tensile force induced in a fastener by a direct tension force of 250 lbf plus the maximum moment from the application of 250 lbf shall be less than the allowable withdrawal load between the fastener and the supporting structure.

Handrails: hazards

HR-10 Are handrails or grab bars and any wall or other surfaces adjacent to them free of any sharp or abrasive elements? (4.26.4)

(AL) Alarms (4.28)

NOTE:

- At a minimum, visual signal appliances shall be provided in buildings and facilities in restrooms and any other general usage areas. **The ADAAG does not define the number of occupants needed to establish a general or common use area.**

ALLOWANCE:

- Emergency warning systems in medical care facilities may be modified to suit standard health care alarm design practice. [4.1.3(14)]

Alarms: general

AL-01 If emergency warning systems are provided, do they include both audible alarms and visual alarms? [4.1.3(14)]

Audible Alarms: general

AL-02 If provided, do the audible alarms meet required operational criteria? (4.28.2)

- Sound level: exceeds the prevailing sound level in the room or space by at least 15 dbA or exceeds any maximum sound level with a duration of 60 sec by 5 dbA, whichever is louder.

- Sound levels for alarm signals shall not exceed 120 dbA.

AL-03 If single station audible alarms are provided, then are single station visual alarm signals also provided? (4.28.3)

Visual Alarms: general

AL-04 If provided, are the visual alarm signal appliances integrated into the building or facility alarm system? (4.28.3)

AL-05 If provided, do the visual alarm signals meet required operational criteria? [4.28.3(1, 2, 3, 4, 5)]

- Lamp: xenon strobe type or equivalent.
- Color: clear or nominal white (i.e., unfiltered or clear filtered white light).

- Pulse duration: maximum shall be 0.2 sec with a maximum duty cycle of 40 percent.
- Intensity: not less than 75 candela.
- Flash rate: not less than 1 Hz and not more than 3 Hz.

AL-07 Are visual alarm signal appliances provided in general usage areas of the building (such as meeting rooms, corridors, and lobbies) or any other area for common use? (4.28.1)

AUTHOR'S INTERPRETATION:

- The authors identified three or more occupants as the minimum number to establish a common use area.

AL-08 Are the visual alarms placed at 80 in. above the highest floor level or 6 in. below the ceiling, whichever is lower? [4.28.3(6)]

Elevators

Introduction. This review guide is used to design or evaluate passenger elevators required to be accessible. Elevators are the most commonly used form of vertical transportation in multilevel buildings and facilities and, therefore, are an integral part of the accessible route. The ADAAG addresses both maneuverability and perception issues in its requirements for access and operation of the elevator and the recognition of signals and signage.

A passenger elevator is generally required to serve all levels of the building including mezzanines. Restaurants in buildings eligible for the elevator exemption do not have to provide access to mezzanines. The ADAAG allows for certain exceptions which may be allowed in renovations, qualified historic buildings or structures, and certain new facilities of limited size. For alterations and additions to accessible buildings there are certain concessions concerning the technical requirements for automatic reopening devices and the allowance of smaller cabs due to existing shaft size or configurations. In buildings of a demonstrated historic significance, alternative solutions may be allowed if it can be shown that compliance with the requirements for accessible routes would threaten or destroy the historic significance of the building or facility. Elevators are not required in certain facilities that are less than three stories or that have less than 3000 ft² of floor space per story. Title II buildings, shopping centers or malls, professional offices of a health care provider, or public transportation terminals are not allowed this exemption. This elevator exemption does not obviate or limit

in any way the obligation to comply with the other accessibility requirements for the accessible ground floor. This would include the provision of accessible toilet rooms and all other listed spaces and elements on the accessible ground floor. Additionally, elevators are required to meet other federal, state, or local codes such as ASME A17.1-1990.

Any elevator provided, even in a building eligible for the elevator exception, must comply with these requirements and service each floor. A full passenger elevator that serves only one floor of a building from a parking garage is not required to serve other levels.

Freight elevators are not subject to the requirements of ADAAG unless the only elevators provided are used as combination passenger and freight elevators for the public and employees.

PRELIMINARY DESIGN OVERVIEW

There is no "Preliminary Design Overview" for elevators because it is a specified manufactured product and not a space. All the associated compliance issues are in the ADAAG section for elevators.

ADAAG APPENDIX

The ADAAG Appendix contains advisory information pertinent to elevators.

- A4.10 Elevators
- See ADAAG Figs. 20-23.

Elevators Checklist

ELEVATORS

EL01	Elevators: exceptions allowed	**EL16**	Elevator door timing: notification time
EL02	Passenger elevators: serve each level	**EL17**	Elevator door timing: full open
EL03	Passenger elevators: all accessible	**EL18**	Elevator car: clear door opening
EL04	Freight elevators: as public elevator	**EL19**	Elevator car clearance: clear floor space
EL05	Elevators: automatic operation	**EL20**	Elevator car: floor surface
EL06	Elevator self-leveling: landing	**EL21**	Elevator car: illumination
EL07	Sill/hoist way clearance	**EL22**	Elev. car controls: button type and size
EL08	Hall call buttons: criteria	**EL23**	Car control indicator designations: criteria
EL09	Elevator lobby: protruding objects	**EL24**	Car control indicators: criteria
EL10	Visible and audible signal: each elevator	**EL25**	Car control panel: button reach ranges
EL11	Audible signal: "up" and "down"	**EL26**	Emergency control: location and grouping
EL12	Hall lanterns: location, size and visibility	**EL27**	Car control panel: location
EL13	Hoist way: floor designation criteria	**EL28**	Car position indicators: criteria
EL14	Elev. doors: automatic w/reopening device	**EL29**	Car emergency comm.: operation
EL15	Elev. door reopening device: duration	**EL30**	Car emergency comm.: criteria
		EL31	Car emergency comm.: identification

ELEVATORS
COMPREHENSIVE CRITERIA

NOTES:

- Accessible elevators shall be on an accessible route and serve each level, including mezzanines, in all multilevel buildings and facilities unless exempted below.

- Accessible elevators shall comply with ASME A17.1-1990, Safety Code for Elevators and Escalators.

EXCEPTIONS:

- New construction elevator exceptions [4.1.3(5)]

  — *Exception 1:* Elevators are not required in facilities that are less than three stories or that have less than 3000 ft² per story unless the building is a shopping center, a shopping mall, the professional office of a health care provider, or another type of facility as determined by the Attorney General. The elevator exemption set forth in this paragraph does not obviate or limit in any way the obligation to comply with the other accessibility requirements established in ADAAG 4.1.3. For example:

    a. Floors above or below the accessible ground floor must meet the requirements of this section except for elevator service.

    b. If toilet or bathing facilities are provided on a level not served by an elevator, then toilet or bathing facilities must be provided on the accessible ground floor.

    c. In new construction, if a building or facility is eligible for this exemption but a full passenger elevator is nonetheless planned, that elevator shall meet the requirements of ADAAG 4.10 and shall serve each level in the building.

    d. A full passenger elevator that provides service from a garage to only one level of a building or facility is not required to serve other levels.

  — *Exception 2:* Elevator pits, elevator penthouses, mechanical rooms, piping, or equipment catwalks are exempted from this requirement.

  — *Exception 3:* Accessible ramps complying with ADAAG 4.8 may be used in lieu of an elevator.

  — *Exception 4:* Platform lifts (wheelchair lifts) complying with ADAAG 4.11 and applicable state or local codes may be used in lieu of an elevator only under the following conditions:

    a. To provide an accessible route to a performing area in an assembly occupancy.

    b. To comply with the wheelchair viewing position line-of-sight and dispersion requirements of ADAAG 4.33.3, "Assembly Areas."

    c. To provide access to incidental occupiable spaces and rooms that are not open to the general public and that house no more than five persons, including, but not limited to, equipment control rooms and projection booths.

    d. To provide access where existing site constraints or other constraints make use of a ramp or an elevator infeasible.

- Alterations elevator exception [4.1.6(1)(k)]

  — *Exception:* These guidelines do not require the installation of an elevator in an altered facility that is less than three stories or has less than 3000 ft² per story unless the building is a shopping center, a shopping mall, the professional office of a health care provider, or another type of facility as determined by the Attorney General.

NOT EXEMPT:

- The exceptions for elevators in ADAAG 4.1.3(5), *Exception 1,* and ADAAG 4.1.6(1)(k) *do not* apply to a terminal, depot, or other station used for specified public transportation, or an airport passenger terminal, or facilities subject to Title II. (10.1)

Elevators: general

EL-01 Where a passenger elevator is not provided, is the building eligible for the elevator exceptions as identified above? [4.1.3(5)]

EL-02 If a building is not eligible for an elevator exception, does a passenger elevator serve each level in the building, including mezzanines? [4.1.3.(5)]

EL-03 Where more than one elevator is provided, does each full passenger elevator meet required elevator accessibility criteria? [4.1.3(5)]

EL-04 If the only elevators provided are freight elevators, are they combination passenger and freight elevators for the public and employees, and do they comply with accessible criteria? (4.10.1)

Elevators: automatic operation

EL-05 Is the elevator operation automatic? (4.10.2)

EL-06 Is the elevator self-leveling and does the floor of the elevator automatically come within 1/2 in. of the floor landing at each stop? (4.10.2)

EL-07 Is the clearance between the car platform sill and the hoist way landing edge not more than 1¼ in.? (4.10.9)

Elevators: hall call buttons

EL-08 Do the hall call buttons meet the required criteria? (4.10.3, Fig. 20)

- Button location: centered at 42 in. above the floor with the "up" button above the "down" button.
- Button size: at least 3/4 in. in the smallest dimension.
- Button type: raised or flush, not recessed.
- Visual call signals: button indicates each call registered and answered.

EL-09 If an object is mounted below the hall call buttons, does it project less than 4 in. into the elevator lobby? (4.10.3)

- This might typically be a wall-mounted ashtray or trash receptacle.

Elevators: hall lanterns and audible signals

EL-10 Is there a visible and audible signal at each hoistway entrance to indicate which car is answering a call? (4.10.4)

EL-11 Do the audible signals sound once for "up" and twice for "down" or does a verbal annunciator say "up" or "down"? (4.10.4)

EL-12 Do the visible signals meet the required criteria?

- Fixture location: centerline is at least 72 in. above the floor. [4.10.4(1), Fig. 20]
- Fixture size: at least 2½ in. in the smallest dimension. [4.10.4(2)]
- Visibility: visible from the vicinity of the hall call button. [4.10.4(3)] In-car lanterns visible from the hall call button and meeting all requirements are also acceptable.

Elevators: floor designation

EL-13 Does each elevator hoistway entrance have floor designations that meet the required criteria? (4.10.5, Fig. 20; 4.30.4)

- Location: on both door jambs centered 60 in. above the floor.

- Character type: raised, upper case, and sans or simple serif.
- Character size: 2 in. high; raised at least 1/32 in.
- Characters are accompanied by Grade II Braille.
- Finish/contrast: nonglare characters and backgrounds with characters contrasting the background (light-on-dark or dark-on-light).

Elevators: door protective and reopening device

EL-14 Does the elevator door open and close automatically and is it provided with an automatic reopening device that complies with the required criteria? (4.10.6, Fig. 20)

- Noncontact: An object or person passing through the opening, between 5 in. and 29 in. above the floor, automatically, without contact, reopens the doors (e.g., light sensor).
- Contact: Safety door edges, as a reopening device, are satisfactory in existing automatic elevators. [4.1.6(3)(c)(i)]

EL-15 Does the door reopening device hold the door open for at least 20 sec? (4.10.6)

Elevators: door and signal timing for hall calls

EL-16 Does the time from when the elevator's arrival is signaled until the doors begin to close fall within acceptable timing ranges? (4.10.7, Fig. 21)

- Minimum notification time is 5 sec or by use of the formula below, whichever is longer.
- $T = D/1.5$ ft/sec T = time in seconds
  D = distance from a point 60 in. in front of the farther call button for the car to the center of the elevator door.
- A graph interpreting this formula is provided in ADAAG Fig. 21.

EL-17 Do the elevator doors remain fully open for at least 3 sec in response to a car call? (4.10.8)

Elevators: floor plan criteria

EL-18 Is the clear door opening into the elevator car at least 36 in.? (4.10.9, Fig. 22)

EL-19 Does the floor area of the car allow maneuvering room for wheelchair users to enter the car, reach the controls, and exit? (4.10.9)

- New construction:
  — Center door type: at least 54 in. of clear depth from the interior face of the door; at least 51 in. of clear depth from the face of the control panel; at least 80 in. of clear width.
  — Side door type: at least 54 in. of clear depth from the interior face of the door; at least 51 in. of clear depth from the face of the control panel; at least 68 in. of clear width.
- Alterations:
  — At least 48 in. × 48 in. of clear floor space is provided inside the elevator car. [4.1.6(3)(ii)]

— Equivalent facilitation can be provided with an elevator car of different dimensions when usability can be demonstrated. [4.1.6(3)(iii)]

Elevators: floor surfaces and illumination

EL-20 Is the elevator floor surface stable, firm, and slip-resistant, or is the carpet or carpet tile securely attached with not more than a 1/2 in. pile thickness and exposed carpet edges trimmed to no more than 1/2 in.? (4.10.10, 4.5)

EL-21 Is the level of illumination at the car controls, the platform, and the car threshold and landing sill at least 5 footcandles? (4.10.11)

Elevators: car controls

EL-22 Are the car control panel buttons at least 3/4 in. in their smallest dimension and raised or flush? [4.10.12(1)]

EL-23 Do the car control indicator designations meet the required character criteria? [4.10.12(2)]

- Character type: raised, upper case, and sans or simple serif.
- Character size: between 5/8 in. and 2 in. high; raised at least 1/32 in.
- Characters are accompanied by Grade II Braille.
- Finish/contrast: nonglare characters and backgrounds with characters contrasting the background (light-on-dark or dark-on-light).

EL-24 Do the car control indicators meet required criteria? [4.10.12(2)]

- Raised designations are immediately to the left of the button to which they apply.
- Floor buttons visually indicate each call registered and are extinguished when each call is answered.
- The main entry floor is designated by a raised star at the left of the floor designation.

EL-25 Are the car control panel buttons within acceptable side and front reach ranges? [4.10.12(3), Fig. 23a–b]

- Side approach: not more than 54 in. above the floor.
- Front approach: not more than 48 in. above the floor.

EL-26 Are the car control panel emergency controls grouped and at the correct height? [4.10.12(3), Fig. 23a–b]

- Emergency controls, including alarm and stop, are grouped at the panel bottom with centerlines no less than 35 in. above the floor.

EL-27 Are the controls located on the front wall when the elevator car has a center opening door or located on the front wall or side wall when the elevator car has a side opening door? [4.10.12(4), Fig. 23c–d]

Elevators: car position indicators

EL-28 Do the visual car position indicators meet required criteria? (4.10.13)

- Location: above the control panel or over the door and indicate the floor level.
- Floor indication: corresponding numbers illuminate and an audible signal sounds as the car passes or stops at a floor. Automatic verbal announcement of the floor number, as the car passes or stops, may be substituted for the audible signal.
- Character height: at least 1/2 in. high.
- Audible signal: at least 20 db with a frequency no higher than 1500 Hz.

Elevators: emergency communications

EL-29 When provided, is the communication system usable without voice communication? (4.10.14)

EL-30 When provided, does the emergency two-way communication system in the elevator car meet the required criteria? (4.10.14)

- Location: highest operable part of the communication system is not higher than 48 in. above the floor.
- Handset: when provided, has a cord at least 29 in. long.
- When located in a closed compartment, the door can be operated with one hand; does not require tight grasping, pinching, or wrist twisting; does not require more than 5 lbf of force to open.

EL-31 When provided, is the emergency two-way communication system in the elevator car identified by an adjacent raised symbol and the characters? (4.10.14)

- Character type: raised, upper case, and sans or simple serif.
- Character size: between 5/8 in. and 2 in. high; raised at least 1/32 in.
- Characters are accompanied by Grade II Braille.
- Finish/contrast: nonglare characters and backgrounds with characters contrasting the background (light-on-dark or dark-on-light).

Laboratories

Introduction. Use this "Space-type Review Guide" to design or evaluate laboratories such as those found in educational environments and used in chemistry, physics, biology, medical research, etc. It can be used to review commercial laboratories, but privately owned labs could be considered "employee only areas" where accessibility would only be necessary in certain areas to accommodate a disabled employee. Laboratories such as those used for computers, languages, math, etc., would typically be evaluated using "Assembly Areas without Fixed Seating or Tables."

When designing an accessible laboratory, it is important to remember that laboratories are multi-functional spaces. They almost simultaneously can be used for research, classroom, meeting room, storage room, and office. Because of these various functions it is important that at least one of each type of work area, fixed storage unit, and built-in equipment be accessible. Different types of work areas can usually be identified by the type of built-in controls and operating mechanisms at a particular location. If one work area is used as a desk and another for experiments, then both must be accessible. If the lab has fixed seating, then a certain proportion of the seating will have to be accessible. When various sinks are used for specialized purposes, one of each type will need to be accessible. Laboratories have many different types of storage systems that range from typical shelves, drawers, and cabinets to specialized drying racks for bottles, test tubes, and flasks. If these units are built-in, then one of each type will need to be accessible.

Laboratories usually have a bewildering array of controls and operating mechanisms that vary from simple emergency shower pull chains to complex groups of switches, handles, and valves located on various pieces of equipment. Fortunately, the majority of these devices occur on equipment that is not built-in and, therefore, not covered under the ADAAG unless its use is required by a disabled employee or student. Equipment is usually considered to be built-in if it is attached to the floor, wall, or counter and/or cannot be readily moved by the user. Equipment such as enclosed fume hoods can be either built-in or placed on counters. In both cases they must be connected to electrical power and exhaust vents as well as water, gas, and air lines. All these connections make them very difficult to move and make accessible to someone in a wheelchair. Thus, if this type of equipment occurs in laboratories used by students, the equipment would need to be located at an accessible work station.

Finally, many laboratories typically have spaces such as offices, darkrooms, temperature control areas, and general storage located directly off the main laboratory. Unless these spaces are "employee only" areas they must be accessible. Not only must they be accessible but, as in the main laboratory, one of each type of storage, work area, and built-in equipment must be accessible. Since these spaces are typically small, someone in a wheelchair will have a maneuvering problem working in and exiting the space. The authors feel that if the accessible route into the room is over 5 ft long, a 180° or a "T"-shaped turning space should be provided. This will allow chair users maneuvering space within the room and also prevent them from having to back out of the room. There must also be the required maneuvering space on both sides of the door leading into each of these spaces.

PRELIMINARY DESIGN OVERVIEW

(AL) Alarms

- Visual alarms must be provided in laboratories that may be occupied by the general public (e.g., educational facilities). Emergency warning systems in medical care facilities may be modified to suit standard health care alarm design practice.

(AR) Accessible Routes

- An accessible route must connect each accessible work area, sink, emergency shower, eyewash, storage unit, and piece of built-in equipment.
- Aisles within the laboratory which are formed by fixed elements such as counters, pieces of equipment, or walls may need to be wider than usual if the aisle is an accessible route which passes through or to an accessible work station.
- Dead end aisles over 5 ft long used as an accessible route to an accessible workstation, accessible equipment, or accessible storage will need a 180° or a "T"-shaped turning space for a wheelchair.
- Aisle widths at U-turns around the ends of counters must meet accessiblity criteria.

(CT) Controls and Operating Mechanisms

- One of each type of control device and operating mechanism (switches, electrical outlets, water, gas, air valves, etc.) should be accessible at each workstation.
- Frequently overlooked controls and operating mechanisms in this space-type are controls on built-in accessible equipment, overhead controls for valves and electrical outlets, controls on window air conditioner units, thermostats, pull cords on overhead projection screens, fans, etc.

(DR) Doors

- If double doors are used as the entrance to the laboratory, one of the doors in the pair must meet all accessibility requirements.

(FS) Floor and Ground Surfaces

- In some areas floor surfaces should be evaluated as if wet. In particular consider the space around sinks, emergency showers, eyewash stations, exterior doors, etc.
- Grates located on the accessible route must meet accessibility requirements.

(LV) Lavatories, Sinks, and Mirrors

- If sinks and/or lavatories are provided and used for different purposes, then one of each use type must be accessible.

(PR) Protruding Objects

- Common elements that are overlooked as protruding objects include upper cabinets, shelves, corners of countertops, gauge valves and pipes on built-in equipment, etc.

(SE) Fixed Seating and Tables and/or Counters

- Laboratories that also serve as classrooms may have fixed seating and/or work areas for students; a minimum of 5 percent of the total number but not fewer than one of either type must be accessible.

(SG) Signage

- Pictograms that are not temporary and provide information about the laboratory (e.g., hazardous warning signs) must be accessible and meet the criteria for pictograms.
- Room identification signage at double doors should be on the wall closest to the accessible door.

(SR) Fixed Storage, Closets, Lockers, and Shelves

- One of each type of fixed storage unit provided must be accessible (e.g., shelves, cabinets, closets, dispensers, drying racks, hooks, towel bars, etc.). The authors consider base cabinets and upper cabinets as the same type of storage unit.

- Walk-in storage closets, including walk-in refrigeration units, which need to be wheelchair accessible must in-clude a turnaround space if they are over 60 in. deep. This will allow the wheelchair user to be able to make a forward exit.

(SS) Emergency Showers and Eyewashes

- Emergency shower and eyewash stations must meet re-quirements for clear floor space, reach ranges, and oper-ation. Forward reach is preferable for eyewash stations.

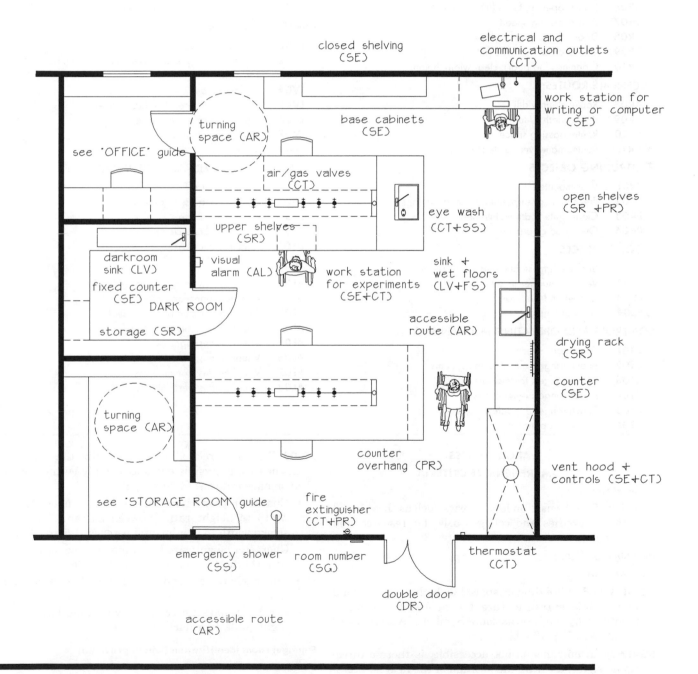

Figure: 3-12. Laboratory.

Laboratories Checklist

SIGNAGE:

SG01	Entry signage: I.S.A. requirement
SG02	Entry signage: inaccessible entrances
SG03	Inaccessible entry signage: criteria
SG04	Room signage: criteria
SG05	Room signage: location
SG08	Directional/informational signage: criteria
SG09	Suspended/projected signs: location

DOORS:

DR04	Doors: maneuvering clearances
DR05	Doors: handle type
DR06	Doors: opening force (interior only)
DR07	Doors: closing speed
DR08	Doors: thresholds
DR09	Doors: clear width/height
DR10	Openings (no door): clear width/height

ACCESSIBLE ROUTES:

AR08	Route: clear width
AR09	Route width: U-turns
AR10	Route: passing space
AR11	Route: maneuvering clearances

PROTRUDING OBJECTS

PR01	Wall-mounted
PR02	Freestanding/suspended on posts/pylons
PR03	Clear route width maintained
PR04	Overhead clearance

FLOOR SURFACES

FS01	Surface: firm, stable, and slip-resistant
FS02	Vertical changes in level
FS03	Carpet and tile floors
FS04	Floor gratings

CONTROLS AND OPERATING MECHANISMS

CT01	Clear floor space
CT02	Reach ranges: elec./comm. systems
CT03	Reach ranges: thermostats
CT04	Reach ranges: other controls
CT05	Reach ranges: life safety devices
CT06	Controls: operation

FIXED TABLES AND/OR COUNTERS

SE01	Fixed seating: number required
SE02	Wheelchairs: clear floor space at tables
SE03	Tables/counters: heights
SE04	Tables/counters: knee clearance criteria

FIXED STORAGE, CLOSETS, LOCKERS, OR SHELVES:

SR01	Accessibility: one of each type
SR02	Clear floor space
SR03	Reach ranges
SR04	Storage closets w/o passage: criteria
SR05	Storage hardware: operation

LAVATORIES AND SINKS:

LV01	Clear floor space
LV02	Rim/apron heights and extension from wall
LV03	Toe clearance
LV04	Insulated pipes
LV05	Controls and operation requirements
LV06	Lavatories: knee clearance
LV07	Sinks: knee clearance
LV08	Sinks: bowl depth

EMERGENCY SHOWERS AND EYEWASHES:

SS06	Shower controls: location
SS07	Shower controls: operation
LV01	Clear floor space
LV06	Lavatories: knee clearance
DF07	Height of eyewasher

ALARMS:

AL01	Emergency warning: audible/visual
AL02	Audible alarms: operation
AL03	Single station audible and visual
AL04	Visual alarms: integration w/building alarm
AL05	Visual alarms: operation
AL06	Visual alarms: public restrooms
AL07	Visual alarms: common use areas
AL08	Visual alarms: vertical placement

LABORATORIES COMPREHENSIVE CRITERIA

General Notes

- This form focuses on laboratories such as those found in universities and colleges used for research and teaching.

(SG) Signage (4.30)

Signage: entry

SG-01 Where a building or space has both accessible and inaccessible entrances, are the accessible entrances identified by the International Symbol of Accessibility? [4.1.2(7)(c), Fig. 43a–b]

SG-02 If an entrance is not accessible, is there a directional sign indicating the location of the nearest accessible entrance? [4.1.2(7)(c), 4.1.3(8)(d)]

SG-03 Does the directional sign indicating the location of the nearest accessible entrance comply with directional signage criteria? (4.30.2, 3, 5)

- Character proportion: letters and numbers have a width to height ratio between 3:5 and 1:1 and a stroke width to height ratio between 1:5 and 1:10.
- Character height: sized according to viewing distance with characters on overhead signs at least 3 in. high.
- Finish: characters and backgrounds have a nonglare finish.
- Contrast: characters contrast with their background (light-on-dark or dark-on-light).

Signage: room identification (where provided)

DEFINITION:

- These signs designate permanent rooms and spaces.

AUTHOR'S INTERPRETATION:

- Signs that designate stairs, exit doors, and toilet rooms generally are associated with permanent spaces, while an "office" sign is not since the room function may change over time. Room numbers also must meet the ADAAG criteria as permanent designations, while personal names do not since the occupant may change over time.

SG-04 Do signs that designate permanent rooms and spaces comply with the following criteria? [4.1.2(7); 4.1.3(16); 4.30.4, 5, 6]

- Character type: raised and accompanied by Grade II Braille.
- Character size: between 5/8 in. and 2 in. high; raised at least 1/32 in.
- Character style: upper case, and sans or simple serif.
- Finish: characters and backgrounds have a nonglare finish.
- Contrast: characters contrast with their background (light-on-dark or dark-on-light).

SG-05 Is the room identification sign mounted in the required location? (4.30.6)

- Mounting location: installed on the wall adjacent to the latch side of the door or where wall space to the latch side of the door is not available, including double doors, placed on the nearest adjacent wall.
- Mounting height: 60 in. above the floor/ground to the centerline of the sign.
- Sign access: approach to within 3 in. of a sign without encountering protruding objects or standing within the swing of the door.

Signage: direction and information (where provided)

DEFINITION:

- Signs that provide direction to or information about functional spaces of the building.

EXCEPTION:

- Building directories, menus, and all other temporary signs are not required to comply. [4.1.3(16)]

SG-08 Do signs that provide direction to, or information about, functional spaces of the building comply with the following criteria? [4.1.2(7); 4.1.3(16); 4.30.1, 2, 3, 5]

- Character proportion: letters and numbers have a width to height ratio between 3:5 and 1:1 and a stroke width to height ratio between 1:5 and 1:10.
- Character height: sized according to viewing distance with characters on overhead signs at least 3 in. high.

NOTE:

- When the sign is mounted below 80 in., there are no prescribed character heights. Only when the sign is mounted 80 in. or higher are the characters required to be at least 3 in. high. (4.30.3)
- Finish: characters and backgrounds have a nonglare finish.
- Contrast: characters contrast with their background (light-on-dark or dark-on-light).

SG-09 Is a sign located so that the overhead clearance or the projection of a suspended or projected sign does not result in a protruding object (free-standing or wall-mounted)?

- Clear height: at least 80 in. (4.4.2, Fig. 8a)
- Overhang for free-standing signs on posts or pylons located between 27 in. and 80 in. high: no more than a 12-in. projection into accessible routes. (4.4.1, Fig. 8c)
- Overhang for wall-mounted signs between 27 in. and 80 in. high: no more than a 4-in. projection into accessible routes. (4.4.1, Fig. 8a)

(DR) Doors (4.13)

NOTE:

- Included in this category are doors, revolving doors, turnstiles, and gates.

AUTHOR'S INTERPRETATION:

- It is suggested that, for purposes of documentation and review, a door be assigned to the space it swings into. Corridors are an exception to this rule and include only entry doors into the corridor or intermediate fire doors.

Doors: maneuvering clearance

DR-04 If the door is not automatic or power assisted, does it have the required maneuvering clearance provided on the push and pull side, and is the floor level and clear within the maneuvering area? (4.13.6)

- A verbal description cannot adequately describe the requirements. See ADAAG Fig. 25a–f for a graphic description.

EXCEPTION:

- Entry doors to acute care hospital bedrooms for inpatients are exempt from maneuvering space at the latch side of the door if the door is at least 44 in. wide.

AUTHOR'S INTERPRETATION:

- While ADAAG does not describe what elements can reduce the required maneuvering clearance, they could include a narrow entry alcove, an adjacent wall, railing, or permanently installed shelving, or a deep recessed door jamb.

Doors: hardware

DR-05 Do all door handles, locks, latches, or other operable devices meet required operational criteria? (4.13.9)

- Hardware operation: operable with one hand without tight grasping, pinching, or wrist twisting.
- Force required to operate the controls: not greater than 5 lbf. This does not apply to the force required to retract latch bolts or to disengage other devices that only hold the door in a closed position.
- Hardware type: "U"-shaped handles, levers, and push type mechanisms are acceptable designs.
- Hardware height: not greater than 48 in. above the floor.
- Sliding doors: hardware is exposed and usable from both sides when the doors are fully open.

Doors: opening force

DR-06 Do interior hinged doors and sliding or folding doors have an opening force of 5 lbf or less? (4.13.11)

- At present, no accessible criteria exist for exterior doors.
- Fire doors shall have the minimum opening force allowable by the appropriate administrative authority.

Doors: closing speed

DR-07 If the door has a closer, is the closer adjusted so that the door does not close too quickly? (4.13.10)

- From an open position of 70° the door will take at least 3 sec to move to a point 3 in. from the latch (measured to the leading edge of the door).

Doors: thresholds

DR-08 Where raised thresholds are provided, do they meet height limitations and are they beveled when required? (4.13.8, 4.5.2, Fig. 7)

- Threshold height: not more than 3/4 in. for exterior sliding doors or 1/2 in. for other types of doors.
- Threshold bevel: thresholds less than 1/4 in. high need no bevel; thresholds between 1/4 and 1/2 in. high shall be beveled at each edge with not more than a 1:2 slope.

EXCEPTION:

- A 3/4-in. high threshold is allowed in existing conditions. [4.1.6(3)(d)(ii)]

Doors: clear opening width and height

DR-09 Is the clear opening for the doorway adequate in width and height? (4.13.3, 4, 5; Fig. 24)

- Door width: at least 32 in. of clear width with the door open at 90°, measured between the face of the door and the door stop on the latch side. This also pertains to the active leaf of a double-leaf door or gate.
- Opening width: openings more than 24 in. deep must provide 36 in. of clear width.
- Height: at least 80 in. of vertical clearance.

EXCEPTIONS:

- Doors not requiring full user passage, such as shallow closets, may have the clear opening reduced to not less than 20 in.
- Where it is technically infeasible to comply with clear opening width requirements, a projection of 5/8 in. maximum will be permitted for the latch side. [4.1.6(d)(i)]

DR-10 Is the clear opening (when there is no door) adequate in width and height? (4.2.1, 4.3.3, 4.4.2)

- Width: at least 32 in. of clear width for depths 24 in. or less and at least 36 in. of clear width for depths greater than 24 in.
- Height: at least 80 in. of vertical clearance.

(AR) Accessible Routes (4.3)

NOTE:

- The accessible route shall, to the maximum extent feasible, coincide with the route for the general public.

Accessible Routes: width

AR-08 Is the minimum clear width along the accessible route adequate for continuous or point passage? (4.2.1; 4.3.3, Fig. 1, Fig. 8e, Fig. 24e)

- Continuous passage (greater than 24 in. long): at least a 36-in. clear width.
- Point passage (not more than 24 in. long): at least a 32-in. clear width.

AUTHOR'S INTERPRETATION:

- Noncompliance with this question generally relates to permanent elements that encroach on the accessible route. Large, heavy equipment that is not readily movable might be considered permanent. If the space is designed so that temporary elements (such as bikes in a bike rack or car bumpers) will consistently encroach, the situation might also be considered a permanent barrier.

AR-09 Is the minimum clear width along the accessible route adequate at a U-turn around an obstruction? (4.3.3, Fig. 7a–b)

- Obstruction 48 in. or greater: at least a 36-in. clear width around the obstruction.
- Obstruction less than 48 in.: at least a 42-in. clear width at each side with at least a 48-in. clear width in the turn.

AR-10 Does the accessible route provide at least 60 in. of clear width for two wheelchairs to pass and, if not, is the required passing space provided? (4.2.2, 4.3.4)

- A 60-in. × 60-in. passing space or "T" intersection should be provided at reasonable intervals not to exceed 200 ft.

AUTHOR'S INTERPRETATION:

- Accessible routes more than 5 ft long (e.g., routes in short hallways, aisles in laboratories, and work/storage areas) should have passing spaces provided.

DEFINITION:

- A *"T" intersection* is defined as the intersection of two corridors or walks, each at least 36 in. wide providing at least a 60-in. depth at the intersection. (Fig. 3b)

Accessible Routes: maneuvering clearances

AR-11 Is the minimum clear floor space for an unobstructed 180° wheelchair turning space or a "T"-shaped turning space provided? (4.2.3, Fig. 3a–b)

- 180° turning space: at least a 60-in. diameter.
- "T"-shaped turning space: at least 36-in. wide legs with a minimum length of 60 in.

(PR) Protruding Objects (4.4)

Protruding Objects: general

PR-01 Do wall-mounted objects having leading edges between 27 in. and 80 in. high project less than 4 in. into walkways, corridors, aisles, or paths of travel? (4.4.1, Fig. 8a–e)

- Objects mounted with their leading edge at or below 27 in. can protrude any amount, as long as they do not reduce the required clear width of an accessible route.

AUTHOR'S INTERPRETATION:

- Protruding objects might include fire extinguishers or cabinets, pencil sharpeners, shelving, counters, built-in equipment overhangs, or various dispensers such as for paper towels or soap.

PR-02 Do free-standing objects, suspended or mounted on posts or pylons with leading edges between 27 in. and 80 in. high, project less than 12 in. into the perpendicular route of travel? (4.4.1, Fig. 8a–e)

AUTHOR'S INTERPRETATION:

- These might include telephone enclosures, drinking fountains, or free-standing signage kiosks.

PR-03 Is the minimum clear route width or maneuvering space still maintained even with the projection of a protruding object? (4.4.1, Fig. 8a–e)

Protruding Objects: overhead clearance

PR-04 Is the minimum overhead clearance of 80 in. provided in accessible areas or along accessible routes? (4.4.2, Fig. 8a)

AUTHOR'S INTERPRETATION:

- Overhead objects that can reduce the required clearance might include structures, pipes, ducts, or light fixtures.

(FS) Floor and Ground Surfaces (4.5)

Floor Surfaces: general

FS-01 Are the floor/ground surfaces on the accessible route stable, firm, and slip-resistant? (4.5.1)

AUTHOR'S INTERPRETATION:

- Exterior spaces, interior circulation, bathrooms, and other spaces where water can collect on the floor around an element (sinks, drinking fountains, hose bibbs, etc.) are reviewed as if wet.
- High gloss surfaces without significant textures that are regularly maintained with waxing (smooth tiles, waxed concrete, etc.) could be considered noncompliant.
- Accessible criteria are not specified for nonpermanent floor surfaces such as mats or rugs.

Floor Surfaces: changes in level

FS-02 Are vertical changes in level between 1/4 in. and 1/2 in. beveled with a slope of 1:2 or less? (4.5.2)

- Changes in level up to 1/4 in. may be vertical without edge treatment.
- Changes in level greater than 1/2 in. should be accomplished by means of a curb ramp, ramp, elevator, or platform lift (as permitted in ADAAG 4.1.3 and 4.1.6).

Floor Surfaces: carpet

FS-03 Does carpet or carpet tile used on the floor comply with accessible criteria?

- Attachment: secured. (4.5.3, Fig. 8f)
- Exposed edges: fastened and trimmed along the entire length.
- Pile type: low pile (1/2 in. maximum).
- Padding: firm pad or no pad underneath.

Floor Surfaces: gratings

FS-04 Do floor gratings in the path of travel comply with accessible criteria? (4.5.4, Fig. 8g–h)

- Opening size: no greater than 1/2 in. in one direction.
- Opening direction: the long dimension is perpendicular to the dominant direction of travel.

(CT) Controls and Operating Mechanisms (4.27)

NOTES:

- Controls or operating mechanisms can include elements such as light switches, pencil sharpeners, manual overhead screens, nonkeyed thermostats, alarm pull stations, fire extinguisher cabinets, A/C window units, microwave ovens, towel dispensers, and wall hooks.
- If controls are to be operated by occupants of the space, they must be accessible. If controls are to be operated by maintenance staff only and not by occupants or other users of the space, they do not have to be accessible. For example, thermostats in auditoriums usually do not have to be accessible, while thermostats in classrooms may need to be accessible.

Controls: clear floor space

CT-01 Is a clear floor space of at least 30 in. × 48 in. provided in front of controls, dispensers, receptacles, and other operable equipment for forward or parallel approach? (4.27.2, Fig. 4a–b)

Controls: reach ranges

NOTES:

- Accessible reach ranges for controls and operating mechanisms are:
  — Forward reach: not less than 15 in. high and not more than 48 in. high without any obstruction or where the obstruction is less than 20 in. deep. For obstructions from 20 in. to 25 in. deep, no forward reach higher than 44 in.
  — Side reach: not less than 9 in. high and not more than 54 in. high. For obstructions not more than 34 in. high or 24 in. deep, no side reach higher than 46 in.
  — Electrical outlets, switches, and communication system receptacles have a minimum outlet height of 15 in. regardless of forward or side reach. See CT-02 below.

CT-02 Are electrical outlets, switches, and communication system receptacles mounted within accessible forward or side reach ranges? (4.27.3)

EXCEPTION:

- These requirements do not apply where the use of special equipment dictates otherwise or where electrical and communications system receptacles are not normally intended for use by building occupants. (4.27.3)

CT-03 Are thermostats or other similar operable equipment mounted within accessible forward or side reach ranges? (4.2.5, 4.2.6, Fig. 5a–b, Fig. 6a–c)

CT-04 Are dispensers or other similar operable equipment mounted within accessible forward or side reach ranges? (4.2.5, 4.2.6, Fig. 5a–b, Fig. 6a–c)

CT-05 Are life safety devices or other similar operable equipment mounted within accessible forward or side reach ranges? (4.2.5, 4.2.6, Fig. 5a–b, Fig. 6a–c)

NOTE:

- This might include fire alarm pull stations, handles to extinguisher cabinets, or wall-mounted extinguishers.

Controls: operation

CT-06 Are controls, dispensers, receptacles, and other operable equipment operable with one hand without tight grasping, pinching, or wrist twisting, and requiring no more than 5 lbf of force? (4.27.4)

(SE) Fixed Tables or Counters (4.32)

Fixed or Built-in Seating and Tables: minimum number

SE-01 Is the minimum number of accessible wheelchair seating locations at fixed tables or counters provided? (4.1.3.18)

- Number required: 5 percent of total number of seats but not fewer than one.

Fixed or Built-in Seating and Tables: clear floor space

AUTHOR'S INTERPRETATION:

- Where the accessible route leads to and through accessible seating adjacent to a wall or another table, the minimum required width for the accessible route will be 65 in. between the table edge and next parallel surface (e.g., wall or another table edge). (4.1.3.18, Fig. 45)

SE-02 Is the clear floor space for a wheelchair at a seating location adequate? (4.32.3, Fig. 4a, Fig. 45)

- Clear floor space: 30 in. × 48 in.
- This clear space can include up to 19 in. under the table/desk.

Fixed or Built-in Seating and Tables: clearances

SE-03 Are the tops of accessible tables and counters between 28 in. and 34 in. from the floor? (4.32.3, Fig. 45)

SE-04 Are the knee clearances at least 27 in. high, 30 in. wide, and 19 in. deep? (4.32.3, Fig. 45)

(SR) STORAGE (4.25)

Storage: general

SR-01 Does at least one of each type of fixed or built-in storage unit comply with accessible criteria? [4.1.3(12)(a); 4.25.1]

NOTE:

- Types of storage facilities might include cabinets, shelves, closets, and drawers.

Storage: clear floor space

SR-02 Is there a clear floor space at least 30 in. × 48 in. at fixed or built-in storage units that allows for either a forward or side approach? (4.25.2, Fig. 4a–b)

Storage: reach ranges

SR-03 Are forward or side reach for each type of accessible storage unit within acceptable reach ranges? (4.2.5-6, Fig. 5a–b, Fig. 6a–c, 4.25.3)

- Forward reach: not less than 15 in. high and not more than 48 in. high without any obstruction or where the obstruction is less than 20 in. deep. For obstructions from 20 in. to 25 in. deep, no forward reach higher than 44 in.
- Side reach: not less than 9 in. high and not more than 54 in. high. For obstructions not more than 34 in. high or 24 in. deep, no side reach higher than 46 in.

SR-04 In a closet where passage is not required to access storage (e.g., door opening is less than 32 in.), are the clothes rod or shelves within required reach ranges? (4.25.3, Fig. 38a–b)

- Door width: at least 20 in. (4.13.5)
- Horizontal reach: not more than 21 in. from the opening.
- Rod reach: if over 10 in. deep, then not more than 48 in. high.
- Shelf reach: if over 10 in. deep, then not more than 48 in. high or less than 9 in. high.

Storage: hardware

SR-05 Is the hardware on the storage unit doors or drawers operable with one hand without tight grasping, pinching, or wrist twisting, and requiring no more than 5 lbf of force? (4.25.4, 4.27.4)

(LV) Lavatories, Sinks, and Mirrors (4.19, 4.24)

NOTE:

- Where lavatories or sinks are provided, at least one of each type must meet accessible requirements.

AUTHOR'S INTERPRETATION:

- While not specifically defined by ADAAG, it appears lavatories are for personal hygiene in bathrooms or toilet rooms, while sinks are for all other situations (e.g., laboratories or kitchens).

Lavatories or Sinks: clearances

LV-01 Is there a clear floor space not less than 30 in. × 48 in. in front of the accessible lavatory or sink allowing a forward approach, and does it adjoin or overlap the accessible route? (4.19.3, 4.24.5, Fig. 32)

- The clear floor space can extend up to 19 in. under the sink or lavatory if adequate knee clearance is provided.

LV-02 Are the accessible lavatory or sink rim or counter height, apron height, and extension from the wall adequate? (4.19.2, 4.24.2, Fig. 31)

- Rim height: not greater than 34 in. above the finish floor.
- Apron height: not less than 29 in. above the finish floor to the bottom of the apron.
- Lavatory extension: not less than 17 in. from the wall.

LV-03 Is toe clearance under the accessible lavatory or sink not less than 9 in. above the finish floor and not deeper than 6 in. from the back wall for the full length of the lavatory or sink? (4.19.2, Fig. 31)

Lavatories or Sinks: pipe shielding

LV-04 Are the hot water and drain pipes at the accessible lavatory or sink insulated or otherwise configured to protect against contact and is the area below the lavatory or sink free of sharp or abrasive surfaces? (4.19.4)

Lavatories or Sinks: controls

LV-05 Do the accessible lavatory or sink controls meet operational requirements? (4.19.5)

- Operation: operable with one hand without tight grasping, pinching, or twisting of the wrist. Acceptable types might include lever operated, push type, touch type, or electronically controlled; no more than 5 lbf of force.
- Self-closing faucets, when used, remain open for at least 10 sec.

Lavatories Only

LV-06 Is adequate knee clearance provided underneath the accessible lavatory? (4.19.2, Fig. 31)

- Lavatory knee clearance: not less than 27 in. high from finish floor to the bottom of the lavatory when measured at a point not less than 8 in. from the front of the lavatory.

Sinks Only

LV-07 Is adequate knee clearance provided underneath the accessible sink? (4.24.3)

- Sink knee clearance: not less than 27 in. high, 30 in. wide, and 19 in. deep under the sink.

LV-08 Is the accessible sink bowl not more than 6½ in. deep? (4.24.4)

(SS) Emergency Showers and Eyewashes (4.21)

AUTHOR'S INTERPRETATION:

- ADAAG has no specific criteria for emergency showers or eyewashes. The guidelines for these elements are taken from the requirements for accessible showers, lavatories, and drinking fountains.

Shower Stalls: controls

SS-06 Are the accessible shower faucets and other controls located in the required area? (4.21.5, Fig. 37a–b)

- Height: between 38 in. and 48 in. above the floor.
- Transfer stall: located on the side wall opposite the seat wall, within 18 in. from the outside edge of the stall.
- Roll-in stall: located on the back wall or on either side wall. If located on the back wall within 27 in. from either side wall with the controls offset to one side; controls located on the side wall are offset to the outside edge of the stall.
- Roll-in stall with folding seat: see control locations shown in ADAAG Fig. 57a–b.

SS-07 In accessible showers, are faucets and other controls operable with one hand without tight grasping, pinching, or wrist twisting, and requiring no more than 5 lbf of force? (4.21.5)

Emergency Eyewash: clear floor space and knee clearance

LV-01 Is there a clear floor space not less than 30 in. × 48 in. in front of the accessible emergency eyewash and does it adjoin or overlap the accessible route? (4.19.3, 4.24.5, Fig. 32)

- The clear floor space can extend up to 19 in. under the emergency eyewash if adequate knee clearance is provided.

LV-06 Is adequate knee clearance provided underneath the accessible emergency eyewash? (4.19.2, Fig. 31)

- Knee clearance: not less than 27 in. high from finished floor to the bottom of the eyewash when measured at a point not less than 8 in. from the front of the eyewash.

AUTHOR'S INTERPRETATION:

- If an eyewash is going to protrude more than 4 in. into an accessible route, then it must be mounted at exactly 27 in. to comply with required knee clearances and not be considered a protruding object.

Emergency Eyewash: height

DF-07 Is the accessible emergency eyewash outlet no higher than 36 in. from the floor? (4.15.2, Fig. 27)

(AL) Alarms (4.28)

NOTE:

- At a minimum, visual signal appliances shall be provided in buildings and facilities in restrooms and any other general usage areas. **The ADAAG does not define the number of occupants needed to establish a general or common use area.**

ALLOWANCE:

- Emergency warning systems in medical care facilities may be modified to suit standard health care alarm design practice. [4.1.3(14)]

Alarms: general

AL-01 If emergency warning systems are provided, do they include both audible alarms and visual alarms? [4.1.3(14)]

Audible Alarms: general

AL-02 If provided, do the audible alarms meet required operational criteria? (4.28.2)

- Sound level: exceeds the prevailing sound level in the room or space by at least 15 dbA or exceeds any maximum sound level with a duration of 60 sec by 5 dbA, whichever is louder.
- Sound levels for alarm signals shall not exceed 120 dbA.

AL-03 If single station audible alarms are provided, then are single station visual alarm signals also provided? (4.28.3)

Visual Alarms: general

AL-04 If provided, are the visual alarm signal appliances integrated into the building or facility alarm system? (4.28.3)

AL-05 If provided, do the visual alarm signals meet required operational criteria? [4.28.3(1, 2, 3, 4, 5)]

- Lamp: xenon strobe type or equivalent.
- Color: clear or nominal white (i.e., unfiltered or clear filtered white light).
- Pulse duration: maximum shall be 0.2 sec with a maximum duty cycle of 40 percent.
- Intensity: not less than 75 candela.
- Flash rate: not less than 1 Hz and not more than 3 Hz.

AL-06 Are visual alarm signal appliances provided in public and common use restrooms? (4.28.1)

AL-07 Are visual alarm signal appliances provided in general usage areas of the building (such as meeting rooms, corridors, and lobbies or any other area for common use)? (4.28.1)

AUTHOR'S INTERPRETATION:

- The authors identified three or more occupants as the minimum number to establish a common use area.

AL-08 Are the visual alarms placed at 80 in. above the highest floor level or 6 in. below the ceiling, whichever is lower? [4.28.3(6)]

Laundries

Introduction. This "Space-type Review Guide" is used to design or evaluate different types of public laundry spaces. Examples of this type of space would include common use laundries in dormitories, boarding houses, social service establishments, and other forms of transient housing, as well as those in apartment complexes or any public laundry facility. The major areas of concern in this type of space are providing an accessible route to all areas of the space, and reach ranges for the different control mechanisms. These reach ranges include not only the laundry equipment but support elements as well. These elements include vending machines, folding counters or tables, sinks, and any other amenity accessible to the general public such as a television set or video games. If any type of professional services are offered (e.g., laundering, dry cleaning, or folding clothes), they must be accessible in an equal manner to all patrons.

PRELIMINARY DESIGN OVERVIEW

(AR) Accessible Routes

- Cross slope requirements for floors sloped for drainage are often overlooked and easily exceeded.
- Frequently overlooked in this space-type are the following maneuvering space problems: approach to all appliances and vending areas; minimum accessible width requirements between aisles, switchbacks, turns around an obstruction, and intersections.
- Route surfaces must meet criteria for vertical changes in level. Problem areas may include transition between materials if, for example, the machines are in a different area from a TV viewing area.
- At turns around obstructions, widths of the accessible route may increase according to the size of the obstruction.

(AL) Alarms

- Visual alarms must be provided in restrooms and any other area of common use.

(BM) Business and Mercantile

- Accessible counters are required at each different area offering sales or services such as retail counters or cleaning services counters.

- If sales and services are located in different parts of the facility, then accessible counters must be dispersed throughout the facility.

(CT) Controls and Operating Mechanisms

- Frequently overlooked in this space-type are controls on window air conditioner units, equipment, dispensers, vending machines, etc.
- One of each type of control device should be accessible and operable.

(DR) Doors

- Typical requirements.

(DF) Drinking Fountains

- Drinking fountains must serve both ambulatory and nonambulatory height requirements; this requires two different spout heights.

(FS) Floor and Ground Surfaces

- Floor surfaces should be evaluated as if wet. In this particular space the possibility of soap on the floor surface increases the potential for slipping.
- Smooth floor surfaces should be evaluated for slip-resistance based on floor finish and maintenance.
- Grates located on the accessible route must meet accessibility requirements.

(LV) Lavatories, Sinks, and Mirrors

- Hot pipes and sharp objects (e.g., valves and drains) must be shielded under lavatories and sinks.
- If sinks are used for different purposes, then one of each use type must be accessible; if they serve the same function only one must be accessible.

(PR) Protruding Objects

- Common wall-mounted elements can be protruding objects, e.g., dispensers, clothes folding counters, infant changing stations.
- Overhead clearances can be an unforeseen compliance problem, e.g., signs and banners, open space under stairs, suspended TV sets, etc.
- Standard fire safety items are often protruding objects, e.g., permanently mounted fire hose cabinets, fire ex-

tinguishers and fire extinguisher cabinets, valves on standpipes, etc.

(SG) Signage

- Permanent directional and informational signage must meet accessibility criteria; letter height varies with mounting height of sign.

(SE) Fixed or Built-in Seating and Tables and/or Counters

- If fixed tables or counters are provided, a minimum of 5 percent of the total number but not fewer than one of either type must be accessible.
- An accessible route must lead to and through accessible seating at fixed tables or counters.
- Frequently overlooked in this space-type are infant changing stations and clothes folding tables.

(SR) Fixed Storage, Closets, Lockers, and Shelves

- When provided, one of each type of storage unit (shelves, dispensers, hooks, etc.) must be accessible.

- Frequently overlooked storage units for this space-type include coat hooks, book storage bins, etc.

(TL) Telephones

- When public telephones are provided, at least one must be on the accessible route and comply with all telephone requirements.

ADAAG APPENDIX

The ADAAG Appendix contains advisory information pertinent to this space-type.

- A4.2.1 Space Allowances and Reach Ranges
- A4.5 Ground and Floor Surfaces

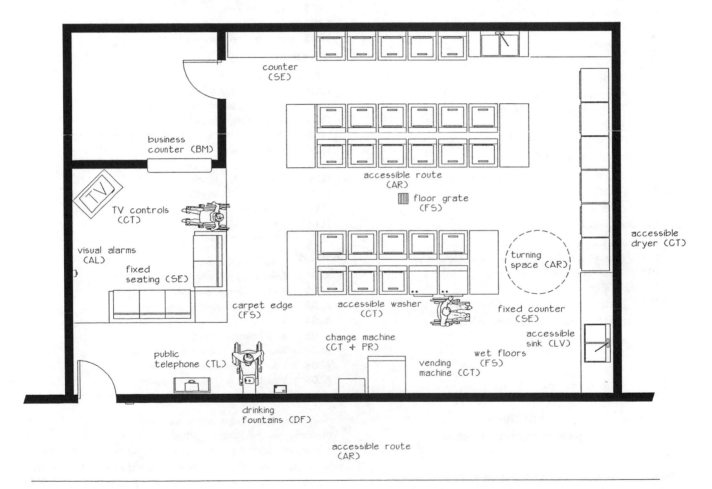

Figure 3-13. Laundry.

Laundries Checklist

SIGNAGE

SG04	Room signage: criteria
SG05	Room signage: location
SG08	Directional/informational signage: criteria
SG09	Suspended/projected signs: location

DOORS

DR02	Automatic doors: ANSI standards
DR03	Automatic doors: operation
DR04	Doors: maneuvering clearances
DR05	Doors: handle type
DR06	Doors: opening force (interior only)
DR07	Doors: closing speed
DR08	Doors: thresholds
DR09	Doors: clear width/height
DR10	Openings (no door): clear width/height
DR11	Doors in series: clear space between

BUSINESS AND MERCANTILE

BM01	Sales/service counters: accessible route
BM02	Counters w/cash registers: criteria
BM03	Counters w/o cash registers: criteria

ACCESSIBLE ROUTES

AR08	Route: clear width
AR09	Route width: U-turns
AR10	Route: passing space
AR11	Route: maneuvering clearances
AR13	Route: cross slope
AR14	Route: changes of level

FLOOR AND GROUND SURFACES

FS01	Surface: firm, stable, and slip-resistant
FS02	Vertical changes in level
FS04	Floor gratings

PROTRUDING OBJECTS

PR01	Wall-mounted
PR02	Freestanding/suspended on posts/pylons
PR03	Clear route width maintained
PR04	Overhead clearance
PR05	Vertical clearance: cane detection barrier

CONTROLS AND OPERATING MECHANISMS

CT01	Clear floor space
CT02	Reach ranges: elec./comm. systems
CT03	Reach ranges: thermostats
CT04	Reach ranges: other controls
CT05	Reach ranges: life safety devices
CT06	Controls: operation

LAVATORIES, SINKS, AND MIRRORS

LV01	Clear floor space
LV02	Rim/apron heights and extension from wall
LV03	Toe clearance
LV04	Insulated pipes
LV05	Controls and operation requirements
LV07	Sinks: knee clearance
LV08	Sinks: bowl depth

FIXED OR BUILT-IN SEATING AND TABLES

SE01	Fixed seating: number required
SE02	Wheelchairs: clear floor space at tables
SE03	Tables/counters: heights
SE04	Tables/counters: knee clearance criteria

STORAGE

SR01	Accessibility: one of each type
SR02	Clear floor space
SR03	Reach ranges
SR04	Storage closets w/o passage: criteria
SR05	Storage hardware: operation

TELEPHONES

TL01	Single public telephone: compliance
TL02	Public telephone bank: one compliant
TL04	Accessible telephone: clear floor space
TL05	Accessible telephone: accessible route
TL06	Wall- or post-mounted: protruding objects
TL07	Reach ranges
TL08	Push-button controls where available
TL09	Telephone book: reach ranges
TL10	Handset cord: length
TL11	Volume control: requirements
TL12	Volume control: amplification
TL13	Telephone: hearing aid compatible

ALARMS

AL01	Emergency warning: audible/visual
AL02	Audible alarms: operation
AL03	Single station audible and visual
AL04	Visual alarms: integration w/building alarm
AL05	Visual alarms: operation
AL07	Visual alarms: common use areas
AL08	Visual alarms: vertical placement
AL09	Visual alarms: horizontal spacing

LAUNDRIES
COMPREHENSIVE CRITERIA

(SG) Signage (4.30)

Signage: room identification (where provided)

DEFINITION:

- These signs designate permanent rooms and spaces.

AUTHOR'S INTERPRETATION:

- Signs that designate stairs, exit doors, and toilet rooms generally are associated with permanent spaces, while an "office" sign is not since the room function may change over time. Room numbers also must meet the ADAAG criteria as permanent designations, while personal names do not since the occupant may change over time.

SG-04 Do signs that designate permanent rooms and spaces comply with the following criteria? [4.1.2(7); 4.1.3(16); 4.30.4, 5, 6]

- Character type: raised and accompanied by Grade II Braille.
- Character size: between 5/8 in. and 2 in. high; raised at least 1/32 in.
- Character style: upper case, and sans or simple serif.

- Finish: characters and backgrounds have a nonglare finish.
- Contrast: characters contrast with their background (light-on-dark or dark-on-light).

SG-05 Is the room identification sign mounted in the required location? (4.30.6)

- Mounting location: installed on the wall adjacent to the latch side of the door or where wall space to the latch side of the door is not available, including double doors, placed on the nearest adjacent wall.
- Mounting height: 60 in. above the floor/ground to the centerline of the sign.
- Sign access: approach to within 3 in. of a sign without encountering protruding objects or standing within the swing of the door.

Signage: direction and information (where provided)

DEFINITION:

- Signs that provide direction to or information about functional spaces of the building.

EXCEPTION:

- Building directories, menus, and all other temporary signs are not required to comply. [4.1.3(16)]

SG-08 Do signs that provide direction to, or information about, functional spaces of the building comply with the following criteria? [4.1.2(7); 4.1.3(16); 4.30.1, 2, 3, 5]

- Character proportion: letters and numbers have a width to height ratio between 3:5 and 1:1 and a stroke width to height ratio between 1:5 and 1:10.
- Character height: sized according to viewing distance with characters on overhead signs at least 3 in. high.

NOTE:

- When the sign is mounted below 80 in., there are no prescribed character heights. Only when the sign is mounted 80 in. or higher are the characters required to be at least 3 in. high. (4.30.3)
- Finish: characters and backgrounds have a nonglare finish.
- Contrast: characters contrast with their background (light-on-dark or dark-on-light).

SG-09 Is a sign located so that the overhead clearance or the projection of a suspended or projected sign does not result in a protruding object (free-standing or wall-mounted)?

- Clear height: at least 80 in. (4.4.2, Fig. 8a)
- Overhang for free-standing signs on posts or pylons located between 27 in. and 80 in. high: no more than a 12-in. projection into accessible routes. (4.4.1, Fig. 8c)
- Overhang for wall-mounted signs between 27 in. and 80 in. high: no more than a 4-in. projection into accessible routes. (4.4.1, Fig. 8a)

(DR) Doors (4.13)

NOTE:

- Included in this category are doors, revolving doors, turnstiles, and gates.

AUTHOR'S INTERPRETATION:

- It is suggested that, for purposes of documentation and review, a door be assigned to the space it swings into. Corridors are an exception to this rule and include only entry doors into the corridor or intermediate fire doors.

Doors: automatic or power assisted

DR-02 If an automatic door or power assisted door is used, does it comply with the appropriate ANSI standard? (4.13.12)

- Automatic door: ANSI/BHMA A156.10-1985.
- Slow opening, low powered automatic door: ANSI A156.19-1984.
- Power assisted door: ANSI A156.19-1984.

DR-03 Do slow opening, low powered automatic doors or power assisted doors comply with opening and closing requirements? (4.13.12)

- Slow opening, low powered automatic doors: do not open to back-check faster than 3 sec and require no more than 15 lbf of force to stop door movement.
- Power assisted doors: no more than 5 lbf of opening force.

Doors: maneuvering clearance

DR-04 If the door is not automatic or power assisted, does it have the required maneuvering clearance provided on the push and pull side, and is the floor level and clear within the maneuvering area? (4.13.6)

- A verbal description cannot adequately describe the requirements. See ADAAG Fig. 25a–f for a graphic description.

EXCEPTION:

- Entry doors to acute care hospital bedrooms for inpatients are exempt from maneuvering space at the latch side of the door if the door is at least 44 in. wide.

AUTHOR'S INTERPRETATION:

- While ADAAG does not describe what elements can reduce the required maneuvering clearance, they could include a narrow entry alcove, an adjacent wall, railing, or permanently installed shelving, or a deep recessed door jamb.

Doors: hardware

DR-05 Do all door handles, locks, latches, or other operable devices meet required operational criteria? (4.13.9)

- Hardware operation: operable with one hand without tight grasping, pinching, or wrist twisting.
- Force required to operate the controls: not greater than 5 lbf. This does not apply to the force required to retract latch bolts or to disengage other devices that only hold the door in a closed position.
- Hardware type: "U"-shaped handles, levers, and push type mechanisms are acceptable designs.
- Hardware height: not greater than 48 in. above the floor.
- Sliding doors: hardware is exposed and usable from both sides when the doors are fully open.

Doors: opening force

DR-06 Do interior hinged doors and sliding or folding doors have an opening force of 5 lbf or less? (4.13.11)

- At present, no accessible criteria exist for exterior doors.

- Fire doors shall have the minimum opening force allowable by the appropriate administrative authority.

Doors: closing speed

DR-07 If the door has a closer, is the closer adjusted so that the door does not close too quickly? (4.13.10)

- From an open position of 70° the door will take at least 3 sec to move to a point 3 in. from the latch (measured to the leading edge of the door).

Doors: thresholds

DR-08 Where raised thresholds are provided, do they meet height limitations and are they beveled when required? (4.13.8, 4.5.2, Fig. 7)

- Threshold height: not more than 3/4 in. for exterior sliding doors or 1/2 in. for other types of doors.

- Threshold bevel: thresholds less than 1/4 in. high need no bevel; thresholds between 1/4 and 1/2 in. high shall be beveled at each edge with not more than a 1:2 slope.

EXCEPTION:

- A 3/4-in. high threshold is allowed in existing conditions. [4.1.6(3)(d)(ii)]

Doors: clear opening width and height

DR-09 Is the clear opening for the doorway adequate in width and height? (4.13.3, 4, 5, Fig. 24)

- Door width: at least 32 in. of clear width with the door open at 90°, measured between the face of the door and the door stop on the latch side. This also pertains to the active leaf of a double-leaf door or gate.

- Opening width: openings more than 24 in. deep must provide 36 in. of clear width.

- Height: at least 80 in. of vertical clearance.

EXCEPTIONS:

- Doors not requiring full user passage, such as shallow closets, may have the clear opening reduced to not less than 20 in.

- Where it is technically infeasible to comply with clear opening width requirements, a projection of 5/8 in. maximum will be permitted for the latch side. [4.1.6(d)(i)]

DR-10 Is the clear opening (when there is no door) adequate in width and height? (4.2.1, 4.3.3, 4.4.2)

- Width: at least 32 in. of clear width for depths 24 in. or less and at least 36 in. of clear width for depths greater than 24 in.

- Height: at least 80 in. of vertical clearance.

Doors: two doors in a series

DR-11 If there are two doors in a series, is the required clear space between the doors provided and do the doors swing in the appropriate direction? (4.13.7, Fig. 26)

- Clear space between the doors: not less than 48 in. plus the width of any door swinging into the space.

- Door swing: must swing in the same direction or away from the space between the doors.

(BM) Business and Mercantile (7.0)

Business: general

BM-01 Are all areas used for business transactions with the public, such as sales and service counters and/or self-service displays, on an accessible route? [4.1.3(12)(b), 7.2.2]

Business: sales counters with cash registers

BM-02 In retail stores where counters with cash registers are provided, is there at least one accessible cash register counter, and where more than one occurs, are they distributed throughout the facility? (7.2.1)

- Main counter: a portion of the counter is at least 36 in. long and is not more than 36 in. high.

- Alterations: where it is technically infeasible to provide an accessible counter, an auxiliary counter meeting these criteria may be provided.

Business: sales or service counters without cash registers

BM-03 At ticketing counters, teller stations, registration counters, and other counters for distributing goods or services to the public without cash registers, is there an accessible counter or alternative provided? (7.2.2)

- Main counter: a portion of the counter is at least 36 in. long and is not more than 36 in. high.

- Auxiliary counter: in close proximity to the main counter and not more than 36 in. high.

- Equivalent facilitation: might consist of a folding shelf attached to the main counter (for an individual with disabilities to write) and use of the space at the side of the counter for handing materials back and forth.

(AR) Accessible Route (4.3)

NOTES:

- All walks, halls, corridors, aisles, skywalks, tunnels, and other spaces that are part of a designated accessible route shall comply with accessible requirements.

  — Any slope on the accessible route that is greater than 1:20 is required to meet all ramp criteria.

  — The accessible route shall, to the maximum extent feasible, coincide with the route for the general public.

  — In historic buildings, accessible routes from an accessible entrance shall be provided to all publicly used spaces on at least the level of the accessible entrance. Access shall be provided to all levels of a building or facility whenever practical. [4.1.7(3)(d)]

AUTHOR'S INTERPRETATION:

- An accessible route "generally coincides" with the route used by the public if:

  — It does not force the user to go out of the way.

  — It is most like the route chosen by the general public.

  — It is direct.

  — It gives the same basic experience as the route preferred by the public.

Accessible Routes: width

AR-08 Is the minimum clear width along the accessible route adequate for continuous or point passage? (4.2.1; 4.3.3, Fig. 1, Fig. 8e, Fig. 24e)

- Continuous passage (greater than 24 in. long): at least a 36-in. clear width.
- Point passage (not more than 24 in. long): at least a 32-in. clear width.

AUTHOR'S INTERPRETATION:

- Noncompliance with this question generally relates to permanent elements that encroach on the accessible route. Large, heavy equipment that is not readily movable might be considered permanent. If the space is designed so that temporary elements (such as bikes in a bike rack or car bumpers) will consistently encroach, the situation might also be considered a permanent barrier.

AR-09 Is the minimum clear width along the accessible route adequate at a U-turn around an obstruction? (4.3.3, Fig. 7a–b)

- Obstruction 48 in. or greater: at least a 36-in. clear width around the obstruction.
- Obstruction less than 48 in.: at least a 42-in. clear width at each side with at least a 48-in. clear width in the turn.

Accessible Routes: passing space

AR-10 Does the accessible route provide at least 60 in. of clear width for two wheelchairs to pass and, if not, is the required passing space provided? (4.2.2, 4.3.4)

- A 60-in. × 60-in. passing space or "T" intersection should be provided at reasonable intervals not to exceed 200 ft.

AUTHOR'S INTERPRETATION:

- Accessible routes more than 5 ft long (e.g., routes in short hallways, aisles in laboratories, and work/storage areas) should have passing spaces provided.

DEFINITION:

- A *"T" intersection* is defined as the intersection of two corridors or walks, each at least 36 in. wide providing at least a 60-in. depth at the intersection. (Fig. 3b)

Accessible Routes: maneuvering clearances

AR-11 Is the minimum clear floor space for an unobstructed 180° wheelchair turning space or a "T"-shaped turning space provided? (4.2.3, Fig. 3a–b)

- 180° turning space: at least a 60-in. diameter.
- "T"-shaped turning space: at least 36-in. wide legs with a minimum length of 60 in.

Accessible Routes: slopes

AR-13 Is the cross slope on the accessible route 1:50 or less? (4.3.7)

Accessible Routes: changes in level

AR-14 Are changes in level greater than 1/2 in. accomplished by means of a curb ramp, ramp, elevator, or platform lift (as permitted in ADAAG 4.1.3 and 4.1.6)? (4.3.8)

(FS) Floor and Ground Surfaces (4.5)

Floor Surfaces: general

FS-01 Are the floor/ground surfaces on the accessible route stable, firm, and slip-resistant? (4.5.1)

AUTHOR'S INTERPRETATION:

- Exterior spaces, interior circulation, bathrooms, and other spaces where water can collect on the floor around an element (sinks, drinking fountains, hose bibbs, etc.) are reviewed as if wet.
- High gloss surfaces without significant textures that are regularly maintained with waxing (smooth tiles, waxed concrete, etc.) could be considered noncompliant.
- Accessible criteria are not specified for nonpermanent floor surfaces such as mats or rugs.

Floor Surfaces: changes in level

FS-02 Are vertical changes in level between 1/4 in. and 1/2 in. beveled with a slope of 1:2 or less? (4.5.2)

- Changes in level up to 1/4 in. may be vertical without edge treatment.
- Changes in level greater than 1/2 in. should be accomplished by means of a curb ramp, ramp, elevator, or platform lift (as permitted in ADAAG 4.1.3 and 4.1.6).

Floor Surfaces: gratings

FS-04 Do floor gratings in the path of travel comply with accessible criteria? (4.5.4, Fig. 8g–h)

- Opening size: no greater than 1/2 in. in one direction.
- Opening direction: the long dimension is perpendicular to the dominant direction of travel.

(PR) Protruding Objects (4.4)

Protruding Objects: general

PR-01 Do wall-mounted objects having leading edges between 27 in. and 80 in. high project less than 4 in. into walkways, corridors, aisles, or paths of travel? (4.4.1, Fig. 8a–e)

- Objects mounted with their leading edge at or below 27 in. can protrude any amount, as long as they do not reduce the required clear width of an accessible route.

AUTHOR'S INTERPRETATION:

- Protruding objects might include fire extinguishers or cabinets, pencil sharpeners, shelving, counters, built-in equipment overhangs, or various dispensers such as for paper towels or soap.

PR-02 Do free-standing objects, suspended or mounted on posts or pylons with leading edges between 27 in. and 80 in. high, project less than 12 in. into the perpendicular route of travel? (4.4.1, Fig. 8a–e)

AUTHOR'S INTERPRETATION:

- These might include telephone enclosures, drinking fountains, or free-standing signage kiosks.

PR-03 Is the minimum clear route width or maneuvering space still maintained even with the projection of a protruding object? (4.4.1, Fig. 8a–e)

Protruding Objects: overhead clearance

PR-04 Is the minimum overhead clearance of 80 in. provided in accessible areas or along accessible routes? (4.4.2, Fig. 8a)

AUTHOR'S INTERPRETATION:

- Overhead objects that can reduce the required clearance might include structures, pipes, ducts, or light fixtures.

PR-05 Where the vertical clearance of a space adjoining the accessible route is less than 80 in. high, is a cane detection barrier less than 27 in. from the floor provided for blind or visually impaired persons? (4.4.2, Fig. 8c-1)

AUTHOR'S INTERPRETATION:

- This condition might be found under a stair, at a sloped ceiling space, or with guy wires from telephone poles along an exterior accessible route.

(CT) Controls and Operating Mechanisms (4.27)

NOTES:

- Controls or operating mechanisms can include elements such as light switches, pencil sharpeners, manual overhead screens, nonkeyed thermostats, alarm pull stations, fire extinguisher cabinets, A/C window units, microwave ovens, towel dispensers, and wall hooks.
  - If controls are to be operated by occupants of the space, they must be accessible. If controls are to be operated by maintenance staff only and not by occupants or other users of the space, they do not have to be accessible. For example, thermostats in auditoriums usually do not have to be accessible, while thermostats in classrooms may need to be accessible.

Controls: clear floor space

CT-01 Is a clear floor space of at least 30 in. × 48 in. provided in front of controls, dispensers, receptacles, and other operable equipment for forward or parallel approach? (4.27.2, Fig. 4a–b)

Controls: reach ranges

NOTES:

- Accessible reach ranges for controls and operating mechanisms are:
  - Forward reach: not less than 15 in. high and not more than 48 in. high without any obstruction or where the obstruction is less than 20 in. deep. For obstructions from 20 in. to 25 in. deep, no forward reach higher than 44 in.
  - Side reach: not less than 9 in. high and not more than 54 in. high. For obstructions not more than 34 in. high or 24 in. deep, no side reach higher than 46 in.
  - Electrical outlets, switches, and communication system receptacles have a minimum outlet height of 15 in. regardless of forward or side reach. See CT-02 below.

CT-02 Are electrical outlets, switches, and communication system receptacles mounted within accessible forward or side reach ranges? (4.27.3)

EXCEPTION:

- These requirements do not apply where the use of special equipment dictates otherwise or where electrical and communications system receptacles are not normally intended for use by building occupants. (4.27.3)

CT-03 Are thermostats or other similar operable equipment mounted within accessible forward or side reach ranges? (4.2.5, 4.2.6, Fig. 5a–b, Fig. 6a–c)

CT-04 Are dispensers or other similar operable equipment mounted within accessible forward or side reach ranges? (4.2.5, 4.2.6, Fig. 5a–b, Fig. 6a–c)

CT-05 Are life safety devices or other similar operable equipment mounted within accessible forward or side reach ranges? (4.2.5, 4.2.6, Fig. 5a–b, Fig. 6a–c)

NOTE:

- This might include fire alarm pull stations, handles to extinguisher cabinets, or wall-mounted extinguishers.

Controls: operation

CT-06 Are controls, dispensers, receptacles, and other operable equipment operable with one hand without tight grasping, pinching, or wrist twisting, and requiring no more than 5 lbf of force? (4.27.4)

(LV) Lavatories, Sinks, and Mirrors (4.19, 4.24)

NOTE:

- Where lavatories or sinks are provided, at least one of each type must meet accessible requirements.

AUTHOR'S INTERPRETATION:

- While not specifically defined by ADAAG, it appears lavatories are for personal hygiene in bathrooms or toilet rooms, while sinks are for all other situations (e.g., laboratories or kitchens).

Lavatories or Sinks: clearances

LV-01 Is there a clear floor space not less than 30 in. × 48 in. in front of the accessible lavatory or sink allowing a forward approach, and does it adjoin or overlap the accessible route? (4.19.3, 4.24.5, Fig. 32)

- The clear floor space can extend up to 19 in. under the sink or lavatory if adequate knee clearance is provided.

LV-02 Are the accessible lavatory or sink rim or counter height, apron height, and extension from the wall adequate? (4.19.2, 4.24.2, Fig. 31)

- Rim height: not greater than 34 in. above the finish floor.
- Apron height: not less than 29 in. above the finish floor to the bottom of the apron.
- Lavatory extension: not less than 17 in. from the wall.

LV-03 Is toe clearance under the accessible lavatory or sink not less than 9 in. above the finish floor and not deeper than 6 in. from the back wall for the full length of the lavatory or sink? (4.19.2, Fig. 31)

Lavatories or Sinks: pipe shielding

LV-04 Are the hot water and drain pipes at the accessible lavatory or sink insulated or otherwise configured to protect against contact and is the area below the lavatory or sink free of sharp or abrasive surfaces? (4.19.4)

Lavatories or Sinks: controls

LV-05 Do the accessible lavatory or sink controls meet operational requirements? (4.19.5)

- Operation: operable with one hand without tight grasping, pinching, or twisting of the wrist. Acceptable types might include lever operated, push type, touch type, or electronically controlled; no more than 5 lbf of force.

- Self-closing faucets, when used, remain open for at least 10 sec.

Sinks Only

LV-07 Is adequate knee clearance provided underneath the accessible sink? (4.24.3)

- Sink knee clearance: not less than 27 in. high, 30 in. wide, and 19 in. deep under the sink.

LV-08 Is the accessible sink bowl not more than 6½ in. deep? (4.24.4)

(SE) Fixed or Built-in Seating and Tables (4.32)

Fixed or Built-in Seating and Tables: minimum number

SE-01 Is the minimum number of accessible wheelchair seating locations at fixed tables or counters provided? (4.1.3.18)

- Number required: 5 percent of total number of seats but not fewer than one.

Fixed or Built-in Seating and Tables: clear floor space

AUTHOR'S INTERPRETATION:

- Where the accessible route leads to and through accessible seating adjacent to a wall or another table, the minimum required width for the accessible route will be 65 in. between the table edge and next parallel surface (e.g., wall or another table edge). (4.1.3.18, Fig. 45)

SE-02 Is the clear floor space for a wheelchair at a seating location adequate? (4.32.3, Fig. 4a, Fig. 45)

- Clear floor space: 30 in. × 48 in.
- This clear space can include up to 19 in. under the table/desk.

Fixed or Built-in Seating and Tables: clearances

SE-03 Are the tops of accessible tables and counters between 28 in. and 34 in. from the floor? (4.32.3, Fig. 45)

SE-04 Are the knee clearances at least 27 in. high, 30 in. wide, and 19 in. deep? (4.32.3, Fig. 45)

(SR) STORAGE (4.25)

NOTE:

- Accessible reach range requirements do not apply to shelves or display units allowing self-service by customers in mercantile occupancies but they must be located on an accessible route. [4.1.3(12)(b)]

Storage: general

SR-01 Does at least one of each type of fixed or built-in storage unit comply with accessible criteria? [4.1.3(12)(a), 4.25.1]

NOTE:

- Types of storage facilities might include cabinets, shelves, closets, and drawers.

Storage: clear floor space

SR-02 Is there a clear floor space at least 30 in. × 48 in. at fixed or built-in storage units that allows for either a forward or side approach? (4.25.2, Fig. 4a–b)

Storage: reach ranges

SR-03 Are forward or side reach for each type of accessible storage unit within acceptable reach ranges? (4.2.5–6, Fig. 5a–b, Fig. 6a–c, 4.25.3)

- Forward reach: not less than 15 in. high and not more than 48 in. high without any obstruction or where the obstruction is less than 20 in. deep. For obstructions from 20 in. to 25 in. deep, no forward reach higher than 44 in.

- Side reach: not less than 9 in. high and not more than 54 in. high. For obstructions not more than 34 in. high or 24 in. deep, no side reach higher than 46 in.

SR-04 In a closet where passage is not required to access storage (e.g., door opening is less than 32 in.), are the clothes rod or shelves within required reach ranges? (4.25.3, Fig. 38a–b)

- Door width: at least 20 in. (4.13.5)
- Horizontal reach: not more than 21 in. from the opening.
- Rod reach: if over 10 in. deep, then not more than 48 in. high.
- Shelf reach: if over 10 in. deep, then not more than 48 in. high or less than 9 in. high.

Storage: hardware

SR-05 Is the hardware on the storage unit doors or drawers operable with one hand without tight grasping, pinching, or wrist twisting, and requiring no more than 5 lbf of force? (4.25.4, 4.27.4)

(TL) Telephones (4.31)

DEFINITION:

- Telephone types include public pay telephones, public closed circuit telephones, or other public telephones.

NOTE:

- Signage related to telephones is found in Section "SG, Signage."

AUTHOR'S INTERPRETATION:

- Frequently, public pay telephones are provided by a contractual agreement with a vendor. The vendor, through the contract, might be made responsible for compliance with all applicable ADAAG criteria.

Telephones: number required

TL-01 If there is only one public telephone on a floor, does it comply with accessible criteria? [4.1.3(17)(a)]

- Unless otherwise specified, accessible telephones may be either forward or side reach telephones.

TL-02 If there is a single bank of public telephones on a floor, does at least one of the telephones in the bank comply with accessible criteria? [4.1.3(17)(a)]

- A bank consists of two or more adjacent public telephones, often installed as a unit.
- Unless otherwise specified, accessible telephones may be either forward or side reach telephones.

Telephones: clear floor or ground space

TL-04 Does the accessible telephone have at least a 30 in. × 48 in. clear floor or ground space that allows either a forward or side approach? (4.31.2, Fig. 44, 4.2.4)

- Bases, enclosures, and fixed seats shall not impede approaches to telephones.
- If this clear floor space is located in an alcove or confined space, see ADAAG Fig. 4d–e for additional maneuvering clearance requirements.

TL-05 Does an accessible route adjoin or overlap the clear floor space for the accessible telephone? (4.31.2, Fig. 44, 4.2.4)

Telephones: protruding object

TL-06 Do wall-mounted or post-mounted telephones with leading edges between 27 in. and 80 in. from the floor have projections that do not result in a protruding object? (4.31.4, 4.4.1)

- Wall-mounted: project less than 4 in. into the pathway.
- Post-mounted: project less than 12 in. into a perpendicular route of travel.

Telephones: mounting height

TL-07 Is the highest operable part of the telephone within forward or side reach ranges? (4.31.3, 4.2.6)

- Forward: not more than 48 in. above the floor.
- Side: not more than 54 in. above the floor.

Telephones: push-button controls

TL-08 Does the telephone have push-button controls where such service is available? (4.31.6)

Telephones: telephone book

TL-09 Is the telephone book, if provided, located in a position that complies with forward or side reach ranges? (4.31.7)

- Forward: not more than 48 in. above the floor.
- Side: not more than 54 in. above the floor.

Telephones: cord length

TL-10 Is the cord from the telephone to the handset at least 29 in. long? (4.31.8)

Telephones: volume control and hearing aid compatibility

TL-11 Do the public telephones comply with volume control requirements? [4.1.3(17)(b)]

- Each accessible telephone is equipped with a volume control.
- In addition, 25 percent, but not fewer than one, of all other public telephones should be equipped with volume controls and dispersed among all types of public telephones.

TL-12 Are volume controls capable of amplification between 12 dbA and 18 dbA above normal? [4.31.5(2)]

- If an automatic reset button is provided, the maximum of 18 dbA may be exceeded.

TL-13 Are telephones hearing aid compatible? [4.31.5(1)]

Telephones: text telephones

NOTE:

- If more than four public telephones are provided, a text telephone may be required. If more than three public telephones are provided, a shelf is required. See (TL) Telephone section for specific requirements.

(AL) Alarms (4.28)

NOTE:

- At a minimum, visual signal appliances shall be provided in buildings and facilities in restrooms and any other general usage areas. **The ADAAG does not define the number of occupants needed to establish a general or common use area.**

ALLOWANCE:

- Emergency warning systems in medical care facilities may be modified to suit standard health care alarm design practice. [4.1.3(14)]

Alarms: general

AL-01 If emergency warning systems are provided, do they include both audible alarms and visual alarms? [4.1.3(14)]

Audible Alarms: general

AL-02 If provided, do the audible alarms meet required operational criteria? (4.28.2)

- Sound level: exceeds the prevailing sound level in the room or space by at least 15 dbA or exceeds any maximum sound level with a duration of 60 sec by 5 dbA, whichever is louder.
- Sound levels for alarm signals shall not exceed 120 dbA.

AL-03 If single station audible alarms are provided, then are single station visual alarm signals also provided? (4.28.3)

Visual Alarms: general

AL-04 If provided, are the visual alarm signal appliances integrated into the building or facility alarm system? (4.28.3)

AL-05 If provided, do the visual alarm signals meet required operational criteria? [4.28.3(1, 2, 3, 4, 5)]

- Lamp: xenon strobe type or equivalent.

- Color: clear or nominal white (i.e., unfiltered or clear filtered white light).
- Pulse duration: maximum shall be 0.2 sec with a maximum duty cycle of 40 percent.
- Intensity: not less than 75 candela.
- Flash rate: not less than 1 Hz and not more than 3 Hz.

AL-07 Are visual alarm signal appliances provided in general usage areas of the building (such as meeting rooms, corridors, and lobbies) or any other area for common use? (4.28.1)

AUTHOR'S INTERPRETATION:

- The authors identified three or more occupants as the minimum number to establish a common use area.

AL-08 Are the visual alarms placed at 80 in. above the highest floor level or 6 in. below the ceiling, whichever is lower? [4.28.3(6)]

AL-09 In spaces required to have visual alarms, are the alarms spaced properly? [4.28.3(7)]

- No place in any space should be more than 50 ft from a visual signal alarm.
- Where a space or large room exceeds 100 ft across, without obstructions 6 ft above the finished floor, visual alarms can be spaced a maximum of 100 ft apart at the perimeter, in lieu of suspending appliances from the ceiling.

Libraries

Introduction. Use this "Space-type Review Guide" to design or evaluate library facilities. Libraries are covered under Title II or Title III, depending on whether they are federally funded or owned, for example, by a private college. If it is a Title II facility, such as a library on a state university campus, then access must be provided for "programs, services, and activities" for disabled users. This may mean that a particular library on campus is not accessible as long as another facility can provide the needed service. In addition to this review guide, please see other individual review guides for "Parking Lots and Passenger Loading Zones," "Lobbies, Corridors, and Interior Accessible Routes," "Toilet Rooms," "Elevators," "Offices," and so on.

A library must have an accessible entrance, regardless of the provision of an electronic book security gate or turnstile. Therefore, if accessibility requirements are not met with an accessible gate, then an accessible door next to a turnstile or security device must be provided for a person in a wheelchair. Directional signage for locating sections of the library, book call numbers, and other elements/facilities such as phones, toilet rooms, elevators, and so on must follow accessibility guidelines. At least 5 percent (but not fewer than one) of fixed seating, tables, and/or study carrels must meet accessibility requirements. These facilities must meet requirements for clear floor space, knee space, height of writing surface, and requirements for aisles leading up to or between the tables or study carrels.

At least one checkout area must be provided with a portion of the counter lowered to accommodate a person who uses a wheelchair. Card catalogs and magazine displays must meet accessible width requirements between aisles. Additionally the card catalog must meet unique reach ranges for the low height requirements (18 in. above the floor surface). The clear aisle width between shelving stacks must meet minimum requirements with a wider preferred measurement suggested, but there is no shelf height restriction for the stacks. A library is not required to have accessible aisles in the stacks if a person is available to retrieve books and other materials for a disabled person who may need assistance.

If provided, computer terminals, microfiche readers, and other audiovisual equipment must be located on accessible work surfaces with accessible controls. Newspapers, current periodicals, new books on display, and frequently used reference materials must be located within reach, or a person must be available to retrieve them for a disabled user. If stairways are freestanding, a cane detection barrier must be provided as a warning to a visually impaired person not to walk into the underside of the stairs. Changes of material from one section of a library to another are common but must not result in an inaccessible level change.

When stairs are included, only stairs that connect levels not connected by an elevator or other accessible means of vertical access are required to comply with ADAAG. Open risers are never permitted on accessible stairs and handrail extensions must be designed so that they will not be a protruding object, especially where the extensions intersect another accessible route.

Often library entrance vestibules have marble or terrazzo flooring that is highly polished. These surfaces can be very slippery when wet so specify a slip-resistant finish to comply with accessibility criteria. Visual emergency alarms must be visible throughout the library to a person who is hearing impaired, especially within a stack area where one may be somewhat isolated from the major traffic areas.

PRELIMINARY DESIGN OVERVIEW

In historic buildings displays and written information, documents, etc., should be located where they can be seen by a seated person. Exhibits and signage displayed horizontally (e.g., open books) should be no higher than 44 in. above the floor surface.

(AR) Accessible Routes

- Frequently overlooked in this space-type are the following maneuvering space problems: with book shelf aisles, minimum accessible width requirements between aisles, switchbacks, turns around an obstruction, and intersections should meet requirements for accessible routes. Electronic security gates must meet requirements for accessible routes.

(AL) Alarms

- Typical requirements.

(AA) Assembly Areas

- An accessible route from each wheelchair seating location must serve as a means of egress in an emergency.

(CT) Controls and Operating Mechanisms

- Controls and operating mechanisms have clear floor space and reach range requirements. Frequently overlooked in this space type are pull cords on fans and lights, outside book return depositories, etc.
- One of each type of control device should be accessible and operable.

(DF) Drinking Fountains and Water Coolers

- Drinking fountains must serve both ambulatory and nonambulatory height requirements; this requires two different spout heights

(DR) Doors

- Two doors in a series must meet both clear space and door swing requirements (e.g., vestibules, entries, etc.).
- Revolving doors, turnstiles, and gates require an adjacent accessible door, gate, or opening providing the same use pattern.

(EX) Exits and Areas of Rescue Assistance

- Typical requirements.

(FS) Floor Surfaces

- In some areas floor surfaces should be evaluated as if wet. In particular consider entrance areas.
- Smooth floor surfaces should be evaluated for slip-resistance based on floor finish and maintenance (e.g., marble, terrazzo, tiles).
- Vertical changes in levels along the accessible route can be an unforeseen barrier, e.g., transition between floor materials. Also of concern are raised objects in the path of travel (e.g., electrical and communication outlets, etc.)

(LB) Libraries

- A percentage (but no fewer than one of each type) of work station (e.g., fixed seating, tables, counters, computer terminals, or study carrels) must be accessible.
- All public areas (such as reading and study areas, stacks, reference rooms, reserve areas, and special facilities or collections) must be physically or programmatically accessible.

- Card catalogs and magazine displays have unique requirements for reach ranges.
- At least one lane at each checkout area must be on the accessible route and meet accessibility criteria.
- Security gates or turnstiles must comply with accessible criteria.

(PR) Protruding Objects

- Common wall-mounted elements can be protruding objects, e.g., pencil sharpeners, bookshelves, drinking fountains, public telephones, signs, display cases, etc.
- Overhead clearances can be an unforeseen compliance problem, e.g., signs and banners, open spaces under stairs, low ceilings around checkout desks and information booths, etc.
- Standard fire safety items are often protruding objects, e.g., permanently mounted fire hose cabinets, fire extinguishers and fire extinguisher cabinets, valves on standpipes, etc.

(SG) Signage

- Permanent directional and informational signage must meet accessibility criteria; letter height varies with mounting height of sign.
- Building directories, menus, and temporary signs are not required to comply. (This is located in 4.1.3.16b Exceptions.)

(SR) Fixed Storage, Closets, Lockers, or Shelves

- When provided, one of each type of storage unit (shelves, hooks, etc.) must be accessible.

(ST) Stairs

- Only stairs that connect levels not connected by an elevator or other accessible means of vertical access are required to comply.
- Open risers are not permitted on accessible stairs.
- Handrail extensions are possible protruding objects, especially where the extensions intersect another accessible route.

ADAAG APPENDIX

The ADAAG Appendix has advisory information pertinent to this space-type.

- A4.2 Space Allowances and Reach Ranges
- A4.13.12 Automatic Doors and Power Assisted Doors
- A4.32 Fixed or Built-in Seating and Tables

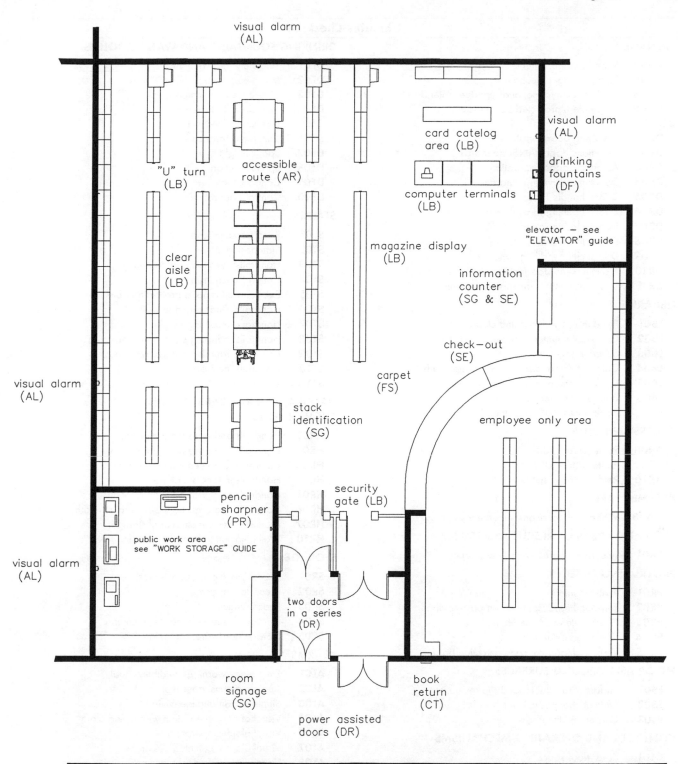

Figure 3-14. Library.

Libraries Checklist

SIGNAGE

SG04	Room signage: criteria
SG05	Room signage: location
SG08	Directional/informational signage: criteria
SG09	Suspended/projected signs: location

DOORS

DR01	Revolving door/turnstile
DR02	Automatic doors: ANSI standards
DR03	Automatic doors: operation
DR04	Doors: maneuvering clearances
DR05	Doors: handle type
DR06	Doors: opening force (interior only)
DR07	Doors: closing speed
DR08	Doors: thresholds
DR09	Doors: clear width/height
DR10	Openings (no door): clear width/height
DR11	Doors in series: clear space between

LIBRARIES

LB01	Fixed tables: number and clearances
LB02	Check-out counter: number and criteria
LB03	Security gate: clearances
LB04	Card cat./mag. display: clear aisle width
LB05	Card cat./mag. display: reach range
LB06	Book stacks: clear aisle width
LB07	Book stacks: "U" turns at end of stack

ACCESSIBLE ROUTE

AR08	Route: clear width
AR09	Route width: "U" turns
AR10	Route: passing space

ASSEMBLY AREAS

AA08	Wheelchair locations: emergency egress

EXITS AND AREAS OF RESCUE ASSISTANCE

EX01	Acc. route: egress/rescue assistance

PROTRUDING OBJECTS

PR01	Wall mounted
PR02	Freestanding/suspended on posts/pylons
PR03	Clear route width maintained
PR04	Overhead clearance
PR05	Vertical clearance: cane detection barrier

FLOOR AND GROUND SURFACES

FS01	Surface: firm, stable, and slip resistant
FS02	Vertical changes in level
FS03	Carpet and tile floors

CONTROLS AND OPERATING MECHANISMS

CT01	Clear floor space
CT02	Reach ranges: elec./comm. systems
CT03	Reach ranges: thermostats
CT04	Reach ranges: other controls
CT05	Reach ranges: life safety devices
CT06	Controls: operation

DRINKING FOUNTAINS AND WATER COOLERS

DF01	Single unit requirements
DF02	Multiple unit requirements
DF03	Alcove location: criteria
DF04	Unit: clear floor space
DF05	Unit: knee clearance
DF06	Unit: toe clearance
DF07	Spout: height
DF08	Spout: location
DF09	Controls: location
DF10	Controls: operation

STAIRS

ST01	Riser/tread: criteria
ST02	Stair nosing: criteria
ST03	Handrails: location and continuity
ST04	Handrails: extensions
ST05	Ext. handrail is not a protruding object
ST06	Handrails: clear space to wall
ST07	Handrails: mounting height
ST08	Handrails: gripping surface uninterrupted
ST09	Handrails: rounded ends or returned
ST10	Handrails: no rotation
ST11	Water does not accumulate

HANDRAILS , GRAB BARS, TUB AND SHOWER SEATS

HR01	Handrails and grab bars: diameter
HR02	Handrails and grab bars: edge radius
HR03	Clearance between handrail & wall
HR04	Handrails in recess: criteria
HR05	Handrails and grab bars: no rotation
HR06	Handrails and grab bars: structural strength
HR07	Mounting devices: structural strength
HR10	Wall adjacent to handrail abrasion free

STORAGE

SR01	Accessibility: one of each type
SR02	Clear floor space
SR03	Reach ranges
SR04	Storage closets w/o passage: criteria
SR05	Storage hardware: operation

ALARMS

AL01	Emergency warning : audible/visual
AL02	Audible alarms: operation
AL03	Single station audible & visual
AL04	Visual alarms: integration w/building alarm
AL05	Visual alarms: operation
AL07	Visual alarms: common use areas
AL08	Visual alarms: vertical placement
AL09	Visual alarms: horizontal spacing
AL10	Visual alarms: corridor spacing

LIBRARIES
COMPREHENSIVE CRITERIA

(SG) Signage (4.30)

Signage: room identification (where provided)

DEFINITION:

- These signs designate permanent rooms and spaces.

AUTHOR'S INTERPRETATION:

- Signs that designate stairs, exit doors, and toilet rooms generally are associated with permanent spaces, while an "office" sign is not since the room function may change over time. Room numbers also must meet the ADAAG criteria as permanent designations, while personal names do not since the occupant may change over time.

SG-04 Do signs that designate permanent rooms and spaces comply with the following criteria? [4.1.2(7); 4.1.3(16); 4.30.4, 5, 6]

- Character type: raised and accompanied by Grade II Braille.
- Character size: between 5/8 in. and 2 in. high; raised at least 1/32 in.
- Character style: upper case, and sans or simple serif.
- Finish: characters and backgrounds have a nonglare finish.
- Contrast: characters contrast with their background (light-on-dark or dark-on-light).

SG-05 Is the room identification sign mounted in the required location? (4.30.6)

- Mounting location: installed on the wall adjacent to the latch side of the door or where wall space to the latch side of the door is not available, including double doors, placed on the nearest adjacent wall.
- Mounting height: 60 in. above the floor/ground to the centerline of the sign.
- Sign access: approach to within 3 in. of a sign without encountering protruding objects or standing within the swing of the door.

Signage: direction and information (where provided)

EXCEPTION:

DEFINITION:

- Signs that provide direction to or information about functional spaces of the building.

EXCEPTION:

- Building directories, menus, and all other temporary signs are not required to comply. [4.1.3(16)]

SG-08 Do signs that provide direction to, or information about, functional spaces of the building comply with the following criteria? [4.1.2(7); 4.1.3(16); 4.30.1, 2, 3, 5]

- Character proportion: letters and numbers have a width to height ratio between 3:5 and 1:1 and a stroke width to height ratio between 1:5 and 1:10.
- Character height: sized according to viewing distance with characters on overhead signs at least 3 in. high.

NOTE:

- When the sign is mounted below 80 in., there are no prescribed character heights. Only when the sign is mounted 80 in. or higher, are the characters required to be at least 3 in. high. (4.30.3)
- Finish: characters and backgrounds have a nonglare finish.
- Contrast: characters contrast with their background (light-on-dark or dark-on-light).

SG-09 Is a sign located so that the overhead clearance or the projection of a suspended or projected sign does not result in a protruding object (free-standing or wall-mounted)?

- Clear height: at least 80 in. (4.4.2, Fig. 8a)
- Overhang for free-standing signs on posts or pylons located between 27 in. and 80 in. high: no more than a 12-in. projection into accessible routes. (4.4.1, Fig. 8c)
- Overhang for wall-mounted signs between 27 in. and 80 in. high: no more than a 4-in. projection into accessible routes. (4.4.1, Fig. 8a)

(DR) Doors (4.13)

NOTE:

- Included in this category are doors, revolving doors, turnstiles, and gates.

AUTHOR'S INTERPRETATION:

- It is suggested that, for purposes of documentation and review, a door be assigned to the space it swings into. Corridors are an exception to this rule and include only entry doors into the corridor or intermediate fire doors.

Doors: revolving doors, turnstiles, and gates

DR-01 Where revolving doors or turnstiles are used on an accessible route, is an adjacent accessible gate or door provided that allows the same use pattern? (4.13.2)

Doors: automatic or power assisted

DR-02 If an automatic door or power assisted door is used, does it comply with the appropriate ANSI standard? (4.13.12)

- Automatic door: ANSI/BHMA A156.10-1985.
- Slow opening, low powered automatic door: ANSI A156.19-1984.
- Power assisted door: ANSI A156.19-1984.

DR-03 Do slow opening, low powered automatic doors or power assisted doors comply with opening and closing requirements? (4.13.12)

- Slow opening, low powered automatic doors: do not open to back-check faster than 3 sec and require no more than 15 lbf of force to stop door movement.
- Power assisted doors: no more than 5 lbf of opening force.

Doors: maneuvering clearance

DR-04 If the door is not automatic or power assisted, does it have the required maneuvering clearance provided on the push and pull side, and is the floor level and clear within the maneuvering area? (4.13.6)

- A verbal description cannot adequately describe the requirements. See ADAAG Fig. 25a–f for a graphic description.

EXCEPTION:

- Entry doors to acute care hospital bedrooms for inpatients are exempt from maneuvering space at the latch side of the door if the door is at least 44 in. wide.

AUTHOR'S INTERPRETATION:

- While ADAAG does not describe what elements can reduce the required maneuvering clearance, they could include a narrow entry alcove, an adjacent wall, railing, or permanently installed shelving, or a deep recessed door jamb.

Doors: hardware

DR-05 Do all door handles, locks, latches, or other operable devices meet required operational criteria? (4.13.9)

- Hardware operation: operable with one hand without tight grasping, pinching, or wrist twisting.
- Force required to operate the controls: not greater than 5 lbf. This does not apply to the force required to retract latch bolts or to disengage other devices that only hold the door in a closed position.
- Hardware type: "U"-shaped handles, levers, and push type mechanisms are acceptable designs.
- Hardware height: not greater than 48 in. above the floor.
- Sliding doors: hardware is exposed and usable from both sides when the doors are fully open.

Doors: opening force

DR-06 Do interior hinged doors and sliding or folding doors have an opening force of 5 lbf or less? (4.13.11)

- At present, no accessible criteria exist for exterior doors.
- Fire doors shall have the minimum opening force allowable by the appropriate administrative authority.

Doors: closing speed

DR-07 If the door has a closer, is the closer adjusted so that the door does not close too quickly? (4.13.10)

- From an open position of 70° the door will take at least 3 sec to move to a point 3 in. from the latch (measured to the leading edge of the door).

Doors: thresholds

DR-08 Where raised thresholds are provided, do they meet height limitations and are they beveled when required? (4.13.8, 4.5.2, Fig. 7)

- Threshold height: not more than 3/4 in. for exterior sliding doors or 1/2 in. for other types of doors.
- Threshold bevel: thresholds less than 1/4 in. high need no bevel; thresholds between 1/4 and 1/2 in. high shall be beveled at each edge with not more than a 1:2 slope.

EXCEPTION:

- A 3/4-in. high threshold is allowed in existing conditions. [4.1.6(3)(d)(ii)]

Doors: clear opening width and height

DR-09 Is the clear opening for the doorway adequate in width and height? (4.13.3, 4, 5, Fig. 24)

- Door width: at least 32 in. of clear width with the door open at 90°, measured between the face of the door and the door stop on the latch side. This also pertains to the active leaf of a double-leaf door or gate.
- Opening width: openings more than 24 in. deep must provide 36 in. of clear width.
- Height: at least 80 in. of vertical clearance.

EXCEPTIONS:

- Doors not requiring full user passage, such as shallow closets, may have the clear opening reduced to not less than 20 in.
- Where it is technically infeasible to comply with clear opening width requirements, a projection of 5/8 in. maximum will be permitted for the latch side. [4.1.6(d)(i)]

DR-10 Is the clear opening (when there is no door) adequate in width and height? (4.2.1, 4.3.3, 4.4.2)

- Width: at least 32 in. of clear width for depths 24 in. or less and at least 36 in. of clear width for depths greater than 24 in.
- Height: at least 80 in. of vertical clearance.

Doors: two doors in a series

DR-11 If there are two doors in a series, is the required clear space between the doors provided and do the doors swing in the appropriate direction? (4.13.7, Fig. 26)

- Clear space between the doors: not less than 48 in. plus the width of any door swinging into the space.
- Door swing: must swing in the same direction or away from the space between the doors.

(LB) Libraries (8.0)

NOTE:

- In historic buildings displays and written information, documents, etc., should be located where they can be seen by a seated person. Exhibits and signage displayed horizontally (e.g., open books) should be no higher than 44 in. above the floor surface. [4.1.7(3)(e)]

Libraries: minimum number

LB-01 Do at least 5 percent (but not fewer than one) of fixed seating, tables, study carrels, and computer terminals meet accessible criteria? (8.2)

- Seating space: at least a 30-in. × 48-in. clear floor space that adjoins or overlaps an accessible route. No more than 19 in. of the clear floor space can be measured under the table.
- Knee space: at least 27 in. high, 30 in. wide, and 19 in. deep.
- Table/counter height: between 28 in. and 34 in. above the floor.
- Aisles leading up to and between the tables or study carrels are at least 36 in. wide.

NOTE:

- Types of seating can include fixed tables, counters, study carrels, computer terminals, or lounge areas.

Libraries: checkout areas

LB-02 Is there at least one lane at each checkout area where a portion of the counter complies with the required length and height? (8.3, 7.2.1)

- A portion of the counter is at least 36 in. long and not more than 36 in. high.
- In alterations where it is technically infeasible to provide an accessible counter, an auxiliary counter meeting these requirements may be provided.

LB-03 Do security gates or turnstiles comply with accessible width and head clearances? (8.3; 4.13.3, 4, 5, Fig. 24)

- Width: at least a 32-in. clear width at 90° for passage less than 24 in. deep.
- Width: at least a 36-in. clear width for passage greater than 24 in. deep.
- Height: at least 80 in. head clearance.

Libraries: card catalogs and magazine displays

LB-04 Is the aisle space between card catalogs and magazine displays at least 36 in. wide? (8.4, Fig. 55)

LB-05 Are the card catalogs and magazine displays within the accessible reach ranges for forward or side approach? (8.4; 4.2, Fig. 55)

- Minimum height: 18 in.
- Maximum height: forward approach is 48 in.; side approach is 54 in. A height of 48 in. is preferred.

Libraries: stacks

LB-06 Is the minimum clear aisle between stacks at least 36 in. wide? (8.5, Fig. 56)

- Shelf height in stack areas is unrestricted. A minimum clear aisle width of 42 in. is preferred, where possible.

LB-07 Is the minimum clear width for U-turns around the end of stacks provided? (4.3.3, Fig. 7a–b)

- Obstruction 48 in. or greater: at least a 36-in. clear width around the obstruction.
- Obstruction less than 48 in.: at least a 42-in. clear width at each side with at least a 48-in. clear width in the turn.

(AR) Accessible Routes (4.3)

NOTES:

- All walks, halls, corridors, aisles, skywalks, tunnels, and other spaces that are part of a designated accessible route shall comply with accessible requirements.
- Any slope on the accessible route that is greater than 1:20 is required to meet all ramp criteria.
- The accessible route shall, to the maximum extent feasible, coincide with the route for the general public.
- In historic buildings, accessible routes from an accessible entrance shall be provided to all publicly used spaces on at least the level of the accessible entrance. Access shall be provided to all levels of a building or facility whenever practical. (4.1.7(3)(d)]

AUTHOR'S INTERPRETATION:

- An accessible route "generally coincides" with the route used by the public if

- It does not force the user to go out of the way
- It is most like the route chosen by the general public
- It is direct
- It gives the same basic experience as the route preferred by the public

Accessible Routes: width

AR-08 Is the minimum clear width along the accessible route adequate for continuous or point passage? (4.2.1, 4.3.3, Fig. 1, Fig. 8e, Fig. 24e)

- Continuous passage (greater than 24 in. long): at least a 36-in. clear width.
- Point passage (not more than 24 in. long): at least a 32-in. clear width.

AUTHOR'S INTERPRETATION:

- Noncompliance with this question generally relates to permanent elements that encroach on the accessible route. Large, heavy equipment that is not readily movable might be considered permanent. If the space is designed so that temporary elements (such as bikes in a bike rack or car bumpers) will consistently encroach, the situation might also be considered a permanent barrier.

AR-09 Is the minimum clear width along the accessible route adequate at a U-turn around an obstruction? (4.3.3, Fig. 7a–b)

- Obstruction 48 in. or greater: at least a 36-in. clear width around the obstruction.
- Obstruction less than 48 in.: at least a 42-in. clear width at each side with at least a 48-in. clear width in the turn.

Accessible routes: passing space

AR-10 Does the accessible route provide at least 60 in. of clear width for two wheelchairs to pass and, if not, is the required passing space provided? (4.2.2, 4.3.4)

- A 60-in. × 60-in. passing space or "T" intersection should be provided at reasonable intervals not to exceed 200 ft.

AUTHOR'S INTERPRETATION:

- Accessible routes more than 5 ft long (e.g., routes in short hallways, aisles in laboratories, and work/storage areas) should have passing spaces provided.

DEFINITION:

- A *"T" intersection* is defined as the intersection of two corridors or walks, each at least 36 in. wide providing at least a 60 in. depth at the intersection. (Fig. 3b)

(AA) Assembly Areas (4.33)

Assembly Areas: location

AA-08 Do wheelchair locations adjoin an accessible route that also serves as a means of emergency egress? (4.33.3)

(EX) Exits and Areas of Rescue Assistance (4.3.11)

DEFINITIONS:

- *Area of Rescue Assistance:* An area with direct access to an exit where people who are unable to use stairs may remain temporarily in safety to await further instructions or assistance during emergency evacuation.

- *Means of Egress:* A continuous and unobstructed way of exit travel from any point in a building or facility to a public way. A means of egress comprises vertical and horizontal travel and may include intervening room spaces, doorways, hallways, corridors, passageways, balconies, ramps, stairs, enclosures, lobbies, horizontal exits, courts, and yards. An accessible means of egress is one that complies with these guidelines and does not include stairs, steps, or escalators. Areas of rescue assistance or evacuation elevators may be included as part of accessible means of egress.

EXCEPTIONS:

- New construction: Areas of rescue assistance are not required in buildings or facilities having a supervised automatic sprinkler system. [4.1.3(9)]
- Alterations: Alterations are not required to provide an area of rescue assistance. [4.1.6(1)(g)]

ALLOWANCE:

- New construction: A horizontal exit can be used as an area of rescue assistance when the exit is designed in accordance with the local building code. [4.1.3(9)]

Exits: number required

EX-01 Does each occupiable level of a building or facility that is required to be accessible have accessible means of egress equal to the number of exits required by local building/life safety regulations? [4.1.3(9)]

- Where a required exit is not accessible, areas of rescue assistance shall be provided equal to the number of inaccessible required exits. [4.1.3(9)]

(PR) Protruding Objects (4.4)

Protruding Objects: general

PR-01 Do wall-mounted objects having leading edges between 27 in. and 80 in. high project less than 4 in. into walkways, corridors, aisles, or paths of travel? (4.4.1, Fig. 8a–e)

- Objects mounted with their leading edge at or below 27 in. can protrude any amount, as long as they do not reduce the required clear width of an accessible route.

AUTHOR'S INTERPRETATION:

- Protruding objects might include fire extinguishers or cabinets, pencil sharpeners, shelving, counters, built-in equipment overhangs, or various dispensers such as for paper towels or soap.

PR-02 Do free-standing objects, suspended or mounted on posts or pylons with leading edges between 27 in. and 80 in. high, project less than 12 in. into the perpendicular route of travel? (4.4.1, Fig. 8a–e)

AUTHOR'S INTERPRETATION:

- These might include telephone enclosures, drinking fountains, or free-standing signage kiosks.

PR-03 Is the minimum clear route width or maneuvering space still maintained even with the projection of a protruding object? (4.4.1, Fig. 8a–e)

Protruding Objects: overhead clearance

PR-04 Is the minimum overhead clearance of 80 in. provided in accessible areas or along accessible routes? (4.4.2, Fig. 8a)

AUTHOR'S INTERPRETATION:

- Overhead objects that can reduce the required clearance might include structures, pipes, ducts, or light fixtures.

PR-05 Where the vertical clearance of a space adjoining the accessible route is less than 80 in. high, is a cane detection barrier less than 27 in. from the floor provided for blind or visually impaired persons? (4.4.2, Fig. 8c-1)

AUTHOR'S INTERPRETATION:

- This condition might be found under a stair, at a sloped ceiling space, or with guy wires from telephone poles along an exterior accessible route.

(FS) Floor and Ground Surfaces (4.5)

Floor Surfaces: general

FS-01 Are the floor/ground surfaces on the accessible route stable, firm, and slip-resistant? (4.5.1)

AUTHOR'S INTERPRETATION:

- Exterior spaces, interior circulation, bathrooms, and other spaces where water can collect on the floor around an element (sinks, drinking fountains, hose bibbs, etc.) are reviewed as if wet.
- High gloss surfaces without significant textures that are regularly maintained with waxing (smooth tiles, waxed concrete, etc.) could be considered noncompliant.
- Accessible criteria are not specified for nonpermanent floor surfaces such as mats or rugs.

Floor Surfaces: changes in level

FS-02 Are vertical changes in level between 1/4 in. and 1/2 in. beveled with a slope of 1:2 or less? (4.5.2)

- Changes in level up to 1/4 in. may be vertical without edge treatment.
- Changes in level greater than 1/2 in. should be accomplished by means of a curb ramp, ramp, elevator, or platform lift (as permitted in ADAAG 4.1.3 and 4.1.6).

Floor Surfaces: carpet

FS-03 Does carpet or carpet tile used on the floor comply with accessible criteria?

- Attachment: secured. (4.5.3, Fig. 8f)
- Exposed edges: fastened and trimmed along the entire length.
- Pile type: low pile (1/2 in. maximum).
- Padding: firm pad or no pad underneath.

(CT) Controls and Operating Mechanisms (4.27)

NOTES:

- Controls or operating mechanisms can include elements such as light switches, pencil sharpeners, manual overhead screens, nonkeyed thermostats, alarm pull stations, fire extinguisher cabinets, A/C window units, microwave ovens, towel dispensers, and wall hooks.

- If controls are to be operated by occupants of the space, they must be accessible. If controls are to be operated by maintenance staff only and not by occupants or other users of the space, they do not have to be accessible. For example, thermostats in auditoriums usually do not have to be accessible, while thermostats in classrooms may need to be accessible.

Controls: clear floor space

CT-01 Is a clear floor space of at least 30 in. × 48 in. provided in front of controls, dispensers, receptacles, and other operable equipment for forward or parallel approach? (4.27.2, Fig. 4a–b)

Controls: reach ranges

NOTES:

- Accessible reach ranges for controls and operating mechanisms are:
  — Forward reach: not less than 15 in. high and not more than 48 in. high without any obstruction or where the obstruction is less than 20 in. deep. For obstructions from 20 in. to 25 in. deep, no forward reach higher than 44 in.
  — Side reach: not less than 9 in. high and not more than 54 in. high. For obstructions not more than 34 in. high or 24 in. deep, no side reach higher than 46 in.
  — Electrical outlets, switches, and communication system receptacles have a minimum outlet height of 15 in. regardless of forward or side reach. See CT-02 below.

CT-02 Are electrical outlets, switches, and communication system receptacles mounted within accessible forward or side reach ranges? (4.27.3)

  EXCEPTION:
  - These requirements do not apply where the use of special equipment dictates otherwise or where electrical and communications system receptacles are not normally intended for use by building occupants. (4.27.3)

CT-03 Are thermostats or other similar operable equipment mounted within accessible forward or side reach ranges? (4.2.5, 4.2.6, Fig. 5a–b, Fig. 6a–c)

CT-04 Are dispensers or other similar operable equipment mounted within accessible forward or side reach ranges? (4.2.5, 4.2.6, Fig. 5a–b, Fig. 6a–c)

CT-05 Are life safety devices or other similar operable equipment mounted within accessible forward or side reach ranges? (4.2.5, 4.2.6, Fig. 5a–b, Fig. 6a–c)

  NOTE:
  - This might include fire alarm pull stations, handles to extinguisher cabinets, or wall-mounted extinguishers.

Controls: operation

CT-06 Are controls, dispensers, receptacles, and other operable equipment operable with one hand without tight grasping, pinching, or wrist twisting, and requiring no more than 5 lbf of force? (4.27.4)

(DF) Drinking Fountains and Water Coolers (4.15)

Drinking Fountains: minimum number

DF-01 Where only one drinking fountain is provided on a floor, is it on an accessible route and is it accessible to both wheelchair users and to persons having difficulty stooping or bending? [4.1.3(10)(a)]

- Drinking fountains are required to be accessible to both wheelchair users (accessible height fountain) and persons having difficulty stooping or bending (standard height fountain).

NOTE:

- Alternate solutions might include a high-low fountain or an accessible height fountain and a water cooler with cups. [4.1.3(10)(a)]

DF-02 Where more than one drinking fountain is provided on a floor, do at least 50 percent but not fewer than one of the fountains meet accessible criteria, and is each accessible fountain on an accessible route? [4.1.3(10)(b)]

- Drinking fountains are required to be accessible to both wheelchair users (accessible height fountain) and persons having difficulty stooping or bending (standard height fountain).

Drinking Fountains: clearances and clear floor space

DF-03 If the accessible drinking fountain is located in an alcove, is the alcove adequate in depth and width? (4.15.5, Fig. 27b)

- Depth: not more than 24 in. deep.
- Width: at least 30 in. wide.

DF-04 Is a clear floor space at least 30 in. × 48 in. provided at accessible drinking fountains? [4.15.5(1, 2), Fig. 27b]

DF-05 Does the knee clearance space for wall- and post-mounted cantilevered accessible drinking fountains meet required criteria? (4.15.5, Fig. 27)

- Height: at least 27 in. high from the floor to the apron bottom and maintaining that height for at least 8 in. under the equipment.
- Width: at least 30 in. wide.
- Depth: between 17 in. and 19 in. deep.

NOTE:

- Wall-mounted fountains with leading edges between 27 in. and 80 in. are protruding objects if they project more than 4 in. into the accessible route. A leading edge at 27 in. or below can project any amount as long as it does not restrict the required clear width of the route. (4.4.1)

AUTHOR'S INTERPRETATION:

- If a water fountain is going to protrude more than 4 in. into an accessible route, then it must be mounted at exactly 27 in. in order to comply with required knee clearances and not be considered a protruding object.

DF-06 Is toe clearance at the base of the accessible drinking fountain at least 9 in. high and not more than 6 in. deep? (4.15.5, Fig. 27)

- See ADAAG Fig. 27 for the permitted equipment or piping area.

Drinking Fountains: spout location

DF-07 Is the accessible drinking fountain spout outlet no higher than 36 in. from the ground or floor? (4.15.2, Fig. 27)

DF-08 Is the spout located near the front of the fountain and does it meet required water flow criteria? (4.15.3)

- Water flow trajectory: nearly parallel to the front edge and at least 4 in. high to allow the insertion of a cup or glass.
- Fountain with a round or oval bowl: flow of water is within 3 in. of the front edge.

Drinking Fountains: controls

DF-09 Are the accessible drinking fountain controls front-mounted and/or side-mounted near the front edge? (4.15.4)

DF-10 Are the accessible drinking fountain controls operable with one hand without tight grasping, pinching, or wrist twisting, and require no more than 5 lbf of force? (4.15.4)

(ST) Stairs (4.9)

NOTE:

- Only stairs that connect levels not connected by an elevator, ramp, or other accessible means of vertical access are required to comply. [4.1.3(4)]
- In new construction, this condition may occur in facilities subject to the elevator exemption [4.1.3(5)—Exception 1] or where mezzanines are exempt in restaurants. (5.4)

Stairs: risers, treads, and nosings

ST-01 Do the stair treads and risers meet the required criteria? (4.9.2, Fig. 18a)

- Uniformity: riser heights and tread widths should remain uniform in any one flight of stairs.
- Treads: not less than 11 in. measured from riser to riser.
- Risers: no open risers are permitted.

ST-02 Do the stair nosings meet the required criteria? See ADAAG Fig. 18 for clarification. (4.9.3)

- Risers: risers slope toward the nosing.
- Radius of the curvature: not more than 1/2-in. radius at the leading edge of the tread.
- Angle nosing: angled underside on nosing is not less than 60° from the horizontal; underside of nosing should not be abrupt.
- Nosing projection: not more than 1½ in.

Stairs: handrails

NOTE:

- Additional criteria for handrails can be found in Section "HR, Handrails."

ST-03 Is the handrail provided on both sides of the stair, and is the inside rail on switchback or dogleg stairs continuous at the landing? [4.9.4(1), Fig. 19a–b]

- The outside handrail along the perimeter wall does not have to be continuous around the landing.

ST-04 At the end of the stair handrails, is there at least 12 in. of handrail parallel to the floor beyond the top riser and is there at least one tread width of sloping handrail plus at least 12 in. of horizontal handrail beyond the bottom riser? [4.9.4(2), Fig. 19c–d.]

- See ADAAG Fig. 19c–d for extension design.

ST-05 If the handrail extension protrudes into an accessible route, is the handrail extension rounded to 27 in. or less from the floor so that it does not create a protruding object? [4.9.4(2)]

ST-06 Is the clearance between the stair handrail and the wall exactly 1½ in.? [4.9.4(3)]

ST-07 Are the tops of stair handrails between 34 in. and 38 in. above the stair nosing? [4.9.4(5)]

ST-08 Is the stair handrail gripping surface uninterrupted by newel posts, other obstructions, or missing segments? [4.9.4(4)]

ST-09 Are the ends of stair handrails rounded or returned smoothly to the floor, wall, or post? [4.9.4(6)]

ST-10 Are handrails fixed so that they do not rotate within their fittings? [4.9.4(7)]

Stairs: water accumulation

ST-11 Are outdoor stairs and their approaches designed so that water does not accumulate on walking surfaces? (4.9.6)

(HR) Handrails, Grab Bars, and Tub and Shower Seats (4.26)

NOTE:

- HR Guidelines may be repeated in other element-based guidelines: (RP) Ramps, (ST) Stairs, (WC) Water Closets, (TS) Toilet Stalls, (BT) Bathtubs, and (SS) Shower Stalls.

Handrails: size and spacing

HR-01 Is the gripping surface of the grab bars or handrails 1¼ to 1½ in. in outside diameter? (4.26.2, Fig. 39)

AUTHOR'S INTERPRETATION:

- Standard pipe sizes designated by the industry as 1¼ in. to 1½ in. are acceptable for purposes of this section.

HR-02 Do the grab bars or handrails have edges with a minimum radius of 1/8 in.? (4.26.4)

HR-03 Is the clearance between the grab bars or handrails and the wall exactly 1½ in.? (4.26.2, Fig. 39)

HR-04 If the handrail is located in a recess, is the recess a maximum of 3 in. deep extending at least 18 in. above the rail? (4.26.2, Fig. 39d)

Handrails: grab bar or handrail structural strength

HR-05 Are the grab bars or handrails secure so that they do not rotate in their fittings? [4.26.3(5)]

HR-06 Do the grab bars and handrails meet the structural strength requirements for bending stress and shear stress? (4.26.3)

- Actual bending stress in the grab bar induced by the maximum bending moment from the application of 250 lbf is less than the allowable bending stress for the material of the grab bar.

- Shear stress induced in a grab bar by the application of 250 lbf shall be less than the allowable shear stress for the material of the grab bar. If the connection between the grab bar and its mounting bracket or other support is considered to be fully restrained, then direct and torsional shear stresses shall be totaled for the combined shear stress, which shall not exceed the allowable shear stress.

HR-07 Do the fasteners and mounting devices for the grab bars or handrails meet the structural strength requirements for shear force and tensile force? (4.26.3)

- Shear force induced in a fastener or mounting device from the application of 250 lbf shall be less than the allowable lateral load of either the fastener or mounting device or the supporting structure, whichever is the smaller allowable load.

- Tensile force induced in a fastener by a direct tension force of 250 lbf plus the maximum moment from the application of 250 lbf shall be less than the allowable withdrawal load between the fastener and the supporting structure.

Handrails: hazards

HR-10 Are handrails or grab bars and any wall or other surfaces adjacent to them free of any sharp or abrasive elements? (4.26.4)

(SR) Storage (4.25)

NOTE:

- Accessible reach range requirements do not apply to shelves or display units allowing self-service by customers in mercantile occupancies but they must be located on an accessible route. [4.1.3(12)(b)]

Storage: general

SR-01 Does at least one of each type of fixed or built-in storage unit comply with accessible criteria? [4.1.3(12)(a), 4.25.1]

  NOTE:

  - Types of storage facilities might include cabinets, shelves, closets, and drawers.

Storage: clear floor space

SR-02 Is there a clear floor space at least 30 in. × 48 in. at fixed or built-in storage units that allows for either a forward or side approach? (4.25.2, Fig. 4a–b)

Storage: reach ranges

SR-03 Are forward or side reach for each type of accessible storage unit within acceptable reach ranges? (4.2.5-6, Fig. 5a–b, Fig. 6a–c, 4.25.3)

- Forward reach: not less than 15 in. high and not more than 48 in. high without any obstruction or where the obstruction is less than 20 in. deep. For obstructions from 20 in. to 25 in. deep, no forward reach higher than 44 in.

- Side reach: not less than 9 in. high and not more than 54 in. high. For obstructions not more than 34 in. high or 24 in. deep, no side reach higher than 46 in.

SR-04 In a closet where passage is not required to access storage (e.g., door opening is less than 32 in.), are the clothes rod or shelves within required reach ranges? (4.25.3, Fig. 38a–b)

- Door width: at least 20 in. (4.13.5)

- Horizontal reach: not more than 21 in. from the opening.

- Rod reach: if over 10 in. deep, then not more than 48 in. high.

- Shelf reach: if over 10 in. deep, then not more than 48 in. high or less than 9 in. high.

Storage: hardware

SR-05 Is the hardware on the storage unit doors or drawers operable with one hand without tight grasping, pinching, or wrist twisting, and requiring no more than 5 lbf of force? (4.25.4, 4.27.4)

(AL) Alarms (4.28)

NOTE:

- At a minimum, visual signal appliances shall be provided in buildings and facilities in restrooms and any other general usage areas. **The ADAAG does not define the number of occupants needed to establish a general or common use area.**

ALLOWANCE:

- Emergency warning systems in medical care facilities may be modified to suit standard health care alarm design practice. [4.1.3(14)]

Alarms: general

AL-01 If emergency warning systems are provided, do they include both audible alarms and visual alarms? [4.1.3(14)]

Audible Alarms: general

AL-02 If provided, do the audible alarms meet required operational criteria? (4.28.2)

- Sound level: exceeds the prevailing sound level in the room or space by at least 15 dBA or exceeds any maximum sound level with a duration of 60 sec by 5 dBA, whichever is louder.

- Sound levels for alarm signals shall not exceed 120 dBA.

AL-03 If single station audible alarms are provided, then are single station visual alarm signals also provided? (4.28.3)

Visual Alarms: general

AL-04 If provided, are the visual alarm signal appliances integrated into the building or facility alarm system? (4.28.3)

AL-05 If provided, do the visual alarm signals meet required operational criteria? [4.28.3(1, 2, 3, 4, 5)]
- Lamp: xenon strobe type or equivalent.
- Color: clear or nominal white (i.e., unfiltered or clear filtered white light).
- Pulse duration: maximum shall be 0.2 sec with a maximum duty cycle of 40 percent.
- Intensity: not less than 75 candela.
- Flash rate: not less than 1 Hz and not more than 3 Hz.

AL-07 Are visual alarm signal appliances provided in general usage areas of the building (such as meeting rooms, corridors, and lobbies) or any other area for common use? (4.28.1)

AUTHOR'S INTERPRETATION:
- The authors identified three or more occupants as the minimum number to establish a common use area.

AL-08 Are the visual alarms placed at 80 in. above the highest floor level or 6 in. below the ceiling, whichever is lower? [4.28.3(6)]

AL-09 In spaces required to have visual alarms, are the alarms spaced properly? [4.28.3(7)]
- No place in any space should be more than 50 ft from a visual signal alarm.
- Where a space or large room exceeds 100 ft across, without obstructions 6 ft above the finished floor, visual alarms can be spaced a maximum of 100 ft apart at the perimeter, in lieu of suspending appliances from the ceiling.

AL-10 Are visual alarms placed so that no area in a common corridor or hallway is more than 50 ft from the signal? [4.28.3(8)]

Lobbies, Corridors, Interior Accessible Routes, and Exits

Introduction. This "Space-type Review Guide" is used for public, common use circulation spaces that are part of the interior accessible route. While both lobbies and corridors are usually reasonably well-defined spaces, there are other less well-defined spaces that can be reviewed with this document. These other interior accessible routes are those spaces that do not seem to belong to a particular space but are primarily used as circulation spaces. They might include designated circulation spaces in a large area using office systems or an area defined by architectural elements but not necessarily a corridor. The reviewer must develop a consistent strategy for determining what constitutes *interior space* vs. *exterior space* to ensure that spaces such as covered walkways, breezeways, balconies, or attached decks are not overlooked in the review process. Accessible routes through specialized use areas such as Auditoriums, Dining Areas, Toilet Rooms, or Dressing Rooms are covered in those specific "Space-type Review Guides."

Common circulation spaces are important because they provide the accessible link between spaces in a facility. The entrances to a facility are generally covered within this form, with the total number of required accessible entrances being tied to the number required by the fire code as well as the total number being designed into the project. Special requirements are found that relate to power assisted doors and revolving doors. Elements that provide orientation to the rest of the facility such as signage and other graphics are found within the interior accessible routes. If the signage is overhead it has specific size requirements. Accessible circulation and gathering spaces frequently contain a number of common use elements that are required to be accessible. Examples include drinking fountains, public telephones, vending and ATM machines, and public seating areas. When multiples of an item are provided, e.g., drinking fountains, fixed seating, or public telephones, refer to the individual item requirements to determine percentages and minimum number required to be accessible. These elements within the accessible route have detailed requirements for access as well as prohibitions to keep them from becoming a barrier in the form of a protruding object. On occasion uncommon items may occur in these spaces. An example we encountered several times within universities and research facilities was emergency showers and eyewash stations. The reviewer will find that type of element-based information within the "Master Guidelines."

In addition to these types of elements for public use, interior circulation and gathering spaces frequently provide for interaction between individuals. These places of interaction may in whole or part be covered by the ADA legislation. Examples of these areas or elements would be transaction counters (such as ticket counters or concession stands), reception desks, information desks, and public seating areas. Handrails are items frequently found in the lobbies and corridors of elderly housing and medical facilities. These handrails are not required to comply with ADAAG unless they are part of a ramp. However, it will add consistency to use the same criteria throughout the facility.

PRELIMINARY DESIGN OVERVIEW

(AR) Accessible Routes
- An accessible route must connect all accessible spaces and elements.

(AL) Alarms
- Visual alarms must be provided in any general usage areas, such as corridors and lobbies.

(AT) Automated Teller Machines
- If ATMs are provided, at least one must be on the accessible route and meet general accessibility requirements in clear floor space, reach range, and operation.

(BM) Business and Mercantile
- Accessible counters are required at each different area offering sales or services such as auditorium lobbies, ticket

booths, reception desks, concession stands, information counters, coat check rooms, etc. Consider different types of services such as hotel check-in counters, courtesy service counters, retail counters, etc. as different types.

- If sales and services are located in different parts of the facility, then accessible counters must be dispersed throughout the facility.

(CT) Controls and Operating Mechanisms

- Controls and operating mechanisms have clear floor space and reach range requirements. Frequently overlooked in this space-type are communication outlets, controls on window air conditioner units, thermostats, vending machines, etc.

(DF) Drinking Fountains

- Drinking fountains must serve both ambulatory and nonambulatory height requirements; this requires two different spout heights.

(DR) Doors

- Revolving doors or turnstiles require an adjacent accessible door, gate, or opening.
- Door clearance requirements must account for the depth of any panic device located on an exit door if the device is at or below the elevation of the wheels on the wheelchair; if it is above that height it is exempt. Designers should make every effort to keep this hardware to a minimum depth.
- All doors within corridors, including fire doors, must meet accessibility requirements.
- Two doors in a series must meet both clear space and door swing requirements (e.g., vestibules, toilet room entries, lobby entrances).

(EN) Entrances

- Half of all public entrances must be accessible, and at least one must be accessible on the ground floor.
- The number of accessible entrances must be equal to the number of exits required by the building/fire code.

(EX) Exits and Areas of Rescue Assistance

- Areas of rescue assistance are not required in buildings with a supervised automatic sprinkler system or in buildings undergoing alterations.

(FS) Floor Surfaces

- Surfaces should be evaluated as if wet. In particular consider spaces around exterior doors, emergency showers, eyewash stations, drinking fountains, concession stands, etc.
- Smooth floor surfaces should be evaluated for slip-resistance based on floor finish and maintenance.
- Vertical changes in levels along the accessible route can be an unforeseen barrier, e.g., transition between floor materials, and construction and expansion joints.

(HR) Handrails, Grab Bars, and Tub and Shower Seats

- Typical requirements.

(PL) Platform Lifts

- Use platform lifts in lieu of elevators only under specific conditions.

(PR) Protruding Objects

- Common wall-mounted elements can be protruding objects, e.g., shelves, upper cabinets, drinking fountains, public telephones, ATM machines, signs, mailboxes, display cases.
- Overhead clearances can be an unforeseen compliance problem, e.g., signs and banners, open space under stairs, low ceilings around concession stands and information booths, utility guy wires, etc.
- Standard fire safety items are often protruding objects, e.g., permanently mounted fire hose cabinets, fire extinguishers and fire extinguisher cabinets, valves on standpipes, etc.

(RP) Ramps

- Any slope along an accessible route greater than 1:20 (5 percent) is considered a ramp and must meet all ramp criteria.
- Handrail extensions are possible protruding objects, especially where the extensions intersect another accessible route.
- Some persons who use walking aids prefer stairs over ramps; consider including both.

(SG) Signage

- If all entrances are not accessible, the accessible entrances must be identified by the ISA symbol; nonaccessible entrances must have signage indicating the accessible route to an accessible entrance.
- Permanent directional and informational signage must meet accessibility criteria; letter height varies with mounting height of sign.
- Building directories, menus, and temporary signs are not required to comply. (This is located in ADAAG 4.1.3.16b Exceptions.)
- The majority of exit signs do not comply with the stroke height to width ratio requirements.

(SA) Space Allowances and Reach Ranges

- Typical requirements.

(ST) Stairs

- Only stairs that connect levels not connected by an elevator or other accessible means of vertical access are required to comply.
- Open risers are not permitted on accessible stairs.
- Handrail extensions are possible protruding objects, especially where the extensions intersect another accessible route.

(SR) Fixed Storage, Closets, Lockers, and Shelves

- One of each type of storage unit (shelves, dispensers, etc.) must be accessible; locked storage used only by employees may not have to be accessible.
- Frequently overlooked storage units for this space-type include coat hooks, brochure racks, mailboxes.

(SE) Fixed Tables and/or Counters
- Typical requirements.

(TL) Telephones

- When public telephones are provided, at least one must be on the accessible route and comply with all telephone requirements.

- Text telephones or equivalent facilitation may be required depending on the number of public telephones provided within the building.

- If a public interior telephone is provided, text telephones must be provided depending on the type of facility. These include stadiums; arenas; convention centers; hotels with convention centers; covered malls; and hospital emergency, recovery, and waiting rooms.

- For text telephones, specific signage is required even if a telephone is not provided.

- An accessible shelf and electrical outlet must be provided for portable text telephones if a bank of three or more interior public telephones is provided.

ADAAG APPENDIX

The ADAAG Appendix contains advisory information pertinent to this space-type.

- A.4.1.3(10)   Drinking Fountains
- A4.1.6(1)(h)   Accessible Entrances
- A4.2.1   Space Allowances and Reach Ranges
- A4.3   Accessible Routes
- A4.5   Ground and Floor Surfaces

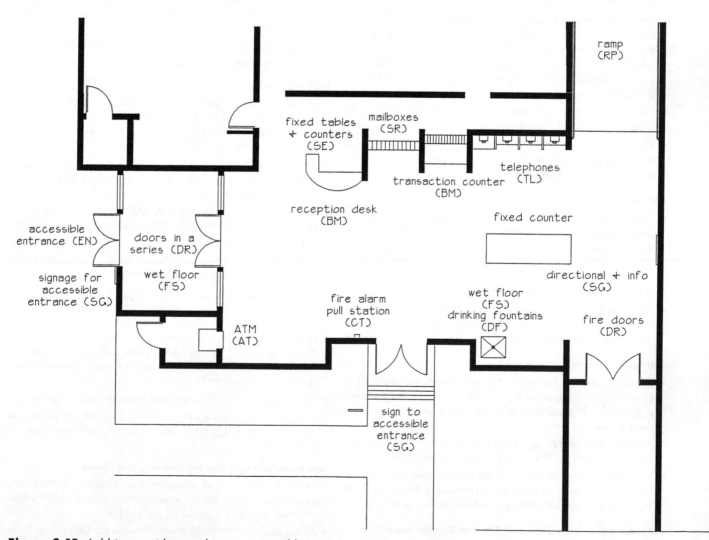

Figure 3-15. Lobbies, corridors, and interior accessible routes.

Lobbies, Corridors, Interior Accessible Routes, and Exits Checklist

SIGNAGE

SG04	Room signage: criteria
SG05	Room signage: location
SG08	Directional/informational signage: criteria
SG09	Suspended/projected signs: location

DOORS

DR01	Revolving door/turnstile
DR02	Automatic doors: ANSI standards
DR03	Automatic doors: operation
DR04	Doors: maneuvering clearances
DR05	Doors: handle type
DR06	Doors: opening force (interior only)
DR07	Doors: closing speed
DR08	Doors: thresholds
DR09	Doors: clear width/height
DR10	Openings (no door): clear width/height
DR11	Doors in series: clear space between

ENTRANCES

EN01	Acc. entrances: 50 percent accessible
EN02	Acc. entrances: ground floor
EN03	Acc. entrances: equal number of exits
EN04	Acc. entrances: public
EN05	Acc. entrances: parking garage
EN06	Acc. entrances: elevated walk or tunnel
EN07	Acc. entrances: service entrance

ACCESSIBLE ROUTES

AR06	Bldg entry to accessible spaces/elements
AR07	Dwelling unit entry to int./ext. spaces
AR08	Route: clear width
AR09	Route width: U-turns
AR10	Route: passing space
AR12	Route: running slope
AR13	Route: cross slope
AR14	Route: changes of level

BUSINESS AND MERCANTILE

BM01	Sales/service counters: accessible route
BM03	Counters w/o cash registers: criteria
BM08	Security bollards: access and egress

PROTRUDING OBJECTS

PR01	Wall-mounted
PR02	Freestanding/suspended on posts/pylons
PR03	Clear route width maintained
PR04	Overhead clearance
PR05	Vertical clearance: cane detection barrier

FLOOR AND GROUND SURFACES

FS01	Surface: firm, stable, and slip-resistant
FS02	Vertical changes in level
FS03	Carpet and tile floors
FS04	Floor gratings

EXITS AND AREAS OF RESCUE ASSISTANCE

EX01	Acc. route: egress/rescue assistance
EX02	Location and construction criteria
EX03	Clear floor space for two wheelchairs
EX04	Wheelchair spaces: total per floor
EX05	Adjacent stairway width
EX06	Two way communication: visual/audible
EX07	Signage

RAMPS

RP01	Maximum running slopes and lengths
RP02	Maximum cross slope
RP03	Minimum clear width
RP04	Landings: location
RP05	Landings: size
RP06	Landings used to change direction
RP07	Handrails: when required
RP08	Handrails: switchbacks
RP09	Handrails: extensions past ramp
RP10	Handrails: clear space to wall
RP11	Handrails: mounting height
RP12	Handrails: continuous gripping surface
RP13	Handrails: rounded end or returned
RP14	Handrails: no rotation
RP15	Ramp edge protection
RP16	Floor surface stability
RP17	Water does not accumulate

STAIRS

ST01	Riser/tread: criteria
ST02	Stair nosing: criteria
ST03	Handrails: location and continuity
ST04	Handrails: extensions
ST05	Ext. handrail is not a protruding object
ST06	Handrails: clear space to wall
ST07	Handrails: mounting height
ST08	Handrails: gripping surface uninterrupted
ST09	Handrails: rounded ends or returned
ST10	Handrails: no rotation

HANDRAILS

HR01	Handrails and grab bars: diameter
HR02	Handrails and grab bars: edge radius
HR04	Handrails in recess: criteria
HR05	Handrails and grab bars: no rotation
HR06	Handrails and grab bars: structural strength
HR07	Mounting devices: structural strength
HR10	Wall adjacent to handrail abrasion free

PLATFORM LIFTS

PL01	Able to use without assistance
PL02	Platform size
PL03	Clear floor area for entry and controls
PL04	Controls: reach ranges
PL05	Controls: operation
PL06	Platform lift on accessible route
PL07	Lift floor and adjacent route: floor criteria
PL08	Changes in level
PL09	ASME A17.1 standards

CONTROLS AND OPERATING MECHANISMS

CT01	Clear floor space
CT02	Reach ranges: elec./comm. systems
CT03	Reach ranges: thermostats

(continued)

Lobbies, Corridors, Interior Accessible Routes, and Exits Checklist (*continued*)

CT04	Reach ranges: other controls		TL03	Multiple banks: one compliant per bank
CT05	Reach ranges: life safety devices		TL04	Accessible telephone: clear floor space
CT06	Controls: operation		TL05	Accessible telephone: accessible route

DRINKING FOUNTAINS

DF01	Single unit requirements		TL06	Wall- or post-mounted: protruding objects
DF02	Multiple unit requirements		TL07	Reach ranges
DF03	Alcove location: criteria		TL08	Push-button controls where available
DF04	Unit: clear floor space		TL09	Telephone book: reach ranges
DF05	Unit: knee clearance		TL10	Handset cord: length
DF06	Unit: toe clearance		TL11	Volume control: requirements
DF07	Spout: height		TL12	Volume control: amplification
DF08	Spout: location		TL13	Telephone: hearing aid compatible
DF09	Controls: location		TL14	Four public telephones: one text
DF10	Controls: operation		TL15	Listed assembly areas: public text tele.

SPACE ALLOWANCES AND REACH RANGES

SA01	Single wheelchair passage: minimum width		TL16	Hospital locations: public text telephone
SA02	Two wheelchair passage: minimum width		TL17	No required text: equivalent facilitation
SA03	Wheelchair 180° turn: min. clear space		TL18	Text telephone: permanently mounted
SA04	Wheelchair: clear floor space		TL19	Acoustic coupler: cord length
SA05	Reach ranges: forward or side		TL20	Three interior tele.: shelf/electrical outlet
			TL21	Shelf: size requirements

STORAGE

AUTOMATED TELLER MACHINES

SR01	Accessibility: one of each type		AT01	ATM: accessible route
SR02	Clear floor space		AT02	ATM: clear floor space
SR03	Reach ranges		AT03	ATM: reach ranges
SR04	Storage closets w/o passage: criteria		AT04	ATM: transaction bins
SR05	Storage hardware: operation		AT05	ATM: controls operation
			AT06	ATM: instructions: visual impairments

FIXED OR BUILT-IN SEATING AND TABLES

ALARMS

SE01	Fixed seating: number required		AL01	Emergency warning: audible/visual
SE02	Wheelchairs: clear floor space at tables		AL02	Audible alarms: operation
SE03	Tables/counters: heights		AL03	Single station audible and visual
SE04	Tables/counters: knee clearance criteria		AL04	Visual alarms: integration w/building alarm
			AL05	Visual alarms: operation

TELEPHONES

			AL07	Visual alarms: common use areas
TL01	Single public telephone: compliance		AL08	Visual alarms: vertical placement
TL02	Public telephone bank: one compliant		AL09	Visual alarms: horizontal spacing
			AL10	Visual alarms: corridor spacing

LOBBIES, CORRIDORS, INTERIOR ACCESSIBLE ROUTES, AND EXITS COMPREHENSIVE CRITERIA

(SG) Signage (4.30)

NOTE:

- In historic buildings displays and written information, documents, etc., should be located where they can be seen by a seated person. Exhibits and signage displayed horizontally (e.g., open books) should be no higher than 44 in. above the floor surface. [4.1.7(3)(e)]

Signage: room identification (where provided)

DEFINITION:

- These signs designate permanent rooms and spaces.

AUTHOR'S INTERPRETATION:

- Signs that designate stairs, exit doors, and toilet rooms generally are associated with permanent spaces, while an "office" sign is not since the room function may change over time. Room numbers also must meet the ADAAG criteria as permanent designations, while personal names do not since the occupant may change over time.

SG-04 Do signs that designate permanent rooms and spaces comply with the following criteria? [4.1.2(7); 4.1.3(16); 4.30.4, 5, 6]

- Character type: raised and accompanied by Grade II Braille.
- Character size: between 5/8 in. and 2 in. high; raised at least 1/32 in.
- Character style: upper case, and sans or simple serif.
- Finish: characters and backgrounds have a nonglare finish.
- Contrast: characters contrast with their background (light-on-dark or dark-on-light).

SG-05 Is the room identification sign mounted in the required location? (4.30.6)

- Mounting location: installed on the wall adjacent to the latch side of the door or where wall space to the latch side of the door is not available, including double doors, placed on the nearest adjacent wall.

- Mounting height: 60 in. above the floor/ground to the centerline of the sign.
- Sign access: approach to within 3 in. of a sign without encountering protruding objects or standing within the swing of the door.

Signage: direction and information (where provided)

DEFINITION:

- Signs that provide direction to or information about functional spaces of the building.

EXCEPTION:

- Building directories, menus, and all other temporary signs are not required to comply. [4.1.3(16)]

SG-08 Do signs that provide direction to, or information about, functional spaces of the building comply with the following criteria? [4.1.2(7); 4.1.3(16); 4.30.1, 2, 3, 5]

- Character proportion: letters and numbers have a width to height ratio between 3:5 and 1:1 and a stroke width to height ratio between 1:5 and 1:10.
- Character height: sized according to viewing distance with characters on overhead signs at least 3 in. high.

NOTE:

- When the sign is mounted below 80 in., there are no prescribed character heights. Only when the sign is mounted 80 in. or higher are the characters required to be at least 3 in. high. (4.30.3)
- Finish: characters and backgrounds have a nonglare finish.
- Contrast: characters contrast with their background (light-on-dark or dark-on-light).

SG-09 Is a sign located so that the overhead clearance or the projection of a suspended or projected sign does not result in a protruding object (free-standing or wall-mounted)?

- Clear height: at least 80 in. (4.4.2, Fig. 8a)
- Overhang for free-standing signs on posts or pylons located between 27 in. and 80 in. high: no more than a 12-in. projection into accessible routes. (4.4.1, Fig. 8c)
- Overhang for wall-mounted signs between 27 in. and 80 in. high: no more than a 4-in. projection into accessible routes. (4.4.1, Fig. 8a)

(DR) Doors (4.13)

NOTE:

- Included in this category are doors, revolving doors, turnstiles, and gates.

AUTHOR'S INTERPRETATION:

- It is suggested that, for purposes of documentation and review, a door be assigned to the space it swings into. Corridors are an exception to this rule and include only entry doors into the corridor or intermediate fire doors.

Doors: revolving doors, turnstiles, and gates

DR-01 Where revolving doors or turnstiles are used on an accessible route, is an adjacent accessible gate or door provided that allows the same use pattern? (4.13.2)

Doors: automatic or power assisted

DR-02 If an automatic door or power assisted door is used, does it comply with the appropriate ANSI standard? (4.13.12)

- Automatic door: ANSI/BHMA A156.10-1985.
- Slow opening, low powered automatic door: ANSI A156.19-1984.
- Power assisted door: ANSI A156.19-1984.

DR-03 Do slow opening, low powered automatic doors or power assisted doors comply with opening and closing requirements? (4.13.12)

- Slow opening, low powered automatic doors: do not open to back-check faster than 3 sec and require no more than 15 lbf of force to stop door movement.
- Power assisted doors: no more than 5 lbf of opening force.

Doors: maneuvering clearance

DR-04 If the door is not automatic or power assisted, does it have the required maneuvering clearance provided on the push and pull side, and is the floor level and clear within the maneuvering area? (4.13.6)

- A verbal description cannot adequately describe the requirements. See ADAAG Fig. 25a–f for a graphic description.

EXCEPTION:

- Entry doors to acute care hospital bedrooms for inpatients are exempt from maneuvering space at the latch side of the door if the door is at least 44 in. wide.

AUTHOR'S INTERPRETATION:

- While ADAAG does not describe what elements can reduce the required maneuvering clearance, they could include a narrow entry alcove, an adjacent wall, railing, or permanently installed shelving, or a deep recessed door jamb.

Doors: hardware

DR-05 Do all door handles, locks, latches, or other operable devices meet required operational criteria? (4.13.9)

- Hardware operation: operable with one hand without tight grasping, pinching, or wrist twisting.
- Force required to operate the controls: not greater than 5 lbf. This does not apply to the force required to retract latch bolts or to disengage other devices that only hold the door in a closed position.
- Hardware type: "U"-shaped handles, levers, and push type mechanisms are acceptable designs.
- Hardware height: not greater than 48 in. above the floor.
- Sliding doors: hardware is exposed and usable from both sides when the doors are fully open.

Doors: opening force

DR-06 Do interior hinged doors and sliding or folding doors have an opening force of 5 lbf or less? (4.13.11)

- At present, no accessible criteria exist for exterior doors.
- Fire doors shall have the minimum opening force allowable by the appropriate administrative authority.

Doors: closing speed

DR-07 If the door has a closer, is the closer adjusted so that the door does not close too quickly? (4.13.10)

- From an open position of 70° the door will take at least 3 sec to move to a point 3 in. from the latch (measured to the leading edge of the door).

Doors: thresholds

DR-08 Where raised thresholds are provided, do they meet height limitations and are they beveled when required? (4.13.8, 4.5.2, Fig. 7)

- Threshold height: not more than 3/4 in. for exterior sliding doors or 1/2 in. for other types of doors.
- Threshold bevel: thresholds less than 1/4 in. high need no bevel; thresholds between 1/4 in. and 1/2 in. high shall be beveled at each edge with not more than a 1:2 slope.

EXCEPTION:

- A 3/4-in. high threshold is allowed in existing conditions. [4.1.6(3)(d)(ii)]

Doors: clear opening width and height

DR-09 Is the clear opening for the doorway adequate in width and height? (4.13.3, 4, 5; Fig. 24)

- Door width: at least 32 in. of clear width with the door open at 90°, measured between the face of the door and the door stop on the latch side. This also pertains to the active leaf of a double-leaf door or gate.
- Opening width: openings more than 24 in. deep must provide 36 in. of clear width.
- Height: at least 80 in. of vertical clearance.

EXCEPTIONS:

- Doors not requiring full user passage, such as shallow closets, may have the clear opening reduced to not less than 20 in.
- Where it is technically infeasible to comply with clear opening width requirements, a projection of 5/8 in. maximum will be permitted for the latch side. [4.1.6(d)(i)]

DR-10 Is the clear opening (when there is no door) adequate in width and height? (4.2.1, 4.3.3, 4.4.2)

- Width: at least 32 in. of clear width for depths 24 in. or less and at least 36 in. of clear width for depths greater than 24 in.
- Height: at least 80 in. of vertical clearance.

Doors: two doors in a series

DR-11 If there are two doors in a series, is the required clear space between the doors provided and do the doors swing in the appropriate direction? (4.13.7, Fig. 26)

- Clear space between the doors: not less than 48 in. plus the width of any door swinging into the space.
- Door swing: must swing in the same direction or away from the space between the doors.

(EN) Entrances (4.14)

EXCEPTION:

- In historic buildings, if it is determined that no entrance used by the public can comply with this section, then access at any entrance not used by the general public but open (unlocked) with directional signage at the primary entrance may be used. The accessible entrance shall also have a notification system. Where security is a problem, remote monitoring may be used. [4.1.7(3)(b)]

Entrances: general

EN-01 Are at least 50 percent of all public entrances accessible? [4.14.1, 4.1.3(8)(a)(i)]

- This does not include service or loading docks, and direct pedestrian access from enclosed parking garages, pedestrian tunnels, or elevated walkways.

EN-02 Is at least one accessible public entrance provided on the ground floor? [4.14.1, 4.1.3(8)(a)(i)]

EN-03 Is the number of accessible entrances at least equivalent to the number of exits required by the applicable fire/building codes? [4.14.1, 4.1.3(8)(a)(ii)]

- This does not require an increase in the total number of entrances planned for the facility.

EN-04 Where feasible, are the accessible entrances used by the majority of the people working and visiting the building? [4.1.3(8)(a)(iii)]

EN-05 If direct pedestrian access is provided into a building from an enclosed parking garage, is at least one accessible entrance directly from the garage provided? [4.14.1, 4.1.3(8)(b)(i)]

EN-06 If pedestrian access is provided into a building from an elevated walkway or pedestrian tunnel, is at least one accessible entrance from the walkway or tunnel provided? [4.14.1, 4.1.3(8)(b)(ii)]

EN-07 If the service entrance is the only entrance into the building or facility, is it accessible? [4.14.1, 4.1.3(8)(c)]

(AR) Accessible Routes (4.3)

NOTES:

- All walks, halls, corridors, aisles, skywalks, tunnels, and other spaces that are part of a designated accessible route shall comply with accessible requirements.
- Any slope on the accessible route that is greater than 1:20 is required to meet all ramp criteria.
- The accessible route shall, to the maximum extent feasible, coincide with the route for the general public.
- In historic buildings, accessible routes from an accessible entrance shall be provided to all publicly used spaces on at least the level of the accessible entrance. Access shall be provided to all levels of a building or facility whenever practical. [4.1.7(3)(d)]

AUTHOR'S INTERPRETATION:

- An accessible route "generally coincides" with the route used by the public if:
  — It does not force the user to go out of the way.
  — It is most like the route chosen by the general public.
  — It is direct.
  — It gives the same basic experience as the route preferred by the public.

Accessible Routes: interior

AR-06 Is the building entrance space connected by an accessible route to all accessible spaces, elements, and all accessible dwelling units within the building or facility? [4.3.2(3)]

Accessible Routes: dwelling units

AR-07 Does an accessible route connect at least one accessible entrance of each accessible dwelling unit with those exterior and interior spaces and facilities that serve the accessible unit? [4.3.2(4)]

Accessible Routes: width

AR-08 Is the minimum clear width along the accessible route adequate for continuous or point passage? (4.2.1, 4.3.3, Fig. 1, Fig. 8e, Fig. 24e)

- Continuous passage (greater than 24 in. long): at least a 36-in. clear width.
- Point passage (not more than 24 in. long): at least a 32-in. clear width.

AUTHOR'S INTERPRETATION:

- Noncompliance with this question generally relates to permanent elements that encroach on the accessible route. Large, heavy equipment that is not readily movable might be considered permanent. If the space is designed so that temporary elements (such as bikes in a bike rack or car bumpers) will consistently encroach, the situation might also be considered a permanent barrier.

AR-09 Is the minimum clear width along the accessible route adequate at a U-turn around an obstruction? (4.3.3, Fig. 7a–b)

- Obstruction 48 in. or greater: at least a 36-in. clear width around the obstruction.
- Obstruction less than 48 in.: at least a 42-in. clear width at each side with at least a 48-in. clear width in the turn.

Accessible Routes: passing space

AR-10 Does the accessible route provide at least 60 in. of clear width for two wheelchairs to pass and, if not, is the required passing space provided? (4.2.2, 4.3.4)

- A 60-in. × 60-in. passing space or "T" intersection should be provided at reasonable intervals not to exceed 200 ft.

AUTHOR'S INTERPRETATION:

- Accessible routes more than 5 ft long (e.g., routes in short hallways, aisles in laboratories, and work/storage areas) should have passing spaces provided.

DEFINITION:

- A *"T" intersection* is defined as the intersection of two corridors or walks, each at least 36 in. wide providing at least a 60-in. depth at the intersection. (Fig. 3b)

Accessible Routes: slopes

AR-12 Is the running slope on the accessible route 1:20 or less? (4.3.7)

- Any slope on the accessible route that is greater than 1:20 is required to meet all ramp criteria.

AR-13 Is the cross slope on the accessible route 1:50 or less? (4.3.7)

Accessible Routes: changes in level

AR-14 Are changes in level greater than 1/2 in. accomplished by means of a curb ramp, ramp, elevator, or platform lift (as permitted in ADAAG 4.1.3 and 4.1.6)? (4.3.8)

(BM) Business and Mercantile (7.0)

Business: general

BM-01 Are all areas used for business transactions with the public, such as sales and service counters and/or self-service displays, on an accessible route? [4.1.3(12)(b), 7.2.2]

Business: sales or service counters without cash registers

BM-03 At ticketing counters, teller stations, registration counters, and other counters for distributing goods or services to the public without cash registers, is there an accessible counter or alternative provided? (7.2.2)

- Main counter: a portion of the counter is at least 36 in. long and is not more than 36 in. high.
- Auxiliary counter: in close proximity to the main counter and not more than 36 in. high.
- Equivalent facilitation: might consist of a folding shelf attached to the main counter (for an individual with disabilities to write) and use of the space at the side of the counter for handing materials back and forth.

Business: security bollards

BM-08 Are security bollards or other such devices installed so that accessible access and egress is provided? (7.4)

NOTE:

- An alternate accessible entry that is equally convenient to that provided for the general public is acceptable.

(PR) Protruding Objects (4.4)

Protruding Objects: general

PR-01 Do wall-mounted objects having leading edges between 27 in. and 80 in. high project less than 4 in. into walkways, corridors, aisles, or paths of travel? (4.4.1, Fig. 8a–e)

- Objects mounted with their leading edge at or below 27 in. can protrude any amount, as long as they do not reduce the required clear width of an accessible route.

AUTHOR'S INTERPRETATION:

- Protruding objects might include fire extinguishers or cabinets, pencil sharpeners, shelving, counters, built-in equipment overhangs, or various dispensers such as for paper towels or soap.

PR-02 Do free-standing objects, suspended or mounted on posts or pylons with leading edges between 27 in. and 80 in. high, project less than 12 in. into the perpendicular route of travel? (4.4.1, Fig. 8a–e)

AUTHOR'S INTERPRETATION:

- These might include telephone enclosures, drinking fountains, or free-standing signage kiosks.

PR-03 Is the minimum clear route width or maneuvering space still maintained even with the projection of a protruding object? (4.4.1, Fig. 8a–e)

Protruding Objects: overhead clearance

PR-04 Is the minimum overhead clearance of 80 in. provided in accessible areas or along accessible routes? (4.4.2, Fig. 8a)

AUTHOR'S INTERPRETATION:

- Overhead objects that can reduce the required clearance might include structures, pipes, ducts, or light fixtures.

PR-05 Where the vertical clearance of a space adjoining the accessible route is less than 80 in. high, is a cane detection barrier less than 27 in. from the floor provided for blind or visually impaired persons? (4.4.2, Fig. 8c-1)

AUTHOR'S INTERPRETATION:

- This condition might be found under a stair, at a sloped ceiling space, or with guy wires from telephone poles along an exterior accessible route.

(FS) Floor and Ground Surfaces (4.5)

Floor Surfaces: general

FS-01 Are the floor/ground surfaces on the accessible route stable, firm, and slip-resistant? (4.5.1)

AUTHOR'S INTERPRETATION:

- Exterior spaces, interior circulation, bathrooms, and other spaces where water can collect on the floor around an element (sinks, drinking fountains, hose bibbs, etc.) are reviewed as if wet.
- High gloss surfaces without significant textures that are regularly maintained with waxing (smooth tiles, waxed concrete, etc.) could be considered noncompliant.
- Accessible criteria are not specified for nonpermanent floor surfaces such as mats or rugs.

Floor Surfaces: changes in level

FS-02 Are vertical changes in level between 1/4 in. and 1/2 in. beveled with a slope of 1:2 or less? (4.5.2)

- Changes in level up to 1/4 in. may be vertical without edge treatment.
- Changes in level greater than 1/2 in. should be accomplished by means of a curb ramp, ramp, elevator, or platform lift (as permitted in ADAAG 4.1.3 and 4.1.6).

Floor Surfaces: carpet

FS-03 Does carpet or carpet tile used on the floor comply with accessible criteria? (4.5.3, Fig. 8f)

- Attachment: secured.
- Exposed edges: fastened and trimmed along the entire length.
- Pile type: low pile (1/2 in. maximum).
- Padding: firm pad or no pad underneath.

Floor Surfaces: gratings

FS-04 Do floor gratings in the path of travel comply with accessible criteria? (4.5.4, Fig. 8g–h)

- Opening size: no greater than 1/2 in. in one direction.
- Opening direction: the long dimension is perpendicular to the dominant direction of travel.

(EX) Exits and Areas of Rescue Assistance (4.3.11)

DEFINITIONS:

- *Area of Rescue Assistance:* An area with direct access to an exit where people who are unable to use stairs may remain temporarily in safety to await further instructions or assistance during emergency evacuation.
- *Means of Egress:* A continuous and unobstructed way of exit travel from any point in a building or facility to a public way. A means of egress comprises vertical and horizontal travel and may include intervening room spaces, doorways, hallways, corridors, passageways, balconies, ramps, stairs, enclosures, lobbies, horizontal exits, courts, and yards. An accessible means of egress is one that complies with these guidelines and does not include stairs, steps, or escalators. Areas of rescue assistance or evacuation elevators may be included as part of accessible means of egress.

EXCEPTIONS:

- New construction: Areas of rescue assistance are not required in buildings or facilities having a supervised automatic sprinkler system. [4.1.3(9)]
- Alterations: Alterations are not required to provide an area of rescue assistance. [4.1.6(1)(g)]

ALLOWANCE:

- New construction: A horizontal exit can be used as an area of rescue assistance when the exit is designed in accordance with the local building code. [4.1.3(9)]

Exits: number required

EX-01 Does each occupiable level of a building or facility that is required to be accessible have accessible means of egress equal to the number of exits required by local building/life safety regulations? [4.1.3(9)]

- Where a required exit is not accessible, areas of rescue assistance shall be provided equal to the number of inaccessible required exits. [4.1.3(9)]

Areas of Rescue Assistance: location and construction

EX-02 Is each of the areas of rescue assistance located and constructed in compliance with the following criteria as well as local building requirements? [4.3.11(1)]

- The general scope for seven different types of areas of rescue assistance allowed follow. See ADAAG 4.3.11(1) for specific details for each type.

— A portion of a stairway landing within a smokeproof enclosure.

— A portion of an exterior exit balcony located immediately adjacent to an exit stairway.

— A portion of a one-hour fire-resistive corridor located immediately adjacent to an exit enclosure.

— A vestibule located immediately adjacent to an exit enclosure and constructed to the same fire-resistive standards as required for corridors and openings.

— A portion of a stairway landing within an exit enclosure that is vented to the exterior and is separated from the interior of the building with not less than one-hour fire-resistive doors.

— A smokeproof, one-hour fire-resistive room provided with direct access to a one-hour exit enclosure.

— An elevator lobby when elevator shafts and adjacent lobbies are pressurized as required for smokeproof enclosures.

Areas of Rescue Assistance: wheelchair criteria

EX-03 Does each area of rescue assistance provide space for at least two wheelchairs? [4.3.11(2)]

- Each of the two wheelchair spaces is not less than 30 in. × 48 in. and does not encroach on any required exit width.

EX-04 Is the total number of required wheelchair spaces per story provided? [4.3.11(2)]

- Total spaces per floor: not fewer than one for every 200 persons of calculated occupant load being served by the area of rescue assistance.

EXCEPTION:

- The appropriate administrative authority may reduce the minimum number to only one for each area of rescue assistance on floors where the occupant load is less than 200.

EX-05 Is each stairway serving an area of rescue assistance at least 48 in. wide between handrails? [4.3.11(3)]

Areas of Rescue Assistance: communications and signage

EX-06 Is a method of two-way communication, with both visual and audible signals, provided between each area of rescue assistance and the primary entry? [4.3.11(4)]

- The fire department or appropriate administrative authority may approve a location other than the primary entry.

EX-07 Does signage relating to areas of rescue assistance meet the criteria listed below? [4.3.11(5)]

- Each area is identified by an illuminated sign (if exit signs are required to be illuminated) which states "AREA OF RESCUE ASSISTANCE" and displays the International Symbol of Accessibility.

- Signage is installed at all inaccessible exits and where otherwise necessary to indicate the direction to areas of rescue assistance.

- Instructions are provided on the use of the area during emergencies and are posted adjacent to the two-way communication system.

(RP) Ramps (4.8)

NOTE:

- Any slope on the accessible route that is greater than 1:20 is considered a ramp and shall comply with accessible requirements.

Ramps: slopes and rises

RP-01 Is the running slope for the ramp within required parameters? (4.8.2, Fig. 16)

- New construction: 1:12 slope or less with not more than a 30-in. rise for any run.
  - 1:12 slope: 30-ft run between landings.
  - 1:16 slope: 40-ft run between landings.
- On existing sites where space limitations prohibit the use of a slope of 1:12 or less, the following slopes can be considered. [4.1.6(3)(a)(i–ii)]
  - Between 1:10 and 1:12 for a maximum rise of 6 in.
  - Between 1:8 and 1:10 for a maximum rise of 3 in.
  - A slope steeper than 1:8 is not allowed.

EXCEPTION:

- In historic buildings, a ramp with a slope no greater than 1:6 for a run not to exceed 2 ft may be used as part of an accessible route to an entrance. [4.1.7(3)(a)]

RP-02 Is the cross slope of the ramp 1:50 or less? (4.8.6)

Ramps: clear width

RP-03 Is the clear width (between handrails) of the ramp at least 36 in.? (4.8.3)

Ramps: landings

RP-04 Is there a level landing at the top and bottom of each ramp and each ramp run? (4.8.4)

- If a doorway is located at a landing, then the area in front of the doorway must meet door maneuvering clearance requirements.

RP-05 Does each ramp landing meet required dimensions? [4.8.4(1–2)]

- Landing width: at least equal to the ramp width.
- Landing length: at least 60 in. long.

RP-06 Where the ramp changes direction, is there a landing of at least 60-in. × 60-in.? [4.8.4(3)]

Ramps: handrails

NOTE:

- Additional criteria for handrails can be found in Section "HR, Handrails."

RP-07 If the ramp rises more than 6 in. or is longer than 72 in., does it have a handrail on each side? (4.8.5)

- Handrails are not required on curb ramps or adjacent to seating in assembly areas.

RP-08 Is the handrail provided on both sides of ramp segments and is the inside rail on switchback or dogleg ramps continuous? [4.8.5(1), Fig. 19a–b]

RP-09 At the end of the ramp handrails, is there at least 12 in. of handrail parallel to the floor or ground surface, extending beyond the top and the bottom of the ramp segments? [4.8.5(2), Fig. 17]

RP-10 Is the clearance between the ramp handrail and the wall exactly 1½ in.? [4.8.5(3)]

- For recesses, see ADAAG Fig. 39.

RP-11 Are the tops of ramp handrails between 34 in. and 38 in. above ramp surfaces? [4.8.5(5)]

RP-12 Is the ramp handrail gripping surface continuous without obstructions or missing segments? [4.8.5(4)]

RP-13 Are the ends of ramp handrails rounded or returned smoothly to the floor, wall, or post? [4.8.5(6)]

RP-14 Are the ramp handrails fixed so that they do not rotate within their fittings? [4.8.5(7)]

Ramps: edge protection and floor surfaces

RP-15 If a ramp or landing has a drop-off, is it protected by an acceptable option? (4.8.7, Fig. 17)

- Acceptable options include: a wall, a minimum 12-in. horizontal floor extension beyond the railing, a minimum 2-in. curb, or a railing design that prevents people from falling or rolling off.

RP-16 Is the ramp floor surface stable, firm, and slip-resistant? (4.5.1)

RP-17 Are outdoor ramps and their approaches designed so that water does not accumulate on walking surfaces? (4.8.8)

(ST) Stairs (4.9)

NOTE:

- Only stairs that connect levels not connected by an elevator, ramp, or other accessible means of vertical access are required to comply. [4.1.3(4)]
  - In new construction, this condition may occur in facilities subject to the elevator exemption [4.1.3(5)—Exception 1] or where mezzanines are exempt in restaurants. (5.4)

Stairs: risers, treads, and nosings

ST-01 Do the stair treads and risers meet the required criteria? (4.9.2, Fig. 18a)

- Uniformity: riser heights and tread widths should remain uniform in any one flight of stairs.
- Treads: not less than 11 in. measured from riser to riser.
- Risers: no open risers are permitted.

ST-02 Do the stair nosings meet the required criteria? See ADAAG Fig. 18 for clarification. (4.9.3)

- Risers: risers slope toward the nosing.
- Radius of the curvature: not more than 1/2-in. radius at the leading edge of the tread.
- Angle nosing: angled underside on nosing is not less than 60° from the horizontal; underside of nosing should not be abrupt.
- Nosing projection: not more than 1½ in.

Stairs: handrails

NOTE:

- Additional criteria for handrails can be found in Section "HR, Handrails."

ST-03 Is the handrail provided on both sides of the stair and is the inside rail on switchback or dogleg stairs continuous at the landing? [4.9.4(1), Fig. 19a–b]

- The outside handrail along the perimeter wall does not have to be continuous around the landing.

ST-04 At the end of the stair handrails, is there at least 12 in. of handrail parallel to the floor beyond the top riser and is there at least one tread width of sloping handrail plus at least 12 in. of horizontal handrail beyond the bottom riser? [4.9.4(2), Fig. 19c–d]

- See ADAAG Fig. 19c–d for extension design.

ST-05 If the handrail extension protrudes into an accessible route, is the handrail extension rounded to 27 in. or less from the floor so that it does not create a protruding object? [4.9.4(2)]

ST-06 Is the clearance between the stair handrail and the wall exactly 1½ in.? [4.9.4(3)]

ST-07 Are the tops of stair handrails between 34 in. and 38 in. above the stair nosing? [4.9.4(5)]

ST-08 Is the stair handrail gripping surface uninterrupted by newel posts, other obstructions, or missing segments? [4.9.4(4)]

ST-09 Are the ends of stair handrails rounded or returned smoothly to the floor, wall, or post? [4.9.4(6)]

ST-10 Are handrails fixed so that they do not rotate within their fittings? [4.9.4(7)]

(HR) Handrails, Grab Bars, and Tub and Shower Seats (4.26)

NOTE:

- HR Guidelines may be repeated in other element-based guidelines: (RP) Ramps, (ST) Stairs, (WC) Water Closets, (TS) Toilet Stalls, (BT) Bathtubs, and (SS) Shower Stalls.

Handrails: size and spacing

HR-01 Is the gripping surface of the grab bars or handrails 1¼ in. to 1½ in. in outside diameter? (4.26.2, Fig. 39)

AUTHOR'S INTERPRETATION:

- Standard pipe sizes designated by the industry as 1¼ in. to 1½ in. are acceptable for purposes of this section.

HR-02 Do the grab bars or handrails have edges with a minimum radius of 1/8 in.? (4.26.4)

HR-04 If the handrail is located in a recess, is the recess a maximum of 3 in. deep extending at least 18 in. above the rail? (4.26.2, Fig. 39d)

Handrails: grab bar or handrail structural strength

HR-05 Are the grab bars or handrails secure so that they do not rotate in their fittings? [4.26.3(5)]

HR-06 Do the grab bars and handrails meet the structural strength requirements for bending stress and shear stress? (4.26.3)

- Actual bending stress in the grab bar induced by the maximum bending moment from the application of 250 lbf is less than the allowable bending stress for the material of the grab bar.

- Shear stress induced in a grab bar by the application of 250 lbf shall be less than the allowable shear stress for the material of the grab bar. If the connection between the grab bar and its mounting bracket or other support is considered to be fully restrained, then direct and torsional shear stresses shall be totaled for the combined shear stress, which shall not exceed the allowable shear stress.

HR-07 Do the fasteners and mounting devices for the grab bars or handrails meet the structural strength requirements for shear force and tensile force? (4.26.3)

- Shear force induced in a fastener or mounting device from the application of 250 lbf shall be less than the allowable lateral load of either the fastener or mounting device or the supporting structure, whichever is the smaller allowable load.
- Tensile force induced in a fastener by a direct tension force of 250 lbf plus the maximum moment from the application of 250 lbf shall be less than the allowable withdrawal load between the fastener and the supporting structure.

Handrails: hazards

HR-10 Are handrails or grab bars and any wall or other surfaces adjacent to them free of any sharp or abrasive elements? (4.26.4)

(PL) Platform Lifts (4.11)

EXCEPTIONS:

- New construction elevator exceptions [4.1.3(5)]:
  — *Exception 4:* Platform lifts (wheelchair lifts) complying with ADAAG 4.11 and applicable state or local codes may be used in lieu of an elevator only under the following conditions:
    a. To provide an accessible route to a performing area in an assembly occupancy.
    b. To comply with the wheelchair viewing position line-of-sight and dispersion requirements of ADAAG 4.33.3.
    c. To provide access to incidental occupiable spaces and rooms that are not open to the general public and that house no more than five persons, including, but not limited to, equipment control rooms and projection booths.
    d. To provide access where existing site constraints or other constraints make use of a ramp or an elevator infeasible.

Platform Lifts: general

PL-01 Can the lift be entered, operated, and exited without assistance? (4.11.3)

PL-02 Is the lift platform at least 30 in. × 48 in.? (4.11.2, 4.2.4)

PL-03 Is there at least a 30-in. × 48-in. clear floor area provided for both entry to the lift and access to the controls? (4.11.2, 4.2.4)

Platform Lifts: controls

PL-04 Are the platform controls within acceptable reach ranges for forward or side approach? (4.11.2, 4.2.5–6, Fig. 5a–b, Fig. 6a–c)

- Forward reach: not less than 15 in. high and not more than 48 in. high without any obstruction or where the obstruction is less than 20 in. deep. For obstructions from 20 in. to 25 in. deep, no forward reach higher than 44 in.
- Side reach: not less than 9 in. high and not more than 54 in. high. For obstructions not more than 34 in. high or 24 in. deep, no side reach higher than 46 in.

PL-05 Are controls operable with one hand without tight grasping, pinching, or wrist twisting, and requiring no more than 5 lbf of force? (4.11.2, 4.27.4)

Platform Lifts: accessible route

PL-06 Is the lift on an accessible route? [4.1.2(1), 4.3.2]

PL-07 Is the floor of the lift and the adjacent accessible route stable, firm, and slip-resistant? (4.11.2, 4.5.1)

PL-08 Between the edge of the platform lift and the accessible route, are vertical changes in level between 1/4 in. and 1/2 in. beveled with a slope of 1:2 or less? (4.11.2, 4.5.2)

- Changes in level: up to 1/4 in. may be vertical without edge treatment.

Platform Lifts: safety code

PL-09 Does the lift meet the ASME A17.1 Safety Code for Elevators and Escalators, Section XX, 1990? (4.11.2)

(CT) Controls and Operating Mechanisms (4.27)

NOTES:

- Controls or operating mechanisms can include elements such as light switches, pencil sharpeners, manual overhead screens, nonkeyed thermostats, alarm pull stations, fire extinguisher cabinets, A/C window units, microwave ovens, towel dispensers, and wall hooks.
- If controls are to be operated by occupants of the space, they must be accessible. If controls are to be operated by maintenance staff only and not by occupants or other users of the space, they do not have to be accessible. For example, thermostats in auditoriums usually do not have to be accessible, while thermostats in classrooms may need to be accessible.

Controls: clear floor space

CT-01 Is a clear floor space of at least 30 in. × 48 in. provided in front of controls, dispensers, receptacles, and other operable equipment for forward or parallel approach? (4.27.2, Fig. 4a–b)

Controls: reach ranges

NOTES:

- Accessible reach ranges for controls and operating mechanisms are:
  — Forward reach: not less than 15 in. high and not more than 48 in. high without any obstruction or where the obstruction is less than 20 in. deep. For

obstructions from 20 in. to 25 in. deep, no forward reach higher than 44 in.

— Side reach: not less than 9 in. high and not more than 54 in. high. For obstructions not more than 34 in. high or 24 in. deep, no side reach higher than 46 in.

— Electrical outlets, switches, and communication system receptacles have a minimum outlet height of 15 in. regardless of forward or side reach. See CT-02 below.

CT-02 Are electrical outlets, switches, and communication system receptacles mounted within accessible forward or side reach ranges? (4.27.3)

EXCEPTION:

- These requirements do not apply where the use of special equipment dictates otherwise or where electrical and communications system receptacles are not normally intended for use by building occupants. (4.27.3)

CT-03 Are thermostats or other similar operable equipment mounted within accessible forward or side reach ranges? (4.2.5, 4.2.6, Fig. 5a–b, Fig. 6a–c)

CT-04 Are dispensers or other similar operable equipment mounted within accessible forward or side reach ranges? (4.2.5, 4.2.6, Fig. 5a–b, Fig. 6a–c)

CT-05 Are life safety devices or other similar operable equipment mounted within accessible forward or side reach ranges? (4.2.5, 4.2.6, Fig. 5a–b, Fig. 6a–c)

NOTE:

- This might include fire alarm pull stations, handles to extinguisher cabinets, or wall-mounted extinguishers.

Controls: operation

CT-06 Are controls, dispensers, receptacles, and other operable equipment operable with one hand without tight grasping, pinching, or wrist twisting, and requiring no more than 5 lbf of force? (4.27.4)

(DF) Drinking Fountains and Water Coolers (4.15)

Drinking Fountains: minimum number

DF-01 Where only one drinking fountain is provided on a floor, is it on an accessible route and is it accessible to both wheelchair users and to persons having difficulty stooping or bending? [4.1.3(10)(a)]

- Drinking fountains are required to be accessible to both wheelchair users (accessible height fountain) and persons having difficulty stooping or bending (standard height fountain).

NOTE:

- Alternate solutions might include a high-low fountain or an accessible height fountain and a water cooler with cups. [4.1.3(10)(a)]

DF-02 Where more than one drinking fountain is provided on a floor, do at least 50 percent but not fewer than one of the fountains meet accessible criteria, and is each accessible fountain on an accessible route? [4.1.3(10)(b)]

- Drinking fountains are required to be accessible to both wheelchair users (accessible height fountain) and persons having difficulty stooping or bending (standard height fountain).

Drinking Fountains: clearances and clear floor space

DF-03 If the accessible drinking fountain is located in an alcove, is the alcove adequate in depth and width? (4.15.5, Fig. 27b)

- Depth: not more than 24 in. deep.
- Width: at least 30 in. wide.

DF-04 Is a clear floor space at least 30 in. × 48 in. provided at accessible drinking fountains? [4.15.5(1, 2); Fig. 27b]

DF-05 Does the knee clearance space for wall- and post-mounted cantilevered accessible drinking fountains meet required criteria? (4.15.5, Fig. 27)

- Height: at least 27 in. high from the floor to the apron bottom and maintaining that height for at least 8 in. under the equipment.
- Width: at least 30 in. wide.
- Depth: between 17 in. and 19 in. deep.

NOTE:

- Wall-mounted fountains with leading edges between 27 in. and 80 in. are protruding objects if they project more than 4 in. into the accessible route. A leading edge at 27 in. or below can project any amount as long as it does not restrict the required clear width of the route. (4.4.1)

AUTHOR'S INTERPRETATION:

- If a water fountain is going to protrude more than 4 in. into an accessible route, then it must be mounted at exactly 27 in. in order to comply with required knee clearances and not be considered a protruding object.

DF-06 Is toe clearance at the base of the accessible drinking fountain at least 9 in. high and not more than 6 in. deep? (4.15.5, Fig. 27)

- See ADAAG Fig. 27 for the permitted equipment or piping area.

Drinking Fountains: spout location

DF-07 Is the accessible drinking fountain spout outlet no higher than 36 in. from the ground or floor? (4.15.2, Fig. 27)

DF-08 Is the spout located near the front of the fountain and does it meet required water flow criteria? (4.15.3)

- Water flow trajectory: nearly parallel to the front edge and at least 4 in. high to allow the insertion of a cup or glass.
- Fountain with a round or oval bowl: flow of water is within 3 in. of the front edge.

Drinking Fountains: controls

DF-09 Are the accessible drinking fountain controls front-mounted and/or side-mounted near the front edge? (4.15.4)

DF-10 Are the accessible drinking fountain controls operable with one hand without tight grasping, pinching, or wrist twisting, and requiring no more than 5 lbf of force? (4.15.4)

(SA) Space Allowance and Reach Ranges (4.2)

NOTE:

- SA guidelines deal with wheelchair passage space, maneuvering space, clear floor space, and reach ranges. While this element is found in the ADAAG, the SA code generally is not used in the space-forms because all of these criteria are included in other element-based guidelines such as (SR) Storage, (CT) Controls and Operating Mechanisms, (SS) Shower Stalls, etc.

Space Allowance

SA-01 Is the minimum clear width along the accessible route adequate for continuous or point passage? (4.2.1, 4.3.3, Fig. 1, Fig. 8e, Fig. 24e)

- Continuous passage (greater than 24 in. long): at least a 36-in. clear width.
- Point passage (not more than 24 in. long): at least a 32-in. clear width.

AUTHOR'S INTERPRETATION:

- Noncompliance with this question generally relates to permanent elements that encroach on the accessible route. Large, heavy equipment that is not readily movable might be considered permanent. If the space is designed so that temporary elements (such as bikes in a bike rack or car bumpers) will consistently encroach, the situation might also be considered a permanent barrier.

SA-02 Does the accessible route provide at least 60 in. of clear width for two wheelchairs to pass and, if not, is the required passing space provided? (4.2.2, 4.3.4)

- A 60-in. × 60-in. passing space or "T" intersection should be provided at reasonable intervals not to exceed 200 ft.

AUTHOR'S INTERPRETATION:

- ADAAG does not state that a route must maintain continuous clear passage for two wheelchairs, but it does require that if a clear width of 60 in. is not maintained, an accessible route more than 5 ft in length must have a passing space provided.

DEFINITION:

- A *"T" intersection* is defined as the intersection of two corridors or walks, each at least 36 in. wide providing at least a 60-in. depth at the intersection. (Fig. 3b)

SA-03 Is the minimum clear floor space for an unobstructed 180° wheelchair turning space or a "T"-shaped turning space provided? (4.2.3, Fig. 3a–b)

- 180° turning space: at least a 60-in. diameter.
- "T"-shaped turning space: at least 36-in. wide legs with a minimum length of 60 in.

SA-04 Is the clear floor space for a wheelchair at least 30 in. × 48 in.? [4.2.4(1), Fig. 4a]

- The clear floor space can extend up to 19 in. under some elements if adequate knee clearance is provided.

Reach Ranges

SA-05 Are forward or side reach within acceptable ranges? (4.2.5–6, Fig. 5a–b, Fig. 6a–c)

- Forward reach: not less than 15 in. high and not more than 48 in. high without any obstruction or where the obstruction is less than 20 in. deep. For obstructions from 20 in. to 25 in. deep, no forward reach higher than 44 in.
- Side reach: not less than 9 in. high and not more than 54 in. high. For obstructions not more than 34 in. high or 24 in. deep, no side reach higher than 46 in.

EXCEPTION:

- These requirements do not apply where the use of special equipment dictates otherwise or where electrical and communications system receptacles are not normally intended for use by building occupants. (4.27.3)

(SR) Storage (4.25)

NOTE:

- Accessible reach range requirements do not apply to shelves or display units allowing self-service by customers in mercantile occupancies but they must be located on an accessible route. [4.1.3(12)(b)]

Storage: general

SR-01 Does at least one of each type of fixed or built-in storage unit comply with accessible criteria? [4.1.3(12)(a), 4.25.1]

NOTE:

- Types of storage facilities might include cabinets, shelves, closets, and drawers.

Storage: clear floor space

SR-02 Is there a clear floor space at least 30 in. × 48 in. at fixed or built-in storage units that allows for either a forward or side approach? (4.25.2, Fig. 4a–b)

Storage: reach ranges

SR-03 Are forward or side reach for each type of accessible storage unit within acceptable reach ranges? (4.2.5–6, Fig. 5a–b, Fig. 6a–c, 4.25.3)

- Forward reach: not less than 15 in. high and not more than 48 in. high without any obstruction or where the obstruction is less than 20 in. deep. For obstructions from 20 in. to 25 in. deep, no forward reach higher than 44 in.
- Side reach: not less than 9 in. high and not more than 54 in. high. For obstructions not more than 34 in. high or 24 in. deep, no side reach higher than 46 in.

SR-04 In a closet where passage is not required to access storage (e.g., door opening is less than 32 in.), are the clothes rod or shelves within required reach ranges? (4.25.3, Fig. 38a–b)

- Door width: at least 20 in. (4.13.5)
- Horizontal reach: not more than 21 in. from the opening.
- Rod reach: if over 10 in. deep, then not more than 48 in. high.

- Shelf reach: if over 10 in. deep, then not more than 48 in. high or less than 9 in. high.

Storage: hardware

SR-05 Is the hardware on the storage unit doors or drawers operable with one hand without tight grasping, pinching, or wrist twisting, and requiring no more than 5 lbf of force? (4.25.4, 4.27.4)

(SE) Fixed or Built-in Seating and Tables (4.32)

Fixed or Built-in Seating and Tables: minimum number

SE-01 Is the minimum number of accessible wheelchair seating locations at fixed tables or counters provided? (4.1.3.18)

- Number required: 5 percent of total number of seats but not fewer than one.

Fixed or Built-in Seating and Tables: clear floor space

AUTHOR'S INTERPRETATION:

- Where the accessible route leads to and through accessible seating adjacent to a wall or another table, the minimum required width for the accessible route will be 65 in. between the table edge and next parallel surface (e.g., wall or another table edge). (4.1.3.18, Fig. 45)

SE-02 Is the clear floor space for a wheelchair at a seating location adequate? (4.32.3, Fig. 4a, Fig. 45)

- Clear floor space: 30 in. × 48 in.
- This clear space can include up to 19 in. under the table/desk.

Fixed or Built-in Seating and Tables: clearances

SE-03 Are the tops of accessible tables and counters between 28 in. and 34 in. from the floor? (4.32.3, Fig. 45)

SE-04 Are the knee clearances at least 27 in. high, 30 in. wide, and 19 in. deep? (4.32.3, Fig. 45)

(TL) Telephones (4.31)

DEFINITION:

- Telephone types include public pay telephones, public closed circuit telephones, or other public telephones.

NOTE:

- Signage related to telephones is found in App. C, "Master Guidelines," "SG, 10-14."

AUTHOR'S INTERPRETATION:

- Frequently, public pay telephones are provided by a contractual agreement with a vendor. The vendor, through the contract, might be made responsible for compliance with all applicable ADAAG criteria.

Telephones: number required

TL-01 If there is only one public telephone on a floor, does it comply with accessible criteria? [4.1.3(17)(a)]

- Unless otherwise specified, accessible telephones may be either forward or side reach telephones.

TL-02 If there is a single bank of public telephones on a floor, does at least one of the telephones in the bank comply with accessible criteria? [4.1.3(17)(a)]

- A bank consists of two or more adjacent public telephones, often installed as a unit.

- Unless otherwise specified, accessible telephones may be either forward or side reach telephones.

TL-03 Where two or more banks of public telephones are provided on a floor, is at least one accessible telephone provided at each bank or within proximity to the bank and does at least one of these accessible telephones comply with forward reach criteria? [4.1.3(17)(a)]

EXCEPTION:

- For exterior installations only, if dial tone first service is available, then a side reach telephone may be installed instead of the required forward reach telephone.

Telephones: clear floor or ground space

TL-04 Does the accessible telephone have at least a 30-in. × 48-in. clear floor or ground space that allows either a forward or side approach? (4.31.2, Fig. 44, 4.2.4)

- Bases, enclosures, and fixed seats shall not impede approaches to telephones.
- If this clear floor space is located in an alcove or confined space, see ADAAG Fig. 4d–e for additional maneuvering clearance requirements.

TL-05 Does an accessible route adjoin or overlap the clear floor space for the accessible telephone? (4.31.2, Fig. 44, 4.2.4)

Telephones: protruding object

TL-06 Do wall-mounted or post-mounted telephones with leading edges between 27 in. and 80 in. from the floor have projections that do not result in a protruding object? (4.31.4, 4.4.1)

- Wall-mounted: project less than 4 in. into the pathway.
- Post-mounted: project less than 12 in. into a perpendicular route of travel.

Telephones: mounting height

TL-07 Is the highest operable part of the telephone within forward or side reach ranges? (4.31.3, 4.2.6)

- Forward: not more than 48 in. above the floor.
- Side: not more than 54 in. above the floor.

Telephones: push-button controls

TL-08 Does the telephone have push-button controls where such service is available? (4.31.6)

Telephones: telephone book

TL-09 Is the telephone book, if provided, located in a position that complies with forward or side reach ranges? (4.31.7)

- Forward: not more than 48 in. above the floor.
- Side: not more than 54 in. above the floor.

Telephones: cord length

TL-10 Is the cord from the telephone to the handset at least 29 in. long? (4.31.8)

Telephones: volume control and hearing aid compatibility

TL-11 Do the public telephones comply with volume control requirements? [4.1.3(17)(b)]

- Each accessible telephone is equipped with a volume control.
- In addition, 25 percent, but not fewer than one, of all other public telephones should be equipped with volume controls and dispersed among all types of public telephones.

TL-12 Are volume controls capable of amplification between 12 dbA and 18 dbA above normal? [4.31.5(2)]

- If an automatic reset button is provided, the maximum of 18 dbA may be exceeded.

TL-13 Are telephones hearing aid compatible? [4.31.5(1)]

Telephones: text telephones

TL-14 If a total of four or more public pay telephones (including both interior and exterior phones) are provided at a site and at least one is in an interior location, is at least one interior public text telephone provided? [4.1.3(17)(c)(i)]

TL-15 If an interior public pay telephone is provided in a stadium or arena, convention center, a hotel with a convention center, or a covered mall, is at least one interior public text telephone provided in the facility? [4.1.3(17)(c)(ii)]

TL-16 If there is a public pay telephone in or adjacent to a hospital emergency room, a hospital recovery room, or a hospital waiting room, is there a public text telephone in each such location? [4.1.3(17)(c)(iii)]

TL-17 If a required text telephone is not provided, is equivalent facilitation provided? [4.31.9(3)]

- A portable text telephone may be made available in a hotel at the registration desk if it is available on a 24-hour basis for use with nearby public pay telephones that can accommodate the accessible requirements for a portable text telephone.

TL-18 Is a required text telephone permanently mounted within, or adjacent to, the telephone enclosure? (4.31.9)

TL-19 If an acoustic coupler is used, is the telephone cord long enough to allow connection of the text telephone to the telephone receiver? [4.31.9(1)]

TL-20 If there are three or more telephones in an interior bank of telephones, does at least one telephone have a shelf and electrical outlet for use with a portable text telephone? [4.1.3(17)(d)]

TL-21 Is the shelf large enough to accommodate a text telephone, provide at least 6 in. of vertical clearance, and allow the telephone handset to be placed flush on the surface of the shelf? [4.31.9(2)]

(AT) Automated Teller Machines (4.34)

NOTES:

- Each automated teller machine required to be accessible shall be on an accessible route.
- Where one or more automated teller machines (ATMs) are provided, at least one must comply with ADAAG 4.34. [4.1.3(20)]

EXCEPTION:

- Drive-up-only automated teller machines are not required to comply with ADAAG 4.27.2 (clear floor space) and ADAAG 4.27.3 (reach ranges). [4.1.3(20)]

Automated Teller Machines: accessible route

AT-01 Is each accessible ATM located on an accessible route? (4.34.1)

Automated Teller Machines: clear floor space

AT-02 Is clear floor space of at least 30 in. × 48 in. provided for a forward or parallel approach to the accessible ATM? (4.34.2, Fig. 4a–c)

Automated Teller Machines: reach ranges

AT-03 Is the highest operable part of the controls on the accessible ATM within the required reach ranges for forward or parallel approach? [4.34.3(1), 4.34.3(2)]

- Forward reach: not less than 15 in. high and not more than 48 in. high without any obstruction or where the obstruction is less than 20 in. deep. For obstructions from 20 in. to 25 in. deep, no forward reach higher than 44 in.
- Side reach:
  — Reach depth not more than 10 in.: not more than 54 in. high above the floor or grade.
  — Reach depth more than 10 in.:
    11 in. depth: not more than 53½ in. high
    12 in. depth: not more than 53 in. high
    13 in. depth: not more than 52½ in. high
    14 in. depth: not more than 51½ in. high
    15 in. depth: not more than 51 in. high
    16 in. depth: not more than 50½ in. high
    17 in. depth: not more than 50 in. high
    18 in. depth: not more than 49½ in. high
    19 in. depth: not more than 49 in. high
    20 in. depth: not more than 48½ in. high
    21 in. depth: not more than 47½ in. high
    22 in. depth: not more than 47 in. high
    23 in. depth: not more than 46½ in. high
    24 in. depth: not more than 46 in. high

EXCEPTION:

- Where a function can be performed in an equivalent manner by using an alternate control, only one of the controls is required to comply. If the controls are identified by tactile markings, such markings shall be provided on both controls.

AT-04 Where bins are provided for envelopes, wastepaper, or other purposes, is at least one of each type provided within the required reach ranges for forward or parallel approach? [4.34.3(4)]

Automated Teller Machines: controls

AT-05 Are controls operable with one hand without tight grasping, pinching, or wrist twisting, and requiring no more than 5 lbf of force? (4.34.4, 4.27.4)

Automated Teller Machines: visual impairments

AT-06 Are instructions and information for use made accessible to and independently usable by people with visual impairments? (4.34.5)

(AL) Alarms (4.28)

NOTE:

- At a minimum, visual signal appliances shall be provided in buildings and facilities in restrooms and any other general usage areas. **The ADAAG does not define the number of occupants needed to establish a general or common use area.**

ALLOWANCE:

- Emergency warning systems in medical care facilities may be modified to suit standard health care alarm design practice. [4.1.3(14)]

Alarms: general

AL-01 If emergency warning systems are provided, do they include both audible alarms and visual alarms? [4.1.3(14)]

Audible Alarms: general

AL-02 If provided, do the audible alarms meet required operational criteria? (4.28.2)
- Sound level: exceeds the prevailing sound level in the room or space by at least 15 dbA or exceeds any maximum sound level with a duration of 60 sec by 5 dbA, whichever is louder.
- Sound levels for alarm signals shall not exceed 120 dbA.

AL-03 If single station audible alarms are provided, then are single station visual alarm signals also provided? (4.28.3)

Visual Alarms: general

AL-04 If provided, are the visual alarm signal appliances integrated into the building or facility alarm system? (4.28.3)

AL-05 If provided, do the visual alarm signals meet required operational criteria? [4.28.3(1, 2, 3, 4, 5)]
- Lamp: xenon strobe type or equivalent.
- Color: clear or nominal white (i.e., unfiltered or clear filtered white light).
- Pulse duration: maximum shall be 0.2 sec with a maximum duty cycle of 40 percent.
- Intensity: not less than 75 candela.
- Flash rate: not less than 1 Hz and not more than 3 Hz.

AL-07 Are visual alarm signal appliances provided in general usage areas of the building (such as meeting rooms, corridors, and lobbies) or any other area for common use? (4.28.1)

AUTHOR'S INTERPRETATION:

- The authors identified three or more occupants as the minimum number to establish a common use area.

AL-08 Are the visual alarms placed at 80 in. above the highest floor level or 6 in. below the ceiling, whichever is lower? [4.28.3(6)]

AL-09 In spaces required to have visual alarms, are the alarms spaced properly? [4.28.3(7)]
- No place in any space should be more than 50 ft from a visual signal alarm.
- Where a space or large room exceeds 100 ft across, without obstructions 6 ft above the finished floor, visual alarms can be spaced a maximum of 100 ft apart at the perimeter, in lieu of suspending appliances from the ceiling.

AL-10 Are visual alarms placed so that no area in a common corridor or hallway is more than 50 ft from the signal? [4.28.3(8)]

Medical Care Facilities
(Patient Rooms and Parking Requirements)

Introduction. Use this "Space-type Review Guide" to design or evaluate medical care facilities. Medical facilities covered by ADAAG 6.0 are those in which people receive physical or medical treatment or care, where persons may need assistance in responding to an emergency, and where the period of stay may exceed 24 hours. In other words, medical facilities may provide outpatient services, be a general purpose hospital, or specialize in treatment or services for persons with mobility impairments or the elderly. In each case, the accessible parking and loading zone facilitation is slightly different. Refer to the Parking Lots and Passenger Loading Zones "Space-type Review Guide." The following brief description focuses mostly on the special requirements for the number and type of accessible patient rooms and parking facilities within medical care facilities.

Refer to other "Space-type Review Guides" for a complete set of accessibility guidelines (e.g., Lobbies, Corridors and Interior Accessible Routes, Toilet Rooms, Business and Mercantile, Elevators, Offices, Libraries, and so on).

Within a general purpose hospital, all common and public use areas must be accessible and at least 10 percent of patient bedrooms and toilets must comply. The distribution of accessible patient bedrooms can vary, based on the anticipated need in different specialized units (e.g., more than 10 percent may be needed in a general surgical unit and fewer than 10 percent in obstetrics and pediatrics). This includes psychiatric facilities and detoxification facilities.

If the facility is a hospital or rehabilitation facility that specializes in treating conditions that affect mobility, or a unit within either that specializes in treating conditions that affect mobility, all common and public use areas must be accessible, as well as all patient bedrooms and toilets.

If the facility is a long-term care facility or nursing home, 50 percent of patient bedrooms and toilets must be accessible. Each accessible bedroom must have adequate space to provide maneuvering space. A 60-in. diameter turning space or "T"-shaped space is required for maneuvering. If the room has two beds, it is preferable that this space be located between the beds. Each accessible bedroom must have adequate space to provide a minimum clear floor space along each side of the bed and an accessible route to each side of the bed. Where toilet/bathrooms are provided as a part of an accessible patient bedroom, the accessible toilet/bathroom must be located on an accessible route.

Where patient bedrooms are added or altered as part of renovation to an entire wing, department, or other discrete area, the percentage of accessible rooms provided must comply with overall minimum requirements. However, no additional accessible rooms are required in an alteration when the overall number of accessible bedrooms provided in the facility would meet or exceed the percentage required. Altered patient accessible bedrooms and toilet/bathrooms must meet accessibility criteria.

In a general purpose hospital, employee-only spaces are not required to be accessible. However, sorting out which spaces are used only by employees may be difficult. For example, in a private hospital volunteers frequently help out by distributing flowers and reading material to patients and by serving as attendants in family members' waiting areas. Although volunteers are considered to be the public, they must have access to many areas that a hospital may consider employee-only spaces. In a teaching hospital located on a university campus a student who is working as a resident doctor also must have access to all programs and services offered within programs. The multiple and overlapping roles that students, volunteers, and employees can fill make it difficult for a designer to separate and/or define individual spaces as employee-only spaces.

PRELIMINARY DESIGN OVERVIEW

Special criteria that apply to only medical care facilities follow. Be sure to check other space-type review guides that apply to spaces in medical care facilities, such as Parking and Passenger Loading Zones; Lobbies, Corridors, and Interior Accessible Routes; Toilet Rooms; Business and Mercantile; Elevators; and so on.

(MD) Medical Care Facilities

- The minimum number of accessible patient bedrooms and toilets depends on the facility type: general hospitals (10 percent), facilities specializing in mobility treatments (100 percent), long-term care facilities (50 percent).
- At least one accessible entrance is protected from weather by canopy or roof overhang and incorporates a compliant passenger loading zone.
- All public and common use areas must be accessible.
- Alterations and additions to patient rooms and toilets must be made accessible until the facility meets its required number of accessible rooms.

- Entry doors to acute care hospital bedrooms may be exempt from certain door maneuvering space requirements if they are at least 44 in. wide.
- Bedrooms must provide adequate wheelchair turning space.
- An accessible route is required along each side of each bed.
- Patient toilet/bathrooms provided as part of an accessible patient room must be accessible.

(PK) Parking and Passenger Loading Zones

In a medical care facility parking area, where only one accessible space is provided, it shall meet van accessible criteria.

- Accessible spaces are required for both vans and cars [see ADAAG 4.1.2(5)(a–b) table]. The minimum number of spaces increases if parking serves the mobility-impaired or outpatients.

ADAAG APPENDIX

The Appendix, found at the end of ADAAG (Federal Register, 1991), includes additional advisory information pertinent to medical care facilities.

- A4.6.3   Parking Spaces
- A4.22.3 Toilet Rooms, Clear Floor Space

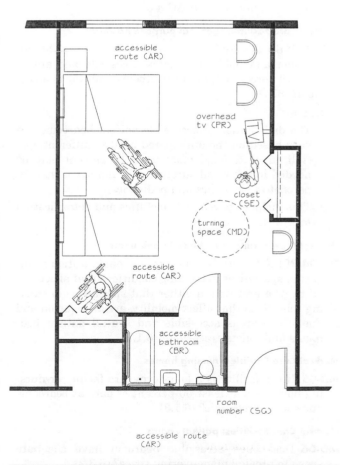

Figure 3-16. Medical care facilities: Patient room with bathroom.

MEDICAL CARE FACILITIES

MD01	Entrances: number required and covering
MD02	Entrances: passenger loading zone
MD03	General hospitals: number required
MD04	Special hospitals: number required
MD05	Nursing homes: number required
MD06	Patient rooms: turning spaces
MD07	Patient rooms: clear floor space at bed
MD08	Patient rooms: acc. toilet/bathrooms
MD09	Alterations: multiple rooms: criteria
MD10	Alterations: acc. toilet/bathrooms
MD11	Alterations: single bedroom: criteria

PARKING AND PASSENGER LOADING ZONES

PK04	Outpatient facilities: number required
PK05	Mobility impairment facilities: number required

MEDICAL CARE FACILITIES
COMPREHENSIVE CRITERIA

Special criteria that apply only to medical care facilities follow. Be sure to check other space-type review guides that apply to spaces in medical care facilities, such as parking, ramps, corridors, lobbies, toilet rooms, business and mercantile, elevators, and so on.

(MD) Medical Care Facilities (6.0)

Medical Care Facilities: entrances

MD-01 Is there at least one accessible entrance covered by a canopy or overhang? (6.2)

MD-02 Is there an accessible passenger loading zone at this entrance that complies with passenger loading zone requirements, ADAAG 4.6.6? (6.2)

Medical Care Facilities: general purpose hospitals

MD-03 If the facility is a general purpose hospital, are all common and public use areas accessible and are at least 10 percent of patient bedrooms and toilets accessible? (6.1.1)

NOTES:

- The distribution of accessible patient bedrooms can vary based on the anticipated need in different specialized units (e.g., more than 10 percent may be needed in a general surgical unit and fewer than 10 percent in obstetrics and pediatrics).
- This includes psychiatric facilities and detoxification facilities.

Medical Care Facilities: mobility impairments

MD-04 If the facility is a hospital or rehabilitation facility that specializes in treating conditions that affect mobility, or a unit within either that specializes in treating conditions that affect mobility, are all common and public use areas accessible and are all patient bedrooms and toilets accessible? (6.1.2)

Medical Care Facilities: nursing homes

MD-05 If the facility is a long-term care facility or nursing home, are at least 50 percent of patient bedrooms and toilets accessible? (6.1.3)

Medical Care Facilities: patient rooms

MD-06 Does each accessible bedroom have adequate space to provide maneuvering space? (6.3.2)

- A 60-in. × 60-in. turning space or "T"-shaped space is required for maneuvering.

NOTE:

- If the room has two beds, it is preferable that this space be located between the beds.

MD-07 Does each accessible bedroom have adequate space to provide a minimum clear floor space of 36 in. along each side of the bed and an accessible route to each side of the bed? (6.3.3)

MD-08 Where toilet/bathrooms are provided as a part of an accessible patient bedroom, is the toilet/bathroom located on an accessible route and does the toilet/bathroom meet accessible criteria? (6.4)

NOTE:

- See space-type review guide, "Transient Housing: Single User Bathrooms," for toilet/bathroom accessible criteria.

Medical Care Facilities: alterations

MD-09 Where patient bedrooms are added or altered as part of renovation to an entire wing, department, or other discrete area, does the percentage of accessible rooms provided comply with ADAAG 6.1.1, 6.1.2, or 6.1.3? [6.1.4(a)] See MD-03, 04, and 05.

NOTE:

- Additional accessible rooms are not required in an alteration when the overall number of accessible bedrooms provided in the facility would meet or exceed the percentage required.

MD-10 Do the altered patient bedrooms and toilet/bathrooms that are required to be accessible meet accessible criteria? [6.1.4(a)]

MD-11 Where patient bedrooms are added or altered individually, do they meet accessible criteria? [6.1.4(b)]

NOTE:

- These patient bedrooms are not required to be accessible when the overall number of accessible bedrooms provided in the facility would meet or exceed the percentage required.

Parking: required number

PK-04 If the parking lot serves an outpatient facility, are 10 percent of the total parking spaces accessible? [4.1.2(5)(d)(i)]

PK-05 If the parking lot serves a mobility impairment facility, are 20 percent of the total parking spaces accessible? [4.1.2(5)(d)(ii)]

Offices

Introduction. This "Space-type Review Guide" is used to design or evaluate public and individual office spaces. Examples of public office space would include reception spaces and their associated waiting areas, and general office spaces that are occupied by more than one person. A consistent element in many of these spaces is a point of business transaction between individuals. Examples of these areas or elements would be business transaction counters where bills are paid, receipts are given, appointments made, or tickets bought. A determination as to whether the general office space is included under the law must be made based on whether it is to be accessed by the general public or by employees with a disability. If a space is determined to be a general or common use area it also is required to meet the alarm criteria.

Included in most waiting or reception areas is a reception or information desk and public seating areas. These elements are addressed in the ADAAG in both the technical requirements and the percentages to be accessible. The importance of these spaces that frequently provide the first point of contact between the individual consumer and the service provider cannot be overstated. Movable furniture is not directly addressed in the ADAAG, but the space that is defined by the furniture is frequently part of an accessible route. The rearrangement of furniture to provide accessible routes or required clear floor space to access a fixed element may seem to be an easy accommodation. However, if the issues are not solved in the design stages, less than desirable solutions may result. Public use telephones, whether or not they are pay telephones, have specific requirements concerning accessibility and types required.

Individual offices are similar to general offices but are frequently smaller, and generally do not have the public transaction functions. Typically individual offices do not have fixed seating and work surfaces that are required to comply with the ADAAG. The applicability of the ADAAG to an individual office is, to a large extent, determined by whether it needs to be accessed by anyone who may have a disability. If the persons requiring access are employees, specific accommodation for those individuals must be made. If the access is by the general public, the full extent of the law comes to bear on the space. In certain Title II facilities such as schools and universities, students or volunteers may use individual offices, which would bring them under the compliance requirements. Since individual offices are not considered common or general use spaces, the alarm compliance criteria found in common use space such as a lobby or reception space do not apply.

PRELIMINARY DESIGN OVERVIEW

(AR) Accessible Routes

- Route surfaces must meet criteria for vertical changes in level. Problem areas may include transition between materials, construction and expansion joints, wood decks, and individual pavers.
- An accessible route must connect all accessible spaces and elements.

(AL) Alarms

- Visual alarms must be provided in any general usage areas, e.g., meeting rooms, hallways, lobbies.

(BM) Business and Mercantile

- Accessible counters are required at each different area offering sales or services such as ticket counters, reception desks, courtesy service counters, concession stands, information counters, coat check rooms, etc.
- If sales and services are located in different parts of the facility, then accessible counters must be dispersed throughout the facility.

(CT) Controls and Operating Mechanisms

- Controls and operating mechanisms have clear floor space and reach range requirements. Frequently overlooked in this space-type are communication outlets; controls on window air conditioner units; thermostats; controls in refrigerators; pull cords on overhead projection screens, fans, and lights; etc.

(DR) Doors

- Typical requirements.

(FS) Floor Surfaces

- Carpets should not be plush; deep pile carpets with thick padding can be a significant obstacle for someone using a manual wheelchair.
- Vertical changes in levels along the accessible route can be an unforeseen barrier, e.g., transition between floor materials, and construction and expansion joints.

(PR) Protruding Objects

- Common wall-mounted elements can be protruding objects, e.g., pencil sharpeners, bookshelves, upper cabinets, drinking fountains, public telephones, ATMs, signs, mailboxes, display cases.

(TL) Public Telephones

- When courtesy public telephones are provided, at least one must be on the accessible route and comply with all telephone requirements.
- Text telephones or equivalent facilitation may be required depending on the number of public telephones provided within the building.

(SE) Fixed Tables and/or Counters

- If fixed tables or counters are provided, a minimum of 5 percent of the total number but not fewer than one of either type must be accessible.

(SG) Signage

- Permanent directional and informational signage, as well as room designations, must meet accessibility criteria.

(SR) Fixed Storage, Closets, Lockers, and Shelves

- One of each type of storage unit (shelves, dispensers, etc.) must be accessible; locked storage used only by employees may not have to be accessible.

- Frequently overlooked storage units for this space-type include coat hooks on doors, brochure racks, mailboxes, etc.

- A4.1.1(3)   Work Areas Used Only by Employees as Work Areas
- A4.5.3   Carpet

ADAAG APPENDIX
The ADAAG Appendix contains advisory information pertinent to offices.

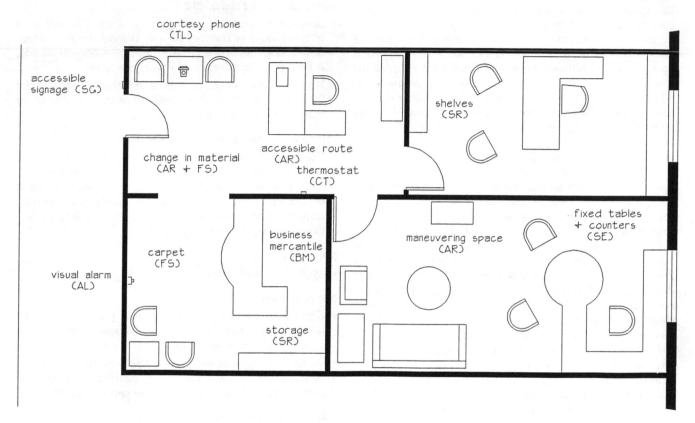

Figure 3-17. Office.

Offices Checklist

SIGNAGE

SG04	Room signage: criteria
SG05	Room signage: location
SG08	Directional/informational signage: criteria
SG09	Suspended/projected signs: location

DOORS

DR04	Doors: maneuvering clearances
DR05	Doors: handle type
DR06	Doors: opening force (interior only)
DR07	Doors: closing speed
DR08	Doors: thresholds
DR09	Doors: clear width/height
DR10	Openings (no door): clear width/height
DR11	Doors in series: clear space between

BUSINESS AND MERCANTILE

BM01	Sales/service counters: accessible route
BM02	Counters w/cash registers: criteria
BM03	Counters w/o cash registers: criteria

ACCESSIBLE ROUTES

AR08	Route: clear width
AR09	Route width: U-turns
AR11	Route: maneuvering clearances
AR14	Route: changes of level

FLOOR AND GROUND SURFACES

FS01	Surface: firm, stable, and slip-resistant
FS02	Vertical changes in level
FS03	Carpet and tile floors

PROTRUDING OBJECTS

PR01	Wall-mounted
PR02	Freestanding/suspended on posts/pylons
PR03	Clear route width maintained
PR04	Overhead clearance
PR05	Vertical clearance: cane detection barrier

CONTROLS AND OPERATING MECHANISMS

CT01	Clear floor space
CT02	Reach ranges: elec./comm. systems
CT03	Reach ranges: thermostats
CT04	Reach ranges: other controls
CT05	Reach ranges: life safety devices
CT06	Controls: operation

FIXED OR BUILT-IN SEATING AND TABLES

SE01	Fixed seating: number required
SE02	Wheelchairs: clear floor space at tables
SE03	Tables/counters: heights
SE04	Tables/counters: knee clearance criteria

STORAGE

SR01	Accessibility: one of each type
SR02	Clear floor space
SR03	Reach ranges
SR04	Storage closets w/o passage: criteria
SR05	Storage hardware: operation

TELEPHONES

TL01	Single public telephone: compliance
TL02	Public telephone bank: one compliant
TL04	Accessible telephone: clear floor space
TL05	Accessible telephone: accessible route
TL06	Wall- or post-mounted: protruding objects
TL07	Reach ranges
TL08	Push-button controls where available
TL09	Telephone book: reach ranges
TL10	Handset cord: length
TL11	Volume control: requirements
TL12	Volume control: amplification
TL13	Telephone: hearing aid compatible

ALARMS

AL01	Emergency warning: audible/visual
AL02	Audible alarms: operation
AL03	Single station audible and visual
AL04	Visual alarms: integration w/building alarm
AL05	Visual alarms: operation
AL07	Visual alarms: common use areas
AL08	Visual alarms: vertical placement
AL09	Visual alarms: horizontal spacing
AL10	Visual alarms: corridor spacing

OFFICES
COMPREHENSIVE CRITERIA

(SG) Signage (4.30)

NOTE:

- In historic buildings displays and written information, documents, etc., should be located where they can be seen by a seated person. Exhibits and signage displayed horizontally (e.g., open books) should be no higher than 44 in. above the floor surface. [4.1.7(3)(e)]

Signage: room identification (where provided)

DEFINITION:

- These signs designate permanent rooms and spaces.

AUTHOR'S INTERPRETATION:

- Signs that designate stairs, exit doors, and toilet rooms generally are associated with permanent spaces, while an "office" sign is not since the room function may change over time. Room numbers also must meet the ADAAG criteria as permanent designations, while personal names do not since the occupant may change over time.

SG-04 Do signs that designate permanent rooms and spaces comply with the following criteria? [4.1.2(7); 4.1.3(16); 4.30.4, 5, 6]

- Character type: raised and accompanied by Grade II Braille.
- Character size: between 5/8 in. and 2 in. high; raised at least 1/32 in.
- Character style: upper case, and sans or simple serif.
- Finish: characters and backgrounds have a nonglare finish.
- Contrast: characters contrast with their background (light-on-dark or dark-on-light).

SG-05 Is the room identification sign mounted in the required location? (4.30.6)

- Mounting location: installed on the wall adjacent to the latch side of the door or where wall space to the latch side of the door is not available, including double doors, placed on the nearest adjacent wall.
- Mounting height: 60 in. above the floor/ground to the centerline of the sign.
- Sign access: approach to within 3 in. of a sign without encountering protruding objects or standing within the swing of the door.

Signage: direction and information (where provided)

DEFINITION:

- Signs that provide direction to or information about functional spaces of the building.

EXCEPTION:

- Building directories, menus, and all other temporary signs are not required to comply. [4.1.3(16)]

SG-08 Do signs that provide direction to, or information about, functional spaces of the building comply with the following criteria? [4.1.2(7); 4.1.3(16); 4.30.1, 2, 3, 5]

- Character proportion: letters and numbers have a width to height ratio between 3:5 and 1:1 and a stroke width to height ratio between 1:5 and 1:10.
- Character height: sized according to viewing distance with characters on overhead signs at least 3 in. high.

NOTE:

- When the sign is mounted below 80 in., there are no prescribed character heights. Only when the sign is mounted 80 in. or higher are the characters required to be at least 3 in. high. (4.30.3)

- Finish: characters and backgrounds have a nonglare finish.
- Contrast: characters contrast with their background (light-on-dark or dark-on-light).

SG-09 Is a sign located so that the overhead clearance or the projection of a suspended or projected sign does not result in a protruding object (free-standing or wall-mounted)?

- Clear height: at least 80 in. (4.4.2, Fig. 8a)
- Overhang for free-standing signs on posts or pylons located between 27 in. and 80 in. high: no more than a 12-in. projection into accessible routes. (4.4.1, Fig. 8c)
- Overhang for wall-mounted signs between 27 in. and 80 in. high: no more than a 4-in. projection into accessible routes. (4.4.1, Fig. 8a)

(DR) Doors (4.13)

NOTE:

- Included in this category are doors, revolving doors, turnstiles, and gates.

AUTHOR'S INTERPRETATION:

- It is suggested that, for purposes of documentation and review, a door be assigned to the space it swings into.

Corridors are an exception to this rule and include only entry doors into the corridor or intermediate fire doors.

Doors: maneuvering clearance

DR-04 If the door is not automatic or power assisted, does it have the required maneuvering clearance provided on the push and pull side, and is the floor level and clear within the maneuvering area? (4.13.6)

- A verbal description cannot adequately describe the requirements. See ADAAG Fig. 25a–f for a graphic description.

EXCEPTION:

- Entry doors to acute care hospital bedrooms for inpatients are exempt from maneuvering space at the latch side of the door if the door is at least 44 in. wide.

AUTHOR'S INTERPRETATION:

- While ADAAG does not describe what elements can reduce the required maneuvering clearance, they could include a narrow entry alcove, an adjacent wall, railing, or permanently installed shelving, or a deep recessed door jamb.

Doors: hardware

DR-05 Do all door handles, locks, latches, or other operable devices meet required operational criteria? (4.13.9)

- Hardware operation: operable with one hand without tight grasping, pinching, or wrist twisting.
- Force required to operate the controls: not greater than 5 lbf. This does not apply to the force required to retract latch bolts or to disengage other devices that only hold the door in a closed position.
- Hardware type: "U"-shaped handles, levers, and push type mechanisms are acceptable designs.
- Hardware height: not greater than 48 in. above the floor.
- Sliding doors: hardware is exposed and usable from both sides when the doors are fully open.

Doors: opening force

DR-06 Do interior hinged doors and sliding or folding doors have an opening force of 5 lbf or less? (4.13.11)

- At present, no accessible criteria exist for exterior doors.
- Fire doors shall have the minimum opening force allowable by the appropriate administrative authority.

Doors: closing speed

DR-07 If the door has a closer, is the closer adjusted so that the door does not close too quickly? (4.13.10)

- From an open position of 70° the door will take at least 3 sec to move to a point 3 in. from the latch (measured to the leading edge of the door).

Doors: thresholds

DR-08 Where raised thresholds are provided, do they meet height limitations and are they beveled when required? (4.13.8, 4.5.2, Fig. 7)

- Threshold height: not more than 3/4 in. for exterior sliding doors or 1/2 in. for other types of doors.
- Threshold bevel: thresholds less than 1/4 in. high need no bevel; thresholds between 1/4 in. and 1/2 in. high shall be beveled at each edge with not more than a 1:2 slope.

EXCEPTION:

- A 3/4-in. high threshold is allowed in existing conditions. [4.1.6(3)(d)(ii)]

Doors: clear opening width and height

DR-09 Is the clear opening for the doorway adequate in width and height? (4.13.3, 4, 5; Fig. 24)

- Door width: at least 32 in. of clear width with the door open at 90°, measured between the face of the door and the door stop on the latch side. This also pertains to the active leaf of a double-leaf door or gate.
- Opening width: openings more than 24 in. deep must provide 36 in. of clear width.
- Height: at least 80 in. of vertical clearance.

EXCEPTIONS:

- Doors not requiring full user passage, such as shallow closets, may have the clear opening reduced to not less than 20 in.
- Where it is technically infeasible to comply with clear opening width requirements, a projection of 5/8 in. maximum will be permitted for the latch side. [4.1.6(d)(i)]

DR-10 Is the clear opening (when there is no door) adequate in width and height? (4.2.1, 4.3.3, 4.4.2)

- Width: at least 32 in. of clear width for depths 24 in. or less and at least 36 in. of clear width for depths greater than 24 in.
- Height: at least 80 in. of vertical clearance.

Doors: two doors in a series

DR-11 If there are two doors in a series, is the required clear space between the doors provided and do the doors swing in the appropriate direction? (4.13.7, Fig. 26)

- Clear space between the doors: not less than 48 in. plus the width of any door swinging into the space.
- Door swing: must swing in the same direction or away from the space between the doors.

(BM) Business and Mercantile (7.0)

Business: general

BM-01 Are all areas used for business transactions with the public, such as sales and service counters and/or self-service displays, on an accessible route? [4.1.3(12)(b), 7.2.2]

Business: sales counters with cash registers

BM-02 In retail stores where counters with cash registers are provided, is there at least one accessible cash register counter, and where more than one occurs, are they distributed throughout the facility? (7.2.1)

- Main counter: a portion of the counter is at least 36 in. long and is not more than 36 in. high.
- Alterations: where it is technically infeasible to provide an accessible counter, an auxiliary counter meeting these criteria may be provided.

Business: sales or service counters without cash registers

BM-03 At ticketing counters, teller stations, registration counters, and other counters for distributing goods or services to the public without cash registers, is there an accessible counter or alternative provided? (7.2.2)

- Main counter: a portion of the counter is at least 36 in. long and is not more than 36 in. high.
- Auxiliary counter: in close proximity to the main counter and not more than 36 in. high.
- Equivalent facilitation: might consist of a folding shelf attached to the main counter (for an individual with disabilities to write) and use of the space at the side of the counter for handing materials back and forth.

(AR) Accessible Routes (4.3)

NOTES:

- All walks, halls, corridors, aisles, skywalks, tunnels, and other spaces that are part of a designated accessible route shall comply with accessible requirements.
- Any slope on the accessible route that is greater than 1:20 is required to meet all ramp criteria.
- The accessible route shall, to the maximum extent feasible, coincide with the route for the general public.
- In historic buildings, accessible routes from an accessible entrance shall be provided to all publicly used spaces on at least the level of the accessible entrance. Access shall be provided to all levels of a building or facility whenever practical. [4.1.7(3)(d)]

AUTHOR'S INTERPRETATION:

- An accessible route "generally coincides" with the route used by the public if:
  - It does not force the user to go out of the way.
  - It is most like the route chosen by the general public.
  - It is direct.
  - It gives the same basic experience as the route preferred by the public.

Accessible Routes: width

AR-08 Is the minimum clear width along the accessible route adequate for continuous or point passage? (4.2.1, 4.3.3, Fig. 1, Fig. 8e, Fig. 24e)

- Continuous passage (greater than 24 in. long): at least a 36-in. clear width.
- Point passage (not more than 24 in. long): at least a 32-in. clear width.

AUTHOR'S INTERPRETATION:

- Noncompliance with this question generally relates to permanent elements that encroach on the accessible route. Large, heavy equipment that is not readily movable might be considered permanent. If the space is designed so that temporary elements (such as bikes in a bike rack or car bumpers) will consistently encroach, the situation might also be considered a permanent barrier.

AR-09 Is the minimum clear width along the accessible route adequate at a U-turn around an obstruction? (4.3.3, Fig. 7a–b)

- Obstruction 48 in. or greater: at least a 36-in. clear width around the obstruction.

- Obstruction less than 48 in.: at least a 42-in. clear width at each side with at least a 48-in. clear width in the turn.

Accessible Routes: maneuvering clearances

AR-11 Is the minimum clear floor space for an unobstructed 180° wheelchair turning space or a "T"-shaped turning space provided? (4.2.3, Fig. 3a–b)

- 180° turning space: at least a 60-in. diameter.

- "T"-shaped turning space: at least 36-in. wide legs with a minimum length of 60 in.

Accessible Routes: changes in level

AR-14 Are changes in level greater than 1/2 in. accomplished by means of a curb ramp, ramp, elevator, or platform lift (as permitted in ADAAG 4.1.3 and 4.1.6)? (4.3.8)

(FS) Floor and Ground Surfaces (4.5)

Floor Surfaces: general

FS-01 Are the floor/ground surfaces on the accessible route stable, firm, and slip-resistant? (4.5.1)

AUTHOR'S INTERPRETATION:

- Exterior spaces, interior circulation, bathrooms, and other spaces where water can collect on the floor around an element (sinks, drinking fountains, hose bibbs, etc.) are reviewed as if wet.

- High gloss surfaces without significant textures that are regularly maintained with waxing (smooth tiles, waxed concrete, etc.) could be considered noncompliant.

- Accessible criteria are not specified for nonpermanent floor surfaces such as mats or rugs.

Floor Surfaces: changes in level

FS-02 Are vertical changes in level between 1/4 in. and 1/2 in. beveled with a slope of 1:2 or less? (4.5.2)

- Changes in level up to 1/4 in. may be vertical without edge treatment.

- Changes in level greater than 1/2 in. should be accomplished by means of a curb ramp, ramp, elevator, or platform lift (as permitted in ADAAG 4.1.3 and 4.1.6).

Floor Surfaces: carpet

FS-03 Does carpet or carpet tile used on the floor comply with accessible criteria? (4.5.3, Fig. 8f)

- Attachment: secured.

- Exposed edges: fastened and trimmed along the entire length.

- Pile type: low pile (1/2 in. maximum).

- Padding: firm pad or no pad underneath.

(PR) Protruding Objects (4.4)

Protruding Objects: general

PR-01 Do wall-mounted objects having leading edges between 27 in. and 80 in. high project less than 4 in. into walkways, corridors, aisles, or paths of travel? (4.4.1, Fig. 8a–e)

- Objects mounted with their leading edge at or below 27 in. can protrude any amount, as long as they do not reduce the required clear width of an accessible route.

AUTHOR'S INTERPRETATION:

- Protruding objects might include fire extinguishers or cabinets, pencil sharpeners, shelving, counters, built-in equipment overhangs, or various dispensers such as for paper towels or soap.

PR-02 Do free-standing objects, suspended or mounted on posts or pylons with leading edges between 27 in. and 80 in. high, project less than 12 in. into the perpendicular route of travel? (4.4.1, Fig. 8a–e)

AUTHOR'S INTERPRETATION:

- These might include telephone enclosures, drinking fountains, or free-standing signage kiosks.

PR-03 Is the minimum clear route width or maneuvering space still maintained even with the projection of a protruding object? (4.4.1, Fig. 8a–e)

Protruding Objects: overhead clearance

PR-04 Is the minimum overhead clearance of 80 in. provided in accessible areas or along accessible routes? (4.4.2, Fig. 8a)

AUTHOR'S INTERPRETATION:

- Overhead objects that can reduce the required clearance might include structures, pipes, ducts, or light fixtures.

PR-05 Where the vertical clearance of a space adjoining the accessible route is less than 80 in. high, is a cane detection barrier less than 27 in. from the floor provided for blind or visually impaired persons? (4.4.2, Fig. 8c-1)

AUTHOR'S INTERPRETATION:

- This condition might be found under a stair, at a sloped ceiling space, or with guy wires from telephone poles along an exterior accessible route.

(CT) Controls and Operating Mechanisms (4.27)

NOTES:

- Controls or operating mechanisms can include elements such as light switches, pencil sharpeners, manual overhead screens, nonkeyed thermostats, alarm pull stations, fire extinguisher cabinets, A/C window units, microwave ovens, towel dispensers, and wall hooks.

- If controls are to be operated by occupants of the space, they must be accessible. If controls are to be operated by maintenance staff only and not by occupants or other users of the space, they do not have to be accessible. For example, thermostats in auditoriums usually do not have to be accessible, while thermostats in classrooms may need to be accessible.

Controls: clear floor space

CT-01 Is a clear floor space of at least 30 in. × 48 in. provided in front of controls, dispensers, receptacles, and other operable equipment for forward or parallel approach? (4.27.2, Fig. 4a–b)

Controls: reach ranges

NOTES:

- Accessible reach ranges for controls and operating mechanisms are:
  — Forward reach: not less than 15 in. high and not more than 48 in. high without any obstruction or where the obstruction is less than 20 in. deep. For obstructions from 20 in. to 25 in. deep, no forward reach higher than 44 in.
  — Side reach: not less than 9 in. high and not more than 54 in. high. For obstructions not more than 34 in. high or 24 in. deep, no side reach higher than 46 in.
  — Electrical outlets, switches, and communication system receptacles have a minimum outlet height of 15 in. regardless of forward or side reach. See CT-02 below.

CT-02 Are electrical outlets, switches, and communication system receptacles mounted within accessible forward or side reach ranges? (4.27.3)

  EXCEPTION:

  - These requirements do not apply where the use of special equipment dictates otherwise or where electrical and communications system receptacles are not normally intended for use by building occupants. (4.27.3)

CT-03 Are thermostats or other similar operable equipment mounted within accessible forward or side reach ranges? (4.2.5, 4.2.6, Fig. 5a–b, Fig. 6a–c)

CT-04 Are dispensers or other similar operable equipment mounted within accessible forward or side reach ranges? (4.2.5, 4.2.6, Fig. 5a–b, Fig. 6a–c)

CT-05 Are life safety devices or other similar operable equipment mounted within accessible forward or side reach ranges? (4.2.5, 4.2.6, Fig. 5a–b, Fig. 6a–c)

  NOTE:

  - This might include fire alarm pull stations, handles to extinguisher cabinets, or wall-mounted extinguishers.

Controls: operation

CT-06 Are controls, dispensers, receptacles, and other operable equipment operable with one hand without tight grasping, pinching, or wrist twisting, and requiring no more than 5 lbf of force? (4.27.4)

(SE) Fixed or Built-in Seating and Tables (4.32)

Fixed or Built-in Seating and Tables: minimum number

SE-01 Is the minimum number of accessible wheelchair seating locations at fixed tables or counters provided? (4.1.3.18)

- Number required: 5 percent of total number of seats but not fewer than one.

Fixed or Built-in Seating and Tables: clear floor space

AUTHOR'S INTERPRETATION:

- Where the accessible route leads to and through accessible seating adjacent to a wall or another table, the minimum required width for the accessible route will be 65 in. between the table edge and next parallel surface (e.g., wall or another table edge). (4.1.3.18, Fig. 45)

SE-02 Is the clear floor space for a wheelchair at a seating location adequate? (4.32.3, Fig. 4a, Fig. 45)

- Clear floor space: 30 in. × 48 in.
- This clear space can include up to 19 in. under the table/desk.

Fixed or Built-in Seating and Tables: clearances

SE-03 Are the tops of accessible tables and counters between 28 in. and 34 in. from the floor? (4.32.3, Fig. 45)

SE-04 Are the knee clearances at least 27 in. high, 30 in. wide, and 19 in. deep? (4.32.3, Fig. 45)

(SR) Storage (4.25)

NOTE:

- Accessible reach range requirements do not apply to shelves or display units allowing self-service by customers in mercantile occupancies but they must be located on an accessible route. [4.1.3(12)(b)]

Storage: general

SR-01 Does at least one of each type of fixed or built-in storage unit comply with accessible criteria? [4.1.3(12)(a), 4.25.1]

  NOTE:

  - Types of storage facilities might include cabinets, shelves, closets, and drawers.

Storage: clear floor space

SR-02 Is there a clear floor space at least 30 in. × 48 in. at fixed or built-in storage units that allows for either a forward or side approach? (4.25.2, Fig. 4a–b)

Storage: reach ranges

SR-03 Are forward or side reach for each type of accessible storage unit within acceptable reach ranges? (4.2.5–6, Fig. 5a–b, Fig. 6a–c, 4.25.3)

- Forward reach: not less than 15 in. high and not more than 48 in. high without any obstruction or where the obstruction is less than 20 in. deep. For obstructions from 20 in. to 25 in. deep, no forward reach higher than 44 in.
- Side reach: not less than 9 in. high and not more than 54 in. high. For obstructions not more than 34 in. high or 24 in. deep, no side reach higher than 46 in.

SR-04 In a closet where passage is not required to access storage (e.g., door opening is less than 32 in.), are the clothes rod or shelves within required reach ranges? (4.25.3, Fig. 38a–b)

- Door width: at least 20 in. (4.13.5)

- Horizontal reach: not more than 21 in. from the opening.
- Rod reach: if over 10 in. deep, then not more than 48 in. high.
- Shelf reach: if over 10 in. deep, then not more than 48 in. high or less than 9 in. high.

Storage: hardware

SR-05 Is the hardware on the storage unit doors or drawers operable with one hand without tight grasping, pinching, or wrist twisting, and requiring no more than 5 lbf of force? (4.25.4, 4.27.4)

(TL) Telephones (4.31)

DEFINITION:

- Telephone types include public pay telephones, public closed circuit telephones, or other public telephones.

AUTHOR'S INTERPRETATION:

- Frequently, public pay telephones are provided by a contractual agreement with a vendor. The vendor, through the contract, might be made responsible for compliance with all applicable ADAAG criteria.

Telephones: number required

TL-01 If there is only one public telephone on a floor, does it comply with accessible criteria? [4.1.3(17)(a)]

- Unless otherwise specified, accessible telephones may be either forward or side reach telephones.

TL-02 If there is a single bank of public telephones on a floor, does at least one of the telephones in the bank comply with accessible criteria? [4.1.3(17)(a)]

- A bank consists of two or more adjacent public telephones, often installed as a unit.
- Unless otherwise specified, accessible telephones may be either forward or side reach telephones.

Telephones: clear floor or ground space

TL-04 Does the accessible telephone have at least a 30 in. × 48 in. clear floor or ground space that allows either a forward or side approach? (4.31.2, Fig. 44, 4.2.4)

- Bases, enclosures, and fixed seats shall not impede approaches to telephones.
- If this clear floor space is located in an alcove or confined space, see ADAAG Fig. 4d–e for additional maneuvering clearance requirements.

TL-05 Does an accessible route adjoin or overlap the clear floor space for the accessible telephone? (4.31.2, Fig. 44, 4.2.4)

Telephones: protruding object

TL-06 Do wall-mounted or post-mounted telephones with leading edges between 27 in. and 80 in. from the floor have projections that do not result in a protruding object? (4.31.4, 4.4.1)

- Wall-mounted: project less than 4 in. into the pathway.
- Post-mounted: project less than 12 in. into a perpendicular route of travel.

Telephones: mounting height

TL-07 Is the highest operable part of the telephone within forward or side reach ranges? (4.31.3, 4.2.6)

- Forward: not more than 48 in. above the floor.
- Side: not more than 54 in. above the floor.

Telephones: push-button controls

TL-08 Does the telephone have push-button controls where such service is available? (4.31.6)

Telephones: telephone book

TL-09 Is the telephone book, if provided, located in a position that complies with forward or side reach ranges? (4.31.7)

- Forward: not more than 48 in. above the floor.
- Side: not more than 54 in. above the floor.

Telephones: cord length

TL-10 Is the cord from the telephone to the handset at least 29 in. long? (4.31.8)

Telephones: volume control and hearing aid compatibility

TL-11 Do the public telephones comply with volume control requirements? [4.1.3(17)(b)]

- Each accessible telephone is equipped with a volume control.
- In addition, 25 percent, but not fewer than one, of all other public telephones should be equipped with volume controls and dispersed among all types of public telephones.

TL-12 Are volume controls capable of amplification between 12 dbA and 18 dbA above normal? [4.31.5(2)]

- If an automatic reset button is provided, the maximum of 18 dbA may be exceeded.

TL-13 Are telephones hearing aid compatible? [4.31.5(1)]

(AL) Alarms (4.28)

NOTE:

- At a minimum, visual signal appliances shall be provided in buildings and facilities in restrooms and any other general usage areas. **The ADAAG does not define the number of occupants needed to establish a general or common use area.**

ALLOWANCE:

- Emergency warning systems in medical care facilities may be modified to suit standard health care alarm design practice. [4.1.3(14)]

Alarms: general

AL-01 If emergency warning systems are provided, do they include both audible alarms and visual alarms? [4.1.3(14)]

Audible Alarms: general

AL-02 If provided, do the audible alarms meet required operational criteria? (4.28.2)

- Sound level: exceeds the prevailing sound level in the room or space by at least 15 dbA or exceeds any maximum sound level with a duration of 60 sec by 5 dbA, whichever is louder.

- Sound levels for alarm signals shall not exceed 120 dbA.

AL-03 If single station audible alarms are provided, then are single station visual alarm signals also provided? (4.28.3)

Visual Alarms: general

AL-04 If provided, are the visual alarm signal appliances integrated into the building or facility alarm system? (4.28.3)

AL-05 If provided, do the visual alarm signals meet required operational criteria? [4.28.3(1, 2, 3, 4, 5)]

- Lamp: xenon strobe type or equivalent.
- Color: clear or nominal white (i.e., unfiltered or clear filtered white light).
- Pulse duration: maximum shall be 0.2 sec with a maximum duty cycle of 40 percent.
- Intensity: not less than 75 candela.
- Flash rate: not less than 1 Hz and not more than 3 Hz.

AL-07 Are visual alarm signal appliances provided in general usage areas of the building (such as meeting rooms, corridors, and lobbies) or any other area for common use? (4.28.1)

AUTHOR'S INTERPRETATION:

- The authors identified three or more occupants as the minimum number to establish a common use area.

AL-08 Are the visual alarms placed at 80 in. above the highest floor level or 6 in. below the ceiling, whichever is lower? [4.28.3(6)]

AL-09 In spaces required to have visual alarms, are the alarms spaced properly? [4.28.3(7)]

- No place in any space should be more than 50 ft from a visual signal alarm.
- Where a space or large room exceeds 100 ft across, without obstructions 6 ft above the finished floor, visual alarms can be spaced a maximum of 100 ft apart at the perimeter, in lieu of suspending appliances from the ceiling.

AL-10 Are visual alarms placed so that no area in a common corridor or hallway is more than 50 ft from the signal? [4.28.3(8)]

Restaurants and Cafeterias
(Dining Halls, Banquet Rooms, Bars)

Introduction. Use this "Space-type Review Guide" to design or evaluate restaurants, cafeterias, and similiar types of dining areas. This would include spaces such as bars, lounges, snack bars, lunch counters, and dining halls in churches and educational facilities. Spaces normally associated with restaurants, such as restrooms, meeting rooms, and waiting areas, should be surveyed using the review guide appropriate for those spaces. Kitchens for these facilities are usually staffed by permanent employees and can be considered "employee-only areas" which would not have to meet accessibility criteria except as needed to accomodate an employee with a disability. Kitchens used by people in organizations such as clubs and churches, or students in a group living situation, should be reviewed using "Kitchens" listed under Transient Housing.

In dining facilities, as in other assembly areas, the primary goal of the ADAAG is to ensure that people with mobility problems are not grouped together but integrated into all seating areas. This gives them the opportunity to enjoy whatever atmosphere, services, and views are available in both the interior and exterior spaces. Accessibility problems in traditional restaurants where all the tables and chairs are movable are minor. Tables and chairs can easily be moved to create as many accessible routes or seating spaces as necessary. The only major concerns are door widths, table heights, floor surfaces, and the correct counter height at the cash register. However, many restaurants today have several areas of fixed seating which may occur on different levels. As in other spaces with fixed

tables, counters, or seating, 5 percent must be accessible and dispersed throughout the dining area. If dining occurs on different levels or loggias, *all* areas must be accessible in new construction and, where practical, in alterations. All areas do not have to be accessible in alterations if the same services, character, atmosphere, etc., are provided in other accessible dining areas.

Self-service lines similar to those used in cafeterias and various counters for buffets, salads, tableware, breverages, and ice cream have added flexibility and diversity in many restaurants but they have also created greater accessibility problems. The required number of shelves and counters for these self-service counters is greater than might be expected. Usually only one of each type of counter would need to be accessible. However, in restaurants, cafeterias, and other dining areas the main food service line and 50 percent of each type of self-service or dispensing devices must be accessible. The controls on the self-service or dispensing devices must also be accessible. In addition, all accessible seating must be located on accessible routes that connect all the self-service areas as well as those areas normally used by the general public, such as restrooms, telephones, and vending machines.

Mezzanines and raised platforms are two other areas of major concern in these types of spaces. Mezzanines, as defined by ADAAG, not serviced by an elevator may or may not have to be accessible depending on their size and whether the same services and decor are provided in accessible dining areas. Raised platforms such as those used for a speaker's lectern or a head table must be accessible by a ramp or a platform lift. If the platform has an open edge, it must be protected by a curb or other barrier, such as tables. If stairs also are provided to the platform, they do not have to be accessible, but some people with mobility problems prefer stairs rather than ramps.

PRELIMINARY DESIGN OVERVIEW

(AL) Alarms

- Visual alarms must be provided and be visible in each common use area such as the main dining area and private dining/meeting rooms.

(AR) Accessible Routes

- An accessible route must connect each wheelchair seating location to all areas including restrooms, telephones, salad bars, vending machines, drinking fountains, self-service counters, stages, speaker platforms, dance floors (both indoor and outdoor), etc.

(BM) Business and Mercantile

- Accessible counters are required at each different area offering sales or services such as reception desks, coat check rooms, and cashier counters.
- If sales and services are located in different parts of the facility, then accessible counters must be dispersed throughout the facility.

(CT) Controls and Operating Mechanisms

- One of each type of control device used by the general public should be accessible and operable.

(DF) Drinking Fountains

- Drinking fountains must serve both ambulatory and nonambulatory height requirements; this requires two different spout heights.

(DR) Doors

- If the restaurant or dining area can be entered from an interior and exterior route, doors leading from both routes may need to be accessible.
- Two doors in a series must meet both clear space and door swing requirements (e.g., vestibules, lobby entrances).
- Glass sliding doors leading to exterior spaces must meet accessibility requirements. Note possible threshold exceptions.

(EN) Entrances

- Half of all public entrances must be accessible, and at least one must be accessible on the ground floor.
- The number of accessible entrances must be equal to the number of exits required by the building/fire code.

(FS) Floor and Ground Surfaces

- In some areas floor surfaces should be evaluated as if wet. In particular consider spaces around exterior doors, exterior dining areas, drinking fountains, etc.
- Smooth floor surfaces should be evaluated for slip-resistance based on floor finish and maintenance.

- Vertical changes in levels can be a particular problem at exterior dining areas, e.g., transition between floor materials, construction and expansion joints, uneven planks in wood decks.

(PL) Platform Lifts

- Platform lifts may be used in lieu of ramps for access to raised platforms (stages).

(PR) Protruding Objects

- Overlooked protruding objects in restaurants are tray slides at self-service counters for food, drinks, tableware, dishware, salad bars, and condiments.
- Common wall-mounted protruding objects can be hanger rods, drinking fountains, public telephones, signs, display cases.

(TL) Public Telephones

- When public telephones are provided, at least one must be on the accessible route and comply with all telephone requirements.
- Text telephones or equivalent facilitation may be required depending on the number of public telephones provided within the building.

(RC) Restaurants and Cafeterias

- In new construction, all spaces and dining areas must be accessible and an accessible route must connect all dining areas, including raised or sunken dining areas, loggias, and outdoor seating areas.
- In alterations of existing spaces, inaccessible areas are allowable if the same services and decor are provided in an accessible space usable by the general public and not restricted to use by people with disabilities.
- At least 5 percent of fixed tables or dining counters must be accessible and proportionally distributed throughout the space between smoking and nonsmoking sections.
- A raised platform or stage used by the general public must be accessible. A ramp or platform lift may be used to make the platform or stage accessible.
- An accessible platform or stage requires edge protection.
- In a nonelevator building, accessibility to the mezzanine is not required if the mezzanine seating area does not exceed 33 percent of the total accessible seating area and if the same services and decor are provided in an accessible space usable by the general public and not restricted to use by people with disabilities.
- At least 50 percent of each type of self-service shelves and dispensing devices for tableware, dishware, condiments, food, and beverages must be accessible.
- Vending machines and other like equipment must be located on an accessible route. A clear floor space for forward or parallel approach to controls or operating mechanisms on the machines must also be provided.
- Counters exceeding 34 in. in height must provide at least 60 in. of accessible counter or service at accessible tables within the same area.
- Accessible fixed tables must be accessible by means of an access aisle between parallel edges of tables or between a wall and the table edges.

(RP) Ramps

- Any slope along an accessible route greater than 1:20 (5 percent) is considered a ramp and must meet all ramp criteria.
- Handrail extensions are possible protruding objects, especially where the extensions intersect another accessible route.
- Some persons who use walking aids prefer stairs over ramps; consider including both.

(SE) Fixed Tables and/or Counters

- If fixed tables or counters are provided, a minimum of 5 percent of the total number but not fewer than one of either type must be accessible.
- An accessible route must lead to and through accessible seating at fixed tables or counters.
- If fixed counters are provided, one of each type must be accessible.

(SG) Signage

- If all entrances are not accessible, the accessible entrances must be identified by the ISA symbol; nonaccessible entrances must have signage indicating the accessible route to an accessible entrance.
- Permanent directional and informational signage such as those indicating direction to restrooms, telephones, and private dining areas must meet accessibility criteria; letter height varies with mounting height of sign.
- Building directories, menus, and temporary signs are not required to comply.

(SR) Fixed Storage, Closets, Lockers, and Shelves

- When provided, one of each type of storage unit (shelves, dispensers, hooks, etc.) must be accessible.

ADAAG APPENDIX

The ADAAG Appendix contains advisory information pertinent to this space-type.

- A5.1 Dining Counters
- A7.3 Checkout Aisles

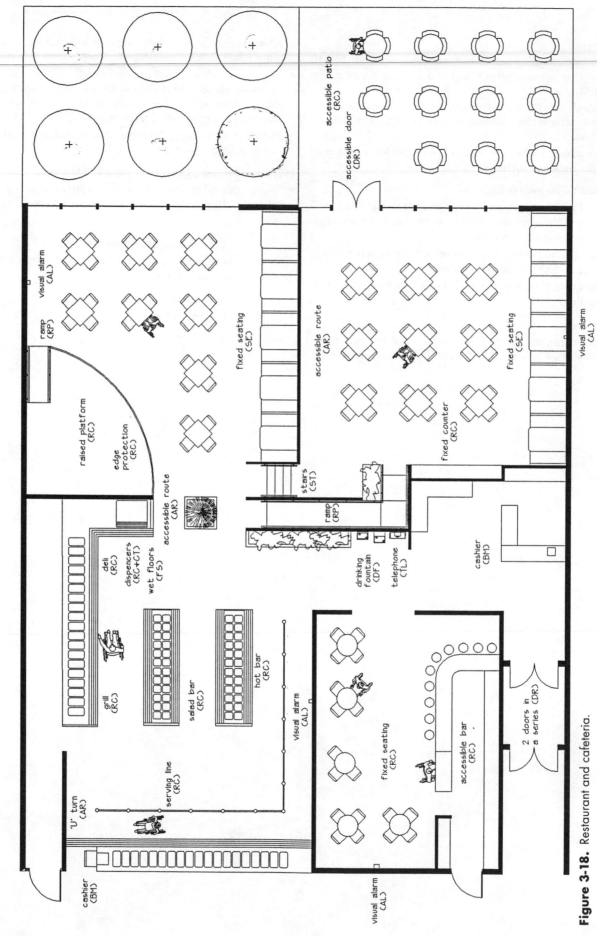

Figure 3-18. Restaurant and cafeteria.

Restaurants and Cafeterias Checklist

SIGNAGE:

SG01	Entry signage: ISA requirement
SG02	Entry signage: inaccessible entrances
SG03	Inaccessible entry signage: criteria
SG04	Room signage: criteria
SG05	Room signage: location
SG08	Directional/informational signage: criteria
SG09	Suspended/projected signs: location

DOORS:

DR02	Automatic doors: ANSI standards
DR03	Automatic doors: operation
DR04	Doors: maneuvering clearances
DR05	Doors: handle type
DR06	Doors: opening force (interior only)
DR07	Doors: closing speed
DR08	Doors: thresholds
DR09	Doors: clear width/height
DR10	Openings (no door): clear width/height
DR11	Doors in series: clear space between

RESTAURANTS AND CAFETERIAS

RC01	Fixed seating: number required and criteria
RC02	Smoking/nonsmoking areas
RC03	Counters/bars: length, height, knee space
RC04	Access aisles: minimum widths
RC05	Dining areas: type req'd to be accessible
RC06	Food service line: clear width
RC07	Food service line: tray slide height
RC08	Shelves/dispen. device: criteria
RC09	Shelves/dispen. device: clear floor space
RC10	Raised platforms: acc. requirements
RC11	Raised platforms: edge protection
RC12	Vending machines: accessible route
RC13	Vending machines: clear floor space

ACCESSIBLE ROUTES

AR08	Route: clear width
AR09	Route width: U-turns
AR10	Route: passing space

RAMPS

RP01	Maximum running slopes and lengths
RP02	Maximum cross slope
RP03	Minimum clear width
RP04	Landings: location
RP05	Landings: size
RP06	Landings used to change direction
RP07	Handrails: when required
RP08	Handrails: switchbacks
RP09	Handrails: extensions past ramp
RP10	Handrails: clear space to wall
RP11	Handrails: mounting height
RP12	Handrails: continuous gripping surface
RP13	Handrails: rounded end or returned
RP14	Handrails: no rotation
RP15	Ramp edge protection
RP16	Floor surface stability

HANDRAILS

HR01	Handrails and grab bars: diameter
HR02	Handrails and grab bars: edge radius
HR03	Clearance between handrail and wall
HR06	Handrails and grab bars: structural strength
HR07	Mounting devices: structural strength
HR10	Wall adjacent to handrail abrasion free

PROTRUDING OBJECTS

PR01	Wall-mounted
PR02	Freestanding/suspended on posts/pylons
PR03	Clear route width maintained
PR04	Overhead clearance

FLOOR SURFACES

FS01	Surface: firm, stable, and slip-resistant
FS02	Vertical changes in level
FS03	Carpet and tile floors

CONTROLS AND OPERATING MECHANISMS

CT01	Clear floor space
CT02	Reach ranges: elec./comm. systems
CT04	Reach ranges: other controls
CT05	Reach ranges: life safety devices
CT06	Controls: operation

TELEPHONES

TL02	Public telephone bank: one compliant
TL04	Accessible telephone: clear floor space
TL05	Accessible telephone: accessible route
TL06	Wall- or post-mounted: protruding objects
TL07	Reach ranges

STORAGE

SR01	Accessibility: one of each type
SR02	Clear floor space
SR03	Reach ranges
SR05	Storage hardware: operation

ALARMS

AL01	Emergency warning: audible/visual
AL02	Audible alarms: operation
AL03	Single station audible and visual
AL04	Visual alarms: integration w/building alarm
AL05	Visual alarms: operation
AL07	Visual alarms: common use areas
AL08	Visual alarms: vertical placement
AL09	Visual alarms: horizontal spacing

RESTAURANTS AND CAFETERIAS
(DINING HALLS, BANQUET ROOMS, BARS)
COMPREHENSIVE CRITERIA

(SG) Signage (4.30)

NOTE:

- In historic buildings displays and written information, documents, etc., should be located where they can be seen by a seated person. Exhibits and signage displayed horizontally (e.g., open books) should be no higher than 44 in. above the floor surface. [4.1.7(3)(e)]

Signage: entry

SG-01 Where a building or space has both accessible and inaccessible entrances, are the accessible entrances identified by the International Symbol of Accessibility? [4.1.2(7)(c), Fig. 43a–b]

SG-02 If an entrance is not accessible, is there a directional sign indicating the location of the nearest accessible entrance? [4.1.2(7)(c), 4.1.3(8)(d)]

SG-03 Does the directional sign indicating the location of the nearest accessible entrance comply with directional signage criteria? (4.30.2, 3, 5)

- Character proportion: letters and numbers have a width to height ratio between 3:5 and 1:1 and a stroke width to height ratio between 1:5 and 1:10.
- Character height: sized according to viewing distance with characters on overhead signs at least 3 in. high.
- Finish: characters and backgrounds have a nonglare finish.
- Contrast: characters contrast with their background (light-on-dark or dark-on-light).

Signage: room identification (where provided)

DEFINITION:

- These signs designate permanent rooms and spaces.

AUTHOR'S INTERPRETATION:

- Signs that designate stairs, exit doors, and toilet rooms generally are associated with permanent spaces, while an "office" sign is not since the room function may change over time. Room numbers also must meet the ADAAG criteria as permanent designations, while personal names do not since the occupant may change over time.

SG-04 Do signs that designate permanent rooms and spaces comply with the following criteria? [4.1.2(7); 4.1.3(16); 4.30.4, 5, 6]

- Character type: raised and accompanied by Grade II Braille.
- Character size: between 5/8 in. and 2 in. high; raised at least 1/32 in.
- Character style: upper case, and sans or simple serif.
- Finish: characters and backgrounds have a nonglare finish.
- Contrast: characters contrast with their background (light-on-dark or dark-on-light).

SG-05 Is the room identification sign mounted in the required location? (4.30.6)

- Mounting location: installed on the wall adjacent to the latch side of the door or where wall space to the latch side of the door is not available, including double doors, placed on the nearest adjacent wall.
- Mounting height: 60 in. above the floor/ground to the centerline of the sign.
- Sign access: approach to within 3 in. of a sign without encountering protruding objects or standing within the swing of the door.

Signage: direction and information (where provided)

DEFINITION:

- Signs that provide direction to or information about functional spaces of the building.

EXCEPTION:

- Building directories, menus, and all other temporary signs are not required to comply. [4.1.3(16)]

SG-08 Do signs that provide direction to, or information about, functional spaces of the building comply with the following criteria? [4.1.2(7); 4.1.3(16); 4.30.1, 2, 3, 5]

- Character proportion: letters and numbers have a width to height ratio between 3:5 and 1:1 and a stroke width to height ratio between 1:5 and 1:10.
- Character height: sized according to viewing distance with characters on overhead signs at least 3 in. high.

NOTE:

- When the sign is mounted below 80 in., there are no prescribed character heights. Only when the sign is mounted 80 in. or higher are the characters required to be at least 3 in. high. (4.30.3)
- Finish: characters and backgrounds have a nonglare finish.
- Contrast: characters contrast with their background (light-on-dark or dark-on-light).

SG-09 Is a sign located so that the overhead clearance or the projection of a suspended or projected sign does not result in a protruding object (free-standing or wall-mounted)?

- Clear height: at least 80 in. (4.4.2, Fig. 8a)
- Overhang for free-standing signs on posts or pylons located between 27 in. and 80 in. high: no more than a 12-in. projection into accessible routes. (4.4.1, Fig. 8c)
- Overhang for wall-mounted signs between 27 in. and 80 in. high: no more than a 4-in. projection into accessible routes. (4.4.1, Fig. 8a)

(DR) Doors (4.13)

NOTE:

- Included in this category are doors, revolving doors, turnstiles, and gates.

AUTHOR'S INTERPRETATION:

- It is suggested that, for purposes of documentation and review, a door be assigned to the space it swings into. Corridors are an exception to this rule and include only entry doors into the corridor or intermediate fire doors.

Doors: automatic or power assisted

DR-02 If an automatic door or power assisted door is used, does it comply with the appropriate ANSI standard? (4.13.12)

- Automatic door: ANSI/BHMA A156.10-1985.
- Slow opening, low powered automatic door: ANSI A156.19-1984.
- Power assisted door: ANSI A156.19-1984.

DR-03 Do slow opening, low powered automatic doors or power assisted doors comply with opening and closing requirements? (4.13.12)

- Slow opening, low powered automatic doors: do not open to back-check faster than 3 sec and require no more than 15 lbf of force to stop door movement.
- Power assisted doors: no more than 5 lbf of opening force.

Doors: maneuvering clearance

DR-04 If the door is not automatic or power assisted, does it have the required maneuvering clearance provided on the push and pull side, and is the floor level and clear within the maneuvering area? (4.13.6)

- A verbal description cannot adequately describe the requirements. See ADAAG Fig. 25a–f for a graphic description.

EXCEPTION:

- Entry doors to acute care hospital bedrooms for inpatients are exempt from maneuvering space at the latch side of the door if the door is at least 44 in. wide.

AUTHOR'S INTERPRETATION:

- While ADAAG does not describe what elements can reduce the required maneuvering clearance, they could include a narrow entry alcove, an adjacent wall, railing, or permanently installed shelving, or a deep recessed door jamb.

Doors: hardware

DR-05 Do all door handles, locks, latches, or other operable devices meet required operational criteria? (4.13.9)

- Hardware operation: operable with one hand without tight grasping, pinching, or wrist twisting.
- Force required to operate the controls: not greater than 5 lbf. This does not apply to the force required to retract latch bolts or to disengage other devices that only hold the door in a closed position.
- Hardware type: "U"-shaped handles, levers, and push type mechanisms are acceptable designs.
- Hardware height: not greater than 48 in. above the floor.
- Sliding doors: hardware is exposed and usable from both sides when the doors are fully open.

Doors: opening force

DR-06 Do interior hinged doors and sliding or folding doors have an opening force of 5 lbf or less? (4.13.11)

- At present, no accessible criteria exist for exterior doors.
- Fire doors shall have the minimum opening force allowable by the appropriate administrative authority.

Doors: closing speed

DR-07 If the door has a closer, is the closer adjusted so that the door does not close too quickly? (4.13.10)

- From an open position of 70° the door will take at least 3 sec to move to a point 3 in. from the latch (measured to the leading edge of the door).

Doors: thresholds

DR-08 Where raised thresholds are provided, do they meet height limitations and are they beveled when required? (4.13.8, 4.5.2, Fig. 7)

- Threshold height: not more than 3/4 in. for exterior sliding doors or 1/2 in. for other types of doors.
- Threshold bevel: thresholds less than 1/4 in. high need no bevel; thresholds between 1/4 in. and 1/2 in. high shall be beveled at each edge with not more than a 1:2 slope.

EXCEPTION:

- A 3/4-in. high threshold is allowed in existing conditions. [4.1.6(3)(d)(ii)]

Doors: clear opening width and height

DR-09 Is the clear opening for the doorway adequate in width and height? (4.13.3, 4, 5; Fig. 24)

- Door width: at least 32 in. of clear width with the door open at 90°, measured between the face of the door and the door stop on the latch side. This also pertains to the active leaf of a double-leaf door or gate.
- Opening width: openings more than 24 in. deep must provide 36 in. of clear width.
- Height: at least 80 in. of vertical clearance.

EXCEPTIONS:

- Doors not requiring full user passage, such as shallow closets, may have the clear opening reduced to not less than 20 in.
- Where it is technically infeasible to comply with clear opening width requirements, a projection of 5/8 in. maximum will be permitted for the latch side. [4.1.6(d)(i)]

DR-10 Is the clear opening (when there is no door) adequate in width and height? (4.2.1, 4.3.3, 4.4.2)

- Width: at least 32 in. of clear width for depths 24 in. or less and at least 36 in. of clear width for depths greater than 24 in.
- Height: at least 80 in. of vertical clearance.

Doors: two doors in a series

DR-11 If there are two doors in a series, is the required clear space between the doors provided and do the doors swing in the appropriate direction? (4.13.7, Fig. 26)

- Clear space between the doors: not less than 48 in. plus the width of any door swinging into the space.

- Door swing: must swing in the same direction or away from the space between the doors.

(RC) Restaurants and Cafeterias (5.0)

Restaurants: fixed tables or dining counters: minimum number and distribution

RC-01 Where fixed tables (or dining counters where food is consumed but there is no service) are provided, do at least 5 percent (but not fewer than 1) of the fixed tables (or a portion of the dining counter) meet accessible criteria? [5.1, 4.1.3(18)]

- Seating space: at least 30 in. × 48 in. of clear floor space that adjoins or overlaps an accessible route. No more than 19 in. of the clear floor space can be measured under the table.
- Knee space: at least 27 in. high, 30 in. wide, and 19 in. deep.
- Table/counter height: between 28 in. and 34 in. above the floor.

RC-02 Where separate areas are designated for smoking and nonsmoking patrons, are accessible tables or counters proportionally distributed between smoking and nonsmoking areas? (5.1)

- In new construction, and where practicable in alterations, the accessible tables or counters shall be distributed throughout the space.

Restaurants: counter and bar lengths

RC-03 Where counter service is provided, is a minimum counter length of 60 in. provided that has a height of not more than 34 in. and knee space at least 27 in. high? (5.2)

NOTE:

- Service provided at accessible tables within the same area can also satisfy this criteria.

Restaurants: access aisles

RC-04 Are all aisles between accessible fixed tables at least 36 in. clear between parallel edges of the tables or between a wall and the table edge? (5.3)

Restaurants: dining areas

RC-05 Are all dining areas (including raised or sunken areas, loggias, and outdoor seating areas) accessible? (5.4)

NOTE:

- In new construction, all spaces and areas must be accessible. However, in alterations or existing spaces, inaccessible areas are allowable if:
  - The same services and decor are provided in an accessible space usable by the general public.
  - The accessible area is not restricted to use by people with disabilities only.

EXCEPTION:

- An accessible means of vertical access to a mezzanine is not required in a building eligible for the elevator exception where the following three conditions exist:

  - The area of mezzanine seating is not larger than 33 percent of the accessible seating area.
  - The same services and decor are provided in an accessible space usable by the general public.
  - The accessible areas are not restricted to use by people with disabilities only.

Restaurants: food service lines

RC-06 Does the food service line have at least 36 in. of clear width between a wall or other obstruction and the face of the tray slide? (5.5, Fig. 53)

RC-07 Are the tray slides mounted no more than 34 in. above the floor? (5.5, Fig. 53)

Restaurants: self-service shelves and dispensing devices

RC-08 Are at least 50 percent of each type of self-service shelves (flatware, trays) or dispensing devices (drink machines, condiments) provided within accessible forward or side reach ranges? (5.5, Fig. 54, 4.2.5–6, Fig. 5a–b, Fig. 6a–c)

- Forward reach: not less than 15 in. high and not more than 48 in. high without any obstruction or where the obstruction is less than 20 in. deep. For obstructions from 20 in. to 25 in. deep, no forward reach higher than 44 in.
- Side reach: not less than 9 in. high and not more than 54 in. high. For obstructions not more than 34 in. high or 24 in. deep, no side reach higher than 46 in.

RC-09 Are self-service shelves and dispensing devices for tableware, dishware, condiments, food, and beverages provided with a minimum clear floor space of 30 in. × 48 in.? (5.6, Fig. 54)

Restaurants: raised platforms

AUTHOR'S INTERPRETATION:

- ADAAG addresses raised platforms only within the restaurant criteria. However, it would seem that raised platforms found in other space-types such as meeting rooms, classrooms, or auditoriums would be required to meet the same criteria.

RC-10 In banquet rooms or spaces where a head table or speaker's lectern is located on a raised platform, is the platform accessible by means of a ramp or platform lift? (5.7)

- Where applicable, review questions related to [(RP) Ramps] or [(PL) Platform Lifts].

RC-11 Are the open edges of a raised platform protected by the placement of tables, a curb, or some other form of edge protection? (5.7)

Restaurants: vending machines

RC-12 Are vending machines and other like equipment located on an accessible route? (5.8)

RC-13 Is clear floor space of at least 30 in. × 48 in. provided for a forward or parallel approach to controls or operating mechanisms on vending machines? (5.8)

(AR) Accessible Routes (4.3)

NOTES

- The interior accessible route is around and through the dining area including the route to the food service lines. However, the food service area is covered in Section RC.
- The accessible route shall, to the maximum extent feasible, coincide with the route for the general public.

AUTHOR'S INTERPRETATION:

- An accessible route "generally coincides" with the route used by the public if:
  — It does not force the user to go out of the way.
  — It is most like the route chosen by the general public.
  — It is direct.
  — It gives the same basic experience as the route preferred by the public.

Accessible Routes: width

AR-08 Is the minimum clear width along the accessible route adequate for continuous or point passage? (4.2.1, 4.3.3, Fig. 1, Fig. 8e, Fig. 24e)

- Continuous passage (greater than 24 in. long): at least a 36-in. clear width.
- Point passage (not more than 24 in. long): at least a 32-in. clear width.

AUTHOR'S INTERPRETATION:

- Noncompliance with this question generally relates to permanent elements that encroach on the accessible route. Large, heavy equipment that is not readily movable might be considered permanent. If the space is designed so that temporary elements (such as bikes in a bike rack or car bumpers) will consistently encroach, the situation might also be considered a permanent barrier.

AR-09 Is the minimum clear width along the accessible route adequate at a U-turn around an obstruction? (4.3.3, Fig. 7a–b)

- Obstruction 48 in. or greater: at least a 36-in. clear width around the obstruction.
- Obstruction less than 48 in.: at least a 42-in. clear width at each side with at least a 48-in. clear width in the turn.

Accessible Routes: passing space

AR-10 Does the accessible route provide at least 60 in. of clear width for two wheelchairs to pass and, if not, is the required passing space provided? (4.2.2, 4.3.4)

- A 60 in. × 60 in. passing space or "T" intersection should be provided at reasonable intervals not to exceed 200 ft.

AUTHOR'S INTERPRETATION:

- Accessible routes more than 5 ft long, e.g., routes in short hallways, aisles in laboratories, and work/storage areas, should have passing spaces provided.

DEFINITION:

- A *"T" intersection* is defined as the intersection of two corridors or walks, each at least 36 in. wide providing at least a 60-in. depth at the intersection. (Fig. 3b)

(RP) Ramps (4.8)

NOTE:

- Any slope on the accessible route that is greater than 1:20 is considered a ramp and shall comply with accessible requirements.

Ramps: slopes and rises

RP-01 Is the running slope for the ramp within required parameters? (4.8.2, Fig. 16)

- New construction: 1:12 slope or less with not more than a 30-in. rise for any run.
  — 1:12 slope: 30-ft run between landings.
  — 1:16 slope: 40-ft run between landings.
- On existing sites where space limitations prohibit the use of a slope of 1:12 or less, the following slopes can be considered. [4.1.6(3)(a)(i–ii)]
  — Between 1:10 and 1:12 for a maximum rise of 6 in.
  — Between 1:8 and 1:10 for a maximum rise of 3 in.
  — A slope steeper than 1:8 is not allowed.

EXCEPTION:

- In historic buildings, a ramp with a slope no greater than 1:6 for a run not to exceed 2 ft may be used as part of an accessible route to an entrance. [4.1.7(3)(a)]

RP-02 Is the cross slope of the ramp 1:50 or less? (4.8.6)

Ramps: clear width

RP-03 Is the clear width (between handrails) of the ramp at least 36 in.? (4.8.3)

Ramps: landings

RP-04 Is there a level landing at the top and bottom of each ramp and each ramp run? (4.8.4)

- If a doorway is located at a landing, then the area in front of the doorway must meet door maneuvering clearance requirements.

RP-05 Does each ramp landing meet required dimensions? [4.8.4(1–2)]

- Landing width: at least equal to the ramp width.
- Landing length: at least 60 in. long.

RP-06 Where the ramp changes direction, is there a landing of at least 60 in. × 60 in.? [4.8.4(3)]

Ramps: handrails

NOTE:

- Additional criteria for handrails can be found in Section "HR, Handrails."

RP-07 If the ramp rises more than 6 in. or is longer than 72 in., does it have a handrail on each side? (4.8.5)

- Handrails are not required on curb ramps or adjacent to seating in assembly areas.

RP-08 Is the handrail provided on both sides of ramp segments and is the inside rail on switchback or dogleg ramps continuous? [4.8.5(1), Fig. 19a–b]

RP-09 At the end of the ramp handrails, is there at least 12 in. of handrail parallel to the floor or ground surface, extending beyond the top and the bottom of the ramp segments? [4.8.5(2), Fig. 17]

RP-10 Is the clearance between the ramp handrail and the wall exactly 1½ in.? [4.8.5(3)]

- For recesses, see ADAAG Fig. 39.

RP-11 Are the tops of ramp handrails between 34 in. and 38 in. above ramp surfaces? [4.8.5(5)]

RP-12 Is the ramp handrail gripping surface continuous without obstructions or missing segments? [4.8.5(4)]

RP-13 Are the ends of ramp handrails rounded or returned smoothly to the floor, wall, or post? [4.8.5(6)]

RP-14 Are the ramp handrails fixed so that they do not rotate within their fittings? [4.8.5(7)]

Ramps: edge protection and floor surfaces

RP-15 If a ramp or landing has a drop-off, is it protected by an acceptable option? (4.8.7, Fig. 17)

- Acceptable options include: a wall, a minimum 12-in. horizontal floor extension beyond the railing, a minimum 2-in. curb, or a railing design that prevents people from falling or rolling off.

RP-16 Is the ramp floor surface stable, firm, and slip-resistant? (4.5.1)

(HR) Handrails (4.26)

NOTE:

- HR Guidelines may be repeated in other element-based guidelines: (RP) Ramps, (ST) Stairs, (WC) Water Closets, (TS) Toilet Stalls, (BT) Bathtubs, and (SS) Shower Stalls.

Handrails: size and spacing

HR-01 Is the gripping surface of the grab bars or handrails 1¼ in. to 1½ in. in outside diameter? (4.26.2, Fig. 39)

AUTHOR'S INTERPRETATION:

- Standard pipe sizes designated by the industry as 1¼ in. to 1½ in. are acceptable for purposes of this section.

HR-02 Do the grab bars or handrails have edges with a minimum radius of 1/8 in.? (4.26.4)

HR-03 Is the clearance between the grab bars or handrails and the wall exactly 1½ in.? (4.26.2, Fig. 39)

Handrails: grab bar or handrail structural strength

HR-06 Do the grab bars and handrails meet the structural strength requirements for bending stress and shear stress? (4.26.3)

- Actual bending stress in the grab bar induced by the maximum bending moment from the application of 250 lbf is less than the allowable bending stress for the material of the grab bar.
- Shear stress induced in a grab bar by the application of 250 lbf shall be less than the allowable shear stress for the material of the grab bar. If the connection between the grab bar and its mounting bracket or other support is considered to be fully restrained, then direct and torsional shear stresses shall be totaled for the combined shear stress, which shall not exceed the allowable shear stress.

HR-07 Do the fasteners and mounting devices for the grab bars or handrails meet the structural strength requirements for shear force and tensile force? (4.26.3)

- Shear force induced in a fastener or mounting device from the application of 250 lbf shall be less than the allowable lateral load of either the fastener or mounting device or the supporting structure, whichever is the smaller allowable load.
- Tensile force induced in a fastener by a direct tension force of 250 lbf plus the maximum moment from the application of 250 lbf shall be less than the allowable withdrawal load between the fastener and the supporting structure.

Handrails: hazards

HR-10 Are handrails or grab bars and any wall or other surfaces adjacent to them free of any sharp or abrasive elements? (4.26.4)

(PR) Protruding Objects (4.4)

Protruding Objects: general

PR-01 Do wall-mounted objects having leading edges between 27 in. and 80 in. high project less than 4 in. into walkways, corridors, aisles, or paths of travel? (4.4.1, Fig. 8a–e)

- Objects mounted with their leading edge at or below 27 in. can protrude any amount, as long as they do not reduce the required clear width of an accessible route.

AUTHOR'S INTERPRETATION:

- Protruding objects might include fire extinguishers or cabinets, pencil sharpeners, shelving, edges of counter tops, built-in equipment, and various dispensers such as for paper towels or soap.

PR-02 Do free-standing objects, suspended or mounted on posts or pylons with leading edges between 27 in. and 80 in. high, project less than 12 in. into the perpendicular route of travel? (4.4.1, Fig. 8a–e)

AUTHOR'S INTERPRETATION:

- These might include telephone enclosures, drinking fountains, or free-standing signage kiosks.

PR-03 Is the minimum clear route width or maneuvering space still maintained even with the projection of a protruding object? (4.4.1, Fig. 8a–e)

Protruding Objects: overhead clearance

PR-04 Is the minimum overhead clearance of 80 in. provided in accessible areas or along accessible routes? (4.4.2, Fig. 8a)

AUTHOR'S INTERPRETATION:

- Overhead objects that can reduce the required clearance might include structures, pipes, ducts, or light fixtures.

(FS) Floor and Ground Surfaces (4.5)

Floor Surfaces: general

FS-01 Are the floor/ground surfaces on the accessible route stable, firm, and slip-resistant? (4.5.1)

AUTHOR'S INTERPRETATION:

- Exterior spaces, interior circulation, bathrooms, and other spaces where water can collect on the floor around an element (sinks, drinking fountains, hose bibbs, etc.) are reviewed as if wet.
- High gloss surfaces without significant textures that are regularly maintained with waxing (smooth tiles, waxed concrete, etc.) could be considered non-compliant.
- Accessible criteria are not specified for nonpermanent floor surfaces such as mats or rugs.

Floor Surfaces: changes in level

FS-02 Are vertical changes in level between 1/4 in. and 1/2 in. beveled with a slope of 1:2 or less? (4.5.2)

- Changes in level up to 1/4 in. may be vertical without edge treatment.
- Changes in level greater than 1/2 in. should be accomplished by means of a curb ramp, ramp, elevator, or platform lift (as permitted in ADAAG 4.1.3 and 4.1.6).

Floor Surfaces: carpet

FS-03 Does carpet or carpet tile used on the floor comply with accessible criteria? (4.5.3, Fig. 8f)

- Attachment: secured.
- Exposed edges: fastened and trimmed along the entire length.
- Pile type: low pile (1/2 in. maximum).
- Padding: firm pad or no pad underneath.

(CT) Controls and Operating Mechanisms (4.27)

NOTES:

- Controls or operating mechanisms can include elements such as light switches, pencil sharpeners, manual overhead screens, nonkeyed thermostats, alarm pull stations, fire extinguisher cabinets, A/C window units, microwave ovens, towel dispensers, and wall hooks.
- If controls are to be operated by occupants of the space, they must be accessible. If controls are to be operated by maintenance staff only and not by occupants or other users of the space, they do not have to be accessible. For example, thermostats in auditoriums usually do not have to be accessible, while thermostats in classrooms may need to be accessible.

Controls: clear floor space

CT-01 Is a clear floor space of at least 30 in. × 48 in. provided in front of controls, dispensers, receptacles, and other operable equipment for forward or parallel approach? (4.27.2, Fig. 4a–b)

Controls: reach ranges

NOTES:

- Accessible reach ranges for controls and operating mechanisms are:
  — Forward reach: not less than 15 in. high and not more than 48 in. high without any obstruction or where the obstruction is less than 20 in. deep. For obstructions from 20 in. to 25 in. deep, no forward reach higher than 44 in.
  — Side reach: not less than 9 in. high and not more than 54 in. high. For obstructions not more than 34 in. high or 24 in. deep, no side reach higher than 46 in.
  — Electrical outlets, switches, and communication system receptacles have a minimum outlet height of 15 in. regardless of forward or side reach. See CT-02 below.

CT-02 Are electrical outlets, switches, and communication system receptacles mounted within accessible forward or side reach ranges? (4.27.3)

EXCEPTION:

- These requirements do not apply where the use of special equipment dictates otherwise or where electrical and communications system receptacles are not normally intended for use by building occupants. (4.27.3)

CT-04 Are dispensers or other similar operable equipment mounted within accessible forward or side reach ranges? (4.2.5, 4.2.6, Fig. 5a–b, Fig. 6a–c)

CT-05 Are life safety devices or other similar operable equipment mounted within accessible forward or side reach ranges? (4.2.5, 4.2.6, Fig. 5a–b, Fig. 6a–c)

NOTE:

- This might include fire alarm pull stations, handles to extinguisher cabinets, or wall-mounted extinguishers.

Controls: operation

CT-06 Are controls, dispensers, receptacles, and other operable equipment operable with one hand without tight grasping, pinching, or wrist twisting, and requiring no more than 5 lbf of force? (4.27.4)

(TL) Telephones (4.31)

DEFINITION:

- Telephone types include public pay telephones, public closed circuit telephones, or other public telephones.

AUTHOR'S INTERPRETATION:

- Frequently, public pay telephones are provided by a contractual agreement with a vendor. The vendor, through the contract, might be made responsible for compliance with all applicable ADAAG criteria.

Telephones: number required

TL-02 If there is a single bank of public telephones on a floor, does at least one of the telephones in the bank comply with accessible criteria? [4.1.3(17)(a)]

- A bank consists of two or more adjacent public telephones, often installed as a unit.
- Unless otherwise specified, accessible telephones may be either forward or side reach telephones.

Telephones: clear floor or ground space

TL-04 Does the accessible telephone have at least a 30 in. × 48 in. clear floor or ground space that allows either a forward or side approach? (4.31.2, Fig. 44, 4.2.4)

- Bases, enclosures, and fixed seats shall not impede approaches to telephones.
  - If this clear floor space is located in an alcove or confined space, see ADAAG Fig. 4d–e for additional maneuvering clearance requirements.

TL-05 Does an accessible route adjoin or overlap the clear floor space for the accessible telephone? (4.31.2, Fig. 44, 4.2.4)

Telephones: protruding object

TL-06 Do wall-mounted or post-mounted telephones with leading edges between 27 in. and 80 in. from the floor have projections that do not result in a protruding object? (4.31.4, 4.4.1)

- Wall-mounted: project less than 4 in. into the pathway.
- Post-mounted: project less than 12 in. into a perpendicular route of travel.

Telephones: mounting height

TL-07 Is the highest operable part of the telephone within forward or side reach ranges? (4.31.3, 4.2.6)

- Forward: not more than 48 in. above the floor.
- Side: not more than 54 in. above the floor.

(SR) Storage (4.25)

NOTE:

- Accessible reach range requirements do not apply to shelves or display units allowing self-service by customers in mercantile occupancies but they must be located on an accessible route. [4.1.3(12)(b)]

Storage: general

SR-01 Does at least one of each type of fixed or built-in storage unit comply with accessible criteria? [4.1.3(12)(a), 4.25.1]

  NOTE:

  - Types of storage facilities might include cabinets, shelves, closets, and drawers.

Storage: clear floor space

SR-02 Is there a clear floor space at least 30 in. × 48 in. at fixed or built-in storage units that allows for either a forward or side approach? (4.25.2, Fig. 4a–b)

Storage: reach ranges

SR-03 Are forward or side reach for each type of accessible storage unit within acceptable reach ranges? (4.2.5–6, Fig. 5a–b, Fig. 6a–c, 4.25.3)

- Forward reach: not less than 15 in. high and not more than 48 in. high without any obstruction or where the obstruction is less than 20 in. deep. For obstructions from 20 in. to 25 in. deep, no forward reach higher than 44 in.
- Side reach: not less than 9 in. high and not more than 54 in. high. For obstructions not more than 34 in. high or 24 in. deep, no side reach higher than 46 in.

Storage: hardware

SR-05 Is the hardware on the storage unit doors or drawers operable with one hand without tight grasping, pinching, or wrist twisting, and requiring no more than 5 lbf of force? (4.25.4, 4.27.4)

(AL) Alarms (4.28)

NOTE:

- At a minimum, visual signal appliances shall be provided in buildings and facilities in restrooms and any other general usage areas. **The ADAAG does not define the number of occupants needed to establish a general or common use area.**

ALLOWANCE:

- Emergency warning systems in medical care facilities may be modified to suit standard health care alarm design practice. [4.1.3(14)]

Alarms: general

AL-01 If emergency warning systems are provided, do they include both audible alarms and visual alarms? [4.1.3(14)]

Audible Alarms: general

AL-02 If provided, do the audible alarms meet required operational criteria? (4.28.2)

- Sound level: exceeds the prevailing sound level in the room or space by at least 15 dbA or exceeds any maximum sound level with a duration of 60 sec by 5 dbA, whichever is louder.
- Sound levels for alarm signals shall not exceed 120 dbA.

AL-03 If single station audible alarms are provided, then are single station visual alarm signals also provided? (4.28.3)

Visual Alarms: general

AL-04 If provided, are the visual alarm signal appliances integrated into the building or facility alarm system? (4.28.3)

AL-05 If provided, do the visual alarm signals meet required operational criteria? [4.28.3(1, 2, 3, 4, 5)]

- Lamp: xenon strobe type or equivalent.
- Color: clear or nominal white (i.e., unfiltered or clear filtered white light).
- Pulse duration: maximum shall be 0.2 sec with a maximum duty cycle of 40 percent.
- Intensity: not less than 75 candela.
- Flash rate: not less than 1 Hz and not more than 3 Hz.

AL-07 Are visual alarm signal appliances provided in general usage areas of the building (such as meeting rooms, corridors, and lobbies) or any other area for common use? (4.28.1)

AUTHOR'S INTERPRETATION:

- The authors identified three or more occupants as the minimum number to establish a common use area.

AL-08 Are the visual alarms placed at 80 in. above the highest floor level or 6 in. below the ceiling, whichever is lower? [4.28.3(6)]

AL-09 In spaces required to have visual alarms, are the alarms spaced properly? [4.28.3(7)]

- No place in any space should be more than 50 ft from a visual signal alarm.

- Where a space or large room exceeds 100 ft across, without obstructions 6 ft above the finished floor, visual alarms can be spaced a maximum of 100 ft apart at the perimeter, in lieu of suspending appliances from the ceiling.

Toilet Rooms

Introduction. Use this "Space-type Review Guide" to design or evaluate public and common use toilet areas in both single and multiple use facilities. Where locker rooms with shower areas are included, use the Dressing, Fitting, and Locker Rooms "Space-type Review Guide." When there is a single or multiple use bathroom with shower(s), bathtub(s), toilet stall(s), and so on refer to Transient Lodging: Single and Multiple User Bathroom "Space-type Review Guide."

Toilet rooms in public buildings and businesses pose special accessibility concerns for designers because of the relatively small area allotted and the large number of individual elements that may be included. For example, toilet rooms often have a vestibule connected to a main corridor by two doors in a series. Adequate space for a person in a wheelchair to open these two doors and to pass into the lavatory and toilet stall areas must be provided. Changes of material from the corridor to the toilet room are common and a threshold dividing these materials must not result in an inaccessible level change. Once inside the main area, clear floor space as well as an unobstructed accessible turning space or a "T"-shaped turning space is required so that a wheelchair user can approach lavatories, urinals, and water closets or toilet stalls. The clear floor space of fixtures and controls, the accessible route, and the turning space may overlap one another. Door swings cannot overlap into the clear floor space of any accessible fixture or element. Toilet rooms require floor surfaces that are slip-resistant.

Another set of factors that complicates toilet rooms is the large number of elements that must be accessible and also allow clear movement between each other (e.g., toilet stalls including grab bars, water closets, urinals, lavatories and mirrors, controls/switches, hand dryers and dispensers). Although the ADAAG does not require that particular elements such as dispensers, receptacles, and coat hooks be placed in toilet rooms, if they are included, then one of each different type must be accessible. Towel and soap dispensers, purse and package shelves, and trash receptacles are often designed to fasten onto a wall surface. Placement of these elements can result in a protruding object or a reduction in required clear floor space or widths. Visual alarm signals must be visible in all areas of a toilet room to a person who is hearing-impaired.

PRELIMINARY DESIGN OVERVIEW

(AR) Accessible Routes
- Typical requirements.

(AL) Alarms
- Visual alarms must be provided in toilet rooms.

(BR) Toilet/Bathrooms
- Typical requirements.

(CT) Controls and Operating Mechanisms
- One of each type of receptacle and dispenser (if provided) must be accessible and operable.

(DR) Doors
- Two doors in a series must meet both clear space and door swing requirements (e.g., vestibules, toilet room entries, etc.).
- Changes in flooring materials from a corridor to a toilet room, with a threshold dividing these materials, must not result in an inaccessible level change.

(FS) Floor Surfaces
- Toilet room floor surfaces should be evaluated as if wet.
- Smooth floor surfaces should be evaluated for slip-resistance based on floor finish and maintenance.
- Vertical changes in levels along the accessible route can be an unforeseen barrier, e.g., transition between floor materials.
- Floor drains located on the accessible route must meet accessibility requirements.

(HR) Handrails, Grab Bars, and Tub and Shower Seats
- Typical requirements.

(LV) Lavatories, Sinks, and Mirrors
- Hot pipes and sharp objects (e.g., valves and drains) must be shielded under lavatories and sinks.
- Sinks or lavatories used for different purposes must be accessible.
- Where mirrors are provided, one must be accessible. The bottom edge of the reflecting surface (slanted or flush-mounted) must meet accessibility requirements.

(PR) Protruding Objects
- Common wall-mounted elements can be protruding objects, e.g., soap and towel dispensers, trash receptacles, wall-mounted lavatories, counters, and infant changing stations.
- Overhead clearances can be an unforeseen compliance problem, e.g., frames of toilet stalls may not meet vertical clearances.

(SG) Signage
- If all toilet rooms are not accessible, the accessible toilet rooms must be identified by the ISA symbol.

(TS) Toilet Stalls

- The direction of approach greatly affects compliance requirements.
- If six or more toilet stalls are provided, one must be a standard accessible stall and one must comply with the requirements for the alternate accessible stall.
- Doors that swing into the stall increase the overall stall dimensions.
- Toilet stall doors must not swing into the clear floor space of any other accessible fixture.

(UR) Urinals

- While the height of the accessible urinal is prescribed, the depth of the rim of an elongated urinal is not currently defined by ADAAG.
- Partitions extending beyond the front edge of the urinal must meet accessibility criteria.
- Reach range criteria for flush valve controls for urinals are restricted to front reach range requirements.

(WC) Water Closets

- Water closets are not centered in the stall; they are located relative to a side wall or partition.
- Flush valve controls are required to be on the wide side of the toilet area.

ADAAG APPENDIX

The ADAAG Appendix has advisory information pertinent to this space-type.

- A4.16.3 Water Closets—Height
- A4.16.4 Water Closet—Grab Bars
- A4.16.5 Water Closet—Flush Controls
- A4.17.3 Toilet Stalls—Size and Arrangement
- A4.17.5 Toilet Stalls—Doors
- A4.19.6 Lavatories and Mirrors—Mirrors
- A4.22.3 Toilet Rooms—Clear Floor Space

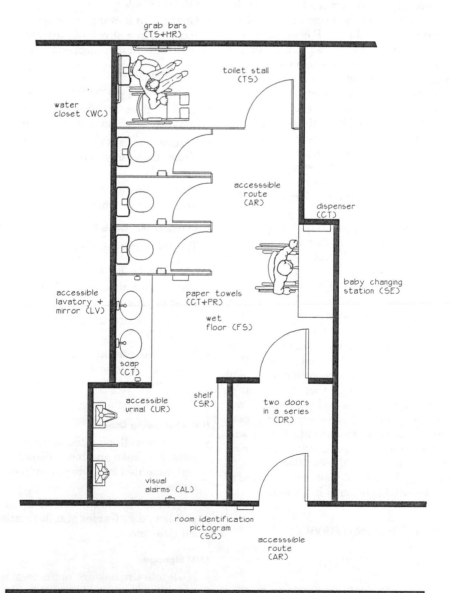

Figure 3-19. Toilet room.

Toilet Rooms Checklist

SIGNAGE

SG02	Entry signage: inaccessible entrances
SG03	Inaccessible entry signage: criteria
SG04	Room signage: criteria
SG05	Room signage: location
SG06	Pictograms: size requirements
SG07	Pictograms: verbal description criteria

DOORS

DR04	Doors: maneuvering clearances
DR05	Doors: handle type
DR06	Doors: opening force (interior only)
DR07	Doors: closing speed
DR08	Doors: thresholds
DR09	Doors: clear width/height
DR10	Openings (no door): clear width/height
DR11	Doors in series: clear space between

BATHROOMS, TOILET ROOMS, BATHING FACILITIES, AND SHOWER ROOMS

BR06	Unisex toilet room: required equipment
BR07	Toilet/bath/shower room: accessible route
BR08	Toilet/bathroom: ISA signage
BR09	Controls and fixtures: accessible route
BR10	Clear floor space: clear of door swing
BR11	Wheelchair turning space
BR18	Controls, dispensers, etc.: accessible
BR20	Medicine cabinet: accessible shelf

ACCESSIBLE ROUTES

AR08	Route: clear width
AR09	Route width: U-turns

PROTRUDING OBJECTS

PR01	Wall-mounted
PR02	Freestanding/suspended on posts/pylons
PR03	Clear route width maintained
PR04	Overhead clearance
PR05	Vertical clearance: cane detection barrier

FLOOR AND GROUND SURFACES

FS01	Surface: firm, stable, and slip-resistant
FS02	Vertical changes in level
FS03	Carpet and tile floors
FS04	Floor gratings

CONTROLS AND OPERATING MECHANISMS

CT01	Clear floor space
CT02	Reach ranges: elec./comm. systems
CT03	Reach ranges: thermostats
CT04	Reach ranges: other controls
CT05	Reach ranges: life safety devices
CT06	Controls: operation

TOILET STALLS

TS01	Accessible route: location
TS02	Required aisle clearance: approach
TS03	Door swings out: maneuvering space
TS04	"Standard": number required
TS05	"Standard": door swing/clear floor space
TS06	"Alternate": number required
TS07	Stall less than 60 in. deep: toe clearance
TS08	Stall doors: dimensions
TS09	Stall doors: hardware and opening force
TS10	"Standard" grab bars: length/placement
TS11	"Alternate" grab bars: length/placement

WATER CLOSETS

WC01	Accessible toilet: centerline location
WC02	Toilet seat: criteria
WC03	Flush controls: location
WC04	Flush controls: operation
WC05	Paper dispensers: location and operation
WC06	Water closet/no stall: clear floor space
WC07	Water closet grab bars/no stall: criteria

HANDRAILS, GRAB BARS, TUB AND SHOWER SEATS

HR01	Handrails and grab bars: diameter
HR02	Handrails and grab bars: edge radius
HR03	Clearance between handrail and wall
HR04	Handrails in recess: criteria
HR05	Handrails and grab bars: no rotation
HR06	Handrails and grab bars: structural strength
HR07	Mounting devices: structural strength
HR10	Wall adjacent to handrail abrasion free

URINALS

UR01	Elongated rim: height above floor
UR02	Clear floor space: forward reach
UR03	Clear width between shields
UR04	Flush controls: reach range
UR05	Flush controls: operation

LAVATORIES, SINKS, AND MIRRORS

LV01	Clear floor space
LV02	Rim/apron heights and extension from wall
LV03	Toe clearance
LV04	Insulated pipes
LV05	Controls and operation requirements
LV06	Lavatories: knee clearance
LV09	Mirror: mounting height

ALARMS

AL04	Visual alarms: integration w/building alarm
AL05	Visual alarms: operation
AL06	Visual alarms: public restrooms
AL07	Visual alarms: common use areas
AL08	Visual alarms: vertical placement

TOILET ROOMS
COMPREHENSIVE CRITERIA

(SG) Signage (4.30)

Signage: entry:

SG-02 If an entrance is not accessible, is there a directional sign indicating the location of the nearest accessible entrance? [4.1.2(7)(c), 4.1.3(8)(d)]

SG-03 Does the directional sign indicating the location of the nearest accessible entrance comply with directional signage criteria? (4.30.2, 3, 5)

- Character proportion: letters and numbers have a width to height ratio between 3:5 and 1:1 and a stroke width to height ratio between 1:5 and 1:10.
- Character height: sized according to viewing distance with characters on overhead signs at least 3 in. high.
- Finish: characters and backgrounds have a nonglare finish.
- Contrast: characters contrast with their background (light-on-dark or dark-on-light).

Signage: room identification (where provided)

DEFINITION:

- These signs designate permanent rooms and spaces.

AUTHOR'S INTERPRETATION:

- Signs that designate stairs, exit doors, and toilet rooms generally are associated with permanent spaces, while an "office" sign is not since the room function may change over time. Room numbers also must meet the ADAAG criteria as permanent designations, while personal names do not since the occupant may change over time.

SG-04 Do signs that designate permanent rooms and spaces comply with the following criteria? [4.1.2(7); 4.1.3(16); 4.30.4, 5, 6]

- Character type: raised and accompanied by Grade II Braille.
- Character size: between 5/8 in. and 2 in. high; raised at least 1/32 in.
- Character style: upper case, and sans or simple serif.
- Finish: characters and backgrounds have a nonglare finish.
- Contrast: characters contrast with their background (light-on-dark or dark-on-light).

SG-05 Is the room identification sign mounted in the required location? (4.30.6)

- Mounting location: installed on the wall adjacent to the latch side of the door or where wall space to the latch side of the door is not available, including double doors, placed on the nearest adjacent wall.
- Mounting height: 60 in. above the floor/ground to the centerline of the sign.
- Sign access: approach to within 3 in. of a sign without encountering protruding objects or standing within the swing of the door.

Signage: pictorial symbol signs (pictograms) (where provided)

AUTHOR'S INTERPRETATION:

- Because the criteria for pictograms are listed in ADAAG 4.30.4, they fall into the category of room identification signage and must meet those criteria that follow.
- While the ISA symbol might be considered to be a pictogram, it does not appear to have the same requirements as pictograms.

SG-06 Is the border dimension of a pictogram, where provided, at least 6 in. high? (4.30.4)

AUTHOR'S INTERPRETATION:

- A pictogram includes both a symbol and the field on which it is displayed. The 6-in. vertical dimension applies to the vertical field, not to the symbol. The required verbal description may not intrude on the 6-in. field.

SG-07 Is a pictogram, where provided, accompanied by the equivalent verbal description placed directly below the pictogram, and does the verbal description meet room identification signage criteria? (4.30.4)

- Character type: raised and accompanied by Grade II Braille.
- Character size: between 5/8 in. and 2 in. high; raised at least 1/32 in.
- Character style: upper case, and sans or simple serif.
- Finish: characters and backgrounds have a nonglare finish.
- Contrast: characters contrast with their background (light-on-dark or dark-on-light).

(DR) Doors (4.13)

AUTHOR'S INTERPRETATION:

- It is suggested that, for purposes of documentation and review, a door be assigned to the space it swings into. Corridors are an exception to this rule and include only entry doors into the corridor or intermediate fire doors.

Doors: maneuvering clearance

DR-04 If the door is not automatic or power assisted, does it have the required maneuvering clearance provided on the push and pull side, and is the floor level and clear within the maneuvering area? (4.13.6)

- A verbal description cannot adequately describe the requirements. See ADAAG Fig. 25a–f for a graphic description.

EXCEPTION:

- Entry doors to acute care hospital bedrooms for inpatients are exempt from maneuvering space at the latch side of the door if the door is at least 44 in. wide.

AUTHOR'S INTERPRETATION:

- While ADAAG does not describe what elements can reduce the required maneuvering clearance, they could include a narrow entry alcove, an adjacent wall, railing, or permanently installed shelving, or a deep recessed door jamb.

Doors: hardware

DR-05 Do all door handles, locks, latches, or other operable devices meet required operational criteria? (4.13.9)

- Hardware operation: operable with one hand without tight grasping, pinching, or wrist twisting.
- Force required to operate the controls: not greater than 5 lbf. This does not apply to the force required to retract latch bolts or to disengage other devices that only hold the door in a closed position.
- Hardware type: "U"-shaped handles, levers, and push type mechanisms are acceptable designs.
- Hardware height: not greater than 48 in. above the floor.
- Sliding doors: hardware is exposed and usable from both sides when the doors are fully open.

Doors: opening force

DR-06 Do interior hinged doors and sliding or folding doors have an opening force of 5 lbf or less? (4.13.11)

- At present, no accessible criteria exist for exterior doors.
- Fire doors shall have the minimum opening force allowable by the appropriate administrative authority.

Doors: closing speed

DR-07 If the door has a closer, is the closer adjusted so that the door does not close too quickly? (4.13.10)

- From an open position of 70° the door will take at least 3 sec to move to a point 3 in. from the latch (measured to the leading edge of the door).

Doors: thresholds

DR-08 Where raised thresholds are provided, do they meet height limitations and are they beveled when required? (4.13.8, 4.5.2, Fig. 7)

- Threshold height: not more than 3/4 in. for exterior sliding doors or 1/2 in. for other types of doors.
- Threshold bevel: thresholds less than 1/4 in. high need no bevel; thresholds between 1/4 in. to 1/2 in. high shall be beveled at each edge with not more than a 1:2 slope.

  EXCEPTION:
- A 3/4-in. high threshold is allowed in existing conditions. [4.1.6(3)(d)(ii)]

Doors: clear opening width and height

DR-09 Is the clear opening for the doorway adequate in width and height? (4.13.3, 4, 5; Fig. 24)

- Door width: at least 32 in. of clear width with the door open at 90°, measured between the face of the door and the door stop on the latch side. This also pertains to the active leaf of a double-leaf door or gate.
- Opening width: openings more than 24 in. deep must provide 36 in. of clear width.
- Height: at least 80 in. of vertical clearance.

  EXCEPTIONS:
- Doors not requiring full user passage, such as shallow closets, may have the clear opening reduced to not less than 20 in.

- Where it is technically infeasible to comply with clear opening width requirements, a projection of 5/8 in. maximum will be permitted for the latch side. [4.1.6(d)(i)]

DR-10 Is the clear opening (when there is no door) adequate in width and height? (4.2.1, 4.3.3, 4.4.2)

- Width: at least 32 in. of clear width for depths 24 in. or less and at least 36 in. of clear width for depths greater than 24 in.
- Height: at least 80 in. of vertical clearance.

Doors: two doors in a series

DR-11 If there are two doors in a series, is the required clear space between the doors provided and do the doors swing in the appropriate direction? (4.13.7, Fig. 26)

- Clear space between the doors: not less than 48 in. plus the width of any door swinging into the space.
- Door swing: must swing in the same direction or away from the space between the doors.

(BR) Bathrooms, Toilet Rooms, Bathing Facilities, and Shower Rooms (4.23)

NOTE:

- In historic buildings, if toilets are provided, at least one toilet facility complying with toilet room accessible criteria shall be provided along an accessible route. Such a toilet facility may be unisex in design. [4.1.7(3)(c)]

Toilet/Bathrooms: alternatives

BR-06 Does each accessible unisex toilet/bathroom contain one accessible water closet, one accessible lavatory, and a door with a privacy latch? [4.1.6(3)(e)(i)]

Toilet/Bathrooms: general

BR-07 Are accessible toilet rooms, bathrooms, bathing facilities, or shower rooms located on an accessible route? (4.22.1, 4.23.1)

BR-08 When some toilet/bathrooms are not accessible, are the accessible toilet/bathrooms identified by the International Symbol of Accessibility? [4.1.2(7)(d), Fig. 3a–b]

BR-09 If provided, are accessible fixtures and controls located on an accessible route? (4.22.2, 4.23.2)

BR-10 Does the door swing not reduce the clear floor space for accessible fixtures? (4.22.2, 4.23.2)

BR-11 Is the minimum clear floor space for an unobstructed 180° turning space or a "T"-shaped turning space provided in the toilet/bathroom? (4.22.3, 4.23.3, Fig. 3)

- 180° turning space has a 60-in. diameter; "T"-shaped space has 36-in. wide legs.
- Clear floor space at fixtures and controls, the accessible route, and the turning space can overlap.

BR-18 Is at least one of each type of control, dispenser, receptacle, or other equipment provided accessible and on an accessible route? (4.22.7, 4.23.7)

BR-20 If medicine cabinets are provided, does at least one cabinet have a usable shelf no higher than 44 in. from the floor and a clear floor space of at least 30 in. × 48 in.? (4.23.9)

(AR) Accessible Routes (4.3)

NOTES:

- All walks, halls, corridors, aisles, skywalks, tunnels, and other spaces that are part of a designated accessible route shall comply with accessible requirements.
- Any slope on the accessible route that is greater than 1:20 is required to meet all ramp criteria.
- The accessible route shall, to the maximum extent feasible, coincide with the route for the general public.
- In historic buildings, accessible routes from an accessible entrance shall be provided to all publicly used spaces on at least the level of the accessible entrance. Access shall be provided to all levels of a building or facility whenever practical. [4.1.7(3)(d)]

AUTHOR'S INTERPRETATION:

- An accessible route "generally coincides" with the route used by the public if:
  — It does not force the user to go out of the way.
  — It is most like the route chosen by the general public.
  — It is direct.
  — It gives the same basic experience as the route preferred by the public.

Accessible Routes: width

AR-08 Is the minimum clear width along the accessible route adequate for continuous or point passage? (4.2.1, 4.3.3, Fig. 1, Fig. 8e, Fig. 24e)

- Continuous passage (greater than 24 in. long): at least a 36-in. clear width.
- Point passage (not more than 24 in. long): at least a 32-in. clear width.

AUTHOR'S INTERPRETATION:

- Noncompliance with this question generally relates to permanent elements that encroach on the accessible route. Large, heavy equipment that is not readily movable might be considered permanent. If the space is designed so that temporary elements (such as bikes in a bike rack or car bumpers) will consistently encroach, the situation might also be considered a permanent barrier.

AR-09 Is the minimum clear width along the accessible route adequate at a U-turn around an obstruction? (4.3.3, Fig. 7a–b)

- Obstruction 48 in. or greater: at least a 36-in. clear width around the obstruction.
- Obstruction less than 48 in.: at least a 42-in. clear width at each side with at least a 48-in. clear width in the turn.

(PR) Protruding Objects (4.4)

Protruding Objects: general

PR-01 Do wall-mounted objects having leading edges between 27 in. and 80 in. high project less than 4 in. into walkways, corridors, aisles, or paths of travel? (4.4.1, Fig. 8a–e)

- Objects mounted with their leading edge at or below 27 in. can protrude any amount, as long as they do not reduce the required clear width of an accessible route.

AUTHOR'S INTERPRETATION:

- Protruding objects might include fire extinguishers or cabinets, pencil sharpeners, shelving, counters, built-in equipment overhangs, or various dispensers such as for paper towels or soap.

PR-02 Do free-standing objects, suspended or mounted on posts or pylons with leading edges between 27 in. and 80 in. high, project less than 12 in. into the perpendicular route of travel? (4.4.1, Fig. 8a–e)

AUTHOR'S INTERPRETATION:

- These might include telephone enclosures, drinking fountains, or free-standing signage kiosks.

PR-03 Is the minimum clear route width or maneuvering space still maintained even with the projection of a protruding object? (4.4.1, Fig. 8a–e)

Protruding Objects: overhead clearance

PR-04 Is the minimum overhead clearance of 80 in. provided in accessible areas or along accessible routes? (4.4.2, Fig. 8a)

AUTHOR'S INTERPRETATION:

- Overhead objects that can reduce the required clearance might include structures, pipes, ducts, or light fixtures.

PR-05 Where the vertical clearance of a space adjoining the accessible route is less than 80 in. high, is a cane detection barrier less than 27 in. from the floor provided for blind or visually impaired persons? (4.4.2, Fig. 8c-1)

AUTHOR'S INTERPRETATION:

- This condition might be found under a stair, at a sloped ceiling space, or with guy wires from telephone poles along an exterior accessible route.

(FS) Floor and Ground Surfaces (4.5)

Floor Surfaces: general

FS-01 Are the floor/ground surfaces on the accessible route stable, firm, and slip-resistant? (4.5.1)

AUTHOR'S INTERPRETATION:

- Exterior spaces, interior circulation, bathrooms, and other spaces where water can collect on the floor around an element (sinks, drinking fountains, hose bibbs, etc.) are reviewed as if wet.
- High gloss surfaces without significant textures that are regularly maintained with waxing (smooth tiles, waxed concrete, etc.) could be considered noncompliant.
- Accessible criteria are not specified for nonpermanent floor surfaces such as mats or rugs.

Floor Surfaces: changes in level

FS-02 Are vertical changes in level between 1/4 in. and 1/2 in. beveled with a slope of 1:2 or less? (4.5.2)

- Changes in level up to 1/4 in. may be vertical without edge treatment.
- Changes in level greater than 1/2 in. should be accomplished by means of a curb ramp, ramp, elevator, or platform lift (as permitted in ADAAG 4.1.3 and 4.1.6).

Floor Surfaces: carpet

FS-03 Does carpet or carpet tile used on the floor comply with accessible criteria?

- Attachment: secured. (4.5.3, Fig. 8f)
- Exposed edges: fastened and trimmed along the entire length.
- Pile type: low pile (1/2 in. maximum).
- Padding: firm pad or no pad underneath.

Floor Surfaces: gratings

FS-04 Do floor gratings in the path of travel comply with accessible criteria? (4.5.4, Fig. 8g–h)

- Opening size: no greater than 1/2 in. in one direction.
- Opening direction: the long dimension is perpendicular to the dominant direction of travel.

(CT) Controls and Operating Mechanisms (4.27)

NOTES:

- Controls or operating mechanisms can include elements such as light switches, pencil sharpeners, manual overhead screens, nonkeyed thermostats, alarm pull stations, fire extinguisher cabinets, A/C window units, microwave ovens, towel dispensers, and wall hooks.
- If controls are to be operated by occupants of the space, they must be accessible. If controls are to be operated by maintenance staff only and not by occupants or other users of the space, they do not have to be accessible. For example, thermostats in auditoriums usually do not have to be accessible, while thermostats in classrooms may need to be accessible.

Controls: clear floor space

CT-01 Is a clear floor space of at least 30 in. × 48 in. provided in front of controls, dispensers, receptacles, and other operable equipment for forward or parallel approach? (4.27.2, Fig. 4a–b)

Controls: reach ranges

NOTES:

- Accessible reach ranges for controls and operating mechanisms are:
  — Forward reach: not less than 15 in. high and not more than 48 in. high without any obstruction or where the obstruction is less than 20 in. deep. For obstructions from 20 in. to 25 in. deep, no forward reach higher than 44 in.
  — Side reach: not less than 9 in. high and not more than 54 in. high. For obstructions not more than 34 in. high or 24 in. deep, no side reach higher than 46 in.
  — Electrical outlets, switches, and communication system receptacles have a minimum outlet height of 15 in. regardless of forward or side reach. See CT-02 below.

CT-02 Are electrical outlets, switches, and communication system receptacles mounted within accessible forward or side reach ranges? (4.27.3)

EXCEPTION:

- These requirements do not apply where the use of special equipment dictates otherwise or where electrical

and communications system receptacles are not normally intended for use by building occupants. (4.27.3)

CT-03 Are thermostats or other similar operable equipment mounted within accessible forward or side reach ranges? (4.2.5, 4.2.6, Fig. 5a–b, Fig. 6a–c)

CT-04 Are dispensers or other similar operable equipment mounted within accessible forward or side reach ranges? (4.2.5, 4.2.6, Fig. 5a–b, Fig. 6a–c)

CT-05 Are life safety devices or other similar operable equipment mounted within accessible forward or side reach ranges? (4.2.5, 4.2.6, Fig. 5a–b, Fig. 6a–c)

NOTE:

- This might include fire alarm pull stations, handles to extinguisher cabinets, or wall-mounted extinguishers.

Controls: operation

CT-06 Are controls, dispensers, receptacles, and other operable equipment operable with one hand without tight grasping, pinching, or wrist twisting, and requiring no more than 5 lbf of force? (4.27.4)

(TS) Toilet Stalls (4.17)

Toilet Stalls: location and approach

TS-01 Are the accessible toilet stalls located on an accessible route? (4.17.1)

TS-02 Is the required aisle clearance provided when approaching the accessible toilet stall? (4.17.5, Fig. 30)

- Aisle clearance if the stall door swings out and the approach is from the *latch side*: not less than 42 in. between the door side of the stall and any obstruction.
- Aisle clearance if the stall door swings out and the approach is from the *hinge side*: not less than 48 in. between the door side of the stall and any obstruction.

Toilet Stalls: maneuvering space

TS-03 If the stall door swings out at the end of an aisle, is at least 18 in. of maneuvering space provided at the latch side of the stall door? (4.17.5, 4.13.5)

Toilet Stalls: size and arrangement

TS-04 If toilet stalls are provided, is at least one a "standard" accessible stall? (4.17.3, 4.22.4, 4.23.4, Fig. 30a)

- "Standard" accessible stall: at least 60 in. wide × 59 in. deep (with floor-mounted water closet) or at least 56 in. deep (with wall-mounted water closet). The door should be located at the open side of the stall.

EXCEPTION:

- In instances of alteration work where a "standard" stall is technically infeasible or where plumbing code requirements prevent combining existing stalls to provide space, either "alternate" stall configuration described as follows may be provided in lieu of the "standard" stall. (4.17.3, Fig. 30b)
  — One: 36 in. wide × 69 in. deep (with floor-mounted water closet) or at least 66 in. deep (with wall-mounted water closet), with an outward swinging, self-closing door and parallel grab bars on side walls.

— Two: At least 48 in. wide × 54 in. deep, with an outward swinging, self-closing door and grab bars on side and rear walls.

TS-05 If the door swings into the "standard" accessible stall, is the additional depth provided in the stall so that the door does not encroach on the clear floor space required at the toilet? (4.17.5, 4.13.5, Fig. 30a-1)

- Additional depth: not less than 36 in.
- At least 18 in. of maneuvering space at the latch side of the door on the inside of the stall is needed.

TS-06 Where six or more stalls are provided, is at least one an "alternate" accessible stall, in addition to the "standard" accessible stall? (4.22.4, 4.23.4, 4.17.3, Fig. 30b)

- "Alternate" accessible stalls for new construction are:
  — Exactly 36 in. wide × at least 69 in. deep (with floor-mounted water closet) or at least 66 in. deep (with wall-mounted water closet), with an outward swinging, self-closing door and parallel grab bars on side walls.

Toilet Stalls: toe clearance

TS-07 If the stall is less than 60 in. deep, does the front partition and at least one side partition have toe clearances of at least 9 in. above the floor? (4.17.4)

Toilet Stalls: doors

TS-08 Does the stall door, including door hardware, or the opening into the accessible stall comply with the minimum width and height requirements? (4.17.5, 4.13.5, 4.4.2)

- Width clearance: not less than 32 in. between the face of the door and the edge of the partition on the latch side when the stall door is open 90°.
- Height clearance: not less than 80 in.

TS-09 Do the toilet stall doors and hardware comply with typical door accessible criteria including handle type, mounting height, and opening force? (4.17.5, 4.4.2)

Toilet Stalls: grab bars

NOTE:

- Additional criteria for grab bars can be found in Section "HR, Handrails."

TS-10 Are the grab bars in the "standard" stall the required length and are they placed in the required location? (4.17.6; Fig. 30a, c, d)

- Rear wall: not less than 36 in. long, starting at no more than 6 in. from the side wall.
- Side wall: not less than 40 in. long, starting at no more than 12 in. from the rear wall.
- Mounting height: 33 in. to 36 in. to centerline above the finish floor and mounted horizontally.

TS-11 Are the grab bars in the "alternate" stall the required length and are they placed in the required location? (4.17.6; Fig. 30b, c, d)

- Rear wall: not less than 36 in. long, starting at no more than 6 in. from the side wall.

- Side wall: not less than 42 in. long, starting at no more than 12 in. from the rear wall.
- Mounting height: 33 in. to 36 in. to centerline above the finish floor and mounted horizontally.

NOTE:

- A rear grab bar is required in stalls wider than 36 in.

(WC) Water Closets (4.16)

Water Closets (general): centerline and toilet seats

WC-01 Is the centerline of the accessible toilet (in or not in a stall) located exactly 18 in. from a side wall or partition? (Fig. 28; Fig. 30a, a-1, b)

WC-02 Is the top of the toilet seat between 17 in. and 19 in. from the top of the finish floor? (4.16.3, Fig. 29b, Fig. 30d)

- Seats shall not automatically return to a lifted position.

Water Closets (general): flush controls

WC-03 Are the flush controls mounted on the wide side of the toilet and no more than 44 in. above the finish floor? (4.16.5)

WC-04 Is the toilet flush valve control automatic or operable with one hand without tight grasping, pinching, or wrist twisting, and requiring no more than 5 lbf of force? (4.16.5)

Water Closets (general): toilet paper dispenser

WC-05 Is the toilet paper dispenser placed in the correct location and does it permit continuous paper flow? (4.16.6, Fig. 29b)

- Location: not less than 19 in. high from finish floor to centerline; not more than 36 in. from the back wall.

Water Closets (not in stalls): clear floor space

WC-06 Is clear floor space provided at the accessible toilet (not in a stall and with a lavatory at the side) for front, side, or dual approach? (4.16.2, Fig. 28)

- Front approach: at least 48 in. wide × 66 in. deep; lavatory may encroach up to 12 in.
- Side approach: at least 48 in. wide × 56 in. deep; lavatory may encroach up to 12 in.
- Dual approach: at least 60 in. wide × 56 in. deep with no lavatory encroachment.

Water Closets (not in stalls)

NOTE:

- Additional criteria for grab bars can be found in Section "HR, Handrails."

WC-07 Are the grab bars for toilets (not in stalls) the correct length and are they placed in the correct location? (4.16.4, Fig. 28–29)

- Rear wall: not less than 36 in. long starting at no more than 6 in. from the side wall.
- Side wall: not less than 42 in. long starting at no more than 12 in. from the rear wall.
- Mounting height: 33 in. to 36 in. to centerline above the finish floor and mounted horizontally.

(HR) Handrails, Grab Bars, and Tub and Shower Seats (4.26)

NOTE:

- HR Guidelines may be repeated in other element-based guidelines: (RP) Ramps, (ST) Stairs, (WC) Water Closets, (TS) Toilet Stalls, (BT) Bathtubs, and (SS) Shower Stalls.

Handrails: size and spacing

HR-01 Is the gripping surface of the grab bars or handrails 1¼ in. to 1½ in. in outside diameter? (4.26.2, Fig. 39)

AUTHOR'S INTERPRETATION:

- Standard pipe sizes designated by the industry as 1¼ in. to 1½ in. are acceptable for purposes of this section.

HR-02 Do the grab bars or handrails have edges with a minimum radius of 1/8 in.? (4.26.4)

HR-03 Is the clearance between the grab bars or handrails and the wall exactly 1½ in.? (4.26.2, Fig. 39)

HR-04 If the handrail is located in a recess, is the recess a maximum of 3 in. deep extending at least 18 in. above the rail? (4.26.2, Fig. 39d)

Handrails: grab bar or handrail structural strength

HR-05 Are the grab bars or handrails secure so that they do not rotate in their fittings? [4.26.3(5)]

HR-06 Do the grab bars and handrails meet the structural strength requirements for bending stress and shear stress? (4.26.3)

- Actual bending stress in the grab bar induced by the maximum bending moment from the application of 250 lbf is less than the allowable bending stress for the material of the grab bar.
- Shear stress induced in a grab bar by the application of 250 lbf shall be less than the allowable shear stress for the material of the grab bar. If the connection between the grab bar and its mounting bracket or other support is considered to be fully restrained, then direct and torsional shear stresses shall be totaled for the combined shear stress, which shall not exceed the allowable shear stress.

HR-07 Do the fasteners and mounting devices for the grab bars or handrails meet the structural strength requirements for shear force and tensile force? (4.26.3)

- Shear force induced in a fastener or mounting device from the application of 250 lbf shall be less than the allowable lateral load of either the fastener or mounting device or the supporting structure, whichever is the smaller allowable load.
- Tensile force induced in a fastener by a direct tension force of 250 lbf plus the maximum moment from the application of 250 lbf shall be less than the allowable withdrawal load between the fastener and the supporting structure.

Handrails: hazards

HR-10 Are handrails or grab bars and any wall or other surfaces adjacent to them free of any sharp or abrasive elements? (4.26.4)

(UR) Urinals (4.18)

Urinals: height

UR-01 Does the accessible urinal have an elongated rim with a maximum height to the rim of no more than 17 in. above the floor? (4.18.2, 4.22.5)

AUTHOR'S INTERPRETATION:

- The ADAAG does not define when a urinal is considered as elongated. However, some codes suggest the face of an elongated rim is at least 14 in. from the wall.

Urinals: clear floor space

UR-02 Is clear floor space provided that allows a forward approach to the accessible urinal? (4.18.3)

- Clear floor space: not less than 30 in. × 48 in. and adjoins or overlaps an accessible route.

UR-03 Is the required clear width provided between the accessible urinal shields? (4.18.3)

- Shields that do not extend beyond the front edge of the urinal rim: at least 29 in. wide between partitions.
- Shields extending beyond the urinal rim: not less than 30 in. wide between partitions.

Urinals: flush controls

UR-04 Is the accessible urinal flush valve control located within reach range? (4.18.4)

- Height: not more than 44 in.

UR-05 Is the accessible urinal flush valve control automatic or operable with one hand without tight grasping, pinching, or wrist twisting, and requiring no more than 5 lbf of force? (4.18.4)

(LV) Lavatories, Sinks, and Mirrors (4.19, 4.24)

NOTE:

- Where lavatories or sinks are provided, at least one of each type must meet accessible requirements.

AUTHOR'S INTERPRETATION:

- While not specifically defined by ADAAG, it appears lavatories are for personal hygiene in bathrooms or toilet rooms, while sinks are for all other situations (e.g., laboratories or kitchens).

Lavatories or Sinks: clearances

LV-01 Is there a clear floor space not less than 30 in. × 48 in. in front of the accessible lavatory or sink allowing a forward approach, and does it adjoin or overlap the accessible route? (4.19.3, 4.24.5, Fig. 32)

- The clear floor space can extend up to 19 in. under the sink or lavatory if adequate knee clearance is provided.

LV-02 Are the accessible lavatory or sink rim or counter height, apron height, and extension from the wall adequate? (4.19.2, 4.24.2, Fig. 31)

- Rim height: not greater than 34 in. above the finish floor.
- Apron height: not less than 29 in. above the finish floor to the bottom of the apron.
- Lavatory extension: not less than 17 in. from the wall.

LV-03 Is toe clearance under the accessible lavatory or sink not less than 9 in. above the finish floor and not deeper than 6 in. from the back wall for the full length of the lavatory or sink? (4.19.2, Fig. 31)

Lavatories or Sinks: pipe shielding

LV-04 Are the hot water and drain pipes at the accessible lavatory or sink insulated or otherwise configured to protect against contact and is the area below the lavatory or sink free of sharp or abrasive surfaces? (4.19.4)

Lavatories or Sinks: controls

LV-05 Do the accessible lavatory or sink controls meet operational requirements? (4.19.5)

- Operation: operable with one hand without tight grasping, pinching, or twisting of the wrist. Acceptable types might include lever operated, push type, touch type, or electronically controlled; no more than 5 lbf of force.
- Self-closing faucets, when used, remain open for at least 10 sec.

Lavatories only

LV-06 Is adequate knee clearance provided underneath the accessible lavatory? (4.19.2, Fig. 31)

- Lavatory knee clearance: not less than 27 in. high from finish floor to the bottom of the lavatory when measured at a point not less than 8 in. from the front of the lavatory.

Lavatories or Sinks: mirrors

LV-09 Where mirrors are provided, does at least one mirror have a bottom edge of the reflecting surface no higher than 40 in. above the floor? (4.19.6, Fig. 31)

AUTHOR'S INTERPRETATION:

- Slanted mirrors located above 40 in. are not recognized as compliant by the ADAAG.

(AL) Alarms (4.28)

NOTE:

- At a minimum, visual signal appliances shall be provided in buildings and facilities in restrooms and any other general usage areas. **The ADAAG does not define the number of occupants needed to establish a general or common use area.**

ALLOWANCE:

- Emergency warning systems in medical care facilities may be modified to suit standard health care alarm design practice. [4.1.3(14)]

Visual Alarms: general

AL-04 If provided, are the visual alarm signal appliances integrated into the building or facility alarm system? (4.28.3)

AL-05 If provided, do the visual alarm signals meet required operational criteria? [4.28.3(1, 2, 3, 4, 5)]

- Lamp: xenon strobe type or equivalent.
- Color: clear or nominal white (i.e., unfiltered or clear filtered white light).
- Pulse duration: maximum shall be 0.2 sec with a maximum duty cycle of 40 percent.
- Intensity: not less than 75 candela.
- Flash rate: not less than 1 Hz and not more than 3 Hz.

AL-06 Are visual alarm signal appliances provided in public and common use restrooms? (4.28.1)

AL-07 Are visual alarm signal appliances provided in general usage areas of the building (such as meeting rooms, corridors, and lobbies) or any other area for common use? (4.28.1)

AUTHOR'S INTERPRETATION:

- The authors identified three or more occupants as the minimum number to establish a common use area.

AL-08 Are the visual alarms placed at 80 in. above the highest floor level or 6 in. below the ceiling, whichever is lower? [4.28.3(6)]

Public Work and Storage Spaces

Introduction. This "Space-type Review Guide" is used to design or evaluate public work or storage spaces. Examples of these types of spaces could include spaces at schools or universities such as copy rooms, mail and storage rooms, or other work rooms that are accessed by more than just employees. In the private sector they would include common storage facilities or any common use room that has been designated as requiring access.

The ADAAG addresses work areas for employees only [4.1.1(3)] by indicating that these types of areas must be designed and constructed so that individuals with disabilities can approach, enter, and exit the areas. Full accessibility is not required. This review guide can be used for this limited requirement as well as for the more complete review of spaces required to be fully accessible due to their mixed usage by persons other than employees. Since these rooms are considered common usage areas and will accommodate several people at any given time, the alarm requirements would apply.

In general, the exact makeup of the elements in this type of multiuse space is difficult to determine, and most of these types of spaces are rather simple. This guide contains the most obvious elements required for general work and storage spaces. Other forms may be more applicable to specialized types of spaces. Any element not covered in this guide but encountered in the actual space would be addressed in the "Master Guidelines," App. C.

PRELIMINARY DESIGN OVERVIEW

(AR) Accessible Routes

- An accessible route must connect all accessible spaces and elements.
- Frequently overlooked in this space-type are the following maneuvering space problems: approach to all equipment; minimum accessible width requirements between aisles, switchbacks, turns around an obstruction, and intersections.
- At turns around obstructions, widths of the accessible route may need to increase according to the size of the obstruction.

(AL) Alarms

- Visual alarms must be provided in general usage areas; this type of common use space would be included.

(DR) Doors

- Typical requirements.

(CT) Controls and Operating Mechanisms

- Controls and operating mechanisms have clear floor space and reach range requirements. Frequently overlooked in this space-type are communication outlets, controls on window air conditioner units, thermostats, fans and lights, equipment, etc.
- One of each type of control device should be accessible and operable.

(FS) Floor Surfaces

- In some areas floor surfaces should be evaluated as if wet. In particular consider spaces around exterior doors, emergency showers, eyewash stations, drinking fountains, etc.

(LV) Lavatories, Sinks, and Mirrors

- If sinks are used for different purposes, then one of each use type must be accessible.

(PR) Protruding Objects

- Common wall-mounted elements can be protruding objects, e.g., pencil sharpeners, book shelves, upper cabinets, drinking fountains, public telephones, signs, mailboxes.
- Overhead clearances can be an unforeseen compliance problem, e.g., signs and banners, open space under stairs, low ceilings, etc.
- Standard fire safety items are often protruding objects, e.g., permanently mounted fire hose cabinets, fire extinguishers and fire extinguisher cabinets, valves on standpipes, etc.

(SG) Signage

- Typical requirements.

(SR) Fixed Storage, Closets, Lockers, and Shelves

- One of each type of storage unit (shelves, clothes hooks, dispensers, etc.) must be accessible; locked storage used only by employees may not have to be accessible.
- Frequently overlooked storage units for this space-type include coat hooks, mailboxes, etc.

(SE) Fixed Tables and/or Counters

- Typical requirements.

ADAAG APPENDIX

The ADAAG Appendix contains advisory information pertinent to this space-type.

- A4.2.1   Space Allowances and Reach Ranges
- A4.5   Ground and Floor Surfaces

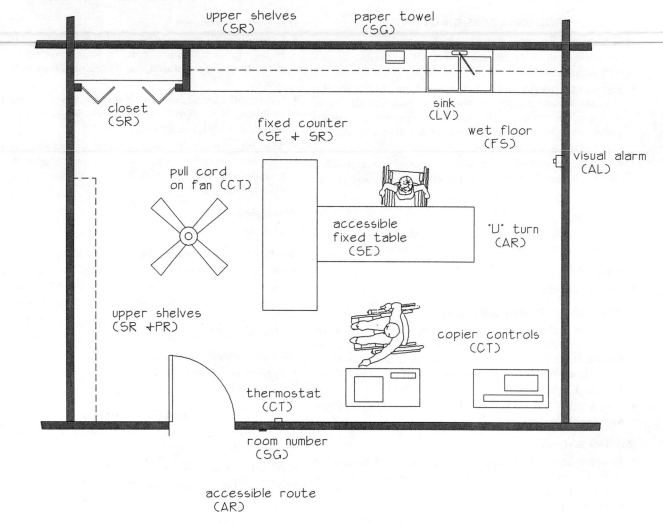

Figure 3-20. Public work and storage area.

Public Work and Storage Spaces Checklist

SIGNAGE

SG04	Room signage: criteria
SG05	Room signage: location
SG08	Directional/informational signage: criteria
SG09	Suspended/projected signs: location

DOORS

DR04	Doors: maneuvering clearances
DR05	Doors: handle type
DR06	Doors: opening force (interior only)
DR07	Doors: closing speed
DR08	Doors: thresholds
DR09	Doors: clear width/height
DR10	Openings (no door): clear width/height

ACCESSIBLE ROUTES

AR08	Route: clear width
AR09	Route width: U-turns
AR11	Route: maneuvering clearances
AR14	Route: changes of level

FLOOR AND GROUND SURFACES

FS01	Surface: firm, stable, and slip-resistant
FS02	Vertical changes in level
FS03	Carpet and tile floors

PROTRUDING OBJECTS

PR01	Wall-mounted
PR02	Freestanding/suspended on posts/pylons
PR03	Clear route width maintained
PR04	Overhead clearance
PR05	Vertical clearance: cane detection barrier

CONTROLS AND OPERATING MECHANISMS

CT01	Clear floor space
CT02	Reach ranges: elec./comm. systems
CT03	Reach ranges: thermostats
CT04	Reach ranges: other controls
CT05	Reach ranges: life safety devices
CT06	Controls: operation

LAVATORIES, SINKS, AND MIRRORS

LV01	Clear floor space
LV02	Rim/apron heights and extension from wall
LV03	Toe clearance
LV04	Insulated pipes
LV05	Controls and operation requirements
LV07	Sinks: knee clearance
LV08	Sinks: bowl depth

FIXED OR BUILT-IN SEATING AND TABLES

SE01	Fixed seating: number required
SE02	Wheelchairs: clear floor space at tables
SE03	Tables/counters: heights
SE04	Tables/counters: knee clearance criteria

STORAGE

SR01	Accessibility: one of each type
SR02	Clear floor space
SR03	Reach ranges
SR04	Storage closets w/o passage: criteria
SR05	Storage hardware: operation

ALARMS

AL01	Emergency warning: audible/visual
AL02	Audible alarms: operation
AL03	Single station audible and visual
AL04	Visual alarms: integration w/building alarm
AL05	Visual alarms: operation
AL07	Visual alarms: common use areas
AL08	Visual alarms: vertical placement
AL09	Visual alarms: horizontal spacing

PUBLIC WORK AND STORAGE SPACES COMPREHENSIVE CRITERIA

(SG) Signage (4.30)

Signage: room identification (where provided)

DEFINITION:

- These signs designate permanent rooms and spaces.

AUTHOR'S INTERPRETATION:

- Signs that designate stairs, exit doors, and toilet rooms generally are associated with permanent spaces, while an "office" sign is not since the room function may change over time. Room numbers also must meet the ADAAG criteria as permanent designations, while personal names do not since the occupant may change over time.

SG-04 Do signs that designate permanent rooms and spaces comply with the following criteria? [4.1.2(7); 4.1.3(16); 4.30.4, 5, 6]

- Character type: raised and accompanied by Grade II Braille.
- Character size: between 5/8 in. and 2 in. high; raised at least 1/32 in.

- Character style: upper case, and sans or simple serif.
- Finish: characters and backgrounds have a nonglare finish.
- Contrast: characters contrast with their background (light-on-dark or dark-on-light).

SG-05 Is the room identification sign mounted in the required location? (4.30.6)

- Mounting location: installed on the wall adjacent to the latch side of the door or where wall space to the latch side of the door is not available, including double doors, placed on the nearest adjacent wall.
- Mounting height: 60 in. above the floor/ground to the centerline of the sign.
- Sign access: approach to within 3 in. of a sign without encountering protruding objects or standing within the swing of the door.

Signage: direction and information (where provided)

DEFINITION:

- Signs that provide direction to or information about functional spaces of the building.

EXCEPTION:

- Building directories, menus, and all other temporary signs are not required to comply. [4.1.3(16)]

SG-08 Do signs that provide direction to, or information about, functional spaces of the building comply with the following criteria? [4.1.2(7); 4.1.3(16); 4.30.1, 2, 3, 5]

- Character proportion: letters and numbers have a width to height ratio between 3:5 and 1:1 and a stroke width to height ratio between 1:5 and 1:10.
- Character height: sized according to viewing distance with characters on overhead signs at least 3 in. high.

NOTE:

- When the sign is mounted below 80 in., there are no prescribed character heights. Only when the sign is mounted 80 in. or higher are the characters required to be at least 3 in. high. (4.30.3)
- Finish: characters and backgrounds have a nonglare finish.
- Contrast: characters contrast with their background (light-on-dark or dark-on-light).

SG-09 Is a sign located so that the overhead clearance or the projection of a suspended or projected sign does not result in a protruding object (free-standing or wall-mounted)?

- Clear height: at least 80 in. (4.4.2, Fig. 8a)
- Overhang for free-standing signs on posts or pylons located between 27 in. and 80 in. high: no more than a 12-in. projection into accessible routes. (4.4.1, Fig. 8c)
- Overhang for wall-mounted signs between 27 in. and 80 in. high: no more than a 4-in. projection into accessible routes. (4.4.1, Fig. 8a)

(DR) Doors (4.13)

NOTE:

- Included in this category are doors, revolving doors, turnstiles, and gates.

AUTHOR'S INTERPRETATION:

- It is suggested that, for purposes of documentation and review, a door be assigned to the space it swings into. Corridors are an exception to this rule and include only entry doors into the corridor or intermediate fire doors.

Doors: maneuvering clearance

DR-04 If the door is not automatic or power assisted, does it have the required maneuvering clearance provided on the push and pull side, and is the floor level and clear within the maneuvering area? (4.13.6)

- A verbal description cannot adequately describe the requirements. See ADAAG Fig. 25a–f for a graphic description.

EXCEPTION:

- Entry doors to acute care hospital bedrooms for inpatients are exempt from maneuvering space at the latch side of the door if the door is at least 44 in. wide.

AUTHOR'S INTERPRETATION:

- While ADAAG does not describe what elements can reduce the required maneuvering clearance, they could include a narrow entry alcove, an adjacent wall, railing, or permanently installed shelving, or a deep recessed door jamb.

Doors: hardware

DR-05 Do all door handles, locks, latches, or other operable devices meet required operational criteria? (4.13.9)

- Hardware operation: operable with one hand without tight grasping, pinching, or wrist twisting.
- Force required to operate the controls: not greater than 5 lbf. This does not apply to the force required to retract latch bolts or to disengage other devices that only hold the door in a closed position.
- Hardware type: "U"-shaped handles, levers, and push type mechanisms are acceptable designs.
- Hardware height: not greater than 48 in. above the floor.
- Sliding doors: hardware is exposed and usable from both sides when the doors are fully open.

Doors: opening force

DR-06 Do interior hinged doors and sliding or folding doors have an opening force of 5 lbf or less? (4.13.11)

- At present, no accessible criteria exist for exterior doors.
- Fire doors shall have the minimum opening force allowable by the appropriate administrative authority.

Doors: closing speed

DR-07 If the door has a closer, is the closer adjusted so that the door does not close too quickly? (4.13.10)

- From an open position of 70° the door will take at least 3 sec to move to a point 3 in. from the latch (measured to the leading edge of the door).

Doors: thresholds

DR-08 Where raised thresholds are provided, do they meet height limitations and are they beveled when required? (4.13.8, 4.5.2, Fig. 7)

- Threshold height: not more than 3/4 in. for exterior sliding doors or 1/2 in. for other types of doors.
- Threshold bevel: thresholds less than 1/4 in. high need no bevel; thresholds between 1/4 in. and 1/2 in. high shall be beveled at each edge with not more than a 1:2 slope.

EXCEPTION:

- A 3/4-in. high threshold is allowed in existing conditions. [4.1.6(3)(d)(ii)]

Doors: clear opening width and height

DR-09 Is the clear opening for the doorway adequate in width and height? (4.13.3, 4, 5; Fig. 24)

- Door width: at least 32 in. of clear width with the door open at 90°, measured between the face of the door and the door stop on the latch side. This also pertains to the active leaf of a double-leaf door or gate.
- Opening width: openings more than 24 in. deep must provide 36 in. of clear width.
- Height: at least 80 in. of vertical clearance.

EXCEPTIONS:

- Doors not requiring full user passage, such as shallow closets, may have the clear opening reduced to not less than 20 in.
- Where it is technically infeasible to comply with clear opening width requirements, a projection of 5/8 in. maximum will be permitted for the latch side. [4.1.6(d)(i)]

DR-10 Is the clear opening (when there is no door) adequate in width and height? (4.2.1, 4.3.3, 4.4.2)

- Width: at least 32 in. of clear width for depths 24 in. or less and at least 36 in. of clear width for depths greater than 24 in.
- Height: at least 80 in. of vertical clearance.

(AR) Accessible Routes (4.3)

NOTES:

- All walks, halls, corridors, aisles, sky walks, tunnels, and other spaces that are part of a designated accessible route shall comply with accessible requirements.
- Any slope on the accessible route that is greater than 1:20 is required to meet all ramp criteria.
- The accessible route shall, to the maximum extent feasible, coincide with the route for the general public.
- In historic buildings, accessible routes from an accessible entrance shall be provided to all publicly used spaces on at least the level of the accessible entrance. Access shall be provided to all levels of a building or facility whenever practical. [4.1.7(3)(d)]

AUTHOR'S INTERPRETATION:

- An accessible route "generally coincides" with the route used by the public if:
  — It does not force the user to go out of the way.
  — It is most like the route chosen by the general public.
  — It is direct.
  — It gives the same basic experience as the route preferred by the public.

Accessible Routes: width

AR-08 Is the minimum clear width along the accessible route adequate for continuous or point passage? (4.2.1, 4.3.3, Fig. 1, Fig. 8e, Fig. 24e)

- Continuous passage (greater than 24 in. long): at least a 36-in. clear width.
- Point passage (not more than 24 in. long): at least a 32-in. clear width.

AUTHOR'S INTERPRETATION:

- Noncompliance with this question generally relates to permanent elements that encroach on the accessi-

ble route. Large, heavy equipment that is not readily movable might be considered permanent. If the space is designed so that temporary elements (such as bikes in a bike rack or car bumpers) will consistently encroach, the situation might also be considered a permanent barrier.

AR-09 Is the minimum clear width along the accessible route adequate at a U-turn around an obstruction? (4.3.3, Fig. 7a–b)

- Obstruction 48 in. or greater: at least a 36-in. clear width around the obstruction.
- Obstruction less than 48 in.: at least a 42-in. clear width at each side with at least a 48-in. clear width in the turn.

Accessible Routes: maneuvering clearances

AR-11 Is the minimum clear floor space for an unobstructed 180° wheelchair turning space or a "T"-shaped turning space provided? (4.2.3, Fig. 3a–b)

- 180° turning space: at least a 60-in. diameter.
- "T"-shaped turning space: at least 36-in. wide legs with a minimum length of 60 in.

Accessible Routes: changes in level

AR-14 Are changes in level greater than 1/2 in. accomplished by means of a curb ramp, ramp, elevator, or platform lift (as permitted in ADAAG 4.1.3 and 4.1.6)? (4.3.8)

(FS) Floor and Ground Surfaces (4.5)

Floor Surfaces: general

FS-01 Are the floor/ground surfaces on the accessible route stable, firm, and slip-resistant? (4.5.1)

AUTHOR'S INTERPRETATION:

- Exterior spaces, interior circulation, bathrooms, and other spaces where water can collect on the floor around an element (sinks, drinking fountains, hose bibbs, etc.) are reviewed as if wet.
- High gloss surfaces without significant textures that are regularly maintained with waxing (smooth tiles, waxed concrete, etc.) could be considered noncompliant.
- Accessible criteria are not specified for nonpermanent floor surfaces such as mats or rugs.

Floor Surfaces: changes in level

FS-02 Are vertical changes in level between 1/4 in. and 1/2 in. beveled with a slope of 1:2 or less? (4.5.2)

- Changes in level up to 1/4 in. may be vertical without edge treatment.
- Changes in level greater than 1/2 in. should be accomplished by means of a curb ramp, ramp, elevator, or platform lift (as permitted in ADAAG 4.1.3 and 4.1.6).

Floor Surfaces: carpet

FS-03 Does carpet or carpet tile used on the floor comply with accessible criteria? (4.5.3, Fig. 8f)

- Attachment: secured.

- Exposed edges: fastened and trimmed along the entire length.
- Pile type: low pile (1/2 in. maximum).
- Padding: firm pad or no pad underneath.

(PR) Protruding Objects (4.4)

Protruding Objects: general

PR-01 Do wall-mounted objects having leading edges between 27 in. and 80 in. high project less than 4 in. into walkways, corridors, aisles, or paths of travel? (4.4.1, Fig. 8a–e)

- Objects mounted with their leading edge at or below 27 in. can protrude any amount, as long as they do not reduce the required clear width of an accessible route.

AUTHOR'S INTERPRETATION:

- Protruding objects might include fire extinguishers or cabinets, pencil sharpeners, shelving, counters, built-in equipment overhangs, or various dispensers such as for paper towels or soap.

PR-02 Do free-standing objects, suspended or mounted on posts or pylons with leading edges between 27 in. and 80 in. high, project less than 12 in. into the perpendicular route of travel? (4.4.1, Fig. 8a–e)

AUTHOR'S INTERPRETATION:

- These might include telephone enclosures, drinking fountains, or free-standing signage kiosks.

PR-03 Is the minimum clear route width or maneuvering space still maintained even with the projection of a protruding object? (4.4.1, Fig. 8a–e)

Protruding Objects: overhead clearance

PR-04 Is the minimum overhead clearance of 80 in. provided in accessible areas or along accessible routes? (4.4.2, Fig. 8a)

AUTHOR'S INTERPRETATION:

- Overhead objects that can reduce the required clearance might include structures, pipes, ducts, or light fixtures.

PR-05 Where the vertical clearance of a space adjoining the accessible route is less than 80 in. high, is a cane detection barrier less than 27 in. from the floor provided for blind or visually impaired persons? (4.4.2, Fig. 8c-1)

AUTHOR'S INTERPRETATION:

- This condition might be found under a stair, at a sloped ceiling space, or with guy wires from telephone poles along an exterior accessible route.

(CT) Controls and Operating Mechanisms (4.27)

NOTES:

- Controls or operating mechanisms can include elements such as light switches, pencil sharpeners, manual overhead screens, nonkeyed thermostats, alarm pull stations, fire extinguisher cabinets, A/C window units, microwave ovens, towel dispensers, and wall hooks.
- If controls are to be operated by occupants of the space, they must be accessible. If controls are to be operated by maintenance staff only and not by occupants or other users of the space, they do not have to be accessible. For example, thermostats in auditoriums usually do not have to be accessible, while thermostats in classrooms may need to be accessible.

Controls: clear floor space

CT-01 Is a clear floor space of at least 30 in. × 48 in. provided in front of controls, dispensers, receptacles, and other operable equipment for forward or parallel approach? (4.27.2, Fig. 4a–b)

Controls: reach ranges

NOTES:

- Accessible reach ranges for controls and operating mechanisms are:
  - Forward reach: not less than 15 in. high and not more than 48 in. high without any obstruction or where the obstruction is less than 20 in. deep. For obstructions from 20 in. to 25 in. deep, no forward reach higher than 44 in.
  - Side reach: not less than 9 in. high and not more than 54 in. high. For obstructions not more than 34 in. high or 24 in. deep, no side reach higher than 46 in.
  - Electrical outlets, switches, and communication system receptacles have a minimum outlet height of 15 in. regardless of forward or side reach. See CT-02 below.

CT-02 Are electrical outlets, switches, and communication system receptacles mounted within accessible forward or side reach ranges? (4.27.3)

EXCEPTION:

- These requirements do not apply where the use of special equipment dictates otherwise or where electrical and communications system receptacles are not normally intended for use by building occupants. (4.27.3)

CT-03 Are thermostats or other similar operable equipment mounted within accessible forward or side reach ranges? (4.2.5, 4.2.6, Fig. 5a–b, Fig. 6a–c)

CT-04 Are dispensers or other similar operable equipment mounted within accessible forward or side reach ranges? (4.2.5, 4.2.6, Fig. 5a–b, Fig. 6a–c)

CT-05 Are life safety devices or other similar operable equipment mounted within accessible forward or side reach ranges? (4.2.5, 4.2.6, Fig. 5a–b, Fig. 6a–c)

NOTE:

- This might include fire alarm pull stations, handles to extinguisher cabinets, or wall-mounted extinguishers.

Controls: operation

CT-06 Are controls, dispensers, receptacles, and other operable equipment operable with one hand without tight grasping, pinching, or wrist twisting, and requiring no more than 5 lbf of force? (4.27.4)

(LV) Lavatories, Sinks, and Mirrors (4.19, 4.24)

NOTE:

- Where lavatories or sinks are provided, at least one of each type must meet accessible requirements.

AUTHOR'S INTERPRETATION:

- While not specifically defined by ADAAG, it appears lavatories are for personal hygiene in bathrooms or toilet rooms, while sinks are for all other situations (e.g., laboratories or kitchens).

Lavatories or Sinks: clearances

LV-01 Is there a clear floor space not less than 30 in. × 48 in. in front of the accessible lavatory or sink allowing a forward approach, and does it adjoin or overlap the accessible route? (4.19.3, 4.24.5, Fig. 32)

- The clear floor space can extend up to 19 in. under the sink or lavatory if adequate knee clearance is provided.

LV-02 Are the accessible lavatory or sink rim or counter height, apron height, and extension from the wall adequate? (4.19.2, 4.24.2, Fig. 31)

- Rim height: not greater than 34 in. above the finish floor.
- Apron height: not less than 29 in. above the finish floor to the bottom of the apron.
- Lavatory extension: not less than 17 in. from the wall.

LV-03 Is toe clearance under the accessible lavatory or sink not less than 9 in. above the finish floor and not deeper than 6 in. from the back wall for the full length of the lavatory or sink? (4.19.2, Fig. 31)

Lavatories or Sinks: pipe shielding

LV-04 Are the hot water and drain pipes at the accessible lavatory or sink insulated or otherwise configured to protect against contact and is the area below the lavatory or sink free of sharp or abrasive surfaces? (4.19.4)

Lavatories or Sinks: controls

LV-05 Do the accessible lavatory or sink controls meet operational requirements? (4.19.5)

- Operation: operable with one hand without tight grasping, pinching, or twisting of the wrist. Acceptable types might include lever operated, push type, touch type, or electronically controlled; no more than 5 lbf of force.
- Self-closing faucets, when used, remain open for at least 10 sec.

Sinks Only

LV-07 Is adequate knee clearance provided underneath the accessible sink? (4.24.3)

- Sink knee clearance: not less than 27 in. high, 30 in. wide, and 19 in. deep under the sink.

LV-08 Is the accessible sink bowl not more than 6½ in. deep? (4.24.4)

(SE) Fixed or Built-in Seating and Tables (4.32)

Fixed or Built-in Seating and Tables: minimum number

SE-01 Is the minimum number of accessible wheelchair seating locations at fixed tables or counters provided? (4.1.3.18)

- Number required: 5 percent of total number of seats but not fewer than one.

Fixed or Built-in Seating and Tables: clear floor space

AUTHOR'S INTERPRETATION:

- Where the accessible route leads to and through accessible seating adjacent to a wall or another table, the minimum required width for the accessible route will be 65 in. between the table edge and next parallel surface (e.g., wall or another table edge). (4.1.3.18, Fig. 45)

SE-02 Is the clear floor space for a wheelchair at a seating location adequate? (4.32.3, Fig. 4a, Fig. 45)

- Clear floor space: 30 in. × 48 in.
- This clear space can include up to 19 in. under the table/desk.

Fixed or Built-in Seating and Tables: clearances

SE-03 Are the tops of accessible tables and counters between 28 in. and 34 in. from the floor? (4.32.3, Fig. 45)

SE-04 Are the knee clearances at least 27 in. high, 30 in. wide, and 19 in. deep? (4.32.3, Fig. 45)

(SR) STORAGE (4.25)

NOTE:

- Accessible reach range requirements do not apply to shelves or display units allowing self-service by customers in mercantile occupancies but they must be located on an accessible route. [4.1.3(12)(b)]

Storage: general

SR-01 Does at least one of each type of fixed or built-in storage unit comply with accessible criteria? [4.1.3(12)(a), 4.25.1]

NOTE:

- Types of storage facilities might include cabinets, shelves, closets, and drawers.

Storage: clear floor space

SR-02 Is there a clear floor space at least 30 in. × 48 in. at fixed or built-in storage units that allows for either a forward or side approach? (4.25.2, Fig. 4a–b)

Storage: reach ranges

SR-03 Are forward or side reach for each type of accessible storage unit within acceptable reach ranges? (4.2.5–6, Fig. 5a–b, Fig. 6a–c, 4.25.3)

- Forward reach: not less than 15 in. high and not more than 48 in. high without any obstruction or where the obstruction is less than 20 in. deep. For obstructions from 20 in. to 25 in. deep, no forward reach higher than 44 in.
- Side reach: not less than 9 in. high and not more than 54 in. high. For obstructions not more than 34 in. high or 24 in. deep, no side reach higher than 46 in.

SR-04 In a closet where passage is not required to access storage (e.g., door opening is less than 32 in.), are the clothes rod or shelves within required reach ranges? (4.25.3, Fig. 38a–b)

- Door width: at least 20 in. (4.13.5)
- Horizontal reach: not more than 21 in. from the opening.

- Rod reach: if over 10 in. deep, then not more than 48 in. high.
- Shelf reach: if over 10 in. deep, then not more than 48 in. high or less than 9 in. high.

Storage: hardware

SR-05 Is the hardware on the storage unit doors or drawers operable with one hand without tight grasping, pinching, or wrist twisting, and requiring no more than 5 lbf of force? (4.25.4, 4.27.4)

(AL) Alarms (4.28)

NOTE:

- At a minimum, visual signal appliances shall be provided in buildings and facilities in restrooms and any other general usage areas. **The ADAAG does not define the number of occupants needed to establish a general or common use area.**

ALLOWANCE:

- Emergency warning systems in medical care facilities may be modified to suit standard health care alarm design practice. [4.1.3(14)]

Alarms: general

AL-01 If emergency warning systems are provided, do they include both audible alarms and visual alarms? [4.1.3(14)]

Audible Alarms: general

AL-02 If provided, do the audible alarms meet required operational criteria? (4.28.2)

- Sound level: exceeds the prevailing sound level in the room or space by at least 15 dbA or exceeds any maximum sound level with a duration of 60 sec by 5 dbA, whichever is louder.
- Sound levels for alarm signals shall not exceed 120 dbA.

AL-03 If single station audible alarms are provided, then are single station visual alarm signals also provided? (4.28.3)

Visual Alarms: general

AL-04 If provided, are the visual alarm signal appliances integrated into the building or facility alarm system? (4.28.3)

AL-05 If provided, do the visual alarm signals meet required operational criteria? [4.28.3(1, 2, 3, 4, 5)]

- Lamp: xenon strobe type or equivalent.
- Color: clear or nominal white (i.e., unfiltered or clear filtered white light).
- Pulse duration: maximum shall be 0.2 sec with a maximum duty cycle of 40 percent.
- Intensity: not less than 75 candela.
- Flash rate: not less than 1 Hz and not more than 3 Hz.

AL-07 Are visual alarm signal appliances provided in general usage areas of the building (such as meeting rooms, corridors, and lobbies) or any other area for common use? (4.28.1)

AUTHOR'S INTERPRETATION:

- The authors identified three or more occupants as the minimum number to establish a common use area.

AL-08 Are the visual alarms placed at 80 in. above the highest floor level or 6 in. below the ceiling, whichever is lower? [4.28.3(6)]

AL-09 In spaces required to have visual alarms, are the alarms spaced properly? [4.28.3(7)]

- No place in any space should be more than 50 ft from a visual signal alarm.
- Where a space or large room exceeds 100 ft across, without obstructions 6 ft above the finished floor, visual alarms can be spaced a maximum of 100 ft apart at the perimeter, in lieu of suspending appliances from the ceiling.

TRANSIENT LODGING: OVERVIEW

"Transient Lodging" is an ADAAG section that covers two types of accommodations:

1. Hotels, motels, inns, resorts, dormitories, and campus student apartments.
2. Social services establishments such as homeless shelters, halfway houses, group homes, and other similar places.

The major differences between these two types are the *number* and *type* of accessible sleeping units or sleeping rooms and suites required by ADAAG in new construction and alterations. ADAAG 9.1 through 9.4 do not apply to an establishment located within a building that contains not more than five rooms for rent or hire and that is actually occupied by the proprietor of such establishment as the residence of such proprietor.

Three of the following five "Space-type Review Guides"—"Bathrooms," "Kitchens," and "Living and Dining"—can be used to review such space-types in either hotels, motels, dormitories, or social services establishments. The compliance requirements are the same for any kitchen that is part of a suite in an accessible room in a hotel or a common-use kitchen in a homeless shelter.

However, there are separate review guides for sleeping accommodations within the two categories. "Transient Lodging Sleeping Rooms and Suites" review guide is used for hotel, motel, inn, resort, and dormitory accommodations; "Transient Lodging Sleeping Units" should be used for reviewing social services establishments. Although requirements are only slightly different, we have two separate review guides to avoid any confusion.

If you are designing a hotel complex, there are numerous "Space-type Review Guides" that you may need to use. These may include "Lobbies, Corridors, and Interior Accessible Routes," "Restaurants and Cafeterias," "Conference Rooms," "Offices," "Toilet Rooms," "Dressing, Fitting, and Locker Rooms," and so on. "Parking Structures" and "Parking Lots and Loading Zones" may likewise be needed. If the facility furnishes a common-use laundry facility for the guests, then a portion of these facilities must meet accessible criteria. If an activity area is provided, then any person with a disability must also be able to use it. These types of occurrences are not covered in the following transient lodging review guides of interior spaces, but you as the designer need to consider them from the outset and make necessary accommodations for the overall facilities.

Bathrooms (Hotels, Inns, Resorts, Dormitories, and Other Places of Accommodation and Social Services Establishments: Homeless Shelters, Halfway Houses, Transient Group Homes, and Others)

Introduction. ADAAG designates two major categories of "Transient Lodging":

1. Private or public inns, resorts, boarding houses, hotels, motels, dormitories, and student campus apartments.
2. Social services establishments such as homeless shelters, halfway houses, transient group homes, and others.

Use this review guide to design or evaluate facilities, or portions thereof, that contain bathroom accommodations within both categories of transient lodging. Note that hotel, inn, and motel bathrooms are most often single user facilities with tub, toilet, and lavatory, while social services establishments and dormitories often have multiple user bathroom accommodations that include toilet stalls and urinals. Although the ADAAG criteria are similar for both types of bathrooms, individual explanations are given below. See other review guides ("Comprehensive Criteria") in transient lodging—"Hotels, Sleeping Rooms and Suites" and "Social Services Establishments, Sleeping Units"—to ascertain the required number of accessible facilities. In addition, other review guides cover

"Kitchens," "Living and Dining Rooms," "Exterior Activity Areas," and "Parking Lots and Loading Zones."

Single user bathrooms must provide an unobstructed accessible turning space or a "T"-shaped turning space to allow wheelchair users maneuverability. The clear floor space of fixtures and controls, the accessible route, and the turning space may overlap one another. Door swings cannot overlap into the clear floor space of any accessible fixture or element. Changes of material from the bedroom to the bathroom are common and a threshold dividing these materials must not result in an inaccessible level change. Flooring surfaces are often wet in bathrooms and shower areas, so a floor surface that is slip-resistant, even when wet, must be specified. When a medicine cabinet is provided, at least one shelf must be accessible to a person in a wheelchair. An electrical outlet combined with a light fixture placed above a lavatory might not be within the accessible reach range for a person in a wheelchair. Provide an additional accessible receptacle within reach ranges in this area for electric razors and hairdryers. Enclosures for bathtubs and showers must not obstruct controls or transfer from a wheelchair onto shower or tub seats. Therefore, do not mount shower enclosure tracks on the rim of a tub. Visual alarm signals must be visible to a person who is hearing-impaired in all areas of an accessible unit including the bathroom.

Multiple user bathrooms, such as those found in dormitories, fraternity and sorority houses, or social services establishments, might have a vestibule connected to a main corridor by two doors in a series. Adequate space for a person in a wheelchair to open these two doors and to pass into and back out of the lavatory, toilet stall, and bathing area must be provided. Once inside the main area, clear floor space is required for approaching all accessible fixtures and elements. These bathrooms might have a number of toilet stalls and urinals in one room, a number of lavatories and counters in another room, and showers stalls or tubs in another. Since areas with various fixtures might be separated by doors, clear floor space is required for a person in a wheelchair to open the doors and to pass into and through the lavatory, toilet stall area, and bathing/shower areas. Lavatory and bathing area floor surfaces that are slip-resistant, even when wet, should be specified. Visual alarm signals must be visible to a person who is hearing-impaired while they are in any portion of the multiple user bathroom.

PRELIMINARY DESIGN OVERVIEW

(AL) Alarms

- Visual emergency alarm signals must be visible in all areas of the unit.

(AR) Accessible Routes

- Typical requirements.

(BR) Bathroom Criteria

- The clear floor space at fixtures or controls, the accessible route, and turning space may overlap.
- Minimum clear floor space for accessible turning spaces is often overlooked in toilet rooms.
- Doors must not swing into the clear floor space of an accessible fixture.

(BT) Bathtub

- Bathtub enclosures must not interfere with transfer or operation of controls.
- Bathtub seating may be built-in or removable; structural and dimensional requirements vary for each.

(CT) Controls and Operating Mechanisms

- Controls and operating mechanisms have clear floor space and reach range requirements. Frequently overlooked in this space-type are controls in showers, tubs, and lavatories, pull cords on fans and lights, etc.
- One of each type of control device must be accessible and operable.

(DR) Doors

- In multiple user bathrooms, two doors in a series must meet both clear space and door swing requirements (e.g., vestibules, toilet rooms, shower room entries, etc.).

(FS) Floor Surfaces

- In some areas floor surfaces should be evaluated as if wet. In particular consider tub and shower areas as well as lavatories.
- Smooth floor surfaces should be evaluated for slip-resistance based on floor finish and maintenance.
- Vertical changes in levels along the accessible route can be an unforeseen barrier, e.g., transitions between floor materials such as carpet and tile.
- Floor grates or drains located on the accessible route must meet accessibility requirements.

(HR) Handrails, Grab Bars, and Tub and Shower Seats

- Typical requirements.

(LV) Lavatories, Sinks, and Mirrors

- Hot pipes and sharp objects (e.g., valves and drains) must be shielded under lavatories and sinks.
- If sinks and/or lavatories are used for different purposes, then one of each use type must be accessible.
- Where mirrors are provided, one must be accessible. The bottom edge of the reflecting surface (slanted or flush-mounted) must meet accessibility requirements.

(PR) Protruding Objects

- Common wall-mounted elements can be protruding objects, e.g., shelves, dispensers, and lighting fixtures, and must be out of the path of travel.

(SG) Signage

- Typical requirements.

(SR) Storage

- One of each type of storage unit (shelves, hooks, dispensers, etc.) must be accessible.

(SS) Shower Stall

- Accessible showers in transient lodging can have requirements that are different from showers found in other space-types (see roll-in showers in TH).
- Shower spray unit must be accessible for both fixed or hand-held operation. (In vandal-prone facilities, a fixed shower head may be used in lieu of a hand-held shower head. The fixed head must meet mounting height requirements.)

(TH) Transient Lodging

- Roll-in showers with a folding seat are required if over fifty sleeping units are provided in hotels, motels, inns, dormitories, and other similar places. See ADAAG table 9.1.2.
- Visual emergency alarms must be visible in all areas of accessible units.
- In addition to general alarm requirements, visual notification devices must be provided in units, sleeping rooms, and suites.

(TS) Toilet Stalls (generally not needed in single user bathrooms)

- The direction of approach greatly affects compliance requirements.

- If six or more toilet stalls are provided, one must be a standard accessible stall and one must comply with the requirements for the additional accessible stall.
- Toilet stall doors that swing into the stall increase the overall stall dimensions.
- Toilet stall doors must not swing into the clear floor space of any other accessible fixture.

(UR) Urinals (generally not found in single user bathrooms)

- The depth of the rim of an elongated urinal is not currently defined by ADAAG.
- Partitions extending beyond the front edge of the urinal must meet accessibility criteria.
- Reach range requirements for flush valve controls are more restrictive than typical reach range requirements.

(WC) Water Closets

- Water closets are not centered in the stall; they are located relative to a side wall or partition.
- Flush valve controls are required to be on the wide side of the toilet area.

- When not in a stall, there are clear floor space criteria for water closets.
- Toilet paper dispenser is often placed out of required reach range.
- Note location, height, size, and wall anchorage of grab bars for water closets that are not in stalls.

ADAAG APPENDIX

The ADAAG Appendix has advisory information pertinent to this space-type.

- A4.16.3 Water Closets—Height
- A4.16.4 Water Closets—Grab Bars
- A4.16.5 Water Closets—Flush Controls
- A4.17.3 Toilet Stalls—Size and Arrangement
- A4.17.5 Toilet Stalls—Doors
- A4.19.6 Lavatories and Mirrors—Mirrors
- A4.22.3 Toilet Rooms—Clear Floor Space
- A4.28.4 Alarms—Auxiliary Alarms

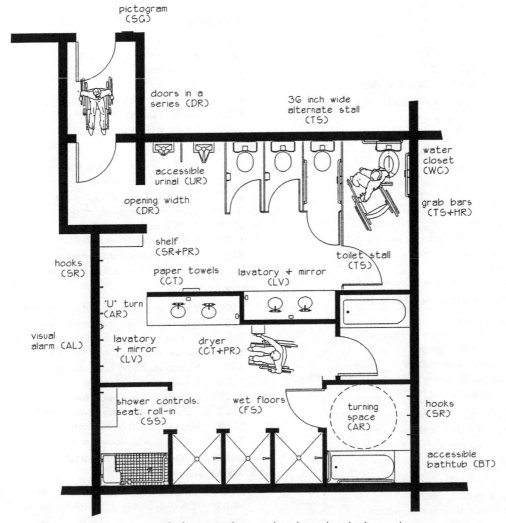

Figure 3.21. Transient lodging: Bathrooms (single and multiple user).

Bathrooms Checklist

SIGNAGE

SG02	Entry signage: inaccessible entrances
SG03	Inaccessible entry signage: criteria
SG04	Room signage: criteria
SG05	Room signage: location
SG06	Pictograms: size requirements
SG07	Pictograms: verbal description criteria

DOORS

DR04	Doors: maneuvering clearances
DR05	Doors: handle type
DR06	Doors: opening force (interior only)
DR07	Doors: closing speed
DR08	Doors: thresholds
DR09	Doors: clear width/height
DR10	Openings (no door): clear width/height
DR11	Doors in series: clear space between

TRANSIENT LODGING: BATHROOMS

TH02	51+ sleeping units: roll-in shower w/seat
TH06	Unit choice: type/class of acc. rooms
TH08	Sleeping unit: linked accessible spaces
TH09	Sleeping unit: linked accessible elements
TH16	Hearing-imp. unit: visual alarm req.
TH17	Hearing-imp. unit: visual alarms in all areas
TH18	Hearing-imp. units: visual notification device
TH19	Hearing-imp. units: telephone

BATHROOMS, TOILET ROOMS,
BATHING FACILITIES, AND SHOWER ROOMS

BR10	Clear floor space: clear of door swing
BR11	Wheelchair turning space
BR20	Medicine cabinet: accessible shelf

ACCESSIBLE ROUTES

AR08	Route: clear width
AR09	Route width: U-turns

PROTRUDING OBJECTS

PR01	Wall-mounted
PR02	Freestanding/suspended on posts/pylons
PR03	Clear route width maintained
PR04	Overhead clearance
PR05	Vertical clearance: cane detection barrier

CONTROLS AND OPERATING MECHANISMS

CT01	Clear floor space
CT02	Reach ranges: elec./comm. systems
CT03	Reach ranges: thermostats
CT04	Reach ranges: other controls
CT05	Reach ranges: life safety devices
CT06	Controls: operation

FLOOR AND GROUND SURFACES

FS01	Surface: firm, stable, and slip-resistant
FS02	Vertical changes in level
FS04	Floor gratings

TOILET STALLS

TS01	Accessible route: location
TS02	Required aisle clearance: approach
TS03	Door swings out: maneuvering space
TS04	"Standard": number required
TS05	"Standard": door swing/clear floor space
TS06	"Alternate": number required
TS07	Stall less than 60 in. deep: toe clearance
TS08	Stall doors: dimensions
TS09	Stall doors: hardware and opening force
TS10	"Standard" grab bars: length/placement
TS11	"Alternate" grab bars: length/placement

WATER CLOSETS

WC01	Accessible toilet: centerline location
WC02	Toilet seat: criteria
WC03	Flush controls: location
WC04	Flush controls: operation
WC05	Paper dispensers: location and operation
WC06	Water closet/no stall: clear floor space
WC07	Water closet grab bars/no stall: criteria

URINALS

UR01	Elongated rim: height above floor
UR02	Clear floor space: forward reach
UR03	Clear width between shields
UR04	Flush controls: reach range
UR05	Flush controls: operation

LAVATORIES, SINKS, AND MIRRORS

LV01	Clear floor space
LV02	Rim/apron heights and extension from wall
LV03	Toe clearance
LV04	Insulated pipes
LV05	Controls and operation requirements
LV06	Lavatories: knee clearance
LV09	Mirror: mounting height

BATHTUBS

BT01	Bathtub approach: clear floor space
BT02	Accessible seating in tub
BT03	Grab bars for seat-in tub: criteria
BT04	Grab bars for built-in tub seat: criteria
BT05	Bathtub controls: location
BT06	Bathtub controls: operation
BT07	Bathtub controls: shower spray
BT08	Enclosures: obstructions/transfer

SHOWER STALLS

SS01	Where provided: at least one accessible
SS02	Min. size criteria and clear floor space
SS03	Shower stall seats: location
SS04	Shower stall seats: type and size
SS05	Shower stall grab bars: criteria
SS06	Shower controls: location
SS07	Shower controls: operation
SS08	Shower stall controls: spray unit criteria
SS09	Shower stall: floor curb criteria
SS10	Shower stall enclosure: criteria

HANDRAILS, GRAB BARS, TUB AND
SHOWER SEATS

HR01	Handrails and grab bars: diameter
HR02	Handrails and grab bars: edge radius

(continued)

Bathrooms Checklist *(continued)*

HR03	Clearance between handrail and wall	**SR03**	Reach ranges
HR04	Handrails in recess: criteria	**SR04**	Storage closets w/o passage: criteria
HR05	Handrails and grab bars: no rotation	**SR05**	Storage hardware: operation
HR06	Handrails and grab bars: structural strength	**ALARMS**	
HR07	Mounting devices: structural strength	**AL04**	Visual alarms: integration w/building alarm
HR08	Tub/shower seat: structural strength	**AL05**	Visual alarms: operation
HR09	Tub/shower fasteners: structural strength	**AL06**	Visual alarms: public restrooms
HR10	Wall adjacent to handrail abrasion free	**AL07**	Visual alarms: common use areas
STORAGE		**AL08**	Visual alarms: vertical placement
SR01	Accessibility: one of each type	**AL12**	Visual alarms: visible throughout unit
SR02	Clear floor space		

BATHROOMS
(HOTELS, INNS, RESORTS, DORMITORIES, AND OTHER PLACES OF ACCOMMODATION AND SOCIAL SERVICES ESTABLISHMENTS: HOMELESS SHELTERS, HALFWAY HOUSES, TRANSIENT GROUP HOMES, AND OTHERS) COMPREHENSIVE CRITERIA

(SG) Signage (4.30)

Signage: room identification (where provided)

DEFINITION:

- These signs designate permanent rooms and spaces.

AUTHOR'S INTERPRETATION:

- Signs that designate stairs, exit doors, and toilet rooms generally are associated with permanent spaces, while an "office" sign is not since the room function may change over time. Room numbers also must meet the ADAAG criteria as permanent designations, while personal names do not since the occupant may change over time.

SG-02 If an entrance is not accessible, is there a directional sign indicating the location of the nearest accessible entrance? [4.1.2(7)(c), 4.1.3(8)(d)]

SG-03 Does the directional sign indicating the location of the nearest accessible entrance comply with directional signage criteria? (4.30.2, 3, 5)

- Character proportion: letters and numbers have a width to height ratio between 3:5 and 1:1 and a stroke width to height ratio between 1:5 and 1:10.
- Character height: sized according to viewing distance with characters on overhead signs at least 3 in. high.
- Finish: characters and backgrounds have a nonglare finish.
- Contrast: characters contrast with their background (light-on-dark or dark-on-light).

SG-04 Do signs that designate permanent rooms and spaces comply with the following criteria? [4.1.2(7); 4.1.3(16); 4.30.4, 5, 6]

- Character type: raised and accompanied by Grade II Braille.
- Character size: between 5/8 in. and 2 in. high; raised at least 1/32 in.

- Character style: upper case, and sans or simple serif.
- Finish: characters and backgrounds have a nonglare finish.
- Contrast: characters contrast with their background (light-on-dark or dark-on-light).

SG-05 Is the room identification sign mounted in the required location? (4.30.6)

- Mounting location: installed on the wall adjacent to the latch side of the door or where wall space to the latch side of the door is not available, including double doors, placed on the nearest adjacent wall.
- Mounting height: 60 in. above the floor/ground to the centerline of the sign.
- Sign access: approach to within 3 in. of a sign without encountering protruding objects or standing within the swing of the door.

Signage: pictorial symbol signs (pictograms) (where provided)

AUTHOR'S INTERPRETATION:

- Because the criteria for pictograms are listed in ADAAG 4.30.4, they fall into the category of room identification signage and must meet those criteria that follow.
- While the ISA symbol might be considered to be a pictogram, it does not appear to have the same requirements as pictograms.

SG-06 Is the border dimension of a pictogram, where provided, at least 6 in. high? (4.30.4)

AUTHOR'S INTERPRETATION:

- A pictogram includes both a symbol and the field on which it is displayed. The 6-in. vertical dimension applies to the vertical field, not to the symbol. The required verbal description may not intrude on the 6-in. field.

SG-07 Is a pictogram, where provided, accompanied by the equivalent verbal description placed directly below the pictogram, and does the verbal description meet room identification signage criteria? (4.30.4)

- Character type: raised and accompanied by Grade II Braille.
- Character size: between 5/8 in. and 2 in. high; raised at least 1/32 in.

- Character style: upper case, and sans or simple serif.
- Finish: characters and backgrounds have a nonglare finish.
- Contrast: characters contrast with their background (light-on-dark or dark-on-light).

(DR) Doors (4.13)

NOTE:

- Included in this category are doors, revolving doors, turnstiles, and gates.

AUTHOR'S INTERPRETATION:

- It is suggested that, for purposes of documentation and review, a door be assigned to the space it swings into. Corridors are an exception to this rule and include only entry doors into the corridor or intermediate fire doors.

Doors: maneuvering clearance

DR-04 If the door is not automatic or power assisted, does it have the required maneuvering clearance provided on the push and pull side, and is the floor level and clear within the maneuvering area? (4.13.6)

- A verbal description cannot adequately describe the requirements. See ADAAG Fig. 25a–f for a graphic description.

EXCEPTION:

- Entry doors to acute care hospital bedrooms for inpatients are exempt from maneuvering space at the latch side of the door if the door is at least 44 in. wide.

AUTHOR'S INTERPRETATION:

- While ADAAG does not describe what elements can reduce the required maneuvering clearance, they could include a narrow entry alcove, an adjacent wall, railing, or permanently installed shelving, or a deep recessed door jamb.

Doors: hardware

DR-05 Do all door handles, locks, latches, or other operable devices meet required operational criteria? (4.13.9)

- Hardware operation: operable with one hand without tight grasping, pinching, or wrist twisting.
- Force required to operate the controls: not greater than 5 lbf. This does not apply to the force required to retract latch bolts or to disengage other devices that only hold the door in a closed position.
- Hardware type: "U"-shaped handles, levers, and push type mechanisms are acceptable designs.
- Hardware height: not greater than 48 in. above the floor.
- Sliding doors: hardware is exposed and usable from both sides when the doors are fully open.

Doors: opening force

DR-06 Do interior hinged doors and sliding or folding doors have an opening force of 5 lbf or less? (4.13.11)

- At present, no accessible criteria exist for exterior doors.

- Fire doors shall have the minimum opening force allowable by the appropriate administrative authority.

Doors: closing speed

DR-07 If the door has a closer, is the closer adjusted so that the door does not close too quickly? (4.13.10)

- From an open position of 70° the door will take at least 3 sec to move to a point 3 in. from the latch (measured to the leading edge of the door).

Doors: thresholds

DR-08 Where raised thresholds are provided, do they meet height limitations and are they beveled when required? (4.13.8, 4.5.2, Fig. 7)

- Threshold height: not more than 3/4 in. for exterior sliding doors or 1/2 in. for other types of doors.
- Threshold bevel: thresholds less than 1/4 in. high need no bevel; thresholds between 1/4 in. and 1/2 in. high shall be beveled at each edge with not more than a 1:2 slope.

EXCEPTION:

- A 3/4-in. high threshold is allowed in existing conditions. [4.1.6(3)(d)(ii)]

Doors: clear opening width and height

DR-09 Is the clear opening for the doorway adequate in width and height? (4.13.3, 4, 5; Fig. 24)

- Door width: at least 32 in. of clear width with the door open at 90°, measured between the face of the door and the door stop on the latch side. This also pertains to the active leaf of a double-leaf door or gate.
- Opening width: openings more than 24 in. deep must provide 36 in. of clear width.
- Height: at least 80 in. of vertical clearance.

EXCEPTIONS:

- Doors not requiring full user passage, such as shallow closets, may have the clear opening reduced to not less than 20 in.
- Where it is technically infeasible to comply with clear opening width requirements, a projection of 5/8 in. maximum will be permitted for the latch side. [4.1.6(d)(i)]

DR-10 Is the clear opening (when there is no door) adequate in width and height? (4.2.1, 4.3.3, 4.4.2)

- Width: at least 32 in. of clear width for depths 24 in. or less and at least 36 in. of clear width for depths greater than 24 in.
- Height: at least 80 in. of vertical clearance.

Doors: two doors in a series

DR-11 If there are two doors in a series, is the required clear space between the doors provided and do the doors swing in the appropriate direction? (4.13.7, Fig. 26)

- Clear space between the doors: not less than 48 in. plus the width of any door swinging into the space.

- Door swing: must swing in the same direction or away from the space between the doors.

(TH) Accessible Transient lodging (9.0)
(Hotels, Motels, Inns, Boarding Houses, Dormitories, and Similar Places)

NOTE:

- Transient lodging is divided into two categories.
  — Hotels, motels, inns, boarding houses, dormitories, and similar places (TH-01 through TH-19).
  — Homeless shelters, halfway houses, transient group homes, and other social services establishments (TH-20 through TH-26 and TH-07 through TH-19).

- Doors and doorways designed to allow passage into and within all transient lodging sleeping units shall comply with accessible door width criteria. This means any sleeping unit in the facility, whether it is designated as accessible or not. (9.4)

AUTHOR'S INTERPRETATION:

- Accessible units, sleeping rooms, and suites are divided into two categories: fully accessible and hearing-impaired. Fully accessible units, sleeping rooms, and suites must comply with accessible criteria for both mobility and hearing impairments. (9.2.8) Hearing-impaired units must comply only with those accessible criteria that relate to visual alarms, notification devices, and telephones. (9.3)

- The total number of accessible units required by ADAAG can be easily misinterpreted if not carefully read. For example, the total number of rooms required for 76–100 hotel rooms is 9, broken down as follows:
  — Four fully accessible rooms with accessible bathrooms.
  — One fully accessible room with accessible bathroom with a roll-in shower with folding seat.
  — Four rooms for the hearing-impaired (other accessible criteria are not required including an accessible bathroom).

- In dormitories or other facilities where bath facilities are multiple user and separate from the sleeping room, the minimum number of accessible tubs or showers required is not clearly prescribed. ADAAG 4.23.8, which indicates a minimum of at least one accessible tub or shower (when provided) in bathrooms, appears to be applicable to this situation.

EXCEPTION:

- ADAAG 9.1 through 9.4 do not apply to an establishment located within a building that contains no more than five rooms for rent or hire and that is actually occupied by the proprietor of such establishment as the residence of such proprietor.

Accessible Transient Lodging/Hotels: number required/ new construction

TH-02 In hotels of 51 or more sleeping rooms and suites, is the required number of additional accessible sleeping rooms with a roll-in shower with folding seat provided? (9.1.2, Fig. 57a–b)

- Accessible rooms with roll-in showers with folding seats: 1 per 51–100, 2 per 101–200, 3 per 201–300, and 4 per 301–400.

- For more than 400 rooms, 4 accessible rooms with roll-in showers with folding seat plus 1 for each 100 over 400.

NOTES:

- Roll-in shower with folding seat design for this type of transient housing differs from transfer and roll-in showers described in Section "SS, Shower Stalls." See ADAAG Fig. 57a–b for dimensional criteria and configurations.

Accessible Transient Lodging/Hotels: room dispersion

TH-06 Are the accessible rooms and suites dispersed among various classes of sleeping accommodations available to all patrons? (9.1.4)

NOTES:

- Factors to be considered include room size, cost, amenities, and number of beds provided.

- Equal facilitation: For purposes of this section, the operator may choose to limit construction of accessible rooms to those designed for multiple occupancy rooms if the multiple occupancy accessible rooms are made available at a single occupancy rate to an individual with a disability who requests a single occupancy room.

Accessible Transient Lodging/Hotels: accessible routes

TH-08 Does an accessible route connect all accessible spaces within the accessible unit? [9.2.2(2, 6, 7)]

- Where provided, this includes the living area, the dining area, a dual occupancy sleeping area, patio or balcony, a full bathroom or half bath (if only half baths are provided), kitchen (also kitchenette or wet bar), and parking space.

NOTE:

- Elevators are not required in a multilevel unit if the previously listed spaces are all on the accessible level and the accessible sleeping area is suitable for dual occupancy.

EXCEPTION:

- The requirements of thresholds at doors (4.13.8) and changes in levels (4.3.8) do not apply where it is necessary to utilize a higher door threshold or a change in level to protect the integrity of the unit from wind/water damage. Where this exception results in patios, terraces, or balconies that are not at an accessible level, equivalent facilitation shall be provided (e.g., equivalent facilitation at a hotel patio or balcony might consist of providing raised decking or a ramp to provide accessibility).

TH-09 Does the accessible route connect all accessible elements within the accessible unit? [9.2.2(3, 4, 5)]

- Accessible elements would include doors and doorways, storage (accessible, fixed, or built-in), controls and operating mechanisms, and telephones.

TH-16 Do accessible living units and sleeping accommodations comply with the requirements for visual alarms? (9.3, 4.28.4)

- Visual alarms meet required operational criteria.
- Visual alarms connect to the building emergency alarm system.
- Or a standard electrical outlet is provided and connected to the facility's central alarm system which enables room occupants to utilize portable devices provided by the operator of the facility.

TH-17 Is the signal from the visual alarm visible in all areas of the living unit or room? (9.3, 4.28.4)

TH-18 Do the living units, sleeping rooms, and suites comply with the requirements for visual notification devices? (9.3.1)

- This includes any space where the occupant would expect to be able to hear a phone or door bell.
- Visual notification devices are to alert the occupant of incoming telephone calls and a door knock or bell.
- This device must *not* be connected to the visual alarm system.

TH-19 Do the living units, sleeping rooms, and suites comply with the requirements for telephones? (9.3.1)

- If provided, permanently installed (hardwired) telephones should have volume controls capable of a minimum of 12 dbA and a maximum of 18 dbA above normal. If an automatic reset is provided, then 18 dbA may be exceeded.
- Outlets: An accessible electrical outlet is within 4 ft of a telephone connection, where provided.

(BR) Bathrooms, Toilet Rooms, Bathing Facilities, and Shower Rooms (4.23)

NOTE:

- In historic buildings, if toilets are provided, at least one toilet facility complying with toilet room accessible criteria shall be provided along an accessible route. Such a toilet facility may be unisex in design. [4.1.7(3)(c)]

BR-10 Does the door swing not reduce the clear floor space for accessible fixtures? (4.22.2, 4.23.2)

BR-11 Is the minimum clear floor space for an unobstructed 180° turning space or a "T"-shaped turning space provided in the toilet/bathroom? (4.22.3, 4.23.3, Fig. 3)

- 180° turning space has a 60-in. diameter; "T"-shaped space has 36-in. wide legs.
- Clear floor space at fixtures and controls, the accessible route, and the turning space can overlap.

BR-20 If medicine cabinets are provided, does at least one cabinet have a usable shelf no higher than 44 in. from the floor and a clear floor space of at least 30 in. × 48 in.? (4.23.9)

(AR) Accessible Routes (4.3)

NOTES:

- All walks, halls, corridors, aisles, skywalks, tunnels, and other spaces that are part of a designated accessible route shall comply with accessible requirements.
- Any slope on the accessible route that is greater than 1:20 is required to meet all ramp criteria.
- The accessible route shall, to the maximum extent feasible, coincide with the route for the general public.
- In historic buildings, accessible routes from an accessible entrance shall be provided to all publicly used spaces on at least the level of the accessible entrance. Access shall be provided to all levels of a building or facility whenever practical. [4.1.7(3)(d)]

AUTHOR'S INTERPRETATION:

- An accessible route "generally coincides" with the route used by the public if:
  — It does not force the user to go out of the way.
  — It is most like the route chosen by the general public.
  — It is direct.
  — It gives the same basic experience as the route preferred by the public.

Accessible Routes: width

AR-08 Is the minimum clear width along the accessible route adequate for continuous or point passage? (4.2.1, 4.3.3, Fig. 1, Fig. 8e, Fig. 24e)

- Continuous passage (greater than 24 in. long): at least a 36-in. clear width.
- Point passage (not more than 24 in. long): at least a 32-in. clear width.

AUTHOR'S INTERPRETATION:

- Noncompliance with this question generally relates to permanent elements that encroach on the accessible route. Large, heavy equipment that is not readily movable might be considered permanent. If the space is designed so that temporary elements (such as bikes in a bike rack or car bumpers) will consistently encroach, the situation might also be considered a permanent barrier.

AR-09 Is the minimum clear width along the accessible route adequate at a U-turn around an obstruction? (4.3.3, Fig. 7a–b)

- Obstruction 48 in. or greater: at least a 36-in. clear width around the obstruction.
- Obstruction less than 48 in.: at least a 42-in. clear width at each side with at least a 48-in. clear width in the turn.

(PR) Protruding Objects (4.4)

Protruding Objects: general

PR-01 Do wall-mounted objects having leading edges between 27 in. and 80 in. high project less than 4 in. into walkways, corridors, aisles, or paths of travel? (4.4.1, Fig. 8a–e)

- Objects mounted with their leading edge at or below 27 in. can protrude any amount, as long as they do not reduce the required clear width of an accessible route.

AUTHOR'S INTERPRETATION:

- Protruding objects might include fire extinguishers or cabinets, pencil sharpeners, shelving, counters, built-in equipment overhangs, or various dispensers such as for paper towels or soap.

PR-02 Do free-standing objects, suspended or mounted on posts or pylons with leading edges between 27 in. and 80 in. high, project less than 12 in. into the perpendicular route of travel? (4.4.1, Fig. 8a–e)

AUTHOR'S INTERPRETATION:

- These might include telephone enclosures, drinking fountains, or free-standing signage kiosks.

PR-03 Is the minimum clear route width or maneuvering space still maintained even with the projection of a protruding object? (4.4.1, Fig. 8a–e)

Protruding Objects: overhead clearance

PR-04 Is the minimum overhead clearance of 80 in. provided in accessible areas or along accessible routes? (4.4.2, Fig. 8a)

AUTHOR'S INTERPRETATION:

- Overhead objects that can reduce the required clearance might include structures, pipes, ducts, or light fixtures.

PR-05 Where the vertical clearance of a space adjoining the accessible route is less than 80 in. high, is a cane detection barrier less than 27 in. from the floor provided for blind or visually impaired persons? (4.4.2, Fig. 8c-1)

AUTHOR'S INTERPRETATION:

- This condition might be found under a stair, at a sloped ceiling space, or with guy wires from telephone poles along an exterior accessible route.

(CT) Controls and Operating Mechanisms (4.27)

NOTES:

- Controls or operating mechanisms can include elements such as light switches, pencil sharpeners, manual overhead screens, nonkeyed thermostats, alarm pull stations, fire extinguisher cabinets, A/C window units, microwave ovens, towel dispensers, and wall hooks.
- If controls are to be operated by occupants of the space, they must be accessible. If controls are to be operated by maintenance staff only and not by occupants or other users of the space, they do not have to be accessible. For example, thermostats in auditoriums usually do not have to be accessible, while thermostats in classrooms may need to be accessible.

Controls: clear floor space

CT-01 Is a clear floor space of at least 30 in. × 48 in. provided in front of controls, dispensers, receptacles, and other operable equipment for forward or parallel approach? (4.27.2, Fig. 4a–b)

Controls: reach ranges

NOTES:

- Accessible reach ranges for controls and operating mechanisms are:
  — Forward reach: not less than 15 in. high and not more than 48 in. high without any obstruction or where the obstruction is less than 20 in. deep. For obstructions from 20 in. to 25 in. deep, no forward reach higher than 44 in.
  — Side reach: not less than 9 in. high and not more than 54 in. high. For obstructions not more than 34 in. high or 24 in. deep, no side reach higher than 46 in.
  — Electrical outlets, switches, and communication system receptacles have a minimum outlet height of 15 in. regardless of forward or side reach. See CT-02 below.

CT-02 Are electrical outlets, switches, and communication system receptacles mounted within accessible forward or side reach ranges? (4.27.3)

EXCEPTION:

- These requirements do not apply where the use of special equipment dictates otherwise or where electrical and communications system receptacles are not normally intended for use by building occupants. (4.27.3)

CT-03 Are thermostats or other similar operable equipment mounted within accessible forward or side reach ranges? (4.2.5, 4.2.6, Fig. 5a–b, Fig. 6a–c)

CT-04 Are dispensers or other similar operable equipment mounted within accessible forward or side reach ranges? (4.2.5, 4.2.6, Fig. 5a–b, Fig. 6a–c)

CT-05 Are life safety devices or other similar operable equipment mounted within accessible forward or side reach ranges? (4.2.5, 4.2.6, Fig. 5a–b, Fig. 6a–c)

NOTE:

- This might include fire alarm pull stations, handles to extinguisher cabinets, or wall-mounted extinguishers.

Controls: operation

CT-06 Are controls, dispensers, receptacles, and other operable equipment operable with one hand without tight grasping, pinching, or wrist twisting, and requiring no more than 5 lbf of force? (4.27.4)

(FS) Floor and Ground Surfaces (4.5)

Floor Surfaces: general

FS-01 Are the floor/ground surfaces on the accessible route stable, firm, and slip-resistant? (4.5.1)

AUTHOR'S INTERPRETATION:

- Exterior spaces, interior circulation, bathrooms, and other spaces where water can collect on the floor around an element (sinks, drinking fountains, hose bibbs, etc.) are reviewed as if wet.
- High gloss surfaces without significant textures that are regularly maintained with waxing (smooth tiles, waxed concrete, etc.) could be considered noncompliant.
- Accessible criteria are not specified for nonpermanent floor surfaces such as mats or rugs.

Floor Surfaces: changes in level

FS-02 Are vertical changes in level between 1/4 in. and 1/2 in. beveled with a slope of 1:2 or less? (4.5.2)

- Changes in level up to 1/4 in. may be vertical without edge treatment.

- Changes in level greater than 1/2 in. should be accomplished by means of a curb ramp, ramp, elevator, or platform lift (as permitted in ADAAG 4.1.3 and 4.1.6).

Floor Surfaces: gratings

FS-04 Do floor gratings in the path of travel comply with accessible criteria? (4.5.4, Fig. 8g–h)

- Opening size: no greater than 1/2 in. in one direction.

- Opening direction: the long dimension is perpendicular to the dominant direction of travel.

(TS) Toilet Stalls (4.17)

Toilet Stalls: location and approach

TS-01 Are the accessible toilet stalls located on an accessible route? (4.17.1)

TS-02 Is the required aisle clearance provided when approaching the accessible toilet stall? (4.17.5, Fig. 30)

- Aisle clearance if the stall door swings out and the approach is from the *latch side*: not less than 42 in. between the door side of the stall and any obstruction.

- Aisle clearance if the stall door swings out and the approach is from the *hinge side*: not less than 48 in. between the door side of the stall and any obstruction.

Toilet Stalls: maneuvering space

TS-03 If the stall door swings out at the end of an aisle, is at least 18 in. of maneuvering space provided at the latch side of the stall door? (4.17.5, 4.13.5)

Toilet Stalls: size and arrangement

TS-04 If toilet stalls are provided, is at least one a "standard" accessible stall? (4.17.3, 4.22.4, 4.23.4, Fig. 30a)

- "Standard" accessible stall: at least 60 in. wide × 59 in. deep (with floor-mounted water closet) or at least 56 in. deep (with wall-mounted water closet). The door should be located at the "open" side of the stall.

EXCEPTION:

- In instances of alteration work where a "standard" stall is technically infeasible or where plumbing code requirements prevent combining existing stalls to provide space, either "alternate" stall configuration described as follows may be provided in lieu of the "standard" stall. (4.17.3, Fig. 30b)

  — One: 36 in. wide × 69 in. deep (with floor-mounted water closet) or at least 66 in. deep (with wall-mounted water closet), with an outward swinging, self-closing door and parallel grab bars on side walls.

  — Two: At least 48 in. wide × 54 in. deep, with an outward swinging, self-closing door and grab bars on side and rear walls.

TS-05 If the door swings into the "standard" accessible stall, is the additional depth provided in the stall so that the door does not encroach on the clear floor space required at the toilet? (4.17.5, 4.13.5, Fig. 30a-1)

- Additional depth: not less than 36 in.

- At least 18 in. of maneuvering space at the latch side of the door on the inside of the stall is needed.

TS-06 Where six or more stalls are provided, is at least one an "alternate" accessible stall, in addition to the "standard" accessible stall? (4.22.4, 4.23.4, 4.17.3, Fig. 30b)

- "Alternate" accessible stalls for new construction are:
  — Exactly 36 in. wide × at least 69 in. deep (with floor-mounted water closet) or at least 66 in. deep (with wall-mounted water closet), with an outward swinging, self-closing door and parallel grab bars on side walls.

Toilet Stalls: toe clearance

TS-07 If the stall is less than 60 in. deep, does the front partition and at least one side partition have toe clearances of at least 9 in. above the floor? (4.17.4)

Toilet Stalls: doors

TS-08 Does the stall door, including door hardware, or the opening into the accessible stall comply with the minimum width and height requirements? (4.17.5, 4.13.5, 4.4.2)

- Width clearance: not less than 32 in. between the face of the door and the edge of the partition on the latch side when the stall door is open 90°.

- Height clearance: not less than 80 in.

TS-09 Do the toilet stall doors and hardware comply with typical door accessible criteria including handle type, mounting height, and opening force? (4.17.5, 4.4.2)

Toilet Stalls: grab bars

NOTE:

- Additional criteria for grab bars can be found in Section "HR, Handrails."

TS-10 Are the grab bars in the "standard" stall the required length and are they placed in the required location? (4.17.6; Fig. 30a, c, d)

- Rear wall: not less than 36 in. long, starting at no more than 6 in. from the side wall.

- Side wall: not less than 40 in. long, starting at no more than 12 in. from the rear wall.

- Mounting height: 33 in. to 36 in. to centerline above the finish floor and mounted horizontally.

TS-11 Are the grab bars in the "alternate" stall the required length and are they placed in the required location? (4.17.6; Fig. 30b, c, d)

- Rear wall: not less than 36 in. long, starting at no more than 6 in. from the side wall.

- Side wall: not less than 42 in. long, starting at no more than 12 in. from the rear wall.

- Mounting height: 33 in. to 36 in. to centerline above the finish floor and mounted horizontally.

NOTE:

- A rear grab bar is required in stalls wider than 36 in.

(WC) Water Closets (4.16)

Water Closets (general): centerline and toilet seats

WC-01 Is the centerline of the accessible toilet (in or not in a stall) located exactly 18 in. from a side wall or partition? (Fig. 28; Fig. 30a, a-1, b)

WC-02 Is the top of the toilet seat between 17 in. and 19 in. from the top of the finish floor? (4.16.3, Fig. 29b, Fig. 30d)

- Seats shall not automatically return to a lifted position.

Water Closets (general): flush controls

WC-03 Are the flush controls mounted on the wide side of the toilet and no more than 44 in. above the finish floor? (4.16.5)

WC-04 Is the toilet flush valve control automatic or operable with one hand without tight grasping, pinching, or wrist twisting, and requiring no more than 5 lbf of force? (4.16.5)

Water Closets (general): toilet paper dispenser

WC-05 Is the toilet paper dispenser placed in the correct location and does it permit continuous paper flow? (4.16.6, Fig. 29b)

- Location: not less than 19 in. high from finish floor to centerline; not more than 36 in. from the back wall.

Water Closets (not in stalls): clear floor space

WC-06 Is clear floor space provided at the accessible toilet (not in a stall and with a lavatory at the side) for front, side, or dual approach? (4.16.2, Fig. 28)

- Front approach: at least 48 in. wide × 66 in. deep; lavatory may encroach up to 12 in.
- Side approach: at least 48 in. wide × 56 in. deep; lavatory may encroach up to 12 in.
- Dual approach: at least 60 in. wide × 56 in. deep with no lavatory encroachment.

Water Closets (not in stalls): grab bars

NOTE:

- Additional criteria for grab bars can be found in Section "HR, Handrails."

WC-07 Are the grab bars for toilets (not in stalls) the correct length and are they placed in the correct location? (4.16.4, Fig. 28–29)

- Rear wall: not less than 36 in. long starting at no more than 6 in. from the side wall.
- Side wall: not less than 42 in. long starting at no more than 12 in. from the rear wall.
- Mounting height: 33 in. to 36 in. to centerline above the finish floor and mounted horizontally.

(UR) Urinals (4.18)

Urinals: height

UR-01 Does the accessible urinal have an elongated rim with a maximum height to the rim of no more than 17 in. above the floor? (4.18.2, 4.22.5)

AUTHOR'S INTERPRETATION:

- The ADAAG does not define when a urinal is considered as elongated. However, some codes suggest the face of an elongated rim is at least 14 in. from the wall.

Urinals: clear floor space

UR-02 Is clear floor space provided that allows a forward approach to the accessible urinal? (4.18.3)

- Clear floor space: not less than 30 in. × 48 in. and adjoins or overlaps an accessible route.

UR-03 Is the required clear width provided between the accessible urinal shields? (4.18.3)

- Shields that do not extend beyond the front edge of the urinal rim: at least 29 in. wide between partitions.
- Shields extending beyond the urinal rim: not less than 30 in. wide between partitions.

Urinals: flush controls

UR-04 Is the accessible urinal flush valve control located within reach range? (4.18.4)

- Height: not more than 44 in.

UR-05 Is the accessible urinal flush valve control automatic or operable with one hand without tight grasping, pinching, or wrist twisting, and requiring no more than 5 lbf of force? (4.18.4)

(LV) Lavatories, Sinks, and Mirrors (4.19, 4.24)

NOTE:

- Where lavatories or sinks are provided, at least one of each type must meet accessible requirements.

AUTHOR'S INTERPRETATION:

- While not specifically defined by ADAAG, it appears lavatories are for personal hygiene in bathrooms or toilet rooms, while sinks are for all other situations (e.g., laboratories or kitchens).

Lavatories or Sinks: clearances

LV-01 Is there a clear floor space not less than 30 in. × 48 in. in front of the accessible lavatory or sink allowing a forward approach, and does it adjoin or overlap the accessible route? (4.19.3, 4.24.5, Fig. 32)

- The clear floor space can extend up to 19 in. under the sink or lavatory if adequate knee clearance is provided.

LV-02 Are the accessible lavatory or sink rim or counter height, apron height, and extension from the wall adequate? (4.19.2, 4.24.2, Fig. 31)

- Rim height: not greater than 34 in. above the finish floor.
- Apron height: not less than 29 in. above the finish floor to the bottom of the apron.
- Lavatory extension: not less than 17 in. from the wall.

LV-03 Is toe clearance under the accessible lavatory or sink not less than 9 in. above the finish floor and not deeper than 6 in. from the back wall for the full length of the lavatory or sink? (4.19.2, Fig. 31)

Lavatories or Sinks: pipe shielding

LV-04 Are the hot water and drain pipes at the accessible lavatory or sink insulated or otherwise configured to protect against contact and is the area below the lavatory or sink free of sharp or abrasive surfaces? (4.19.4)

Lavatories or Sinks: controls

LV-05 Do the accessible lavatory or sink controls meet operational requirements? (4.19.5)

- Operation: operable with one hand without tight grasping, pinching, or twisting of the wrist. Acceptable types might include lever operated, push type, touch type, or electronically controlled; no more than 5 lbf of force.
- Self-closing faucets, when used, remain open for at least 10 sec.

Lavatories Only

LV-06 Is adequate knee clearance provided underneath the accessible lavatory? (4.19.2, Fig. 31)

- Lavatory knee clearance: not less than 27 in. high from finish floor to the bottom of the lavatory when measured at a point not less than 8 in. from the front of the lavatory.

Lavatories or Sinks: mirrors

LV-09 Where mirrors are provided, does at least one mirror have a bottom edge of the reflecting surface no higher than 40 in. above the floor? (4.19.6, Fig. 31)

AUTHOR'S INTERPRETATION:

- Slanted mirrors located above 40 in. are not recognized as compliant by the ADAAG.

(BT) Bathtubs (4.20)

Bathtubs: clear floor space

BT-01 Is the clear floor space for a parallel or perpendicular approach to the accessible bathtub provided? (4.20.2, Fig. 33)

- Seat-in tub with approach from head of tub and parallel to tub length: at least 30 in. wide × 60 in. long.
- Seat-in tub with approach perpendicular to tub length: at least 48 in. wide × 60 in. long.
- Built-in seat located at head of tub: at least 30 in. wide × 75 in. long.

NOTES:

- Head of tub is the end opposite from the controls.
- The lavatory may encroach into clear floor space at control end of tub.

Bathtubs: seats

BT-02 Does the tub seat comply with accessibility requirements? (4.20.3, Fig. 33–34)

- Size for seat at the head end of tub: at least 15 in. wide.
- Location: opposite end from controls.
- Securely mounted and does not slip during use.

Bathtubs: grab bars

NOTE:

- Additional criteria for grab bars can be found in Section "HR, Handrails."

BT-03 Do the grab bars for seat-in tubs comply with accessible criteria for length and placement? (4.20.4, Fig. 33–34, 4.26, Fig. 39)

- At control wall (foot): at least 24 in. long, beginning at the outside edge of the tub; mounted at 33 in. to 36 in. above the floor.
- At back wall: a double row of bars, at least 24 in. long, beginning not more than 12 in. from the control end and not more than 24 in. from the head end; top bar is 33 in. to 36 in. above the floor; lower bar at 9 in. above the tub rim.
- At head wall: at least 12 in. long beginning at the outside edge of the tub; mounted at 33 in. to 36 in. above the floor.

BT-04 Do the grab bars for built-in seats at head of tub comply with accessible criteria for length and placement? (4.20.4, Fig. 33–34, 4.26, Fig. 39)

- At control wall (foot): at least 24 in. long, beginning at the outside edge of the tub; mounted at 33 in. to 36 in. above the floor.
- At back wall: a double row of bars, at least 48 in. long, beginning not more than 12 in. from the control end and not more than 15 in. from the head end; top bar is 33 in. to 36 in. above the floor; lower bar at 9 in. above the tub rim.
- At head wall: none required.

Bathtubs: controls

BT-05 Are the controls for accessible bathtubs located on the foot wall of the tub, below the grab bar, and offset to the outside edge of the tub? (4.20.5)

BT-06 In accessible bathtubs, are faucets and other controls operable with one hand without tight grasping, pinching, or wrist twisting, and requiring no more than 5 lbf of force? (4.20.5)

BT-07 In accessible bathtubs, is a shower spray unit provided that can be used as both a fixed shower head and a hand-held unit, and does the unit have a hose at least 60 in. long? (4.20.6)

Bathtubs: enclosure

BT-08 Is the bathtub enclosure designed so that it does not obstruct operation of the controls or transfer from a wheelchair onto the bathtub seat or into the bathtub? (4.20.7)

- Enclosures on bathtubs shall not have tracks mounted on their rims.

(SS) Shower Stalls (4.21)

NOTE:

- Requirements for the following shower stalls are for public or common use bathing facilities. Requirements for shower stalls in transient housing may differ. See Section "TH, Transient Housing."

DEFINITIONS:

- *Transfer stall:* a shower stall exactly 36 in. × 36 in.
- *Roll-in stall:* a shower stall at least 30 in. × 60 in.
- *Roll-in stall with folding seat:* two configurations shown in ADAAG Fig. 57a–b. This type is required only in transient housing. See TH-01 and TH-02 in Section "TH, Transient Housing."

Shower Stalls: general

SS-01 Where showers are provided, does at least one comply with accessibility requirements? (4.21.1)

Shower Stalls: stall and clear floor space dimensions

SS-02 Does the accessible shower stall meet the minimum size criteria and provide the required clear floor space? (4.21.2, Fig. 35a–b)

- Transfer stall: a shower stall exactly 36 in. × 36 in. with a clear floor space at least 36 in. wide × 48 in. long extending at least 12 in. beyond the seat wall. A lavatory may not encroach into the clear floor space.
- Roll-in stall: a shower stall at least 30 in. × 60 in. with a clear floor space of at least 36 in. wide × 60 in. long. A lavatory may encroach into the clear floor space.
- Roll-in stall with folding seat: two configurations shown in ADAAG Fig. 57a–b. This type may be required in transient housing.

Shower Stalls: seats

NOTE:

- Depending on the situation, a seat in a roll-in shower may be required only if located in transient housing. For seating in a roll-in shower with folding seat, see ADAAG Fig. 57a–b.

SS-03 Is the seat required in the transfer type shower mounted in the required location? (4.21.3, Fig. 37)

- Height: between 17 in. and 19 in. from the floor.
- Location: mounted on the wall opposite the control wall.

SS-04 Does the seat required in the transfer type shower meet size and shape requirements? (4.21.3, Fig. 36)

- Extends the full width of the stall.
- See ADAAG Fig. 36 for dimensional criteria.

Shower Stalls: grab bars

NOTE:

- Additional criteria for grab bars can be found in Section "HR, Handrails."

SS-05 Do the shower stall grab bars comply with accessible criteria? (4.21.4, Fig. 37a–b)

- Height: between 33 in. and 36 in. above the floor.
- Transfer stall: bar runs along the control wall and is continuous for 18 in. on the back wall. Does not run behind the seat.
- Roll-in stall: continuous bar on all three walls.
- Roll-in stall with folding seat: see grab bar locations shown in ADAAG Fig. 57a–b.

Shower Stalls: controls

SS-06 Are the accessible shower faucet and other controls located in the required area? (4.21.5, Fig. 37a–b)

- Height: between 38 in. and 48 in. above the floor.
- Transfer stall: located on the side wall opposite the seat wall, within 18 in. from the outside edge of the stall.
- Roll-in stall: located on the back wall or on either side wall. If located on the back wall within 27 in. from either side wall with the controls offset to one side; controls located on the side wall are offset to the outside edge of the stall.
- Roll-in stall with folding seat: see control locations shown in ADAAG Fig. 57a–b.

SS-07 In accessible showers, are faucets and other controls operable with one hand without tight grasping, pinching, or wrist twisting, and requiring no more than 5 lbf of force? (4.21.5)

SS-08 In accessible showers, is a shower spray unit provided that can be used as both a fixed shower head and a hand-held unit and does the unit have a hose at least 60 in. long? (4.21.6)

EXCEPTION:

- In unmonitored facilities where vandalism is a consideration, a fixed shower head mounted at 48 in. above the floor may be used in lieu of the hand-held shower head.

Shower Stalls: curbs and enclosure

SS-09 Where floor curbs are provided, do they comply with accessibility requirements? (4.21.7)

- Transfer stall: curbs can be no higher than 1/2 in.
- Roll-in stall: no curb is allowed.

SS-10 Where a shower stall enclosure is provided, is it located so that it does not obstruct the controls or obstruct the transfer from a wheelchair to the shower seat? (4.21.8)

(HR) Handrails, Grab Bars, and Tub and Shower Seats (4.26)

NOTE:

- HR Guidelines may be repeated in other element-based guidelines: (RP) Ramps, (ST) Stairs, (WC) Water Closets, (TS) Toilet Stalls, (BT) Bathtubs, and (SS) Shower Stalls.

Handrails: size and spacing

HR-01 Is the gripping surface of the grab bars or handrails 1¼ in. to 1½ in. in outside diameter? (4.26.2, Fig. 39)

AUTHOR'S INTERPRETATION:

- Standard pipe sizes designated by the industry as 1¼ in. to 1½ in. are acceptable for purposes of this section.

HR-02 Do the grab bars or handrails have edges with a minimum radius of 1/8 in.? (4.26.4)

HR-03 Is the clearance between the grab bars or handrails and the wall exactly 1½ in.? (4.26.2, Fig. 39)

HR-04 If the handrail is located in a recess, is the recess a maximum of 3 in. deep extending at least 18 in. above the rail? (4.26.2, Fig. 39d)

Handrails: grab bar or handrail structural strength

HR-05 Are the grab bars or handrails secure so that they do not rotate in their fittings? [4.26.3(5)]

HR-06 Do the grab bars and handrails meet the structural strength requirements for bending stress and shear stress? (4.26.3)

- Actual bending stress in the grab bar induced by the maximum bending moment from the application of 250 lbf is less than the allowable bending stress for the material of the grab bar.

- Shear stress induced in a grab bar by the application of 250 lbf shall be less than the allowable shear stress for the material of the grab bar. If the connection between the grab bar and its mounting bracket or other support is considered to be fully restrained, then direct and torsional shear stresses shall be totaled for the combined shear stress, which shall not exceed the allowable shear stress.

HR-07 Do the fasteners and mounting devices for the grab bars or handrails meet the structural strength requirements for shear force and tensile force? (4.26.3)

- Shear force induced in a fastener or mounting device from the application of 250 lbf shall be less than the allowable lateral load of either the fastener or mounting device or the supporting structure, whichever is the smaller allowable load.

- Tensile force induced in a fastener by a direct tension force of 250 lbf plus the maximum moment from the application of 250 lbf shall be less than the allowable withdrawal load between the fastener and the supporting structure.

Handrails: tub and shower seat structural strength

HR-08 Do the tub and shower seats meet the structural strength requirements for bending stress and shear stress? (4.26.3)

- Actual bending stress in the seat induced by the maximum bending moment from the application of 250 lbf is less than the allowable bending stress for the material of the grab bar.

- Shear stress induced in a seat by the application of 250 lbf shall be less than the allowable shear stress for the material of the seat. If the connection between the seat and its mounting bracket or other support is considered to be fully restrained, then direct and torsional shear stresses shall be totaled for the combined shear stress, which shall not exceed the allowable shear stress.

HR-09 Do the fasteners and mounting devices for the tub and shower seats meet the structural strength requirements for shear force and tensile force? (4.26.3)

- Shear force induced in a fastener or mounting device from the application of 250 lbf shall be less than the allowable lateral load of either the fastener or mounting device or the supporting structure, whichever is the smaller allowable load.

- Tensile force induced in a fastener by a direct tension force of 250 lbf plus the maximum moment from the application of 250 lbf shall be less than the allowable withdrawal load between the fastener and the supporting structure.

Handrails: hazards

HR-10 Are handrails or grab bars and any wall or other surfaces adjacent to them free of any sharp or abrasive elements? (4.26.4)

(SR) Storage (4.25)

NOTE:

- Accessible reach range requirements do not apply to shelves or display units allowing self-service by customers in mercantile occupancies but they must be located on an accessible route. [4.1.3(12)(b)]

Storage: general

SR-01 Does at least one of each type of fixed or built-in storage unit comply with accessible criteria? [4.1.3(12)(a), 4.25.1]

NOTE:

- Types of storage facilities might include cabinets, shelves, closets, and drawers.

Storage: clear floor space

SR-02 Is there a clear floor space at least 30 in. × 48 in. at fixed or built-in storage units that allows for either a forward or side approach? (4.25.2, Fig. 4a–b)

Storage: reach ranges

SR-03 Are forward or side reach for each type of accessible storage unit within acceptable reach ranges? (4.2.5–6, Fig. 5a–b, Fig. 6a–c, 4.25.3)

- Forward reach: not less than 15 in. high and not more than 48 in. high without any obstruction or where the obstruction is less than 20 in. deep. For obstructions from 20 in. to 25 in. deep, no forward reach higher than 44 in.

- Side reach: not less than 9 in. high and not more than 54 in. high. For obstructions not more than 34 in. high or 24 in. deep, no side reach higher than 46 in.

SR-04 In a closet where passage is not required to access storage (e.g., door opening is less than 32 in.), are the clothes rod or shelves within required reach ranges? (4.25.3, Fig. 38a–b)

- Door width: at least 20 in. (4.13.5)

- Horizontal reach: not more than 21 in. from the opening.

- Rod reach: if over 10 in. deep, then not more than 48 in. high.

- Shelf reach: if over 10 in. deep, then not more than 48 in. high or less than 9 in. high.

Storage: hardware

SR-05 Is the hardware on the storage unit doors or drawers operable with one hand without tight grasping, pinching, or wrist twisting, and requiring no more than 5 lbf of force? (4.25.4, 4.27.4)

(AL) Alarms (4.28)

NOTE:

- At a minimum, visual signal appliances shall be provided in buildings and facilities in restrooms and any other general usage areas. **The ADAAG does not define the number of occupants needed to establish a general or common use area.**

ALLOWANCE:

- Emergency warning systems in medical care facilities may be modified to suit standard health care alarm design practice. [4.1.3(14)]

Visual Alarms: general

AL-04 If provided, are the visual alarm signal appliances integrated into the building or facility alarm system? (4.28.3)

AL-05 If provided, do the visual alarm signals meet required operational criteria? [4.28.3(1, 2, 3, 4, 5)]

- Lamp: xenon strobe type or equivalent.

- Color: clear or nominal white (i.e., unfiltered or clear filtered white light).
- Pulse duration: maximum shall be 0.2 sec with a maximum duty cycle of 40 percent.
- Intensity: not less than 75 candela.
- Flash rate: not less than 1 Hz and not more than 3 Hz.

AL-06 Are visual alarm signal appliances provided in public and common use restrooms? (4.28.1)

AL-07 Are visual alarm signal appliances provided in general usage areas of the building (such as meeting rooms, corridors, and lobbies) or any other area for common use? (4.28.1)

AUTHOR'S INTERPRETATION:

- The authors identified three or more occupants as the minimum number to establish a common use area.

AL-08 Are the visual alarms placed at 80 in. above the highest floor level or 6 in. below the ceiling, whichever is lower? [4.28.3(6)]

Visual Alarms: living units

AL-12 Is the signal from the visual alarm visible in all areas of the living unit or room? (4.28.4)

Kitchens (Single Unit or Common Use)
(Hotels, Inns, Resorts, Dormitories and Other Places of Accommodation and Social Services Establishments: Homeless Shelters, Halfway Houses, Transient Group Homes, and Others)

Introduction. ADAAG designates two major categories of "Transient Lodging":

1. Private or public inns, resorts, boarding houses, hotels, motels, dormitories, and student campus apartments.
2. Social services establishments such as homeless shelters, halfway houses, transient group homes, and others.

Use this review guide to design or evaluate facilities, or portions thereof, that provide accessible single or common-use kitchen accommodations in both categories of transient lodging. See other review guides in transient lodging (hotels and social services establishments)—"Bathrooms," "Living and Dining Rooms," "Exterior Activity Areas," "Parking Lots and Loading Zones," and so on—as needed.

The kitchen, kitchenette, or wet bar must be accessible if provided as part of an accessible unit, a dormitory, student apartment, suite, homeless shelter, group home, or other social services establishment. Clear floor space for front and side approaches at base cabinets, counter tops, or appliances must be provided for a person in a wheelchair. If an eating space is placed within the kitchen, verify that clear floor space is not compromised.

Accessible reach ranges must be followed for all appliances including the range or cook top, oven, refrigera-

tor/freezer, dishwasher, and trash compactor. Placement of controls and operating mechanisms must be carefully planned to allow for adequate and safe reaching as well as accessible operation. Verify that the controls on stoves, ventilation fans, dishwashers, and so on have operating mechanisms that comply with ADAAG. Accessibility criteria do not apply to movable equipment like microwave ovens, toaster ovens, and so on.

Refrigerators, freezers, and shelves in cabinets must have at least 50 percent of the storage within accessible reach ranges. The refrigerator and freezer operating controls must be within accessible reach ranges. Door pulls and handles on all appliances and wall cabinets must comply with accessibility criteria. Upper and lower cabinets can be considered together as one type of storage unit even though base cabinets are generally deeper than wall hung cabinets.

Visual emergency alarm and visual notification device signals must be visible in all areas of the unit. If the signals in another portion of the unit are not visible in the kitchen, then they also must be installed within the kitchen.

PRELIMINARY DESIGN OVERVIEW

(AL) Alarms

- Visual emergency alarm signals must be visible in all areas of the unit.

(AR) Accessible Routes

- Clear floor space must be provided at appliances, base cabinets, and counter tops.

AUTHOR'S INTERPRETATION:

- If the kitchen is greater than 5 ft deep, then a turning space should be provided.

(CT) Controls and Operating Mechanisms

- Controls and operating mechanisms have clear floor space and reach range requirements. When there are controls in refrigerators/freezers, pull cords on fans and lights, and switches and electrical outlets mounted over base cabinets and sinks, provide clear floor space and required reach ranges.

(DR) Doors

- Typical requirements.

(FS) Floor Surfaces

- Smooth floor surfaces should be evaluated for slip-resistance based on floor finish and maintenance.

(LV) Sinks

- Knee clearance must be provided at sinks.
- Sinks have a maximum rim height.

(PR) Protruding Objects

- Common wall-mounted elements can be protruding objects, e.g., shelves, upper cabinets, racks, and lighting fixtures, and must be placed out of the path of travel.

(SE) Fixed Tables and/or Counters

- All kitchen counters have a maximum height.

(SG) Signage (common-use kitchens)

- Typical requirements.

(SR) Storage

- One of each type of storage unit (shelves, pantries, drawers, towel racks, and hooks), if present, must be accessible.

(TH) Transient Lodging/Housing

- In kitchens, kitchenettes, or wet bars, all cabinet doors and appliance doors must be accessible.
- At least 50 percent of shelf space in cabinets, refrigerator, and freezer must comply with reach range criteria.
- All controls and operating mechanisms in accessible units must be accessible and usable.
- Counter tops and sinks have a maximum height requirement in addition to meeting other typical accessible requirements.
- In new construction, at least one of each amenity (i.e., washer, dryer) in each public and common area must be accessible.
- In addition to general alarm requirements, visual notification devices must be provided in units, sleeping rooms, and suites.

ADAAG APPENDIX

The ADAAG Appendix includes additional advisory information pertinent to transient lodging facilities.

- A2.2   Equivalent Facilitation—9.1.4 and 9.2.2(6)(d)

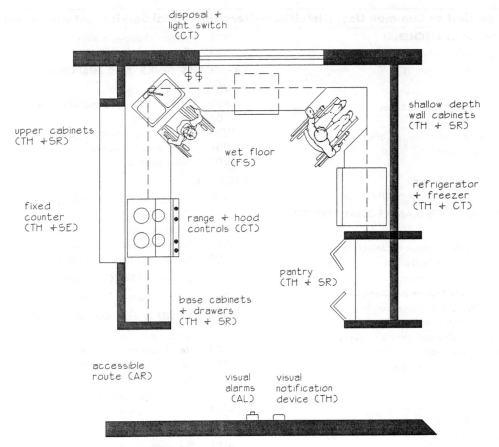

disposal +
light switch
(CT)

upper cabinets
(TH +SR)

shallow depth
wall cabinets
(TH + SR)

wet floor
(FS)

fixed
counter
(TH +SE)

range + hood
controls (CT)

refrigerator
+ freezer
(TH + CT)

pantry
(TH + SR)

base cabinets
+ drawers
(TH + SR)

accessible
route (AR)

visual
alarms
(AL)

visual
notification
device (TH)

Figure 3-22. Transient lodging: Kitchen.

Kitchens (Single Unit or Common Use) (Hotel/Dormitory and Social Services Establishments) Checklist

SIGNAGE (COMMON-USE KITCHENS)

SG04	Room signage: criteria
SG05	Room signage: location

DOORS

DR04	Doors: maneuvering clearances
DR05	Doors: handle type
DR06	Doors: opening force (interior only)
DR07	Doors: closing speed
DR08	Doors: thresholds
DR09	Doors: clear width/height
DR10	Openings (no door): clear width/height

TRANSIENT LODGING: HOTELS AND SOCIAL SERVICES ESTB. KITCHENS

TH11	Kitchen: clear floor space: counters/sinks
TH12	Kitchen counter tops/sinks: mounting height
TH13	Kitchen shelf space: criteria
TH14	Kitchen controls/disp.: reach ranges
TH15	Kitchen controls/disp.: operation
TH16	Hearing-imp. unit: visual alarm required
TH17	Hearing-imp. unit: visual alarms in all areas
TH18	Hearing-imp. units: visual notification device
TH19	Hearing-imp. units: telephone

ACCESSIBLE ROUTES

AR08	Route: clear width
AR09	Route width: U-turns
AR10	Route: passing space

PROTRUDING OBJECTS

PR01	Wall-mounted
PR03	Clear route width maintained
PR04	Overhead clearance
PR05	Vertical clearance: cane detection barrier

FLOOR SURFACES

FS01	Surface: firm, stable, and slip-resistant
FS02	Vertical changes in level
FS03	Carpet and tile floors

LAVATORIES, SINKS, AND MIRRORS

LV01	Clear floor space
LV02	Rim/apron heights and extension from wall
LV04	Insulated pipes
LV05	Controls and operation requirements
LV07	Sinks: knee clearance
LV08	Sinks: bowl depth

STORAGE

SR01	Accessibility: one of each type
SR02	Clear floor space
SR03	Reach ranges
SR04	Storage closets w/o passage: criteria
SR05	Storage hardware: operation

FIXED TABLES AND/OR COUNTERS

SE03	Tables/counters: heights

CONTROLS AND OPERATING MECHANISMS

CT01	Clear floor space
CT02	Reach ranges: elec./comm. systems
CT03	Reach ranges: thermostats
CT04	Reach ranges: other controls
CT05	Reach ranges: life safety devices
CT06	Controls: operation

ALARMS

AL01	Emergency warning: audible/visual
AL02	Audible alarms: operation
AL03	Single station audible and visual
AL04	Visual alarms: integration w/building alarm
AL05	Visual alarms: operation
AL08	Visual alarms: vertical placement
AL11	Visual alarms: acc. living and sleeping units

KITCHENS (SINGLE UNIT OR COMMON USE) (HOTELS, INNS, RESORTS, DORMITORIES, AND OTHER PLACES OF ACCOMMODATION AND SOCIAL SERVICES ESTABLISHMENTS: HOMELESS SHELTERS, HALFWAY HOUSES, TRANSIENT GROUP HOMES, AND OTHERS) COMPREHENSIVE CRITERIA

(SG) Signage (4.30)

Signage: room identification (where provided)

DEFINITION:

- These signs designate permanent rooms and spaces.

AUTHOR'S INTERPRETATION:

- Signs that designate stairs, exit doors, and toilet rooms generally are associated with permanent spaces, while an "office" sign is not since the room function may change over time. Room numbers also must meet the ADAAG criteria as permanent designations, while personal names do not since the occupant may change over time.

SG-04 Do signs that designate permanent rooms and spaces comply with the following criteria? [4.1.2(7); 4.1.3(16); 4.30.4, 5, 6]

- Character type: raised and accompanied by Grade II Braille.
- Character size: between 5/8 in. and 2 in. high; raised at least 1/32 in.
- Character style: upper case, and sans or simple serif.
- Finish: characters and backgrounds have a nonglare finish.
- Contrast: characters contrast with their background (light-on-dark or dark-on-light).

SG-05 Is the room identification sign mounted in the required location? (4.30.6)

- Mounting location: installed on the wall adjacent to the latch side of the door or where wall space to the latch side of the door is not available, including double doors, placed on the nearest adjacent wall.
- Mounting height: 60 in. above the floor/ground to the centerline of the sign.

- Sign access: approach to within 3 in. of a sign without encountering protruding objects or standing within the swing of the door.

(DR) Doors (4.13)

NOTE:

- Included in this category are doors, revolving doors, turnstiles, and gates.

AUTHOR'S INTERPRETATION:

- It is suggested that, for purposes of documentation and review, a door be assigned to the space it swings into. Corridors are an exception to this rule and include only entry doors into the corridor or intermediate fire doors.

Doors: maneuvering clearance

DR-04 If the door is not automatic or power assisted, does it have the required maneuvering clearance provided on the push and pull side, and is the floor level and clear within the maneuvering area? (4.13.6)

- A verbal description cannot adequately describe the requirements. See ADAAG Fig. 25a–f for a graphic description.

EXCEPTION:

- Entry doors to acute care hospital bedrooms for inpatients are exempt from maneuvering space at the latch side of the door if the door is at least 44 in. wide.

AUTHOR'S INTERPRETATION:

- While ADAAG does not describe what elements can reduce the required maneuvering clearance, they could include a narrow entry alcove, an adjacent wall, railing, or permanently installed shelving, or a deep recessed door jamb.

Doors: hardware

DR-05 Do all door handles, locks, latches, or other operable devices meet required operational criteria? (4.13.9)

- Hardware operation: operable with one hand without tight grasping, pinching, or wrist twisting.
- Force required to operate the controls: not greater than 5 lbf. This does not apply to the force required to retract latch bolts or to disengage other devices that only hold the door in a closed position.
- Hardware type: "U"-shaped handles, levers, and push type mechanisms are acceptable designs.
- Hardware height: not greater than 48 in. above the floor.
- Sliding doors: hardware is exposed and usable from both sides when the doors are fully open.

Doors: opening force

DR-06 Do interior hinged doors and sliding or folding doors have an opening force of 5 lbf or less? (4.13.11)

- At present, no accessible criteria exist for exterior doors.
- Fire doors shall have the minimum opening force allowable by the appropriate administrative authority.

Doors: closing speed

DR-07 If the door has a closer, is the closer adjusted so that the door does not close too quickly? (4.13.10)

- From an open position of 70° the door will take at least 3 sec to move to a point 3 in. from the latch (measured to the leading edge of the door).

Doors: thresholds

DR-08 Where raised thresholds are provided, do they meet height limitations and are they beveled when required? (4.13.8, 4.5.2, Fig. 7)

- Threshold height: not more than 3/4 in. for exterior sliding doors or 1/2 in. for other types of doors.
- Threshold bevel: thresholds less than 1/4 in. high need no bevel; thresholds between 1/4 in. and 1/2 in. high shall be beveled at each edge with not more than a 1:2 slope.

EXCEPTION:

- A 3/4-in. high threshold is allowed in existing conditions. [4.1.6(3)(d)(ii)]

Doors: clear opening width and height

DR-09 Is the clear opening for the doorway adequate in width and height? (4.13.3, 4, 5; Fig. 24)

- Door width: at least 32 in. of clear width with the door open at 90°, measured between the face of the door and the door stop on the latch side. This also pertains to the active leaf of a double-leaf door or gate.
- Opening width: openings more than 24 in. deep must provide 36 in. of clear width.
- Height: at least 80 in. of vertical clearance.

EXCEPTIONS:

- Doors not requiring full user passage, such as shallow closets, may have the clear opening reduced to not less than 20 in.
- Where it is technically infeasible to comply with clear opening width requirements, a projection of 5/8 in. maximum will be permitted for the latch side. [4.1.6(d)(i)]

DR-10 Is the clear opening (when there is no door) adequate in width and height? (4.2.1, 4.3.3, 4.4.2)

- Width: at least 32 in. of clear width for depths 24 in. or less and at least 36 in. of clear width for depths greater than 24 in.
- Height: at least 80 in. of vertical clearance.

(TH) Accessible Transient lodging (9.0)
(Hotels, Motels, Inns, Boarding Houses, Dormitories, and Similar Places and Homeless Shelters, Halfway Houses, Transient Group Homes, and Other Social Services Establishments)

NOTE:

- Transient lodging is divided into two categories:
  - Hotels, motels, inns, boarding houses, dormitories, and similar places (TH-01 through TH-19).
  - Homeless shelters, halfway houses, transient group homes, and other social services establishments (TH-20 through TH-26 and TH-07 through TH-19).

- Doors and doorways designed to allow passage into and within all transient lodging sleeping units shall comply with accessible door width criteria. This applies to every sleeping unit in the facility, whether it is designated as accessible or not. (9.4)

AUTHOR'S INTERPRETATION:

- Accessible units, sleeping rooms, and suites are divided into two categories: fully accessible and hearing-impaired. Fully accessible units, sleeping rooms, and suites must comply with accessible criteria for both mobility and hearing impairments. (9.2.8) Hearing-impaired units must comply only with those accessible criteria that relate to visual alarms, notification devices, and telephones. (9.3)

- The total number of accessible units required by ADAAG can be easily misinterpreted if not carefully read. For example, the total number of rooms required for 76–100 hotel rooms is 9, broken down as follows:

— Four fully accessible rooms with accessible bathrooms.

— One fully accessible room with accessible bathroom with a roll-in shower with folding seat.

— Four rooms for the hearing-impaired (other accessible criteria are not required including an accessible bathroom).

- In dormitories or other facilities where bath facilities are multiple user and separate from the sleeping room, the minimum number of accessible tubs or showers required is not clearly prescribed. ADAAG 4.23.8, which indicates a minimum of at least one accessible tub or shower (when provided) in bathrooms, appears to be applicable to this situation.

EXCEPTION:

- ADAAG 9.1 through 9.4 do not apply to an establishment located within a building that contains no more than five rooms for rent or hire and that is actually occupied by the proprietor of such establishment as the residence of such proprietor.

Accessible Transient Lodging/S.S.: kitchens (if provided)

NOTE:

- The following questions are the same as those found in accessible transient lodging for hotels.

TH-11 Is a clear floor space of 30 in. × 48 in. provided at kitchen cabinets, counters, sinks, and appliances for front or parallel approach? [9.5.3, 9.2.2(7)]

- Clear floor space for individual appliances and use areas may overlap.

- No more than 19 in. of the clear floor space can be measured under counters.

TH-12 Are kitchen counter tops and sinks mounted no more than 34 in. above the floor? [9.5.3, 9.2.2(7)]

- The 34 in. is a maximum height for all counter tops.

TH-13 Is at least 50 percent of shelf space in all cabinets or refrigerators/freezers within acceptable reach ranges for forward or side approach? [9.5.3, 9.2.2(7)]

- Forward reach: not less than 15 in. high and not more than 48 in. high without any obstruction or where the obstruction is less than 20 in. deep. For

obstructions from 20 in. to 25 in. deep, no forward reach higher than 44 in.

- Side reach: not less than 9 in. high and not more than 54 in. high. For obstructions not more than 34 in. high or 24 in. deep, no side reach higher than 46 in.

TH-14 Are the controls and operating mechanisms on major kitchen appliances (ranges, ovens) within acceptable reach ranges for forward or side approach? [9.5.3, 9.2.2(7)]

- Forward reach: not less than 15 in. high and not more than 48 in. high without any obstruction or where the obstruction is less than 20 in. deep. For obstructions from 20 in. to 25 in. deep, no forward reach higher than 44 in.

- Side reach: not less than 9 in. high and not more than 54 in. high. For obstructions not more than 34 in. high or 24 in. deep, no side reach higher than 46 in.

NOTE:

- Small, movable appliances such as microwave ovens are not considered.

TH-15 Are controls, dispensers, receptacles, and other operable equipment operable with one hand without tight grasping, pinching, or wrist twisting, and requiring no more than 5 lbf of force? [9.5.3, 9.2.2(7), 4.27.4]

Accessible Transient Lodging/S.S.: hearing-impaired rooms

NOTE:

- The following questions are the same as those found in accessible transient lodging for hotels.

TH-16 Do accessible living units and sleeping accommodations comply with the requirements for visual alarms? (9.5.3, 9.3, 4.28.4)

- Visual alarms meet required operational criteria.

- Visual alarms connect to the building emergency alarm system;

- Or a standard electrical outlet is provided and connected to the facility's central alarm system which enables room occupants to utilize portable devices provided by the operator of the facility.

TH-17 Is the signal from the visual alarm visible in all areas of the living unit or room? (9.5.3, 9.3, 4.28.4)

TH-18 Do the living units and sleeping rooms comply with the requirements for visual notification devices? (9.5.3, 9.3.1)

- This includes any space where the occupant would expect to be able to hear a phone or door bell.

- Visual notification devices are to alert the occupant of incoming telephone calls and a door knock or bell.

- This device must *not* be connected to the visual alarm system.

TH-19 Do the living units and sleeping rooms comply with the requirements for telephones? (9.5.3, 9.3.1)

- If provided, permanently installed (hardwired) telephones should have volume controls capable of a minimum of 12 dbA and a maximum of 18 dbA above normal. If an automatic reset is provided, then 18 dbA may be exceeded.

▪ Outlets: An accessible electrical outlet is within 4 ft of a telephone connection, where provided.

(AR) Accessible Routes (4.3)

NOTES:

▪ All walks, halls, corridors, aisles, skywalks, tunnels, and other spaces that are part of a designated accessible route shall comply with accessible requirements.

▪ The accessible route shall, to the maximum extent feasible, coincide with the route for the general public.

AUTHOR'S INTERPRETATION:

▪ An accessible route "generally coincides" with the route used by the public if:
  — It does not force the user to go out of the way.
  — It is most like the route chosen by the general public.
  — It is direct.
  — It gives the same basic experience as the route preferred by the public.

Accessible Routes: width

AR-08 Is the minimum clear width along the accessible route adequate for continuous or point passage? (4.2.1, 4.3.3, Fig. 1, Fig. 8e, Fig. 24e)

▪ Continuous passage (greater than 24 in. long): at least a 36-in. clear width.

▪ Point passage (not more than 24 in. long): at least a 32-in. clear width.

AUTHOR'S INTERPRETATION:

▪ Noncompliance with this question generally relates to permanent elements that encroach on the accessible route. Large, heavy equipment that is not readily movable might be considered permanent. If the space is designed so that temporary elements (such as bikes in a bike rack or car bumpers) will consistently encroach, the situation might also be considered a permanent barrier.

AR-09 Is the minimum clear width along the accessible route adequate at a U-turn around an obstruction? (4.3.3, Fig. 7a–b)

▪ Obstruction 48 in. or greater: at least a 36-in. clear width around the obstruction.

▪ Obstruction less than 48 in.: at least a 42-in. clear width at each side with at least a 48-in. clear width in the turn.

Accessible Routes: passing space

AR-10 Does the accessible route provide at least 60 in. of clear width for two wheelchairs to pass and, if not, is the required passing space provided? (4.2.2, 4.3.4)

▪ A 60-in. × 60-in. passing space or "T" intersection should be provided at reasonable intervals not to exceed 200 ft.

AUTHOR'S INTERPRETATION:

▪ Accessible routes more than 5 ft long (e.g., routes in short hallways, aisles in laboratories, and work/storage areas) should have passing spaces provided.

DEFINITION:

▪ A *"T" intersection* is defined as the intersection of two corridors or walks, each at least 36 in. wide providing at least a 60-in. depth at the intersection. (Fig. 3b)

(PR) Protruding Objects (4.4)

Protruding Objects: general

PR-01 Do wall-mounted objects having leading edges between 27 in. and 80 in. high project less than 4 in. into walkways, corridors, aisles, or paths of travel? (4.4.1, Fig. 8a–e)

▪ Objects mounted with their leading edge at or below 27 in. can protrude any amount, as long as they do not reduce the required clear width of an accessible route.

AUTHOR'S INTERPRETATION:

▪ Protruding objects might include fire extinguishers or cabinets, pencil sharpeners, shelving, counters, built-in equipment overhangs, or various dispensers such as for paper towels or soap.

PR-03 Is the minimum clear route width or maneuvering space still maintained even with the projection of a protruding object? (4.4.1, Fig. 8a–e)

Protruding Objects: overhead clearance

PR-04 Is the minimum overhead clearance of 80 in. provided in accessible areas or along accessible routes? (4.4.2, Fig. 8a)

AUTHOR'S INTERPRETATION:

▪ Overhead objects that can reduce the required clearance might include structures, pipes, ducts, or light fixtures.

PR-05 Where the vertical clearance of a space adjoining the accessible route is less than 80 in. high, is a cane detection barrier less than 27 in. from the floor provided for blind or visually impaired persons? (4.4.2, Fig. 8c-1)

AUTHOR'S INTERPRETATION:

▪ This condition might be found under a stair, at a sloped ceiling space, or with guy wires from telephone poles along an exterior accessible route.

(FS) Floor and Ground Surfaces (4.5)

Floor Surfaces: general

FS-01 Are the floor/ground surfaces on the accessible route stable, firm, and slip-resistant? (4.5.1)

AUTHOR'S INTERPRETATION:

▪ Exterior spaces, interior circulation, bathrooms, and other spaces where water can collect on the floor around an element (sinks, drinking fountains, hose bibbs, etc.) are reviewed as if wet.

▪ High gloss surfaces without significant textures that are regularly maintained with waxing (smooth tiles, waxed concrete, etc.) could be considered noncompliant.

▪ Accessible criteria are not specified for nonpermanent floor surfaces such as mats or rugs.

Floor Surfaces: changes in level

FS-02 Are vertical changes in level between 1/4 in. and 1/2 in. beveled with a slope of 1:2 or less? (4.5.2)

- Changes in level up to 1/4 in. may be vertical without edge treatment.
  - Changes in level greater than 1/2 in. should be accomplished by means of a curb ramp, ramp, elevator, or platform lift (as permitted in ADAAG 4.1.3 and 4.1.6).

Floor Surfaces: carpet

FS-03 Does carpet or carpet tile used on the floor comply with accessible criteria? (4.5.3, Fig. 8f)

- Attachment: secured.
- Exposed edges: fastened and trimmed along the entire length.
- Pile type: low pile (1/2 in. maximum).
- Padding: firm pad or no pad underneath.

(LV) Lavatories, Sinks, and Mirrors (4.19, 4.24)

NOTE:

- Where lavatories or sinks are provided, at least one of each type must meet accessible requirements.

AUTHOR'S INTERPRETATION:

- While not specifically defined by ADAAG, it appears lavatories are for personal hygiene in bathrooms or toilet rooms, while sinks are for all other situations (e.g., laboratories or kitchens).

Lavatories or Sinks: clearances

LV-01 Is there a clear floor space not less than 30 in. × 48 in. in front of the accessible lavatory or sink allowing a forward approach, and does it adjoin or overlap the accessible route? (4.19.3, 4.24.5, Fig. 32)

- The clear floor space can extend up to 19 in. under the sink or lavatory if adequate knee clearance is provided.

LV-02 Are the accessible lavatory or sink rim or counter height, apron height, and extension from the wall adequate? (4.19.2, 4.24.2, Fig. 31)

- Rim height: not greater than 34 in. above the finish floor.
- Apron height: not less than 29 in. above the finish floor to the bottom of the apron.
- Lavatory extension: not less than 17 in. from the wall.

Lavatories or Sinks: pipe shielding

LV-04 Are the hot water and drain pipes at the accessible lavatory or sink insulated or otherwise configured to protect against contact and is the area below the lavatory or sink free of sharp or abrasive surfaces? (4.19.4)

Lavatories or Sinks: controls

LV-05 Do the accessible lavatory or sink controls meet operational requirements? (4.19.5)

- Operation: operable with one hand without tight grasping, pinching, or twisting of the wrist. Acceptable types might include lever operated, push type, touch type, or electronically controlled; no more than 5 lbf of force.
- Self-closing faucets, when used, remain open for at least 10 sec.

Sinks Only

LV-07 Is adequate knee clearance provided underneath the accessible sink? (4.24.3)

- Sink knee clearance: not less than 27 in. high, 30 in. wide, and 19 in. deep under the sink.

LV-08 Is the accessible sink bowl not more than 6½ in. deep? (4.24.4)

(SR) Storage (4.25)

NOTE:

- Accessible reach range requirements do not apply to shelves or display units allowing self-service by customers in mercantile occupancies but they must be located on an accessible route. [4.1.3(12)(b)]

Storage: general

SR-01 Does at least one of each type of fixed or built-in storage unit comply with accessible criteria? [4.1.3(12)(a), 4.25.1]

NOTE:

- Types of storage facilities might include cabinets, shelves, closets, and drawers.

Storage: clear floor space

SR-02 Is there a clear floor space at least 30 in. × 48 in. at fixed or built-in storage units that allows for either a forward or side approach? (4.25.2, Fig. 4a–b)

Storage: reach ranges

SR-03 Are forward or side reach for each type of accessible storage unit within acceptable reach ranges? (4.2.5–6, Fig. 5a–b, Fig. 6a–c, 4.25.3)

- Forward reach: not less than 15 in. high and not more than 48 in. high without any obstruction or where the obstruction is less than 20 in. deep. For obstructions from 20 in. to 25 in. deep, no forward reach higher than 44 in.
- Side reach: not less than 9 in. high and not more than 54 in. high. For obstructions not more than 34 in. high or 24 in. deep, no side reach higher than 46 in.

SR-04 In a closet where passage is not required to access storage (e.g., door opening is less than 32 in.), are the clothes rod or shelves within required reach ranges? (4.25.3, Fig. 38a–b)

- Door width: at least 20 in. (4.13.5)
- Horizontal reach: not more than 21 in. from the opening.
- Rod reach: if over 10 in. deep, then not more than 48 in. high.
- Shelf reach: if over 10 in. deep, then not more than 48 in. high or less than 9 in. high.

Storage: hardware

SR-05 Is the hardware on the storage unit doors or drawers operable with one hand without tight grasping, pinching, or wrist twisting, and requiring no more than 5 lbf of force? (4.25.4, 4.27.4)

(SE) Fixed or Built-in Seating and Tables (4.32)

Fixed or Built-in Seating and Tables: clearances

SE-03 Are the tops of accessible tables and counters between 28 in. and 34 in. from the floor? (4.32.3, Fig. 45)

(CT) Controls and Operating Mechanisms (4.27)

NOTES:

- Controls or operating mechanisms can include elements such as light switches, pencil sharpeners, manual overhead screens, nonkeyed thermostats, alarm pull stations, fire extinguisher cabinets, A/C window units, microwave ovens, towel dispensers, and wall hooks.
- If controls are to be operated by occupants of the space, they must be accessible. If controls are to be operated by maintenance staff only and not by occupants or other users of the space, they do not have to be accessible. For example, thermostats in auditoriums usually do not have to be accessible, while thermostats in classrooms may need to be accessible.

Controls: clear floor space

CT-01 Is a clear floor space of at least 30 in. × 48 in. provided in front of controls, dispensers, receptacles, and other operable equipment for forward or parallel approach? (4.27.2, Fig. 4a–b)

Controls: reach ranges

NOTES:

- Accessible reach ranges for controls and operating mechanisms are:
- — Forward reach: not less than 15 in. high and not more than 48 in. high without any obstruction or where the obstruction is less than 20 in. deep. For obstructions from 20 in. to 25 in. deep, no forward reach higher than 44 in.
- — Side reach: not less than 9 in. high and not more than 54 in. high. For obstructions not more than 34 in. high or 24 in. deep, no side reach higher than 46 in.
- — Electrical outlets, switches, and communication system receptacles have a minimum outlet height of 15 in. regardless of forward or side reach. See CT-02 below.

CT-02 Are electrical outlets, switches, and communication system receptacles mounted within accessible forward or side reach ranges? (4.27.3)

EXCEPTION:

- These requirements do not apply where the use of special equipment dictates otherwise or where electrical and communications system receptacles are not normally intended for use by building occupants. (4.27.3)

CT-03 Are thermostats or other similar operable equipment mounted within accessible forward or side reach ranges? (4.2.5, 4.2.6, Fig. 5a–b, Fig. 6a–c)

CT-04 Are dispensers or other similar operable equipment mounted within accessible forward or side reach ranges? (4.2.5, 4.2.6, Fig. 5a–b, Fig. 6a–c)

CT-05 Are life safety devices or other similar operable equipment mounted within accessible forward or side reach ranges? (4.2.5, 4.2.6, Fig. 5a–b, Fig. 6a–c)

NOTE:

- This might include fire alarm pull stations, handles to extinguisher cabinets, or wall-mounted extinguishers.

Controls: operation

CT-06 Are controls, dispensers, receptacles, and other operable equipment operable with one hand without tight grasping, pinching, or wrist twisting, and requiring no more than 5 lbf of force? (4.27.4)

(AL) Alarms (4.28)

NOTE:

- At a minimum, visual signal appliances shall be provided in buildings and facilities in restrooms and any other general usage areas. **The ADAAG does not define the number of occupants needed to establish a general or common use area.**

ALLOWANCE:

- Emergency warning systems in medical care facilities may be modified to suit standard health care alarm design practice. [4.1.3(14)]

Alarms: general

AL-01 If emergency warning systems are provided, do they include both audible alarms and visual alarms? [4.1.3(14)]

Audible Alarms: general

AL-02 If provided, do the audible alarms meet required operational criteria? (4.28.2)

- Sound level: exceeds the prevailing sound level in the room or space by at least 15 dbA or exceeds any maximum sound level with a duration of 60 sec by 5 dbA, whichever is louder.
- Sound levels for alarm signals shall not exceed 120 dbA.

AL-03 If single station audible alarms are provided, then are single station visual alarm signals also provided? (4.28.3)

Visual Alarms: general

AL-04 If provided, are the visual alarm signal appliances integrated into the building or facility alarm system? (4.28.3)

AL-05 If provided, do the visual alarm signals meet required operational criteria? [4.28.3(1, 2, 3, 4, 5)]

- Lamp: xenon strobe type or equivalent.
- Color: clear or nominal white (i.e., unfiltered or clear filtered white light).
- Pulse duration: maximum shall be 0.2 sec with a maximum duty cycle of 40 percent.
- Intensity: not less than 75 candela.
- Flash rate: not less than 1 Hz and not more than 3 Hz.

AL-08 Are the visual alarms placed at 80 in. above the highest floor level or 6 in. below the ceiling, whichever is lower? [4.28.3(6)]

Visual Alarms: living units

AL-11 Do accessible living units and sleeping accommodations have a visual alarm connected to the building emergency alarm system or do they have a standard 110-volt electrical receptacle into which such an alarm can be connected, and a means by which a signal from the building emergency alarm system can trigger such an auxiliary alarm? (4.28.4)

Living and Dining Rooms
(Hotels, Inns, Resorts, Dormitories, and Other Places of Accommodation and Social Services Establishments: Homeless Shelters, Halfway Houses, Transient Group Homes, and Others)

Introduction. ADAAG designates two major categories of "Transient Lodging":

1. Private or public inns, resorts, boarding houses, hotels, motels, dormitories, and student campus apartments.
2. Social services establishments such as homeless shelters, halfway houses, transient group homes, and others.

Use this review guide to design or evaluate facilities, or portions thereof, that contain accessible living and dining room accommodations within both categories of transient lodging. See other review guides in transient lodging (hotels and social services establishments)—"Bathrooms," "Kitchens" (kitchenettes and/or wet bars), "Exterior Activity Areas," "Parking Lots and Loading Zones," and so on—as needed.

At first glance, accessible living and dining rooms seem to be a simple design task in terms of meeting ADAAG requirements, since movable furniture is not an ADAAG consideration. Nonetheless, the furnishings and the room arrangements must be carefully planned so that a wide range of activities as well as people with different types of disabilities can be accommodated.

The accessible entrance must be on an accessible route. Maneuvering space for a wheelchair user is critical within the entry or foyer area leading to a living room. If there is a storage closet or coat hooks, they must be accessible. When planning the living room, anticipate where large furnishings may be placed either as built-ins or freestanding pieces. Doors and doorways designed to allow passage into and within all transient lodging sleeping units and suites must comply with accessible door width criteria. Plan the placement of controls (light switches and electrical outlets) and operating mechanisms so they will not be blocked by large, heavy pieces of furniture. Carpeting in living rooms must not limit accessibility for a person in a wheelchair in terms of pile height and pad thickness and firmness.

Consider the number of persons who will use a dining room so that an adequately sized table with chairs still allows for continuous and point passage between the kitchen and living room. If the dining space is within the kitchen, verify that a table and chairs do not restrict clear floor space, accessible turning space, or access to counter areas.

In accessible units with a balcony, porch, or seating area, access may be provided with a sliding glass door. In this case, the threshold must be compliant in terms of height and design, unless it is necessary to utilize a higher door threshold to protect the integrity of the unit from wind or water damage. Place visual notification devices and alarms in living or dining areas so that a hearing-impaired person can readily see the signal.

PRELIMINARY DESIGN OVERVIEW

(AR) Accessible Routes

- Typical requirements.

(AL) Alarms

- Visual emergency alarm signals must be visible in all areas of the unit.

(CT) Controls and Operating Mechanisms

- Controls and operating mechanisms have clear floor space and reach range requirements. If communication outlets, controls on window air conditioner units, thermostats, pull cords on lights, switches, and electrical outlets are provided, then clear floor space and reach range requirements must be met. Plan placement of outlets and controls so they are not behind or under heavy or fixed pieces of furniture.

(DR) Doors

- Glass sliding doors must meet accessibility requirements. Note possible threshold exceptions.
- Doors and doorways designed to allow passage into and within all transient lodging sleeping units must comply with accessible door width criteria.

(FS) Floor Surfaces

- Smooth floor surfaces should be evaluated for slip-resistance based on floor finish and maintenance.
- Vertical changes in levels along the accessible route can be an unforeseen barrier, e.g., transition between floor materials such as carpet and resilient flooring.
- Carpets must meet accessibility requirements of pile height and pad thickness and firmness.

(PR) Protruding Objects

- Common wall-mounted elements can be protruding objects, e.g., bookshelves, display cases, and wall-mounted lighting fixtures, and must be placed out of the path of travel.

(SE) Fixed Tables and/or Counters

- Typical requirements.

(SG) Signage

- Typical requirements.

(SR) Storage

- One of each type of storage unit that is present (shelves, closets, coat hooks) must be accessible.

(TH) Transient Lodging

- In accessible living and dining rooms, one of each type of permanent storage (cabinet shelves, closets, and drawers) must be accessible.

- All controls (switches and outlets) in accessible living and dining rooms must be accessible.

- In addition to general alarm requirements, visual notification devices must be provided in units, sleeping rooms, and suites and must be visible throughout.

Other

- If provided, peepholes on doors should be mounted at high and low accessible heights.

ADAAG APPENDIX

The ADAAG Appendix includes additional advisory information pertinent to transient lodging facilities.

- A2.2   Equivalent Facilitation—9.1.4 and 9.2.2(6)(d)
- A4.5.3   Floor Surfaces—Carpet

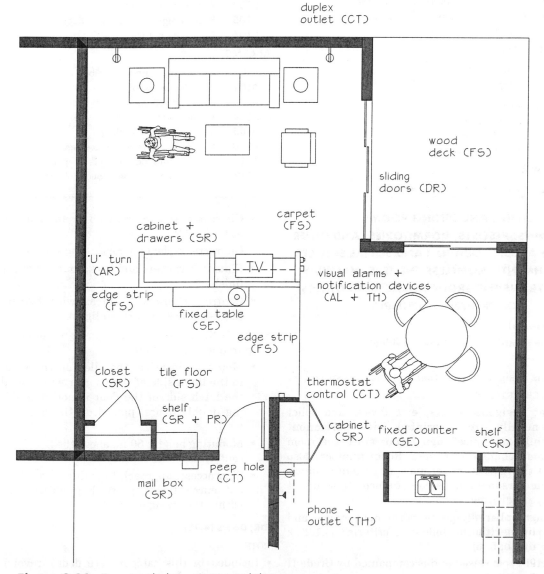

Figure 3-23. Transient lodging: Living and dining.

Living and Dining Rooms Checklist

SIGNAGE

SG04	Room signage: criteria
SG05	Room signage: location

DOORS

DR04	Doors: maneuvering clearances
DR05	Doors: handle type
DR06	Doors: opening force (interior only)
DR07	Doors: closing speed
DR08	Doors: thresholds
DR09	Doors: clear width/height
DR10	Openings (no door): clear width/height

TRANSIENT LODGING: HOTELS—SLEEPING ROOMS AND SUITES

TH07	Sleeping unit: accessible route
TH08	Sleeping unit: linked accessible spaces
TH09	Sleeping unit: linked accessible elements
TH16	Hearing-imp. unit: visual alarm required
TH17	Hearing-imp. unit: visual alarms in all areas
TH18	Hearing-imp. units: visual notification device
TH19	Hearing-imp. units: telephone

ACCESSIBLE ROUTES

AR08	Route: clear width

PROTRUDING OBJECTS

PR01	Wall-mounted
PR03	Clear route width maintained
PR04	Overhead clearance
PR05	Vertical clearance: cane detection barrier

FLOOR SURFACES

FS01	Surface: firm, stable, and slip-resistant

FS02	Vertical changes in level
FS03	Carpet and tile floors

STORAGE

SR01	Accessibility: one of each type
SR02	Clear floor space
SR03	Reach ranges
SR04	Storage closets w/o passage: criteria
SR05	Storage hardware: operation

FIXED TABLES AND/OR COUNTERS

SE01	Fixed seating: number required
SE02	Wheelchairs: clear floor space at tables
SE03	Tables/counters: heights
SE04	Tables/counters: knee clearance criteria

CONTROLS AND OPERATING MECHANISMS

CT01	Clear floor space
CT02	Reach ranges: elec./comm. systems
CT03	Reach ranges: thermostats
CT04	Reach ranges: other controls
CT05	Reach ranges: life safety devices
CT06	Controls: operation

ALARMS

AL01	Emergency warning: audible/visual
AL02	Audible alarms: operation
AL03	Single station audible and visual
AL04	Visual alarms: integration w/building alarm
AL05	Visual alarms: operation
AL08	Visual alarms: vertical placement
AL11	Visual alarms: acc. living & sleeping units
AL12	Visual alarms: visible throughout unit

LIVING AND DINING ROOMS
(HOTELS, INNS, RESORTS, DORMITORIES, AND OTHER PLACES OF ACCOMMODATION AND SOCIAL SERVICES ESTABLISHMENTS: HOMELESS SHELTERS, HALFWAY HOUSES, TRANSIENT GROUP HOMES, AND OTHERS) COMPREHENSIVE CRITERIA

(SG) Signage (4.30)

Signage: room identification (where provided)

DEFINITION:

- These signs designate permanent rooms and spaces.

AUTHOR'S INTERPRETATION:

- Signs that designate stairs, exit doors, and toilet rooms generally are associated with permanent spaces, while an "office" sign is not since the room function may change over time. Room numbers also must meet the ADAAG criteria as permanent designations, while personal names do not since the occupant may change over time.

SG-04 Do signs that designate permanent rooms and spaces comply with the following criteria? [4.1.2(7); 4.1.3(16); 4.30.4, 5, 6]

- Character type: raised and accompanied by Grade II Braille.

- Character size: between 5/8 in. and 2 in. high; raised at least 1/32 in.

- Character style: upper case, and sans or simple serif.

- Finish: characters and backgrounds have a nonglare finish.

- Contrast: characters contrast with their background (light-on-dark or dark-on-light).

SG-05 Is the room identification sign mounted in the required location? (4.30.6)

- Mounting location: installed on the wall adjacent to the latch side of the door or where wall space to the latch side of the door is not available, including double doors, placed on the nearest adjacent wall.

- Mounting height: 60 in. above the floor/ground to the centerline of the sign.

- Sign access: approach to within 3 in. of a sign without encountering protruding objects or standing within the swing of the door.

(DR) Doors (4.13)

NOTE:

- Included in this category are doors, revolving doors, turnstiles, and gates.

AUTHOR'S INTERPRETATION:

- It is suggested that, for purposes of documentation and review, a door be assigned to the space it swings into. Corridors are an exception to this rule and include only entry doors into the corridor or intermediate fire doors.

Doors: maneuvering clearance

DR-04 If the door is not automatic or power assisted, does it have the required maneuvering clearance provided on the push and pull side, and is the floor level and clear within the maneuvering area? (4.13.6)

- A verbal description cannot adequately describe the requirements. See ADAAG Fig. 25a–f for a graphic description.

EXCEPTION:

- Entry doors to acute care hospital bedrooms for in-patients are exempt from maneuvering space at the latch side of the door if the door is at least 44 in. wide.

AUTHOR'S INTERPRETATION:

- While ADAAG does not describe what elements can reduce the required maneuvering clearance, they could include a narrow entry alcove, an adjacent wall, railing, or permanently installed shelving, or a deep recessed door jamb.

Doors: hardware

DR-05 Do all door handles, locks, latches, or other operable devices meet required operational criteria? (4.13.9)

- Hardware operation: operable with one hand without tight grasping, pinching, or wrist twisting.
- Force required to operate the controls: not greater than 5 lbf. This does not apply to the force required to retract latch bolts or to disengage other devices that only hold the door in a closed position.
- Hardware type: "U"-shaped handles, levers, and push type mechanisms are acceptable designs.
- Hardware height: not greater than 48 in. above the floor.
- Sliding doors: hardware is exposed and usable from both sides when the doors are fully open.

Doors: opening force

DR-06 Do interior hinged doors and sliding or folding doors have an opening force of 5 lbf or less? (4.13.11)

- At present, no accessible criteria exist for exterior doors.
- Fire doors shall have the minimum opening force allowable by the appropriate administrative authority.

Doors: closing speed

DR-07 If the door has a closer, is the closer adjusted so that the door does not close too quickly? (4.13.10)

- From an open position of 70° the door will take at least 3 sec to move to a point 3 in. from the latch (measured to the leading edge of the door).

Doors: thresholds

DR-08 Where raised thresholds are provided, do they meet height limitations and are they beveled when required? (4.13.8, 4.5.2, Fig. 7)

- Threshold height: not more than 3/4 in. for exterior sliding doors or 1/2 in. for other types of doors.
- Threshold bevel: thresholds less than 1/4 in. high need no bevel; thresholds between 1/4 in. and 1/2 in. high shall be beveled at each edge with not more than a 1:2 slope.

EXCEPTION:

- A 3/4-in. high threshold is allowed in existing conditions. [4.1.6(3)(d)(ii)]

Doors: clear opening width and height

DR-09 Is the clear opening for the doorway adequate in width and height? (4.13.3, 4, 5; Fig. 24)

- Door width: at least 32 in. of clear width with the door open at 90°, measured between the face of the door and the door stop on the latch side. This also pertains to the active leaf of a double-leaf door or gate.
- Opening width: openings more than 24 in. deep must provide 36 in. of clear width.
- Height: at least 80 in. of vertical clearance.

EXCEPTIONS:

- Doors not requiring full user passage, such as shallow closets, may have the clear opening reduced to not less than 20 in.
- Where it is technically infeasible to comply with clear opening width requirements, a projection of 5/8 in. maximum will be permitted for the latch side. [4.1.6(d)(i)]

DR-10 Is the clear opening (when there is no door) adequate in width and height? (4.2.1, 4.3.3, 4.4.2)

- Width: at least 32 in. of clear width for depths 24 in. or less and at least 36 in. of clear width for depths greater than 24 in.
- Height: at least 80 in. of vertical clearance.

(TH) Accessible Transient lodging (9.0)
(Hotels, Motels, Inns, Boarding Houses, Dormitories, and Similar Places)

NOTE:

- Transient lodging is divided into two categories:
  - Hotels, motels, inns, boarding houses, dormitories, and similar places (TH-01 through TH-19).
  - Homeless shelters, halfway houses, transient group homes, and other social services establishments (TH-20 through TH-26 and TH-07 through TH-19).
- Doors and doorways designed to allow passage into and within all transient lodging sleeping units shall comply with accessible door width criteria. This means any sleeping unit in the facility, whether it is designated as accessible or not. (9.4)

AUTHOR'S INTERPRETATION:

- Accessible units, sleeping rooms, and suites are divided into two categories: fully accessible and hearing-impaired. Fully accessible units, sleeping rooms, and suites must comply with accessible criteria for both mobility and hearing impairments. (9.2.8) Hearing-impaired units must comply only with those accessible criteria that relate to visual alarms, notification devices, and telephones. (9.3)

- The total number of accessible units required by ADAAG can be easily misinterpreted if not carefully read. For example, the total number of rooms required for 76–100 hotel rooms is 9, broken down as follows:
  - Four fully accessible rooms with accessible bathrooms.
  - One fully accessible room with accessible bathroom with a roll-in shower with folding seat.
  - Four rooms for the hearing-impaired (other accessible criteria are not required including an accessible bathroom).
- In dormitories or other facilities where bath facilities are multiple user and separate from the sleeping room, the minimum number of accessible tubs or showers required is not clearly prescribed. ADAAG 4.23.8, which indicates a minimum of at least one accessible tub or shower (when provided) in bathrooms, appears to be applicable to this situation.

EXCEPTION:

- ADAAG 9.1 through 9.4 do not apply to an establishment located within a building that contains no more than five rooms for rent or hire and that is actually occupied by the proprietor of such establishment as the residence of such proprietor.

Accessible Transient Lodging/Hotels: accessible routes

TH-07 Are accessible sleeping rooms or suites located on an accessible route? (9.2.2)

TH-08 Does an accessible route connect all accessible spaces within the accessible unit? [9.2.2(2, 6, 7)]

- Where provided, this includes the living area, the dining area, a dual occupancy sleeping area, patio or balcony, a full bathroom or half bath (if only half baths are provided), kitchen (also kitchenette or wet bar), and parking space.

  NOTE:

- Elevators are not required in a multilevel unit if the previously listed spaces are all on the accessible level and the accessible sleeping area is suitable for dual occupancy.

  EXCEPTION:

- The requirements of thresholds at doors (4.13.8) and changes in levels (4.3.8) do not apply where it is necessary to utilize a higher door threshold or a change in level to protect the integrity of the unit from wind/water damage. Where this exception results in patios, terraces or balconies that are not at an accessible level, equivalent facilitation shall be provided (e.g., equivalent facilitation at a hotel patio or balcony might consist of providing raised decking or a ramp to provide accessibility).

TH-09 Does the accessible route connect all accessible elements within the accessible unit? [9.2.2(3, 4, 5)]

- Accessible elements would include doors and doorways, storage (accessible, fixed, or built-in), controls and operating mechanisms, and telephones.

Accessible Transient Lodging/Hotels: hearing-impaired rooms

TH-16 Do accessible living units and sleeping accommodations comply with the requirements for visual alarms? (9.3, 4.28.4)

- Visual alarms meet required operational criteria.
- Visual alarms connect to the building emergency alarm system.
- Or a standard electrical outlet is provided and connected to the facility's central alarm system which enables room occupants to utilize portable devices provided by the operator of the facility.

TH-17 Is the signal from the visual alarm visible in all areas of the living unit or room? (9.3, 4.28.4)

TH-18 Do the living units, sleeping rooms, and suites comply with the requirements for visual notification devices? (9.3.1)

- This includes any space where the occupant would expect to be able to hear a phone or door bell.
- Visual notification devices are to alert the occupant of incoming telephone calls and a door knock or bell.
- This device must *not* be connected to the visual alarm system.

TH-19 Do the living units, sleeping rooms, and suites comply with the requirements for telephones? (9.3.1)

- If provided, permanently installed (hardwired) telephones should have volume controls capable of a minimum of 12 dbA and a maximum of 18 dbA above normal. If an automatic reset is provided, then 18 dbA may be exceeded.
- Outlets: An accessible electrical outlet is within 4 ft of a telephone connection, where provided.

(AR) Accessible Routes (4.3)

NOTES:

- All walks, halls, corridors, aisles, skywalks, tunnels, and other spaces that are part of a designated accessible route shall comply with accessible requirements.
- The accessible route shall, to the maximum extent feasible, coincide with the route for the general public.

AUTHOR'S INTERPRETATION:

- An accessible route "generally coincides" with the route used by the public if:
  - It does not force the user to go out of the way.
  - It is most like the route chosen by the general public.
  - It is direct.
  - It gives the same basic experience as the route preferred by the public.

Accessible Routes: width

AR-08 Is the minimum clear width along the accessible route adequate for continuous or point passage? (4.2.1, 4.3.3, Fig. 1, Fig. 8e, Fig. 24e)

- Continuous passage (greater than 24 in. long): at least a 36-in. clear width.
- Point passage (not more than 24 in. long): at least a 32-in. clear width.

AUTHOR'S INTERPRETATION:

- Noncompliance with this question generally relates to permanent elements that encroach on the accessible route. Large, heavy equipment that is not readily movable might be considered permanent. If the space is designed so that temporary elements (such as bikes in a bike rack or car bumpers) will consistently encroach, the situation might also be considered a permanent barrier.

(PR) Protruding Objects (4.4)

Protruding Objects: general

PR-01 Do wall-mounted objects having leading edges between 27 in. and 80 in. high project less than 4 in. into walkways, corridors, aisles, or paths of travel? (4.4.1, Fig. 8a–e)

- Objects mounted with their leading edge at or below 27 in. can protrude any amount, as long as they do not reduce the required clear width of an accessible route.

AUTHOR'S INTERPRETATION:

- Protruding objects might include fire extinguishers or cabinets, pencil sharpeners, shelving, counters, built-in equipment overhangs, or various dispensers such as for paper towels or soap.

PR-03 Is the minimum clear route width or maneuvering space still maintained even with the projection of a protruding object? (4.4.1, Fig. 8a–e)

Protruding Objects: overhead clearance

PR-04 Is the minimum overhead clearance of 80 in. provided in accessible areas or along accessible routes? (4.4.2, Fig. 8a)

AUTHOR'S INTERPRETATION:

- Overhead objects that can reduce the required clearance might include structures, pipes, ducts, or light fixtures.

PR-05 Where the vertical clearance of a space adjoining the accessible route is less than 80 in. high, is a cane detection barrier less than 27 in. from the floor provided for blind or visually impaired persons? (4.4.2, Fig. 8c-1)

AUTHOR'S INTERPRETATION:

- This condition might be found under a stair, at a sloped ceiling space, or with guy wires from telephone poles along an exterior accessible route.

(FS) Floor and Ground Surfaces (4.5)

Floor Surfaces: general

FS-01 Are the floor/ground surfaces on the accessible route stable, firm, and slip-resistant? (4.5.1)

AUTHOR'S INTERPRETATION:

- Exterior spaces, interior circulation, bathrooms, and other spaces where water can collect on the floor around an element (sinks, drinking fountains, hose bibbs, etc.) are reviewed as if wet.
- High gloss surfaces without significant textures that are regularly maintained with waxing (smooth tiles, waxed concrete, etc.) could be considered non-compliant.
- Accessible criteria are not specified for nonpermanent floor surfaces such as mats or rugs.

Floor Surfaces: changes in level

FS-02 Are vertical changes in level between 1/4 in. and 1/2 in. beveled with a slope of 1:2 or less? (4.5.2)

- Changes in level up to 1/4 in. may be vertical without edge treatment.
- Changes in level greater than 1/2 in. should be accomplished by means of a curb ramp, ramp, elevator, or platform lift (as permitted in ADAAG 4.1.3 and 4.1.6).

Floor Surfaces: carpet

FS-03 Does carpet or carpet tile used on the floor comply with accessible criteria? (4.5.3, Fig. 8f)

- Attachment: secured.
- Exposed edges: fastened and trimmed along the entire length.
- Pile type: low pile (1/2 in. maximum).
- Padding: firm pad or no pad underneath.

(SR) Storage (4.25)

NOTE:

- Accessible reach range requirements do not apply to shelves or display units allowing self-service by customers in mercantile occupancies but they must be located on an accessible route. [4.1.3(12)(b)]

Storage: general

SR-01 Does at least one of each type of fixed or built-in storage unit comply with accessible criteria? [4.1.3(12)(a), 4.25.1]

NOTE:

- Types of storage facilities might include cabinets, shelves, closets, and drawers.

Storage: clear floor space

SR-02 Is there a clear floor space at least 30 in. × 48 in. at fixed or built-in storage units that allows for either a forward or side approach? (4.25.2, Fig. 4a–b)

Storage: reach ranges

SR-03 Are forward or side reach for each type of accessible storage unit within acceptable reach ranges? (4.2.5–6, Fig. 5a–b, Fig. 6a–c, 4.25.3)

- Forward reach: not less than 15 in. high and not more than 48 in. high without any obstruction or where the obstruction is less than 20 in. deep. For obstructions from 20 in. to 25 in. deep, no forward reach higher than 44 in.
- Side reach: not less than 9 in. high and not more than 54 in. high. For obstructions not more than

34 in. high or 24 in. deep, no side reach higher than 46 in.

SR-04 In a closet where passage is not required to access storage (e.g., door opening is less than 32 in.), are the clothes rod or shelves within required reach ranges? (4.25.3, Fig. 38a–b)

- Door width: at least 20 in. (4.13.5)
- Horizontal reach: not more than 21 in. from the opening.
- Rod reach: if over 10 in. deep, then not more than 48 in. high.
- Shelf reach: if over 10 in. deep, then not more than 48 in. high or less than 9 in. high.

Storage: hardware

SR-05 Is the hardware on the storage unit doors or drawers operable with one hand without tight grasping, pinching, or wrist twisting, and requiring no more than 5 lbf of force? (4.25.4, 4.27.4)

(SE) Fixed or Built-in Seating and Tables (4.32)

Fixed or Built-in Seating and Tables: minimum number

SE-01 Is the minimum number of accessible wheelchair seating locations at fixed tables or counters provided? (4.1.3.18)

- Number required: 5 percent of total number of seats but not fewer than one.

Fixed or Built-in Seating and Tables: clear floor space

AUTHOR'S INTERPRETATION:

- Where the accessible route leads to and through accessible seating adjacent to a wall or another table, the minimum required width for the accessible route will be 65 in. between the table edge and next parallel surface (e.g., wall or another table edge). (4.1.3.18, Fig. 45)

SE-02 Is the clear floor space for a wheelchair at a seating location adequate? (4.32.3, Fig. 4a, Fig. 45)

- Clear floor space: 30 in. × 48 in.
- This clear space can include up to 19 in. under the table/desk.

Fixed or Built-in Seating and Tables: clearances

SE-03 Are the tops of accessible tables and counters between 28 in. and 34 in. from the floor? (4.32.3, Fig. 45)

SE-04 Are the knee clearances at least 27 in. high, 30 in. wide, and 19 in. deep? (4.32.3, Fig. 45)

(CT) Controls and Operating Mechanisms (4.27)

NOTES:

- Controls or operating mechanisms can include elements such as light switches, pencil sharpeners, manual overhead screens, nonkeyed thermostats, alarm pull stations, fire extinguisher cabinets, A/C window units, microwave ovens, towel dispensers, and wall hooks.
- If controls are to be operated by occupants of the space, they must be accessible. If controls are to be operated by maintenance staff only and not by occupants or other users of the space, they do not have to be accessible. For example, thermostats in auditoriums usually do not have to be accessible, while thermostats in classrooms may need to be accessible.

Controls: clear floor space

CT-01 Is a clear floor space of at least 30 in. × 48 in. provided in front of controls, dispensers, receptacles, and other operable equipment for forward or parallel approach? (4.27.2, Fig. 4a–b)

Controls: reach ranges

NOTES:

- Accessible reach ranges for controls and operating mechanisms are:
  — Forward reach: not less than 15 in. high and not more than 48 in. high without any obstruction or where the obstruction is less than 20 in. deep. For obstructions from 20 in. to 25 in. deep, no forward reach higher than 44 in.
  — Side reach: not less than 9 in. high and not more than 54 in. high. For obstructions not more than 34 in. high or 24 in. deep, no side reach higher than 46 in.
  — Electrical outlets, switches, and communication system receptacles have a minimum outlet height of 15 in. regardless of forward or side reach. See CT-02 below.

CT-02 Are electrical outlets, switches, and communication system receptacles mounted within accessible forward or side reach ranges? (4.27.3)

EXCEPTION:

- These requirements do not apply where the use of special equipment dictates otherwise or where electrical and communications system receptacles are not normally intended for use by building occupants. (4.27.3)

CT-03 Are thermostats or other similar operable equipment mounted within accessible forward or side reach ranges? (4.2.5, 4.2.6, Fig. 5a–b, Fig. 6a–c)

CT-04 Are dispensers or other similar operable equipment mounted within accessible forward or side reach ranges? (4.2.5, 4.2.6, Fig. 5a–b, Fig. 6a–c)

CT-05 Are life safety devices or other similar operable equipment mounted within accessible forward or side reach ranges? (4.2.5, 4.2.6, Fig. 5a–b, Fig. 6a–c)

NOTE:

- This might include fire alarm pull stations, handles to extinguisher cabinets, or wall-mounted extinguishers.

Controls: operation

CT-06 Are controls, dispensers, receptacles, and other operable equipment operable with one hand without tight grasping, pinching, or wrist twisting, and requiring no more than 5 lbf of force? (4.27.4)

(AL) Alarms (4.28)

NOTE:

- At a minimum, visual signal appliances shall be provided in buildings and facilities in restrooms and any other general usage areas. **The ADAAG does not de-**

fine the number of occupants needed to establish a general or common use area.

ALLOWANCE:

- Emergency warning systems in medical care facilities may be modified to suit standard health care alarm design practice. [4.1.3(14)]

Alarms: general

AL-01 If emergency warning systems are provided, do they include both audible alarms and visual alarms? [4.1.3(14)]

Audible Alarms: general

AL-02 If provided, do the audible alarms meet required operational criteria? (4.28.2)

- Sound level: exceeds the prevailing sound level in the room or space by at least 15 dbA or exceeds any maximum sound level with a duration of 60 sec by 5 dbA, whichever is louder.
- Sound levels for alarm signals shall not exceed 120 dbA.

AL-03 If single station audible alarms are provided, then are single station visual alarm signals also provided? (4.28.3)

Visual Alarms: general

AL-04 If provided, are the visual alarm signal appliances integrated into the building or facility alarm system? (4.28.3)

AL-05 If provided, do the visual alarm signals meet required operational criteria? [4.28.3(1, 2, 3, 4, 5)]

- Lamp: xenon strobe type or equivalent.
- Color: clear or nominal white (i.e., unfiltered or clear filtered white light).
- Pulse duration: maximum shall be 0.2 sec with a maximum duty cycle of 40 percent.
- Intensity: not less than 75 candela.
- Flash rate: not less than 1 Hz and not more than 3 Hz.

AL-08 Are the visual alarms placed at 80 in. above the highest floor level or 6 in. below the ceiling, whichever is lower? [4.28.3(6)]

Visual Alarms: living units

AL-11 Do accessible living units and sleeping accommodations have a visual alarm connected to the building emergency alarm system or do they have a standard 110-volt electrical receptacle into which such an alarm can be connected, and a means by which a signal from the building emergency alarm system can trigger such an auxiliary alarm? (4.28.4)

AL-12 Is the signal from the visual alarm visible in all areas of the living unit or room? (4.28.4)

Sleeping Rooms and Suites
(Hotels, Inns, Resorts, Dormitories, and Other Places of Accommodation)

Introduction. ADAAG designates two major categories of "Transient Lodging":

1. Private or public inns, resorts, boarding houses, hotels, motels, dormitories, and student campus apartments.
2. Social services establishments such as homeless shelters, halfway houses, transient group homes, and others.

This review guide is used for buildings, facilities, or portions thereof, that contain one or more publicly or privately operated sleeping accommodations within a hotel, inn, motel, student campus apartment, and so on. See other review guides in transient lodging (hotels)—"Living and Dining Rooms," "Bathrooms," "Kitchens" (kitchenettes and/or wet bars), "Exterior Activity Areas," "Parking Lots and Loading Zones," and so on—as needed.

ADAAG requires that a proportion of the total number of sleeping rooms within hotels, inns, resorts, dormitories, and other places of accommodation must be accessible to persons with disabilities. Accessible units, sleeping rooms, and suites are grouped into two categories: fully accessible and hearing-impaired. (The required number of accessible sleeping units is different for social services establishments.) Also the available accessible sleeping accommodations must provide persons with disabilities a range of options such as size, cost, amenities, and the number of beds provided. Large facilities with more than 50 sleeping rooms are required to have additional facilities (e.g., wheelchair accessible rooms shall provide an accessible roll-in shower with folding seat). The sleeping rooms and suites for hearing-impaired persons must provide visual alarms, notification devices, and telephones, but are not required to be fully accessible.

Accessible units must be located on an accessible route connected with other amenities provided by the facility such as conference rooms, vending machines, lobbies, and so on. Doors and doorways designed to allow passage into and within all transient lodging sleeping units must comply with accessible door width criteria. In other words, all sleeping units in the facility, whether designated as accessible or not, must comply with accessible door width criteria. Maneuvering space for a wheelchair user is a critical issue in sleeping rooms where large pieces of furniture such as dressers and beds are frequently fixed in place. When two beds are placed in a room, maneuvering space between the beds, as well as between the adjacent walls and the beds, must be provided. In accessible units with a balcony, porch, or seating area, access may be provided with a sliding glass door. In this case, the threshold must be compliant in terms of height and design, unless it is necessary to utilize a higher door threshold to protect the integrity of the unit from wind or water damage. Where this exception results in balconies or patios that are not at an accessible level, then equivalent facilities must be provided.

Place all controls and operating mechanisms within accessible reach ranges and verify, for example, that electrical outlets are not located behind a fixed dresser, desk, or night stand. In addition, thermostats on walls and security latches on doors must not be placed too high for a person in a wheelchair to reach. The controls on air conditioning and heating units generally have operating mechanisms that are difficult to manipulate; verify their accessibility. Designers may consider specifying luxurious plush carpeting in sleeping rooms to add comfort. However, carpeting in sleeping rooms must not limit accessibility for a person in a wheelchair in terms of pile height and pad thickness and firmness. For wheelchair users, permanently mounted mirrors within the room and counter alcove must be mounted at an accessible height. When provided, lavatories must comply with accessibility criteria.

Visual emergency alarm signals must be visible in all areas of the unit. In addition, visual notification devices and volume controlled telephones must be provided in units, sleeping rooms, and suites for hearing-impaired persons.

If provided, a security peephole in the door itself needs to be placed with both the wheelchair user and the nonwheelchair user in mind; two peepholes may be needed at different distances above the finished floor.

PRELIMINARY DESIGN OVERVIEW

(AR) Accessible Routes

- Sleeping rooms must be on an accessible route and guests need access to facilities such as ice and vending machines, conference rooms, lobbies, and so on.

(AL) Alarms

- Visual emergency alarm signals must be visible in all areas of the unit.

(CT) Controls and Operating Mechanisms

- If provided, communication outlets, controls on window air conditioner units, thermostats, fans, lights, electrical outlets (placed behind fixed furniture), and radio, TV, and coffee makers permanently attached to fixed furniture must be accessible and operable.

(DR) Doors

- Glass sliding doors must meet accessibility requirements. Note possible threshold exceptions.
- Doors and doorways designed to allow passage into and within all transient lodging sleeping units must comply with accessible door width criteria.

(FS) Floor Surfaces

- Vertical changes in levels along the accessible route can be an unforeseen barrier, e.g., transition between floor materials such as tile and carpet.
- Carpets must meet accessibility requirements of pile height and pad thickness and firmness.

(LV) Lavatories, Sinks, and Mirrors

- Hot pipes and sharp objects (i.e., valves and drains) must be shielded under lavatories and sinks.
- If lavatories are used for different purposes, then one of each use type must be accessible.
- Where mirrors are provided, one must be accessible. The bottom edge of the reflecting surface (slanted or flush-mounted) must meet accessibility requirements.

(PR) Protruding Objects

- Common wall-mounted elements can be protruding objects, e.g., shelving and lighting fixtures.

(SE) Fixed Tables and/or Counters

- Frequently overlooked are fixed tables, counters, and dressers that do not allow a person in a wheelchair adequate kneespace under the top surface.

(SG) Signage

- Typical requirements.

(SR) Storage

- One of each type of storage unit (shelves, closets, drawers, dispensers, and racks) must be accessible.

(TH) Transient Lodging

- A minimum number of accessible units within a building or facility is determined by using the tables provided by ADDAG 9.1.2. Requirements and numbers differ for mobility impairments and hearing impairments.
- Additional rooms with a roll-in shower with folding seat are required as the total number of sleeping units provided increase over 50. See ADAAG table 9.1.2.
- In new construction, at least one of each amenity (e.g., washer, dryer) in each public and common area must be accessible.
- The accessible sleeping room must provide clear width for maneuvering along or between beds.
- In sleeping rooms, one of each type of storage (cabinet shelves, closets, and drawers), if provided, must be accessible.
- All controls in accessible units, sleeping rooms, and suites must be accessible.
- In addition to general alarm requirements, visual notification devices must be provided in units, sleeping rooms, and suites and must be visible throughout.

Other

- If provided, peepholes on doors should be mounted at high and low accessible heights.

ADAAG APPENDIX

The ADAAG Appendix includes additional advisory information pertinent to transient lodging facilities.

- A2.2   Equivalent Facilitation—9.1.4 and 9.2.2(6)(d)
- A4.5.3 Floor Surfaces—Carpet

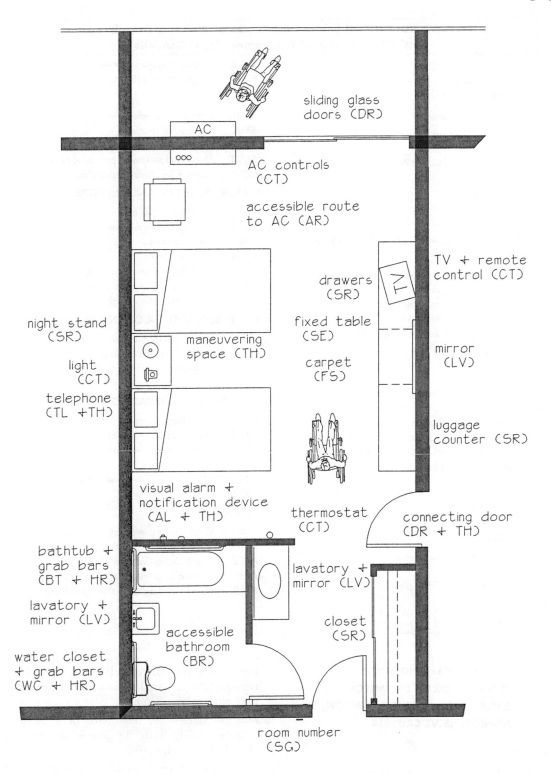

sliding glass
doors (DR)

AC

AC controls
(CT)

accessible route
to AC (AR)

TV + remote
control (CT)

drawers
(SR)

night stand
(SR)

fixed table
(SE)

mirror
(LV)

maneuvering
space (TH)

carpet
(FS)

light
(CT)

telephone
(TL +TH)

luggage
counter (SR)

visual alarm +
notification device
(AL + TH)

thermostat
(CT)

connecting door
(DR + TH)

bathtub +
grab bars
(BT + HR)

lavatory +
mirror (LV)

lavatory +
mirror (LV)

closet
(SR)

accessible
bathroom
(BR)

water closet
+ grab bars
(WC + HR)

room number
(SG)

accessible route (AR)

Figure 3-24. Transient lodging: Sleeping room and suite (hotels, inns, dorms).

Sleeping Rooms and Suites (Hotels , Inns, Resorts, Dormitories and Other Places of Accommodation) Checklist

SIGNAGE

SG04	Room signage: criteria
SG05	Room signage: location

DOORS

DR04	Doors: maneuvering clearances
DR05	Doors: handle type
DR06	Doors: opening force (interior only)
DR07	Doors: closing speed
DR08	Doors: thresholds
DR09	Doors: clear width/height
DR10	Openings (no door): clear width/height

TRANSIENT LODGING: HOTELS—SLEEPING ROOMS AND SUITES

TH01	Sleeping units: number required (New)
TH02	51+ Sleeping units: roll-in shower w/seat
TH03	Hearing-impaired units: number req'd (New)
TH04	Sleeping units: number required (Alt.)
TH05	Hearing-impaired units: number req'd (Alt.)
TH06	Unit choice: type/class of acc. rooms
TH07	Sleeping unit: accessible route
TH08	Sleeping unit: linked accessible spaces
TH09	Sleeping unit: linked accessible elements
TH10	Sleeping unit: maneuv. space at beds/wall
TH16	Hearing-imp. unit: visual alarm req.
TH17	Hearing-imp. unit: visual alarms in all areas
TH18	Hearing-imp. units: visual notification device
TH19	Hearing-imp. units: telephone

ACCESSIBLE ROUTES

AR08	Route: clear width

PROTRUDING OBJECTS

PR01	Wall-mounted
PR03	Clear route width maintained
PR04	Overhead clearance
PR05	Vertical clearance: cane detection barrier

FLOOR SURFACES

FS01	Surface: firm, stable, and slip-resistant

FS02	Vertical changes in level
FS03	Carpet and tile floors

STORAGE

SR01	Accessibility: one of each type
SR02	Clear floor space
SR03	Reach ranges
SR04	Storage closets w/o passage: criteria
SR05	Storage hardware: operation

LAVATORIES, SINKS, AND MIRRORS

LV01	Clear floor space
LV02	Rim/apron heights and extension from wall
LV03	Toe clearance
LV04	Insulated pipes
LV05	Controls and operation requirements
LV06	Lavatories: knee clearance
LV09	Mirror: mounting height

FIXED TABLES AND/OR COUNTERS

SE01	Fixed seating: number required
SE02	Wheelchairs: clear floor space at tables
SE03	Tables/counters: heights
SE04	Tables/counters: knee clearance criteria

CONTROLS AND OPERATING MECHANISMS

CT01	Clear floor space
CT02	Reach ranges: elec./comm. systems
CT03	Reach ranges: thermostats
CT04	Reach ranges: other controls
CT05	Reach ranges: life safety devices
CT06	Controls: operation

ALARMS

AL04	Visual alarms: integration w/building alarm
AL05	Visual alarms: operation
AL08	Visual alarms: vertical placement
AL11	Visual alarms: acc. living and sleeping units
AL12	Visual alarms: visible throughout unit

SLEEPING ROOMS AND SUITES (HOTELS , INNS, RESORTS, DORMITORIES, AND OTHER PLACES OF ACCOMMODATION) COMPREHENSIVE CRITERIA

(SG) Signage (4.30)

Signage: room identification (where provided)

DEFINITION:

- These signs designate permanent rooms and spaces.

AUTHOR'S INTERPRETATION:

- Signs that designate stairs, exit doors, and toilet rooms generally are associated with permanent spaces, while an "office" sign is not since the room function may change over time. Room numbers also must meet the ADAAG criteria as permanent designations, while personal names do not since the occupant may change over time.

SG-04 Do signs that designate permanent rooms and spaces comply with the following criteria? [4.1.2(7); 4.1.3(16); 4.30.4, 5, 6]

- Character type: raised and accompanied by Grade II Braille.
- Character size: between 5/8 in. and 2 in. high; raised at least 1/32 in.
- Character style: upper case, and sans or simple serif.
- Finish: characters and backgrounds have a nonglare finish.
- Contrast: characters contrast with their background (light-on-dark or dark-on-light).

SG-05 Is the room identification sign mounted in the required location? (4.30.6)

- Mounting location: installed on the wall adjacent to the latch side of the door or where wall space to the latch side of the door is not available, including double doors, placed on the nearest adjacent wall.
- Mounting height: 60 in. above the floor/ground to the centerline of the sign.
- Sign access: approach to within 3 in. of a sign without encountering protruding objects or standing within the swing of the door.

(DR) Doors (4.13)

NOTE:

- Included in this category are doors, revolving doors, turnstiles, and gates.

AUTHOR'S INTERPRETATION:

- It is suggested that, for purposes of documentation and review, a door be assigned to the space it swings into. Corridors are an exception to this rule and include only entry doors into the corridor or intermediate fire doors.

Doors: maneuvering clearance

DR-04 If the door is not automatic or power assisted, does it have the required maneuvering clearance provided on the push and pull side, and is the floor level and clear within the maneuvering area? (4.13.6)

- A verbal description cannot adequately describe the requirements. See ADAAG Fig. 25a–f for a graphic description.

EXCEPTION:

- Entry doors to acute care hospital bedrooms for inpatients are exempt from maneuvering space at the latch side of the door if the door is at least 44 in. wide.

AUTHOR'S INTERPRETATION:

- While ADAAG does not describe what elements can reduce the required maneuvering clearance, they could include a narrow entry alcove, an adjacent wall, railing, or permanently installed shelving, or a deep recessed door jamb.

Doors: hardware

DR-05 Do all door handles, locks, latches, or other operable devices meet required operational criteria? (4.13.9)

- Hardware operation: operable with one hand without tight grasping, pinching, or wrist twisting.
- Force required to operate the controls: not greater than 5 lbf. This does not apply to the force required to retract latch bolts or to disengage other devices that only hold the door in a closed position.
- Hardware type: "U"-shaped handles, levers, and push type mechanisms are acceptable designs.
- Hardware height: not greater than 48 in. above the floor.

- Sliding doors: hardware is exposed and usable from both sides when the doors are fully open.

Doors: opening force

DR-06 Do interior hinged doors and sliding or folding doors have an opening force of 5 lbf or less? (4.13.11)

- At present, no accessible criteria exist for exterior doors.
- Fire doors shall have the minimum opening force allowable by the appropriate administrative authority.

Doors: closing speed

DR-07 If the door has a closer, is the closer adjusted so that the door does not close too quickly? (4.13.10)

- From an open position of 70° the door will take at least 3 sec to move to a point 3 in. from the latch (measured to the leading edge of the door).

Doors: thresholds

DR-08 Where raised thresholds are provided, do they meet height limitations and are they beveled when required? (4.13.8, 4.5.2, Fig. 7)

- Threshold height: not more than 3/4 in. for exterior sliding doors or 1/2 in. for other types of doors.
- Threshold bevel: thresholds less than 1/4 in. high need no bevel; thresholds between 1/4 in. and 1/2 in. high shall be beveled at each edge with not more than a 1:2 slope.

EXCEPTION:

- A 3/4-in. high threshold is allowed in existing conditions. [4.1.6(3)(d)(ii)]

Doors: clear opening width and height

DR-09 Is the clear opening for the doorway adequate in width and height? (4.13.3, 4, 5; Fig. 24)

- Door width: at least 32 in. of clear width with the door open at 90°, measured between the face of the door and the door stop on the latch side. This also pertains to the active leaf of a double-leaf door or gate.
- Opening width: openings more than 24 in. deep must provide 36 in. of clear width.
- Height: at least 80 in. of vertical clearance.

EXCEPTIONS:

- Doors not requiring full user passage, such as shallow closets, may have the clear opening reduced to not less than 20 in.
- Where it is technically infeasible to comply with clear opening width requirements, a projection of 5/8 in. maximum will be permitted for the latch side. [4.1.6(d)(i)]

DR-10 Is the clear opening (when there is no door) adequate in width and height? (4.2.1, 4.3.3, 4.4.2)

- Width: at least 32 in. of clear width for depths 24 in. or less and at least 36 in. of clear width for depths greater than 24 in.
- Height: at least 80 in. of vertical clearance.

(TH) Accessible Transient Lodging (9.0)
(Hotels, Motels, Inns, Boarding Houses, Dormitories, and Similar Places)

NOTE:

- Transient lodging is divided into two categories:
  — Hotels, motels, inns, boarding houses, dormitories, and similar places (TH-01 through TH-19).
  — Homeless shelters, halfway houses, transient group homes, and other social services establishments (TH-20 through TH-26 and TH-07 through TH-19).

- Doors and doorways designed to allow passage into and within all transient lodging sleeping units shall comply with accessible door width criteria. This means any sleeping unit in the facility, whether it is designated as accessible or not. (9.4)

AUTHOR'S INTERPRETATION:

- Accessible units, sleeping rooms, and suites are divided into two categories: fully accessible and hearing-impaired. Fully accessible units, sleeping rooms, and suites must comply with accessible criteria for both mobility and hearing impairments. (9.2.8) Hearing-impaired units must comply only with those accessible criteria that relate to visual alarms, notification devices, and telephones. (9.3)

- The total number of accessible units required by ADAAG can be easily misinterpreted if not carefully read. For example, the total number of rooms required for 76–100 hotel rooms is 9, broken down as follows:
  — Four fully accessible rooms with accessible bathrooms.
  — One fully accessible room with accessible bathroom with a roll-in shower with folding seat.
  — Four rooms for the hearing-impaired (other accessible criteria are not required including an accessible bathroom).

- In dormitories or other facilities where bath facilities are multiple user and separate from the sleeping room, the minimum number of accessible tubs or showers required is not clearly prescribed. ADAAG 4.23.8, which indicates a minimum of at least one accessible tub or shower (when provided) in bathrooms, appears to be applicable to this situation.

EXCEPTION:

- ADAAG 9.1 through 9.4 do not apply to an establishment located within a building that contains no more than five rooms for rent or hire and that is actually occupied by the proprietor of such establishment as the residence of such proprietor.

Accessible Transient Lodging/Hotels: number required/ new construction

TH-01 Are the required number of accessible sleeping rooms and suites provided? (9.1.2)

- Accessible rooms: 1 per 1–25, 2 per 26–50, 3 per 51–75, 4 per 76–100, 5 per 101–150, 6 per 151–200, 7 per 201–300, 8 per 301–400, 9 per 401–500, and 501–1000 is 2 percent of total.

- For more than 1000 rooms, 20 accessible rooms plus 1 for each 100 over 1000.

AUTHOR'S INTERPRETATION:

- When the total number of rooms is fewer than 50, the type of shower that can be provided relates to the criteria shown in Section "SS, Shower Stalls." However, when the number of rooms exceeds 50, the type of shower required is a roll-in shower with folding seat—see TH-02 below.

TH-02 In hotels of 51 or more sleeping rooms and suites, is the required number of additional accessible sleeping rooms with a roll-in shower with folding seat provided? (9.1.2, Fig. 57a–b)

- Accessible rooms with roll-in showers with folding seats: 1 per 51–100, 2 per 101–200, 3 per 201–300, and 4 per 301–400.

- For more than 400 rooms, 4 accessible rooms with roll-in showers with folding seat plus 1 for each 100 over 400.

NOTES:

- Roll-in shower with folding seat design for this type of transient housing differs from transfer and roll-in showers described in Section "SS, Shower Stalls." See ADAAG Fig. 57a–b for dimensional criteria and configurations.

TH-03 In addition to accessible units required for mobility disabilities, are the required number of sleeping rooms and suites also provided that meet accessibility requirements for the hearing-impaired? (9.1.3)

- Accessible rooms: 1 per 1–25, 2 per 26–50, 3 per 51–75, 4 per 76–100, 5 per 101–150, 6 per 151–200, 7 per 201–300, 8 per 301–400, 9 per 401–500, and 501–1000 is 2 percent of total.

- For more than 1000 rooms, 20 accessible rooms plus 1 for each 100 over 1000.

Accessible Transient Lodging/Hotels: number required/alterations

TH-04 When sleeping rooms or suites are altered, is at least one accessible room or suite provided for each 25 altered rooms (or portion thereof) until the number equals that in TH-01? (9.1.5)

TH-05 In addition, when sleeping rooms or suites are altered, is at least one accessible room or suite provided for each 25 altered rooms (or portion thereof) until the number equals that in TH-03 that meets accessibility requirements for the hearing-impaired? (9.1.5)

Accessible Transient Lodging/Hotels: room dispersion

TH-06 Are the accessible rooms and suites dispersed among various classes of sleeping accommodations available to all patrons? (9.1.4)

NOTES:

- Factors to be considered include room size, cost, amenities, and number of beds provided.

- Equal facilitation: For purposes of this section, the operator may choose to limit construction of accessible rooms to those designed for multiple occupancy rooms if the multiple occupancy accessible rooms are made available at a single occupancy rate to an individual with a disability who requests a single occupancy room.

Accessible Transient Lodging/Hotels: accessible routes

TH-07 Are accessible sleeping rooms or suites located on an accessible route? (9.2.2)

TH-08 Does an accessible route connect all accessible spaces within the accessible unit? [9.2.2(2, 6, 7)]

- Where provided, this includes the living area, the dining area, a dual occupancy sleeping area, patio or balcony, a full bathroom or half bath (if only half baths are provided), kitchen (also kitchenette or wet bar), and parking space.

NOTE:

- Elevators are not required in a multilevel unit if the previously listed spaces are all on the accessible level and the accessible sleeping area is suitable for dual occupancy.

EXCEPTION:

- The requirements of thresholds at doors (4.13.8) and changes in levels (4.3.8) do not apply where it is necessary to utilize a higher door threshold or a change in level to protect the integrity of the unit from wind/water damage. Where this exception results in patios, terraces, or balconies that are not at an accessible level, equivalent facilitation shall be provided (e.g., equivalent facilitation at a hotel patio or balcony might consist of providing raised decking or a ramp to provide accessibility).

TH-09 Does the accessible route connect all accessible elements within the accessible unit? [9.2.2(3, 4, 5)]

- Accessible elements would include doors and doorways, storage (accessible, fixed, or built-in), controls and operating mechanisms, and telephones.

Accessible Transient Lodging/Hotels: sleeping rooms

TH-10 Does the accessible sleeping room provide clear width for maneuvering along or between fixed, built-in, or movable beds? [9.2.2(1)]

- Width:
  - 36 in. clear width maneuvering space along both sides of a fixed or built-in bed;
  - or 36 in. clear width maneuvering space along either side of a movable bed;
  - or 36 in. clear width maneuvering space between two fixed beds.

Accessible Transient Lodging/Hotels: hearing-impaired rooms

TH-16 Do accessible living units and sleeping accommodations comply with the requirements for visual alarms? (9.3, 4.28.4)

- Visual alarms meet required operational criteria.
- Visual alarms connect to the building emergency alarm system.

- Or a standard electrical outlet is provided and connected to the facility's central alarm system which enables room occupants to utilize portable devices provided by the operator of the facility.

TH-17 Is the signal from the visual alarm visible in all areas of the living unit or room? (9.3, 4.28.4)

TH-18 Do the living units, sleeping rooms, and suites comply with the requirements for visual notification devices? (9.3.1)

- This includes any space where the occupant would expect to be able to hear a phone or door bell.
- Visual notification devices are to alert the occupant of incoming telephone calls and a door knock or bell.
- This device must *not* be connected to the visual alarm system.

TH-19 Do the living units, sleeping rooms, and suites comply with the requirements for telephones? (9.3.1)

- If provided, permanently installed (hardwired) telephones should have volume controls capable of a minimum of 12 dbA and a maximum of 18 dbA above normal. If an automatic reset is provided, then 18 dbA may be exceeded.
- Outlets: An accessible electrical outlet is within 4 ft of a telephone connection, where provided.

(AR) Accessible Routes (4.3)

NOTES:

- All walks, halls, corridors, aisles, skywalks, tunnels, and other spaces that are part of a designated accessible route shall comply with accessible requirements.
- The accessible route shall, to the maximum extent feasible, coincide with the route for the general public.

AUTHOR'S INTERPRETATION:

- An accessible route "generally coincides" with the route used by the public if:
  - It does not force the user to go out of the way.
  - It is most like the route chosen by the general public.
  - It is direct.
  - It gives the same basic experience as the route preferred by the public.

Accessible Routes: width

AR-08 Is the minimum clear width along the accessible route adequate for continuous or point passage? (4.2.1, 4.3.3, Fig. 1, Fig. 8e, Fig. 24e)

- Continuous passage (greater than 24 in. long): at least a 36-in. clear width.
- Point passage (not more than 24 in. long): at least a 32-in. clear width.

AUTHOR'S INTERPRETATION:

- Noncompliance with this question generally relates to permanent elements that encroach on the accessible route. Large, heavy equipment that is not readily movable might be considered permanent. If the space is designed so that temporary elements (such as bikes in a bike rack or car bumpers) will consistently encroach, the situation might also be considered a permanent barrier.

(PR) Protruding Objects (4.4)

Protruding Objects: general

PR-01 Do wall-mounted objects having leading edges between 27 in. and 80 in. high project less than 4 in. into walkways, corridors, aisles, or paths of travel? (4.4.1, Fig. 8a–e)

- Objects mounted with their leading edge at or below 27 in. can protrude any amount, as long as they do not reduce the required clear width of an accessible route.

AUTHOR'S INTERPRETATION:

- Protruding objects might include fire extinguishers or cabinets, pencil sharpeners, shelving, counters, built-in equipment overhangs, or various dispensers such as for paper towels or soap.

PR-03 Is the minimum clear route width or maneuvering space still maintained even with the projection of a protruding object? (4.4.1, Fig. 8a–e)

Protruding Objects: overhead clearance

PR-04 Is the minimum overhead clearance of 80 in. provided in accessible areas or along accessible routes? (4.4.2, Fig. 8a)

AUTHOR'S INTERPRETATION:

- Overhead objects that can reduce the required clearance might include structures, pipes, ducts, or light fixtures.

PR-05 Where the vertical clearance of a space adjoining the accessible route is less than 80 in. high, is a cane detection barrier less than 27 in. from the floor provided for blind or visually impaired persons? (4.4.2, Fig. 8c-1)

AUTHOR'S INTERPRETATION:

- This condition might be found under a stair, at a sloped ceiling space, or with guy wires from telephone poles along an exterior accessible route.

(FS) Floor and Ground Surfaces (4.5)

Floor Surfaces: general

FS-01 Are the floor/ground surfaces on the accessible route stable, firm, and slip-resistant? (4.5.1)

AUTHOR'S INTERPRETATION:

- Exterior spaces, interior circulation, bathrooms, and other spaces where water can collect on the floor around an element (sinks, drinking fountains, hose bibbs, etc.) are reviewed as if wet.

- High gloss surfaces without significant textures that are regularly maintained with waxing (smooth tiles, waxed concrete, etc.) could be considered noncompliant.

- Accessible criteria are not specified for nonpermanent floor surfaces such as mats or rugs.

Floor Surfaces: changes in level

FS-02 Are vertical changes in level between 1/4 in. and 1/2 in. beveled with a slope of 1:2 or less? (4.5.2)

- Changes in level up to 1/4 in. may be vertical without edge treatment.

- Changes in level greater than 1/2 in. should be accomplished by means of a curb ramp, ramp, elevator, or platform lift (as permitted in ADAAG 4.1.3 and 4.1.6).

Floor Surfaces: carpet

FS-03 Does carpet or carpet tile used on the floor comply with accessible criteria? (4.5.3, Fig. 8f)

- Attachment: secured.
- Exposed edges: fastened and trimmed along the entire length.
- Pile type: low pile (1/2 in. maximum).
- Padding: firm pad or no pad underneath.

(SR) Storage (4.25)

NOTE:

- Accessible reach range requirements do not apply to shelves or display units allowing self-service by customers in mercantile occupancies but they must be located on an accessible route. [4.1.3(12)(b)]

Storage: general

SR-01 Does at least one of each type of fixed or built-in storage unit comply with accessible criteria? [4.1.3(12)(a), 4.25.1]

NOTE:

- Types of storage facilities might include cabinets, shelves, closets, and drawers.

Storage: clear floor space

SR-02 Is there a clear floor space at least 30 in. × 48 in. at fixed or built-in storage units that allows for either a forward or side approach? (4.25.2, Fig. 4a–b)

Storage: reach ranges

SR-03 Are forward or side reach for each type of accessible storage unit within acceptable reach ranges? (4.2.5–6, Fig. 5a–b, Fig. 6a–c, 4.25.3)

- Forward reach: not less than 15 in. high and not more than 48 in. high without any obstruction or where the obstruction is less than 20 in. deep. For obstructions from 20 in. to 25 in. deep, no forward reach higher than 44 in.

- Side reach: not less than 9 in. high and not more than 54 in. high. For obstructions not more than 34 in. high or 24 in. deep, no side reach higher than 46 in.

SR-04 In a closet where passage is not required to access storage (e.g., door opening is less than 32 in.), are the clothes rod or shelves within required reach ranges? (4.25.3, Fig. 38a–b)

- Door width: at least 20 in. (4.13.5)
- Horizontal reach: not more than 21 in. from the opening.
- Rod reach: if over 10 in. deep, then not more than 48 in. high.
- Shelf reach: if over 10 in. deep, then not more than 48 in. high or less than 9 in. high.

Storage: hardware

SR-05 Is the hardware on the storage unit doors or drawers operable with one hand without tight grasping, pinching, or wrist twisting, and requiring no more than 5 lbf of force? (4.25.4, 4.27.4)

(LV) Lavatories, Sinks, and Mirrors (4.19, 4.24)

NOTE:

- Where lavatories or sinks are provided, at least one of each type must meet accessible requirements.

AUTHOR'S INTERPRETATION:

- While not specifically defined by ADAAG, it appears lavatories are for personal hygiene in bathrooms or toilet rooms, while sinks are for all other situations (e.g., laboratories or kitchens).

Lavatories or Sinks: clearances

LV-01 Is there a clear floor space not less than 30 in. × 48 in. in front of the accessible lavatory or sink allowing a forward approach, and does it adjoin or overlap the accessible route? (4.19.3, 4.24.5, Fig. 32)

- The clear floor space can extend up to 19 in. under the sink or lavatory if adequate knee clearance is provided.

LV-02 Are the accessible lavatory or sink rim or counter height, apron height, and extension from the wall adequate? (4.19.2, 4.24.2, Fig. 31)

- Rim height: not greater than 34 in. above the finish floor.
- Apron height: not less than 29 in. above the finish floor to the bottom of the apron.
- Lavatory extension: not less than 17 in. from the wall.

LV-03 Is toe clearance under the accessible lavatory or sink not less than 9 in. above the finish floor and not deeper than 6 in. from the back wall for the full length of the lavatory or sink? (4.19.2, Fig. 31)

Lavatories or Sinks: pipe shielding

LV-04 Are the hot water and drain pipes at the accessible lavatory or sink insulated or otherwise configured to protect against contact and is the area below the lavatory or sink free of sharp or abrasive surfaces? (4.19.4)

Lavatories or Sinks: controls

LV-05 Do the accessible lavatory or sink controls meet operational requirements? (4.19.5)

- Operation: operable with one hand without tight grasping, pinching, or twisting of the wrist. Acceptable types might include lever operated, push type, touch type, or electronically controlled; no more than 5 lbf of force.
- Self-closing faucets, when used, remain open for at least 10 sec.

Lavatories Only

LV-06 Is adequate knee clearance provided underneath the accessible lavatory? (4.19.2, Fig. 31)

- Lavatory knee clearance: not less than 27 in. high from finish floor to the bottom of the lavatory when

measured at a point not less than 8 in. from the front of the lavatory.

Lavatories or Sinks: mirrors

LV-09 Where mirrors are provided, does at least one mirror have a bottom edge of the reflecting surface no higher than 40 in. above the floor? (4.19.6, Fig. 31)

AUTHOR'S INTERPRETATION:

- Slanted mirrors located above 40 in. are not recognized as compliant by the ADAAG.

(SE) Fixed or Built-in Seating and Tables (4.32)

Fixed or Built-in Seating and Tables: minimum number

SE-01 Is the minimum number of accessible wheelchair seating locations at fixed tables or counters provided? (4.1.3.18)

- Number required: 5 percent of total number of seats but not fewer than one.

Fixed or Built-in Seating and Tables: clear floor space

AUTHOR'S INTERPRETATION:

- Where the accessible route leads to and through accessible seating adjacent to a wall or another table, the minimum required width for the accessible route will be 65 in. between the table edge and next parallel surface (e.g., wall or another table edge). (4.1.3.18, Fig. 45)

SE-02 Is the clear floor space for a wheelchair at a seating location adequate? (4.32.3, Fig. 4a, Fig. 45)

- Clear floor space: 30 in. × 48 in.
- This clear space can include up to 19 in. under the table/desk.

Fixed or Built-in Seating and Tables: clearances

SE-03 Are the tops of accessible tables and counters between 28 in. and 34 in. from the floor? (4.32.3, Fig. 45)

SE-04 Are the knee clearances at least 27 in. high, 30 in. wide, and 19 in. deep? (4.32.3, Fig. 45)

(CT) Controls and Operating Mechanisms (4.27)

NOTES:

- Controls or operating mechanisms can include elements such as light switches, pencil sharpeners, manual overhead screens, nonkeyed thermostats, alarm pull stations, fire extinguisher cabinets, A/C window units, microwave ovens, towel dispensers, and wall hooks.
- If controls are to be operated by occupants of the space, they must be accessible. If controls are to be operated by maintenance staff only and not by occupants or other users of the space, they do not have to be accessible. For example, thermostats in auditoriums usually do not have to be accessible, while thermostats in classrooms may need to be accessible.

Controls: clear floor space

CT-01 Is a clear floor space of at least 30 in. × 48 in. provided in front of controls, dispensers, receptacles, and other operable equipment for forward or parallel approach? (4.27.2, Fig. 4a–b)

Controls: reach ranges

NOTES:

- Accessible reach ranges for controls and operating mechanisms are:
  — Forward reach: not less than 15 in. high and not more than 48 in. high without any obstruction or where the obstruction is less than 20 in. deep. For obstructions from 20 in. to 25 in. deep, no forward reach higher than 44 in.
  — Side reach: not less than 9 in. high and not more than 54 in. high. For obstructions not more than 34 in. high or 24 in. deep, no side reach higher than 46 in.
  — Electrical outlets, switches, and communication system receptacles have a minimum outlet height of 15 in. regardless of forward or side reach. See CT-02 below.

CT-02 Are electrical outlets, switches, and communication system receptacles mounted within accessible forward or side reach ranges? (4.27.3)

EXCEPTION:

- These requirements do not apply where the use of special equipment dictates otherwise or where electrical and communications system receptacles are not normally intended for use by building occupants. (4.27.3)

CT-03 Are thermostats or other similar operable equipment mounted within accessible forward or side reach ranges? (4.2.5, 4.2.6, Fig. 5a–b, Fig. 6a–c)

CT-04 Are dispensers or other similar operable equipment mounted within accessible forward or side reach ranges? (4.2.5, 4.2.6, Fig. 5a–b, Fig. 6a–c)

CT-05 Are life safety devices or other similar operable equipment mounted within accessible forward or side reach ranges? (4.2.5, 4.2.6, Fig. 5a–b, Fig. 6a–c)

NOTE:

- This might include fire alarm pull stations, handles to extinguisher cabinets, or wall-mounted extinguishers.

Controls: operation

CT-06 Are controls, dispensers, receptacles, and other operable equipment operable with one hand without tight grasping, pinching, or wrist twisting, and requiring no more than 5 lbf of force? (4.27.4)

(AL) Alarms (4.28)

NOTE:

- At a minimum, visual signal appliances shall be provided in buildings and facilities in restrooms and any other general usage areas. **The ADAAG does not define the number of occupants needed to establish a general or common use area.**

ALLOWANCE:

- Emergency warning systems in medical care facilities may be modified to suit standard health care alarm design practice. [4.1.3(14)]

Visual Alarms: general

AL-04 If provided, are the visual alarm signal appliances integrated into the building or facility alarm system? (4.28.3)

AL-05 If provided, do the visual alarm signals meet required operational criteria? [4.28.3(1, 2, 3, 4, 5)]

- Lamp: xenon strobe type or equivalent.
- Color: clear or nominal white (i.e., unfiltered or clear filtered white light).
- Pulse duration: maximum shall be 0.2 sec with a maximum duty cycle of 40 percent.
- Intensity: not less than 75 candela.
- Flash rate: not less than 1 Hz and not more than 3 Hz.

AL-08 Are the visual alarms placed at 80 in. above the highest floor level or 6 in. below the ceiling, whichever is lower? [4.28.3(6)]

Visual Alarms: living units

AL-11 Do accessible living units and sleeping accommodations have a visual alarm connected to the building emergency alarm system or have a standard 110-volt electrical receptacle into which such an alarm can be connected, and a means by which a signal from the building emergency alarm system can trigger such an auxiliary alarm? (4.28.4)

AL-12 Is the signal from the visual alarm visible in all areas of the living unit or room? (4.28.4)

Sleeping Units
(Social Services Establishments: Homeless Shelters, Halfway Houses, Transient Group Homes, and Others)

Introduction. ADAAG designates two major categories of "Transient Lodging":

1. Private or public inns, resorts, boarding houses, hotels, motels, dormitories, and student campus apartments.
2. Social services establishments such as homeless shelters, halfway houses, transient group homes, and others.

This review guide is used for buildings, facilities, or portions thereof, that contain one or more publicly or privately operated sleeping accommodation within social service establishments such as homeless shelters, halfway houses, or transient group homes. See other review guides in transient lodging (hotels)—"Living and Dining Rooms," "Bathrooms," "Kitchens" (kitchenettes and/or wet bars), "Exterior Activity Areas," "Parking Lots and Loading Zones," and so on—as needed.

ADAAG requires that a proportion of the total number of sleeping rooms/beds within homeless shelters, halfway houses, transient group homes, and other social service establishments must be fully accessible to persons with disabilities. Accessible sleeping units are grouped into two categories: fully accessible and hearing-impaired. (The required number of accessible sleeping units is different for hotels, inns, resorts, dormitories, and so on.) Additionally, a proportion of the standard sleeping rooms or multibed rooms must provide visual alarms, notification devices, and telephones for hearing-impaired persons. Accessible units must be located on an accessible route that connects with other amenities provided by the facility such as washers, dryers, and similar equipment. Where a building is exempt from the elevator requirement, accessible amenities are not required on inaccessible floors as long as one of each type is provided in common areas on accessible floors.

Maneuvering space for a wheelchair user is a critical issue in sleeping rooms or rooms with multibed facilities where large pieces of furniture such as dressers and beds are frequently fixed in place. Accessible sleeping rooms need maneuvering space along both sides of a bed or, when two beds or more are placed in a room, maneuvering space is required between the beds. Doors and doorways designed to allow passage into and within all transient lodging sleeping units must comply with accessible door width criteria. In other words, all sleeping units in the facility, whether designated as accessible or not, must comply with accessible door width criteria.

Place controls and operating mechanisms within accessible reach ranges and verify, for example, that electrical outlets are not located behind a fixed dresser, desk, or night stand. In addition, thermostats on walls and security latches on doors must not be placed too high for a person in a wheelchair to reach. The controls on air conditioning and heating units generally have operating mechanisms that are difficult to manipulate; verify their accessibility. Carpeting in sleeping rooms must not limit accessibility for a person in a wheelchair in terms of pile height and pad thickness and firmness. Permanently mounted mirrors within the room must be mounted at an accessible height.

Visual emergency alarm signals must be visible in all areas of the unit. In addition, visual notification devices and telephones must be provided in units, sleeping rooms, and suites for hearing-impaired persons.

If a security peephole is provided in the door, it needs to be placed with both the wheelchair user and the nonwheelchair user in mind; two peepholes may be needed at different distances above the finished floor.

PRELIMINARY DESIGN OVERVIEW

NOTE:

- Verify the required number of sleeping units based on ADAAG table 9.1.2.
- Sleeping rooms must be on an accessible route and residents need access to facilities such as washers, dryers, and similar equipment.

(AR) Accessible Routes

- Typical requirements.

(AL) Alarms

- Visual emergency alarm signals must be visible in all areas of the unit.

(CT) Controls and Operating Mechanisms

- If provided, communication outlets, controls on window air conditioner units, thermostats, fans, lights, electrical outlets (placed behind fixed furniture), and radio, TV, and coffee makers permanently attached to fixed furniture must be accessible and operable.

(DR) Doors

- Doors and doorways designed to allow passage into and within all transient lodging sleeping units must comply with accessible door width criteria.

(FS) Floor Surfaces

- Smooth floor surfaces should be evaluated for slip-resistance based on floor finish and maintenance.
- Vertical changes in levels along the accessible route can be an unforeseen barrier, e.g., transition between floor materials.

(LV) Lavatories, Sinks, and Mirrors

- Where mirrors are provided, one must be accessible. The bottom edge of the reflecting surface (slanted or flush-mounted) must meet accessibility requirements.

(PR) Protruding Objects

- Common wall-mounted elements can be protruding objects, e.g., shelving and lighting fixtures.

(SE) Fixed Tables and/or Counters

- Frequently overlooked are fixed tables, counters, and dressers that allow a person in a wheelchair knee space under the top surface.

(SG) Signage

- Typical requirements.

(SR) Storage

- One of each type of storage unit (shelves, closets, drawers, dispensers, and racks) must be accessible.

(TH) Transient Lodging

- A minimum number of accessible units within a building or facility is determined by using the tables provided by ADDAG. Requirements and numbers differ for mobility impairments and hearing impairments.
- In new construction, at least one of each amenity (i.e., washer, dryer) in each public and common area must be accessible.
- The accessible sleeping room/beds must provide clear width for maneuvering along or between beds.
- In sleeping rooms, one of each type of storage (cabinet shelves, closets, and drawers), if provided, must be accessible.
- All controls in accessible units, sleeping rooms, and suites must be accessible.
- In addition to general alarm requirements, visual notification devices must be provided in units, sleeping rooms, and suites.

ADAAG APPENDIX

The ADAAG Appendix includes additional advisory information pertinent to transient lodging facilities.

- A2.2   Equivalent Facilitation—9.1.4 and 9.2.2(6)(d)
- A4.5.3   Floor Surfaces—Carpet

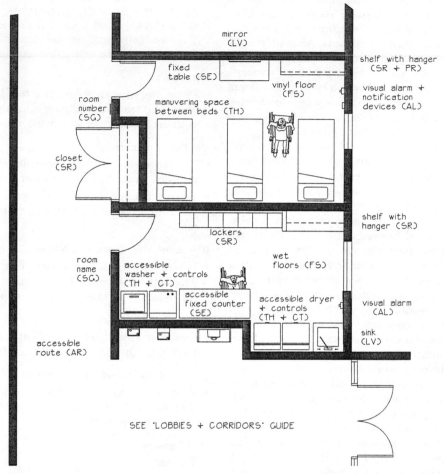

Figure 3-25. Transient lodging: Sleeping unit (social services establishment).

Sleeping Units (Social Services Establishments: Homeless Shelters, Halfway Houses, Transient Group Homes, and Others) Checklist

SIGNAGE

SG04	Room signage: criteria
SG05	Room signage: location

DOORS

DR04	Doors: maneuvering clearances
DR05	Doors: handle type
DR06	Doors: opening force (interior only)
DR07	Doors: closing speed
DR08	Doors: thresholds
DR09	Doors: clear width/height
DR10	Openings (no door): clear width/height

TRANSIENT LODGING: SOCIAL SERVICES SLEEPING UNITS

TH20	Sleeping rooms: number req'd (New)
TH21	Multibed rooms: number req'd (New)
TH22	Hearing-imp. rooms: number req'd (New)
TH23	Sleeping rooms (not homeless shelters): number req'd (Alt.)
TH24	Multibed rooms: number req'd (Alt.)
TH25	Hearing-imp. rooms: number req'd (Alt.)
TH26	Amenities: acc. and on acc. route
TH07	Sleeping unit: accessible route
TH08	Sleeping unit: linked accessible spaces
TH09	Sleeping unit: linked accessible elements
TH10	Sleeping unit: maneuv. space at beds/wall
TH16	Hearing-imp. unit: visual alarm req.
TH17	Hearing-imp. unit: visual alarms in all areas
TH18	Hearing-imp. units: visual notification device
TH19	Hearing-imp. units: telephone

ACCESSIBLE ROUTES

AR08	Route: clear width

PROTRUDING OBJECTS

PR01	Wall-mounted
PR03	Clear route width maintained
PR04	Overhead clearance
PR05	Vertical clearance: cane detection barrier

FLOOR SURFACES

FS01	Surface: firm, stable, and slip-resistant
FS02	Vertical changes in level
FS03	Carpet and tile floors

STORAGE

SR01	Accessibility: one of each type
SR02	Clear floor space
SR03	Reach ranges
SR04	Storage closets w/o passage: criteria
SR05	Storage hardware: operation

LAVATORIES, SINKS, AND MIRRORS

LV09	Mirror: mounting height

FIXED TABLES AND/OR COUNTERS

SE01	Fixed seating: number required
SE02	Wheelchairs: clear floor space at tables
SE03	Tables/counters: heights
SE04	Tables/counters: knee clearance criteria

CONTROLS AND OPERATING MECHANISMS

CT01	Clear floor space
CT02	Reach ranges: elec./comm. systems
CT03	Reach ranges: thermostats
CT04	Reach ranges: other controls
CT05	Reach ranges: life safety devices
CT06	Controls: operation

ALARMS

AL04	Visual alarms: integration w/building alarm
AL05	Visual alarms: operation
AL08	Visual alarms: vertical placement
AL11	Visual alarms: acc. living and sleeping units
AL12	Visual alarms: visible throughout unit

SLEEPING UNITS (SOCIAL SERVICES ESTABLISHMENTS: HOMELESS SHELTERS, HALFWAY HOUSES, TRANSIENT GROUP HOMES, AND OTHERS) COMPREHENSIVE CRITERIA

(SG) Signage (4.30)

NOTE:

- In historic buildings displays and written information, documents, etc., should be located where they can be seen by a seated person. Exhibits and signage displayed horizontally (e.g., open books) should be no higher than 44 in. above the floor surface. [4.1.7(3)(e)]

Signage: room identification (where provided)

DEFINITION:

- These signs designate permanent rooms and spaces.

AUTHOR'S INTERPRETATION:

- Signs that designate stairs, exit doors, and toilet rooms generally are associated with permanent spaces, while an "office" sign is not since the room function may change over time. Room numbers also must meet the ADAAG criteria as permanent designations, while personal names do not since the occupant may change over time.

SG-04 Do signs that designate permanent rooms and spaces comply with the following criteria? [4.1.2(7); 4.1.3(16); 4.30.4, 5, 6]

- Character type: raised and accompanied by Grade II Braille.

- Character size: between 5/8 in. and 2 in. high; raised at least 1/32 in.

- Character style: upper case, and sans or simple serif.

- Finish: characters and backgrounds have a nonglare finish.
- Contrast: characters contrast with their background (light-on-dark or dark-on-light).

SG-05 Is the room identification sign mounted in the required location? (4.30.6)

- Mounting location: installed on the wall adjacent to the latch side of the door or where wall space to the latch side of the door is not available, including double doors, placed on the nearest adjacent wall.
- Mounting height: 60 in. above the floor/ground to the centerline of the sign.
- Sign access: approach to within 3 in. of a sign without encountering protruding objects or standing within the swing of the door.

(DR) Doors (4.13)

NOTE:

- Included in this category are doors, revolving doors, turnstiles, and gates.

AUTHOR'S INTERPRETATION:

- It is suggested that, for purposes of documentation and review, a door be assigned to the space it swings into. Corridors are an exception to this rule and include only entry doors into the corridor or intermediate fire doors.

Doors: maneuvering clearance

DR-04 If the door is not automatic or power assisted, does it have the required maneuvering clearance provided on the push and pull side, and is the floor level and clear within the maneuvering area? (4.13.6)

- A verbal description cannot adequately describe the requirements. See ADAAG Fig. 25a–f for a graphic description.

EXCEPTION:

- Entry doors to acute care hospital bedrooms for inpatients are exempt from maneuvering space at the latch side of the door if the door is at least 44 in. wide.

AUTHOR'S INTERPRETATION:

- While ADAAG does not describe what elements can reduce the required maneuvering clearance, they could include a narrow entry alcove, an adjacent wall, railing, or permanently installed shelving, or a deep recessed door jamb.

Doors: hardware

DR-05 Do all door handles, locks, latches, or other operable devices meet required operational criteria? (4.13.9)

- Hardware operation: operable with one hand without tight grasping, pinching, or wrist twisting.
- Force required to operate the controls: not greater than 5 lbf. This does not apply to the force required to retract latch bolts or to disengage other devices that only hold the door in a closed position.
- Hardware type: "U"-shaped handles, levers, and push type mechanisms are acceptable designs.

- Hardware height: not greater than 48 in. above the floor.
- Sliding doors: hardware is exposed and usable from both sides when the doors are fully open.

Doors: opening force

DR-06 Do interior hinged doors and sliding or folding doors have an opening force of 5 lbf or less? (4.13.11)

- At present, no accessible criteria exist for exterior doors.
- Fire doors shall have the minimum opening force allowable by the appropriate administrative authority.

Doors: closing speed

DR-07 If the door has a closer, is the closer adjusted so that the door does not close too quickly? (4.13.10)

- From an open position of 70° the door will take at least 3 sec to move to a point 3 in. from the latch (measured to the leading edge of the door).

Doors: thresholds

DR-08 Where raised thresholds are provided, do they meet height limitations and are they beveled when required? (4.13.8, 4.5.2, Fig. 7)

- Threshold height: not more than 3/4 in. for exterior sliding doors or 1/2 in. for other types of doors.
- Threshold bevel: thresholds less than 1/4 in. high need no bevel; thresholds between 1/4 in. and 1/2 in. high shall be beveled at each edge with not more than a 1:2 slope.

EXCEPTION:

- A 3/4-in. high threshold is allowed in existing conditions. [4.1.6(3)(d)(ii)]

Doors: clear opening width and height

DR-09 Is the clear opening for the doorway adequate in width and height? (4.13.3, 4, 5; Fig. 24)

- Door width: at least 32 in. of clear width with the door open at 90°, measured between the face of the door and the door stop on the latch side. This also pertains to the active leaf of a double-leaf door or gate.
- Opening width: openings more than 24 in. deep must provide 36 in. of clear width.
- Height: at least 80 in. of vertical clearance.

EXCEPTIONS:

- Doors not requiring full user passage, such as shallow closets, may have the clear opening reduced to not less than 20 in.
- Where it is technically infeasible to comply with clear opening width requirements, a projection of 5/8 in. maximum will be permitted for the latch side. [4.1.6(d)(i)]

DR-10 Is the clear opening (when there is no door) adequate in width and height? (4.2.1, 4.3.3, 4.4.2)

- Width: at least 32 in. of clear width for depths 24 in. or less and at least 36 in. of clear width for depths greater than 24 in.
- Height: at least 80 in. of vertical clearance.

(TH) Accessible Transient Lodging (9.0)
(Homeless Shelters, Halfway Houses, Transient Group Homes, and Other Social Services Establishments)

NOTE:

- Transient lodging is divided into two categories:
  - Hotels, motels, inns, boarding houses, dormitories, and similar places (TH-01 through TH-19).
  - Homeless shelters, halfway houses, transient group homes, and other social services establishments (TH-20 through TH-26 and TH-07 through TH-19).
- Doors and doorways designed to allow passage into and within all transient lodging sleeping units shall comply with accessible door width criteria. This applies to every sleeping unit in the facility, whether it is designated as accessible or not. (9.4)

AUTHOR'S INTERPRETATION:

- Accessible units, sleeping rooms, and suites are divided into two categories: fully accessible and hearing-impaired. Fully accessible units, sleeping rooms, and suites must comply with accessible criteria for both mobility and hearing impairments. (9.2.8) Hearing-impaired units must comply only with those accessible criteria that relate to visual alarms, notification devices, and telephones. (9.3)
- The total number of accessible units required by ADAAG can be easily misinterpreted if not carefully read. For example, the total number of rooms in social services required for 76–100 sleeping rooms is 8, broken down as follows:
  - Four fully accessible rooms with accessible bathrooms.
  - Four rooms for the hearing-impaired (other accessible criteria are not required including an accessible bathroom).
- In facilities where bath facilities are multiple user and separate from the sleeping room or multibed rooms, the minimum number of accessible tubs or showers required is not clearly prescribed. ADAAG 4.23.8, which indicates a minimum of at least one accessible tub or shower (when provided) in bathrooms, appears to be applicable to this situation.

Accessible Transient Lodging/S.S.: number required/ new construction

TH-20 Is the required number of accessible sleeping rooms provided? (9.5.3, 9.1.2)

- Accessible rooms: 1 per 1–25, 2 per 26–50, 3 per 51–75, 4 per 76–100, 5 per 101–150, 6 per 151–200, 7 per 201–300, 8 per 301–400, 9 per 401–500, and 501–1000 is 2 percent of total.
- For more than 1000 rooms, 20 accessible rooms plus 1 for each 100 over 1000.

TH-21 In facilities with multibed sleeping rooms or spaces, is the required number of accessible beds provided? (9.5.3, 9.1.2)

- Accessible beds: 1 per 1–25, 2 per 26–50, 3 per 51–75, 4 per 76–100, 5 per 101–150, 6 per 151–200, 7 per 201–300, 8 per 301–400, 9 per 401–500, and 501–1000 is 2 percent of total.
- For more than 1000 beds, 20 accessible beds plus 1 for each 100 over 1000.

TH-22 In addition to accessible rooms required for mobility disabilities, is the required number of sleeping rooms also provided that meet accessibility requirements for the hearing-impaired? (9.1.3)

- Accessible rooms: 1 per 1–25, 2 per 26–50, 3 per 51–75, 4 per 76–100, 5 per 101–150, 6 per 151–200, 7 per 201–300, 8 per 301–400, 9 per 401–500, and 501–1000 is 2 percent of total.
- For more than 1000 rooms, 20 accessible rooms plus 1 for each 100 over 1000.

Accessible Transient Lodging/S.S.: number required/alterations

TH-23 In alterations to social service establishments that are not homeless shelters, is at least one accessible sleeping room provided for each 25 altered rooms (or portion thereof) until the number equals that in TH-20 or TH-21? [9.5.2(1), 9.5.3, 9.1.5]

TH-24 In alterations to homeless shelters where sleeping rooms are provided, is at least one accessible sleeping room provided for each 25 altered rooms (or portion thereof) until the number equals that in TH-20 or TH-21? [9.5.2(1), 9.5.3, 9.1.5]

TH-25 In addition, when sleeping rooms are altered, is at least one accessible room or suite provided for each 25 altered rooms (or portion thereof) until the number equals that in TH-22 that meets accessibility requirements for the hearing-impaired? (9.1.5)

Accessible Transient Lodging/S.S.: amenities

TH-26 Is at least one of each type of amenity (e.g., washer, dryer, and similar equipment) in each common area accessible and located on an accessible route to any accessible sleeping room? (9.5.1)

EXCEPTION:

- Where a building is exempt from the elevator requirement, accessible amenities are not required on inaccessible floors as long as one of each type is provided in common areas on accessible floors.

Accessible Transient Lodging/S.S.: accessible routes

NOTE:

- The following questions are the same as those found in accessible transient lodging for hotels.

TH-07 Are accessible sleeping rooms or suites located on an accessible route? (9.5.3, 9.2.2)

TH-08 Does an accessible route connect all accessible spaces within the accessible unit? [9.5.3; 9.2.2(2, 6, 7)]

- Where provided, this includes the living area, the dining area, a dual occupancy sleeping area, patio or balcony, a full bathroom or half bath (if only half baths are provided), kitchen (also kitchenette or wet bar), and parking space.

NOTE:

- Elevators are not required in a multilevel unit if the previously listed spaces are all on the accessible level and the accessible sleeping area is suitable for dual occupancy.

EXCEPTION:

- The requirements of thresholds at doors (4.13.8) and changes in levels (4.3.8) do not apply where it is necessary to utilize a higher door threshold or a change in level to protect the integrity of the unit from wind/water damage. Where this exception results in patios, terraces or balconies that are not at an accessible level, equivalent facilitation shall be provided (e.g., equivalent facilitation at a hotel patio or balcony might consist of providing raised decking or a ramp to provide accessibility).

TH-09 Does the accessible route connect all accessible elements within the accessible unit? [9.2.2(3, 4, 5)]

- Accessible elements would include doors and doorways, storage (accessible, fixed, or built-in), controls and operating mechanisms, and telephones.

Accessible Transient Lodging/S.S.: sleeping rooms

NOTE:

- The following questions are the same as those found in accessible transient lodging for hotels.

TH-10 Does the accessible sleeping room provide clear width for maneuvering along or between fixed, built-in, or movable beds? [9.5.3, 9.2.2(1)]

- Width:
  - 36 in. clear width maneuvering space along both sides of a fixed or built-in bed;
  - or 36 in. clear width maneuvering space along either side of a movable bed;
  - or 36 in. clear width maneuvering space between two fixed beds.

Accessible Transient Lodging/S.S.: hearing-impaired rooms

NOTE:

- The following questions are the same as those found in accessible transient lodging for hotels.

TH-16 Do accessible living units and sleeping accommodations comply with the requirements for visual alarms? (9.5.3, 9.3, 4.28.4)

- Visual alarms meet required operational criteria.
- Visual alarms connect to the building emergency alarm system.
- Or a standard electrical outlet is provided and connected to the facility's central alarm system which enables room occupants to utilize portable devices provided by the operator of the facility.

TH-17 Is the signal from the visual alarm visible in all areas of the living unit or room? (9.5.3, 9.3, 4.28.4)

TH-18 Do the living units and sleeping rooms comply with the requirements for visual notification devices? (9.5.3, 9.3.1)

- This includes any space where the occupant would expect to be able to hear a phone or door bell.
- Visual notification devices are to alert the occupant of incoming telephone calls and a door knock or bell.
- This device must *not* be connected to the visual alarm system.

TH-19 Do the living units and sleeping rooms comply with the requirements for telephones? (9.5.3, 9.3.1)

- If provided, permanently installed (hardwired) telephones should have volume controls capable of a minimum of 12 dbA and a maximum of 18 dbA above normal. If an automatic reset is provided, then 18 dbA may be exceeded.
- Outlets: An accessible electrical outlet is within 4 ft of a telephone connection, where provided.

(AR) Accessible Routes (4.3)

NOTES:

- All walks, halls, corridors, aisles, skywalks, tunnels, and other spaces that are part of a designated accessible route shall comply with accessible requirements.
- The accessible route shall, to the maximum extent feasible, coincide with the route for the general public.

AUTHOR'S INTERPRETATION:

- An accessible route "generally coincides" with the route used by the public if:
  - It does not force the user to go out of the way.
  - It is most like the route chosen by the general public.
  - It is direct.
  - It gives the same basic experience as the route preferred by the public.

Accessible Routes: width

AR-08 Is the minimum clear width along the accessible route adequate for continuous or point passage? (4.2.1, 4.3.3, Fig. 1, Fig. 8e, Fig. 24e)

- Continuous passage (greater than 24 in. long): at least a 36-in. clear width.
- Point passage (not more than 24 in. long): at least a 32-in. clear width.

AUTHOR'S INTERPRETATION:

- Noncompliance with this question generally relates to permanent elements that encroach on the accessible route. Large, heavy equipment that is not readily movable might be considered permanent. If the space is designed so that temporary elements (such as bikes in a bike rack or car bumpers) will consistently encroach, the situation might also be considered a permanent barrier.

(PR) Protruding Objects (4.4)

Protruding Objects: general

PR-01 Do wall-mounted objects having leading edges between 27 in. and 80 in. high project less than 4 in. into walkways, corridors, aisles, or paths of travel? (4.4.1, Fig. 8a–e)

- Objects mounted with their leading edge at or below 27 in. can protrude any amount, as long as they do not reduce the required clear width of an accessible route.

AUTHOR'S INTERPRETATION:

- Protruding objects might include fire extinguishers or cabinets, pencil sharpeners, shelving, counters, built-in equipment overhangs, or various dispensers such as for paper towels or soap.

PR-03 Is the minimum clear route width or maneuvering space still maintained even with the projection of a protruding object? (4.4.1, Fig. 8a–e)

Protruding Objects: overhead clearance

PR-04 Is the minimum overhead clearance of 80 in. provided in accessible areas or along accessible routes? (4.4.2, Fig. 8a)

AUTHOR'S INTERPRETATION:

- Overhead objects that can reduce the required clearance might include structures, pipes, ducts, or light fixtures.

PR-05 Where the vertical clearance of a space adjoining the accessible route is less than 80 in. high, is a cane detection barrier less than 27 in. from the floor provided for blind or visually impaired persons? (4.4.2, Fig. 8c-1)

AUTHOR'S INTERPRETATION:

- This condition might be found under a stair, at a sloped ceiling space, or with guy wires from telephone poles along an exterior accessible route.

(FS) Floor and Ground Surfaces (4.5)

Floor Surfaces: general

FS-01 Are the floor/ground surfaces on the accessible route stable, firm, and slip-resistant? (4.5.1)

AUTHOR'S INTERPRETATION:

- Exterior spaces, interior circulation, bathrooms, and other spaces where water can collect on the floor around an element (sinks, drinking fountains, hose bibbs, etc.) are reviewed as if wet.
- High gloss surfaces without significant textures that are regularly maintained with waxing (smooth tiles, waxed concrete, etc.) could be considered noncompliant.
- Accessible criteria are not specified for nonpermanent floor surfaces such as mats or rugs.

Floor Surfaces: changes in level

FS-02 Are vertical changes in level between 1/4 in. and 1/2 in. beveled with a slope of 1:2 or less? (4.5.2)

- Changes in level up to 1/4 in. may be vertical without edge treatment.
- Changes in level greater than 1/2 in. should be accomplished by means of a curb ramp, ramp, elevator, or platform lift (as permitted in ADAAG 4.1.3 and 4.1.6).

Floor Surfaces: carpet

FS-03 Does carpet or carpet tile used on the floor comply with accessible criteria? (4.5.3, Fig. 8f)

- Attachment: secured.

- Exposed edges: fastened and trimmed along the entire length.
- Pile type: low pile (1/2 in. maximum).
- Padding: firm pad or no pad underneath.

(SR) Storage (4.25)

NOTE:

- Accessible reach range requirements do not apply to shelves or display units allowing self-service by customers in mercantile occupancies but they must be located on an accessible route. [4.1.3(12)(b)]

Storage: general

SR-01 Does at least one of each type of fixed or built-in storage unit comply with accessible criteria? [4.1.3(12)(a), 4.25.1]

NOTE:

- Types of storage facilities might include cabinets, shelves, closets, and drawers.

Storage: clear floor space

SR-02 Is there a clear floor space at least 30 in. × 48 in. at fixed or built-in storage units that allows for either a forward or side approach? (4.25.2, Fig. 4a–b)

Storage: reach ranges

SR-03 Are forward or side reach for each type of accessible storage unit within acceptable reach ranges? (4.2.5–6, Fig. 5a–b, Fig. 6a–c, 4.25.3)

- Forward reach: not less than 15 in. high and not more than 48 in. high without any obstruction or where the obstruction is less than 20 in. deep. For obstructions from 20 in. to 25 in. deep, no forward reach higher than 44 in.
- Side reach: not less than 9 in. high and not more than 54 in. high. For obstructions not more than 34 in. high or 24 in. deep, no side reach higher than 46 in.

SR-04 In a closet where passage is not required to access storage (e.g., door opening is less than 32 in.), are the clothes rod or shelves within required reach ranges? (4.25.3, Fig. 38a–b)

- Door width: at least 20 in. (4.13.5)
- Horizontal reach: not more than 21 in. from the opening.
- Rod reach: if over 10 in. deep, then not more than 48 in. high.
- Shelf reach: if over 10 in. deep, then not more than 48 in. high or less than 9 in. high.

Storage: hardware

SR-05 Is the hardware on the storage unit doors or drawers operable with one hand without tight grasping, pinching, or wrist twisting, and requiring no more than 5 lbf of force? (4.25.4, 4.27.4)

(LV) Lavatories, Sinks, and Mirrors (4.19, 4.24)

Lavatories or Sinks: mirrors

LV-09 Where mirrors are provided, does at least one mirror have a bottom edge of the reflecting surface no higher than 40 in. above the floor? (4.19.6, Fig. 31)

AUTHOR'S INTERPRETATION:

- Slanted mirrors located above 40 in. are not recognized as compliant by the ADAAG.

(SE) Fixed or Built-in Seating and Tables (4.32)

Fixed or Built-in Seating and Tables: minimum number

SE-01 Is the minimum number of accessible wheelchair seating locations at fixed tables or counters provided? (4.1.3.18)

- Number required: 5 percent of total number of seats but not fewer than one.

Fixed or Built-in Seating and Tables: clear floor space

AUTHOR'S INTERPRETATION:

- Where the accessible route leads to and through accessible seating adjacent to a wall or another table, the minimum required width for the accessible route will be 65 in. between the table edge and next parallel surface (e.g., wall or another table edge). (4.1.3.18, Fig. 45)

SE-02 Is the clear floor space for a wheelchair at a seating location adequate? (4.32.3, Fig. 4a, Fig. 45)

- Clear floor space: 30 in. × 48 in.
- This clear space can include up to 19 in. under the table/desk.

Fixed or Built-in Seating and Tables: clearances

SE-03 Are the tops of accessible tables and counters between 28 in. and 34 in. from the floor? (4.32.3, Fig. 45)

SE-04 Are the knee clearances at least 27 in. high, 30 in. wide, and 19 in. deep? (4.32.3, Fig. 45)

(CT) Controls and Operating Mechanisms (4.27)

NOTES:

- Controls or operating mechanisms can include elements such as light switches, pencil sharpeners, manual overhead screens, nonkeyed thermostats, alarm pull stations, fire extinguisher cabinets, A/C window units, microwave ovens, towel dispensers, and wall hooks.
- If controls are to be operated by occupants of the space, they must be accessible. If controls are to be operated by maintenance staff only and not by occupants or other users of the space, they do not have to be accessible. For example, thermostats in auditoriums usually do not have to be accessible, while thermostats in classrooms may need to be accessible.

Controls: clear floor space

CT-01 Is a clear floor space of at least 30 in. × 48 in. provided in front of controls, dispensers, receptacles, and other operable equipment for forward or parallel approach? (4.27.2, Fig. 4a–b)

Controls: reach ranges

NOTES:

- Accessible reach ranges for controls and operating mechanisms are:
  - Forward reach: not less than 15 in. high and not more than 48 in. high without any obstruction or where the obstruction is less than 20 in. deep. For obstructions from 20 in. to 25 in. deep, no forward reach higher than 44 in.
  - Side reach: not less than 9 in. high and not more than 54 in. high. For obstructions not more than 34 in. high or 24 in. deep, no side reach higher than 46 in.
  - Electrical outlets, switches, and communication system receptacles have a minimum outlet height of 15 in. regardless of forward or side reach. See CT-02 below.

CT-02 Are electrical outlets, switches, and communication system receptacles mounted within accessible forward or side reach ranges? (4.27.3)

EXCEPTION:

- These requirements do not apply where the use of special equipment dictates otherwise or where electrical and communications system receptacles are not normally intended for use by building occupants. (4.27.3)

CT-03 Are thermostats or other similar operable equipment mounted within accessible forward or side reach ranges? (4.2.5, 4.2.6, Fig. 5a–b, Fig. 6a–c)

CT-04 Are dispensers or other similar operable equipment mounted within accessible forward or side reach ranges? (4.2.5, 4.2.6, Fig. 5a–b, Fig. 6a–c)

CT-05 Are life safety devices or other similar operable equipment mounted within accessible forward or side reach ranges? (4.2.5, 4.2.6, Fig. 5a–b, Fig. 6a–c)

NOTE:

- This might include fire alarm pull stations, handles to extinguisher cabinets, or wall-mounted extinguishers.

Controls: operation

CT-06 Are controls, dispensers, receptacles, and other operable equipment operable with one hand without tight grasping, pinching, or wrist twisting, and requiring no more than 5 lbf of force? (4.27.4)

(AL) Alarms (4.28)

NOTE:

- At a minimum, visual signal appliances shall be provided in buildings and facilities in restrooms and any other general usage areas. **The ADAAG does not define the number of occupants needed to establish a general or common use area.**

ALLOWANCE:

- Emergency warning systems in medical care facilities may be modified to suit standard health care alarm design practice. [4.1.3(14)]

Visual Alarms: general

AL-04 If provided, are the visual alarm signal appliances integrated into the building or facility alarm system? (4.28.3)

AL-05 If provided, do the visual alarm signals meet required operational criteria? [4.28.3(1, 2, 3, 4, 5)]

- Lamp: xenon strobe type or equivalent.

- Color: clear or nominal white (i.e., unfiltered or clear filtered white light).
- Pulse duration: maximum shall be 0.2 sec with a maximum duty cycle of 40 percent.
- Intensity: not less than 75 candela.
- Flash rate: not less than 1 Hz and not more than 3 Hz.

AL-08 Are the visual alarms placed at 80 in. above the highest floor level or 6 in. below the ceiling, whichever is lower? [4.28.3(6)]

Visual Alarms: living units

AL-11 Do accessible living units and sleeping accommodations have a visual alarm connected to the building emergency alarm system or have a standard 110-volt electrical receptacle into which such an alarm can be connected, and a means by which a signal from the building emergency alarm system can trigger such an auxiliary alarm? (4.28.4)

AL-12 Is the signal from the visual alarm visible in all areas of the living unit or room? (4.28.4)

Transportation Facilities are divided into three separate "Space-type Review Guides."

- Bus Stops (TF-01 through TF-06).
- Airports (TF-07 through TF-19).
- Fixed Facilities, Terminals, and Stations (TF-20 through TF-69).

Boat and ferry docks are reserved as of the publication of this book.

Transportation facilities have very specific requirements that are unique to these spaces. Escalators, people movers, public address systems, and clocks are not mentioned elsewhere in ADAAG. Baggage check in and retrieval will rarely be found outside transportation facilities. Some common elements and issues have different and/or additional requirements if in a transportation facility (e.g., vertical changes, number of accessible entrances, telephones, signage). Detectable warnings have not been suspended at platform edges. Elevators, if provided, are not exempt from typical exceptions and include additional criteria. A very careful reading of Section 10 of ADAAG is recommended before using these guides.

Transportation facilities vary significantly—from a bus shelter to a small one-gate commuter airport to complex urban developments involving many transportation modes and services. It is necessary that the transportation facilities review guides be used in conjunction with other review guides. In most cases, the transportation facilities review guides will be supplements that address only the issues associated with transportation facilities. For example, ticketing often occurs in a lobby space; refer to "Lobbies, Corridors, and Interior Accessible Routes" as well as the appropriate transportation facility "Space-type Review Guide." When evaluating a boarding platform, use an accessible route review guide (interior or exterior as appropriate), because ADAAG's criteria for boarding areas reflect only where compliance differs from general accessibility. A space may encompass several different space-types at once. Newsstands, snack bars, and small retail areas are commonly found adjacent to or within passenger boarding areas.

The "Building" review guide will be necessary in many cases. Refer to other "Space-type Review Guides" as needed for associated common use spaces such as dining facilities, rest rooms, exterior passenger loading zones, offices, etc. Because of their location in a transportation facility, these spaces may have to meet compliance criteria above their general requirements. If, for example, public address systems or other information systems are audible or visible in rest rooms or dining areas, they too must meet Section 10 requirements for equivalent facilitation.

Airports

Introduction. This particular "Space-type Review Guide" addresses airports only, and it only covers specific criteria unique to these facilities. These include ticketing areas, baggage check in and retrieval areas, and other elements found in airports. ADAAG includes airport criteria for new construction only. Accessibility concerns for existing facilities must comply with all typical ADAAG criteria (routes, reach ranges, protruding objects, business and mercantile, etc.). However, for the following transportation issues, existing airports may be addressed on a case by case basis.

This review guide must be used in conjunction with other "Space-type Review Guides." For example, baggage retrieval, ticketing, and baggage check in usually occur in lobby areas; consequently, refer to "Lobbies, Corridors, and Interior Accessible Routes" to complete the evaluation of those spaces. It may be necessary to refer to additional guides or to the "Master Guidelines" if waiting areas, car rental booths, and other retail areas are in the space. Associated common use spaces such as restaurants, rest rooms, exterior passenger loading zones, etc., may need to be evaluated using this review guide. For example, if public address systems are provided in rest rooms, dining facilities, etc., equivalent facilitation may need be required in these spaces. Combine the appropriate review guides as needed.

Equivalent facilitation and access in all aspects of the operation of the facility must be considered, including, but not limited to, ticketing, entrance and egress from all public spaces, baggage check in and retrieval, terminal information systems, signage, clocks, and public telephones. If provided, drinking fountains, ATMs, and other elements must meet accessibility requirements. Refer to the "Master Guidelines" as needed.

The general concerns of accessible routes apply to these facilities. Universal or barrier-free access throughout the facility may not be feasible; therefore, the accessible routes (as well as accessible spaces and elements) must be identified. The distances that users must negotiate should be minimized, and, as much as possible, the routes should coincide with those used by the general public. If the accessible route and/or entrance must be different, compliant directional signage must be provided. Although accessibility for escalators and people movers is not specifically mandated under ADAAG 10.4, "Airports," their criteria are given in ADAAG 10.3, "Fixed Facilities and Stations." Making all escalators and people movers accessible should be considered. ADAAG does not give any specific criteria for compliant boarding or exiting of planes.

Many airports include rail systems as part of the public circulation system. Refer to "Transportation Facilities: Fixed Facilities, Terminals, and Stations" as needed. If buses are part of the circulation system (internal or as part of a citywide system), refer to "Transportation Facilities: Bus Stops."

Terminal information systems (public address systems, visual paging, etc.) must provide the same or equivalent information to the hearing-impaired. Clocks, if provided, must meet specific criteria as to placement and legibility.

Security systems were reserved at the time of publication. However, if unattended security barriers are used, at least one accessible gate must be provided. If turnstiles, gates, revolving doors, etc., are used, an accessible alternative must be provided. If gates are not automatic (i.e., the user must push against it to open it), there are criteria governing the surface of the gate.

The number and type of accessible seating for this space-type is not clearly defined in ADAAG. However, the "Assembly Areas" and "Fixed Tables and Seating" sections of the "Master Guidelines" can serve as guides. Consider seating in waiting areas, gate boarding areas, lobbies, and other public seating areas. Many airports place the ISA symbol over seats closest to the boarding gate to serve users with certain mobility and/or stamina impairments. For chair users, provide clear floor space that is distributed throughout the seating area and adjacent to companion seating.

PRELIMINARY DESIGN OVERVIEW

This is an overview of compliance issues associated specifically with airports. Refer to other review guides as appropriate (e.g., "Lobbies, Corridors, and Interior Accessible Routes"; "Toilet Rooms"; "Business and Mercantile"; "Office"; "Restaurants and Cafeterias"; etc.).

(AL) Alarms
- Typical requirements.

(AR) Accessible Routes
- Maneuvering space problems include ticketing areas, kiosks, roped-off waiting lanes, baggage check in and retrieval, security gates, bollards, and turnstiles.
- Route surfaces must meet criteria for vertical changes in level. Problem areas include transition between materials and docking facilities that connect waiting areas with the plane. ADAAG does not provide accessibility criteria for boarding or disembarking from airplanes.
- Provide access and clear floor space to ticketing, telephones, baggage check in and retrieval, and lockers (if provided to the general public).
- If the accessible route must be different from that of the general public, compliant directional signage must be provided.
- A number of transportation modes may be provided. People movers and escalator criteria are given in ADAAG 10.3, "Fixed Facilities and Stations"; refer to "Transportation Facilities: Fixed Facilities and Stations." If bus stops are provided, see "Transportation Facilities: Bus Stops."

(AA) Assembly Areas
- The minimum number of wheelchair locations in facilities with fixed seating is determined by using ADAAG table 4.1.3(19)(a). Consider waiting areas, lobbies, and other areas with fixed seating.

(BM) Business and Mercantile
- Ticketing areas must be compliant. Also consider any auxiliary areas such as newsstands, food courts, gift shops, car rental booths, etc.

(DR) Doors
- Revolving doors or turnstiles require an adjacent accessible door, gate, or opening.
- Unattended security barriers must provide at least one compliant gate.
- In transportation facilities, nonautomatic gates that must be pushed open by the user have specific requirements.

(DW) Detectable Warnings
- Detectable warnings are currently suspended except for platform edges in new and altered rapid, light, commuter, and inner-city rail stations. Additionally, key rapid, light and commuter rail stations and all inner-city rail stations must install detectable warnings where platform edges are not otherwise protected by screens or guardrails. (As of April 24, 1994 to July 26, 1996.)

(EL) Elevators
- The exceptions for both new construction and alterations do not apply in transportation facilities.
- Placement must minimize the distance that users must travel. Their path of travel should not be longer than that of the general public.

(SE) Fixed or Built-in Seating and Tables and/or Counters
- The minimum number of wheelchair locations in facilities with fixed seating but no fixed writing surface (tables, counters, folding arms, etc.) may be determined by using the ADAAG table 4.1.3(19)(a). For seating with fixed surfaces, a minimum of 5 percent of the total number but not fewer than one of either type must be accessible.

(TL) Public Telephones
- If public pay telephones are provided (and at least one is located in the interior), at least one compliant public text telephone must be provided.
- If four or more interior public phones are provided at certain areas (main terminal outside security areas, concourse within security areas, or baggage claim), at least one public text telephone must be provided at that location.

(SG) Signage
- Compliant directional signage must be provided if the accessible route differs from that used by the general public.

(SR) Fixed Storage, Closets, Lockers, and Shelves
- Typical requirements.

(TF) Transportation Facilities (Airports)

- Information systems providing information to the general public must provide the same or equivalent information to the disabled.
- If provided, clocks must meet accessibility criteria for placement and legibility.

ADAAG APPENDIX

The ADAAG Appendix includes additional advisory information pertinent to this space-type:

- A10.3 Fixed Facilities and Stations

Airports Checklist

This supplemental review guide contains only the ADAAG criteria that are specific to airports. Refer to the appropriate "Space-type Review Guides" (such as "Lobbies, Corridors, and Interior Accessible Routes"; "Business and Mercantile," etc.) to complete evaluation of these spaces.

TRANSPORTATION FACILITIES (AIRPORTS)

TF07	Distance traveled: minimize
TF08	Acc. circulation: coincide w/general public
TF09	Acc. route signage: criteria

TF10	Accessible ticket and baggage check in
TF11	Ticketing counter: criteria
TF12	Bag check in/retrieval: on acc. route
TF13	Bag check in/retrieval: clear floor space
TF14	Unattended security barriers: acc. gate
TF15	Acc. gate: criteria
TF16	Text telephones: minimum number
TF17	Text telephones: location
TF18	Public address systems: equiv. facilitation
TF19	Clocks: criteria

AIRPORTS
COMPREHENSIVE CRITERIA

This supplemental review guide addresses issues specifically described only for airports. Other review guides ("Lobbies, Corridors, and Interior Accessible Routes"; "Business and Mercantile"; etc.) must be used with this guide for complete evaluation of the entire building.

(TF) Transportation Facilities (10.0)

NOT EXEMPT:

- The exception for elevators in facilities that are less than three stories or that have less than 3000 ft² per story [4.1.3(5) Exception 1 and 4.1.6 (1)(k)] *do not* apply to a terminal, depot, or other station used for specified public transportation, an airport passenger terminal, or facilities subject to Title II.

Transportation Facilities/Airports: circulation

TF-07 Are elements such as ramps, elevators, or other circulation devices, ticketing areas, security checkpoints, or passenger waiting areas placed so as to minimize the distance that wheelchair users and other persons who cannot negotiate steps must travel, as compared to the general public? [10.4, 10.4.1(1)]

TF-08 To the maximum extent practicable, does the circulation path, including an accessible entrance and an accessible route, coincide with the circulation path for the general public? [10.4.1(2)]

TF-09 Where the accessible circulation path is different from that of the general public, does directional signage indicate the location of the nearest accessible entrance and accessible route, and does it meet applicable directional signage criteria? [10.4.1(2)]

Transportation Facilities/Airports: ticketing areas

TF-10 Are ticketing areas designed in such a way that persons with disabilities can obtain tickets and check baggage? [10.4.1(3)]

TF-11 Are ticketing counters provided with a portion of the main counter at least 36 in. long and not more than 36 in. high? [10.4.1(3), 7.2.2]

- Equivalent facilitation may be provided by:
  - an auxiliary counter with a maximum height of 36 in., located in close proximity to the main counter; or
  - a folding shelf attached to the main counter that provides a writing surface for individuals with disabilities; or
  - a space provided on the side of the counter or desk that allows materials to be passed back and forth.

Transportation Facilities/Airports: baggage check in and retrieval

TF-12 Are baggage check in and retrieval systems on an accessible route? [10.4.1(5)]

TF-13 Is a clear floor space at least 30 in. × 48 in. provided in the space immediately adjacent for parallel or forward approach? [10.4.1(5)]

Transportation Facilities/Airports: terminal gates

TF-14 Where unattended security barriers are provided, is an accessible gate provided? [10.4.1(5)]

- Accessible gates must meet accessible door criteria.

TF-15 If gates must be pushed open by wheelchair or mobility aid users, do they have a smooth, continuous surface extending from 2 in. above the floor to at least 27 in. above the floor? [10.4.1(5)]

Transportation Facilities/Airports: text telephones

TF-16 Where public pay telephones are provided at an interior location, is at least one interior public text telephone provided? [10.4.1(4), 4.31.9]

TF-17 If at least four or more public pay telephones are located in any of the areas identified below, is at least one public text telephone provided in that location? [10.4.1(4)]

- Locations: a main terminal outside the security area; a concourse within the security areas; or a baggage claim area in a terminal.
- These telephones are in addition to TF-16.

Transportation Facilities/Airports: public address system

TF-18 Where terminal information systems broadcast information to the general public through a public address system, is there a way to provide the same or equivalent information to persons with hearing impairments? [10.4.1(6)]

AUTHOR'S INTERPRETATION:

- Acceptable solutions might include a visual paging system or an Assistive Listening System.

Transportation Facilities/Airports: clocks

TF-19 If clocks are provided for use by the public, do they comply with accessible criteria? [10.4.1(7)]

- Clock faces are uncluttered, resulting in elements that are clearly visible.
- Hands, numerals, and/or digits contrast with the background.
- Where clocks are mounted overhead, the numerals and/or digits are at least 3 in. high.
- Clocks are placed in uniform locations throughout the facility to the maximum extent practicable.

Bus Stops

Introduction. Use this review guide to evaluate bus stops, bus shelters, and other areas where passengers board and alight from buses. These spaces usually occur in conjunction with an exterior accessible route or parking lot. Refer to the appropriate "Space-type Review Guides" as necessary to complete the evaluation of the entire space. Bus stations and terminals should be reviewed using "Fixed Facilities, Terminals, and Stations" review guide.

Bus stop pads have specific criteria concerning slope, stability, and clear floor space. The minimum clear space is different from that of most other spaces. In addition, the orientation of the pad to the roadway is important. Positive drainage may be problematic given the slight slope allowed.

Obviously, bus stops and shelters must connect to an accessible route in the public way. Such shelters must not encroach on the clear width of the accessible route. Protruding objects (route brochure racks, signage, mounted trash cans, etc.) and low roof overhangs are often overlooked.

Bus schedules, timetables, or maps posted at bus stops or bays are not required to be compliant. Bus route identification signage is required to meet criteria for finish and contrast, and, to the maximum extent practicable, to meet signage criteria for character. Other local, state, or federal regulations concerning maximum size may impact accessibility compliance.

PRELIMINARY DESIGN OVERVIEW

This is an overview of compliance issues associated with bus stops, bus stop pads, and bus shelters only. As they are elements and/or spaces generally associated with accessible routes, passenger loading zones, or parking lots, refer to those review guides as appropriate.

(PR) Protruding Objects

- Common wall-mounted elements can be protruding objects, e.g., signs, display cases, brochure dispensers.

- Overhead clearances can be an unforeseen compliance problem, e.g., signs and banners, low ceilings, utility guy wires, etc.

(SE) Fixed or Built-in Seating and Tables and/or Counters

- If fixed seating is provided, a minimum of 5 percent of the total number but not fewer than one must be accessible.

(SR) Fixed Storage, Closets, Lockers, and Shelves

- Frequently overlooked storage units include racks or dispensers for bus schedules, route information, and maps.

(TF) Transportation Facilities (Bus Stops)

- An accessible route must connect the bus stop pad to streets, sidewalks, and pedestrian paths.
- The bus stop pad must be compliant in surface and, to the extent practicable, width and length. A slight maximum slope is allowed for drainage. Note dimensional criteria and positioning of the pad.
- If covered shelter is provided, minimum clear floor space must be provided entirely within the perimeter of the shelter. It must be accessed from the public way and connect to the boarding area by an accessible route. If fixed seating is provided, consider how this clear floor space relates to it.
- The bus stop floor surface must be firm, stable, and slip-resistant. Evaluate as if wet.
- Where provided, all new and replaced route identification signs must be compliant in finish and contrast, and, to the maximum extent practicable, in character proportion and height. Posted bus schedules, timetables, and maps are an exception.

Bus Stops Checklist

TRANSPORTATION FACILITIES

TF01	Bus stop pad: on accessible route
TF02	Bus stop pad: slope and surface criteria
TF03	Bus stop pad: size
TF04	Bus shelters: clear floor space/route to boarding area

TF05	Bus stop signs: lettering
TF06	Bus stop signs not protruding objects

Refer to **SE**, **ST**, **PR**, and other sections as necessary.

BUS STOPS
COMPREHENSIVE CRITERIA

Any element not found on this review guide but necessary to complete the evaluation of the site should be selected from the "Master Guidelines." These may include fixed seating, protruding objects, storage, etc.

(TF) Transportation Facilities (10.0)
(Bus Stops and Terminals)

Transportation Facilities/Bus Stops: bus stop pad

TF-01 Is the bus stop pad connected to streets, sidewalks, or pedestrian paths by an accessible route? [10.2.1(1)]

TF-02 Does the surface of the bus stop pad comply with accessible criteria? [10.2.1(1)]

- Pad surface: firm and stable.
- Pad slope: slope is parallel to the roadway and, to the extent feasible, the same as that of the roadway.

NOTE:

- A maximum slope of 1:50 perpendicular to the roadway is allowed for water drainage.

TF-03 Do the dimensions of the bus stop pad comply with accessible criteria? [10.2.1(1)]

- Length: at least 96 in. (measured perpendicular to the curb or vehicle roadway).
- Width: at least 60 in. (measured parallel to the vehicle roadway).

NOTE:

- Both of the preceding dimensions should comply to the maximum extent as allowed by legal or site constraints (e.g., a retaining wall or adjacent building).

Transportation Facilities/Bus Stops: bus shelters

TF-04 Does the bus stop shelter comply with accessible criteria? [10.2.1(2)]

- Position: permits a wheelchair or mobility aid user to enter from the public way and reach a location having a clear floor area of 30 in. × 48 in., entirely within the perimeter of the shelter.

- Connection: connected by an accessible route to the boarding area provided.

Transportation Facilities/Bus Stops: bus stop signage

TF-05 Where provided, do all new signs identifying bus routes comply with accessible criteria? (4.30.2, 4.30.3, 4.30.5)

- Character proportion: letters and numbers have a width to height ratio between 3:5 and 1:1 and a stroke width to height ratio between 1:5 and 1:10.
- Character height: sized according to viewing distance with characters on overhead signs at least 3 in. high.
- Finish: characters and backgrounds have a nonglare finish.
- Contrast: characters contrast with their background (light-on-dark or dark-on-light).

NOTE:

- Signs that are sized to the maximum dimensions permitted under legitimate local, state, or federal regulations or ordinances shall be considered in compliance.

EXCEPTION:

- Bus schedules, timetables, or maps that are posted at the bus stop or bus bay are not required to comply with this provision.

TF-06 Is the sign located so that the overhead clearance or the projection of a suspended or projected sign does not result in a protruding object (free-standing or wall-mounted)?

- Clear height: at least 80 in. (4.4.2, Fig. 8a)
- Overhang for free-standing signs on posts or pylons located between 27 in. and 80 in. high: no more than a 12-in. projection into walks, corridors, or aisles. (4.4.1, Fig. 8c)
- Overhang for wall-mounted signs between 27 in. and 80 in. high: no more than a 4-in. projection into walks, corridors, or aisles. (4.4.1, Fig. 8a)

Fixed Facilities, Terminals, and Stations

Introduction. Use this review guide to evaluate various spaces associated with rapid rail, light rail, commuter rail, intercity bus, intercity rail, high speed rail, and other fixed guideway systems. These include boarding areas, fare vending areas, specific issues of accessible route, and unique requirements for common elements if they are provided in these spaces. Compliance criteria differ for new construction and for alterations in existing facilities.

The types of facilities and spaces evaluated with this guide may vary greatly—from simple covered or uncovered boarding platforms to subway stations to complex transit centers. Associated common use spaces such as dining facilities, lobbies, rest rooms, exterior passenger loading zones, offices, etc., may need to be evaluated using this guide as well as their usual "Space-type Review Guide," as telephones, entrances, elevators, and other elements have additional requirements if provided in this space-type. The "Building Review Guide" should be used in conjunction with this guide as well, not only because many of these facilities are buildings, but because fixed facilities and stations have unique entrance requirements. Combine the appropriate review guides with this guide as needed.

Fixed facilities and stations must consider equivalent facilitation and access in all aspects of the operation of the facility, including, but not limited to, fare vending and collection, entrance and egress from all public spaces (including vehicles), baggage check in and retrieval, public address systems, signage, clocks, and public telephones. If provided, drinking fountains, seating, ATMs, and other elements must be compliant. Refer to the "Master Guidelines" or the appropriate review guides as needed.

The general concerns of accessible routes apply to these facilities. However, there are specific route issues unique to these space-types. Lighting along the circulation routes must be uniform. Platform-to-vehicle vertical change requirements are different in new and existing transportation stations; they also vary from the typical vertical change requirements for other spaces. Platform edges bordering a drop-off must have detectable warnings. Detectable warnings have not been suspended for transportation facilities as they have in other situations. It may not be feasible to provide universal or barrier-free access throughout the entire facility; therefore, the accessible route as well as accessible spaces and elements must be identified. The distances users must negotiate should be minimized, and, as much as possible, the routes should coincide with those used by the general public. Disabled users must not be forced to board or alight at locations different from those used by the general public. If possible, users should not be forced to cross tracks. However, ADAAG realizes that this is not always possible and describes a compliant solution. Criteria for escalators and people movers are given only for this space-type.

At least one entrance to the facility should be compliant. However, if different entrances serve different sets of routes, then at least one entrance to each set of routes must be accessible. If passenger loading zones are provided at these entrances, then logically at least one such loading zone at each different entrance should be accessible.

If automatic fare systems are provided, at least one entrance and exit must be accessible. Gates and turnstiles at security points, fare collection, baggage check in and retrieval, etc., must meet the usual door requirements of clear width, overhead clearance, etc., or provide an accessible alternative immediately adjacent. Additionally, if the gate is not automatic (i.e., the user must push against it to open it), there are criteria governing the surface of the gate.

Illumination levels on signage, as well as other signage requirements, are unique to fixed facilities and stations.

Clocks, escalators, people movers, and other elements are described in ADAAG only under transportation facilities.

The number and type of accessible seating for this space-type is not clearly defined in ADAAG. However, the "Assembly Areas" and "Fixed Tables and Seating" sections of the "Master Guidelines" can serve as guides. Consider seating in waiting areas, boarding platforms, lobbies, and other public seating areas. Many facilities place the ISA symbol over seats closest to boarding gates or doors to serve users with certain mobility and/or stamina impairments. For chair users, provide clear floor space in seating areas that is dispersed and adjacent to companion seating.

PRELIMINARY DESIGN OVERVIEW

This is a supplemental overview of compliance issues associated specifically with fixed facilities and stations. Refer to other review guides as appropriate (e.g., "Lobbies, Corridors, and Interior Accessible Routes"; "Offices"; "Business and Mercantile"; etc.).

(AA) Assembly Areas

- The minimum number of wheelchair locations in facilities with fixed seating is determined by using ADAAG table 4.1.3(10)(a). Consider waiting areas, lobbies, and other areas with fixed seating.

(AR) Accessible Routes

- Maneuvering space problems include ticketing areas, fare vending and collection devices, security gates, bollards, and turnstiles.

- Route surfaces must meet criteria for vertical changes in level. The criteria for fixed facilities and stations differ greatly from the maximum changes allowed in other spaces. The criteria for new construction and existing facilities differ as well.

- Provide access to ticket counters, automatic fare vending and collection, baggage check in and retrieval, and storage units (i.e., lockers) if provided.

- If the accessible route is not the same as that used by the general public, compliant directional signage must be provided. If the accessible route does not coincide with that of the general public, accessible fare collection systems must be provided at or adjacent to the accessible point of entry or exit.

- When boarding or disembarking from vehicles, persons with disabilities must not be required to do so at locations different from those used by the general public.

- Where users must cross tracks, one of several accessible alternatives may be used.

- If provided, direct connections (existing or future) to residential, commercial, or retail facilities must be accessible.

- Automatic and/or self-service fare systems must provide access and clear floor space. Specific criteria apply.

- ADAAG 10.3, "Fixed Facilities and Stations," is the only section of ADAAG that addresses compliance issues for escalators and people movers.

- Lighting (both type and configuration) along circulation routes must be uniform.

(AL) Alarms
- Typical requirements.

(DR) Doors
- Gates that must be pushed open have specific compliance criteria.

(DW) Detectable Warnings
- Detectable warnings are currently suspended except for platform edges in new and altered rapid, light, commuter, and inner-city rail stations. Additionally, key rapid, light, and commuter rail stations and all inner-city rail stations must install detectable warnings where platform edges are not otherwise protected by screens or guardrails.

(EL) Elevators
- In transportation facilities, the exceptions for both new construction and alterations do not apply.
- Elevators must have glazed or transparent panels that allow an unobstructed view both into and out of the car.
- In fixed facilities and stations, different dimensions may be substituted for the typical minimum car dimensions.

(EN) Entrances
- At least one entrance must be compliant. However, if different entrances serve different sets of routes, at least one entrance to each set of routes must be accessible.
- Where signs are provided at entrances, at least one sign at each entrance must be compliant. If there is no defined entrance, but identification signage is still provided, place compliant signage in a central location.

(FS) Floor and Ground Surfaces
- Compliant ranges for changes in level are different when dealing with the relationship of passenger cars to platforms. Consider new construction vs. existing facilities, as well as numerous exceptions.
- Horizontal gap and vertical difference are both concerns. Consider how passenger cars meet platforms, people movers, and escalators.

(PK) Parking and Passenger Loading Zones
- Refer to "Parking Lots and Passenger Loading Zones" or to "Parking Structures: Parking Garages."
- If different entrances serve different sets of routes, at least one entrance to each set of routes must be accessible. If provided, at least one passenger loading zone at each different entrance should be accessible.

(PL) Platform Lifts
- Platform lifts or other means of meeting horizontal gap and vertical difference requirements may be used in certain situations.

(TL) Public Telephones
- If an interior public pay phone is provided in a transit facility, at least one interior compliant public text telephone must be provided.

- If four or more public pay telephones serve a particular entrance, and if at least one of those is located in the interior, at least one interior compliant public text telephone must also be provided.

(SE) Fixed or Built-in Seating and Tables and/or Counters
- Consider waiting areas, lobbies, and other seating areas.

(SG) Signage
- Compliant station identification signage is required for at least one entrance to the station.
- Placement of identification signage must consider views from passenger cars, uniform placement within the transit system, and other issues specific to fixed facilities and stations.
- If the accessible route differs from that used by the public, compliant signage must be provided.
- Illumination levels on signage must be uniform and minimize glare.

(TF) Transportation Facilities (Fixed Facilities and Stations)
- Where public address systems are used, the same or equivalent information must be made available to the disabled.
- Where clocks are provided for the public, they must be legible and clearly visible. Compliance requirements vary slightly with their location.
- If provided, baggage check in and retrieval systems must be on an accessible route and provide compliant clear floor space immediately adjacent to the system. Security measures (unattended barriers, gates, etc.) must also meet accessibility requirements.
- Connections to other facilities (retail, residential, etc.) have compliance criteria. Existing and future connections must comply.
- Fare vending, ticketing, and baggage check in and retrieval systems must meet compliance criteria.
- Gates that must be pushed open have specific criteria.
- Platform edges must be protected or have detectable warnings.
- Gaps between cars and boarding platforms and in people mover systems have specific criteria unique to this space-type.
- A number of issues are only addressed in this section of ADAAG. These include illumination levels, automatic fare vending systems, gaps between cars and platforms, people movers, crossing of tracks, escalators.

ADAAG APPENDIX
The ADAAG Appendix includes additional advisory information pertinent to this space-type:

- A4.29 Detectable Warnings
- A10.3 Fixed Facilities and Stations

Fixed Facilities, Terminals, and Stations Checklist

This supplemental review guide contains only the ADAAG criteria that are specific to fixed facilities, terminals, and stations. Refer to the appropriate "Space-type Review Guides" (such as "Lobbies, Corridors, and Interior Accessible Routes"; "Business and Mercantile," etc.) to complete evaluation of these spaces.

TRANSPORTATION FACILITIES
(Fixed Facilities, Terminals, and Stations)

TF20	Distance traveled: minimize
TF21	Acc. circulation: coincide w/general public
TF22	Acc. route signage: criteria
TF23	Accessible entrance: linkages
TF24	Acc. entrance for each different set of routes
TF25	Acc. entrances: coincide w/general public
TF26	Entry signage: criteria
TF27	Entry signage: uniform locations
TF28	Acc. connections to adjacent facilities
TF29	Access to future direct connections
TF30	Station/platform signage: criteria
TF31	Station/platform signs: visibility and placement
TF32	Station/platform signs: relationship to windows
TF33	Route signs: height, proportion, contrast
TF34	Route signs: mounting location, Braille or raised
TF35	Route signs: uniform locations
TF36	Accessible ticket and baggage check in
TF37	Ticketing counter: criteria
TF38	Baggage: on acc. route
TF39	Baggage: clear floor space
TF40	Baggage: acc. gate
TF41	Baggage: gate criteria
TF42	Fare systems: comply w/ATM criteria
TF43	Automatic fare machines on acc. route
TF44	Self-service fares: number req'd/location
TF45	Fare systems: clear width
TF46	Fare systems: controls
TF47	Fare systems: gate
TF48	Fare system: adjacent route
TF49	Detectable warnings at platform edge
TF50	Detectable warnings : width and length
TF51	Detectable warnings: criteria
TF52	Detectable warnings: resiliency and sound
TF53	Rail-to-platform: vertical difference
TF54	Vehicle-to-platform: horizontal gap
TF55	People mover: horizontal gap
TF56	All users board or alight at same place
TF57	Illumination: uniform on signage
TF58	Illumination: minimize glare on signs
TF59	Illumination: unif. along circulation routes
TF60	Text telephone: minimum number
TF61	Text telephones: location
TF62	Track crossings: criteria
TF63	Public address systems: equiv. facilitation
TF64	Clocks: criteria
TF65	Escalator: clear width
TF66	Escalator: top and bottom of run
TF67	Escalator: contrasting nose on step
TF68	Escalator: slip resistance
TF69	Elevators: transparent panels for viewing

FIXED FACILITIES, TERMINALS, AND STATIONS COMPREHENSIVE CRITERIA

This guide covers only transportation issues and must be used in conjunction with other "Space-type Review Guides." Included in this space-type are rapid rail, light rail, commuter rail, intercity bus, intercity rail, high speed rail, and other fixed guideway systems (e.g., automated guideway transit, monorails, etc.).

(TF) Transportation Facilities (10.0)
(Fixed Facilities and Stations)

NOT EXEMPT:

- The exception for elevators in facilities that are less than three stories or that have less than 3000 ft² per story [4.1.3(5) Exception 1 and 4.1.6 (1)(k)] *do not* apply to a terminal, depot, or other station used for specified public transportation, an airport passenger terminal, or facilities subject to Title II.

Transportation Facilities/Rail Stations
and Bus Terminals: circulation

TF-20 Are elements such as ramps, elevators, or other circulation devices, fare vending, ticketing areas, fare collection, security checkpoints, or passenger waiting areas placed so as to minimize the distance that wheelchair users and other persons who cannot negotiate steps must travel as compared to the general public? [10.3, 10.3.1(1)]

TF-21 Does the circulation path, including an accessible entrance and an accessible route, to the maximum extent practicable, coincide with the circulation path for the general public? [10.3.1(1)]

TF-22 Where the accessible circulation path is different from that of the general public, does directional signage indicate the location of the nearest accessible entrance and accessible route, and does it meet applicable directional signage criteria? [10.3.1(1)]

Transportation Facilities/Rail Stations
and Bus Terminals: entrances

TF-23 Is at least one entrance connected by an accessible route to public transportation stops, accessible parking, passenger loading zones, and public streets or sidewalks, if available, and to all accessible spaces or elements with the facility? [10.3.1(2)]

TF-24 If different entrances to the station serve different transportation fixed routes or groups of fixed routes, does at least one accessible entrance serving each group or route comply with accessible criteria? [10.3.1(2)]

TF-25 Do all accessible entrances coincide with those used by the majority of the general public, to the maximum extent possible? [10.3.1(2)]

Transportation Facilities/Rail Stations and Bus Terminals: entrance signs

TF-26 Where signs are provided at station entrances that identify the station, the entrance, or both, does at least one sign meet accessible criteria for raised and Braille letters and mounting location? [10.3.1(4), 4.30.4, 4.30.6]

TF-27 Is entrance signage, when provided, placed in uniform locations at the entrances to the maximum extent feasible? [10.3.1(4)]

EXCEPTION:

- Where the station has no defined entrance, but signage is provided, then the accessible signage shall be placed in a central location.

Transportation Facilities/Rail Stations and Bus Terminals: connections

TF-28 If there are direct connections to commercial, retail, or residential facilities, is there an accessible route from the point of connection to boarding platforms and all transportation system elements used by the public? [10.3.1(3)]

NOTE:

- If it is a new connection in an existing facility, then compliance with connection to the accessible route is to the "maximum extent feasible." [10.3.2(5)]

TF-29 Where elements are provided to facilitate future direct connections, are they on an accessible route connecting boarding platforms and all transportation system elements used by the public? [10.3.1(3)]

Transportation Facilities/Rail Stations and Bus Terminals: station/platform signs

TF-30 Do stations/platforms have identification signs that comply with information signage criteria for letter height, proportion, and contrast? [10.3.1(5)]

TF-31 Are station/platform identification signs placed at frequent intervals and clearly visible from inside the vehicle on both sides (when not obstructed by another train)? [10.3.1(5)]

TF-32 When station/platform identification signs are placed close to vehicle windows, is the top of the highest letter or symbol below the top of the vehicle window and the bottom of the lowest letter or symbol above the horizontal midline of the vehicle window? [10.3.1(5)]

Transportation Facilities/Rail Stations and Bus Terminals: route signs

TF-33 Do route signs located on boarding areas, platforms, or mezzanines that list stations, routes, or destinations served by the station comply with information signage criteria for letter height, proportion, and contrast? [10.3.1(6)]

TF-34 Does at least one sign on each platform or boarding area that identifies the specific station comply with room identification criteria for raised or Braille letters and mounting location? [10.3.1(6)]

TF-35 Are all signs that list stations, routes, or destinations served by the station placed in uniform locations within the transit system to the maximum extent practicable? [10.3.1(6)]

Transportation Facilities/Rail Stations and Bus Terminals: ticketing areas

TF-36 Where provided, are ticketing areas designed in such a way that persons with disabilities can obtain tickets and check baggage? [10.3.1(18), 7.2]

TF-37 Are ticketing counters provided with a portion of the main counter at least 36 in. long and not more than 36 in. high? [10.3.1(18), 7.2.2]

- Equivalent facilitation may be provided by:
  — an auxiliary counter with a maximum height of 36 in., located in close proximity to the main counter; or
  — a folding shelf attached to the main counter that provides a writing surface for individuals with disabilities; or
  — a space provided on the side of the counter or desk that allows materials to be passed back and forth.

Transportation Facilities/Rail Stations and Bus Terminals: baggage check in and retrieval

TF-38 If provided, are baggage check in and retrieval systems on an accessible route? [10.3.1(19)]

TF-39 Is a clear floor space at least 30 in. × 48 in. provided in the space immediately adjacent for parallel or forward approach? [10.3.1(19)]

TF-40 Where unattended security barriers are provided, is an accessible gate provided? [10.3.1(19)]

- Accessible gates comply with accessible door/gate criteria.

TF-41 If gates must be pushed open by wheelchair or mobility aid users, do they have a smooth, continuous surface extending from 2 in. above the floor to at least 27 in. above the floor? [10.3.1(19)]

Transportation Facilities/Rail Stations and Bus Terminals: fare vending and collection

TF-42 Do automatic fare vending, collection, and adjustment systems comply with automated teller machine criteria for control requirements, clearances, reach ranges, and persons with visual impairments? [10.3.1(7)]

TF-43 Are automatic fare vending machines located on an accessible route? [10.3.1(7)]

TF-44 If self-service fare collection devices are provided for the public, is there at least one accessible device for entering and exiting at each accessible point of entry or exit (unless one device serves both functions)? [10.3.1(7)]

TF-45 Does each accessible fare collection device provide a minimum clear width of at least 32 in. to allow passage of a wheelchair? [10.3.1(7)]

TF-46 Where provided, do self-service fare collection devices (coin or card slots) comply with control mechanisms criteria for clear floor space, reach range, and operation? [10.3.1(7)]

TF-47 If gates must be pushed open by wheelchair or mobility aid users, do they have a smooth, continuous surface extending from 2 in. above the floor to at least 27 in. above the floor? [10.3.1(7)]

- Accessible gates comply with accessible door/gate criteria.

TF-48 Where the circulation path does not coincide with that used by the general public, is the accessible fare collection system located at, or adjacent to, the accessible point of entry or exit? [10.3.1(7)]

NOTE:

- In existing stations, where a technical infeasibility requires the accessible route to lead from the public way to a paid area of the transit system, an accessible fare collection system should be provided along the accessible route. [10.3.2(3)]

Transportation Facilities/Rail Stations and Bus Terminals: detectable warnings

NOTE:

- The suspension action for truncated domes, suspended until July 26, 1996, does not affect the requirement for detectable warnings (truncated domes) on transit platforms.

TF-49 When not protected by platform screens or guardrails, do platform edges, bordering a drop-off, have a detectable warning? [10.3.1(8)]

TF-50 Are the detectable warnings 24 in. wide, running the full length of the platform drop-off? [10.3.1(8)]

TF-51 Do the detectable warnings consist of raised truncated domes and do they meet the required criteria? [10.3.1(8)]

- Diameter: nominal 0.9 in.
- Height: nominal 0.2 in.
- Spacing: nominal 2.35 in., center to center, offset every other row.
- Contrast: contrast visually with adjoining surface (light-on-dark or dark-on-light).
- The material used to provide contrast shall be an integral part of the walking surface. Detectable warnings used on interior surfaces shall differ from adjoining walking surfaces in resiliency or sound-on-cane contact.

TF-52 Where the platform is in an interior location, do the detectable warnings differ from the adjoining walking surface in resiliency or sound-on-cane contact? [10.3.1(8)]

Transportation Facilities/Rail Stations and Bus Terminals: platform change in levels and gaps

EXCEPTION:

- Existing vehicles retrofitted to meet the requirements of 49 CFR 37.93 (one car per train rule) shall be coordi-

nated with the platform such that, for at least one door, the vertical difference between the vehicle floor and the platform (measured when the vehicle is at rest with 50 percent normal passenger capacity) is within plus or minus 2 in. and the horizontal gap is no greater than 4 in. [10.3.2(4)]

TF-53 Is the rail-to-platform height coordinated with the floor height of new vehicles so that the vertical difference (measured when the vehicle is at rest) is within plus or minus 5/8 in. under normal passenger load conditions? [10.3.1(9)]

EXCEPTION:

- Existing vehicles operating in new stations may have a vertical difference with respect to the new platform within plus or minus 1½ in. [10.3.1(9)]
- Existing stations may have a vertical difference with respect to the existing platform within plus or minus 1½ in. [10.3.2(4)]

TF-54 For rapid rail, light rail, commuter rail, high speed rail, and intercity rail systems, is the horizontal gap (measured when the new vehicle is at rest) no greater than 3 in.? [10.3.1(9)]

EXCEPTION:

- In light rail, commuter rail, and intercity rail systems where it is not operationally or structurally feasible to meet the horizontal gap or vertical difference requirements, mini-high platforms, car-borne or platform-mounted lifts, ramps or bridge plates, or similar manually deployed devices, meeting the applicable requirements of 36 CFR Part 1192 or 49 CFR Part 38 shall suffice.

TF-55 For slow moving automated guideway people mover transit systems, is the horizontal gap (measured when the new vehicle is at rest) no greater than 1 in.? [10.3.1(9)]

Transportation Facilities/Rail Stations and Bus Terminals: boarding and alighting

TF-56 Is the station designed so that persons with disabilities are able to board or alight from a vehicle at the same location as that used by the general public? [10.3.1(10)]

Transportation Facilities/Rail Stations and Bus Terminals: illumination

TF-57 Are illumination levels uniform in the areas where signage is located? [10.3.1(11)]

TF-58 Does the method of illumination minimize excessive glare on signs? [10.3.1(11)]

TF-59 Does the lighting type and configuration provide uniform illumination along accessible circulation routes ? [10.3.1(11)]

Transportation Facilities/Rail Stations and Bus Terminals: text telephones

TF-60 If an interior public pay telephone is provided in a transit facility, is at least one interior public text telephone provided? [10.3.1(12)(a)]

NOTE:

- Transit facility [as defined in 49 CFR 37.3 for purposes of applying ADAAG 10.3.1(12)] is any physical structure whose primary function is to facilitate access to and from a transportation system that has scheduled stops at the structure. It does not include an open structure or a physical structure whose primary purpose is providing services other than transportation services.

TF-61 If there are four or more public pay telephones serving a particular entrance to a rail station and at least one is in an interior location, is at least one text telephone provided to serve that entrance? [10.3.1(12)(b)]

NOTE:

- Text telephones shall comply with all required criteria.

Transportation Facilities/Rail Stations and Bus Terminals: track crossings

TF-62 Where it is necessary to cross tracks to reach boarding platforms, is the surface of the route level and flush with the rail top at the outer edge and between the rails except for a maximum 2½-in. gap on the inner edge of each rail to permit passage of wheel flanges? [10.3.1(13)]

NOTE:

- Where gap reduction is not practicable, there should be an above-grade or below-grade accessible route.

Transportation Facilities/Rail Stations and Bus Terminals: public address system

TF-63 Where terminal information systems broadcast information to the general public through a public address system, is there a way to provide the same or equivalent information to persons with hearing impairments? [10.3.1(14)]

AUTHOR'S INTERPRETATION:

- Acceptable solutions might include a visual paging system or an Assistive Listening System.

Transportation Facilities/Rail Stations and Bus Terminals: clocks

TF-64 If clocks are provided for use by the public, do they comply with accessible criteria? [10.3.1(15)]

- Clock faces are uncluttered, resulting in elements that are clearly visible.

- Hands, numerals, and/or digits contrast with the background.
- Where clocks are mounted overhead, the numerals and/or digits are at least 3 in. high.
- Clocks are placed in uniform locations throughout the facility to the maximum extent practicable.

Transportation Facilities/Rail Stations and Bus Terminals: escalators

TF-65 Where provided in below grade stations, do escalators have a clear width of at least 32 in.? [10.3.1(16)]

TF-66 At the top and bottom of each escalator run, are at least two continuous treads level beyond the comb plate before the risers begin to form? [10.3.1(16)]

TF-67 Are all escalator treads marked by a strip of clearly contrasting color 2 in. wide, parallel to and on the nose of each step? [10.3.1(16)]

- The edge of the tread must be apparent from both ascending and descending directions.

TF-68 Is the contrasting strip of material at least as slip-resistant as the remainder of the tread? [10.3.1(16)]

Transportation Facilities/Rail Stations and Bus Terminals: elevators

NOTE:

- Including the following criteria, elevators should comply with required criteria. See the review guide on elevators for compliance criteria.

EXCEPTION:

- Elevator cars with a clear floor area in which a 60-in. diameter circle can be inscribed may be substituted for the minimum car dimensions of ADAAG 4.10, Fig. 22.

NOT EXEMPT:

- The exception for elevators in facilities that are less than three stories or that have less than 3000 ft^2 per story [4.1.3(5) Exception 1 and 4.1.6 (1)(k)] *do not* apply to a terminal, depot, or other station used for specified public transportation, an airport passenger terminal, or facilities subject to Title II.

TF-69 Where provided, do elevators have glass or transparent panels to allow an unobstructed view both into and out of the car? [10.3.1(17)]

Introduction. This review guide should be used to evaluate the site and building after all the individual rooms and exterior spaces have been designed or evaluated. A few of the ADAAG criteria apply to the overall site and building, and they cannot be properly reviewed by using the previous site or individual room guides. For example, if all entrances to a building are not accessible, at least 50 percent must be accessible, and each accessible entrance must have the proper ADAAG signage. Another issue concerns the overall site: If there is more than one building on the same site, such as a university or college campus, all accessible facilities must be connected by an accessible route.

The importance of an overall review of a building is probably best exemplified by the proper location of accessible toilet/bathrooms in buildings without elevators. In these facilities if a toilet/bathroom is provided on an upper or lower floor level, then one must also be provided on the accessible ground floor. This requirement could easily be missed using only the toilet/bathroom review guide that basically only checks for accessibility issues within the space.

Since there are so few criteria to be reviewed, the "Preliminary Design Overview" and "Checklist" used with the other review guides have been excluded from this guide.

SITE AND BUILDING SUMMARY
COMPREHENSIVE CRITERIA

- This review guide focuses on the overall building and site.

(AR) Accessible Routes (4.3)

Accessible Routes: site

AR-01 If on-site parking is provided, does at least one accessible route within the boundaries of the site connect accessible parking spaces to the accessible building entrance? [4.1.2(1), 4.3.2(1)]

AR-02 Does at least one accessible route within the boundaries of the site connect public streets and sidewalks to the accessible building entrance? [4.1.2(1), 4.3.2(1)]

AR-03 If public transportation stops are available, does at least one accessible route within the boundaries of the site connect public transportation stops to the accessible building entrance? [4.1.2(1), 4.3.2(1)]

AR-04 If passenger loading zones are provided, does at least one accessible route within the boundaries of the site connect a passenger loading zone to the accessible building entrance? [4.1.2(1), 4.3.2(1)]

AR-05 Is there an accessible route connecting all accessible buildings, facilities, elements and spaces on the same site? (4.1.2(2), 4.3.2(2)]

Accessible Routes: interior

AR-06 Is the building entrance space connected by an accessible route to all accessible spaces, elements, and all accessible dwelling units within the building or facility? [4.3.2(3)]

Accessible Routes: dwelling units

AR-07 Does an accessible route connect at least one accessible entrance of each accessible dwelling unit with those exterior and interior spaces and facilities that serve the accessible unit? [4.3.2(4)]

(EN) Entrances (4.14)

EXCEPTION:

- In historic buildings, if it is determined that no entrance used by the public can comply with this section, then access at any entrance not used by the general public but open (unlocked) with directional signage at the primary entrance may be used. The accessible entrance shall also have a notification system. Where security is a problem, remote monitoring may be used. [4.1.7(3)(b)]

Entrances: general

EN-01 Are at least 50 percent of all public entrances accessible? [4.14.1, 4.1.3.(8)(a)(i)]

- This does not include service or loading docks, and direct pedestrian access from enclosed parking garages, pedestrian tunnels, or elevated walkways.

EN-02 Is at least one accessible public entrance provided on the ground floor? [4.14.1, 4.1.3.(8)(a)(i)]

EN-03 Is the number of accessible entrances at least equivalent to the number of exits required by the applicable fire/building codes? [4.14.1, 4.1.3.(8)(a)(ii)]

- This does not require an increase in the total number of entrances planned for the facility.

EN-04 Where feasible, are the accessible entrances used by the majority of the people working in and visiting the building? [4.1.3(8)(a)(iii)]

EN-05 If direct pedestrian access is provided into a building from an enclosed parking garage, is at least one accessible entrance directly from the garage provided? [4.14.1, 4.1.3(8)(b)(i)]

EN-06 If pedestrian access is provided into a building from an elevated walkway or pedestrian tunnel, is at least one accessible entrance from the walkway or tunnel provided? [4.14.1, 4.1.3(8)(b)(ii)]

EN-07 If the service entrance is the only entrance into the building or facility, is it accessible? [4.14.1, 4.1.3(8)(c)]

(MD) Medical Care Facilities (6.0)

Medical Care Facilities: entrances

MD-01 Is there at least one accessible entrance covered by a canopy or overhang? (6.2)

MD-02 Is there an accessible passenger loading zone at this entrance that complies with passenger loading zone requirements, ADAAG 4.6.6? (6.2)

Medical Care Facilities: general purpose hospitals

MD-03 If the facility is a general purpose hospital, are all common and public use areas accessible and are at least 10 percent of patient bedrooms and toilets accessible? (6.1.1)

NOTES:

- The distribution of accessible patient bedrooms can vary based on the anticipated need in different specialized units (e.g., more than 10 percent may be needed in a general surgical unit and fewer than 10 percent in obstetrics and pediatrics).

- This includes psychiatric facilities and detoxification facilities.

(TH) Accessible Transient Lodging (9.0)

NOTE:

- Doors and doorways designed to allow passage into and within all transient lodging sleeping units shall comply with accessible door width criteria. This means any sleeping unit in the facility, whether it is designated as accessible or not. (9.4)

(SG) Signage (4.30)

Signage: entry

NOTE:

- Building directories, and all other temporary signs are not required to comply. (4.1.3.16)

SG-01 Where a building or space has both accessible and inaccessible entrances, are the accessible entrances identified by the International Symbol of Accessibility? [4.1.2(7)(c), Fig. 43a–b]

SG-02 If an entrance is not accessible, is there a directional sign indicating the location of the nearest accessible entrance? [4.1.2(7)(c), 4.1.3(8)(d)]

SG-03 Does the directional sign indicating the location of the nearest accessible entrance comply with directional signage criteria? (4.30.2, 3, 5)

- Character proportion: letters and numbers have a width to height ratio between 3:5 and 1:1 and a stroke width to height ratio between 1:5 and 1:10.

- Character height: sized according to viewing distance with characters on overhead signs at least 3 in. high.

- Finish: characters and backgrounds have a nonglare finish.

- Contrast: characters contrast with their background (light-on-dark or dark-on-light).

(EL) Elevators (4.10)

NOTES:

- Accessible elevators shall be on an accessible route and serve each level, including mezzanines, in all multilevel buildings and facilities unless exempted below.

- Accessible elevators shall comply with ASME A17.1-1990, Safety Code for Elevators and Escalators.

EXCEPTIONS:

- New construction elevator exceptions [4.1.3(5)]

  — *Exception 1:* Elevators are not required in facilities that are less than three stories or that have less than 3000 ft^2 per story unless the building is a shopping center, a shopping mall, or the professional office of a health care provider, or another type of facility as determined by the Attorney General. The elevator exemption set forth in this paragraph does not obviate or limit in any way the obligation to comply with the other accessibility requirements established in ADAAG 4.1.3. For example:

    a. Floors above or below the accessible ground floor must meet the requirements of this section except for elevator service.

    b. If toilet or bathing facilities are provided on a level not served by an elevator, then toilet or bathing facilities must be provided on the accessible ground floor.

    c. In new construction, if a building or facility is eligible for this exemption but a full passenger elevator is nonetheless planned, that elevator shall meet the requirements of ADAAG 4.10 and shall serve each level in the building.

    d. A full passenger elevator that provides service from a garage to only one level of a building or facility is not required to serve other levels.

  — *Exception 2:* Elevator pits, elevator penthouses, mechanical rooms, piping, or equipment catwalks are exempted from this requirement.

  — *Exception 3:* Accessible ramps complying with ADAAG 4.8 may be used in lieu of an elevator.

  — *Exception 4:* Platform lifts (wheelchair lifts) complying with ADAAG 4.11 and applicable state or local codes may be used in lieu of an elevator only under the following conditions:

    a. To provide an accessible route to a performing area in an assembly occupancy.

    b. To comply with the wheelchair viewing position line-of-sight and dispersion requirements of ADAAG 4.33.3, "Assembly Areas."

    c. To provide access to incidental occupiable spaces and rooms that are not open to the general public and that house no more than five persons, including, but not limited to, equipment control rooms and projection booths.

    d. To provide access where existing site constraints or other constraints make use of a ramp or an elevator infeasible.

- Alterations elevator exception [4.1.6(1)(k)]:

  — *Exception:* These guidelines do not require the installation of an elevator in an altered facility that is less than three stories or has less than 3000 ft^2 per story unless the building is a shopping center, a shopping mall, the professional office of a health care provider, or another type of facility as determined by the Attorney General.

NOT EXEMPT:

- The exceptions for elevators in ADAAG 4.1.3(5), *Exception 1,* and ADAAG 4.1.6(1)(k) *do not* apply to a terminal, depot, or other station used for specified public transportation, or an airport passenger terminal, or facilities subject to Title II. (10.1)

Elevators: general

EL-01 Where a passenger elevator is not provided, is the building eligible for the elevator exceptions as identified above? [4.1.3(5)]

EL-02 If a building is not eligible for the elevator exception, does a passenger elevator serve each level in the building, including mezzanines? [4.1.3(5)]

EL-03 Where more than one elevator is provided, does each full passenger elevator meet required elevator accessibility criteria? [4.1.3(5)]

EL-04 If the only elevators provided are freight elevators, are they combination passenger and freight elevators for the public and employees, and do they comply with accessible criteria? (4.10.1)

(TL) Telephones (4.31)

Telephones: number required

TL-01 If there is only one public telephone on a floor, does it comply with accessible criteria? [4.1.3(17)(a)]

- Unless otherwise specified, accessible telephones may be either forward or side reach telephones.

TL-02 If there is a single bank of public telephones on a floor, does at least one of the telephones in the bank comply with accessible criteria? [4.1.3(17)(a)]

- A bank consists of two or more adjacent public telephones, often installed as a unit.
- Unless otherwise specified, accessible telephones may be either forward or side reach telephones.

TL-03 Where two or more banks of public telephones are provided on a floor, is at least one accessible telephone provided at each bank or within proximity to the bank and does at least one of these accessible telephones comply with forward reach criteria? [4.1.3(17)(a)]

EXCEPTION:

- For exterior installations only, if dial tone first service is available, then a side reach telephone may be installed instead of the required forward reach telephone.

Telephones: text telephones

TL-14 If a total of four or more public pay telephones (including both interior and exterior phones) are provided at a site and at least one is in an interior location, is at least one interior public text telephone provided? [4.1.3(17)(c)(i)]

TL-15 If an interior public pay telephone is provided in a stadium or arena, convention center, a hotel with a convention center, or a covered mall, is at least one interior public text telephone provided in the facility? [4.1.3(17)(c)(ii)]

TL-16 If there is a public pay telephone in or adjacent to a hospital emergency room, a hospital recovery room, or a hospital waiting room, is there a public text telephone in each such location? [4.1.3(17)(c)(iii)]

TL-17 If a required text telephone is not provided, is equivalent facilitation provided? [4.31.9(3)]

- A portable text telephone may be made available in a hotel at the registration desk if it is available on a 24-hour basis for use with nearby public pay telephones that can accommodate the accessible requirements for a portable text telephone.

(BR) Toilet Rooms, Bathrooms (4.23)

NOTE:

- In historic buildings, if toilets are provided, at least one toilet facility complying with toilet room accessible criteria shall be provided along an accessible route. Such a toilet facility may be unisex in design. [4.1.7(3)(c)]

Toilet Rooms: public and common use

BR-01 If toilet rooms are provided, does each public and common use toilet room comply with accessible criteria? [4.1.2(6), 4.1.3(11), 4.22.1]

DEFINITION:

- A *common use toilet room* is one used for a restricted group of people, such as occupants of a building or employees of a company.

BR-02 If other toilet rooms are provided for the use of an occupant of a specific space (such as a private toilet room for a company president) is each toilet room adaptable (e.g., door clearance, clear floor space at fixtures, and maneuvering space)? [4.1.2(6), 4.1.3(11), 4.22.1]

Bathrooms: public and common use

BR-03 If bathrooms or bathing facilities are provided, does each public and common use bathroom or bathing facility comply with accessible criteria? [4.1.2(6), 4.1.3(11), 4.23.1]

Toilet/Bathrooms: alternatives

BR-04 In buildings eligible for the elevator exception, if toilet/bathrooms are provided on a level not served by an elevator is an accessible toilet/bathroom located on the accessible ground floor? [4.1.3(5)]

NOTE:

- If toilet or bathing facilities are also provided on floors above or below the ground level, they must be accessible.

BR-05 Where it is technically infeasible to comply with ADAAG 4.22 or ADAAG 4.23, is at least one unisex toilet/bathroom provided per floor, located in the same area as existing toilet facilities? [4.1.6(3)(e)(i)]

NOTE:

- This is permitted in lieu of modifying existing toilet facilities to be accessible.

Toilet/Bathrooms: general

BR-07 Are accessible toilet rooms, bathrooms, bathing facilities, or shower rooms located on an accessible route? (4.22.1, 4.23.1)

(EX) Exits and Areas of Rescue Assistance (4.3.11)

DEFINITIONS:

- *Area of Rescue Assistance:* An area with direct access to an exit where people who are unable to use stairs may remain temporarily in safety to await further instructions or assistance during emergency evacuation.

- *Means of Egress:* A continuous and unobstructed way of exit travel from any point in a building or facility to a public way. A means of egress comprises vertical and horizontal travel and may include intervening room spaces, doorways, hallways, corridors, passageways, balconies, ramps, stairs, enclosures, lobbies, horizontal exits, courts, and yards. An accessible means of egress is one that complies with these guidelines and does not include stairs, steps, or escalators. Areas of rescue assistance or evacuation elevators may be included as part of accessible means of egress.

EXCEPTIONS:

- New construction: Areas of rescue assistance are not required in buildings or facilities having a supervised automatic sprinkler system. [4.1.3(9)]

- Alterations: Alterations are not required to provide an area of rescue assistance. [4.1.6(1)(g)]

ALLOWANCES:

- New construction: A horizontal exit can be used as an area of rescue assistance when the exit is designed in accordance with the local building /life safety code. [4.1.3(9)]

Exits: number required

EX-01 Does each occupiable level of a building or facility that is required to be accessible have accessible means of egress equal to the number of exits required by local building/life safety regulations? [4.1.3(9)]

- Where a required exit is not accessible, areas of rescue assistance shall be provided equal to the number of inaccessible required exits. [4.1.3(9)]

(AL) Alarms (4.28)

NOTE:

- At a minimum, visual signal appliances shall be provided in buildings and facilities in restrooms and any other general usage areas. **The ADAAG does not define the number of occupants needed to establish a general or common use area.**

ALLOWANCE:

- Emergency warning systems in medical care facilities may be modified to suit standard health care alarm design practice. [4.1.3(14)]

Alarms: general

AL-01 If emergency warning systems are provided, do they include both audible alarms and visual alarms? [4.1.3(14)]

4

Specifications, Schedules, and Details

INTRODUCTION

The "Space-type Review Guides" found in the previous chapter provide the compliance criteria necessary for a comprehensive plan review. However, numerous elements affected by ADAAG will appear in specifications, on various schedules, or in sections and enlarged details. For example, stairs drawn on a floor plan may reveal little dimensional information about landings, treads, or handrails. Such information is generally found on an enlarged floor plan of the stair and accompanied by detailed sections through the stair. Audible and visual alarms may be located on a plan while their performance criteria, including mounting heights, will be described in the specifications. The purpose of this chapter is to identify those compliance criteria that may not be easily described on typical floor plans.

Placement of information in construction documents can vary depending on office practices. Specifications may be found in a project manual or placed directly on the drawings; pertinent dimensions may be included in a specification or found on an elevation or sectional detail. To accommodate these variations in office procedures, this chapter provides an alphabetical list of categories based on the ADAAG elements. Each category is organized by section as "Specifications," "Schedules," or "Details." Items required to meet compliance criteria are listed within each section. Frequently, an item is listed in both the specification and detail sections and also repeated in another category in an effort to accommodate variations in office practice.

Each compliance item is followed by the code number used in the "Master Guidelines" so that the reviewer can reference the necessary criteria. We recommend that the ADAAG Appendix be reviewed in conjunction with this chapter. While the ADAAG Appendix is supplemental and only advisory, it provides additional information that might influence your specification or detail. Sections of the ADAAG Appendix that relate to the compliance item are identified.

The format used in this chapter is as follows.

Alarms

Specifications
- Audible alarms
  — operational criteria (AL-02)

Details: drawings
- Alarm system layout
  — alarm spacing and vertical location (AL-08, AL-09, AL-10)

ADAAG Appendix
- A4.28: audible alarms, visual alarms, and auxiliary alarms

This chapter does not contain an exhaustive listing of all possible building elements, but instead represents those elements predominantly identified in the ADAAG. For example, fume hoods used in scientific experimentation and found in laboratories are not specifically covered by ADAAG. Nevertheless, the controls and counter top for this equipment need to meet compliance criteria at an accessible work station. It is up to the reader to find compatible analogies within the categories provided.

"Exceptions" provided for certain elements by ADAAG are not noted in the categorical items, but are located instead with the compliance criteria in the "Master Guidelines." In addition, building codes or other regulations outside of the ADAAG, and applicable to your project, have not been considered.

Categories

Accessible Routes	Dressing, Fitting, and Locker Rooms	Rail and Bus Station Platforms
Air Conditioning Units	Drinking Fountains	Ramps
Alarms	Electrical and Communication	Ranges and Ovens
Alarm Pull Stations	Devices	Refrigerators/Freezers
Areas of Rescue Assistance	Elevators	Restaurants and Cafeterias
Assistive Listening Systems	Entrances and Storefronts	Security Gates
Automated Teller Machines	Escalators	Shelves
Baggage Check in and Retrieval Areas	Fare Vending and Collection	Shower Stalls
Bathrooms and Toilet Rooms	Fire Extinguishers and Cabinets	Sidewalks
Bathtubs	Fixed or Built-in Seating and Tables	Signage
Benches and Seats	Floor and Ground Surfaces	Sinks
Boards: Chalk, Marker, and Bulletin	Gates	Sleeping Rooms
Bus Stop Pads	Handrails and Grab Bars	Stages
Cabinets	Kitchens	Stairs
Carpets	Lavatories	Storage Units
Clocks	Libraries	Telephones
Closets	Life Safety Controls	Thermostats
Controls and Operating Mechanisms	Lighting	Thresholds
Corridors	Mirrors and Medicine Cabinets	Ticketing Areas
Counters	Notification Devices	Toilet and Bath Accessories
Curb Ramps	Parking	Toilet Stalls
Detectable Warnings	Passenger Loading Zones	Urinals
Doors	Platform Lifts	Vending Machines
Door Finish Hardware	Plumbing Fixtures	Washers and Dryers
Door Frames	Projection Screens	Water Closets
Drawers	Public Address Systems	Windows

CATEGORIES WITH MASTER GUIDELINES REFERENCES

Accessible Routes

Details: drawings

- Accessible route criteria and layout
  - minimum clear width (AR-08, AR-09)
  - passing space (AR-10)
  - maneuvering clearances (AR-11)
  - running and cross slopes (AR-12, AR-13)
  - changes in level (AR-14)

ADAAG Appendix

- A4.2.1: additional information on wheelchair passage widths
- A4.2.3: wheelchair turning space
- A.4.2.4: clear floor or ground space for wheelchairs
- A4.3.1: travel distances and site slopes
- A4.3.10: egress

Air Conditioning Units: controls
See "Controls and Operating Mechanisms."

Alarms
This category includes criteria for both audible and visual alarms.

Specifications

- Audible alarms
  - operational criteria (AL-02)
  - single station alarm units: audible and visual (AL-03)

- Visual alarms
  - operational criteria (AL-05)
  - alarm vertical location (AL-08)
  - sleeping room criteria (TH-16)
  - visual alarm system integration into the building emergency alarm system (AL-04, AL-11)
- Visual notification device placement
  - living unit and sleeping criteria (TH-18)

Details: drawings

- Alarm system layout
  - alarm spacing and vertical location (AL-08, AL-09, AL-10)
  - visual alarm system integration into the building emergency alarm system (AL-04, AL-11)
  - living unit criteria (AL-12, TH-17)
- Visual notification device placement
  - living unit and sleeping criteria (TH-18)

ADAAG Appendix

- A4.28: audible alarms, visual alarms, and auxiliary alarms

Alarm Pull Stations
See "Controls and Operating Mechanisms."

Areas of Rescue Assistance
An area of rescue assistance is an area with direct access to an exit where people who are unable to use stairs may remain temporarily in safety to await further instructions

or assistance during emergency evacuation. The general scope for seven different types of areas of rescue assistance allowed are outlined in the "Master Guidelines," "Exits, EX-02."

Specifications
- Communications
  — type (EX-06)
- Signage
  — criteria (EX-07)

Details: drawings
- Area of rescue assistance design criteria and layout
  — types (EX-02)
  — size (EX-03)
  — wheelchair spaces required (EX-04)
  — stairway width (EX-05)
  — communications (EX-06)
  — signage (EX-07)

ADAAG Appendix
- A4.3.10: additional information on egress
- A4.3.11.3: stairway widths
- A.4.3.11.4: two-way communication

Assistive Listening Systems

Specifications
- Assembly and other areas, where required
  — operational criteria (AA-16)

Details: drawings
- Assistive Listening System layout
  — required number (AA-14)
  — location (AA-15)

ADAAG Appendix
- A4.33, Table A2: summary of Assistive Listening Devices
- A4.33.6 and A4.33.7: placement of listening systems and types of listening systems
- A4.7: Assistive Listening Devices at sales and service counters, teller windows, and other areas where a physical barrier separates service personnel from customers

Automated Teller Machines

Because this equipment is usually selected for a particular project and is manufactured to industry standards, it is assumed that their accessible specifications will be in compliance with ADAAG. The reviewer, however, can use the following criteria to review product selection for compliance.

Specifications
- ATM
  — reach ranges for controls and bins (AT-03, AT-04)
  — controls (AT-05)
  — visual information (AT-06)

Details: drawings
- ATM layout

  — clear floor space (AT-02)
  — reach ranges for controls and bins (AT-03, AT-04)

Baggage Check in and Retrieval Areas
See "Counters" and "Doors (Security Gates)."

Bathrooms and Toilet Rooms
See individual fixtures and elements for additional design information: toilet stalls, water closets, urinals, lavatories, shower stalls, bathtubs, mirrors, medicine cabinets, and other toilet and bath accessories.

Details: drawings
- Bathroom and toilet room design
  — unisex criteria (BR-06)
  — signage (BR-08)
  — accessible routes for fixtures and controls (BR-09)
  — door swing (BR-10)
  — turning space (BR-11)
  — two doors in a series (DR-11)

ADAAG Appendix
- A4.22: clear floor space in toilet rooms
- A4.23: clear floor space and medicine cabinets in bathrooms

Bathtubs
Specifications
- Seats
  — size and location (BT-02)
  — structural requirements: material and mounting (HR-08, HR-09)
- Grab bars
  — length and location (BT-03, BT-04)
  — size and spacing (HR-01, HR-02, HR-03)
  — structural requirements: material and mounting (HR-05, HR-06, HR-07)
  — hazards (HR-10)
- Controls
  — location (BT-05)
  — operation (BT-06)
  — shower spray unit (BT-07)
  — enclosure (BT-08)

Details: drawings
- Bathtub layout
  — clear floor space (BT-01)
- Seats
  — size and location (BT-02)
- Grab bars
  — length and location (BT-03, BT-04)
  — structural requirements: wall anchors (HR-07)
- Controls
  — location (BT-05)
  — enclosure (BT-08)

Benches and Seats
See "Bathtubs," "Shower Stalls," or "Dressing and Fitting Rooms."

Boards: Chalk, Marker, and Bulletin
See "Controls and Operating Mechanisms."

Bus Stop Pads and Bus Shelters
Details: drawings
- Bus stop pad layout
  — location (TF-01)
  — surface and slope (TF-02)
  — minimum dimensions (TF-03)
- Bus shelter
  — clear floor area (TF-04)
  — connection (TF-04)

Cabinets
See "Storage."

Carpets
See "Floor and Ground Surfaces."

Closets
See "Storage."

Clocks
ADAAG compliance criteria for clocks are only identified in airports, bus stations, and rail terminals. The authors suggest that these same criteria might apply in other public areas where clocks are present.

Specifications
- Clock criteria
  — clock faces (TF-19, TF-64)
  — contrast (TF-19, TF-64)
  — numeral or digit size (TF-19, TF-64)

Details: drawings
- Clock layout
  — location (TF-19, TF-64)

Controls and Operating Mechanisms
Controls and operating mechanisms can include elements such as electrical outlets, light switches, communication system receptacles, pencil sharpeners, manual overhead screens, nonkeyed thermostats, alarm pull stations, fire extinguisher cabinets, emergency showers or eyewashes, A/C window units, kitchen or laundry appliances, vending machines, and a variety of other dispensing devices.

Specifications
- Controls and operating mechanisms
  — reach ranges: side and forward (CT-02, CT-03, CT-04, CT-05)
  — operation (CT-06)

Details: drawings
- Controls and operating mechanisms criteria
  — clear floor space (CT-01)
  — reach ranges: side and forward (CT-02, CT-03, CT-04, CT-05)

ADAAG Appendix
- A4.27: control and operating mechanism heights

Corridors
See "Accessible Routes."

Counters
See "Fixed Seating and Tables" for seating at tables.
Details: drawings
- Checkout aisle and counter layout: retail
  — number required (BM-05, BM-06)
  — dimensional criteria (BM-07)
- Counter design: general (e.g., laboratories)
  — height, length, and knee clearance (SE-03, SE-04)
- Sales counters with cash register design: retail
  — height and length (BM-02)
- Sales or service counters without cash register design: retail, service, or reception
  — height and length (BM-03)
- Checkout counters design: libraries
  — height and length (LB-02)
- Food service counters design: restaurants, cafeterias, and bars
  — height, length, and knee clearance (RC-03)
- Ticketing, baggage check in, and retrieval counter design: transportation facilities
  — height and length (TF-11, TF-37)
- Kitchen counters and cabinets: social services
  — heights and reach ranges (TH-12, TF-13)

ADAAG Appendix
- A.4.2.5 and A4.2.6: horizontal reach ranges
- A7.3: checkout aisles in business and mercantile

Curb Ramps
Details: drawings
- Curb ramp layout
  — built-up curb ramp projections (CR-09)
  — curb ramp obstructions (CR-12)
- Curb ramp design criteria
  — running and cross slopes (CR-02)
  — transition to adjacent surfaces (CR-03)
  — minimum width (CR-05)
  — surface condition (CR-06)
  — side flares (CR-07, CR-08)
  — detectable warnings—suspended until July 26, 1996 (CR-10, CR-11)
  — location at marked crossings (CR-13)
  — diagonal or corner type (CR-14, CR-15, CR-16)
  — islands (CR-17)

Detectable Warnings
Requirements for detectable warnings (truncated domes) at curb ramps, hazardous vehicular areas, and reflecting ponds have been suspended until July 26, 1996. This action does not affect the requirement for detectable warnings (truncated domes) at transit platforms, which remains in effect.

Specifications
- Detectable warning criteria
  — diameter, height, spacing, contrast, and material (DW-03, TF-51)

Details: drawings
- Hazardous vehicular areas
  — location and width (DW-01)
  — **Suspended until July 26, 1996**
- Reflecting ponds
  — location (DW-02)
  — **Suspended until July 26, 1996**
- Transit platforms: rail stations and bus terminals
  — location (TF-49, TF-52)
  — width (TF-50)
  — adjacent surfaces (TF-52)

ADAAG Appendix
- A4.29: detectable warnings on walking surfaces

Doors

Included in this category are metal, wood, and plastic doors; sliding doors; special doors including revolving doors and automatic or power assisted doors; turnstiles; gates; and entrances and storefronts.

At present ADAAG has no compliance requirements on door opening force for exterior doors. It has a "reserved" status.

Specifications
- Automatic or power assisted doors
  — ANSI standards (DR-02)
  — opening and closing requirements (DR-03)

Details or Schedules: drawings
- General door criteria
  — maneuvering clearance (DR-04)
  — clear opening width and height (DR-09)
- Revolving doors, turnstiles, and gates
  — adjacent accessible entry (DR-01)
- Gates: airports
  — surface criteria (TF-15)
- Terminal, baggage check in and retrieval gates: airports, rail and bus stations
  — surface criteria (TF-15, TF-41)
- Fare collection: rail and bus terminals
  — surface criteria (TF-47)
- Two doors in a series
  — clear space between doors (DR-11)
  — door swing (DR-11)

ADAAG Appendix
- A.4.13: thresholds at doors, door hardware, door closers, door opening force, and automatic doors and power assisted doors

Door Finish Hardware

Door hardware, not specified or detailed in a very particular way, can result in a noncompliance. Some areas of concern follow.
- Shape and mounting heights of door handles, locks, latches, bolts, pull units, sliding door and bi-fold hardware are important to accessible operation of the door.

- Certain types of hinges that provide door closure and other types of closers must meet required closing speeds.
- If mounted improperly, overhead closers might violate overhead clearances and result in a protruding object.
- Drop seals or sweeps on door bottoms may increase the opening resistance of a door.
- Door trim units, astragals, or meeting seals can reduce the effective opening size required for passage.
- Exit devices such as push bars generally occur above the wheel height on the chair and are not considered when measuring the opening size. This is an author's interpretation.
- Threshold height and profile are critical for passage.

Specifications and Schedules
- Handles, locks, latches, or other operable devices
  — operational criteria (DR-05)
  — type (DR-05)
  — mounting height (DR-05)
- Closers
  — opening force (DR-06)
  — closing speed (DR-07)
  — clearance height (PR-04)
- Thresholds
  — height (DR-08)
  — bevel (DR-08)

ADAAG Appendix
- A.4.13: thresholds at doors, door hardware, door closers, door opening force, and automatic doors and power assisted doors

Door Frames

Details or Schedules: drawings
- General frame criteria
  — maneuvering clearance (DR-04)
  — clear opening width and height (DR-09)

Drawers

See "Storage."

Dressing, Fitting, and Locker Rooms

Specifications
- Benches: dressing and fitting room
  — structural requirements: material and mounting (DL-06)
  — surfaces (DL-07, DL-08)

Details: drawings
- Room layout
  — minimum number (DL-01)
  — accessible routes (DL-02)
  — maneuvering clearance (DL-03)
  — bench size, height, and location (DL-04)
  — clear floor space (DL-05)
  — mirror: size and location (DL-09, DL-10)

Drinking Fountains

Drinking fountains are required to be accessible to both wheelchair users (accessible height fountain) and persons having difficulty stooping or bending (standard height fountain). In addition, if the bottom edge of an accessible fountain is mounted higher than 27 in., it might be a protruding object depending on its design.

Because this equipment is usually selected for a particular project and is manufactured to industry standards, it is assumed that their accessible specifications will be in compliance with ADAAG. The reviewer, however, can use the following criteria to review product selection for compliance.

Specifications

- Drinking fountain design criteria
  - spout height and location (DF-07, DF-08)
  - control location (DF-09)
  - control operation (DF-10)
  - mounting height/protruding object (PR-01)

Details: drawings

- Drinking fountain layout
  - minimum number (DF-01, DF-02)
  - alcoves (DF-03)
  - clear floor space (DF-04)
  - knee and toe clearance (DF-05, DF-06)
  - mounting height/protruding object (PR-01)

ADAAG Appendix

- A4.1.3(10) and A4.15: drinking fountains and water coolers

Electrical and Communication Devices

See "Controls and Operating Mechanisms."

Elevators

Because this equipment is usually selected for a particular project and is manufactured to industry standards, it is assumed that their accessible specifications will be in compliance with ADAAG. The reviewer, however, can use the following criteria to review product selection for compliance. In addition to compliance with ADAAG, accessible elevators must also comply with ASME A17.1-1990, Safety Code for Elevators and Escalators.

Specifications

- Elevator design criteria
  - automatic operation, self-leveling, edge clearance (EL-05, EL-06, El-07)
  - hall call buttons (EL-08)
  - hall lanterns and audible signals (EL-10, EL-11)
  - visible signals (EL-12)
  - floor designation (EL-13)
  - door protective and reopening device (EL-14, EL-15)
  - door and signal timing for hall calls (EL-16, EL-17)
  - floor surfaces (EL-20)
  - illumination (EL-21)
  - car controls (EL-22, EL-23, EL-24, EL-25, EL-26, EL-27)
  - car position indicators (EL-28)
  - emergency communication (EL-29, EL-30, EL-31)
  - glass or transparent panels: rail and intercity bus stations only (TF-69)

Details: drawings

- Elevator design criteria and layout
  - hall call buttons (EL-08)
  - protruding objects (EL-09)
  - hall lanterns and audible signals (EL-10)
  - visible signal (EL-12)
  - floor designation (EL-13)
  - floor plan criteria (EL-18, EL-19)
  - floor surfaces (EL-20)
  - glass or transparent panels: rail and intercity bus stations only (TF-69)

ADAAG Appendix

- A4.1.3(5): elevator types
- A4.10: door protective and reopening devices, door and signal timing for hall calls, car controls, car position indicators, and emergency communications

Entrances and Storefronts

See "Doors and Door Frames."

Escalators

This element is only mandated for below grade stations identified in "Fixed Facilities and Stations," ADAAG 10.3.

Because this equipment is usually selected for a particular project and is manufactured to industry standards, it is assumed that their accessible specifications will be in compliance with ADAAG. The reviewer, however, can use the following criteria to review product selection for compliance.

Specifications

- Escalator criteria
  - clear width (TF-65)
  - continuous treads (TF-66)
  - tread markings (TF-67)
  - slip resistance (TF-68)

Fare Vending and Collection Devices

Because this equipment is usually selected for a particular project and is manufactured to industry standards, it is assumed that their accessible specifications will be in compliance with ADAAG. The reviewer, however, can use the following criteria to review product selection for compliance.

Specifications

- Automatic fare vending and self-service collection device criteria
  - controls (TF-42)
  - reach ranges for controls (TF-42)
  - visual information (TF-42)
  - minimum width (TF-45)

Details: drawings
- Automatic fare vending and self-service collection device layout
  — minimum clear floor space (TF-42)
  — accessible routes (TF-43)
  — entry or exit at self-service collection devices (TF-44)

Fire Extinguishers and Cabinets
See "Controls and Operating Mechanisms."

Fixed or Built-in Seating and Tables
Criteria for seating may vary depending on the space type. For example, performance type auditoriums with fixed seating generally do not provide writing surfaces, while a lecture/seminar auditorium with fixed seating may include a writing tablet or fixed table; libraries may have study carrels or computer terminals; restaurants may have fixed tables or booths and tables; exterior activity areas may be provided with fixed seating and tables.

Specifications
- Fixed seating with writing tables
  — minimum table heights (SE-03)
  — knee clearance (SE-04)
- Fixed seating: assembly areas
  — aisle seats without armrest or with removable armrest (AA-02)
- Fixed tables, study carrels, and computer terminals: libraries
  — minimum table heights (LB-01)
  — knee clearance (LB-01)
- Fixed dining tables: restaurants
  — minimum table heights (RC-01)
  — knee clearance (RC-01)

Details: drawings
- Fixed seating and table layout
  — required number of wheelchair spaces (AA-01, LB-01, RC-01)
  — required number of aisle seats (without fixed armrests or removable armrest on the aisle side) (AA-02)
  — clear floor space (AA-05, LB-01, RC-01)
  — wheelchair locations (AA-06, RC-02)
  — fixed companion seating (AA-07)
  — accessible routes (AA-08, AA-09)
  — aisles between tables (LB-01, RC-04)
- Fixed seating with writing tables
  — minimum table heights (SE-03)
  — knee clearance (SE-04)
- Fixed tables, study carrels, and computer terminals: libraries
  — minimum table heights (LB-01)
  — knee clearance (LB-01)
- Fixed dining tables: restaurants
  — minimum table heights (RC-01)

  — knee clearance (RC-01)
- Fixed counter and bars: restaurants
  — counter length, height, and knee clearance (RC-01, RC-03)
  — counter height and knee clearance (RC-03)

ADAAG Appendix
- A4.1.3(19)(a): removable seating and signage for seating with removable or folding arm rests
- A4.32.4: heights of tables or counters

Floor and Ground Surfaces
Specifications that might be affected by criteria for this area include cast-in-place concrete, precast concrete, cementitious decks and toppings, tile, terrazzo, wood flooring, stone flooring, pavers, resilient flooring, carpet, and a variety of interior or exterior gratings.

A major item found throughout ADAAG relates to accessible routes being stable, firm, and slip-resistant. None of these terms has specific performance criteria identified for them. However, the ADAAG Appendix, A4.5, "Ground and Floor Surfaces" provides recommended criteria particularly for static coefficients of friction for different surfaces and A4.5.3 includes carpet information.

Specifications
- Floor surface design criteria
  — changes in level (FS-02)
- Carpet criteria
  — attachment, edges, pile type, and padding (FS-03)
- Grating criteria
  — opening size (FS-04)

Details: drawings
- Floor surface design criteria
  — changes in level (FS-02)
- Grating criteria
  — opening direction (FS-04)

ADAAG Appendix
- A4.5: ground and floor surfaces with recommended criteria for static coefficients of friction for different surfaces
- A4.5.3: carpet information

Gates
See "Doors."

Handrails and Grab Bars
Specifications
- Handrails and grab bars
  — size (HR-01)
  — edge (HR-02)
  — structural requirements: material and mounting (HR-05, HR-06, HR-07)
  — hazards (HR-10)

Details: drawings
- Handrail and grab bar design
  — size (HR-01)

— edge (HR-02)

— wall clearances (HR-03)

— recessed handrail design (HR-04)

— hazards (HR-10)

- Shower stall grab bar design
  — height and location (SS-05)
- Water closet grab bar design
  — location and length (WC-07)
- Toilet stall grab bar design
  — length and location: "standard" stall (TS-10)
  — length and location: "alternate" stall (TS-11)

ADAAG Appendix

- A4.26: size and spacing of grab bars and handrails

Kitchens

See "Counters" and "Sinks" for additional information.

Details: drawings

- Kitchen layout
  — clear floor space (TH-11)
  — countertop and sink heights (TH-12)
  — reach ranges for cabinets and refrigerators/freezers (TH-13)
  — control reach ranges on major appliances (TH-14)

ADAAG Appendix

- A.4.2.5 and A4.2.6: horizontal reach ranges

Lavatories

While not specifically defined by ADAAG, it appears that lavatories are for personal hygiene in bathrooms or toilet rooms, while sinks are for all other situations (e.g., laboratories or kitchens).

Specifications

- Lavatory criteria
  — extension from wall (LV-02)
  — toe clearance (LV-03)
  — knee clearance (LV-06)
- Lavatory trim
  — operation (LV-05)
  — self-closing faucet (LV-05)
  — pipe shielding (LV-04)

Details: drawings

- Lavatory design criteria
  — clear floor space (LV-01)
  — counter and apron height (LV-02)
  — extension from wall (LV-02)
  — toe clearance (LV-03)
  — knee clearance (LV-06)

Libraries

Details: drawings

- Library design criteria and layout
  — number required for fixed seating (LB-01)
  — checkout counters (LB-02)

— security gates (LB-03)

— card catalogs and magazine displays (LB-04, LB-05)

— stacks (LB-06, LB-07)

Life Safety Controls

See "Controls and Operating Mechanisms."

Lighting

Generally, ADAAG does not provide specific data as to exact levels of illumination or lighting types. It frequently uses expressions such as "uniform levels of illumination" or "minimize excessive glare." However, there are some instances where footcandles are prescribed.

Specifications

- Illumination criteria
  — elevators (EL-21)
  — transportation facilities: rail stations and intercity bus stations (TF-57, TF-58, TF-59)

Mirrors and Medicine Cabinets

Specifications

- Dressing, fitting, and locker rooms
  — size (DL-09)
- Medicine cabinets
  — mounting heights (BR-20)

Details: drawings

- Dressing, fitting, and locker rooms
  — location (DL-10)
- Bathrooms and toilet rooms
  — mounting height (LV-09)
- Medicine cabinets
  — mounting heights (BR-20)

ADAAG Appendix

- A.4.19: mirrors

Notification Devices

See "Alarms."

Parking

Details: drawings

- Parking lot layout
  — required number of accessible car parking spaces (PK-01, PK-03)
  — required number at medical facilities (PK-04, PK-05)
  — required number of accessible van parking spaces (PK-02)
  — car parking space dimensions (PK-09)
  — van parking space dimensions (PK-10)
  — cross slopes (PK-11)
  — paving surfaces (PK-12)
  — access aisle (PK-14)
  — route width (PK-15)
  — signage for car parking spaces (PK-16)
  — signage for van parking spaces (PK-17)

- Parking structure layout: in addition to the requirements listed above, parking garages would also include:
  — vertical clearances for vans (PK-13)
  — facility connection (EN-05)

ADAAG Appendix
- A4.1.2(5)(e): valet parking
- A4.6: parking spaces, parking signage, and vertical clearances

Passenger Loading Zones

Details: drawings
- Passenger loading zone layout
  — ISA signage (PK-19)
  — access aisle dimensions (PK-20)
  — aisle slopes (PK-21)
  — vertical clearance (PK-22)
  — medical facilities (MD-01, MD-02)

ADAAG Appendix
- A4.1.2(5)(e): valet parking
- A4.6: parking spaces, parking signage, and vertical clearances

Platform Lifts

Because this equipment is usually selected for a particular project and is manufactured to industry standards, it is assumed that their accessible specifications will be in compliance with ADAAG. The reviewer, however, can use the following criteria to review product selection for compliance.

Specifications
- Platform lift criteria
  — controls (PL-04, PL-05)
  — safety code standards (PL-09)

Details: drawings
- Platform lift layout
  — platform dimensions (PL-02)
  — clear floor area (PL-03)
  — controls (PL-04, PL-05)
  — changes in level (PL-08)

ADAAG Appendix
- A4.1.3(5) and A4.11: additional information on platform lifts

Plumbing Fixtures

See individual fixtures: "Sinks," "Lavatories," "Urinals," or "Water Closets."

Projection Screens

See "Controls and Operating Mechanisms."

Public Address Systems

See "Assisted Listening Systems" for additional information.

Specifications
- Information systems: airports, rail stations, and intercity bus stations (TF-18, TF-63)

Rail and Bus Station Platforms

Details: drawings
- Platform levels and gaps
  — platform height/vehicle floor height (TF-53)
  — horizontal gap: rail systems (TF-54)
  — horizontal gap: people mover (TF-55)
- Track crossings
  — route surface and horizontal gap (TF-62)
- Raised platform design: restaurants
  — accessibility (RC-10)
  — edge protection (RC-11)

Ramps

Specifications
- Ramp criteria
  — ramp and landing surfaces (RP-16)
- Ramp handrail criteria
  — size (HR-01)
  — edge (HR-02)
  — structural requirements: material and mounting (HR-05, HR-06, HR-07)
  — handrail rotation (RP-14)
  — hazards (HR-10)

Details: drawings
- Ramp design
  — running and cross slopes and rises (RP-01, RP-02)
  — clear width (RP-03)
  — landing design and location (RP-04, RP-05, RP-06)
  — ramp drop-off (RP-15)
  — ramp and landing surfaces (RP-16, RP-17)
- Ramp handrail design
  — recessed handrail design (HR-04)
  — structural requirements: wall anchors (HR-07)
  — hazards (HR-10)
  — handrail location (RP-07, RP-08)
  — handrail extension (RP-09)
  — wall clearances (RP-10)
  — handrail mounting height (RP-11)
  — gripping surface (RP-12)
  — handrail ends (RP-13)

ADAAG Appendix
- A4.8: ramp slope and rise, landings, and handrails

Ranges and Ovens

See "Controls and Operating Mechanisms."

Refrigerators/Freezers

Specifications
- Appliance criteria
  — shelf space (TH-13)
  — controls (TH-14)

Restaurants and Cafeterias

Details: drawings

- Restaurant layout
  - required number of accessible seating for fixed tables or dining counters (RC-01)
  - distribution of seating (RC-02)
  - aisle dimensions (RC-04)
  - accessible areas (RC-05)
  - mezzanines (RC-05)
- Counter and bar design
  - counter height, length, and knee clearance (RC-03)
- Food service line design
  - clear width (RC-06)
  - tray slide height (RC-07)
- Shelving and dispensing devices
  - required number accessible (RC-08)
  - reach ranges (RC-08)
  - clear floor space (RC-09)
- Raised platform or stage
  - accessibility (RC-10)
  - edge protection (RC-11)
- Vending machine location
  - accessible route (RC-12)
  - clear floor space (RC-13)

ADAAG Appendix

- A5.0: restaurants and cafeterias

Security Gates

See "Doors" and "Transportation Facilities."

Shelves

See "Storage."

Shower Stalls

Two types of accessible shower stalls are identified: transfer stalls and roll-in stalls. Specific criteria are required for each type.

Specifications

- Seats
  - size, height, and location (SS-03, SS-04)
  - structural requirements: material and mounting (HR-08, HR-09)
- Grab bars
  - height and location (SS-05)
  - size and spacing (HR-01, HR-02, HR-03)
  - structural requirements: material and mounting (HR-05, HR-06, HR-07)
  - hazards (HR-10)
- Controls
  - height and location (SS-06)
  - operation (SS-07)
  - shower spray (SS-08)
- Curbs and enclosure
  - floor curbs (SS-09)
  - enclosure (SS-10)

Details: drawings

- Shower stall layout
  - size and clear floor space (SS-02)
- Seats
  - size, height, and location (SS-03, SS-04)
- Grab bars
  - height and location (SS-05)
  - structural requirements: wall anchors (HR-07)
- Controls
  - height and location (SS-06)
  - operation (SS-07)
  - vandalism exception (SS-08)
- Curbs and enclosure
  - floor curbs (SS-09)
  - enclosure (SS-10)

ADAAG Appendix

- A.4.21: shower stalls

Sidewalks

See "Accessible Routes."

Signage

Criteria for signage vary because there are several different categories, each having different requirements. These categories, as defined by ADAAG are:

- Room identification signage: designates permanent rooms and spaces.
- Pictorial symbol signs (pictograms).
- Direction and information signage: provides direction to or information about functional spaces of the building.
- Specific international symbols: International Symbol for Accessibility, International TDD Symbol for text telephones, and the International Symbol for Hearing Loss.

Specifications

- Room identification signage
  - character type, size, style, finish, and contrast (SG-04)
  - location (SG-05)
- Pictograms
  - border dimensions (SG-06)
  - verbal description and character criteria (SG-07)
- Direction and information signage
  - character proportion, height, finish, and contrast (SG-08)
  - location (SG-09)

Details: particular types other than general room identification or direction and information signage

- Entrances
  - accessible entrances are identified by the International Symbol of Accessibility, where required (SG-01)
  - if an entrance is not accessible, a directional sign indicating the location of the nearest accessible entrance (SG-02)

- Assembly areas
  - aisle seating without fixed armrests or removable armrest on the aisle side identified by signage (AA-03)
  - notification of accessible seating posted at the ticket office (AA-04)
  - informational signage installed to notify patrons of the availability of Assistive Listening Systems that includes the International Symbol for Hearing Loss (AA-11)
- Business mercantile
  - checkout aisles (BM-04)
- Elevators
  - floor designations (EL-13)
  - car control indicators (EL-23)
  - car position indicators (EL-28)
  - emergency two-way communication system designation (EL-31)
- Telephones
  - volume controlled telephones identified by a sign showing a handset with radiating sound waves (SG-10)
  - text telephones identified by the International TDD Symbol (SG-11)
  - directional signage provided to indicate the location of the text telephone (SG-12)
- Areas of rescue assistance
  - illuminated sign (EX-07)
  - instructions (EX-07)
  - signage at inaccessible exits to indicate the direction to areas of rescue assistance (EX-07)
- Parking
  - accessible car parking sign (PK-16)
  - accessible van parking sign (PK-17)
  - accessible passenger loading zone (PK-19)
- Bus stops
  - bus routes (TF-05)
  - bus schedules, timetables, or maps that are posted at the bus stop or bus bay are not required to comply
- Rail stations and intercity bus stations
  - accessible circulation (TF-22)
  - entry signs (TF-26, TF-27)
  - station/platform signs (TF-30, TF-31, TF-32)
  - route signs (TF-33, TF-34, TF-35)
  - bus schedules, timetables, or maps that are posted at the bus stop or bus bay are not required to comply
- Airports
  - entry signs (TF-09)
- Protruding objects
  - frequently, signs that are wall-mounted, free-standing, or mounted overhead can result in a protruding object (PR-05)

- Exits signs
  - exit signs located 80 in. or higher must be at least 3 in. high and meet required character proportions, while exit signs mounted below 80 in. do not have a prescribed height

ADAAG Appendix

- A4.30: general information on signage, character proportion, raised and brailled characters and pictograms, finish and contrast, symbols of accessibility for different types of listening systems, and illumination levels for signage

Sinks

While not specifically defined by ADAAG, it appears that lavatories are for personal hygiene in bathrooms or toilet rooms, while sinks are for all other situations (e.g., laboratories or kitchens).

Specifications

- Sink criteria
  - extension from wall (LV-02)
  - toe clearance (LV-03)
  - operation: trim (LV-05)
  - self-closing faucet (LV-05)
  - knee clearance (LV-07)
  - sink depth (LV-08)

Details: drawings

- Sink design
  - clear floor space (LV-01)
  - counter and apron height (LV-02)
  - extension from wall (LV-02)
  - toe clearance (LV-03)
  - pipe shielding (LV-04)
  - knee clearance (LV-07)
  - sink depth (LV-08)

Sleeping Rooms

Details: drawings

- Sleeping room layout: social services and hotels, dormitories, etc.
  - maneuvering space (TH-10)

Stages

ADAAG only addresses raised platforms within the restaurant criteria. However, it would seem that raised platforms found in other space-types such as meeting rooms, classrooms, or auditoriums would be required to meet the same criteria.

Details: drawings

- Raised platform design: restaurants
  - accessibility (RC-10)
  - edge protection (RC-11)

Stairs

Specifications

- Stair criteria
  - treads and risers (ST-01)

— nosings (ST-02)
— floor and landing surfaces (ST-11)
- Stair handrail criteria
  — size (HR-01)
  — edge (HR-02)
  — structural requirements: material and mounting (HR-05, HR-06, HR-07)
  — handrail rotation (ST-10)
  — hazards (HR-10)

Details: drawings
- Stair design
  — treads and risers (ST-01)
  — nosings (ST-02)
  — floor and landing surfaces (ST-11)
- Landing design
  — U-turn around an obstruction (AR-09)
- Stair handrail design
  — recessed handrail design (HR-04)
  — structural requirements: wall anchors (HR-07)
  — hazards (HR-10)
  — handrail location (ST-03)
  — handrail extension (ST-04, ST-05)
  — wall clearances (ST-06)
  — handrail mounting height (ST-07)
  — gripping surface (ST-08)
  — handrail ends (ST-09)

ADAAG Appendix
- A4.3.11.3: stairway widths and A4.9.1 for minimum number

Storage Units

Types of storage facilities might include cabinets, drawers, shelves, closets, clothes rods, hooks, and bins.

Specifications
- Storage criteria
  — hardware criteria (SR-05)

Details: drawings
- Storage design
  — clear floor space (SR-02)
  — reach ranges (SR-03)
  — closets where passage into is not required to access storage (SR-04)
  — hardware criteria (SR-05)

Telephones

Because this equipment is usually selected for a particular project and is manufactured to industry standards, it is assumed that their accessible specifications will be in compliance with ADAAG. The reviewer, however, can use the following criteria to review product selection for compliance.

Specifications
- Telephone criteria
  — mounting height (TL-07)
  — pushbutton controls (TL-08)

— telephone book (TL-09)
— handset cord length (TL-10)
— volume control and dbA (TL-11, TL-12)
— volume control and dbA: living units and sleeping rooms (TH-19)
— hearing aid compatibility (TL-13)
- Text telephones
  — acoustic coupler connection (TL-19)

Details: drawings
- Telephone: general
  — number required (TL-02, TL-03)
  — clear floor space (TL-04)
  — accessible routes (TL-05)
  — protruding objects (TL-06)
  — mounting height (TL-07)
  — telephone book (TL-09)
  — outlet locations: living units and sleeping rooms (TH-19)
- Text telephones
  — number required: general (TL-14)
  — number required: stadiums, arenas, convention centers, and malls (TL-15)
  — number required: medical facilities (TL-16)
  — number required: transportation facilities (TF-16, TF-17, TF-60, TF-61)
  — equivalent facilitation (TL-17)
  — location (TL-18)
  — portable text telephone criteria (TL-20)
  — shelf size (TL-21)

ADAAG Appendix
- A4.1.3(17)(b): volume controls
- A4.31: telephone mounting heights and text telephones

Thermostats
See "Controls and Operating Mechanisms."

Thresholds
Specifications
- Door thresholds
  — height (DR-08)
  — bevel (DR-08)

Ticketing Areas
See "Counters."

Toilet and Bath Accessories
Specifications
- Toilet paper dispenser criteria
  — paper flow (WC-05)

Details: drawings
- Medicine cabinets
  — shelf height (BR-20)
  — clear floor space (BR-20)

- Dispensers (soap, towel, seat cover, facial tissue), waste receptacles, shelves and racks, vending machines, and ash urns
  - clear floor space (CT-01)
  - reach ranges (CT-04)
- Toilet paper dispenser
  - location (WC-05)
  - clear floor space (WC-06)

Toilet Stalls

Specifications
- Stall grab bars
  - size and spacing (HR-01, HR-02, HR-03)
  - structural requirements: material and mounting (HR-05, HR-06, HR-07)
  - hazards (HR-10)

Details: drawings
- Stall design
  - accessible routes (TS-01)
  - aisle clearance (TS-02)
  - maneuvering space (TS-03)
  - "standard" accessible size (TS-04, TS-05)
  - "alternate" accessible size (TS-06)
  - toe clearance (TS-07)
- Stall doors
  - door maneuvering space (TS-03)
  - door opening size (TS-08)
  - door hardware (TS-09)
- Stall grab bars
  - length and location: "standard" stall (TS-10)
  - length and location: "alternate" stall (TS-11)
  - structural requirements: wall anchors (HR-07)

ADAAG Appendix
- A.4.17: toilet stall size and arrangement and stall doors

Urinals

Specifications
- Urinal criteria
  - rim type and height (UR-01)
  - flush control mounting height (UR-04)
  - flush control operation (UR-05)

Details: drawings
- Urinal layout
  - rim height (UR-01)
  - clear floor space (UR-02)

- clear width between urinal shields (UR-03)
- flush control mounting height (UR-04)

Vending Machines

Because this equipment is usually selected for a particular project and provided by a vendor, it is assumed that their accessible specifications will be in compliance with ADAAG. The reviewer, however, can use the following criteria to review product selection for compliance. See also "Fare Vending and Collection Devices" for additional information.

Details: drawings
- Vending machine locations
  - accessible routes (RC-12)
  - clear floor space (RC-13)

Washers and Dryers

See "Controls and Operating Mechanisms."

Water Closets

Specifications
- Water closet criteria
  - location (WC-01)
  - toilet seat height (WC-02)
  - flush control location and mounting height (WC-03)
  - flush control operation (WC-04)
- Grab bars
  - size and spacing (HR-01, HR-02, HR-03)
  - structural requirements: material and mounting (HR-05, HR-06, HR-07)
  - hazards (HR-10)

Details: drawings
- Water closet criteria
  - location (WC-01)
  - flush control location and mounting height (WC-03)
  - clear floor space (WC-06)
- Grab bars
  - location and length (WC-07)
  - structural requirements: wall anchors (HR-07)

ADAAG Appendix
- A.4.16: water closet heights, grab bars, and flush controls

Windows

At present ADAAG has no compliance requirements for this section for "Windows, 4.12." It has a "reserved" status.

ADAAG Appendix
- A4.12: window hardware

Bibliography and Resources

BIBLIOGRAPHY

Adaptive Environments Center. The Americans with Disabilities Act Fact Sheet Series, *Fact Sheet 6: Resources for More Information* (NIDRR grant # H133D10122), Barrier Free Environments, 1992.

American Association of Museums. *Accessible Museum: Model Programs of Accessibility for Persons with Disabilities and Older Persons,* 1992.

Applied Concepts Corporation. *A Comparison of Domestic and Selected Foreign Standards and Codes for Accessible Facilities* (Contract # QA 880099001), Washington, D.C.: United States Architectural and Transportation Barriers Compliance Board (USATBCB), 1989.

Applied Concepts. *Technical Paper on Accessibility Codes and Standards* (Contract # QA 88009001), Washington, D.C.: United States Architectural and Transportation Barriers Compliance Board (USATBCB), 1989.

Applied Concepts Corp. *Visual Alarms to Alert Persons with Hearing Loss,* Washington, D.C.: USATBCB, 1989

Architects and Builders: Are You in Compliance with the Fair Housing Act? Washington, D.C.: U.S. Department of Housing and Urban Development, 1994.

Barrier Free Environments. In conjunction with Adaptive Environments Center. *UFAS Accessibility Checklist,* Washington, D.C.: United States Architectural and Transportation Barriers Compliance Board (USATBCB), 1990.

Barrier Free Environments. *Uniform Federal Accessibility Standards Retrofit Manual* (Contract # QA 89002001), Washington, D.C.: United States Architectural and Transportation Barriers Compliance Board (USATBCB), 1991.

Barrier Free Environments. Staff. *UFAS Retrofit Guide: Accessibility Modifications for Existing Buildings,* Van Nostrand Reinhold, 1993.

Barrier Free Environments. Staff. *Accessible Housing Design File,* Van Nostrand Reinhold, 1991.

BOMA International. *ADA Compliance Guidebook: A Checklist for Your Building,* Washington, D.C., 1991.

BOMA International. *The ADA Answer Book: Answers to the 146 Most Critical Questions About the Americans with Disabilities Act, Title III,* Washington, D.C., 1992.

Cash-Callahan & Company, Inc. Staff. *Accessible Design Handbook: The ADA Troubleshooter Guide and Workbook,* Cash-Callahan, 1991.

Corporate Services for the Deaf, Inc. *Airport TDD Access: Two Case Studies,* Washington, D.C.: United States Architectural and Transportation Barriers Compliance Board (USATBCB), 1990.

Council on Tall Buildings and Urban Habitat Committee 56. *Building Design for Handicapped and Aged Persons,* McGraw-Hill, Inc., 1992.

Daucher, D.E. *Securement of Wheelchairs and Other Mobility Aids on Transit Vehicles,* Washington, D.C.: USATBCB, 1990.

Davies, Jr., D. Thomas, and Kim A. Beasley. *Accessible Design for Hospitality, 2nd Edition: ADA Guidelines for Planning Accessible Hotels, Motels and Other Recreational Facilities,* McGraw-Hill, 1994.

Department of Justice, Office of Attorney General. *Non Discrimination on Basis of Disability by Public Accommodations and Commercial Facilities; Final Rule* (28 CFR Part 36, FR Vol. 56, No. 144), Washington, D.C., 1991.

General Services Administration, Department of Defense, Department of Housing and Urban Development, U.S. Postal Service. *Uniform Federal Accessibility Standards* (FED STD 795), Washington, D.C.: United States Architectural and Transportation Barriers Compliance Board (USATBCB), 1988.

Goltsman, Susan M. *Accessibility Checklist: An Evaluation System for Buildings and Outdoor Settings,* Berkeley, Calif.: MIG Communications, 1992.

Haber, Gilda M. and Thomas O. Blank, ed. *Council on Tall Buildings and Urban Habitat: Building Design for Handicapped and Aged Persons,* 1992.

Herman Miller Product Research Group. *Think About It: Addressing The Needs of People with Different Abilities,* Zeeland, Mich.: Herman Miller, Inc., 1992.

Herman Miller, Inc. *Designing for Accessibility: Publications* (MI 49464, M.MS1902-1), Zeeland, Mich.: 1992.

Herman Miller, Inc. *Designing for Accessibility: Resource Directory* (M.MS1902-2), Zeeland, Mich.: 1991.

Herman Miller, Inc. *Equal Opportunity Facilities: Designing for Accessibility* (O.MS2916), Zeeland, Mich.: 1991.

Kearney, Deborah. *New ADA: Compliance & Costs,* R.S. Means, 1992.

Lebovitch, William L. *Design for Dignity: Accessible Environments for People with Disabilities,* Wiley, 1993.

Leibrock, Cynthia A. *Beautiful Barrier Free: A Visual Guide to Accessibility,* Van Nostrand Reinhold, 1992.

Mayo, Kathleen and Ruth O'Donnell, ed. "The ADA library kit: sample ADA-related documents to help you implement the law." Chicago, Ill.: Association of Specialized and Cooperative Library Agencies, American Library Association, 1994.

Peloquin, Albert A. *Barrier-Free Residential Design,* McGraw Hill, 1993.

Pennsylvania Transportation Institute. *Slip Resistant Surfaces Advisory Guidelines,* Washington, D.C.: USATBCB, 1991.

Perry, Lawrence. *BOMA International's ADA Compliance Guidebook: A Checklist for Your Building,* Washington, D.C.: Building Owners and Managers Association International, 1992.

Raschko, Bettyann Boetticher. *Housing Interiors for the Disabled and Elderly,* Van Nostrand Reinhold, 1991.

Readable Reports. *Toward an Accessible Environment: Effective Research,* Washington, D.C.: U.S. Department of Education, National Institute on Disability and Rehabilitation Research, Interagency Committee on Disability Research, USATBCB, 1988.

Regnier, Victor A. *Assisted Living Housing for the Elderly: Design Innovations from the United States and Europe,* New York: Van Nostrand Reinhold, 1994.

Terry, Evan, Associates Staff. *Americans with Disabilities Act Facilities Compliance: A Practical Guide,* Wiley, 1992.

Terry, Evan, Associates Staff. *Americans with Disabilities Act: Facilities Compliance Workbook,* Wiley, 1992.

Terry, Evan, Associates Staff. *Americans with Disabilities Act: Facilities Compliance Workbook Supplement,* Wiley, 1993.

United States Architectural and Transportation Barriers Compliance Board (USATBCB) Access America. *Minimum Guidelines and Requirements for Accessible Design* (Federal Register Vol. 47, No. 150), Washington, D.C., 1982.

—— *Accessibility Guidelines for Buildings and Facilities, Transportation Facilities, Transportation Vehicles* (36 CFR Part 1191), (36 CFR Part 1191), (36 CFR Part 1192), Washington, D.C., 1992.

—— *Americans with Disabilities Act Accessibility Guidelines Checklist for Buildings and Facilities,* 1331 F Street N.W., Suite 1000, Washington, D.C. 22004-1111, 1992.

—— *Americans with Disabilities Act Accessibility Requirements,* Washington, D.C., 1991.

—— *Americans with Disabilities Act: Accessibility Guidelines for Buildings and Facilities* (Federal Register Vol. 56, No. 144), Washington, D.C., 1991.

—— *Assistive Listening Systems,* Raybrook, NY, 1991.

—— *The Access Board 1991 Annual Report,* Washington, D.C., 1991.

USDA Forest Service. *Design Guide for Accessible Outdoor Recreation* (2300-Recreation, Sept. 1990, 9023-1803), Washington, D.C., United States Department of Agriculture and United States Department of Interior, 1990.

Wilkoff, William L. and Laura W. Abed. *Practicing Universal Design: An Interpretation of the ADA,* Van Nostrand Reinhold, 1994.

RESOURCES

American Foundation for the Blind
1615 M Street, NW, Suite 250
Washington, D.C. 20036
Tele.: (202) 223-0101 (V/TDD)

BOMA International
1201 New York Avenue NW, Suite 300
Washington, D.C. 20005
Tele.: (202) 408-2662
Fax: (202) 371-0181

Gallaudet University—National Center for Law and Deafness
1615 M Street, NW, Suite 250
Washington, D. C. 20036
Tele.: (202) 651-5343 (V/TDD)

Office on the Americans with Disabilities Act
Civil Rights Division
U.S. Department of Justice
PO Box 66118
Washington, D.C. 20035-6118
Tele.: (202) 514-0301

U.S. Architectural and Transportation Barriers Compliance Board
Suite 1000, 1331 F Street, NW
Washington, D.C. 20004-1111
Fax: (202) 653-7863

Technical Assistance on ADAAG:
Tele.: (800) 872-2253 (voice), (800) 993-2882 (TDD)
Electronic bulletin board: (202) 272-5448

U.S. Department of Justice
U.S. Department of Justice
Office of ADA
PO Box 66738
Washington, D.C. 20035
Tele.: (800) 514-0301

INTERNET RESOURCES ARE AVAILABLE THROUGH THESE ADDRESSES:

- Disability Resources:
  http://www.icdi.wvu.edu/others.htm
- ADA and Disability Information:
  http://www.public.iastate.edu/~sbilling/ada.html

B

Recording Sheets

ADAAG Recording Sheet

JOB NUMBER	PROJECT NAME		DATE	REVIEWER
ROOM/SPACE	**CODE**	**REMARKS**		**COST**

ADAAG Recording Sheet:
Exterior Routes, Spaces, and Parking

| PROJECT NAME | | | DATE | REVIEWER |
| JOB NUMBER | EXTERIOR USE | | LEVEL | SHEET _____ OF _____ |

NOTES

AA 01	AR 09	BR 16	CT 05	**DW** 01	**EN** 01	**PK** 01	**RC** 01	**SE** 01	**ST** 01
AA 02	AR 10	BR 17	CT 06	DW 02	EN 02	PK 02	RC 02	SE 02	ST 02
AA 03	AR 11	BR 18	CT 07	DW 03	EN 03	PK 03	RC 03	SE 03	ST 03
AA 04	AR 12	BR 19			EN 04	PK 04	RC 04	SE 04	ST 04
AA 05	AR 13	BR 20	**DF** 01	**EL** 01	EN 05	PK 05	RC 05		ST 05
AA 06	AR 14		DF 02	EL 02	EN 06	PK 06	RC 06	**SG** 01	ST 06
AA 07		**BT** 01	DF 03	EL 03	EN 07	PK 07	RC 07	SG 02	ST 07
AA 08	**AT** 01	BT 02	DF 04	EL 04		PK 08	RC 08	SG 03	ST 08
AA 09	AT 02	BT 03	DF 05	EL 05	**FS** 01	PK 09	RC 09	SG 04	ST 09
AA 10	AT 03	BT 04	DF 06	EL 06	FS 02	PK 10	RC 10	SG 05	ST 10
AA 11	AT 04	BT 05	DF 07	EL 07	FS 03	PK 11	RC 11	SG 06	ST 11
AA 12	AT 05	BT 06	DF 08	EL 08	FS 04	PK 12	RC 12	SG 07	
AA 13	AT 06	BT 07	DF 09	EL 09		PK 13	RC 13	SG 08	**TL** 01
AA 14		BT 08	DF 10	EL 10	**HR** 01	PK 14		SG 09	TL 02
AA 15	**BM** 01			EL 11	HR 02	PK 15	**RP** 01	SG 10	TL 03
AA 16	BM 02	**CR** 01	**DL** 01	EL 12	HR 03	PK 16	RP 02	SG 11	TL 04
	BM 03	CR 02	DL 02	EL 13	HR 04	PK 17	RP 03	SG 12	TL 05
AL 01	BM 04	CR 03	DL 03	EL 14	HR 05	PK 18	RP 04	SG 13	TL 06
AL 02	BM 05	CR 04	DL 04	EL 15	HR 06	PK 19	RP 05	SG 14	TL 07
AL 03	BM 06	CR 05	DL 05	EL 16	HR 07	PK 20	RP 06		TL 08
AL 04	BM 07	CR 06	DL 06	EL 17	HR 08	PK 21	RP 07	**SR** 01	TL 09
AL 05	BM 08	CR 07	DL 07	EL 18	HR 09	PK 22	RP 08	SR 02	TL 10
AL 06		CR 08	DL 08	EL 19	HR 10		RP 09	SR 03	TL 11
AL 07	**BR** 01	CR 09	DL 09	EL 20		**PL** 01	RP 10	SR 04	TL 12
AL 08	BR 02	CR 10	DL 10	EL 21	**LV** 01	PL 02	RP 11	SR 05	TL 13
AL 09	BR 03	CR 11		EL 22	LV 02	PL 03	RP 12		TL 14
AL 10	BR 04	CR 12	**DR** 01	EL 23	LV 03	PL 04	RP 13	**SS** 01	TL 15
AL 11	BR 05	CR 13	DR 02	EL 24	LV 04	PL 05	RP 14	SS 02	TL 16
AL 12	BR 06	CR 14	DR 03	EL 25	LV 05	PL 06	RP 15	SS 03	TL 17
	BR 07	CR 15	DR 04	EL 26	LV 06	PL 07	RP 16	SS 04	TL 18
AR 01	BR 08	CR 16	DR 05	EL 27	LV 07	PL 08	RP 17	SS 05	TL 19
AR 02	BR 09	CR 17	DR 06	EL 28	LV 08	PL 09		SS 06	TL 20
AR 03	BR 10	CR 18	DR 07	EL 29	LV 09		**SA** 01	SS 07	TL 21
AR 04	BR 11		DR 08	EL 30		**PR** 01	SA 02	SS 08	
AR 05	BR 12	**CT** 01	DR 09	EL 31	**MD** 01	PR 02	SA 03	SS 09	
AR 06	BR 13	CT 02	DR 10		MD 02	PR 03	SA 04	SS 10	
AR 07	BR 14	CT 03	DR 11			PR 04	SA 05		
AR 08	BR 15	CT 04				PR 05			

ADAAG Recording Sheet:
Interior Spaces (excluding Lodging and Transportation Facilities)

PROJECT NAME		DATE	REVIEWER
JOB NUMBER	ROOM NUMBER-USE	FLOOR	SHEET _____ OF _____

NOTES

AA	01	AR	09	BR	16	DL	05	EL	20	HR	05	**PL**	01	RP	09	**SR**	01	TL	10
AA	02	AR	10	BR	17	DL	06	EL	21	HR	06	PL	02	RP	10	SR	02	TL	11
AA	03	AR	11	BR	18	DL	07	EL	22	HR	07	PL	03	RP	11	SR	03	TL	12
AA	04	AR	12	BR	19	DL	08	EL	23	HR	08	PL	04	RP	12	SR	04	TL	13
AA	05	AR	13	BR	20	DL	09	EL	24	HR	09	PL	05	RP	13	SR	05	TL	14
AA	06	AR	14			DL	10	EL	25	HR	10	PL	06	RP	14			TL	15
AA	07			**BT**	01			EL	26			PL	07	RP	15	**SS**	01	TL	16
AA	08	**AT**	01	BT	02	**DR**	01	EL	27	**LB**	01	PL	08	RP	16	SS	02	TL	17
AA	09	AT	02	BT	03	DR	02	EL	28	LB	02	PL	09	RP	17	SS	03	TL	18
AA	10	AT	03	BT	04	DR	03	EL	29	LB	03					SS	04	TL	19
AA	11	AT	04	BT	05	DR	04	EL	30	LB	04	**PR**	01	**SA**	01	SS	05	TL	20
AA	12	AT	05	BT	06	DR	05	EL	31	LB	05	PR	02	SA	02	SS	06	TL	21
AA	13	AT	06	BT	07	DR	06			LB	06	PR	03	SA	03	SS	07		
AA	14			BT	08	DR	07	**EN**	01	LB	07	PR	04	SA	04	SS	08	**TS**	01
AA	15	**BM**	01			DR	08	EN	02			PR	05	SA	05	SS	09	TS	02
AA	16	BM	02	**CT**	01	DR	09	EN	03							SS	10	TS	03
		BM	03	CT	02	DR	10	EN	04	**LV**	01	**RC**	01	**SE**	01			TS	04
AL	01	BM	04	CT	03	DR	11	EN	05	LV	02	RC	02	SE	02	**ST**	01	TS	05
AL	02	BM	05	CT	04			EN	06	LV	03	RC	03	SE	03	ST	02	TS	06
AL	03	BM	06	CT	05	**EL**	01	EN	07	LV	04	RC	04	SE	04	ST	03	TS	07
AL	04	BM	07	CT	06	EL	02			LV	05	RC	05			ST	04	TS	08
AL	05	BM	08	CT	07	EL	03	**EX**	01	LV	06	RC	06	**SG**	01	ST	05	TS	09
AL	06					EL	04	EX	02	LV	07	RC	07	SG	02	ST	06	TS	10
AL	07	**BR**	01	**DF**	01	EL	05	EX	03	LV	08	RC	08	SG	03	ST	07	TS	11
AL	08	BR	02	DF	02	EL	06	EX	04	LV	09	RC	09	SG	04	ST	08		
AL	09	BR	03	DF	03	EL	07	EX	05			RC	10	SG	05	ST	09	**UR**	01
AL	10	BR	04	DF	04	EL	08	EX	06	**MD**	01	RC	11	SG	06	ST	10	UR	02
AL	11	BR	05	DF	05	EL	09	EX	07	MD	02	RC	12	SG	07	ST	11	UR	03
AL	12	BR	06	DF	06	EL	10			MD	03	RC	13	SG	08			UR	04
		BR	07	DF	07	EL	11	**FS**	01	MD	04			SG	09	**TL**	01	UR	05
AR	01	BR	08	DF	08	EL	12	FS	02	MD	05	**RP**	01	SG	10	TL	02		
AR	02	BR	09	DF	09	EL	13	FS	03	MD	06	RP	02	SG	11	TL	03	**WC**	01
AR	03	BR	10	DF	10	EL	14	FS	04	MD	07	RP	03	SG	12	TL	04	WC	02
AR	04	BR	11			EL	15			MD	08	RP	04	SG	13	TL	05	WC	03
AR	05	BR	12	**DL**	01	EL	16	**HR**	01	MD	09	RP	05	SG	14	TL	06	WC	04
AR	06	BR	13	DL	02	EL	17	HR	02	MD	10	RP	06			TL	07	WC	05
AR	07	BR	14	DL	03	EL	18	HR	03	MD	11	RP	07			TL	08	WC	06
AR	08	BR	15	DL	04	EL	19	HR	04			RP	08			TL	09	WC	07

ADAAG Recording Sheet:
All Spaces (including Lodging and Transportation Facilities)

PROJECT NAME			DATE	REVIEWER
JOB NUMBER	ROOM NUMBER-USE		FLOOR	SHEET _____ OF _____

AA 01	BM 01	CR 14	EL 01	GN 01	PK 09	RP 08	ST 01	TF 41	TH 23
AA 02	BM 02	CR 15	EL 02	GN 02	PK 10	RP 09	ST 02	TF 42	TH 24
AA 03	BM 03	CR 16	EL 03		PK 11	RP 10	ST 03	TF 43	TH 25
AA 04	BM 04	CR 17	EL 04	HR 01	PK 12	RP 11	ST 04	TF 44	TH 26
AA 05	BM 05	CR 18	EL 05	HR 02	PK 13	RP 12	ST 05	TF 45	
AA 06	BM 06		EL 06	HR 03	PK 14	RP 13	ST 06	TF 46	TL 01
AA 07	BM 07	CT 01	EL 07	HR 04	PK 15	RP 14	ST 07	TF 47	TL 02
AA 08	BM 08	CT 02	EL 08	HR 05	PK 16	RP 15	ST 08	TF 48	TL 03
AA 09		CT 03	EL 09	HR 06	PK 17	RP 16	ST 09	TF 49	TL 04
AA 10	BR 01	CT 04	EL 10	HR 07	PK 18	RP 17	ST 10	TF 50	TL 05
AA 11	BR 02	CT 05	EL 11	HR 08	PK 19		ST 11	TF 51	TL 06
AA 12	BR 03	CT 06	EL 12	HR 09	PK 20	SA 01		TF 52	TL 07
AA 13	BR 04	CT 07	EL 13	HR 10	PK 21	SA 02	TF 01	TF 53	TL 08
AA 14	BR 05		EL 14		PK 22	SA 03	TF 02	TF 54	TL 09
AA 15	BR 06	DF 01	EL 15	LB 01		SA 04	TF 03	TF 55	TL 10
AA 16	BR 07	DF 02	EL 16	LB 02	PL 01	SA 05	TF 04	TF 56	TL 11
	BR 08	DF 03	EL 17	LB 03	PL 02		TF 05	TF 57	TL 12
AL 01	BR 09	DF 04	EL 18	LB 04	PL 03	SE 01	TF 06	TF 58	TL 13
AL 02	BR 10	DF 05	EL 19	LB 05	PL 04	SE 02	TF 07	TF 59	TL 14
AL 03	BR 11	DF 06	EL 20	LB 06	PL 05	SE 03	TF 08	TF 60	TL 15
AL 04	BR 12	DF 07	EL 21	LB 07	PL 06	SE 04	TF 09	TF 61	TL 16
AL 05	BR 13	DF 08	EL 22		PL 07		TF 10	TF 62	TL 17
AL 06	BR 14	DF 09	EL 23	LV 01	PL 08	SG 01	TF 11	TF 63	TL 18
AL 07	BR 15	DF 10	EL 24	LV 02	PL 09	SG 02	TF 12	TF 64	TL 19
AL 08	BR 16		EL 25	LV 03		SG 03	TF 13	TF 65	TL 20
AL 09	BR 17	DL 01	EL 26	LV 04	PR 01	SG 04	TF 14	TF 66	TL 21
AL 10	BR 18	DL 02	EL 27	LV 05	PR 02	SG 05	TF 15	TF 67	
AL 11	BR 19	DL 03	EL 28	LV 06	PR 03	SG 06	TF 16	TF 68	TS 01
AL 12	BR 20	DL 04	EL 29	LV 07	PR 04	SG 07	TF 17	TF 69	TS 02
		DL 05	EL 30	LV 08	PR 05	SG 08	TF 18		TS 03
AR 01	BT 01	DL 06	EL 31	LV 09		SG 09	TF 19	TH 01	TS 04
AR 02	BT 02	DL 07			RC 01	SG 10	TF 20	TH 02	TS 05
AR 03	BT 03	DL 08	EN 01	MD 01	RC 02	SG 11	TF 21	TH 03	TS 06
AR 04	BT 04	DL 09	EN 02	MD 02	RC 03	SG 12	TF 22	TH 04	TS 07
AR 05	BT 05	DL 10	EN 03	MD 03	RC 04	SG 13	TF 23	TH 05	TS 08
AR 06	BT 06		EN 04	MD 04	RC 05	SG 14	TF 24	TH 06	TS 09
AR 07	BT 07	DR 01	EN 05	MD 05	RC 06		TF 25	TH 07	TS 10
AR 08	BT 08	DR 02	EN 06	MD 06	RC 07	SR 01	TF 26	TH 08	TS 11
AR 09		DR 03	EN 07	MD 07	RC 08	SR 02	TF 27	TH 09	
AR 10	CR 01	DR 04		MD 08	RC 09	SR 03	TF 28	TH 10	UR 01
AR 11	CR 02	DR 05	EX 01	MD 09	RC 10	SR 04	TF 29	TH 11	UR 02
AR 12	CR 03	DR 06	EX 02	MD 10	RC 11	SR 05	TF 30	TH 12	UR 03
AR 13	CR 04	DR 07	EX 03	MD 11	RC 12		TF 31	TH 13	UR 04
AR 14	CR 05	DR 08	EX 04		RC 13	SS 01	TF 32	TH 14	UR 05
	CR 06	DR 09	EX 05	PK 01		SS 02	TF 33	TH 15	
AT 01	CR 07	DR 10	EX 06	PK 02	RP 01	SS 03	TF 34	TH 16	WC 01
AT 02	CR 08	DR 11	EX 07	PK 03	RP 02	SS 04	TF 35	TH 17	WC 02
AT 03	CR 09			PK 04	RP 03	SS 05	TF 36	TH 18	WC 03
AT 04	CR 10	DW 01	FS 01	PK 05	RP 04	SS 06	TF 37	TH 19	WC 04
AT 05	CR 11	DW 02	FS 02	PK 06	RP 05	SS 07	TF 38	TH 20	WC 05
AT 06	CR 12	DW 03	FS 03	PK 07	RP 06	SS 08	TF 39	TH 21	WC 06
	CR 13		FS 04	PK 08	RP 07	SS 09	TF 40	TH 22	WC 07
						SS 10			

ADAAG Recording Sheet:
Building and Site

PROJECT NAME		DATE	REVIEWER
JOB NUMBER			SHEET _____ OF _____

			NOTES
AL	**01**		
AR	**01**		
AR	02		
AR	03		
AR	04		
AR	05		
AR	06		
AR	07		
BR	**01**		
BR	02		
BR	03		
BR	04		
BR	05		
BR	07		
EL	**01**		
EL	02		
EL	03		
EL	04		
EN	**01**		
EN	02		
EN	03		
EN	04		
EN	05		
EN	06		
EN	07		
EX	**01**		
MD	**01**		
MD	02		
MD	03		
SG	**01**		
SG	02		
SG	03		
TH	**00**		
TL	**14**		
TL	15		
TL	16		
TL	17		

C

Master Guidelines

(AR) Accessible Routes (4.3)

NOTES:

- All walks, halls, corridors, aisles, skywalks, tunnels, and other spaces that are part of a designated accessible route shall comply with accessible requirements.
- Any slope on the accessible route that is greater than 1:20 is required to meet all ramp criteria.
- The accessible route shall, to the maximum extent feasible, coincide with the route for the general public.
- In historic buildings, accessible routes from an accessible entrance shall be provided to all publicly used spaces on at least the level of the accessible entrance. Access shall be provided to all levels of a building or facility whenever practical. [4.1.7(3)(d)]

AUTHOR'S INTERPRETATION:

- An accessible route "generally coincides" with the route used by the public if:
  — It does not force the user to go out of the way.
  — It is most like the route chosen by the general public.
  — It is direct.
  — It gives the same basic experience as the route preferred by the public.

Accessible Routes: site

AR-01 If on-site parking is provided, does at least one accessible route within the boundaries of the site connect accessible parking spaces to the accessible building entrance? [4.1.2(1), 4.3.2(1)]

AR-02 Does at least one accessible route within the boundaries of the site connect public streets and sidewalks to the accessible building entrance? [4.1.2(1), 4.3.2(1)]

AR-03 If public transportation stops are available, does at least one accessible route within the boundaries of the site connect public transportation stops to the accessible building entrance? [4.1.2(1), 4.3.2(1)]

AR-04 If passenger loading zones are provided, does at least one accessible route within the boundaries of the site connect a passenger loading zone to the accessible building entrance? [4.1.2(1), 4.3.2(1)]

AR-05 Is there an accessible route connecting all accessible buildings, facilities, elements and spaces on the same site? [4.1.2(2), 4.3.2(2)]

Accessible Routes: interior

AR-06 Is the building entrance space connected by an accessible route to all accessible spaces, elements, and all accessible dwelling units within the building or facility? [4.3.2(3)]

Accessible Routes: dwelling units

AR-07 Does an accessible route connect at least one accessible entrance of each accessible dwelling unit with those exterior and interior spaces and facilities that serve the accessible unit? [4.3.2(4)]

Accessible Routes: width

AR-08 Is the minimum clear width along the accessible route adequate for continuous or point passage? (4.2.1, 4.3.3, Fig. 1, Fig. 8e, Fig. 24e)

- Continuous passage (greater than 24 in. long): at least a 36-in. clear width.
- Point passage (not more than 24 in. long): at least a 32-in. clear width.

AUTHOR'S INTERPRETATION:

- Noncompliance with this question generally relates to permanent elements that encroach on the accessible route. Large, heavy equipment that is not readily movable might be considered permanent. If the space is designed so that temporary elements (such as bikes in a bike rack or car bumpers) will consistently encroach, the situation might also be considered a permanent barrier.

AR-09 Is the minimum clear width along the accessible route adequate at a U-turn around an obstruction? (4.3.3, Fig. 7a–b)

- Obstruction 48 in. or greater: at least a 36-in. clear width around the obstruction.
- Obstruction less than 48 in.: at least a 42-in. clear width at each side with at least a 48-in. clear width in the turn.

Accessible Routes: passing space

AR-10 Does the accessible route provide at least 60 in. of clear width for two wheelchairs to pass and, if not, is the required passing space provided? (4.2.2, 4.3.4)

- A 60-in. × 60-in. passing space or "T" intersection should be provided at reasonable intervals not to exceed 200 ft.

AUTHOR'S INTERPRETATION:

- Accessible routes more than 5 ft long, e.g., routes in short hallways, aisles in laboratories, and work/storage areas, should have passing spaces provided.

DEFINITION:

- A *"T" intersection* is defined as the intersection of two corridors or walks, each at least 36 in. wide providing at least a 60-in. depth at the intersection. (Fig. 3b)

Accessible Routes: maneuvering clearances

AR-11 Is the minimum clear floor space for an unobstructed 180° wheelchair turning space or a "T"-shaped turning space provided? (4.2.3, Fig. 3a–b)

- 180° turning space: at least a 60-in. diameter.
- "T"-shaped turning space: at least 36-in. wide legs with a minimum length of 60 in.

Accessible Routes: slopes

AR-12 Is the running slope on the accessible route 1:20 or less? (4.3.7)

- Any slope on the accessible route that is greater than 1:20 is required to meet all ramp criteria.

AR-13 Is the cross slope on the accessible route 1:50 or less? (4.3.7)

Accessible Routes: changes in level

AR-14 Are changes in level greater than 1/2 in. accomplished by means of a curb ramp, ramp, elevator, or platform lift (as permitted in ADAAG 4.1.3 and ADAAG 4.1.6)? (4.3.8)

(AL) Alarms (4.28)

NOTE:

- At a minimum, visual signal appliances shall be provided in buildings and facilities in restrooms and any other general usage areas. **The ADAAG does not define the number of occupants needed to establish a general or common use area.**

ALLOWANCE:

- Emergency warning systems in medical care facilities may be modified to suit standard health care alarm design practice. [4.1.3(14)]

Alarms: general

AL-01 If emergency warning systems are provided, do they include both audible alarms and visual alarms? [4.1.3(14)]

Audible Alarms: general

AL-02 If provided, do the audible alarms meet required operational criteria? (4.28.2)

- Sound level: exceeds the prevailing sound level in the room or space by at least 15 dbA or exceeds any maximum sound level with a duration of 60 sec by 5 dbA, whichever is louder.
- Sound levels for alarm signals shall not exceed 120 dbA.

AL-03 If single station audible alarms are provided, then are single station visual alarm signals also provided? (4.28.3)

Visual Alarms: general

AL-04 If provided, are the visual alarm signal appliances integrated into the building or facility alarm system? (4.28.3)

AL-05 If provided, do the visual alarm signals meet required operational criteria? [4.28.3(1, 2, 3, 4, 5)]

- Lamp: xenon strobe type or equivalent.
- Color: clear or nominal white (i.e., unfiltered or clear filtered white light).
- Pulse duration: maximum shall be 0.2 sec with a maximum duty cycle of 40 percent.
- Intensity: not less than 75 candela.
- Flash rate: not less than 1 Hz and not more than 3 Hz.

AL-06 Are visual alarm signal appliances provided in public and common use restrooms? (4.28.1)

AL-07 Are visual alarm signal appliances provided in general usage areas of the building (such as meeting rooms, corridors, and lobbies) or any other area for common use? (4.28.1)

AUTHOR'S INTERPRETATION:

- The authors identified three or more occupants as the minimum number to establish a common use area.

AL-08 Are the visual alarms placed at 80 in. above the highest floor level or 6 in. below the ceiling, whichever is lower? [4.28.3(6)]

AL-09 In spaces required to have visual alarms, are the alarms spaced properly? [4.28.3(7)]

- No place in any space should be more than 50 ft from a visual signal alarm.
- Where a space or large room exceeds 100 ft across, without obstructions 6 ft above the finished floor, visual alarms can be spaced a maximum of 100 ft apart at the perimeter, in lieu of suspending appliances from the ceiling.

AL-10 Are visual alarms placed so that no area in a common corridor or hallway is more than 50 ft from the signal? [4.28.3(8)]

Visual Alarms: living units

AL-11 Do accessible living units and sleeping accommodations have a visual alarm connected to the building emergency alarm system or do they have a standard 110-volt electrical receptacle into which such an alarm can be connected, and a means by which a signal from the building emergency alarm system can trigger such an auxiliary alarm? (4.28.4)

AL-12 Is the signal from the visual alarm visible in all areas of the living unit or room? (4.28.4)

(AA) Assembly Areas (4.33)

Assembly Areas: minimum number and notification

AA-01 In assembly areas with fixed seating, is the minimum number of required wheelchair spaces provided? [4.1.3(19)(a), 4.33.1]

- Number of spaces required: one per 4–25 seats, two per 26–50 seats, four per 51–300 seats, six per 301–500 seats, over 500 seats requires six plus one per additional 100 seats. [4.1.3(19)(a)]

AA-02 In addition to required wheelchair spaces, is the required number of aisle seats (without fixed armrests or with removable armrest on the aisle side) provided? [4.1.3(19)(a)]

- Number of spaces required: 1 percent of all fixed seating but not fewer than one.

AA-03 Is the aisle seating without fixed armrests or with removable armrest on the aisle side identified by signage? [4.1.3(19)(a)]

AA-04 Is notification of accessible seating posted at the ticket office? [4.1.3(19)(a)]

Assembly Areas: wheelchair seating size

AA-05 Is the clear floor space adequate for forward, rear, or side access to a wheelchair space? (4.33.2, Fig. 46)

- Width: not less than 33 in. for an individual space or 66 in. for paired spaces.
- Depth: not less than 48 in. for forward and rear access or 60 in. for side access.

Assembly Areas: location

AA-06 Are wheelchair spaces located so that they provide variety in price and view comparable to those for the general public? (4.33.3)

- If the seating capacity is over 300, provide spaces in more than one location.

EXCEPTION:

- These spaces may be clustered for bleachers, balconies, and other areas where sight lines require slopes greater than 5 percent.

AA-07 Is a fixed companion seat provided next to a wheelchair space in each wheelchair area? (4.33.3)

AA-08 Do wheelchair locations adjoin an accessible route that also serves as a means of emergency egress? (4.33.3)

AA-09 Is there an accessible route connecting wheelchair seating locations and performance areas including stages, arena floors, dressing rooms, locker rooms, and other spaces used by performers? (4.33.5)

- In alterations, where it is technically infeasible to alter all performing areas to be on an accessible route, at least one of each type of performing area shall be made accessible. [4.1.6(3)(f)(ii)]

Assembly Areas: floor surfaces

AA-10 Is the floor surface at each wheelchair location level, stable, firm, and slip-resistant? (4.33.4, 4.5)

Assembly Areas: Assistive Listening System (ALS)

AA-11 Where a permanently installed Assistive Listening System is provided, is there informational signage installed to notify patrons of the availability of such a system and does the signage include the International Symbol for hearing loss? [4.1.3(19)(b), 4.30.7(4), Fig. 43d]

AA-12 In assembly areas where audible communications are integral to the use of the space (e.g., concert and lecture halls, playhouses, movie theaters, etc.), is there a permanently installed Assistive Listening System (ALS)? [4.1.3(19)(b)]

- The permanently installed ALS is required in assembly areas where there is fixed seating and one of the following:
  - the space seats more than 50 people, or
  - audio amplification is provided.

NOTE:

- See AA-13 if the assembly area does not meet the preceding criteria.

AA-13 For assembly areas not covered in AA-12, is there a permanently installed or portable Assistive Listening System (ALS) available? [4.1.3(19)(b)]

- This provision can be meet by a permanently installed ALS or by an adequate number of outlets for a portable ALS.
- A portable ALS might be an FM type broadcast system with volume controlled, portable headphones.

AA-14 Is the required number of Assistive Listening System (ALS) receivers provided? [4.1.3(19)(b)]

- Receivers required: 4 percent of total number of seats but not fewer than two receivers.

AA-15 If the Assistive Listening System (ALS) serves individual fixed seats, are these seats located within an unobstructed 50-ft viewing distance of the stage? (4.33.6)

AA-16 Does the Assistive Listening System (ALS) provided meet required operational criteria? (4.33.7)

- Operational criteria: provide signals that can be received directly by persons with special receivers or their own hearing aids and that eliminate or filter background noise.
- Magnetic induction loops, infrared, and radio frequency systems are types of listening systems that are appropriate for various applications.

(AT) Automated Teller Machines (4.34)

NOTES:

- Each automated teller machine required to be accessible shall be on an accessible route.
- Where one or more automated teller machines (ATMs) are provided, at least one must comply with ADAAG 4.34. [4.1.3(20)]

EXCEPTION:

- Drive-up-only automated teller machines are not required to comply with ADAAG 4.27.2 (clear floor space) and ADAAG 4.27.3 (reach ranges). [4.1.3(20)]

Automated Teller Machines: accessible route

AT-01 Is each accessible ATM located on an accessible route? (4.34.1)

Automated Teller Machines: clear floor space

AT-02 Is clear floor space of at least 30 in. × 48 in. provided for a forward or parallel approach to the accessible ATM? (4.34.2, Fig. 4a–c)

Automated Teller Machines: reach ranges

AT-03 Is the highest operable part of the controls on the accessible ATM within the required reach ranges for forward or parallel approach? [4.34.3(1), 4.34.3(2)]

- Forward reach: not less than 15 in. high and not more than 48 in. high without any obstruction or where the obstruction is less than 20 in. deep. For obstructions from 20 in. to 25 in. deep, no forward reach higher than 44 in.

- Side reach:
  — Reach depth not more than 10 in.: not more than 54 in. high above the floor or grade.
  — Reach depth more than 10 in.:
    11 in. depth: not more than 53½ in. high
    12 in. depth: not more than 53 in. high
    13 in. depth: not more than 52½ in. high
    14 in. depth: not more than 51½ in. high
    15 in. depth: not more than 51 in. high
    16 in. depth: not more than 50½ in. high
    17 in. depth: not more than 50 in. high
    18 in. depth: not more than 49½ in. high
    19 in. depth: not more than 49 in. high
    20 in. depth: not more than 48½ in. high
    21 in. depth: not more than 47½ in. high
    22 in. depth: not more than 47 in. high
    23 in. depth: not more than 46½ in. high
    24 in. depth: not more than 46 in. high

AT-04 Where bins are provided for envelopes, wastepaper, or other purposes, is at least one of each type provided within the required reach ranges for forward or parallel approach? [4.34.3(4)]

EXCEPTION:

- Where a function can be performed in an equivalent manner by using an alternate control, only one of the controls is required to comply. If the controls are identified by tactile markings, such markings shall be provided on both controls.

Automated Teller Machines: controls

AT-05 Are controls operable with one hand without tight grasping, pinching, or wrist twisting, and requiring no more than 5 lbf of force? (4.34.4, 4.27.4)

Automated Teller Machines: visual impairments

AT-06 Are instructions and information for use made accessible to and independently usable by people with visual impairments? (4.34.5)

(BR) Bathrooms, Toilet Rooms, Bathing Facilities, and Shower Rooms (4.23)

NOTE:

- In historic buildings, if toilets are provided, at least one toilet facility complying with toilet room accessible criteria shall be provided along an accessible route. Such a toilet facility may be unisex in design. [4.1.7(3)(c)]

Toilet Rooms: public and common use

BR-01 If toilet rooms are provided, does each public and common use toilet room comply with accessible criteria? [4.1.2(6), 4.1.3(11), 4.22.1]

DEFINITION:

- A *common use toilet room* is one used for a restricted group of people, such as occupants of a building or employees of a company.

BR-02 If other toilet rooms are provided for the use of an occupant of a specific space (such as a private toilet room for a company president) is each toilet room adaptable (e.g., door clearance, clear floor space at fixtures, and maneuvering space)? [4.1.2(6), 4.1.3(11), 4.22.1]

Bathrooms: public and common use

BR-03 If bathrooms or bathing facilities are provided, does each public and common use bathroom or bathing facility comply with accessible criteria? [4.1.2(6), 4.1.3(11), 4.23.1]

Toilet/Bathrooms: alternatives

BR-04 In buildings eligible for the elevator exception, if toilet/bathrooms are provided on a level not served by an elevator, is an accessible toilet/bathroom located on the accessible ground floor? [4.1.3(5)]

NOTE:

- If toilet or bathing facilities are also provided on floors above or below the ground level, they must be accessible.

BR-05 Where it is technically infeasible to comply with ADAAG 4.22 or ADAAG 4.23, is at least one unisex toilet/bathroom provided per floor, located in the same area as existing toilet facilities? [4.1.6(3)(e)(i)]

NOTE:

- This is permitted in lieu of modifying existing toilet facilities to be accessible.

BR-06 Does each accessible unisex toilet/bathroom contain one accessible water closet, one accessible lavatory, and a door with a privacy latch? [4.1.6(3)(e)(i)]

Toilet/Bathrooms: general

BR-07 Are accessible toilet rooms, bathrooms, bathing facilities, or shower rooms located on an accessible route? (4.22.1, 4.23.1)

BR-08 When some toilet/bathrooms are not accessible, are the accessible toilet/bathrooms identified by the International Symbol of Accessibility? [4.1.2(7)(d), Fig. 3a–b]

BR-09 If provided, are accessible fixtures and controls located on an accessible route? (4.22.2, 4.23.2)

BR-10 Does the door swing not reduce the clear floor space for accessible fixtures? (4.22.2, 4.23.2)

BR-11 Is the minimum clear floor space for an unobstructed 180° turning space or a "T"-shaped turning space provided in the toilet/bathroom? (4.22.3, 4.23.3, Fig. 3)

- 180° turning space has a 60-in. diameter; "T"-shaped space has 36-in. wide legs.

  - Clear floor space at fixtures and controls, the accessible route, and the turning space can overlap.

BR-12 Do "standard" toilet stalls comply with accessible criteria? (4.22.4, 4.23.4, Fig. 30a–b) See Section "TS" for criteria.

BR-13 Where "alternate" toilet stalls are provided, do they comply with accessible criteria? (4.22.4, 4.23.4, Fig. 30d) See Section "TS" for criteria.

BR-14 Do water closets comply with accessible criteria? (4.22.4, 4.23.4, Fig. 30a–b) See Section "WC" for criteria.

BR-15 Where urinals are provided, does at least one urinal comply with accessible criteria? (4.22.5, 4.23.5) See Section "UR" for criteria.

BR-16 If lavatories are provided, does at least one lavatory comply with accessible criteria? (4.22.6, 4.23.6) See Section "LV" for criteria.

BR-17 Where mirrors are provided, does at least one mirror comply with accessible criteria? (4.22.6, 4.23.6) See Section "LV" for criteria.

BR-18 Is at least one of each type of control, dispenser, receptacle, or other equipment provided accessible and on an accessible route? (4.22.7, 4.23.7)

BR-19 Where bathtubs or showers are provided, does at least one comply with accessible criteria? (4.23.8) See Section "SS" for criteria.

BR-20 If medicine cabinets are provided, does at least one cabinet have a usable shelf no higher than 44 in. from the floor and a clear floor space of at least 30 in. × 48 in.? (4.23.9)

(BT) Bathtubs (4.20)

Bathtubs: clear floor space

BT-01 Is the clear floor space for a parallel or perpendicular approach to the accessible bathtub provided? (4.20.2, Fig. 33)

- Seat-in tub with approach from head of tub and parallel to tub length: at least 30 in. wide × 60 in. long.

- Seat-in tub with approach perpendicular to tub length: at least 48 in. wide × 60 in. long.

- Built-in seat located at head of tub: at least 30 in. wide × 75 in. long.

  NOTES:

  - Head of tub is the end opposite from the controls.

  - The lavatory may encroach into clear floor space at control end of tub.

Bathtubs: seats

BT-02 Does the tub seat comply with accessibility requirements? (4.20.3, Fig. 33–34)

- Size for seat at the head end of tub: at least 15 in. wide.

- Location: opposite end from controls.

- Securely mounted and does not slip during use.

Bathtubs: grab bars

NOTE:

- Additional criteria for grab bars can be found in Section "HR, Handrails."

BT-03 Do the grab bars for seat-in tubs comply with accessible criteria for length and placement? (4.20.4, Fig. 33–34, 4.26, Fig. 39)

- At control wall (foot): at least 24 in. long, beginning at the outside edge of the tub; mounted at 33 in. to 36 in. above the floor.

- At back wall: a double row of bars, at least 24 in. long, beginning not more than 12 in. from the control end and not more than 24 in. from the head end; top bar is 33 in. to 36 in. above the floor; lower bar at 9 in. above the tub rim.

- At head wall: at least 12 in. long beginning at the outside edge of the tub; mounted at 33 in. to 36 in. above the floor.

BT-04 Do the grab bars for built-in seats at head of tub comply with accessible criteria for length and placement? (4.20.4, Fig. 33–34, 4.26, Fig. 39)

- At control wall (foot): at least 24 in. long, beginning at the outside edge of the tub; mounted at 33 in. to 36 in. above the floor.

- At back wall: a double row of bars, at least 48 in. long, beginning not more than 12 in. from the control end and not more than 15 in. from the head end; top bar is 33 in. to 36 in. above the floor; lower bar at 9 in. above the tub rim.

- At head wall: none required.

Bathtubs: controls

BT-05 Are the controls for accessible bathtubs located on the foot wall of the tub, below the grab bar, and offset to the outside edge of the tub? (4.20.5)

BT-06 In accessible bathtubs, are faucets and other controls operable with one hand without tight grasping, pinching, or wrist twisting, and requiring no more than 5 lbf of force? (4.20.5)

BT-07 In accessible bathtubs, is a shower spray unit provided that can be used as both a fixed shower head and a hand-held unit, and does the unit have a hose at least 60 in. long? (4.20.6)

Bathtubs: enclosure

BT-08 Is the bathtub enclosure designed so that it does not obstruct operation of the controls or transfer from a wheelchair onto the bathtub seat or into the bathtub? (4.20.7)

- Enclosures on bathtubs shall not have tracks mounted on their rims.

(BM) Business and Mercantile (7.0)

Business: general

BM-01 Are all areas used for business transactions with the public, such as sales and service counters and/or self-service displays, on an accessible route? [4.1.3(12)(b), 7.2.2]

Business: sales counters with cash registers

BM-02 In retail stores where counters with cash registers are provided, is there at least one accessible cash register counter, and where more than one occurs, are they distributed throughout the facility? (7.2.1)

- Main counter: a portion of the counter is at least 36 in. long and is not more than 36 in. high.

- Alterations: where it is technically infeasible to provide an accessible counter, an auxiliary counter meeting these criteria may be provided.

Business: sales or service counters without cash registers

BM-03 At ticketing counters, teller stations, registration counters, and other counters for distributing goods or services to the public without cash registers, is there an accessible counter or alternative provided? (7.2.2)

- Main counter: a portion of the counter is at least 36 in. long and is not more than 36 in. high.

- Auxiliary counter: in close proximity to the main counter and not more than 36 in. high.

- Equivalent facilitation: might consist of a folding shelf attached to the main counter (for an individual with disabilities to write) and use of the space at the side of the counter for handing materials back and forth.

Business: checkout aisles

BM-04 Is there a sign identifying each accessible checkout aisle that is mounted above the checkout aisle and does the sign include the International Symbol of Accessibility (ISA)? (4.30.7, 7.3.3, Fig. 43a–b)

BM-05 For facilities (new or altered) with under 5000 ft² of selling space, is at least one accessible checkout aisle provided? (7.3.1)

BM-06 For facilities with 5000 or more ft² of selling space, is the required number of accessible checkout aisles provided? (7.3.1)

- New construction and alterations: minimum number for each type of checkout aisle design
  — one accessible aisle for each 1–4
  — two accessible aisles for each 5–8
  — three accessible aisles for each 9–15
  — three plus 20 percent of additional aisles for over 15

NOTE:

- Types might be belted vs. nonbelted or permanently designated express lane vs. regular lane.

BM-07 Is the required clear aisle width provided for accessible checkout aisles and is the adjoining counter within the required height? (7.3.2)

- Aisle width: at least 36 in. for lengths greater than 24 in. and at least 32 in. for lengths 24 in. or less. (4.2.1, F1)

- Counter height: no more than 38 in. above the floor or no more than 40 in. above the floor if the counter has a lip on the edge.

Business: security bollards

BM-08 Are security bollards or other such devices installed so that accessible access and egress is provided? (7.4)

NOTE:

- An alternate accessible entry that is equally convenient to that provided for the general public is acceptable.

(CT) Controls and Operating Mechanisms (4.27)

NOTES:

- Controls or operating mechanisms can include elements such as light switches, pencil sharpeners, manual overhead screens, nonkeyed thermostats, alarm pull stations, fire extinguisher cabinets, A/C window units, microwave ovens, towel dispensers, and wall hooks.

- If controls are to be operated by occupants of the space, they must be accessible. If controls are to be operated by maintenance staff only and not by occupants or other users of the space, they do not have to be accessible. For example, thermostats in auditoriums usually do not have to be accessible, while thermostats in classrooms may need to be accessible.

Controls: clear floor space

CT-01 Is a clear floor space of at least 30 in. × 48 in. provided in front of controls, dispensers, receptacles, and other operable equipment for forward or parallel approach? (4.27.2, Fig. 4a–b)

Controls: reach ranges

NOTES:

- Accessible reach ranges for controls and operating mechanisms are:
  — Forward reach: not less than 15 in. high and not more than 48 in. high without any obstruction or where the obstruction is less than 20 in. deep. For obstructions from 20 in. to 25 in. deep, no forward reach higher than 44 in.
  — Side reach: not less than 9 in. high and not more than 54 in. high. For obstructions not more than 34 in. high or 24 in. deep, no side reach higher than 46 in.
  — Electrical outlets, switches, and communication system receptacles have a minimum outlet height of 15 in. regardless of forward or side reach. See CT-02 below.

CT-02 Are electrical outlets, switches, and communication system receptacles mounted within accessible forward or side reach ranges? (4.27.3)

EXCEPTION:

- These requirements do not apply where the use of special equipment dictates otherwise or where electrical and communications system receptacles are not normally intended for use by building occupants. (4.27.3)

CT-03 Are thermostats or other similar operable equipment mounted within accessible forward or side reach ranges? (4.2.5, 4.2.6, Fig. 5a–b, Fig. 6a–c)

CT-04 Are dispensers or other similar operable equipment mounted within accessible forward or side reach ranges? (4.2.5, 4.2.6, Fig. 5a–b, Fig. 6a–c)

CT-05 Are life safety devices or other similar operable equipment mounted within accessible forward or side reach ranges? (4.2.5, 4.2.6, Fig. 5a–b, Fig. 6a–c)

NOTE:

- This might include fire alarm pull stations, handles to extinguisher cabinets, or wall-mounted extinguishers.

Controls: operation

CT-06 Are controls, dispensers, receptacles, and other operable equipment operable with one hand without tight grasping, pinching, or wrist twisting, and requiring no more than 5 lbf of force? (4.27.4)

Controls: exterior conditions

CT-07 Are the controls for fixtures or equipment located on the exterior accessible route mounted within accessible forward or side reach ranges? (4.2.5, 4.2.6, Fig. 5a–b, Fig. 6a–c)

(CR) Curb Ramps (4.7)

Curb Ramps: location

CR-01 Is there a curb ramp wherever an accessible route crosses a curb? (4.7.1)

Curb Ramps: slopes

CR-02 Is the running slope of the curb ramp 1:12 or less? (4.7.2)

- On existing sites where space limitations prohibit the use of a slope of 1:12 or less, the following slopes can be considered. [4.1.6(3)(a)(i–ii)]
  — Between 1:10 and 1:12 for a maximum rise of 6 in.
  — Between 1:8 and 1:10 for a maximum rise of 3 in.
  — A slope steeper than 1:8 is not allowed.

CR-03 Is the transition from the curb ramp to the walkway and to the road or gutter flush and free of abrupt changes? (4.7.2)

CR-04 Are the running slopes of the road, gutter, or accessible route adjoining the ramp no greater than 1:20? (4.7.2, Fig. 11)

Curb Ramps: width

CR-05 Is the width of the curb ramp, not including the flared sides, at least 36 in.? (4.7.3)

Curb Ramps: surface

CR-06 Is the surface of the curb ramp stable, firm, and slip-resistant? (4.5.1, 4.7.4)

Curb Ramps: side flares

CR-07 If the curb ramp is located where pedestrians must walk across it or where it is not protected by handrails or guardrails, does it have flared sides? (4.7.5, Fig. 12a)

- Flared sides shall have a slope of 1:10 or less.
- If the space at the top of the ramp is less than 48 in. and wheelchair users must use the side flares for access, the flared sides shall have a slope of 1:12 or less.

CR-08 If return curb cuts are provided, are the sides flanked by nonwalking surfaces that prevent pedestrian cross traffic? (4.7.5, Fig. 12b)

AUTHOR'S INTERPRETATION:

- "Nonwalking surfaces" such as plantings, raised planters, or raised curbs prevent pedestrian movement. Signage, impermanent objects such as newspaper boxes, and movable planters do not qualify.

Curb Ramps: built-up

CR-09 If built-up curb ramps are provided, are they located so that they do not project into vehicular traffic lanes or parking access aisles? (4.7.6, Fig. 13)

Curb Ramps: detectable warnings

NOTE:

- Requirements for detectable warnings (truncated domes) at curb ramps (4.7.7) have been suspended until July 26, 1996.

CR-10 Does the curb ramp have a detectable warning? (4.7.7)

- **Suspended until July 26, 1996.**

CR-11 Does the detectable warning consist of raised truncated domes and do they comply with the required criteria? (4.29.2)

- Diameter: nominal 0.9 in.
- Height: nominal 0.2 in.
- Spacing: nominal 2.35 in., center to center, offset every other row.
- Contrast: contrast visually with adjoining surface (light-on-dark or dark-on-light).
- The material used to provide contrast shall be an integral part of the walking surface. Detectable warnings used on interior surfaces shall differ from adjoining walking surfaces in resiliency or sound-on-cane contact.

- **Suspended until July 26, 1996.**

Curb Ramps: obstructions

CR-12 Are curb ramps located or protected to prevent obstruction by parked vehicles? (4.7.8)

Curb Ramps: location at marked crossings

CR-13 Are curb ramps at marked crossings wholly contained (excluding flared sides) within the marked crossing? See ADAAG Fig. 15. (4.7.9)

Curb Ramps: diagonal or corner type

CR-14 If diagonal (or corner type) curb ramps have returned curbs or other well-defined edges, are these curbs or edges parallel to the direction of pedestrian flow? (4.7.10)

CR-15 Is there at least 48 in. of clear space within the crosswalk lines at the bottom of a diagonal curb ramp? (4.7.10, Fig. 15c–d)

CR-16 If the diagonal curb ramp has flared sides, is there at least a 24-in. segment of straight curb located on each side of the diagonal curb ramp within the crosswalk lines? (4.7.10, Fig. 15c)

Curb Ramps: islands

CR-17 Are raised islands in crossings cut through level with the street or are curb ramps provided on each side of the island with at least 48 in. of level area between the curb ramps? (4.7.11, Fig. 15a–b)

(DW) Detectable Warnings (4.29)

NOTE:

▪ Requirements for detectable warnings (truncated domes) at curb ramps (4.7.7), hazardous vehicular areas (4.29.5), and reflecting ponds (4.29.6) have been suspended until July 26, 1996. This action does not affect the requirement for detectable warnings (truncated domes) at transit platforms [10.3.1(8)], which remains in effect.

Detectable Warnings: hazardous vehicular areas

DW-01 If a walk crosses or adjoins a vehicular way, and the pedestrian and vehicular paths are not separated by curbs, railings, or other elements, is the boundary of the pedestrian path defined by a continuous detectable warning (truncated domes), 36 in. wide on the edge of the pedestrian area? (4.29.5)

▪ **Suspended until July 26, 1996.**

Detectable Warnings: reflecting pools

DW-02 Are edges of reflecting pools protected by railings, walls, curbs, or detectable warnings (truncated domes)? (4.29.6)

▪ **Suspended until July 26, 1996.**

Detectable Warnings: criteria

DW-03 Do detectable warnings consist of raised truncated domes and do they meet the required criteria? (4.29.2)

▪ Diameter: nominal 0.9 in.
▪ Height: nominal 0.2 in.
▪ Spacing: nominal 2.35 in., center to center, offset every other row.
▪ Contrast: contrast visually with adjoining surface (light-on-dark or dark-on-light).
▪ The material used to provide contrast shall be an integral part of the walking surface. Detectable warnings used on interior surfaces shall differ from adjoining walking surfaces in resiliency or sound-on-cane contact.

(DR) Doors (4.13)

NOTE:

▪ Included in this category are doors, revolving doors, turnstiles, and gates.

AUTHOR'S INTERPRETATION:

▪ It is suggested that, for purposes of documentation and review, a door be assigned to the space it swings into. Corridors are an exception to this rule and include only entry doors into the corridor or intermediate fire doors.

Doors: revolving doors, turnstiles, and gates

DR-01 Where revolving doors or turnstiles are used on an accessible route, is an adjacent accessible gate or door provided that allows the same use pattern? (4.13.2)

Doors: automatic or power assisted

DR-02 If an automatic door or power assisted door is used, does it comply with the appropriate ANSI standard? (4.13.12)

▪ Automatic door: ANSI/BHMA A156.10-1985.
▪ Slow opening, low powered automatic door: ANSI A156.19-1984.
▪ Power assisted door: ANSI A156.19-1984.

DR-03 Do slow opening, low powered automatic doors or power assisted doors comply with opening and closing requirements? (4.13.12)

▪ Slow opening, low powered automatic doors: do not open to back-check faster than 3 sec and require no more than 15 lbf of force to stop door movement.
▪ Power assisted doors: no more than 5 lbf of opening force.

Doors: maneuvering clearance

DR-04 If the door is not automatic or power assisted, does it have the required maneuvering clearance provided on the push and pull side, and is the floor level and clear within the maneuvering area? (4.13.6)

▪ A verbal description cannot adequately describe the requirements. See ADAAG Fig. 25a–f for a graphic description.

EXCEPTION:

▪ Entry doors to acute care hospital bedrooms for inpatients are exempt from maneuvering space at the latch side of the door if the door is at least 44 in. wide.

AUTHOR'S INTERPRETATION:

▪ While ADAAG does not describe what elements can reduce the required maneuvering clearance, they could include a narrow entry alcove, an adjacent wall, railing, or permanently installed shelving, or a deep recessed door jamb.

Doors: hardware

DR-05 Do all door handles, locks, latches, or other operable devices meet required operational criteria? (4.13.9)

▪ Hardware operation: operable with one hand without tight grasping, pinching, or wrist twisting.
▪ Force required to operate the controls: not greater than 5 lbf. This does not apply to the force required to retract latch bolts or to disengage other devices that only hold the door in a closed position.
▪ Hardware type: "U"-shaped handles, levers, and push type mechanisms are acceptable designs.
▪ Hardware height: not greater than 48 in. above the floor.
▪ Sliding doors: hardware is exposed and usable from both sides when the doors are fully open.

Doors: opening force

DR-06 Do interior hinged doors and sliding or folding doors have an opening force of 5 lbf or less? (4.13.11)

▪ At present, no accessible criteria exist for exterior doors.

- Fire doors shall have the minimum opening force allowable by the appropriate administrative authority.

Doors: closing speed

DR-07 If the door has a closer, is the closer adjusted so that the door does not close too quickly? (4.13.10)

- From an open position of 70°, the door will take at least 3 sec to move to a point 3 in. from the latch (measured to the leading edge of the door).

Doors: thresholds

DR-08 Where raised thresholds are provided, do they meet height limitations and are they beveled when required? (4.13.8, 4.5.2, Fig. 7)

- Threshold height: not more than 3/4 in. for exterior sliding doors or 1/2 in. for other types of doors.
- Threshold bevel: thresholds less than 1/4 in. high need no bevel; thresholds between 1/4 in. and 1/2 in. high shall be beveled at each edge with not more than a 1:2 slope.

EXCEPTION:

- A 3/4-in. high threshold is allowed in existing conditions. [4.1.6(3)(d)(ii)]

Doors: clear opening width and height

DR-09 Is the clear opening for the doorway adequate in width and height? (4.13.3, 4, 5; Fig. 24)

- Door width: at least 32 in. of clear width with the door open at 90°, measured between the face of the door and the door stop on the latch side. This also pertains to the active leaf of a double-leaf door or gate.
- Opening width: openings more than 24 in. deep must provide 36 in. of clear width.
- Height: at least 80 in. of vertical clearance.

EXCEPTIONS:

- Doors not requiring full user passage, such as shallow closets, may have the clear opening reduced to not less than 20 in.
- Where it is technically infeasible to comply with clear opening width requirements, a projection of 5/8 in. maximum will be permitted for the latch side. [4.1.6(d)(i)]

DR-10 Is the clear opening (when there is no door) adequate in width and height? (4.2.1, 4.3.3, 4.4.2)

- Width: at least 32 in. of clear width for depths 24 in. or less and at least 36 in. of clear width for depths greater than 24 in.
- Height: at least 80 in. of vertical clearance.

Doors: two doors in a series

DR-11 If there are two doors in a series, is the required clear space between the doors provided and do the doors swing in the appropriate direction? (4.13.7, Fig. 26)

- Clear space between the doors: not less than 48 in. plus the width of any door swinging into the space.
- Door swing: must swing in the same direction or away from the space between the doors.

(DL) Dressing and Fitting Rooms (4.35)

AUTHOR'S INTERPRETATION:

- ADAAG does not specifically address locker rooms within this category. However, it appears that a number of items identified below are applicable in locker room situations.

Dressing and Fitting Rooms: general criteria

DL-01 Where dressing and fitting rooms are provided for use by the general public, patients, customers, or employees, is the minimum number of rooms complying with accessibility requirements provided? [4.1.3(21), 4.35.1]

- Number: 5 percent (but not fewer than one) of each type (gender or use) in each cluster.

DL-02 Are the accessible dressing and fitting rooms located on an accessible route? (4.35.1)

DL-03 In a dressing or fitting room with a swinging or sliding door, are required maneuvering clearances provided? (4.35.2)

- Turning space: 180° turning space with at least a 60-in. diameter or a "T"-shaped space with at least 36-in. wide legs.
- The clear turning space should not be obstructed by the door swing.

NOTE:

- Turning space is not required in a private dressing room entered through a curtained opening at least 32 in. wide and where clear floor space at least 30 in. × 48 in. is provided.

Dressing and Fitting Rooms: benches

DL-04 Does every accessible dressing and fitting room have a bench that complies with accessible criteria? (4.35.4)

- Size: 24 in. × 48 in.
- Height: mounted 17 in. to 19 in. above the floor.
- Location: affixed to the wall along the longer dimension.

DL-05 Is a clear floor space at least 30 in. × 48 in. provided alongside the accessible bench to allow a person using a wheelchair to make a parallel transfer onto the bench? (4.35.4)

DL-06 Do the accessible bench and its attachments comply with structural strength requirements? (4.35.4)

- Actual bending stress in the seat induced by the maximum bending moment from the application of 250 lbf is less than the allowable bending stress for the material of the grab bar.
- Shear stress induced in a seat by the application of 250 lbf shall be less than the allowable shear stress for the material of the seat. If the connection between the seat and its mounting bracket or other support is considered to be fully restrained, then direct and torsional shear stresses shall be totaled for the combined shear stress, which shall not exceed the allowable shear stress.

- Shear force induced in a fastener or mounting device from the application of 250 lbf shall be less than the allowable lateral load of either the fastener or mounting device or the supporting structure, whichever is the smaller allowable load.
- Tensile force induced in a fastener by a direct tension force of 250 lbf plus the maximum moment from the application of 250 lbf shall be less than the allowable withdrawal load between the fastener and the supporting structure.

DL-07 When installed in conjunction with wet locations, does the surface of the accessible bench have a slip-resistant surface? (4.35.4)

DL-08 When installed in conjunction with wet locations, is the accessible bench constructed so that water does not accumulate on the surface? (4.35.4)

Dressing and Fitting Rooms: mirrors

DL-09 Where a mirror is provided, is it a full length mirror at least 18 in. × 54 in. high? (4.35.5)

DL-10 Is the mirror mounted in a position affording a view to a person on the accessible bench as well as to a person in a standing position? (4.35.5)

(DF) Drinking Fountains and Water Coolers (4.15)

Drinking Fountains: minimum number

DF-01 Where only one drinking fountain is provided on a floor, is it on an accessible route and is it accessible to both wheelchair users and to persons having difficulty stooping or bending? [4.1.3(10)(a)]

- Drinking fountains are required to be accessible to both wheelchair users (accessible height fountain) and persons having difficulty stooping or bending (standard height fountain).

NOTE:

- Alternate solutions might include a high-low fountain or an accessible height fountain and a water cooler with cups. [4.1.3(10)(a)]

DF-02 Where more than one drinking fountain is provided on a floor, do at least 50 percent but not fewer than one of the fountains meet accessible criteria, and is each accessible fountain on an accessible route? [4.1.3(10)(b)]

- Drinking fountains are required to be accessible to both wheelchair users (accessible height fountain) and persons having difficulty stooping or bending (standard height fountain).

Drinking Fountains: clearances and clear floor space

DF-03 If the accessible drinking fountain is located in an alcove, is the alcove adequate in depth and width? (4.15.5, Fig. 27b)

- Depth: not more than 24 in. deep.
- Width: at least 30 in. wide.

DF-04 Is a clear floor space at least 30 in. × 48 in. provided at accessible drinking fountains? [4.15.5(1, 2); Fig. 27b]

DF-05 Does the knee clearance space for wall- and post-mounted cantilevered accessible drinking fountains meet required criteria? (4.15.5, Fig. 27)

- Height: at least 27 in. high from the floor to the apron bottom and maintaining that height for at least 8 in. under the equipment.
- Width: at least 30 in. wide.
- Depth: between 17 in. and 19 in. deep.

NOTE:

- Wall-mounted fountains with leading edges between 27 in. and 80 in. are protruding objects if they project more than 4 in. into the accessible route. A leading edge at 27 in. or below can project any amount as long as it does not restrict the required clear width of the route. (4.4.1)

AUTHOR'S INTERPRETATION:

- If a water fountain is going to protrude more than 4 in. into an accessible route, then it must be mounted at exactly 27 in. in order to comply with required knee clearances and not be considered a protruding object.

DF-06 Is toe clearance at the base of the accessible drinking fountain at least 9 in. high and not more than 6 in. deep? (4.15.5, Fig. 27)

- See ADAAG Fig. 27 for the permitted equipment or piping area.

Drinking Fountains: spout location

DF-07 Is the accessible drinking fountain spout outlet no higher than 36 in. from the ground or floor? (4.15.2, Fig. 27)

DF-08 Is the spout located near the front of the fountain and does it meet required water flow criteria? (4.15.3)

- Water flow trajectory: nearly parallel to the front edge and at least 4 in. high to allow the insertion of a cup or glass.
- Fountain with a round or oval bowl: flow of water is within 3 in. of the front edge.

Drinking Fountains: controls

DF-09 Are the accessible drinking fountain controls front-mounted and/or side-mounted near the front edge? (4.15.4)

DF-10 Are the accessible drinking fountain controls operable with one hand without tight grasping, pinching, or wrist twisting, and requiring no more than 5 lbf of force? (4.15.4)

(EL) Elevators (4.10)

NOTES:

- Accessible elevators shall be on an accessible route and serve each level, including mezzanines, in all multilevel buildings and facilities unless exempted below.
- Accessible elevators shall comply with ASME A17.1-1990, Safety Code for Elevators and Escalators.

EXCEPTIONS:

- New construction elevator exceptions [4.1.3(5)]:

— *Exception 1:* Elevators are not required in facilities that are less than three stories or that have less than 3000 ft² per story unless the building is a shopping center, a shopping mall, the professional office of a health care provider, or another type of facility as determined by the Attorney General. The elevator exemption set forth in this paragraph does not obviate or limit in any way the obligation to comply with the other accessibility requirements established in ADAAG 4.1.3. For example:

a. Floors above or below the accessible ground floor must meet the requirements of this section except for elevator service.

b. If toilet or bathing facilities are provided on a level not served by an elevator, then toilet or bathing facilities must be provided on the accessible ground floor.

c. In new construction, if a building or facility is eligible for this exemption but a full passenger elevator is nonetheless planned, that elevator shall meet the requirements of ADAAG 4.10 and shall serve each level in the building.

d. A full passenger elevator that provides service from a garage to only one level of a building or facility is not required to serve other levels.

— *Exception 2:* Elevator pits, elevator penthouses, mechanical rooms, piping, or equipment catwalks are exempted from this requirement.

— *Exception 3:* Accessible ramps complying with ADAAG 4.8 may be used in lieu of an elevator.

— *Exception 4:* Platform lifts (wheelchair lifts) complying with ADAAG 4.11 and applicable state or local codes may be used in lieu of an elevator only under the following conditions:

a. To provide an accessible route to a performing area in an assembly occupancy.

b. To comply with the wheelchair viewing position line-of-sight and dispersion requirements of ADAAG 4.33.3., "Assembly Areas."

c. To provide access to incidental occupiable spaces and rooms that are not open to the general public and that house no more than five persons, including but not limited to equipment control rooms and projection booths.

d. To provide access where existing site constraints or other constraints make use of a ramp or an elevator infeasible.

▪ Alterations elevator exception [4.1.6(1)(k)]:

— *Exception:* These guidelines do not require the installation of an elevator in an altered facility that is less than three stories or has less than 3000 ft² per story unless the building is a shopping center, a shopping mall, the professional office of a health care provider, or another type of facility as determined by the Attorney General.

NOT EXEMPT:

▪ The exceptions for elevators in ADAAG 4.1.3(5), *Exception 1,* and ADAAG 4.1.6(1)(k) *do not* apply to a terminal, depot, or other station used for specified public transportation, or an airport passenger terminal, or facilities subject to Title II. (10.1)

Elevators: general

EL-01 Where a passenger elevator is not provided, is the building eligible for the elevator exceptions as identified above? [4.1.3(5)]

EL-02 If a building is not eligible for an elevator exception, does a passenger elevator serve each level in the building, including mezzanines? [4.1.3(5)]

EL-03 Where more than one elevator is provided, does each full passenger elevator meet required elevator accessibility criteria? [4.1.3(5)]

EL-04 If the only elevators provided are freight elevators, are they combination passenger and freight elevators for the public and employees, and do they comply with accessible criteria? (4.10.1)

Elevators: automatic operation

EL-05 Is the elevator operation automatic? (4.10.2)

EL-06 Is the elevator self-leveling and does the floor of the elevator automatically come within 1/2 in. of the floor landing at each stop? (4.10.2)

EL-07 Is the clearance between the car platform sill and the hoistway landing edge not more than 1¼ in.? (4.10.9)

Elevators: hall call buttons

EL-08 Do the hall call buttons meet the required criteria? (4.10.3, Fig. 20)

▪ Button location: centered at 42 in. above the floor with the "up" button above the "down" button.

▪ Button size: at least 3/4 in. in the smallest dimension.

▪ Button type: raised or flush, not recessed.

▪ Visual call signals: button indicates each call registered and answered.

EL-09 If an object is mounted below the hall call buttons, does it project less than 4 in. into the elevator lobby? (4.10.3)

▪ This might typically be a wall-mounted ashtray or trash receptacle.

Elevators: hall lanterns and audible signals

EL-10 Is there a visible and audible signal at each hoistway entrance to indicate which car is answering a call? (4.10.4)

EL-11 Do the audible signals sound once for "up" and twice for "down" or does a verbal annunciator say "up" or "down"? (4.10.4)

EL-12 Do the visible signals meet the required criteria?

▪ Fixture location: centerline is at least 72 in. above the floor. [4.10.4(1), Fig. 20]

▪ Fixture size: at least 2½ in. in the smallest dimension. [4.10.4(2)]

▪ Visibility: visible from the vicinity of the hall call button. [4.10.4(3)] In-car lanterns visible from the hall call button and meeting all requirements are also acceptable.

Elevators: floor designation

EL-13 Does each elevator hoistway entrance have floor designations that meet the required criteria? (4.10.5, Fig. 20, 4.30.4)

- Location: on both door jambs centered 60 in. above the floor.
- Character type: raised, upper case, and sans or simple serif.
- Character size: 2 in. high; raised at least 1/32 in.
- Characters are accompanied by Grade II Braille.
- Finish/contrast: nonglare characters and backgrounds with characters contrasting the background (light-on-dark or dark-on-light).

Elevators: door protective and reopening device

EL-14 Does the elevator door open and close automatically and is it provided with an automatic reopening device that complies with the required criteria? (4.10.6, Fig. 20)

- Noncontact: An object or person passing through the opening, between 5 in. and 29 in. above the floor, automatically, without contact, reopens the doors (e.g., light sensor).
- Contact: Safety door edges, as a reopening device, are satisfactory in existing automatic elevators. [4.1.6(3)(c)(i)]

EL-15 Does the door reopening device hold the door open for at least 20 sec? (4.10.6)

Elevators: door and signal timing for hall calls

EL-16 Does the time from when the elevator's arrival is signaled until the doors begin to close fall within acceptable timing ranges? (4.10.7, Fig. 21)

- Minimum notification time is 5 sec or by use of the formula below, whichever is longer.
- $T = D/1.5$ ft/sec T = time in seconds

    D = distance from a point 60 in. in front of the farthest call button for the car to the center of the elevator door.
- A graph interpreting this formula is provided in ADAAG Fig. 21.

EL-17 Do the elevator doors remain fully open for at least 3 sec in response to a car call? (4.10.8)

Elevators: floor plan criteria

EL-18 Is the clear door opening into the elevator car at least 36 in.? (4.10.9, Fig. 22)

EL-19 Does the floor area of the car allow maneuvering room for wheelchair users to enter the car, reach the controls, and exit? (4.10.9)

- New construction:
  - Center door type: at least 54 in. of clear depth from the interior face of the door; at least 51 in. of clear depth from the face of the control panel; at least 80 in. of clear width.
  - Side door type: at least 54 in. of clear depth from the interior face of the door; at least 51 in. of clear depth from the face of the control panel; at least 68 in. of clear width.
- Alterations:
  - At least 48 in. × 48 in. of clear floor space is provided inside the elevator car. [4.1.6(3)(ii)]
  - Equivalent facilitation can be provided with an elevator car of different dimensions when usability can be demonstrated. [4.1.6(3)(iii)]

Elevators: floor surfaces and illumination

EL-20 Is the elevator floor surface stable, firm, and slip-resistant, or is the carpet or carpet tile securely attached with not more than a 1/2 in. pile thickness and exposed carpet edges trimmed to no more than 1/2 in.? (4.10.10, 4.5)

EL-21 Is the level of illumination at the car controls, the platform, and the car threshold and landing sill at least 5 footcandles? (4.10.11)

Elevators: car controls

EL-22 Are the car control panel buttons at least 3/4 in. in their smallest dimension and raised or flush? [4.10.12(1)]

EL-23 Do the car control indicator designations meet the required character criteria? [4.10.12(2)]

- Character type: raised, upper case, and sans or simple serif.
- Character size: between 5/8 in. and 2 in. high; raised at least 1/32 in.
- Characters are accompanied by Grade II Braille.
- Finish/contrast: nonglare characters and backgrounds with characters contrasting the background (light-on-dark or dark-on-light).

EL-24 Do the car control indicators meet required criteria? [4.10.12(2)]

- Raised designations are immediately to the left of the button to which they apply.
- Floor buttons visually indicate each call registered and are extinguished when each call is answered.
- The main entry floor is designated by a raised star at the left of the floor designation.

EL-25 Are the car control panel buttons within acceptable side and front reach ranges? [4.10.12(3), Fig. 23a–b]

- Side approach: not more than 54 in. above the floor.
- Front approach: not more than 48 in. above the floor.

EL-26 Are the car control panel emergency controls grouped and at the correct height? [4.10.12(3), Fig. 23a–b)

- Emergency controls, including alarm and stop, are grouped at the panel bottom with centerlines no less than 35 in. above the floor.

EL-27 Are the controls located on the front wall when the elevator car has a center opening door or located on the front wall or side wall when the elevator car has a side opening door? [4.10.12(4), Fig. 23c–d]

Elevators: car position indicators

EL-28 Do the visual car position indicators meet required criteria? (4.10.13)

- Location: above the control panel or over the door and indicate the floor level.
- Floor indication: corresponding numbers illuminate and an audible signal sounds as the car passes or stops at a floor. Automatic verbal announcement of the floor number, as the car passes or stops, may be substituted for the audible signal.
- Character height: at least 1/2 in. high.
- Audible signal: at least 20 db with a frequency no higher than 1500 Hz.

Elevators: emergency communications

EL-29 When provided, is the communication system usable without voice communication? (4.10.14)

EL-30 When provided, does the emergency two-way communication system in the elevator car meet the required criteria? (4.10.14)

- Location: highest operable part of the communication system is not higher than 48 in. above the floor.
- Handset: when provided, has a cord at least 29 in. long.
- When located in a closed compartment, the door can be operated with one hand, does not require tight grasping, pinching, or wrist twisting; does not require more than 5 lbf of force to open.

EL-31 When provided, is the emergency two-way communication system in the elevator car identified by an adjacent raised symbol and the characters? (4.10.14)

- Character type: raised, upper case, and sans or simple serif.
- Character size: between 5/8 in. and 2 in. high; raised at least 1/32 in.
- Characters are accompanied by Grade II Braille.
- Finish/contrast: nonglare characters and backgrounds with characters contrasting the background (light-on-dark or dark-on-light).

(EN) Entrances (4.14)

EXCEPTION:

- In historic buildings, if it is determined that no entrance used by the public can comply with this section, then access at any entrance not used by the general public but open (unlocked) with directional signage at the primary entrance may be used. The accessible entrance shall also have a notification system. Where security is a problem, remote monitoring may be used. [4.1.7(3)(b)]

Entrances: general

EN-01 Are at least 50 percent of all public entrances accessible? [4.14.1, 4.1.3(8)(a)(i)]

- This does not include service or loading docks, and direct pedestrian access from enclosed parking garages, pedestrian tunnels, or elevated walkways.

EN-02 Is at least one accessible public entrance provided on the ground floor? [4.14.1, 4.1.3(8)(a)(i)]

EN-03 Is the number of accessible entrances at least equivalent to the number of exits required by the applicable fire/building codes? [4.14.1, 4.1.3(8)(a)(ii)]

- This does not require an increase in the total number of entrances planned for the facility.

EN-04 Where feasible, are the accessible entrances used by the majority of the people working in and visiting the building? [4.1.3(8)(a)(iii)]

EN-05 If direct pedestrian access is provided into a building from an enclosed parking garage, is at least one accessible entrance directly from the garage provided? [4.14.1, 4.1.3(8)(b)(i)]

EN-06 If pedestrian access is provided into a building from an elevated walkway or pedestrian tunnel, is at least one accessible entrance from the walkway or tunnel provided? [4.14.1, 4.1.3(8)(b)(ii)]

EN-07 If the service entrance is the only entrance into the building or facility, is it accessible? [4.14.1, 4.1.3(8)(c)]

(EX) Exits and Areas of Rescue Assistance (4.3.11)

DEFINITIONS:

- *Area of Rescue Assistance.* An area with direct access to an exit where people who are unable to use stairs may remain temporarily in safety to await further instructions or assistance during emergency evacuation.
- *Means of Egress.* A continuous and unobstructed way of exit travel from any point in a building or facility to a public way. A means of egress comprises vertical and horizontal travel and may include intervening room spaces, doorways, hallways, corridors, passageways, balconies, ramps, stairs, enclosures, lobbies, horizontal exits, courts, and yards. An accessible means of egress is one that complies with these guidelines and does not include stairs, steps, or escalators. Areas of rescue assistance or evacuation elevators may be included as part of accessible means of egress.

EXCEPTIONS:

- New construction: Areas of rescue assistance are not required in buildings or facilities having a supervised automatic sprinkler system. [4.1.3(9)]
- Alterations: Alterations are not required to provide an area of rescue assistance. [4.1.6(1)(g)]

ALLOWANCES:

- New construction: A horizontal exit can be used as an area of rescue assistance when the exit is designed in accordance with the local building code. [4.1.3(9)]

Exits: number required

EX-01 Does each occupiable level of a building or facility that is required to be accessible have accessible means of egress equal to the number of exits required by local building/life safety regulations? [4.1.3(9)]

- Where a required exit is not accessible, areas of rescue assistance shall be provided equal to the number of inaccessible required exits. [4.1.3(9)]

Areas of Rescue Assistance: location and construction

EX-02 Is each of the areas of rescue assistance located and constructed in compliance with the following criteria as well as local building requirements? [4.3.11(1)]

- The general scope for seven different types of areas of rescue assistance allowed follow. See ADAAG 4.3.11(1) for specific details for each type.
  - A portion of a stairway landing within a smokeproof enclosure.
  - A portion of an exterior exit balcony located immediately adjacent to an exit stairway.
  - A portion of a one-hour fire-resistive corridor located immediately adjacent to an exit enclosure.
  - A vestibule located immediately adjacent to an exit enclosure and constructed to the same fire-resistive standards as required for corridors and openings.
  - A portion of a stairway landing within an exit enclosure that is vented to the exterior and is separated from the interior of the building with not less than one-hour fire-resistive doors.
  - A smokeproof, one-hour fire-resistive room provided with direct access to a one-hour exit enclosure.
  - An elevator lobby when elevator shafts and adjacent lobbies are pressurized as required for smokeproof enclosures.

Areas of Rescue Assistance: wheelchair criteria

EX-03 Does each area of rescue assistance provide space for at least two wheelchairs? [4.3.11(2)]

- Each of the two wheelchair spaces is not less than 30 in. × 48 in. and does not encroach on any required exit width.

EX-04 Is the total number of required wheelchair spaces per story provided? [4.3.11(2)]

- Total spaces per floor: not fewer than one for every 200 persons of calculated occupant load being served by the area of rescue assistance.

EXCEPTION:

- The appropriate administrative authority may reduce the minimum number to only one for each area of rescue assistance on floors where the occupant load is less than 200.

EX-05 Is each stairway serving an area of rescue assistance at least 48 in. wide between handrails? [4.3.11(3)]

Areas of Rescue Assistance: communications and signage

EX-06 Is a method of two-way communication, with both visual and audible signals, provided between each area of rescue assistance and the primary entry? [4.3.11(4)]

- The fire department or appropriate administrative authority may approve a location other than the primary entry.

EX-07 Does signage relating to areas of rescue assistance meet the criteria listed below? [4.3.11(5)]

- Each area is identified by an illuminated sign (if exit signs are required to be illuminated) which states "AREA OF RESCUE ASSISTANCE" and displays the International Symbol of Accessibility.
- Signage is installed at all inaccessible exits and where otherwise necessary to indicate the direction to areas of rescue assistance.
- Instructions are provided on the use of the area during emergencies and are posted adjacent to the two-way communication system.

(FS) Floor and Ground Surfaces (4.5)

Floor Surfaces: general

FS-01 Are the floor/ground surfaces on the accessible route stable, firm, and slip-resistant? (4.5.1)

AUTHOR'S INTERPRETATION:

- Exterior spaces, interior circulation, bathrooms, and other spaces where water can collect on the floor around an element (sinks, drinking fountains, hose bibbs, etc.) are reviewed as if wet.
- High gloss surfaces without significant textures that are regularly maintained with waxing (smooth tiles, waxed concrete, etc.) could be considered noncompliant.
- Accessible criteria are not specified for nonpermanent floor surfaces such as mats or rugs.

Floor Surfaces: changes in level

FS-02 Are vertical changes in level between 1/4 in. and 1/2 in. beveled with a slope of 1:2 or less? (4.5.2)

- Changes in level up to 1/4 in. may be vertical without edge treatment.
- Changes in level greater than 1/2 in. should be accomplished by means of a curb ramp, ramp, elevator, or platform lift (as permitted in ADAAG 4.1.3 and ADAAG 4.1.6).

Floor Surfaces: carpet

FS-03 Does carpet or carpet tile used on the floor comply with accessible criteria? (4.5.3, Fig. 8f)

- Attachment: secured.
- Exposed edges: fastened and trimmed along the entire length.
- Pile type: low pile (1/2 in. maximum).
- Padding: firm pad or no pad underneath.

Floor Surfaces: gratings

FS-04 Do floor gratings in the path of travel comply with accessible criteria? (4.5.4, Fig. 8g–h)

- Opening size: no greater than 1/2 in. in one direction.
- Opening direction: the long dimension is perpendicular to the dominant direction of travel.

(GN) General Information (4.1)

General Information: building barriers

GN-01 Is the building free of any major barriers just before, at, or after the entrance? [4.1.3(1)]

- Examples of these barriers might include steps/stairs, steep slopes/ramps, or unstable ground surfaces.

General Information: space or room barriers

GN-02 Is the space free of any major barriers just before, at, or after the entrance? [4.1.3(1)]

- Examples of these barriers might include steps/stairs, steep slopes/ramps, or unstable ground surfaces.

(HR) Handrails, Grab Bars, and Tub and Shower Seats (4.26)

NOTE:

- HR guidelines may be repeated in other element-based guidelines: (RP) Ramps, (ST) Stairs, (WC) Water Closets, (TS) Toilet Stalls, (BT) Bathtubs, and (SS) Shower Stalls.

Handrails: size and spacing

HR-01 Is the gripping surface of the grab bars or handrails 1¼ in. to 1½ in. in outside diameter? (4.26.2, Fig. 39)

AUTHOR'S INTERPRETATION:

- Standard pipe sizes designated by the industry as 1¼ in. to 1½ in. are acceptable for purposes of this section.

HR-02 Do the grab bars or handrails have edges with a minimum radius of 1/8 in.? (4.26.4)

HR-03 Is the clearance between the grab bars or handrails and the wall exactly 1½ in.? (4.26.2, Fig. 39)

HR-04 If the handrail is located in a recess, is the recess a maximum of 3 in. deep extending at least 18 in. above the rail? (4.26.2, Fig. 39d)

Handrails: grab bar or handrail structural strength

HR-05 Are the grab bars or handrails secure so that they do not rotate in their fittings? [4.26.3(5)]

HR-06 Do the grab bars and handrails meet the structural strength requirements for bending stress and shear stress? (4.26.3)

- Actual bending stress in the grab bar induced by the maximum bending moment from the application of 250 lbf is less than the allowable bending stress for the material of the grab bar.
- Shear stress induced in a grab bar by the application of 250 lbf shall be less than the allowable shear stress for the material of the grab bar. If the connection between the grab bar and its mounting bracket or other support is considered to be fully restrained, then direct and torsional shear stresses shall be totaled for the combined shear stress, which shall not exceed the allowable shear stress.

HR-07 Do the fasteners and mounting devices for the grab bars or handrails meet the structural strength requirements for shear force and tensile force? (4.26.3)

- Shear force induced in a fastener or mounting device from the application of 250 lbf shall be less than the allowable lateral load of either the fastener or mounting device or the supporting structure, whichever is the smaller allowable load.

- Tensile force induced in a fastener by a direct tension force of 250 lbf plus the maximum moment from the application of 250 lbf shall be less than the allowable withdrawal load between the fastener and the supporting structure.

Handrails: tub and shower seat structural strength

HR-08 Do the tub and shower seats meet the structural strength requirements for bending stress and shear stress? (4.26.3)

- Actual bending stress in the seat induced by the maximum bending moment from the application of 250 lbf is less than the allowable bending stress for the material of the grab bar.
- Shear stress induced in a seat by the application of 250 lbf shall be less than the allowable shear stress for the material of the seat. If the connection between the seat and its mounting bracket or other support is considered to be fully restrained, then direct and torsional shear stresses shall be totaled for the combined shear stress, which shall not exceed the allowable shear stress.

HR-09 Do the fasteners and mounting devices for the tub and shower seats meet the structural strength requirements for shear force and tensile force? (4.26.3)

- Shear force induced in a fastener or mounting device from the application of 250 lbf shall be less than the allowable lateral load of either the fastener or mounting device or the supporting structure, whichever is the smaller allowable load.
- Tensile force induced in a fastener by a direct tension force of 250 lbf plus the maximum moment from the application of 250 lbf shall be less than the allowable withdrawal load between the fastener and the supporting structure.

Handrails: hazards

HR-10 Are handrails or grab bars and any wall or other surfaces adjacent to them free of any sharp or abrasive elements? (4.26.4)

(LV) Lavatories, Sinks, and Mirrors (4.19, 4.24)

NOTE:

- Where lavatories or sinks are provided, at least one of each type must meet accessible requirements.

AUTHOR'S INTERPRETATION:

- While not specifically defined by ADAAG, it appears lavatories are for personal hygiene in bathrooms or toilet rooms, while sinks are for all other situations (e.g., laboratories or kitchens).

Lavatories or Sinks: clearances

LV-01 Is there a clear floor space not less than 30 in. × 48 in. in front of the accessible lavatory or sink allowing a forward approach, and does it adjoin or overlap the accessible route? (4.19.3, 4.24.5, Fig. 32)

- The clear floor space can extend up to 19 in. under the sink or lavatory if adequate knee clearance is provided.

LV-02 Are the accessible lavatory or sink rim or counter height, apron height, and extension from the wall adequate? (4.19.2, 4.24.2, Fig. 31)

- Rim height: not greater than 34 in. above the finish floor.
- Apron height: not less than 29 in. above the finish floor to the bottom of the apron.
- Lavatory extension: not less than 17 in. from the wall.

LV-03 Is toe clearance under the accessible lavatory or sink not less than 9 in. above the finish floor and not deeper than 6 in. from the back wall for the full length of the lavatory or sink? (4.19.2, Fig. 31)

Lavatories or Sinks: pipe shielding

LV-04 Are the hot water and drain pipes at the accessible lavatory or sink insulated or otherwise configured to protect against contact, and is the area below the lavatory or sink free of sharp or abrasive surfaces? (4.19.4)

Lavatories or Sinks: controls

LV-05 Do the accessible lavatory or sink controls meet operational requirements? (4.19.5)

- Operation: operable with one hand without tight grasping, pinching, or twisting of the wrist. Acceptable types might include lever operated, push type, touch type, or electronically controlled; no more than 5 lbf of force.
- Self-closing faucets, when used, remain open for at least 10 sec.

Lavatories only

LV-06 Is adequate knee clearance provided underneath the accessible lavatory? (4.19.2, Fig. 31)

- Lavatory knee clearance: not less than 27 in. high from finish floor to the bottom of the lavatory when measured at a point not less than 8 in. from the front of the lavatory.

Sinks only

LV-07 Is adequate knee clearance provided underneath the accessible sink? (4.24.3)

- Sink knee clearance: not less than 27 in. high, 30 in. wide, and 19 in. deep under the sink.

LV-08 Is the accessible sink bowl not more than 6½ in. deep? (4.24.4)

Lavatories or Sinks: mirrors

LV-09 Where mirrors are provided, does at least one mirror have a bottom edge of the reflecting surface no higher than 40 in. above the floor? (4.19.6, Fig. 31)

AUTHOR'S INTERPRETATION:

- Slanted mirrors located above 40 in. are not recognized as compliant by the ADAAG.

(LB) Libraries (8.0)

NOTE:

- In historic buildings displays and written information, documents, etc., should be located where they can be seen by a seated person. Exhibits and signage displayed horizontally (e.g., open books) should be no higher than 44 in. above the floor surface. [4.1.7(3)(e)]

Libraries: minimum number

LB-01 Do at least 5 percent (but not fewer than one) of fixed seating, tables, study carrels, and computer terminals meet accessible criteria? (8.2)

- Seating space: at least a 30 in. × 48 in. clear floor space that adjoins or overlaps an accessible route. No more than 19 in. of the clear floor space can be measured under the table.
- Knee space: at least 27 in. high, 30 in. wide, and 19 in. deep.
- Table/counter height: between 28 in. and 34 in. above the floor.
- Aisles leading up to and between the tables or study carrels are at least 36 in. wide.

NOTE:

- Types of seating can include fixed tables, counters, study carrels, computer terminals, or lounge areas.

Libraries: checkout areas

LB-02 Is there at least one lane at each checkout area where a portion of the counter complies with the required length and height? (8.3, 7.2.1)

- A portion of the counter is at least 36 in. long and not more than 36 in. high.
- In alterations where it is technically infeasible to provide an accessible counter, an auxiliary counter meeting these requirements may be provided.

LB-03 Do security gates or turnstiles comply with accessible width and head clearances? (8.3; 4.13.3, 4, 5; Fig. 24)

- Width: at least a 32-in. clear width at 90° for passage less than 24 in. deep.
- Width: at least a 36-in. clear width for passage greater than 24 in. deep.
- Height: at least 80 in. head clearance.

Libraries: card catalogs and magazine displays

LB-04 Is the aisle space between card catalogs and magazine displays at least 36 in. wide? (8.4, Fig. 55)

LB-05 Are the card catalogs and magazine displays within the accessible reach ranges for forward or side approach? (8.4, 4.2, Fig. 55)

- Minimum height: 18 in.
- Maximum height: forward approach is 48 in.; side approach is 54 in. A height of 48 in. is preferred.

Libraries: stacks

LB-06 Is the minimum clear aisle between stacks at least 36 in. wide? (8.5, Fig. 56)

- Shelf height in stack areas is unrestricted. A minimum clear aisle width of 42 in. is preferred, where possible.

LB-07 Is the minimum clear width for U-turns around the end of stacks provided? (4.3.3, Fig. 7a–b)

- Obstruction 48 in. or greater: at least a 36-in. clear width around the obstruction.
- Obstruction less than 48 in.: at least a 42-in. clear width at each side with at least a 48-in. clear width in the turn.

(MD) Medical Care Facilities (6.0)

Medical Care Facilities: entrances

MD-01 Is there at least one accessible entrance covered by a canopy or overhang? (6.2)

MD-02 Is there an accessible passenger loading zone at this entrance that complies with passenger loading zone requirements, ADAAG 4.6.6? (6.2)

Medical Care Facilities: general purpose hospitals

MD-03 If the facility is a general purpose hospital, are all common and public use areas accessible and are at least 10 percent of patient bedrooms and toilets accessible? (6.1.1)

NOTES:

- The distribution of accessible patient bedrooms can vary based on the anticipated need in different specialized units (e.g., more than 10 percent may be needed in a general surgical unit and less than 10 percent in obstetrics and pediatrics).
- This includes psychiatric facilities and detoxification facilities.

Medical Care Facilities: mobility impairments

MD-04 If the facility is a hospital or rehabilitation facility that specializes in treating conditions that affect mobility, or a unit within either that specializes in treating conditions that affect mobility, are all common and public use areas accessible and are all patient bedrooms and toilets accessible? (6.1.2)

Medical Care Facilities: nursing homes

MD-05 If the facility is a long-term care facility or nursing home, are at least 50 percent of patient bedrooms and toilets accessible? (6.1.3)

Medical Care Facilities: patient rooms

MD-06 Does each accessible bedroom have adequate space to provide maneuvering space? (6.3.2)

- A 60-in. × 60-in. turning space or "T"-shaped space is required for maneuvering.

NOTE:

- If the room has two beds, it is preferable that this space be located between the beds.

MD-07 Does each accessible bedroom have adequate space to provide a minimum clear floor space of 36 in. along each side of the bed and an accessible route to each side of the bed? (6.3.3)

MD-08 Where toilet/bathrooms are provided as a part of an accessible patient bedroom, is the toilet/bathroom located on an accessible route and does the toilet/bathroom meet accessible criteria? (6.4)

NOTE:

- See space-type guide, "Transient Housing: Single User Bathrooms," for toilet/bathroom accessible criteria.

Medical Care Facilities: alterations

MD-09 Where patient bedrooms are added or altered as part of renovation to an entire wing, department, or other discrete area, does the percentage of accessible rooms provided comply with ADAAG 6.1.1, ADAAG 6.1.2, or ADAAG 6.1.3? [6.1.4(a)] See MD-03, 04, and 05.

NOTE:

- Additional accessible rooms are not required in an alteration when the overall number of accessible bedrooms provided in the facility would meet or exceed the percentage required.

MD-10 Do the altered patient bedrooms and toilet/bathrooms that are required to be accessible meet accessible criteria? [6.1.4(a)]

MD-11 Where patient bedrooms are added or altered individually, do they meet accessible criteria? [6.1.4(b)]

NOTE:

- These patient bedrooms are not required to be accessible when the overall number of accessible bedrooms provided in the facility would meet or exceed the percentage required.

(PK) Parking and Passenger Loading Zones (4.6)

NOTE:

- Where only one accessible space is provided, it shall meet van accessible criteria. [4.1.2(5)(b)]

Parking: required number

PK-01 Where parking spaces are provided for self-parking by employees, visitors, or both, is the required number of accessible car parking spaces provided? [4.1.2(5)(a)]

- 1–25:1, 26–50:2, 51–75:3, 76–100:4, 101–150:5, 151–200:6, 201–300:7, 301–400:8, 401–500:9, 501–1000:2 percent of the total, greater than 1000:20+1 for each 100 over 1000.
- All or some of the accessible parking spaces may be in a different location if equivalent or greater accessibility is ensured.

PK-02 Is the minimum number of accessible van spaces provided? [4.1.2(5)(b)]

- One in every eight spaces must be served by an access aisle at least 96 in. wide and must be designated "van accessible." Where only one accessible space is provided, it must meet van accessible criteria.

PK-03 Are accessible parking spaces provided in every specific area/lot? [4.1.2(5)(a)]

- All or some of the accessible parking spaces may be provided in a different location if equivalent or greater accessibility (in terms of distance from an accessible entrance), cost, and convenience are ensured.

PK-04 If the parking lot serves an outpatient facility, are 10 percent of the total parking spaces accessible? [4.1.2(5)(d)(i)]

PK-05 If the parking lot serves a mobility impairment facility, are 20 percent of the total parking spaces accessible? [4.1.2(5)(d)(ii)]

Parking: location

NOTE:

- Van accessible spaces may be grouped on one level of a parking structure.

PK-06 Where accessible parking spaces serve a particular building, are the accessible parking spaces located on the shortest accessible route of travel to an accessible entrance? (4.6.2)

PK-07 In parking facilities that do not serve any particular building, are the accessible parking spaces located on the shortest accessible route of travel to an accessible pedestrian entrance of the parking facility? (4.6.2)

PK-08 If multiple accessible entrances in a building are served by adjacent parking, are the accessible parking spaces dispersed and located closest to the accessible entrances? (4.6.2)

Parking: space dimensions and clearances

PK-09 Do the designated accessible car parking spaces comply with accessible criteria? (4.6.3, Fig. 9, Fig. 10)

- Car parking space width: at least 96 in. wide with a clearly demarcated access aisle.
- Adjacent access aisle width: at least 60 in. wide.
- Two adjacent accessible parking spaces may share a common access aisle.

PK-10 Do the designated accessible van parking spaces comply with accessible criteria? [4.1.2(5)(b), 4.6.3, Fig. 9]

- Van parking space width: at least 96 in. wide with a clearly demarcated access aisle.
- Adjacent access aisle width: at least 96 in. wide.
- Two adjacent accessible parking spaces may share a common access aisle.

PK-11 Are the accessible parking spaces and access aisles level with surface slopes of 1:50 or less in all directions? (4.6.3)

NOTE:

- This means a curb ramp cannot project in to the access aisle.

PK-12 Are the access aisles stable, firm, and slip-resistant? (4.6.3)

PK-13 Does the accessible van parking space have vertical clearance of at least 98 in. at the parking space and along one vehicular route to the parking space (including entry and exiting from the parking lot)? [4.6.5, 4.1.2(5)(b)]

NOTE:

- Van accessible spaces may be grouped on one level of a parking structure.

Parking: access aisle and accessible route

PK-14 Does the access aisle for each accessible parking space connect directly to the accessible route? (4.6.3)

PK-15 Is the clear width (36 in.) of the accessible route maintained and not reduced by potential vehicle bumper overhang? (4.6.3, Fig. 9)

AUTHOR'S INTERPRETATION:

- A bumper overhang of 30 in. is assumed. The 30 in. is measured from the curb or wheel stop.

Parking: signage

PK-16 Does each accessible car parking space have a vertical sign, not obscured by a parked vehicle, showing the International Symbol of Accessibility (ISA)? (4.6.4)

PK-17 Does each accessible van parking space have a vertical sign, not obscured by a parked vehicle, showing the International Symbol of Accessibility (ISA) and an additional sign, "Van Accessible," mounted below the ISA sign? (4.6.4)

Passenger Loading

PK-18 Where passenger loading zones are provided, does at least one meet accessibility requirements? [4.1.2(5)(c)]

PK-19 Is the accessible passenger loading zone marked by the International Symbol of Accessibility (ISA)? [4.1.2(7)(b)]

PK-20 Is there an access aisle adjacent and parallel to the vehicular pull-up space, and is it at least 60 in. wide and 20 ft long? (4.6.6, Fig. 10)

PK-21 Is the vehicle standing space and access aisle in accessible passenger loading zones level with no slope greater than 1:50 (2 percent) in all directions? (4.6.6)

PK-22 Is a minimum vertical clearance of 114 in. provided at the passenger loading zone (including vehicle pull-up space and access aisle) and along the vehicular route to the vehicle pull-up space from site entrances and exits? (4.6.5)

(PL) Platform Lifts (4.11)

EXCEPTIONS:

- New construction elevator exceptions [4.1.3(5)]:
  — *Exception 4:* Platform lifts (wheelchair lifts) complying with ADAAG 4.11 and applicable state or local codes may be used in lieu of an elevator only under the following conditions:
    a. To provide an accessible route to a performing area in an assembly occupancy.
    b. To comply with the wheelchair viewing position line-of-sight and dispersion requirements of ADAAG 4.33.3.
    c. To provide access to incidental occupiable spaces and rooms that are not open to the general public and that house no more than five persons, including, but not limited to, equipment control rooms and projection booths.

d. To provide access where existing site constraints or other constraints make use of a ramp or an elevator infeasible.

Platform Lifts: general

PL-01 Can the lift be entered, operated, and exited without assistance? (4.11.3)

PL-02 Is the lift platform at least 30 in. × 48 in.? (4.11.2, 4.2.4)

PL-03 Is there at least a 30-in. × 48-in. clear floor area provided for both entry to the lift and access to the controls? (4.11.2, 4.2.4)

Platform Lifts: controls

PL-04 Are the platform controls within acceptable reach ranges for forward or side approach? (4.11.2, 4.2.5–6, Fig. 5a–b, Fig. 6a–c)

- Forward reach: not less than 15 in. high and not more than 48 in. high without any obstruction or where the obstruction is less than 20 in. deep. For obstructions from 20 in. to 25 in. deep, no forward reach higher than 44 in.

- Side reach: not less than 9 in. high and not more than 54 in. high. For obstructions not more than 34 in. high or 24 in. deep, no side reach higher than 46 in.

PL-05 Are controls operable with one hand without tight grasping, pinching, or wrist twisting, and requiring no more than 5 lbf of force? (4.11.2, 4.27.4)

Platform Lifts: accessible route

PL-06 Is the lift on an accessible route? [4.1.2(1), 4.3.2]

PL-07 Are the floor of the lift and the adjacent accessible route stable, firm, and slip-resistant? (4.11.2, 4.5.1)

PL-08 Between the edge of the platform lift and the accessible route, are vertical changes in level between 1/4 in. and 1/2 in. beveled with a slope of 1:2 or less? (4.11.2, 4.5.2)

- Changes in level: up to 1/4 in. may be vertical without edge treatment.

Platform Lifts: safety code

PL-09 Does the lift meet the ASME A17.1 Safety Code for Elevators and Escalators, Section XX, 1990? (4.11.2)

(PR) Protruding Objects (4.4)

Protruding Objects: general

PR-01 Do wall-mounted objects having leading edges between 27 in. and 80 in. high project less than 4 in. into walkways, corridors, aisles, or paths of travel? (4.4.1, Fig. 8a–e)

- Objects mounted with their leading edge at or below 27 in. can protrude any amount, as long as they do not reduce the required clear width of an accessible route.

AUTHOR'S INTERPRETATION:

- Protruding objects might include fire extinguishers or cabinets, pencil sharpeners, shelving, counters, built-in equipment overhangs, or various dispensers such as for paper towels or soap.

PR-02 Do free-standing objects, suspended or mounted on posts or pylons with leading edges between 27 in. and 80 in. high, project less than 12 in. into the perpendicular route of travel? (4.4.1, Fig. 8a–e)

AUTHOR'S INTERPRETATION:

- These might include telephone enclosures, drinking fountains, or free-standing signage kiosks.

PR-03 Is the minimum clear route width or maneuvering space still maintained even with the projection of a protruding object? (4.4.1, Fig. 8a–e)

Protruding Objects: overhead clearance

PR-04 Is the minimum overhead clearance of 80 in. provided in accessible areas or along accessible routes? (4.4.2, Fig. 8a)

AUTHOR'S INTERPRETATION:

- Overhead objects that can reduce the required clearance might include structures, pipes, ducts, or light fixtures.

PR-05 Where the vertical clearance of a space adjoining the accessible route is less than 80 in. high, is a cane detection barrier less than 27 in. from the floor provided for blind or visually impaired persons? (4.4.2, Fig. 8c-1)

AUTHOR'S INTERPRETATION:

- This condition might be found under a stair, at a sloped ceiling space, or with guy wires from telephone poles along an exterior accessible route.

(RP) Ramps (4.8)

NOTE:

- Any slope greater than 1:20 is considered a ramp and shall comply with accessible requirements.

Ramps: slopes and rises

RP-01 Is the running slope for the ramp within required parameters? (4.8.2, Fig. 16)

- New construction: 1:12 slope or less with not more than a 30-in. rise for any run.
  - 1:12 slope: 30-ft run between landings.
  - 1:16 slope: 40-ft run between landings.

- On existing sites where space limitations prohibit the use of a slope of 1:12 or less, the following slopes can be considered. [4.1.6(3)(a)(i–ii)]
  - Between 1:10 and 1:12 for a maximum rise of 6 in.
  - Between 1:8 and 1:10 for a maximum rise of 3 in.
  - A slope steeper than 1:8 is not allowed.

EXCEPTION:

- In historic buildings, a ramp with a slope no greater than 1:6 for a run not to exceed 2 ft may be used as part of an accessible route to an entrance. [4.1.7(3)(a)]

RP-02 Is the cross slope of the ramp 1:50 or less? (4.8.6)

Ramps: clear width

RP-03 Is the clear width (between handrails) of the ramp at least 36 in.? (4.8.3)

Ramps: landings

RP-04 Is there a level landing at the top and bottom of each ramp and each ramp run? (4.8.4)

- If a doorway is located at a landing, then the area in front of the doorway must meet door maneuvering clearance requirements.

RP-05 Does each ramp landing meet required dimensions? [4.8.4(1–2)]

- Landing width: at least equal to the ramp width.
- Landing length: at least 60 in. long.

RP-06 Where the ramp changes direction, is there a landing of at least 60 in. × 60 in.? [4.8.4(3)]

Ramps: handrails

NOTE:

- Additional criteria for handrails can be found in Section "HR, Handrails."

RP-07 If the ramp rises more than 6 in. or is longer than 72 in., does it have a handrail on each side? (4.8.5)

- Handrails are not required on curb ramps or adjacent to seating in assembly areas.

RP-08 Is the handrail provided on both sides of ramp segments and is the inside rail on switchback or dogleg ramps continuous? [4.8.5(1), Fig. 19a–b]

RP-09 At the end of the ramp handrails, is there at least 12 in. of handrail parallel to the floor or ground surface, extending beyond the top and the bottom of the ramp segments? [4.8.5(2), Fig. 17]

RP-10 Is the clearance between the ramp handrail and the wall exactly 1½ in.? [4.8.5(3)]

- For recesses, see ADAAG Fig. 39.

RP-11 Are the tops of ramp handrails between 34 in. and 38 in. above ramp surfaces? [4.8.5(5)]

RP-12 Is the ramp handrail gripping surface continuous without obstructions or missing segments? [4.8.5(4)]

RP-13 Are the ends of ramp handrails rounded or returned smoothly to the floor, wall, or post? [4.8.5(6)]

RP-14 Are the ramp handrails fixed so that they do not rotate within their fittings? [4.8.5(7)]

Ramps: edge protection and floor surfaces

RP-15 If a ramp or landing has a drop-off, is it protected by an acceptable option? (4.8.7, Fig. 17)

- Acceptable options include: a wall, a minimum 12-in. horizontal floor extension beyond the railing, a minimum 2-in. curb, or a railing design that prevents people from falling or rolling off.

RP-16 Is the ramp floor surface stable, firm, and slip-resistant? (4.5.1)

RP-17 Are outdoor ramps and their approaches designed so that water does not accumulate on walking surfaces? (4.8.8)

(RC) Restaurants and Cafeterias (5.0)

Restaurants: fixed tables or dining counters: minimum number and distribution

RC-01 Where fixed tables (or dining counters where food is consumed but there is no service) are provided, do at least 5 percent (but not fewer than 1) of the fixed tables (or a portion of the dining counter) meet accessible criteria? [5.1, 4.1.3(18)]

- Seating space: at least 30 in. × 48 in. of clear floor space that adjoins or overlaps an accessible route. No more than 19 in. of the clear floor space can be measured under the table.
- Knee space: at least 27 in. high, 30 in. wide, and 19 in. deep.
- Table/counter height: between 28 in. and 34 in. above the floor.

RC-02 Where separate areas are designated for smoking and nonsmoking patrons, are accessible tables or counters proportionally distributed between smoking and nonsmoking areas? (5.1)

- In new construction, and where practicable in alterations, the accessible tables or counters shall be distributed throughout the space.

Restaurants: counter and bar lengths

RC-03 Where counter service is provided, is a minimum counter length of 60 in. provided that has a height of not more than 34 in. and knee space at least 27 in. high? (5.2)

NOTE:

- Service provided at accessible tables within the same area can also satisfy this criteria.

Restaurants: access aisles

RC-04 Are all aisles between accessible fixed tables at least 36 in. clear between parallel edges of the tables or between a wall and the table edge? (5.3)

Restaurants: dining areas

RC-05 Are all dining areas (including raised or sunken areas, loggias, and outdoor seating areas) accessible? (5.4)

NOTE:

- In new construction, all spaces and areas must be accessible. However, in alterations or existing spaces, inaccessible areas are allowable if
  — The same services and decor are provided in an accessible space usable by the general public.
  — The accessible area is not restricted to use by people with disabilities only.

EXCEPTION:

- An accessible means of vertical access to a mezzanine is not required in a building eligible for the elevator exception where the following three conditions exist.
  — The area of mezzanine seating is not larger than 33 percent of the accessible seating area.
  — The same services and decor are provided in an accessible space usable by the general public.
  — The accessible areas are not restricted to use by people with disabilities only.

Restaurants: food service lines

RC-06 Does the food service line have at least 36 in. of clear width between a wall or other obstruction and the face of the tray slide? (5.5, Fig. 53)

RC-07 Are the tray slides mounted no more than 34 in. above the floor? (5.5, Fig. 53)

Restaurants: self-service shelves and dispensing devices

RC-08 Are at least 50 percent of each type of self-service shelves (flatware, trays) or dispensing devices (drink machines, condiments) provided within accessible forward or side reach ranges? (5.5, Fig. 54, 4.2.5–6, Fig. 5a–b, Fig. 6a–c)

- Forward reach: not less than 15 in. high and not more than 48 in. high without any obstruction or where the obstruction is less than 20 in. deep. For obstructions from 20 in. to 25 in. deep, no forward reach higher than 44 in.
- Side reach: not less than 9 in. high and not more than 54 in. high. For obstructions not more than 34 in. high or 24 in. deep, no side reach higher than 46 in.

RC-09 Are self-service shelves and dispensing devices for tableware, dishware, condiments, food, and beverages provided with a minimum clear floor space of 30 in. × 48 in.? (5.6, Fig. 54)

Restaurants: raised platforms

AUTHOR'S INTERPRETATION:

- ADAAG addresses raised platforms only within the restaurant criteria. However, it would seem that raised platforms found in other space-types such as meeting rooms, classrooms, or auditoriums would be required to meet the same criteria.

RC-10 In banquet rooms or spaces where a head table or speaker's lectern is located on a raised platform, is the platform accessible by means of a ramp or platform lift? (5.7)

- Where applicable, review questions related to [(RP) Ramps] or [(PL) Platform Lifts].

RC-11 Are the open edges of a raised platform protected by the placement of tables, a curb, or some other form of edge protection? (5.7)

Restaurants: vending machines

RC-12 Are vending machines and other like equipment located on an accessible route? (5.8)

RC-13 Is clear floor space of at least 30 in. × 48 in. provided for a forward or parallel approach to controls or operating mechanisms on vending machines? (5.8)

(SE) Fixed or Built-in Seating and Tables (4.32)

Fixed or Built-in Seating and Tables: minimum number

SE-01 Is the minimum number of accessible wheelchair seating locations at fixed tables or counters provided? (4.1.3.18)

- Number required: 5 percent of total number of seats but not fewer than one.

Fixed or Built-in Seating and Tables: clear floor space

AUTHOR'S INTERPRETATION:

- Where the accessible route leads to and through accessible seating adjacent to a wall or another table, the minimum required width for the accessible route will be 65 in. between the table edge and next parallel surface (e.g., wall or another table edge). (4.1.3.18, Fig. 45)

SE-02 Is the clear floor space for a wheelchair at a seating location adequate? (4.32.3, Fig. 4a, Fig. 45)

- Clear floor space: 30 in. × 48 in.
- This clear space can include up to 19 in. under the table/desk.

Fixed or Built-in Seating and Tables: clearances

SE-03 Are the tops of accessible tables and counters between 28 in. and 34 in. from the floor? (4.32.3, Fig. 45)

SE-04 Are the knee clearances at least 27 in. high, 30 in. wide, and 19 in. deep? (4.32.3, Fig. 45)

(SS) Shower Stalls (4.21)

NOTE:

- Requirements for the following shower stalls are for public or common use bathing facilities. Requirements for shower stalls in transient housing may differ. See Section "TH, Transient Housing."

DEFINITIONS:

- *Transfer stall:* a shower stall exactly 36 in. × 36 in.
- *Roll-in stall:* a shower stall at least 30 in. × 60 in.
- *Roll-in stall with folding seat:* two configurations shown in ADAAG Fig. 57a–b. This type is required only in transient housing. See TH-01 and TH-02 in Section "TH, Transient Housing."

Shower Stalls: general

SS-01 Where showers are provided, does at least one comply with accessibility requirements? (4.21.1)

Shower Stalls: stall and clear floor space dimensions

SS-02 Does the accessible shower stall meet the minimum size criteria and provide the required clear floor space? (4.21.2, Fig. 35a–b)

- Transfer stall: a shower stall exactly 36 in. × 36 in. with a clear floor space at least 36 in. wide × 48 in. long extending at least 12 in. beyond the seat wall. A lavatory may not encroach into the clear floor space.
- Roll-in stall: a shower stall at least 30 in. × 60 in. with a clear floor space of at least 36 in. wide × 60 in. long. A lavatory may encroach into the clear floor space.
- Roll-in stall with folding seat: two configurations shown in ADAAG Fig. 57a–b. This type may be required in transient housing.

Shower Stalls: seats

NOTE:

- Depending on the situation, a seat in a roll-in shower may be required only if located in transient housing. For seating in a roll-in shower with folding seat, see ADAAG Fig. 57a–b.

SS-03 Is the seat required in the transfer type shower mounted in the required location? (4.21.3, Fig. 37)

- Height: between 17 in. and 19 in. from the floor.

- Location: mounted on the wall opposite the control wall.

SS-04 Does the seat required in the transfer type shower meet size and shape requirements? (4.21.3, Fig. 36)

- Extends the full width of the stall.
- See ADAAG Fig. 36 for dimensional criteria.

Shower Stalls: grab bars

NOTE:

- Additional criteria for grab bars can be found in Section "HR, Handrails."

SS-05 Do the shower stall grab bars comply with accessible criteria? (4.21.4, Fig. 37a–b)

- Height: between 33 in. and 36 in. above the floor.
- Transfer stall: bar runs along the control wall and is continuous for 18 in. on the back wall; does not run behind the seat.
- Roll-in stall: continuous bar on all three walls.
- Roll-in stall with folding seat: see grab bar locations shown in ADAAG Fig. 57a–b.

Shower Stalls: controls

SS-06 Are the accessible shower faucets and other controls located in the required area? (4.21.5, Fig. 37a–b)

- Height: between 38 in. and 48 in. above the floor.
- Transfer stall: located on the side wall opposite the seat wall, within 18 in. from the outside edge of the stall.
- Roll-in stall: located on the back wall or on either side wall. If located on the back wall within 27 in. from either side wall with the controls offset to one side; controls located on the side wall are offset to the outside edge of the stall.
- Roll-in stall with folding seat: see control locations shown in ADAAG Fig. 57a–b.

SS-07 In accessible showers, are faucets and other controls operable with one hand without tight grasping, pinching, or wrist twisting, and requiring no more than 5 lbf of force? (4.21.5)

SS-08 In accessible showers, is a shower spray unit provided that can be used as both a fixed shower head and a hand-held unit and does the unit have a hose at least 60 in. long? (4.21.6)

EXCEPTION:

- In unmonitored facilities where vandalism is a consideration, a fixed shower head mounted at 48 in. above the floor may be used in lieu of the hand-held shower head.

Shower Stalls: curbs and enclosure

SS-09 Where floor curbs are provided, do they comply with accessibility requirements? (4.21.7)

- Transfer stall: curbs can be no higher than 1/2 in.
- Roll-in stall: no curb is allowed.

SS-10 Where a shower stall enclosure is provided, is it located so that it does not obstruct the controls or obstruct the transfer from a wheelchair to the shower seat? (4.21.8)

(SG) Signage (4.30)

NOTE:

- In historic buildings displays and written information, documents, etc., should be located where they can be seen by a seated person. Exhibits and signage displayed horizontally (e.g., open books) should be no higher than 44 in. above the floor surface. [4.1.7(3)(e)]

Signage: entry

SG-01 Where a building or space has both accessible and inaccessible entrances, are the accessible entrances identified by the International Symbol of Accessibility? [4.1.2(7)(c), Fig. 43a–b]

SG-02 If an entrance is not accessible, is there a directional sign indicating the location of the nearest accessible entrance? [4.1.2(7)(c), 4.1.3(8)(d)]

SG-03 Does the directional sign indicating the location of the nearest accessible entrance comply with directional signage criteria? (4.30.2, 3, 5)

- Character proportion: letters and numbers have a width to height ratio between 3:5 and 1:1 and a stroke width to height ratio between 1:5 and 1:10.
- Character height: sized according to viewing distance with characters on overhead signs at least 3 in. high.
- Finish: characters and backgrounds have a nonglare finish.
- Contrast: characters contrast with their background (light-on-dark or dark-on-light).

Signage: room identification (where provided)

DEFINITION:

- These signs designate permanent rooms and spaces.

AUTHOR'S INTERPRETATION:

- Signs that designate stairs, exit doors, and toilet rooms generally are associated with permanent spaces, while an "office" sign is not since the room function may change over time. Room numbers also must meet the ADAAG criteria as permanent designations, while personal names do not since the occupant may change over time.

SG-04 Do signs that designate permanent rooms and spaces comply with the following criteria? [4.1.2(7); 4.1.3(16); 4.30.4, 5, 6]

- Character type: raised and accompanied by Grade II Braille.
- Character size: between 5/8 in. and 2 in. high; raised at least 1/32 in.
- Character style: upper case, and sans or simple serif.
- Finish: characters and backgrounds have a nonglare finish.
- Contrast: characters contrast with their background (light-on-dark or dark-on-light).

SG-05 Is the room identification sign mounted in the required location? (4.30.6)

- Mounting location: installed on the wall adjacent to the latch side of the door or where wall space to the latch side of the door is not available, including double doors, placed on the nearest adjacent wall.
- Mounting height: 60 in. above the floor/ground to the centerline of the sign.
- Sign access: approach to within 3 in. of a sign without encountering protruding objects or standing within the swing of the door.

Signage: pictorial symbol signs (pictograms) (where provided)

AUTHOR'S INTERPRETATION:

- Because the criteria for pictograms are listed in ADAAG 4.30.4, they fall into the category of room identification signage and must meet those criteria.
- While the ISA symbol might be considered to be a pictogram, it does not appear to have the same requirements as pictograms.

SG-06 Is the border dimension of a pictogram, where provided, at least 6 in. high? (4.30.4)

AUTHOR'S INTERPRETATION:

- A pictogram includes both a symbol and the field on which it is displayed. The 6-in. vertical dimension applies to the vertical field, not to the symbol. The required verbal description may not intrude on the 6-in. field.

SG-07 Is a pictogram, where provided, accompanied by the equivalent verbal description placed directly below the pictogram, and does the verbal description meet room identification signage criteria? (4.30.4)

- Character type: raised and accompanied by Grade II Braille.
- Character size: between 5/8 in. and 2 in. high; raised at least 1/32 in.
- Character style: upper case, and sans or simple serif.
- Finish: characters and backgrounds have a nonglare finish.
- Contrast: characters contrast with their background (light-on-dark or dark-on-light).

Signage: direction and information (where provided)

DEFINITION:

- Signs that provide direction to or information about functional spaces of the building.

EXCEPTION:

- Building directories, menus, and all other temporary signs are not required to comply. [4.1.3(16)]

SG-08 Do signs that provide direction to, or information about, functional spaces of the building comply with the criteria below? [4.1.2(7); 4.1.3(16); 4.30.1, 2, 3, 5]

- Character proportion: letters and numbers have a width to height ratio between 3:5 and 1:1 and a stroke width to height ratio between 1:5 and 1:10.
- Character height: sized according to viewing distance with characters on overhead signs at least 3 in. high.

NOTE:

- When the sign is mounted below 80 in., there are no prescribed character heights. Only when the sign is mounted 80 in. or higher are the characters required to be at least 3 in. high. (4.30.3)
- Finish: characters and backgrounds have a nonglare finish.
- Contrast: characters contrast with their background (light-on-dark or dark-on-light).

SG-09 Is a sign located so that the overhead clearance or the projection of a suspended or projected sign does not result in a protruding object (free-standing or wall-mounted)?

- Clear height: at least 80 in. (4.4.2, Fig. 8a)
- Overhang for free-standing signs on posts or pylons located between 27 in. and 80 in. high: no more than a 12-in. projection into accessible routes. (4.4.1, Fig. 8c)
- Overhang for wall-mounted signs between 27 in. and 80 in. high: no more than a 4-in. projection into accessible routes. (4.4.1, Fig. 8a)

Signage: volume control telephones

SG-10 Are volume controlled telephones identified by a sign showing a handset with radiating sound waves? [4.30.7(2)]

Signage: text telephones

SG-11 Are required text telephones identified by the international TDD symbol? [4.30.7(3), Fig. 43c]

SG-12 Is directional signage provided to indicate the location of the text telephone and is that signage placed adjacent to all telephone banks that do not contain a text telephone? [4.30.7(3)]

- If the facility does not have any telephone banks, the directional signage must be provided at the entrance (e.g., in a building directory).

SG-13 Does the directional signage to text telephones comply with directional signage criteria? [4.30.7(3)]

- Character proportion: letters and numbers have a width to height ratio between 3:5 and 1:1 and a stroke width to height ratio between 1:5 and 1:10.
- Character height: sized according to viewing distance with characters on overhead signs at least 3 in. high.
- Finish: characters and backgrounds have a nonglare finish.
- Contrast: characters contrast with their background (light-on-dark or dark-on-light).

SG-14 Where a permanently installed Assistive Listening System is provided, is there informational signage installed to notify patrons of the availability of such a system, and does the signage include the International Symbol for hearing loss? [4.30.7(4), Fig. 43d]

(SA) Space Allowance and Reach Ranges (4.2)

NOTE:

- SA guidelines deal with wheelchair passage space, maneuvering space, clear floor space, and reach ranges.

While this element is found in the ADAAG, the SA code generally is not used in the space forms because each of these criteria are included in other element-based guidelines such as (SR) Storage, (CT) Controls and Operating Mechanisms, (SS) Shower Stalls, etc.

Space Allowance

SA-01 Is the minimum clear width along the accessible route adequate for continuous or point passage? (4.2.1, 4.3.3, Fig. 1, Fig. 8e, Fig. 24e)

- Continuous passage (greater than 24 in. long): at least a 36-in. clear width.
- Point passage (not more than 24 in. long): at least a 32-in. clear width.

AUTHOR'S INTERPRETATION:

- Noncompliance with this question generally relates to permanent elements that encroach on the accessible route. Large, heavy equipment that is not readily movable might be considered permanent. If the space is designed so that temporary elements (such as bikes in a bike rack or car bumpers) will consistently encroach, the situation might also be considered a permanent barrier.

SA-02 Does the accessible route provide at least 60 in. of clear width for two wheelchairs to pass and, if not, is the required passing space provided? (4.2.2, 4.3.4)

- A 60-in. × 60-in. passing space or "T" intersection should be provided at reasonable intervals not to exceed 200 ft.

AUTHOR'S INTERPRETATION:

- ADAAG does not state that a route must maintain continuous clear passage for two wheelchairs, but it does require that if a clear width of 60 in. is not maintained, an accessible route more than 5 ft long must have a passing space provided.

DEFINITION:

- A *"T" intersection* is defined as the intersection of two corridors or walks, each at least 36 in. wide providing at least a 60-in. depth at the intersection. (Fig. 3b)

SA-03 Is the minimum clear floor space for an unobstructed 180° wheelchair turning space or a "T"-shaped turning space provided? (4.2.3, Fig. 3a–b)

- 180° turning space: at least a 60-in. diameter.
- "T"-shaped turning space: at least 36-in. wide legs with a minimum length of 60 in.

SA-04 Is the clear floor space for a wheelchair at least 30 in. × 48 in.? [4.2.4(1), Fig. 4a]

- The clear floor space can extend up to 19 in. under some elements if adequate knee clearance is provided.

Reach Ranges

SA-05 Are forward or side reach within acceptable ranges? (4.2.5–6, Fig. 5a–b, Fig. 6a–c)

- Forward reach: not less than 15 in. high and not more than 48 in. high without any obstruction or where the obstruction is less than 20 in. deep. For obstructions from 20 in. to 25 in. deep, no forward reach higher than 44 in.
- Side reach: not less than 9 in. high and not more than 54 in. high. For obstructions not more than 34 in. high or 24 in. deep, no side reach higher than 46 in.

EXCEPTION:

- These requirements do not apply where the use of special equipment dictates otherwise or where electrical and communications system receptacles are not normally intended for use by building occupants. (4.27.3)

(ST) Stairs (4.9)

NOTE:

- Only stairs that connect levels not connected by an elevator, ramp, or other accessible means of vertical access are required to comply. [4.1.3(4)]
  — In new construction, this condition may occur in facilities subject to the elevator exemption [4.1.3(5)— Exception 1] or where mezzanines are exempt in restaurants. (5.4)

Stairs: risers, treads, and nosings

ST-01 Do the stair treads and risers meet the required criteria? (4.9.2, Fig. 18a)

- Uniformity: riser heights and tread widths should remain uniform in any one flight of stairs.
- Treads: not less than 11 in. measured from riser to riser.
- Risers: no open risers are permitted.

ST-02 Do the stair nosings meet the required criteria? See ADAAG Fig. 18 for clarification. (4.9.3)

- Risers: risers slope toward the nosing.
- Radius of the curvature: not more than 1/2-in. radius at the leading edge of the tread.
- Angle nosing: angled underside on nosing is not less than 60° from the horizontal; underside of nosing should not be abrupt.
- Nosing projection: not more than 1½ in.

Stairs: handrails

NOTE:

- Additional criteria for handrails can be found in Section "HR, Handrails."

ST-03 Is the handrail provided on both sides of the stair and is the inside rail on switchback or dogleg stairs continuous at the landing? [4.9.4(1), Fig. 19a–b]

- The outside handrail along the perimeter wall does not have to be continuous around the landing.

ST-04 At the end of the stair handrails, is there at least 12 in. of handrail parallel to the floor beyond the top riser and is there at least one tread width of sloping handrail plus at least 12 in. of horizontal handrail beyond the bottom riser? [4.9.4(2), Fig. 19c–d]

- See ADAAG Fig. 19c–d for extension design.

ST-05 If the handrail extension protrudes into an accessible route, is the handrail extension rounded to 27 in. or less from the floor so that it does not create a protruding object? [4.9.4(2)]

ST-06 Is the clearance between the stair handrail and the wall exactly 1½ in.? [4.9.4(3)]

ST-07 Are the tops of stair handrails between 34 in. and 38 in. above the stair nosing? [4.9.4(5)]

ST-08 Is the stair handrail gripping surface uninterrupted by newel posts, other obstructions, or missing segments? [4.9.4(4)]

ST-09 Are the ends of stair handrails rounded or returned smoothly to the floor, wall, or post? [4.9.4(6)]

ST-10 Are handrails fixed so that they do not rotate within their fittings? [4.9.4(7)]

Stairs: water accumulation

ST-11 Are outdoor stairs and their approaches designed so that water does not accumulate on walking surfaces? (4.9.6)

(SR) STORAGE (4.25)

NOTE:

- Accessible reach range requirements do not apply to shelves or display units allowing self-service by customers in mercantile occupancies but they must be located on an accessible route. [4.1.3(12)(b)]

Storage: general

SR-01 Does at least one of each type of fixed or built-in storage unit comply with accessible criteria? [4.1.3(12)(a), 4.25.1]

   NOTE:

   - Types of storage facilities might include cabinets, shelves, closets, and drawers.

Storage: clear floor space

SR-02 Is there a clear floor space at least 30 in. × 48 in. at fixed or built-in storage units that allows for either a forward or side approach? (4.25.2, Fig. 4a–b)

Storage: reach ranges

SR-03 Are forward or side reach for each type of accessible storage unit within acceptable reach ranges? (4.2.5–6, Fig. 5a–b, Fig. 6a–c, 4.25.3)

   - Forward reach: not less than 15 in. high and not more than 48 in. high without any obstruction or where the obstruction is less than 20 in. deep. For obstructions from 20 in. to 25 in. deep, no forward reach higher than 44 in.

   - Side reach: not less than 9 in. high and not more than 54 in. high. For obstructions not more than 34 in. high or 24 in. deep, no side reach higher than 46 in.

SR-04 In a closet where passage is not required to access storage (e.g., door opening is less than 32 in.), are the clothes rod or shelves within required reach ranges? (4.25.3, Fig. 38a–b)

- Door width: at least 20 in. (4.13.5)
- Horizontal reach: not more than 21 in. from the opening.
- Rod reach: if over 10 in. deep, then not more than 48 in. high.
- Shelf reach: if over 10 in. deep, then not more than 48 in. high or less than 9 in. high.

Storage: hardware

SR-05 Is the hardware on the storage unit doors or drawers operable with one hand without tight grasping, pinching, or wrist twisting, and requiring no more than 5 lbf of force? (4.25.4, 4.27.4)

(TL) Telephones (4.31)

DEFINITION:

- Telephone types include public pay telephones, public closed circuit telephones, or other public telephones.

NOTE:

- Signage related to telephones is found in Section "SG, Signage."

AUTHOR'S INTERPRETATION:

- Frequently, public pay telephones are provided by a contractual agreement with a vendor. The vendor, through the contract, might be made responsible for compliance with all applicable ADAAG criteria.

Telephones: number required

TL-01 If there is only one public telephone on a floor, does it comply with accessible criteria? [4.1.3(17)(a)]

   - Unless otherwise specified, accessible telephones may be either forward or side reach telephones.

TL-02 If there is a single bank of public telephones on a floor, does at least one of the telephones in the bank comply with accessible criteria? [4.1.3(17)(a)]

   - A bank consists of two or more adjacent public telephones, often installed as a unit.

   - Unless otherwise specified, accessible telephones may be either forward or side reach telephones.

TL-03 Where two or more banks of public telephones are provided on a floor, is at least one accessible telephone provided at each bank or within proximity to the bank and does at least one of these accessible telephones comply with forward reach criteria? [4.1.3(17)(a)]

   EXCEPTION:

   - For exterior installations only, if dial tone first service is available, then a side reach telephone may be installed instead of the required forward reach telephone.

Telephones: clear floor or ground space

TL-04 Does the accessible telephone have at least a 30-in. × 48-in. clear floor or ground space that allows either a forward or side approach? (4.31.2, Fig. 44, 4.2.4)

   - Bases, enclosures, and fixed seats shall not impede approaches to telephones.

   - If this clear floor space is located in an alcove or confined space, see ADAAG Fig. 4d–e for additional maneuvering clearance requirements.

TL-05 Does an accessible route adjoin or overlap the clear floor space for the accessible telephone? (4.31.2, Fig. 44, 4.2.4)

Telephones: protruding object

TL-06 Do wall-mounted or post-mounted telephones with leading edges between 27 in. and 80 in. from the floor have projections that do not result in a protruding object? (4.31.4, 4.4.1)

- Wall-mounted: project less than 4 in. into the pathway.
- Post-mounted: project less than 12 in. into a perpendicular route of travel.

Telephones: mounting height

TL-07 Is the highest operable part of the telephone within forward or side reach ranges? (4.31.3, 4.2.6)

- Forward: not more than 48 in. above the floor.
- Side: not more than 54 in. above the floor.

Telephones: push-button controls

TL-08 Does the telephone have push-button controls where such service is available? (4.31.6)

Telephones: telephone book

TL-09 Is the telephone book, if provided, located in a position that complies with forward or side reach ranges? (4.31.7)

- Forward: not more than 48 in. above the floor.
- Side: not more than 54 in. above the floor.

Telephones: cord length

TL-10 Is the cord from the telephone to the handset at least 29 in. long? (4.31.8)

Telephones: volume control and hearing aid compatibility

TL-11 Do the public telephones comply with volume control requirements? [4.1.3(17)(b)]

- Each accessible telephone is equipped with a volume control.
- In addition, 25 percent, but not fewer than one, of all other public telephones should be equipped with volume controls and dispersed among all types of public telephones.

TL-12 Are volume controls capable of amplification between 12 dbA and 18 dbA above normal? [4.31.5(2)]

- If an automatic reset button is provided, the maximum of 18 dbA may be exceeded.

TL-13 Are telephones hearing aid compatible? [4.31.5(1)]

Telephones: text telephones

TL-14 If a total of four or more public pay telephones (including both interior and exterior phones) are provided at a site and at least one is in an interior location, is at least one interior public text telephone provided? [4.1.3(17)(c)(i)]

TL-15 If an interior public pay telephone is provided in a stadium or arena, convention center, a hotel with a convention center, or a covered mall, is at least one interi-or public text telephone provided in the facility? [4.1.3(17)(c)(ii)]

TL-16 If there is a public pay telephone in or adjacent to a hospital emergency room, a hospital recovery room, or a hospital waiting room, is there a public text telephone in each such location? [4.1.3(17)(c)(iii)]

TL-17 If a required text telephone is not provided, is equivalent facilitation provided? [4.31.9(3)]

- A portable text telephone may be made available in a hotel at the registration desk if it is available on a 24-hour basis for use with nearby public pay telephones that can accommodate the accessible requirements for a portable text telephone.

TL-18 Is a required text telephone permanently mounted within, or adjacent to, the telephone enclosure? (4.31.9)

TL-19 If an acoustic coupler is used, is the telephone cord long enough to allow connection of the text telephone to the telephone receiver? [4.31.9(1)]

TL-20 If there are three or more telephones in an interior bank of telephones, does at least one telephone have a shelf and electrical outlet for use with a portable text telephone? [4.1.3(17)(d)]

TL-21 Is the shelf large enough to accommodate a text telephone, provide at least 6 in. of vertical clearance, and allow the telephone handset to be placed flush on the surface of the shelf? [4.31.9(2)]

(TS) Toilet Stalls (4.17)

Toilet Stalls: location and approach

TS-01 Are the accessible toilet stalls located on an accessible route? (4.17.1)

TS-02 Is the required aisle clearance provided when approaching the accessible toilet stall? (4.17.5, Fig. 30)

- Aisle clearance if the stall door swings out and the approach is from the *latch side*: not less than 42 in. between the door side of the stall and any obstruction.
- Aisle clearance if the stall door swings out and the approach is from the *hinge side*: not less than 48 in. between the door side of the stall and any obstruction.

Toilet Stalls: maneuvering space

TS-03 If the stall door swings out at the end of an aisle, is at least 18 in. of maneuvering space provided at the latch side of the stall door? (4.17.5, 4.13.5)

Toilet Stalls: size and arrangement

TS-04 If toilet stalls are provided, is at least one a "standard" accessible stall? (4.17.3, 4.22.4, 4.23.4, Fig. 30a)

- "Standard" accessible stall: at least 60 in. wide × 59 in. deep (with floor-mounted water closet) or at least 56 in. deep (with wall-mounted water closet). The door should be located at the open side of the stall.

EXCEPTION:

- In instances of alteration work where a "standard" stall is technically infeasible or where plumbing code requirements prevent combining existing stalls to provide space, either "alternate" stall configuration described as follows may be provided in lieu of the "standard" stall. (4.17.3, Fig. 30b)

— One: 36 in. wide × 69 in. deep (with floor-mounted water closet) or at least 66 in. deep (with wall-mounted water closet), with an outward swinging, self-closing door and parallel grab bars on side walls.

— Two: At least 48 in. wide × 54 in. deep, with an outward swinging, self-closing door and grab bars on side and rear walls.

TS-05 If the door swings into the "standard" accessible stall, is the additional depth provided in the stall so that the door does not encroach on the clear floor space required at the toilet? (4.17.5, 4.13.5, Fig. 30a–1)

- Additional depth: not less than 36 in.
- At least 18 in. of maneuvering space at the latch side of the door on the inside of the stall is needed.

TS-06 Where six or more stalls are provided, is at least one an "alternate" accessible stall, in addition to the "standard" accessible stall? (4.22.4, 4.23.4, 4.17.3, Fig. 30b)

- "Alternate" accessible stalls for new construction are:
  — Exactly 36 in. wide × at least 69 in. deep (with floor-mounted water closet) or at least 66 in. deep (with wall-mounted water closet), with an outward swinging, self-closing door and parallel grab bars on side walls.

Toilet Stalls: toe clearance

TS-07 If the stall is less than 60 in. deep, does the front partition and at least one side partition have toe clearances of at least 9 in. above the floor? (4.17.4)

Toilet Stalls: doors

TS-08 Does the stall door, including door hardware, or the opening into the accessible stall comply with the minimum width and height requirements? (4.17.5, 4.13.5, 4.4.2)

- Width clearance: not less than 32 in. between the face of the door and the edge of the partition on the latch side when the stall door is open 90°.
- Height clearance: not less than 80 in.

TS-09 Do the toilet stall doors and hardware comply with typical door accessible criteria including handle type, mounting height, and opening force? (4.17.5, 4.4.2)

Toilet Stalls: grab bars

NOTE:

- Additional criteria for grab bars can be found in Section "HR, Handrails."

TS-10 Are the grab bars in the "standard" stall the required length and are they placed in the required location? (4.17.6; Fig. 30a, c, d)

- Rear wall: not less than 36 in. long, starting at no more than 6 in. from the side wall.
- Side wall: not less than 40 in. long, starting at no more than 12 in. from the rear wall.

- Mounting height: 33 in. to 36 in. to centerline above the finish floor and mounted horizontally.

TS-11 Are the grab bars in the "alternate" stall the required length and are they placed in the required location? (4.17.6; Fig. 30b, c, d)

- Rear wall: not less than 36 in. long, starting at no more than 6 in. from the side wall.
- Side wall: not less than 42 in. long, starting at no more than 12 in. from the rear wall.
- Mounting height: 33 in. to 36 in. to centerline above the finish floor and mounted horizontally.

NOTE:

- A rear grab bar is required in stalls wider than 36 in.

(TF) Transportation Facilities (10.0): Airports

NOTE:

- Transportation facilities are divided into three categories:
  — Bus Stops (TF-01 through TF-06).
  — Airports (TF-07 through TF-19).
  — Fixed Facilities, Terminals, and Stations (TF-20 through TF-69).

NOT EXEMPT:

- The exception for elevators in facilities that are less than three stories or that have less than 3000 ft^2 per story [4.1.3(5) Exception 1 and 4.1.6 (1)(k)] *do not* apply to a terminal, depot, or other station used for specified public transportation, an airport passenger terminal, or facilities subject to Title II.

Transportation Facilities/Airports: circulation

TF-07 Are elements such as ramps, elevators, or other circulation devices, ticketing areas, security checkpoints, or passenger waiting areas placed so as to minimize the distance that wheelchair users and other persons who cannot negotiate steps must travel, as compared to the general public? [10.4, 10.4.1(1)]

TF-08 To the maximum extent practicable, does the circulation path, including an accessible entrance and an accessible route, coincide with the circulation path for the general public? [10.4.1(2)]

TF-09 Where the accessible circulation path is different from that of the general public, does directional signage indicate the location of the nearest accessible entrance and accessible route, and does it meet applicable directional signage criteria? [10.4.1(2)]

Transportation Facilities/Airports: ticketing areas

TF-10 Are ticketing areas designed in such a way that persons with disabilities can obtain tickets and check baggage? [10.4.1(3)]

TF-11 Are ticketing counters provided with a portion of the main counter at least 36 in. long and not more than 36 in. high? [10.4.1(3), 7.2.2]

- Equivalent facilitation may be provided by:
  — an auxiliary counter with a maximum height of 36 in., located in close proximity to the main counter; or

— a folding shelf attached to the main counter that provides a writing surface for individuals with disabilities; or

— a space provided on the side of the counter or desk that allows materials to be passed back and forth.

Transportation Facilities/Airports: baggage check in and retrieval

TF-12 Are baggage check in and retrieval systems on an accessible route? [10.4.1(5)]

TF-13 Is a clear floor space at least 30 in. × 48 in. provided in the space immediately adjacent for parallel or forward approach? [10.4.1(5)]

Transportation Facilities/Airports: terminal gates

TF-14 Where unattended security barriers are provided, is an accessible gate provided? [10.4.1(5)]

- Accessible gates must meet accessible door criteria.

TF-15 If gates must be pushed open by wheelchair or mobility aid users, do they have a smooth, continuous surface extending from 2 in. above the floor to at least 27 in. above the floor? [10.4.1(5)]

Transportation Facilities/Airports: text telephones

TF-16 Where public pay telephones are provided at an interior location, is at least one interior public text telephone provided? [10.4.1(4), 4.31.9]

TF-17 If at least four or more public pay telephones are located in any of the areas identified below, is at least one public text telephone provided in that location? [10.4.1(4)]

- Locations: a main terminal outside the security area; a concourse within the security areas; or a baggage claim area in a terminal.
- These telephones are in addition to TF-16.

Transportation Facilities/Airports: public address system

TF-18 Where terminal information systems broadcast information to the general public through a public address system, is there a way to provide the same or equivalent information to persons with hearing impairments? [10.4.1(6)]

AUTHOR'S INTERPRETATION:

- Acceptable solutions might include a visual paging system or an Assistive Listening System.

Transportation Facilities/Airports: clocks

TF-19 If clocks are provided for use by the public, do they comply with accessible criteria? [10.4.1(7)]

- Clock faces are uncluttered, resulting in elements that are clearly visible.
- Hands, numerals, and/or digits contrast with the background.
- Where clocks are mounted overhead, the numerals and/or digits are at least 3 in. high.
- Clocks are placed in uniform locations throughout the facility to the maximum extent practicable.

(TF) Transportation Facilities (10.0): Bus Stops and Terminals

NOTE:

- Transportation facilities are divided into three categories:
  — Bus Stops (TF-01 through TF-06).
  — Airports (TF-07 through TF-19).
  — Fixed Facilities, Terminals, and Stations (TF-20 through TF-69).

Transportation Facilities/Bus Stops: bus stop pad

TF-01 Is the bus stop pad connected to streets, sidewalks, or pedestrian paths by an accessible route? [10.2.1(1)]

TF-02 Does the surface of the bus stop pad comply with accessible criteria? [10.2.1(1)]

- Pad surface: firm and stable.
- Pad slope: slope is parallel to the roadway and, to the extent feasible, the same as that of the roadway.

NOTE:

- A maximum slope of 1:50 perpendicular to the roadway is allowed for water drainage.

TF-03 Do the dimensions of the bus stop pad comply with accessible criteria? [10.2.1(1)]

- Length: at least 96 in. (measured perpendicular to the curb or vehicle roadway).
- Width: at least 60 in. (measured parallel to the vehicle roadway).

NOTE:

- Both of the preceding dimensions should comply to the maximum extent as allowed by legal or site constraints (e.g., a retaining wall or adjacent building).

Transportation Facilities/Bus Stops: bus shelters

TF-04 Does the bus stop shelter comply with accessible criteria? [10.2.1(2)]

- Position: permits a wheelchair or mobility aid user to enter from the public way and reach a location having a clear floor area of 30 in. × 48 in., entirely within the perimeter of the shelter.
- Connection: connected by an accessible route to the boarding area provided.

Transportation Facilities/Bus Stops: bus stop signage

TF-05 Where provided, do all new signs identifying bus routes comply with accessible criteria? (4.30.2, 4.30.3, 4.30.5)

- Character proportion: letters and numbers have a width to height ratio between 3:5 and 1:1 and a stroke width to height ratio between 1:5 and 1:10.
- Character height: sized according to viewing distance with characters on overhead signs at least 3 in. high.
- Finish: characters and backgrounds have a nonglare finish.
- Contrast: characters contrast with their background (light-on-dark or dark-on-light).

NOTE:

- Signs that are sized to the maximum dimensions permitted under legitimate local, state, or federal regulations or ordinances shall be considered in compliance.

EXCEPTION:

- Bus schedules, timetables, or maps that are posted at the bus stop or bus bay are not required to comply with this provision.

TF-06 Is the sign located so that the overhead clearance or the projection of a suspended or projected sign does not result in a protruding object (free-standing or wall-mounted)?

- Clear height: at least 80 in. (4.4.2, Fig. 8a)
- Overhang for free-standing signs on posts or pylons located between 27 in. and 80 in. high: no more than a 12-in. projection into walks, corridors, or aisles. (4.4.1, Fig. 8c)
- Overhang for wall-mounted signs between 27 in. and 80 in. high: no more than a 4-in. projection into walks, corridors, or aisles. (4.4.1, Fig. 8a)

(TF) Transportation Facilities (10.0): Fixed Facilities and Stations

NOTES:

- Transportation facilities are divided into three categories:
  — Bus Stops (TF-01 through TF-06).
  — Airports (TF-07 through TF-19).
  — Fixed Facilities, Terminals, and Stations (TF-20 through TF-69).

- Included in this space-type are rapid rail, light rail, commuter rail, intercity bus, intercity rail, high speed rail, and other fixed guideway systems (e.g., automated guideway transit, monorails, etc.).

NOT EXEMPT:

- The exception for elevators in facilities that are less than three stories or that have less than 3000 ft^2 per story [4.1.3(5) Exception 1 and 4.1.6 (1)(k)] *do not* apply to a terminal, depot, or other station used for specified public transportation, an airport passenger terminal, or facilities subject to Title II.

Transportation Facilities/Rail Stations and Bus Terminals: circulation

TF-20 Are elements such as ramps, elevators, or other circulation devices, fare vending, ticketing areas, fare collection, security checkpoints, or passenger waiting areas placed so as to minimize the distance that wheelchair users and other persons who cannot negotiate steps must travel as compared to the general public? [10.3, 10.3.1(1)]

TF-21 Does the circulation path, including an accessible entrance and an accessible route, to the maximum extent practicable, coincide with the circulation path for the general public? [10.3.1(1)]

TF-22 Where the accessible circulation path is different from that of the general public, does directional signage indicate the location of the nearest accessible entrance and accessible route, and does it meet applicable directional signage criteria? [10.3.1(1)]

Transportation Facilities/Rail Stations and Bus Terminals: entrances

TF-23 Is at least one entrance connected by an accessible route to public transportation stops, accessible parking, passenger loading zones, and public streets or sidewalks, if available, and to all accessible spaces or elements with the facility? [10.3.1(2)]

TF-24 If different entrances to the station serve different transportation fixed routes or groups of fixed routes, does at least one accessible entrance serving each group or route comply with accessible criteria? [10.3.1(2)]

TF-25 Do all accessible entrances coincide with those used by the majority of the general public, to the maximum extent possible? [10.3.1(2)]

Transportation Facilities/Rail Stations and Bus Terminals: entrance signs

TF-26 Where signs are provided at station entrances that identify the station, the entrance, or both, does at least one sign meet accessible criteria for raised and Braille letters and mounting location? [10.3.1(4), 4.30.4, 4.30.6]

TF-27 Is entrance signage, when provided, placed in uniform locations at the entrances to the maximum extent feasible? [10.3.1(4)]

EXCEPTION:

- Where the station has no defined entrance, but signage is provided, then the accessible signage shall be placed in a central location.

Transportation Facilities/Rail Stations and Bus Terminals: connections

TF-28 If there are direct connections to commercial, retail, or residential facilities, is there an accessible route from the point of connection to boarding platforms and all transportation system elements used by the public? [10.3.1(3)]

NOTE:

- If it is a new connection in an existing facility, then compliance with connection to the accessible route is to the "maximum extent feasible." [10.3.2(5)]

TF-29 Where elements are provided to facilitate future direct connections, are they on an accessible route connecting boarding platforms and all transportation system elements used by the public? [10.3.1(3)]

Transportation Facilities/Rail Stations and Bus Terminals: station/platform signs

TF-30 Do stations/platforms have identification signs that comply with information signage criteria for letter height, proportion, and contrast? [10.3.1(5)]

TF-31 Are station/platform identification signs placed at frequent intervals and clearly visible from inside the vehicle on both sides (when not obstructed by another train)? [10.3.1(5)]

TF-32 When station/platform identification signs are placed close to vehicle windows, is the top of the highest letter or symbol below the top of the vehicle window and the bottom of the lowest letter or symbol above the horizontal midline of the vehicle window? [10.3.1(5)]

Transportation Facilities/Rail Stations and Bus Terminals: route signs

TF-33 Do route signs located on boarding areas, platforms, or mezzanines that list stations, routes, or destinations served by the station comply with information signage criteria for letter height, proportion, and contrast? [10.3.1(6)]

TF-34 Does at least one sign on each platform or boarding area that identifies the specific station comply with room identification criteria for raised or Braille letters and mounting location? [10.3.1(6)]

TF-35 Are all signs that list stations, routes, or destinations served by the station placed in uniform locations within the transit system to the maximum extent practicable? [10.3.1(6)]

Transportation Facilities/Rail Stations and Bus Terminals: ticketing areas

TF-36 Where provided, are ticketing areas designed in such a way that persons with disabilities can obtain tickets and check baggage? [10.3.1(18), 7.2]

TF-37 Are ticketing counters provided with a portion of the main counter at least 36 in. long and not more than 36 in. high? [10.3.1(18), 7.2.2]

- Equivalent facilitation may be provided by:
  — an auxiliary counter with a maximum height of 36 in., located in close proximity to the main counter; or
  — a folding shelf attached to the main counter that provides a writing surface for individuals with disabilities; or
  — a space provided on the side of the counter or desk that allows materials to be passed back and forth.

Transportation Facilities/Rail Stations and Bus Terminals: baggage check in and retrieval

TF-38 If provided, are baggage check in and retrieval systems on an accessible route? [10.3.1(19)]

TF-39 Is a clear floor space at least 30 in. × 48 in. provided in the space immediately adjacent for parallel or forward approach? [10.3.1(19)]

TF-40 Where unattended security barriers are provided, is an accessible gate provided? [10.3.1(19)]

- Accessible gates comply with accessible door/gate criteria.

TF-41 If gates must be pushed open by wheelchair or mobility aid users, do they have a smooth, continuous surface extending from 2 in. above the floor to at least 27 in. above the floor? [10.3.1(19)]

Transportation Facilities/Rail Stations and Bus Terminals: fare vending and collection

TF-42 Do automatic fare vending, collection, and adjustment systems comply with automated teller machine criteria for control requirements, clearances, reach ranges, and persons with visual impairments? [10.3.1(7)]

TF-43 Are automatic fare vending machines located on an accessible route? [10.3.1(7)]

TF-44 If self-service fare collection devices are provided for the public, is there at least one accessible device for entering and exiting at each accessible point of entry or exit (unless one device serves both functions)? [10.3.1(7)]

TF-45 Does each accessible fare collection device provide a minimum clear width of at least 32 in. to allow passage of a wheelchair? [10.3.1(7)]

TF-46 Where provided, do self-service fare collection devices (coin or card slots) comply with control mechanisms criteria for clear floor space, reach range, and operation? [10.3.1(7)]

TF-47 If gates must be pushed open by wheelchair or mobility aid users, do they have a smooth, continuous surface extending from 2 in. above the floor to at least 27 in. above the floor? [10.3.1(7)]

- Accessible gates comply with accessible door/gate criteria.

TF-48 Where the circulation path does not coincide with that used by the general public, is the accessible fare collection system located at, or adjacent to, the accessible point of entry or exit? [10.3.1(7)]

NOTE:

- In existing stations, where a technical infeasibility requires the accessible route to lead from the public way to a paid area of the transit system, an accessible fare collection system should be provided along the accessible route. [10.3.2(3)]

Transportation Facilities/Rail Stations and Bus Terminals: detectable warnings

NOTE:

- The suspension action for truncated domes, suspended until July 26, 1996, does not affect the requirement for detectable warnings (truncated domes) on transit platforms.

TF-49 When not protected by platform screens or guardrails, do platform edges, bordering a drop-off, have a detectable warning? [10.3.1(8)]

TF-50 Are the detectable warnings 24 in. wide, running the full length of the platform drop-off? [10.3.1(8)]

TF-51 Do the detectable warnings consist of raised truncated domes and do they meet the required criteria? [10.3.1(8)]

- Diameter: nominal 0.9 in.
- Height: nominal 0.2 in.

- Spacing: nominal 2.35 in., center to center, offset every other row.
- Contrast: contrast visually with adjoining surface (light-on-dark or dark-on-light).
- The material used to provide contrast shall be an integral part of the walking surface. Detectable warnings used on interior surfaces shall differ from adjoining walking surfaces in resiliency or sound-on-cane contact.

TF-52 Where the platform is in an interior location, do the detectable warnings differ from the adjoining walking surface in resiliency or sound-on-cane contact? [10.3.1(8)]

Transportation Facilities/Rail Stations and Bus Terminals: platform change in levels and gaps

EXCEPTION:

- Existing vehicles retrofitted to meet the requirements of 49 CFR 37.93 (one car per train rule) shall be coordinated with the platform such that, for at least one door, the vertical difference between the vehicle floor and the platform (measured when the vehicle is at rest with 50 percent normal passenger capacity) is within plus or minus 2 in. and the horizontal gap is no greater than 4 in. [10.3.2(4)]

TF-53 Is the rail-to-platform height coordinated with the floor height of new vehicles so that the vertical difference (measured when the vehicle is at rest) is within plus or minus 5/8 in. under normal passenger load conditions? [10.3.1(9)]

EXCEPTION:

- Existing vehicles operating in new stations may have a vertical difference with respect to the new platform within plus or minus 1½ in. [10.3.1(9)]
- Existing stations may have a vertical difference with respect to the existing platform within plus or minus 1½ in. [10.3.2(4)]

TF-54 For rapid rail, light rail, commuter rail, high speed rail, and intercity rail systems, is the horizontal gap (measured when the new vehicle is at rest) no greater than 3 in.? [10.3.1(9)]

EXCEPTION:

- In light rail, commuter rail, and intercity rail systems where it is not operationally or structurally feasible to meet the horizontal gap or vertical difference requirements, mini-high platforms, car-borne or platform-mounted lifts, ramps or bridge plates, or similar manually deployed devices, meeting the applicable requirements of 36 CFR Part 1192 or 49 CFR Part 38 shall suffice.

TF-55 For slow moving automated guideway people mover transit systems, is the horizontal gap (measured when the new vehicle is at rest) no greater than 1 in.? [10.3.1(9)]

Transportation Facilities/Rail Stations and Bus Terminals: boarding and alighting

TF-56 Is the station designed so that persons with disabilities are able to board or alight from a vehicle at the same location as that used by the general public? [10.3.1(10)]

Transportation Facilities/Rail Stations and Bus Terminals: illumination

TF-57 Are illumination levels uniform in the areas where signage is located? [10.3.1(11)]

TF-58 Does the method of illumination minimize excessive glare on signs? [10.3.1(11)]

TF-59 Does the lighting type and configuration provide uniform illumination along accessible circulation routes ? [10.3.1(11)]

Transportation Facilities/Rail Stations and Bus Terminals: text telephones

TF-60 If an interior public pay telephone is provided in a transit facility, is at least one interior public text telephone provided? [10.3.1(12)(a)]

NOTE:

- Transit facility [as defined in 49 CFR 37.3 for purposes of applying ADAAG 10.3.1(12)] is any physical structure whose primary function is to facilitate access to and from a transportation system that has scheduled stops at the structure. It does not include an open structure or a physical structure whose primary purpose is providing services other than transportation services.

TF-61 If there are four or more public pay telephones serving a particular entrance to a rail station and at least one is in an interior location, is at least one text telephone provided to serve that entrance? [10.3.1(12)(b)]

NOTE:

- Text telephones shall comply with all required criteria.

Transportation Facilities/Rail Stations and Bus Terminals: track crossings

TF-62 Where it is necessary to cross tracks to reach boarding platforms, is the surface of the route level and flush with the rail top at the outer edge and between the rails except for a maximum 2½ in. gap on the inner edge of each rail to permit passage of wheel flanges? [10.3.1(13)]

NOTE:

- Where gap reduction is not practicable, there should be an above-grade or below-grade accessible route.

Transportation Facilities/Rail Stations and Bus Terminals: public address system

TF-63 Where terminal information systems broadcast information to the general public through a public address system, is there a way to provide the same or equivalent information to persons with hearing impairments? [10.3.1(14)]

AUTHOR'S INTERPRETATION:

- Acceptable solutions might include a visual paging system or an Assistive Listening System.

Transportation Facilities/Rail Stations and Bus Terminals: clocks

TF-64 If clocks are provided for use by the public, do they comply with accessible criteria? [10.3.1(15)]

- Clock faces are uncluttered, resulting in elements that are clearly visible.
- Hands, numerals, and/or digits contrast with the background.
- Where clocks are mounted overhead, the numerals and/or digits are at least 3 in. high.
- Clocks are placed in uniform locations throughout the facility to the maximum extent practicable.

Transportation Facilities/Rail Stations and Bus Terminals: escalators

TF-65 Where provided in below-grade stations, do escalators have a clear width of at least 32 in.? [10.3.1(16)]

TF-66 At the top and bottom of each escalator run, are at least two continuous treads level beyond the comb plate before the risers begin to form? [10.3.1(16)]

TF-67 Are all escalator treads marked by a strip of clearly contrasting color 2 in. wide, parallel to and on the nose of each step? [10.3.1(16)]

- The edge of the tread must be apparent from both ascending and descending directions.

TF-68 Is the contrasting strip of material at least as slip-resistant as the remainder of the tread? [10.3.1(16)]

Transportation Facilities/Rail Stations and Bus Terminals: elevators

NOTE:

- Including the following criteria, elevators should comply with required criteria. See the review guide on elevators for compliance criteria.

EXCEPTION:

- Elevator cars with a clear floor area in which a 60-in. diameter circle can be inscribed may be substituted for the minimum car dimensions of ADAAG 4.10, Fig. 22.

NOT EXEMPT:

- The exception for elevators in facilities that are less than three stories or that have less than 3000 ft^2 per story [4.1.3(5) Exception 1 and 4.1.6 (1)(k)] *do not* apply to a terminal, depot, or other station used for specified public transportation, an airport passenger terminal, or facilities subject to Title II.

TF-69 Where provided, do elevators have glass or transparent panels to allow an unobstructed view both into and out of the car? [10.3.1(17)]

(TH) Accessible Transient Lodging (9.0) (Hotels, Motels, Inns, Boarding Houses, Dormitories, and Similar Places)

NOTE:

- Transient lodging is divided into two categories:
  - Hotels, motels, inns, boarding houses, dormitories, and similar places (TH-01 through TH-19).

  - Homeless shelters, halfway houses, transient group homes, and other social services establishments (TH-20 through TH-26 and TH-07 through TH-19).

- Doors and doorways designed to allow passage into and within all transient lodging sleeping units shall comply with accessible door width criteria. This applies to every sleeping unit in the facility, whether it is designated as accessible or not. (9.4)

AUTHOR'S INTERPRETATION:

- Accessible units, sleeping rooms, and suites are divided into two categories: fully accessible and hearing-impaired. Fully accessible units, sleeping rooms, and suites must comply with accessible criteria for both mobility and hearing impairments. (9.2.8) Hearing-impaired units must comply only with those accessible criteria that relate to visual alarms, notification devices, and telephones. (9.3)

- The total number of accessible units required by ADAAG can be easily misinterpreted if not carefully read. For example, the total number of rooms required for 76–100 hotel rooms is 9, broken down as follows:
  - Four fully accessible rooms with accessible bathrooms.
  - One fully accessible room with accessible bathroom with a roll-in shower with folding seat.
  - Four rooms for the hearing-impaired (other accessible criteria are not required including an accessible bathroom).

- In dormitories or other facilities where bath facilities are multiple user and separate from the sleeping room, the minimum number of accessible tubs or showers required is not clearly prescribed. ADAAG 4.23.8, which indicates a minimum of at least one accessible tub or shower (when provided) in bathrooms, appears to be applicable to this situation.

EXCEPTION:

- ADAAG 9.1 through 9.4 do not apply to an establishment located within a building that contains no more than five rooms for rent or hire and that is actually occupied by the proprietor of such establishment as the residence of such proprietor.

Accessible Transient Lodging/Hotels: number required /new construction

TH-01 Is the required number of accessible sleeping rooms and suites provided? (9.1.2)

- Accessible rooms: 1 per 1–25, 2 per 26–50, 3 per 51–75, 4 per 76–100, 5 per 101–150, 6 per 151–200, 7 per 201–300, 8 per 301–400, 9 per 401–500, and 501–1000 is 2 percent of total.
- For more than 1000 rooms, 20 accessible rooms plus 1 for each 100 over 1000.

AUTHOR'S INTERPRETATION:

- When the total number of rooms is fewer than 50, the type of shower that can be provided relates to the criteria shown in Section "SS, Shower Stalls." However, when the number of rooms exceeds 50, the type of shower required is a roll-in shower with folding seat—see TH-02 below.

TH-02 In hotels of 51 or more sleeping rooms and suites, is the required number of additional accessible sleeping rooms with a roll-in shower with folding seat provided? (9.1.2, Fig. 57a–b)

- Accessible rooms with roll-in showers with folding seats: 1 per 51–100, 2 per 101–200, 3 per 201–300, and 4 per 301–400.

- For more than 400 rooms, 4 accessible rooms with roll-in showers with folding seat plus 1 for each 100 over 400.

NOTES:

- Roll-in shower with folding seat design for this type of transient housing differs from transfer and roll-in showers described in Section "SS, Shower Stalls." See ADAAG Fig. 57a–b for dimensional criteria and configurations.

TH-03 In addition to accessible units required for mobility disabilities, is the required number of sleeping rooms and suites also provided that meet accessibility requirements for the hearing-impaired? (9.1.3)

- Accessible rooms: 1 per 1–25, 2 per 26–50, 3 per 51–75, 4 per 76–100, 5 per 101–150, 6 per 151–200, 7 per 201–300, 8 per 301–400, 9 per 401–500, and 501–1000 is 2 percent of total.

- For more than 1000 rooms, 20 accessible rooms plus 1 for each 100 over 1000.

Accessible Transient Lodging/Hotels: number required/alterations

TH-04 When sleeping rooms or suites are altered, is at least one accessible room or suite provided for each 25 altered rooms (or portion thereof) until the number equals that in TH-01? (9.1.5)

TH-05 In addition, when sleeping rooms or suites are altered, is at least one accessible room or suite provided for each 25 altered rooms (or portion thereof) until the number equals that in TH-03 that meet accessibility requirements for the hearing-impaired? (9.1.5)

Accessible Transient Lodging/Hotels: room dispersion

TH-06 Are the accessible rooms and suites dispersed among various classes of sleeping accommodations available to all patrons? (9.1.4)

NOTES:

- Factors to be considered include room size, cost, amenities, and number of beds provided.

- Equal facilitation: For purposes of this section, the operator may choose to limit construction of accessible rooms to those designed for multiple occupancy rooms if the multiple occupancy accessible rooms are made available at a single occupancy rate to an individual with a disability who requests a single occupancy room.

Accessible Transient Lodging/Hotels: accessible routes

TH-07 Are accessible sleeping rooms or suites located on an accessible route? (9.2.2)

TH-08 Does an accessible route connect all accessible spaces within the accessible unit? [9.2.2(2, 6, 7)]

- Where provided, this includes the living area, the dining area, a dual occupancy sleeping area, patio or balcony, a full bathroom or half bath (if only half baths are provided), kitchen (also kitchenette or wet bar), and parking space.

NOTE:

- Elevators are not required in a multilevel unit if the previously listed spaces are all on the accessible level and the accessible sleeping area is suitable for dual occupancy.

EXCEPTION:

- The requirements of thresholds at doors (4.13.8) and changes in levels (4.3.8) do not apply where it is necessary to utilize a higher door threshold or a change in level to protect the integrity of the unit from wind/water damage. Where this exception results in patios, terraces, or balconies that are not at an accessible level, equivalent facilitation shall be provided (e.g., equivalent facilitation at a hotel patio or balcony might consist of providing raised decking or a ramp to provide accessibility).

TH-09 Does the accessible route connect all accessible elements within the accessible unit? [9.2.2(3, 4, 5)]

- Accessible elements would include doors and doorways, storage (accessible, fixed, or built-in), controls and operating mechanisms, and telephones.

Accessible Transient Lodging/Hotels: sleeping rooms

TH-10 Does the accessible sleeping room provide clear width for maneuvering along or between fixed, built-in, or movable beds? [9.2.2(1)]

- Width:
  — 36 in. clear width maneuvering space along both sides of a fixed or built-in bed;
  — or 36 in. clear width maneuvering space along either side of a movable bed;
  — or 36 in. clear width maneuvering space between two fixed beds.

Accessible Transient Lodging/Hotels: kitchens (if provided)

TH-11 Is a clear floor space of 30 in. × 48 in. provided at kitchen cabinets, counters, sinks, and appliances for front or parallel approach? [9.2.2(7)]

- Clear floor space for individual appliances and use areas may overlap.

- No more than 19 in. of the clear floor space can be measured under counters.

TH-12 Are kitchen counter tops and sinks mounted no more than 34 in. above the floor? [9.2.2(7)]

- The 34 in. is a maximum height for all counter tops.

TH-13 Is at least 50 percent of shelf space in all cabinets or refrigerator/freezers within acceptable reach ranges for forward or side approach? [9.2.2(7)]

- Forward reach: not less than 15 in. high and not more than 48 in. high without any obstruction or where the obstruction is less than 20 in. deep. For obstructions from 20 in. to 25 in. deep, no forward reach higher than 44 in.

- Side reach: not less than 9 in. high and not more than 54 in. high. For obstructions not more than 34 in. high or 24 in. deep, no side reach higher than 46 in.

TH-14 Are the controls and operating mechanisms on major kitchen appliances (ranges, ovens) within acceptable reach ranges for forward or side approach? [9.2.2(7)]

- Forward reach: not less than 15 in. high and not more than 48 in. high without any obstruction or where the obstruction is less than 20 in. deep. For obstructions from 20 in. to 25 in. deep, no forward reach higher than 44 in.

- Side reach: not less than 9 in. high and not more than 54 in. high. For obstructions not more than 34 in. high or 24 in. deep, no side reach higher than 46 in.

NOTE:

- Small, movable appliances such as microwave ovens are not considered.

TH-15 Are controls, dispensers, receptacles, and other operable equipment operable with one hand without tight grasping, pinching, or wrist twisting, and requiring no more than 5 lbf of force? [9.2.2(7), 4.27.4]

Accessible Transient Lodging/Hotels: hearing-impaired rooms

TH-16 Do accessible living units and sleeping accommodations comply with the requirements for visual alarms? (9.3, 4.28.4)

- Visual alarms meet required operational criteria.
- Visual alarms connect to the building emergency alarm system.
- Or a standard electrical outlet is provided and connected to the facility's central alarm system which enables room occupants to utilize portable devices provided by the operator of the facility.

TH-17 Is the signal from the visual alarm visible in all areas of the living unit or room? (9.3, 4.28.4)

TH-18 Do the living units, sleeping rooms, and suites comply with the requirements for visual notification devices? (9.3.1)

- This includes any space where the occupant would expect to be able to hear a phone or door bell.
- Visual notification devices are to alert the occupant of incoming telephone calls and a door knock or bell.
- This device must *not* be connected to the visual alarm system.

TH-19 Do the living units, sleeping rooms, and suites comply with the requirements for telephones? (9.3.1)

- If provided, permanently installed (hardwired) telephones should have volume controls capable of a minimum of 12 dbA and a maximum of 18 dbA above normal. If an automatic reset is provided, then 18 dbA may be exceeded.
- Outlets: An accessible electrical outlet is within 4 ft of a telephone connection, where provided.

(TH) Accessible Transient Lodging (9.0)
(Homeless Shelters, Halfway Houses, Transient Group Homes, and Other Social Services Establishments)

NOTE:

- Transient lodging is divided into two categories:
  - Hotels, motels, inns, boarding houses, dormitories, and similar places (TH-01 through TH-19).
  - Homeless shelters, halfway houses, transient group homes, and other social services establishments (TH-20 through TH-26 and TH-07 through TH-19).

- Doors and doorways designed to allow passage into and within all transient lodging sleeping units shall comply with accessible door width criteria. This applies to every sleeping unit in the facility, whether it is designated as accessible or not. (9.4)

AUTHOR'S INTERPRETATION:

- Accessible units, sleeping rooms, and suites are divided into two categories: fully accessible and hearing-impaired. Fully accessible units, sleeping rooms, and suites must comply with accessible criteria for both mobility and hearing impairments. (9.2.8) Hearing-impaired units must comply only with those accessible criteria that relate to visual alarms, notification devices, and telephones. (9.3)

- The total number of accessible units required by ADAAG can be easily misinterpreted if not carefully read. For example, the total number of rooms in social services required for 76–100 hotel rooms is 8, broken down as follows:
  - Four fully accessible rooms with accessible bathrooms.
  - Four rooms for the hearing-impaired (other accessible criteria are not required including an accessible bathroom).

- In facilities where bath facilities are multiple user and separate from the sleeping room or multibed rooms, the minimum number of accessible tubs or showers required is not clearly prescribed. ADAAG 4.23.8, which indicates a minimum of at least one accessible tub or shower (when provided) in bathrooms, appears to be applicable to this situation.

Accessible Transient Lodging/S.S.: number required/ new construction

TH-20 Is the required number of accessible sleeping rooms provided? (9.5.3, 9.1.2)

- Accessible rooms: 1 per 1–25, 2 per 26–50, 3 per 51–75, 4 per 76–100, 5 per 101–150, 6 per 151–200, 7 per 201–300, 8 per 301–400, 9 per 401–500, and 501–1000 is 2 percent of total.
- For more than 1000 rooms, 20 accessible rooms plus 1 for each 100 over 1000.

TH-21 In facilities with multibed sleeping rooms or spaces, is the required number of accessible beds provided? (9.5.3, 9.1.2)

- Accessible beds: 1 per 1–25, 2 per 26–50, 3 per 51–75, 4 per 76–100, 5 per 101–150, 6 per 151–200, 7 per

201–300, 8 per 301–400, 9 per 401–500, and 501–1000 is 2 percent of total.

- For more than 1000 beds, 20 accessible beds plus 1 for each 100 over 1000.

TH-22 In addition to accessible rooms required for mobility disabilities, is the required number of sleeping rooms also provided that meet accessibility requirements for the hearing-impaired? (9.1.3)

- Accessible rooms: 1 per 1–25, 2 per 26–50, 3 per 51–75, 4 per 76–100, 5 per 101–150, 6 per 151–200, 7 per 201–300, 8 per 301–400, 9 per 401–500, and 501–1000 is 2 percent of total.

- For more than 1000 rooms, 20 accessible rooms plus 1 for each 100 over 1000.

Accessible Transient Lodging/S.S.: number required/alterations

TH-23 In alterations to social service establishments that are not homeless shelters, is at least one accessible sleeping room provided for each 25 altered rooms (or portion thereof) until the number equals that in TH-20 or TH-21? [9.5.2(1), 9.5.3, 9.1.5]

TH-24 In alterations to homeless shelters where sleeping rooms are provided, is at least one accessible sleeping room provided for each 25 altered rooms (or portion thereof) until the number equals that in TH-20 or TH-21? [9.5.2(1), 9.5.3, 9.1.5]

TH-25 In addition, when sleeping rooms are altered, is at least one accessible room or suite provided for each 25 altered rooms (or portion thereof) until the number equals that in TH-22 that meet accessibility requirements for the hearing-impaired? (9.1.5)

Accessible Transient Lodging/S.S.: amenities

TH-26 Is at least one of each type of amenity (e.g., washer, dryer, and similar equipment) in each common area accessible and located on an accessible route to any accessible sleeping room? (9.5.1)

EXCEPTION:

- Where a building is exempt from the elevator requirement, accessible amenities are not required on inaccessible floors as long as one of each type is provided in common areas on accessible floors.

Accessible Transient Lodging/S.S.: accessible routes

NOTE:

- The following questions are the same as those found in accessible transient lodging for hotels.

TH-07 Are accessible sleeping rooms or suites located on an accessible route? (9.5.3, 9.2.2)

TH-08 Does an accessible route connect all accessible spaces within the accessible unit? [9.5.3; 9.2.2(2, 6, 7)]

- Where provided, this includes the living area, the dining area, a dual occupancy sleeping area, patio or balcony, a full bathroom or half bath (if only half baths are provided), kitchen (also kitchenette or wet bar), and parking space.

NOTE:

- Elevators are not required in a multilevel unit if the previously listed spaces are all on the accessible level and the accessible sleeping area is suitable for dual occupancy.

EXCEPTION:

- The requirements of thresholds at doors (4.13.8) and changes in levels (4.3.8) do not apply where it is necessary to utilize a higher door threshold or a change in level to protect the integrity of the unit from wind/water damage. Where this exception results in patios, terraces or balconies that are not at an accessible level, equivalent facilitation shall be provided (e.g., equivalent facilitation at a hotel patio or balcony might consist of providing raised decking or a ramp to provide accessibility).

TH-09 Does the accessible route connect all accessible elements within the accessible unit? [9.2.2(3, 4, 5)]

- Accessible elements would include doors and doorways, storage (accessible, fixed, or built-in), controls and operating mechanisms, and telephones.

Accessible Transient Lodging/S.S.: sleeping rooms

NOTE:

- The following questions are the same as those found in accessible transient lodging for hotels.

TH-10 Does the accessible sleeping room provide clear width for maneuvering along or between fixed, built-in, or movable beds? [9.5.3, 9.2.2(1)]

- Width:
  - 36 in. clear width maneuvering space along both sides of a fixed or built-in bed;
  - or 36 in. clear width maneuvering space along either side of a movable bed;
  - or 36 in. clear width maneuvering space between two fixed beds.

Accessible Transient Lodging/S.S.: kitchens (if provided)

NOTE:

- The following questions are the same as those found in accessible transient lodging for hotels.

TH-11 Is a clear floor space of 30 in. × 48 in. provided at kitchen cabinets, counters, sinks, and appliances for front or parallel approach? [9.5.3, 9.2.2(7)]

- Clear floor space for individual appliances and use areas may overlap.
- No more than 19 in. of the clear floor space can be measured under counters.

TH-12 Are kitchen counter tops and sinks mounted no more than 34 in. above the floor? [9.5.3; 9.2.2(7)]

- The 34 in. is a maximum height for all counter tops.

TH-13 Is at least 50 percent of shelf space in cabinets or refrigerators/freezers within acceptable reach ranges for forward or side approach? [9.5.3, 9.2.2(7)]

- Forward reach: not less than 15 in. high and not more than 48 in. high without any obstruction or where the obstruction is less than 20 in. deep. For obstructions from 20 in. to 25 in. deep, no forward reach higher than 44 in.

- Side reach: not less than 9 in. high and not more than 54 in. high. For obstructions not more than 34 in. high or 24 in. deep, no side reach higher than 46 in.

TH-14 Are the controls and operating mechanisms on major kitchen appliances (ranges, ovens) within acceptable reach ranges for forward or side approach? [9.5.3, 9.2.2(7)]

- Forward reach: not less than 15 in. high and not more than 48 in. high without any obstruction or where the obstruction is less than 20 in. deep. For obstructions from 20 in. to 25 in. deep, no forward reach higher than 44 in.
- Side reach: not less than 9 in. high and not more than 54 in. high. For obstructions not more than 34 in. high or 24 in. deep, no side reach higher than 46 in.

NOTE:

- Small, movable appliances such as microwave ovens are not considered.

TH-15 Are controls, dispensers, receptacles, and other operable equipment operable with one hand without tight grasping, pinching, or wrist twisting, and requiring no more than 5 lbf of force? [9.5.3, 9.2.2(7), 4.27.4]

Accessible Transient Lodging/S.S.: hearing-impaired rooms

NOTE:

- The following questions are the same as those found in accessible transient lodging for hotels.

TH-16 Do accessible living units and sleeping accommodations comply with the requirements for visual alarms? (9.5.3, 9.3, 4.28.4)

- Visual alarms meet required operational criteria.
- Visual alarms connect to the building emergency alarm system.
- Or a standard electrical outlet is provided and connected to the facility's central alarm system which enables room occupants to utilize portable devices provided by the operator of the facility.

TH-17 Is the signal from the visual alarm visible in all areas of the living unit or room? (9.5.3, 9.3, 4.28.4)

TH-18 Do the living units and sleeping rooms comply with the requirements for visual notification devices? (9.5.3, 9.3.1)

- This includes any space where the occupant would expect to be able to hear a phone or door bell.
- Visual notification devices are to alert the occupant of incoming telephone calls and a door knock or bell.
- This device must *not* be connected to the visual alarm system.

TH-19 Do the living units and sleeping rooms comply with the requirements for telephones? (9.5.3, 9.3.1)

- If provided, permanently installed (hardwired) telephones should have volume controls capable of a minimum of 12 dbA and a maximum of 18 dbA above

normal. If an automatic reset is provided, then 18 dbA may be exceeded.

- Outlets: An accessible electrical outlet is within 4 ft of a telephone connection, where provided.

(UR) Urinals (4.18)

Urinals: height

UR-01 Does the accessible urinal have an elongated rim with a maximum height to the rim of no more than 17 in. above the floor? (4.18.2, 4.22.5)

AUTHOR'S INTERPRETATION:

- The ADAAG does not define when a urinal is considered as elongated. However, some codes suggest the face of an elongated rim is at least 14 in. from the wall.

Urinals: clear floor space

UR-02 Is clear floor space provided that allows a forward approach to the accessible urinal? (4.18.3)

- Clear floor space: not less than 30 in. × 48 in. and adjoins or overlaps an accessible route.

UR-03 Is the required clear width provided between the accessible urinal shields? (4.18.3)

- Shields that do not extend beyond the front edge of the urinal rim: at least 29 in. wide between partitions.
- Shields extending beyond the urinal rim: not less than 30 in. wide between partitions.

Urinals: flush controls

UR-04 Is the accessible urinal flush valve control located within reach range? (4.18.4)

- Height: not more than 44 in.

UR-05 Is the accessible urinal flush valve control automatic or operable with one hand without tight grasping, pinching, or wrist twisting, and requiring no more than 5 lbf of force? (4.18.4)

(WC) Water Closets (4.16)

Water Closets (general): centerline and toilet seats

WC-01 Is the centerline of the accessible toilet (in or not in a stall) located exactly 18 in. from a side wall or partition? (Fig. 28; Fig. 30a, a-1, b)

WC-02 Is the top of the toilet seat between 17 in. and 19 in. from the top of the finish floor? (4.16.3, Fig. 29b, Fig. 30d)

- Seats shall not automatically return to a lifted position.

Water Closets (general): flush controls

WC-03 Are the flush controls mounted on the wide side of the toilet and no more than 44 in. above the finish floor? (4.16.5)

WC-04 Is the toilet flush valve control automatic or operable with one hand without tight grasping, pinching, or wrist twisting, and requiring no more than 5 lbf of force? (4.16.5)

Water Closets (general): toilet paper dispenser

WC-05 Is the toilet paper dispenser placed in the correct location and does it permit continuous paper flow? (4.16.6, Fig. 29b)

- Location: not less than 19 in. high from finish floor to centerline; not more than 36 in. from the back wall.

Water Closets (not in stalls): clear floor space

WC-06 Is clear floor space provided at the accessible toilet (not in a stall and with a lavatory at the side) for front, side, or dual approach? (4.16.2, Fig. 28)

- Front approach: at least 48 in. wide × 66 in. deep; lavatory may encroach up to 12 in.
- Side approach: at least 48 in. wide × 56 in. deep; lavatory may encroach up to 12 in.

- Dual approach: at least 60 in. wide × 56 in. deep with no lavatory encroachment.

Water Closets (not in stalls): grab bars

NOTE:

- Additional criteria for grab bars can be found in Section "HR, Handrails."

WC-07 Are the grab bars for toilets (not in stalls) the correct length and are they placed in the correct location? (4.16.4, Fig. 28–29)

- Rear wall: not less than 36 in. long starting at no more than 6 in. from the side wall.
- Side wall: not less than 42 in. long starting at no more than 12 in. from the rear wall.
- Mounting height: 33 in. to 36 in. to centerline above the finish floor and mounted horizontally.

D

ADAAG Graphics

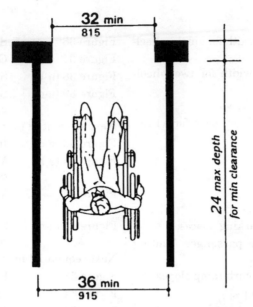

Figure 1. Minimum clear width for single wheelchair.

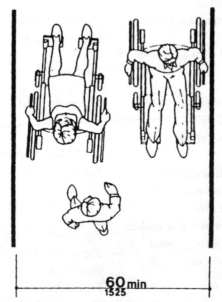

Figure 2. Minimum clear width for two wheelchairs.

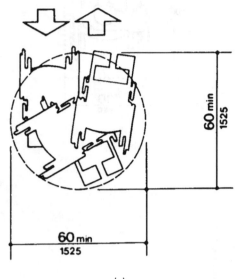

(a)
60-in. (1525-mm) Diameter Space

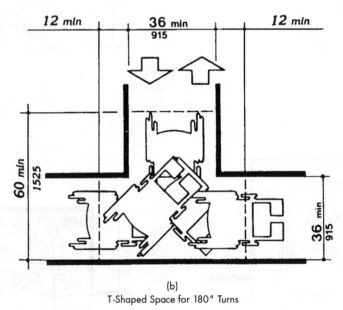

(b)
T-Shaped Space for 180° Turns

Figure 3. Wheelchair turning space.

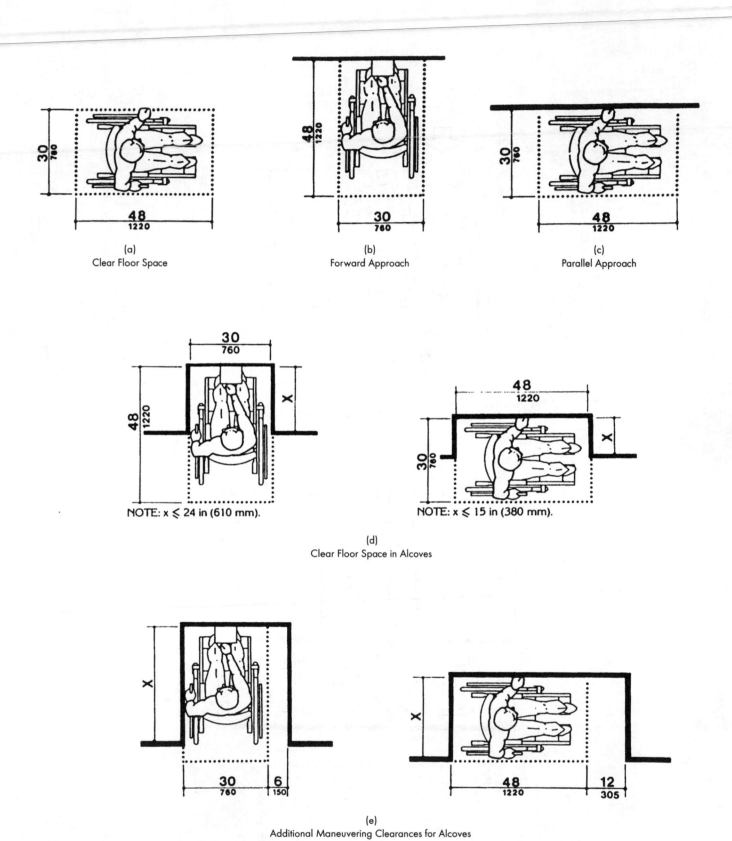

(a)
Clear Floor Space

(b)
Forward Approach

(c)
Parallel Approach

NOTE: x ⩽ 24 in (610 mm).

NOTE: x ⩽ 15 in (380 mm).

(d)
Clear Floor Space in Alcoves

(e)
Additional Maneuvering Clearances for Alcoves

Figure 4. Minimum clear floor space for wheelchairs.

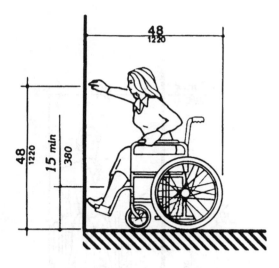
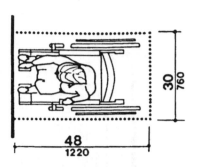

(a)
High Forward Reach Limit

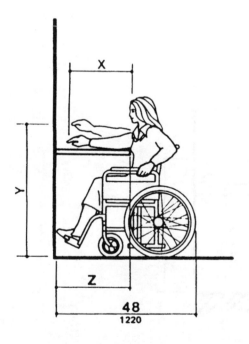
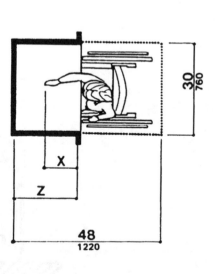

NOTE: x shall be ≤ 25 in (635 mm); z shall be ≥ x. When x < 20 in (510 mm), then y shall be 48 in (1220 mm) maximum. When x is 20 to 25 in (510 to 635 mm), then y shall be 44 in (1120 mm) maximum.

(b)
Maximum Forward Reach over an Obstruction

Figure 5. Forward reach.

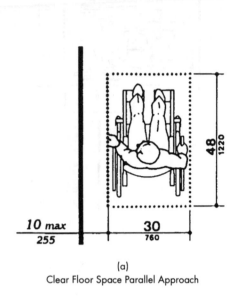

(a)

Clear Floor Space Parallel Approach

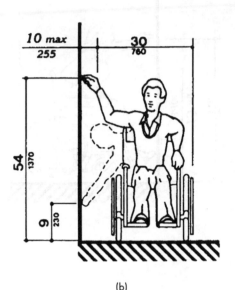

(b)

High and Low Side Reach Limits

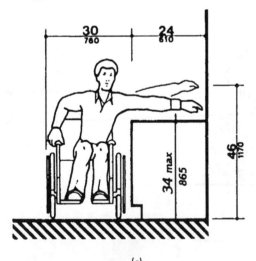

(c)

Maximum Side Reach over an Obstruction

Figure 6. Side reach.

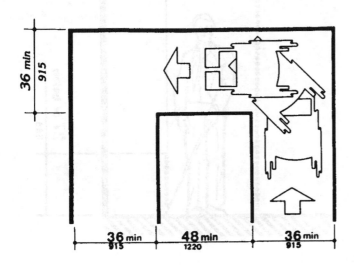

(a)
90° Turn

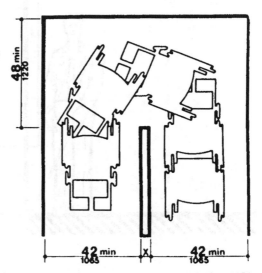

NOTE: Dimensions shown apply when x < 48 in (122

(b)
Turns around an Obstruction

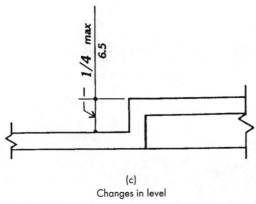

(c)
Changes in level

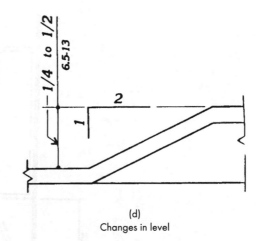

(d)
Changes in level

Figure 7. Accessible route.

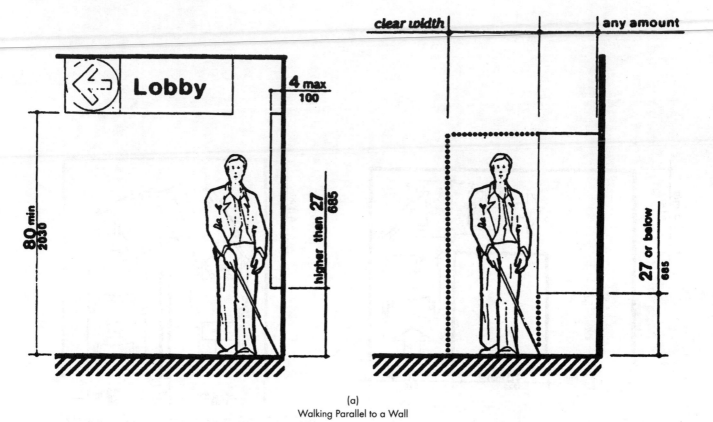

(a)
Walking Parallel to a Wall

(b)
Walking Perpendicular to a Wall

Figure 8. Protruding objects.

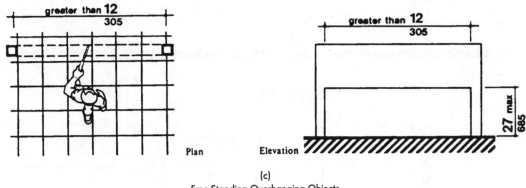

(c)
Free-Standing Overhanging Objects

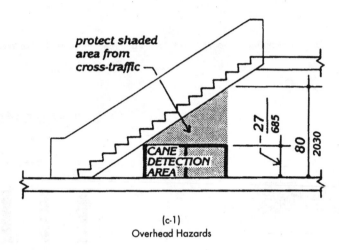

(c-1)
Overhead Hazards

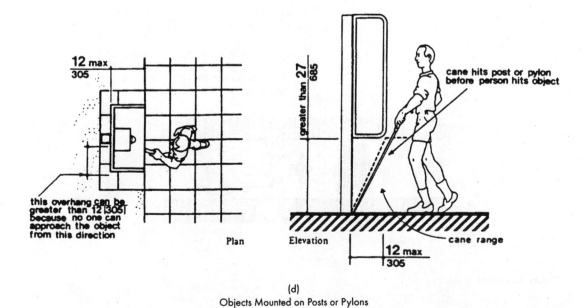

(d)
Objects Mounted on Posts or Pylons

Figure 8. Protruding objects *(cont.)*.

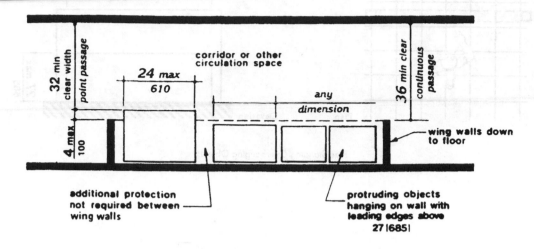

32 min clear width point passage

corridor or other circulation space

24 max
610

any dimension

36 min clear continuous passage

4 max
100

wing walls down to floor

additional protection not required between wing walls

protruding objects hanging on wall with leading edges above 27 [685]

(e)
Example of Protection around Wall-Mounted Objects and Measurements of Clear Widths

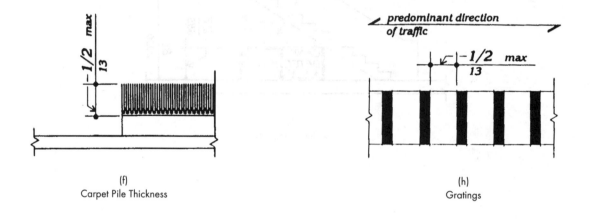

1/2 max
13

(f)
Carpet Pile Thickness

predominant direction of traffic

1/2 max
13

(h)
Gratings

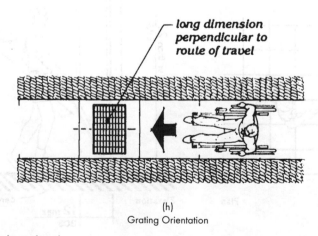

long dimension perpendicular to route of travel

(h)
Grating Orientation

Figure 8. Protruding objects *(cont.).*

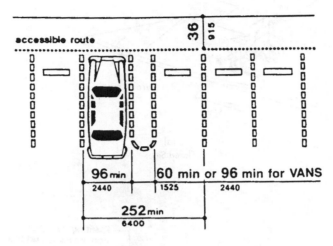

Figure 9. Dimensions of parking spaces.

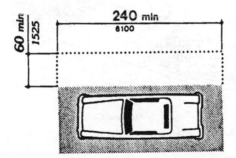

Figure 10. Access aisle at passenger loading zones.

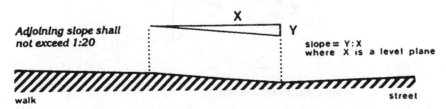

Figure 11. Measurement of curb ramp slopes.

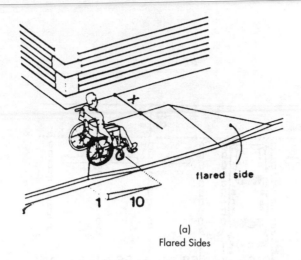

(a)
Flared Sides

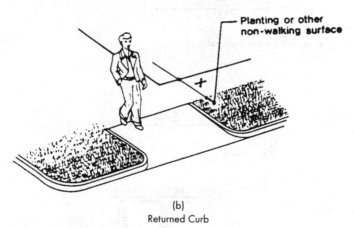

(b)
Returned Curb

Figure 12. Sides of curb ramps.

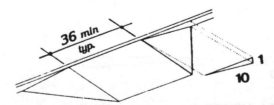

Figure 13. Built-up curb ramp.

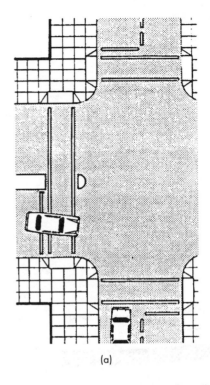

(a)

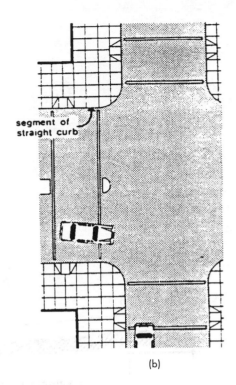

segment of
straight curb

(b)

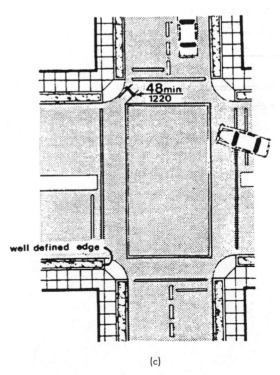

48min
1220

well defined edge

(c)

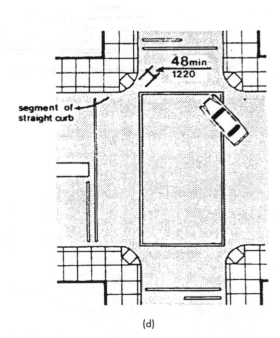

48min
1220

segment of
straight curb

(d)

Figure 15. Curb ramps at marked crossings.

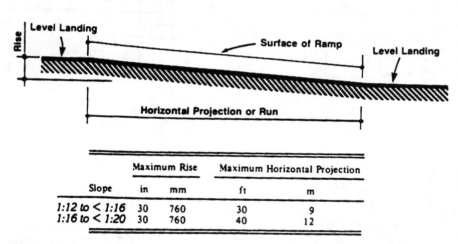

Slope	Maximum Rise		Maximum Horizontal Projection	
	in	mm	ft	m
1:12 to < 1:16	30	760	30	9
1:16 to < 1:20	30	760	40	12

Figure 16. Components of a single ramp run and sample ramp dimensions.

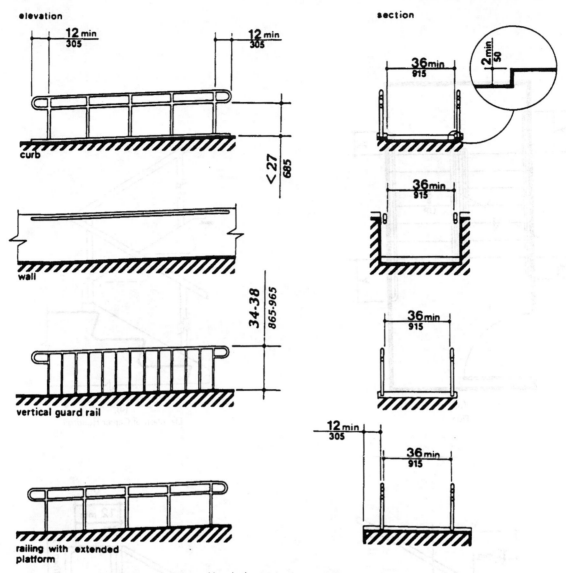

Figure 17. Examples of edge protection and handrail extensions.

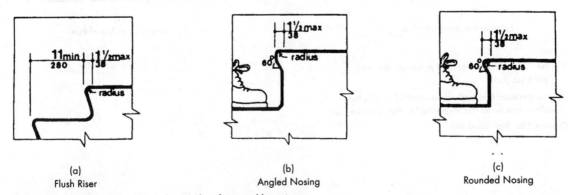

Figure 18. Usable tread width and examples of acceptable nosings.

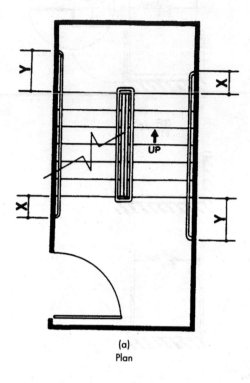

(a)
Plan

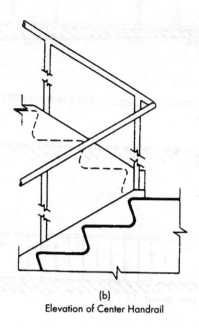

(b)
Elevation of Center Handrail

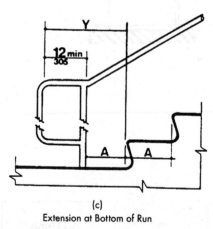

(c)
Extension at Bottom of Run

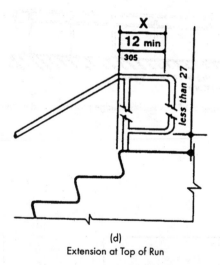

(d)
Extension at Top of Run

NOTE:

X is the 12 in minimum handrail extension required at each top riser.

Y is the minimum handrail extension of 12 in plus the width of one tread that is required at each bottom riser.

Figure 19. Stair handrails.

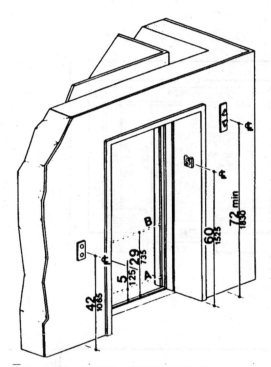

Figure 20. Hoistway and elevator entrances.

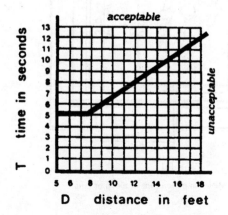

Figure 21. Graph of timing equation.

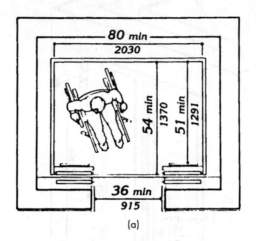

(a)

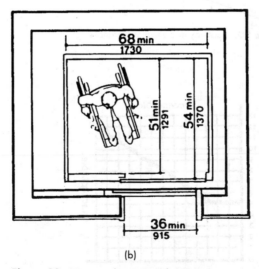

(b)

Figure 22. Minimum dimensions of elevator cars.

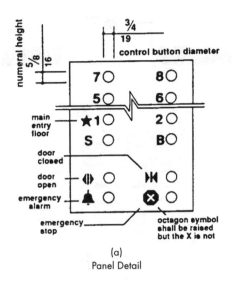

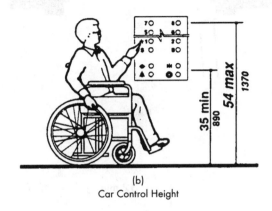

(a)
Panel Detail

(b)
Car Control Height

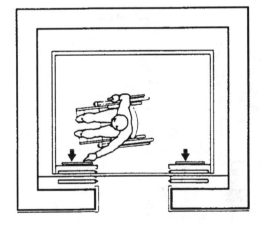

(c)
Alternate Locations of Panel
with Center Opening Door

(d)
Alternate Locations of Panel
with Side Opening Door

Figure 23. Car controls.

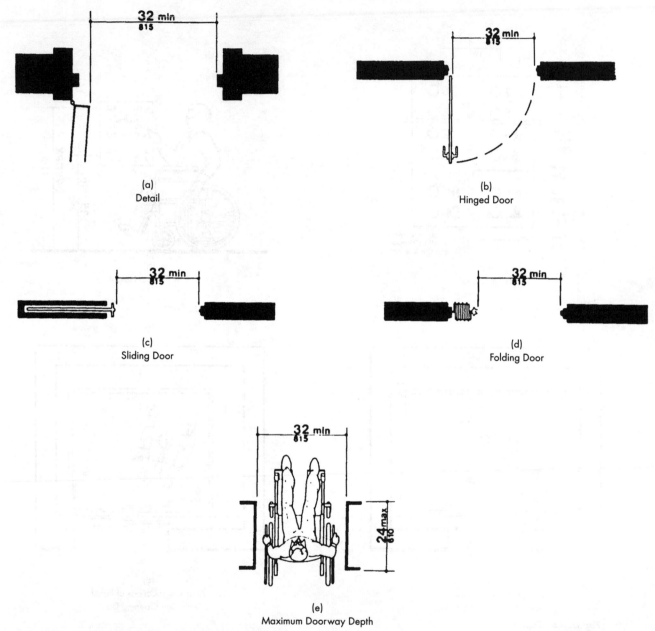

(a)
Detail

(b)
Hinged Door

(c)
Sliding Door

(d)
Folding Door

(e)
Maximum Doorway Depth

Figure 24. Clear doorway width and depth.

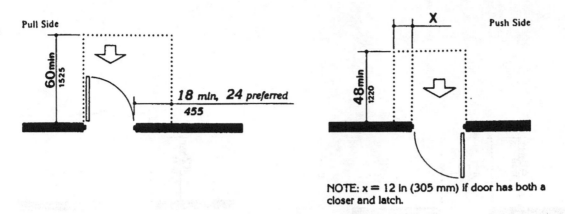

NOTE: x = 12 in (305 mm) if door has both a closer and latch.

(a)
Latch Side Approaches — Swinging Doors

NOTE: All doors in alcoves shall comply with the clearances for front approaches.

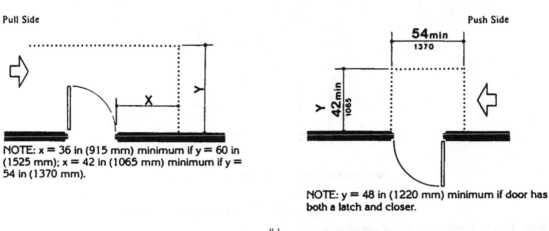

NOTE: x = 36 in (915 mm) minimum if y = 60 in (1525 mm); x = 42 in (1065 mm) minimum if y = 54 in (1370 mm).

NOTE: y = 48 in (1220 mm) minimum if door has both a latch and closer.

(b)
Hinge Side Approaches — Swinging Doors

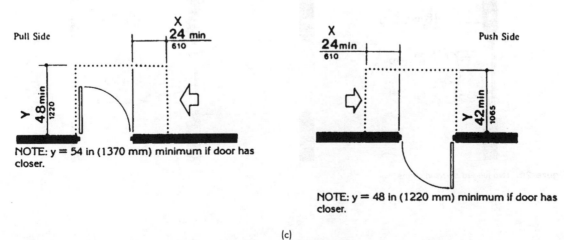

NOTE: y = 54 in (1370 mm) minimum if door has closer.

NOTE: y = 48 in (1220 mm) minimum if door has closer.

(c)
Front Approaches — Swinging Doors

Figure 25. Maneuvering clearances at doors.

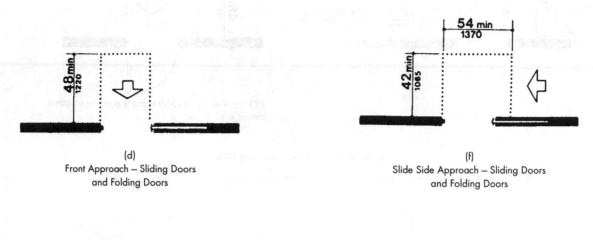

(d)
Front Approach — Sliding Doors
and Folding Doors

(f)
Slide Side Approach — Sliding Doors
and Folding Doors

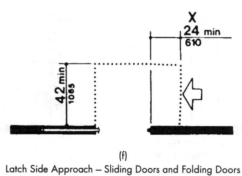

(f)
Latch Side Approach — Sliding Doors and Folding Doors

NOTE: All doors in alcoves shall comply with the clearances for front approaches.

Figure 25. Maneuvering clearances at doors *(cont.)*.

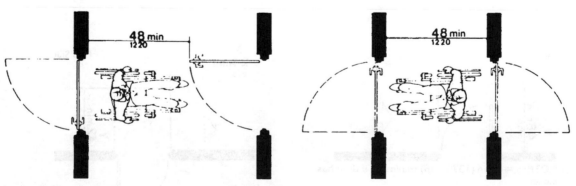

Figure 26. Two hinged doors in series.

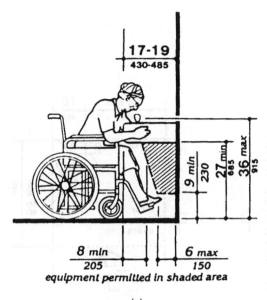

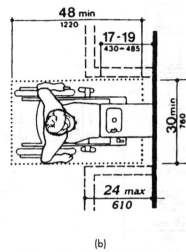

(a)
Spout Height and
Knee Clearance

(b)
Clear Floor Space

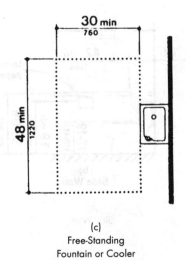

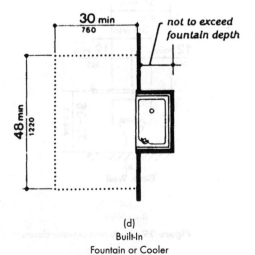

(c)
Free-Standing
Fountain or Cooler

(d)
Built-In
Fountain or Cooler

Figure 27. Drinking fountains and water coolers.

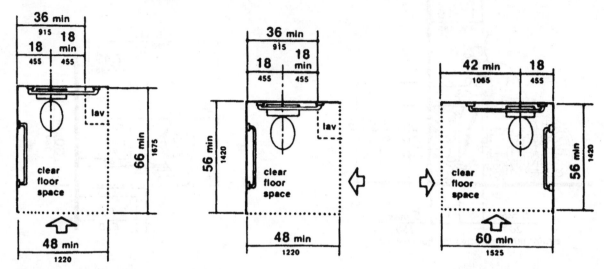

Figure 28. Clear floor space at water closets.

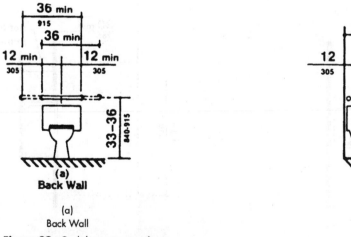

(a)
Back Wall

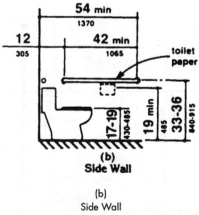

(b)
Side Wall

Figure 29. Grab bars at water closets.

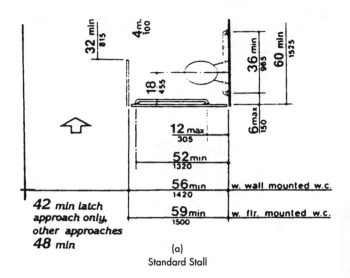

(a)
Standard Stall

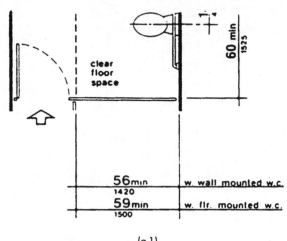

(a-1)
Standard Stall (end of row)

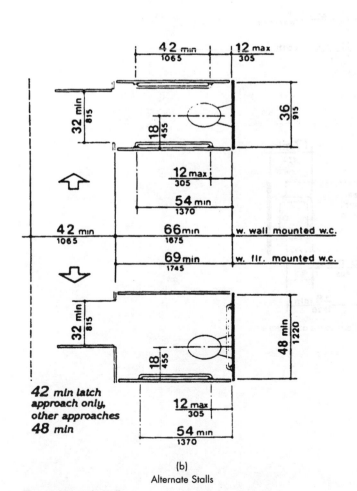

(b)
Alternate Stalls

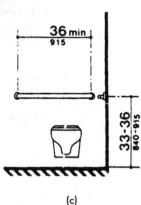

(c)
Rear Wall of Standard Stall

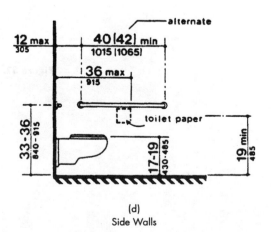

(d)
Side Walls

Figure 30. Toilet stalls.

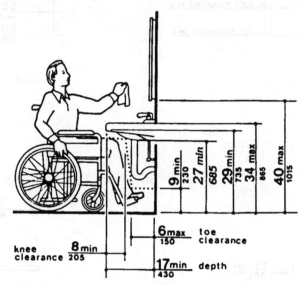

Figure 31. Lavatory clearances.

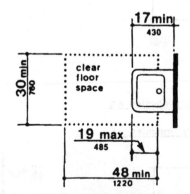

Figure 32. Clear floor space at lavatories.

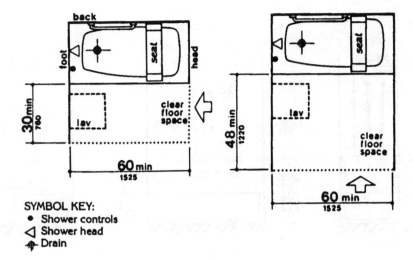

SYMBOL KEY:
- ● Shower controls
- ◁ Shower head
- ⊕ Drain

(a)
With Seat in Tub

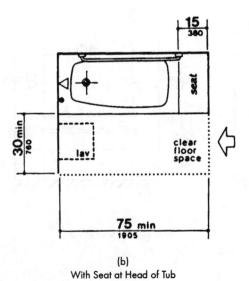

(b)
With Seat at Head of Tub

Figure 33. Clear floor space at bathtubs.

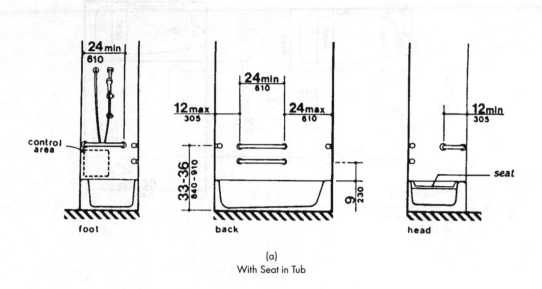

(a)
With Seat in Tub

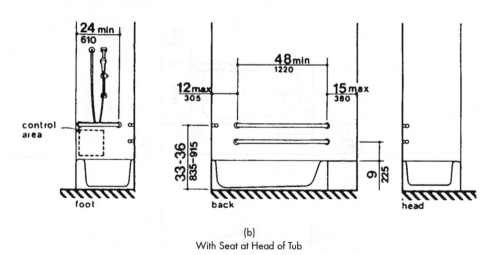

(b)
With Seat at Head of Tub

Figure 34. Grab bars at bathtubs.

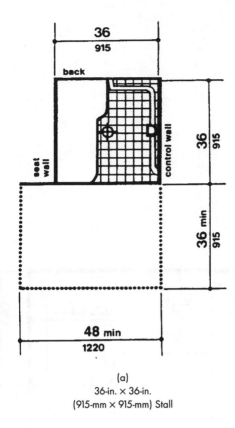

(a)
36-in. × 36-in.
(915-mm × 915-mm) Stall

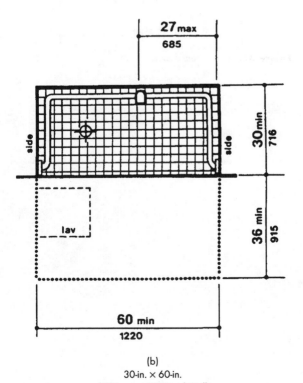

(b)
30-in. × 60-in.
(760-mm × 1525-mm) Stall

Figure 35. Shower size and clearance.

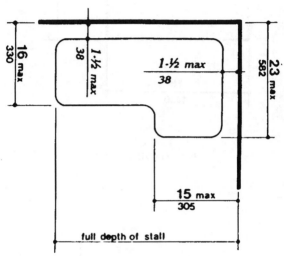

Figure 36. Shower seat design.

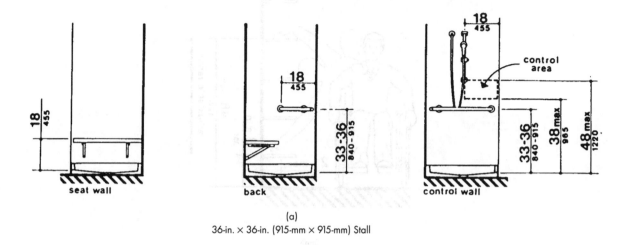

(a)
36-in. × 36-in. (915-mm × 915-mm) Stall

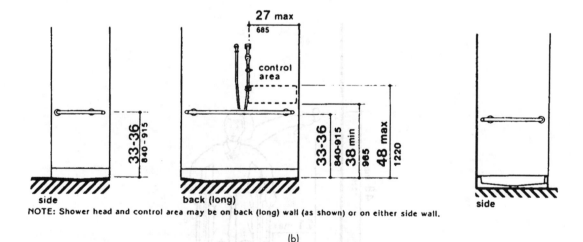

NOTE: Shower head and control area may be on back (long) wall (as shown) or on either side wall.

(b)
36-in. × 60-in. (760-mm × 1525-mm) Stall

Figure 37. Grab bars at shower stalls.

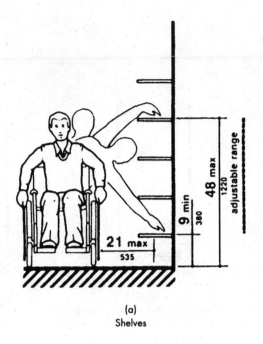

(a)
Shelves

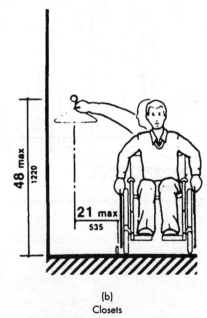

(b)
Closets

Figure 38. Storage shelves and closets.

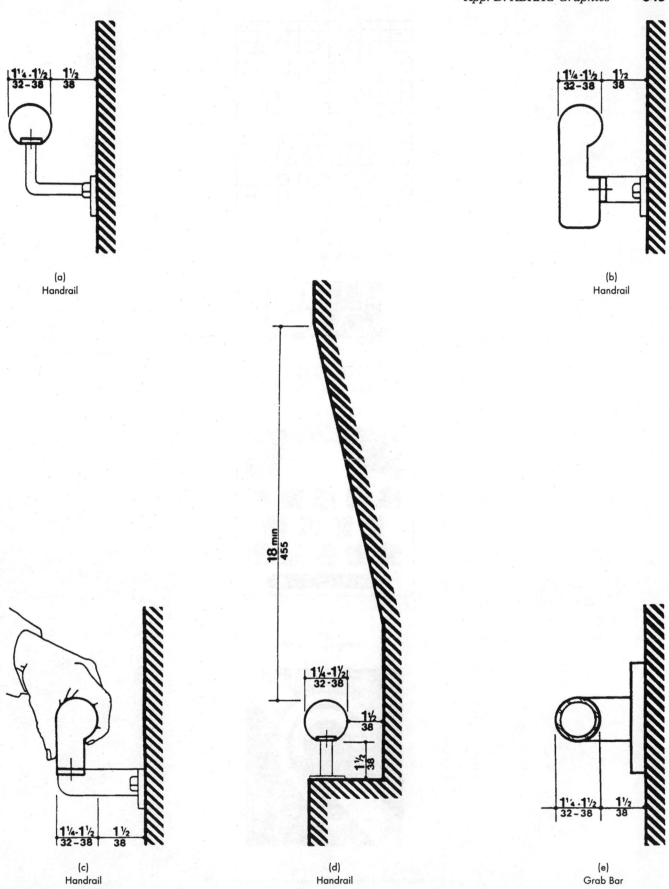

(a)
Handrail

(b)
Handrail

(c)
Handrail

(d)
Handrail

(e)
Grab Bar

Figure 39. Size and spacing of handrails and grab bars.

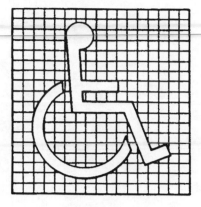

(a)
Proportions
International Symbol of Accessibility

(b)
Display Conditions
International Symbol of Accessibility

(c)
International TDD Symbol

(d)
International Symbol of Access for Hearing Loss

Figure 43. International symbols.

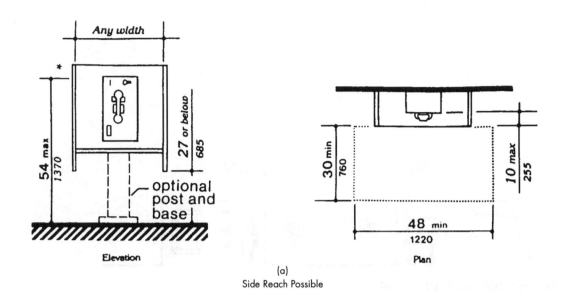

(a)
Side Reach Possible

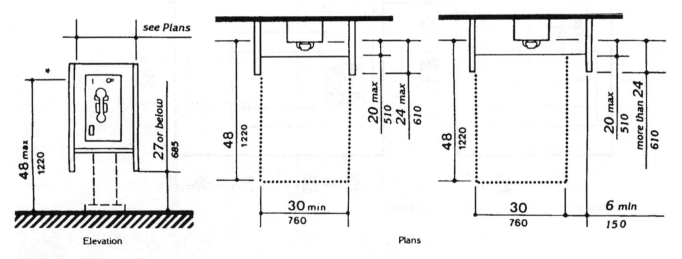

Elevation

Plans

*Height to highest operable
parts which are essential to
basic operation of telephone.

(b)
Forward Reach Required

Figure 44. Mounting heights and clearances for telephones.

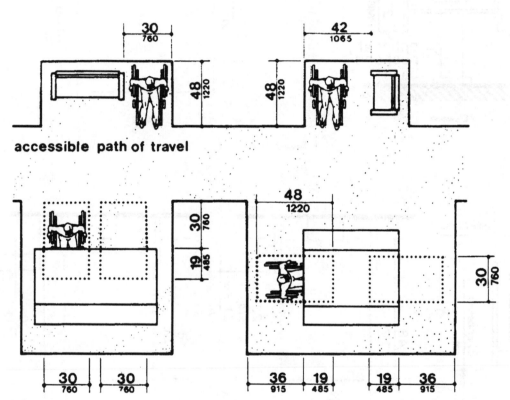

accessible path of travel

Figure 45. Minimum clearances for seating and tables.

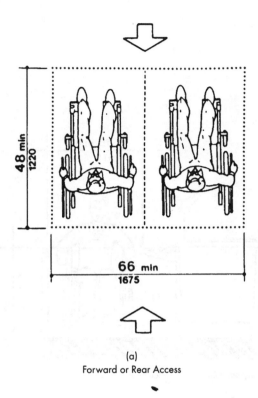

(a)
Forward or Rear Access

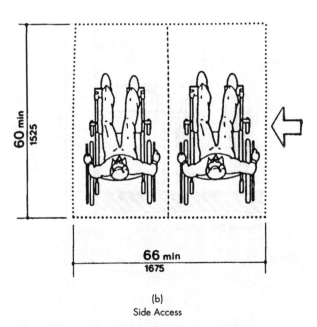

(b)
Side Access

Figure 46. Space requirements for wheelchair seating spaces in series.

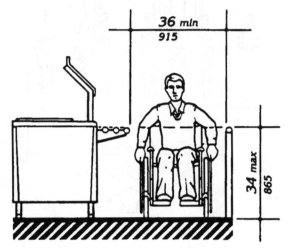

Figure 53. Food service lines.

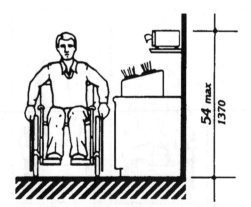

Figure 54. Tableware areas.

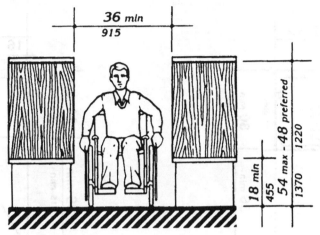

Figure 55. Card catalog.

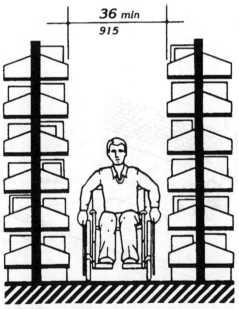

Figure 56. Stacks.

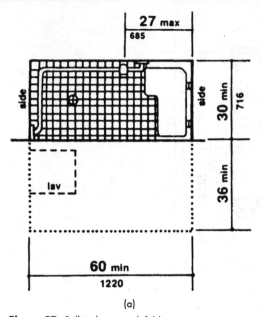

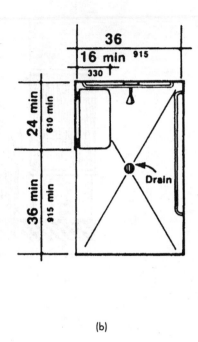

(a)

(b)

Figure 57. Roll-in shower with folding seat.

Figure 58. Level landing at top of perpendicular public sidewalk curb ramp.

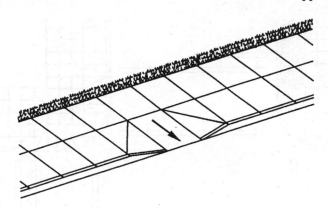

(a)
Perpendicular Public Sidewalk Curb Ramp

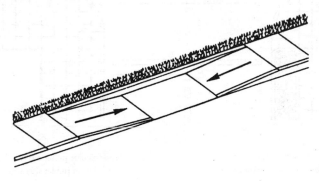

(b)
Parallel Public Sidewalk Curb Ramp

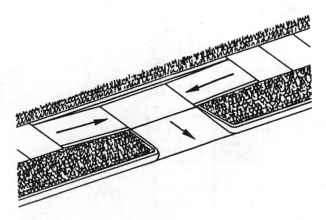

(c)
Combined (Parallel/Perpendicular) Public
Sidewalk Curb Ramp

Figure 59. Public sidewalk curb ramps.

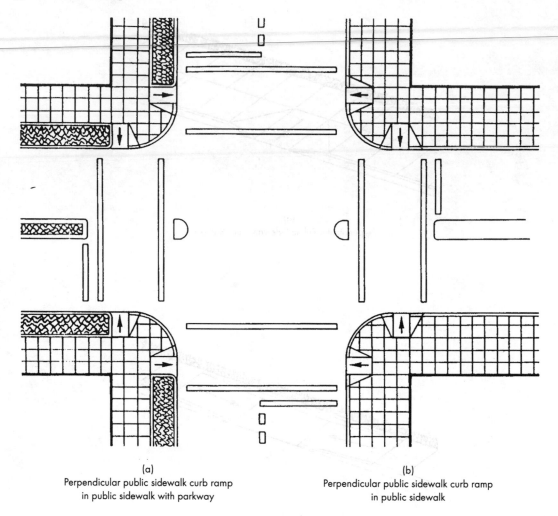

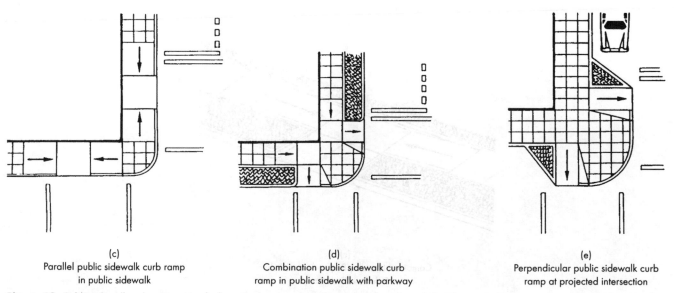

(a)
Perpendicular public sidewalk curb ramp
in public sidewalk with parkway

(b)
Perpendicular public sidewalk curb ramp
in public sidewalk

(c)
Parallel public sidewalk curb ramp
in public sidewalk

(d)
Combination public sidewalk curb
ramp in public sidewalk with parkway

(e)
Perpendicular public sidewalk curb
ramp at projected intersection

Figure 60. Public sidewalk curb ramps at marked crossings.

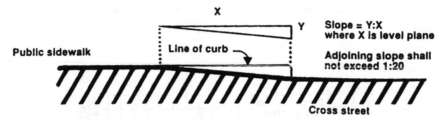

Figure 61. Measurement of public sidewalk curb ramp slope.

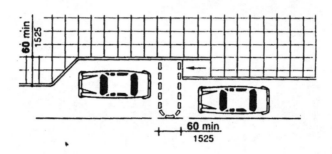

(a)

Single accessible parking space with parallel public
sidewalk curb ramp

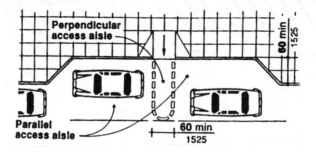

(b)

Single accessible parking space with parallel public
sidewalk curb ramp

Figure 62. Examples of accessible parellel on-street parking spaces.

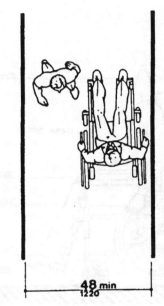

48 min
1220

Figure A1. Minimum passage width for one wheelchair and one ambulatory person.

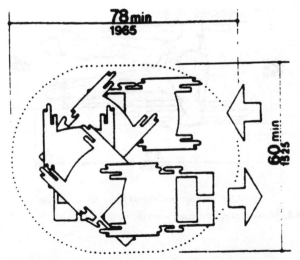

78 min
1965

60 min
1525

Figure A2. Space needed for smooth U-turn in a wheelchair.

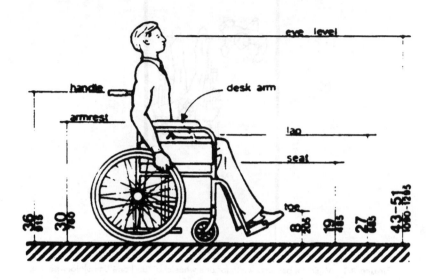

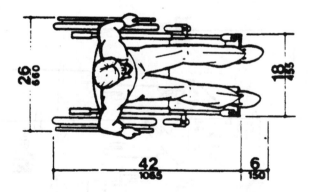

NOTE: Footrests may extend further for tall people

Figure A3. Dimensions of adult-sized wheelchairs.

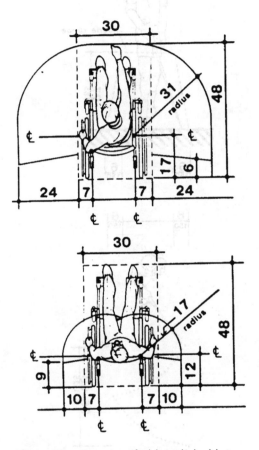

Figure A3a. Dimensions of adult-sized wheelchairs.

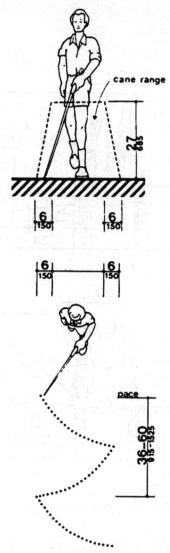

cane range

27
685

6
150

6
150

6
150

6
150

pace

36—60
915—1525

Figure A4. Cane technique.

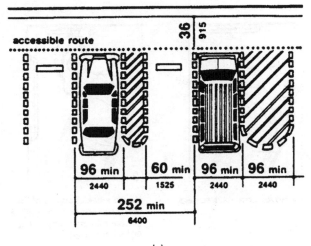

(a)
Van Accessible Space at End Row

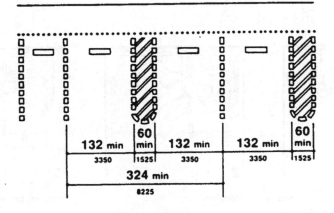

(b)
Universal Parking Space Design

Figure A5. Parking space alternatives.

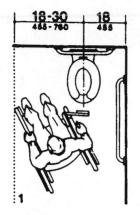

18-30
455-760

18
455

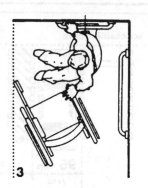

1 Takes transfer position, swings footrest out of the way, sets brakes.

2 Removes armrest, transfers.

3 Moves wheelchair out of the way, changes position (some people fold chair or pivot it 90° to the toilet).

4 Positions on toilet, releases brake.

(a)
Diagonal Approach

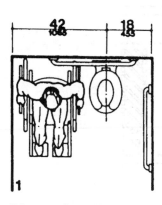

42
1065

18
455

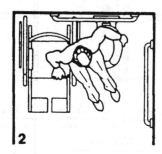

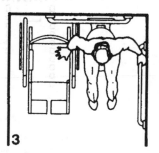

1 Takes transfer position, removes armrest, sets brakes.

2 Transfers.

3 Positions on toilet.

(b)
Side Approach

Figure A6. Wheelchair transfers.

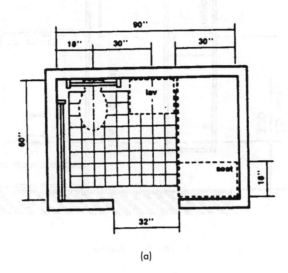

(a)

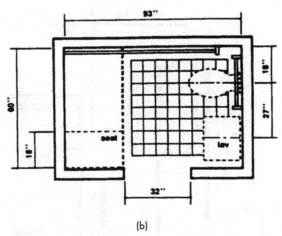

(b)

Figure A7. Clear floor space for toilet rooms.

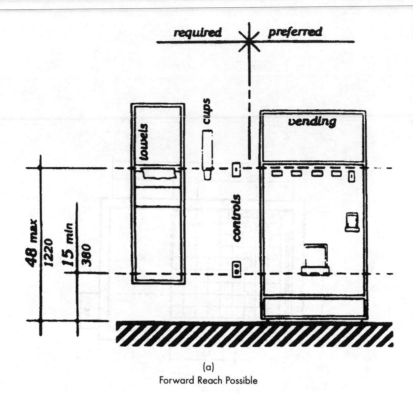

(a)
Forward Reach Possible

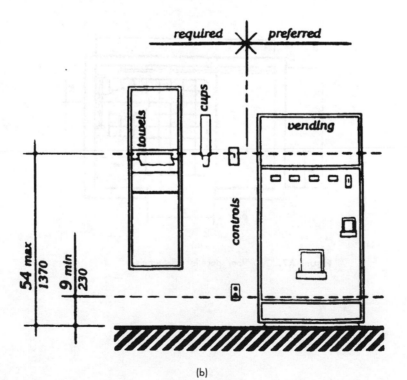

(b)
Side Reach Possible

Figure A8. Control reach limitations.

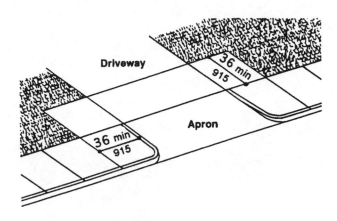

(a)
Sidewalk without parkway where
continuous passage bypasses apron

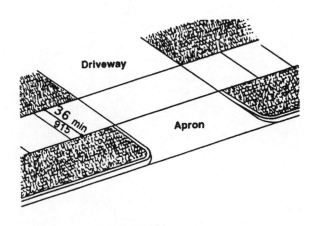

(b)
Sidewalk with parkway

Figure A9. Sidewalks at driveway aprons.

About the Authors

The Accessible Space Team is an interdisciplinary team of design faculty in the College of Architecture at the University of Florida. The principal members and authors of this book are Robert R. Grist, Mary Joyce Hasell, Rocke Hill, James L. West, Tony R. White, and Sara Katherine Williams. In addition to their academic credentials, Hill, White, and West are licensed architects; Hasell is a licensed interior designer; and Grist and Williams are licensed landscape architects.

The team has been responsible for the survey of over 4000 buildings with more than 85,000 spaces that include more than 40 million square feet of interior space. The survey also included all exterior spaces, accessible routes, and parking associated with these facilities.